Entrepreneurship
Text, Cases and Notes

Robert Ronstadt, A.B., M.A., D.B.A.

Associate Professor and Academic Head
of Entrepreneurial Studies

Babson College

First Edition 1984
Lord Publishing, Dover, Massachusetts 02030

Case material is made possible by the cooperation of entrepreneurs who may wish to remain anonymous by having names, quantities, and other identifying details disguised while basic relationships are maintained. Cases are prepared as the basis for class discussion rather than to illustrate either effective or ineffective handling of entrepreneurial situations.

The following materials are reprinted with express permission: *Blue Mountain Resorts, Ltd.,* © Willard Ellis, 1980; *Copyproof Paper,* © Rudolph Winston, 1980; *Country Shop Partnership,* © Cheryl L. Safer, Wendi Innocent Rocheleau, and Robert Ronstadt, 1981; *Couples,* © Rudolph Winston, 1980; *Energy Products A, B and C,* © Michael Merenda, 1981; *How I Overcame the Handicap of a College Education,* © Mrs. John Hendrick, 1981; *Laurel Grove Tennis Center,* © John Pearce, II, 1980; *L.L.Bean, Inc.,* © President and Fellows of Harvard University, 1965.

In addition, excerpts from the following are reprinted with permission:

1) J. Mossinghoff's "Streamlining Patent and Trademark Operations," in *Enterprise,* May, 1983; 2) "Cox Study Sees Big FM Growth", *Television/Radio Age,* September 13, 1976; 3) Kelly, Campanella and McKiernan, *Venture Capital: A Guidebook for New Enterprises,* Management Institute, School of Management, Boston College, Chestnut Hill, Ma. pp 5-6; 4) "External Sources of Funds", in *Assisting Small Business Clients in Obtaining Funds,* pp. 27-35, © 1982 by the American Institute of Certified Public Accountants, Inc.; 5) "Equality Minded Club Med Turns Advisor to Nations", *Advertising Age,* February 12, 1979, p. 5-16.© 1979, Crain Communications, Inc.; 6) William E. Wetzel, Jr., "Informal Risk Capital in New England", in *Frontiers of Entrepreneurship Research, 1981,* Center for Entrepreneurial Studies, Babson College, Wellesley, Ma., 1981.

ISBN: 0-930204-11-5

Printed in the United States of America.

Dedication

For our parents, Bob and Marlene Ronstadt, and Irene Aaron, who helped make this book a reality.

And to the memory of our grandparents, Joseph and Loretta Varen, Susan Carrillo Ronstadt, and William and Edna Rosenzweig, who paid the price so that we could grow, learn, and entrepreneur.

Table of Contents

Part Two   Cases: Initiating Entrepreneurial Activities

ships; general partnerships — limited partnerships, silent partners, joint stock companies, REIT's; incorporations — incorporating yourself, professional corporations, closely-held corporations, sub-chapter S corporations / Special advantages for small business: 1244 stock; new regulation laws; new investment laws / Tax issues for entrepreneurs.

Preface and Acknowledgements

Let me first provide you with a brief overview of this book. Part One presents five chapters of text designed to help you to build a base of knowledge about entrepreneurship. However, this treatment goes beyond other efforts in this area by revealing "a way of thinking" about entrepreneurial activities which is referred to as "an entrepreneurial perspective."

The cases in Parts Two, Three, and Four of the book allow students to develop particular entrepreneurial skills associated with different phases of an entrepreneurial career. Part Two focuses on the pre-startup and early startup stages of initial ventures-- i.e., the first few years preceding and following the launching of an entrepreneurial career. Part Three examines mid-career isues as well as issues associated with operating a new venture. Part Four looks at strategic problems and opportunities, including diversification, turnaround situations, and entrepreneurial succession.

Part Five provides students with access to a wealth of practical information which is especially useful to entrepreneurs throughout their careers. This "technical" information is arranged in a series of notes covering specific areas of interest. A distinguishing feature of these notes is that, where appropriate, the technical information is either related to concepts introduced in Part One or organized around new concepts introduced in the notes themselves. Also, some technical notes provide pertinent background information which is useful for analyzing and discussing issues presented in particular cases.

Most of the materials in this book have been developed over the last five years. During this period, a virtual explosion of knowledge has occurred in the field of entrepreneurial studies. Scholars and informed practitioners have access to this information; however, it is not readily available to students and prospective entrepreneurs. Consequently, I believe a book that incorporates this new knowledge will be timely and beneficial to those seeking more information about entrepreneurship.

But the book includes more than research-based knowledge of entrepreneurial activities. It also incorporates my own experiences as an entrepreneur, as well as the experiences of many other entrepreneurs. Hopefully, the end product has been enhanced through the marriage of academic activities (research and development of teaching materials) with the personal experiences of practicing entrepreneurs. Of course, the deficiencies that exist are mine alone, despite the excellent support and contributions of many other individuals.

And no undertaking of this magnitude becomes a published reality without the support and assistance of many fine people. The book would not have been possible without the generous financial support provided by Babson's Board of Research. I want to thank particularly the Board's Chairman, Professor Edward Handler, whose encouragement and understanding made my task much easier than it otherwise might have been.

I must also acknowledge the outstanding participation of the entrepreneurs who contributed to the case studies and responded to my many requests for interviews. I personally profited from their many insights and I hope this work conveys to some extent their words of wisdom.

Along with the entrepreneurs who provided the case studies, I would like to thank the many students in my classes who read and discussed earlier versions of the cases. Developing quality cases involves class testing and retesting. On several occasions, class discussions revealed ways to improve the cases and I appreciate the efforts of those who helped me to refine them.

I was indeed fortunate to have some outstanding research and staff support during this project. Nancy Tieken was invaluable as a case writer *par excellence*. I have no doubt the book was enhanced greatly by her skill and professionalism. Mrs. Tieken was assisted at various times by Patricia Martin and Keith Humber who worked with both course development and research projects associated with this book. Additional assistance was provided by Marlon Schneider and Panaylotis Vlassiadis. Other case writers who made fine contributions were Edward "Ned" Crecelius, Audrey Uchill, Christine Kazo, Harold Dubin, Wendi Innocent Rocheleau, and Cheryl Avers Safer. In addition, Susan Dennis helped with the historical research underlying Chapter One. Early work on one of the technical notes, Private Placements, was performed by Anne Rafferty, Chris Sommerhoff, and William Waddill. Similar work was performed on the Direct Marketing Note by Harriet Collins and Michael J. Stedman.

I wish to extend special thanks to Mrs. John Hendrick for permission to reprint her husband's short classic on "Overcoming the Handicap of a College Education." The Harvard Business School also granted permission to reprint another classic: L.L. Bean, Inc., and their support is gratefully acknowledged. Similarly, I must acknowledge the excellent cases or other materials contributed by some of my colleagues--Michael Merenda, John Pearce II, Willard Ellis, William Wetzel, as well as Jeffrey Shuman, and Rudy Winston. A special note of appreciation is due to the latter two individuals, who freely offered their entrepreneurial insights as both teachers and practitioners over the last few years. In similar fashion, I received positive support and encouragement from Jeffrey Alves, Jeffry Timmons, and Robert Pavan, all of whom have taught in our entrepreneurship program at Babson College. John Marthinsen of Babson College and William Wetzel of the University of New Hampshire also provided good assistance...the former with some early chapters he read and the latter with a review of the technical note on Private Placements. Finally, I would also be remiss if I failed to acknowledge the early encouragement and guidance I received from John A. Hornaday, Ralph Z. Sorenson and the late Walter Carpenter for helping me to develop my interest in the field of entrepreneurial studies.

As always, Ann Lyons did a superb job coordinating the secretarial effort. She typed numerous drafts and provided cheerful assistance despite many other projects. She was supported expertly by Nancy Libby, Beri Ellis, and Sandy Teixera, along with a top-notch group in Word Processing led by Janet Manter and later by Connie Stumpf. Also, Victoria DelBono, Joanne Solomon, Carol Poirier, Patty Millen and Kimberly Wells supported their efforts. Mrs. Dottie Callaghan handled the typesetting with extraordinary efficiency and aplomb, while art and composition activities were performed expertly by Tina Gottesman-Alves. Rebecca Lord shepherded the whole project through the writing and publishing cycle with care, persistence, and professionalism. More than anyone else, she "made it all happen."

Robert Ronstadt
Wellesley, Massachusetts
1984

Special Acknowledgement

Every project has its ups and downs, its moments of good fortune and bad. A special time of immense good fortune for this endeavor was the day three years ago when Nancy Tieken began working for me as a casewriter. Her contributions since then have been extremely significant and warrant special acknowledgement.

Ms. Tieken is principally responsible for writing several complete cases under my supervision. In addition she has edited many of the remaining cases. She has also helped me develop most of the technical notes in this book. Her insights and sensitivities as an editor were an unexpected but welcome and valuable addition to her contribution as casewriter. Anyone who has been involved with developing a textbook of this size understands full well the difficulty and magnitude of such an undertaking. I am convinced that the project would be as yet unfinished without her invaluable and professional support.

Part One

DEVELOPING AN ENTREPRENEURIAL PERSPECTIVE

Part One

Beyond Folk Wisdom:

Developing an Entrepreneurial Perspective

Doctors, lawyers, economists, even managers are trained to think and act in effective ways that are unique and beneficial to their professions. Entrepreneurs can make no such claim. For no common body of normative standards exists that either entrepreneurs or teachers of the subject accept as the principles that entrepreneurs "ought" to follow when thinking about and acting upon entrepreneurial issues.

To be sure, the skeptics among us will argue that norms for entrepreneurs cannot help but be misleading or at least counterproductive since the very notion of a standard represents no more than an average, a clustering or regression toward some median value. Hence, the very notion of a norm flies in the face of entrepreneurial creativity, nonconformity, and rebellion. Undoubtedly, the same logic was applied years ago to the study of medicine, the law, management, and any number of other fields. However, the fatal flaw in this reasoning is the fact that norms do exist and continue to emerge which are learned and followed by entrepreneurs. But these "guidelines," "maxims," or "rules of thumb" are based, as a colleague recently noted, *not* upon "knowledge" produced by systematic research but "normative folk wisdom." Consequently, the real issue is not the existence of norms *per se* but whether we wish to limit the learning, teaching, and practice of entrepreneurship to the realm of folk wisdom. This book argues for a movement beyond "normative folk wisdom," beyond *de facto* "principles" of entrepreneurship that all too often are based on the singular or limited experiences of individual entrepreneurs.

Sadly we cannot move too far beyond the folklore of entrepreneurship. Research-based knowledge has mushroomed in the last decade, but remains in an infant state. And folk knowledge should not be abandoned too quickly nor dismissed outright by prospective entrepreneurs. It exists, after all, because it is often better than no knowledge. In short, it is better than nothing. Consequently, my recommendation to you is to learn the folklore, but to move *through* and then beyond it.

This movement beyond entrepreneurial folklore requires a bridge. The concept of an entrepreneurial perspective represents the causeway between folklore and knowledge. For whatever the source of information, an entrepreneurial perspective means an awareness of and an ability to apply existing knowledge about entrepreneurship to your specific situation in order to make better decisions about your entrepreneurial activities.

Besides knowing the folklore, you need to acquire two types of knowledge to build and apply an entrepreneurial perspective. One type of knowledge is factual. Factual knowledge involves understanding simple facts about entrepreneurs and their activities, plus understanding how these facts are interrelated. Some examples are: the different types of goals that entrepreneurs have at venture startup and the likelihood these goals will change over time; the varying ages when entrepreneurs initiate their first ventures and the likely problems and opportunities they encounter at these different ages; the propensity to start a new venture from scratch, versus acquire one, and the skills and resources associated with each approach.

The other type of knowledge is conceptual. It is consequently more general and abstract than knowledge about facts and their simple or first order interrelationships. Yet these concepts are based on facts and are consistent with them. Our ability to comprehend meaningful concepts about entrepreneurial activities is vital if we are to be able to predict and plan for certain occurrences that tend to arise frequently during the entrepreneurial process. Some concepts important to our understanding of entrepreneurship include:

1. The concept of displacement.
2. The concept of venture incubation.
3. The concept of "veracity" or veridical perception.
4. The concept of operating leverage.
5. The concept of entrepreneurial (versus managerial) succession.
6. The corridor (multiple venture) principle.

How does one make sense of what can be an ever-extending list of facts and concepts about entrepreneurship? My hope is that the chapters that follow will add some order to this collection of information. The philosopher Leibnitz once said that "the knowledge we have acquired ought not to resemble a great shop without order, and without an inventory; we ought to know what we possess, and be able to make it serve us in our need."

In terms of specific format, the early chapters let us know "what we possess." They lay the intellectual and historical groundwork for developing an entrepreneurial perspective. First we scrutinize the changing concept of entrepreneruship from an historical vantage point in order to identify some basic characteristics of entrepreneurial activity. We then extend these evolving notions in Chapter Two in order to discuss the concept of entrepreneurial perspective from a dynamic or process orientiation while identifying some myths about entrepreneurship that work against developing an entrepreneurial perspective. In Chapter Three we begin building an entrepreneurial perspective by discussing existing factual and conceptual knowledge about entrepreneurs, their ventures, and their environments in terms of the decisions to start, continue, and end an entrepreneurial career. The final two chapters suggest how to apply the notion of an entrepreneurial perspective so that it may "serve us in our need." These chapters provide information on several assessment approaches for entrepreneurs.

In this regard, Chapter Four is unlike the other chapters. It charts new territory in terms of a conceptual framework and procedure for assessing entrepreneurial endeavors by utilizing systematic research as its knowledge base. Given the embryonic state of systematic knowledge about entrepreneurial activity, it is a somewhat speculative endeavor. It is not easy to say what "ought to be," for practitioners, especially in this field. But we have reached a point in the history of entrepreneurship which beckons a beginning. Hopefully, this chapter will enable practitioners to apply with positive results new knowledge to their entrepreneurial pursuits as more research data become available.

Specifically, Chapter Four provides a number of qualitative assessment techniques for prospective and practicing entrepreneurs. These include:

1. The assessment of entrepreneurs.
2. The assessment of their ventures.
3. The assessment of their entrepreneurial environments.
4. The strategic assessment of entrepreneurial situations.
5. The ethical assessment of entrepreneurial situations.

Like Chapter Four, Chapter Five possesses a practical applications value for prospective and practicing entrepreneurs. It describes the tools needed for the *quantitative* assessment of entrepreneurial situations. This Chapter is unique insofar as these quantitative tools are described in terms of a critical and unifying concept for entrepreneurs -- the concept of cash flow.

Finally, let me say that acquiring this knowledge about qualitative and quantitative techniques, as well as developing an entrepreneurial perspective, can be a difficult undertaking. Nor is it honest to say that the need for an entrepreneurial perspective is intuitively obvious or without risk. Knowledge can breed doubt. But it can also bring power and the ability to act decisively. In the pages that follow, you will comprehend further what is meant by an entrepreneurial perspective. However, I believe you will only reach a full understanding of the concept through practice with actual entrepreneurial situations, first vicariously with cases of real life entrepreneurs, and later with your own entrepreneurial experiences. Of course, no one can guarantee you success--with or without an entrepreneurial perspective. But I believe a commitment to develop this special capability will be worth the effort. An entrepreneurial perspective will shift the odds of experiencing entrepreneurial success in your favor. In fact, the concept itself will help you define the type of entrepreneurial success you are seeking. The rest will be up to you...and so it should be.

ENTREPRENEURSHIP:
AN EVOLVING CONCEPT

What is entrepreneurship? Who is an entrepreneur? And who sets the boundaries to determine who is one and, in so doing, defines what constitutes entrepreneurship? These are the critical questions whose answers are also circumscribing an entirely new field of inquiry. The new field is called Entrepreneurial Studies and its emergence is part of a swelling surge of national interest in entrepreneurs.

Entrepreneurship and Entrepreneurial Studies are of course the subject matter of this book; yet, I should warn you that the boundaries of this field remain unfixed and no more stable than the concept of entrepreneurship itself. But such instability should not be considered necessarily bad; in fact, it is quite healthy. In one sense, the vagueness of boundaries only reflects the change of purpose among the actors themselves...the entrepreneurs. And as our perception of "who" is an entrepreneur changes to conform better to reality, so the concept of entrepreneurship will shift with the times. Hopefully, our new field of study will keep pace with the change, for new kinds of entrepreneurs seem to emerge with new times.

But who are they now? Who are the entrepreneurs, both new and old, whom we seek to know, understand, praise, and perhaps emulate? Our own definition will be provided in due course, along with many others. But for now, one thing is certain; unlike individuals who readily claim to be lawyers, doctors, engineers, etc., those who practice entrepreneurship are not so easily identified. The reason is quite simple: people who pursue their entire lives as entrepreneurs do not use the term to describe their activities, for hardly anyone who is an entrepreneur thinks of entrepreneurship as an occupation or a career.

Yet it is.

Why has entrepreneurship been denied career status even among entrepreneurs? A good part, if not all, of the reason resides in our social values which have created a cultural and intellectual bias against entrepreneurs. It is a bias not totally without cause, yet it is nevertheless a biased view that too often completely ignores the social good produced by entrepreneurs. Even today the term "entrepreneur" is considered, shall we say, somewhat disreputable as an occupational description...particularly among the "older generation" of entrepreneurs. For instance, I have had the good fortune to meet many distinguished men and women over the years who are unquestionably entrepreneurs. In fact, their entrepreneurial feats are legend to the point they can be called "celebrity entrepreneurs." But even here their tendency is to identify themselves as owners, founders, creators, chairmen, presidents, etc...anything but "entrepreneurs." It's important to note that these people think of themselves as entrepreneurs. They just refuse to adopt the label. And this rejection isn't grounded in modesty or shyness. For example, they will claim:

Ray Kroc: I *am* MacDonald's.

Armand Hammer: I am the head of Occidental Petroleum, among other things.

Nolan Bushnell: I started Atari and Pizza Time Theaters and am now working with embryonic startups.

Nor is there any reason for false modesty. Ray Kroc was and will continue to be Macdonald's. It is his rightful and good legacy to the world.

But perceptions and descriptions are changing among newer entrepreneurs, particularly the younger ones who are just launching their entrepreneurial careers. For instance, a few years ago a former student dropped by my office to let me know he was still starting new ventures. Actually I wasn't terribly surprised to hear that this particular student, David Lockwood, was continuing his entrepreneurial career. David had been an entrepreneur most of his young life, having started several new ventures before college. He had continued to run his businesses from college while taking an eclectic group of courses which included our offerings in entrepreneurship.

Nor was there anything particularly surprising in David's revelations about his current activities. And after our meeting ended, without any fanfare or comment, he left his business card with me so I could contact him about a case study we had discussed. It was only after David left my office that I read his card, and here's what I saw:

BUY • SELL • TRADE ——————— **WHEEL and DEAL**
BARN DOORS — BUGGY WHIPS — SNOWMOBILES
RIOTS STARTED — REVOLUTIONS QUELLED

CAPT. DAVID LOCKWOOD
ENTREPRENEUR

SKATEBOARDS • NAILS • MANURE • RETREAD TIRES
PLUMBING SUPPLIES • SPORTING GOODS
EDUCATIONAL TESTING

HOME .... OFFICE
222-1234 222-2222

Naturally, I was amused--but I was also surprised. For despite David's varied lines of work, he had not identified himself with any of them. He had simply stated, "I am an entrepreneur." At the same time, I remembered how often I'd met other entrepreneurs who, when asked their profession, generally responded with ... "Well, I'm in computers, or chemicals, or insurance...or some other industry label. At most they might say, "I'm a businessman," but never, never, "I'm an entrepreneur."

And so that simple but rare declaration by David Lockwood surprised me. Sure, it was an amusing, even a brash presentation. But it was also a proud statement which, in a way, marked a shift in the perception of a great many people about the concept of entrepreneurship and the realities of being an entrepreneur.

One of our goals in this chapter is to examine closely how this concept has changed over many decades. A number of definitions are presented and compared to one another. But they are "serious" definitions and somewhere along the line they miss some of the fun and spark... "of riots started and revolutions quelled" ...that permeates David Lockwood's business card.

So, before venturing any farther let me paraphrase what some contemporaries, mostly entrepreneurs, have said about their perception of entrepreneurship.

> "Entrepreneurship is a little like coming to a traffic light which is red and not necessarily stopping."

> "Entrepreneurship is starting a business; and starting a business is the most fun you can possibly have with your clothes on."

> "The *job* of an entrepreneur in our 'competitive' economy is to create an *unfair* advantage."

> "The three letter word entrepreneurs hate the most is j-o-b."

> "I can smell the Ferrari."

Taken together, these statements have the mark of the rebel; certainly they are a little mischievous and even irreverent; but they are also fun. Most important they bear the mark of free minds; and freedom, we are told, is one hallmark of entrepreneurial life.

And so it is, but not without a price. For even the most free of enterprises - those free of debt, or troublesome partners and difficult employees, or those free from direct or cutthroat competition as well as the millstones of everyday ethical dilemmas - even these fortunate ventures are subject to the constraint imposed by the fund of knowledge which ultimately shapes society and the entrepreneurial environment. It is this knowledge constraint that limits the latitude of thought and action available to even the most skilled entrepreneurs.

Yet it is a constraint most entrepreneurs deny. The paradox is that the denial can be healthy. Sometimes doing the impossible occurs when you don't know it can't be done. Here the words of the philosopher, Johann Wolfgang von Goethe, form the action basis of entrepreneurship. He wrote:

> Whatever you can do,
> or dream you can,
> begin it.
> Boldness has genius, power
> and magic in it.

And so it does; momentum and execution can mean everything for the success of a venture. But the other side of the paradox is that all too often the "magic" doesn't work. Entrepreneurs who remain ignorant of the growing storehouse of knowledge about the elements of entrepreneurial success are more apt to be less selective and commit fundamental errors that can derail their entrepreneurial ventures and, more seriously, terminate prematurely their entrepreneurial careers. An important tenet of this book is that knowledge, specifically *entrepreneurial know-how* is as vital to success as technical know-how, product know-how, market know-how, and industry know-how.

Yet entrepreneurial know-how, knowledge of the process of entrepreneurship, tends to be ignored or undervalued by many involved in such pursuits. Even entrepreneurs who value such knowledge have had unfortunately a tendency to rediscover the wheel. For instance, many entrepreneurs that I know socially or have interviewed professionally seem to think (and in fact almost enjoy thinking) they are free of intellectual boundaries, particularly academic ideas. They presume that the ivory towered theorists know nothing of their entrepreneurial pursuits. Unfortunately, all too often they are right. The rare exceptions, however, are theorists who have produced the ideas or knowledge which entrepreneurs unwittingly rediscover when they generalize about their experiences. Years ago the economist John Maynard Keynes addressed this issue when he spoke about he power of "academic" ideas. Here's what he had to say:

> ...the ideas of economists and political philosophers, both when they are right and when they are wrong, are more powerful than is commonly understood. Indeed the world is ruled by little else. Practical men, who believe themselves to be quite exempt from any intellectual influences, are usually the slaves of some defunct economist. Madmen in authority, who hear voices in the air, are distilling their frenzy from some academic scribbler of a few years back. I am sure that the power of vested interests is vastly exaggerated compared with the gradual encroachment of ideas. Not, indeed, immediately, but after a certain interval; for in the field of economic and political philosophy there are not many who are influenced by new theories after they are twenty-five or thirty years of age, so that the ideas which civil servants and politicians and even agitators apply to current events are not

likely to be the newest. But, soon or late, it is ideas, not
vested interests, which are dangerous for good or evil.

(from The General Theory of Employment)*

Keynes' words came alive for me not long ago when an acquaintance and long time
entrepreneur turned to me and said: "I've given the whole issue of what constitutes
entrepreneurial success a great deal of thought. I'm convinced from my own experience,
as well as observing other entrepreneurs, that the critical element is "perserverance." For
the next five minutes he explained his reasoning which does not require repeating here.
What does bear mentioning is that his "discovery" and explanation were essentially the
same as the one made by the French political economist, Jean Baptiste Say. . .the only
difference being that Professor Say made his observations about 180 years earlier. (His
exact comments are presented a little later in this chapter).

My hope of course is that your study of entrepreneurship will allow you to move
beyond the discoveries of nineteenth century political philosophers. Certainly the role of
perserverance is important as a component of entrepreneurial success. I would not deny it
but underscore it. Yet so much more is known about entrepreneurship that it is improper
to center on a single element as the *sine qua non* of entrepreneurial life.

This story also has another message. We would do well to know what other "defunct
economists and academic scribblers" (some of whom were or are practicing
entrepreneurs) have said about entrepreneurship. Why? Because their pronouncements
may help us to understand a complex subject, and with greater understanding resides
greater opportunity for entrepreneurial success in the future.

But the subject is complex. The reason it is complex is that we are dealing with
imperfect knowledge and the knowledge we possess about entrepreneurial pursuits is
based on a variety of different interpretations of the concept. For instance, the concept of
entrepreneurship, and consequently the definition of who is an entrepreneur, have
undergone many evolutionary changes since observers first started recording their ideas
on the topic. Several critical distinctions have been made over the last two hundred years
and people are still finding new ways to interpret and define entrepreneurship, as well as
who is an entrepreneur. I should emphasize that understanding these different definitions
is not simply a semantic or academic exercise. From a practical standpoint, one should
know at least what others mean when discussing the concept, given the variety of possible
meanings and their potential impact on your own entrepreneurial pursuits.

For example, we will see shortly how early writers on the subjects of entrepreneurship
made no distinction (prior to the early 1800's) between investors and entrepreneurs. And
it wasn't until the early 1960's that some researchers began to distinguish carefully

---

*John Maynard Keynes: *The General Theory of Employment, Interest and Money.* The
Collected Writings of John Maynard Keynes. Volume VII: London: MacMillan Press,
1973, pp. 383-384.

between independent or autonomous entrepreneurs who owned their own businesses and managers who made "entrepreneurial" decisions for established corporations. Even more recently, observers have started to distinguish between various kinds of independent entrepreneurs, acquiring entrepreneurs, and corporate entrepreneurs.

Potentially even more significant is the recent shift in focus from characteristics and functions of entrepreneurs as a means of identifying them to a study of the process of entrepreneurship. Over the last two centuries, serious inquiries into the nature of entrepreneurship have focused on either the functions of the entrepreneur, the traits or behavioral characteristics that differentiated entrepreneurs from the rest of mankind, or the environmental conditions that caused entrepreneurs to flower or wither on the vine. Only recently have investigations started to examine the *process of entrepreneurship as a way to distinguish between entrepreneurs*. Thus far the early evidence suggests that how entrepreneurs pursue their entrepreneurial activities can distinguish one from another as much as differences in traits or functions. These findings possess special importance for entrepreneurs who often are in a better position to affect how, where, and when they pursue their entrepreneurial activities versus their capabilities to alter personal traits and characteristics. . .at least over the short term.

But whatever your current view of entrepreneurs and entrepreneurship, you should realize you've probably inherited these notions from one or more sources of varying vintage. Moreover, they are no doubt the consequence of an evolving concept of what constitutes entrepreneurial pursuits. Since the concept of entrepreneurship will continue to change, let us look at how it has evolved in the past so that we may better understand the phenomenon now and in the future.

A HISTORICAL VIEW OF THE CONCEPT OF ENTREPRENEURSHIP

Let's begin with the word itself. The term "entrepreneur" stems from the French (literally, "between-taker," or "go-between") with early references having been traced to the eighteenth century economists Richard Cantillon, Anne-Robert-Jacques Turgot, and Francois Quesnay. The term was even used as early as the Middle Ages to denote an *actor* (with reference to warlike action) or in particular, a person "in charge of large-scale construction projects such as cathedrals, bearing no risks but simply carrying the task forward until resources were exhausted."[1] By the seventeenth century, the term was associated with risk bearing, with the entrepreneur being "a person who entered into a contractual relationship with the government for the performance of a service or the supply of goods. The price at which the contract was valued was fixed and the entrepreneur bore the risks of profit and loss from the bargain."[2]

In France, during the eighteenth century, the term was used in a variety of ways. Cantillon, in 1725, associated entrepreneurs with risk-bearing, yet Cantillon clearly distinguished between entrepreneurs who provided capital versus those who relied on their own labor and resources. "Each was an entrepreneur to Cantillon, which suggested an entrepreneurial role independent of the capitalist's role."[3]

For Quesnay, an entrepreneur was "simply a tenant farmer who rents property at a fixed rent and produces a given output with given factors at given prices." Beaudeau, in 1797, and Turgot also recognized the risk-bearing element of the entrepreneur yet added the concepts of planning, supervising, organizing, and ownership.[4]

In England during this same time period, the concept of entrepreneurship evolved along with the Industrial Revolution of the sixteenth and seventeenth centuries, with its demands for expanding industrial skills, and the rise of the combination landowner/entrepreneur who exploited the resources on their lands. As early as 1697, Daniel DeFoe used the term "projector" in the sense of a "creative entrepreneur" and Postlethwayt's *Universal Dictionary of Trade and Commerce* (London, 1751-55) went a step further and introduced ethical notions. For example, the term "honest projector" included both the inventor and creative entrepreneur as compared to the "idle, roguish and enthusiastical projectors" whose activities reflected "whim and knavery."[5]

By this time, the term "undertaker", which originated in the sixteenth century and referred to contractors, usually large govenment contractors, had became synonymous with "projectors," serving as an English counterpart to the French term entrepreneur. Undertaker, by the middle of the eighteenth century became a name for a big businessman or an ordinary businessman. Eventually, by the time of Postlethwayt and Adam Smith, the term undertaker was reserved primarily for the arranger of funerals. The term gave way to the term capitalist which toward the end of the nineteenth century again gave way to the term entrepreneur.[6] Adam Smith, however, did make passing references to both the undertaker and the projector, and identified the capitalist as one who risked his wealth in establishing a business, yet "his discussion of profits on stock tended to confuse any possible distinction between the pure interest of the capitalist and the pure profit of the entrepreneur."[7]

In the beginning of the nineteenth century, the French political economist, Jean Baptiste Say, criticized Adam Smith for not separating the profits of the entrepreneur from the profits of capital[8] and proceeded to outline his own thoughts on the subject.

Unfortunately, thereafter theorists virtually ignored the entrepreneur for most of the remainder of the nineteenth century. Classical economists at this time made no distinction between the manager and the entrepreneur, between the person who brought necessary resources together, land, labor, and capital, and the person who put these resources to work for himself. Classical economics had a fixation during this period on automatic and impersonal market forces--forces in which the entrepreneur either did not fit or remained an invisible figure.

As more theorists challenged classical theory and a more activist view of human forces in economics developed, there appeared a more focused view on the entrepreneur. In 1876, the American economist, Francis A. Walker, clearly outlined the distinction between those who supplied funds and took their profits in interest (the capitalists) and those whose profit was the compensation for capable managerial abilities (the entrepreneurs). Walker cited "the new captains of industry as the principal agents of production and industrial process."[9]

This distinction, although recognized in the nineteenth century, did not take hold in the literature until 1933, with its appearance in Adolph Berle and Gardiner Means, *The Modern Corporation and Private Property*. The authors ably demonstrated that in most U.S. corporations the owners (stockholders) played no direct role in managing the business and that the managers generally held insignificant amounts of stock.[10] It was at this point that it became obvious that classical theories of economics and management had little, if anything, to do with understanding the behavior of entrepreneurship. It is from this realization that modern scholars have taken their roots and have consequently developed ways to view and understand the concept of entrepreneurs as separate and distinct from the concept of managers.

The dean of the modern scholars was Joseph Schumpeter, whose writings on the topic first appeared in 1934. Schumpeter introduced the notion of entrepreneur as innovator. "Everyone is an entrepreneur only when he actually 'carries out new combinations,' and loses that character as soon as he has built up this business." He is motivated by "the joy of creating, of getting things done."[11] In addition to defining the entrepreneur as the indispensible motivating force which spurred economic growth, Schumpeter characterized entrepreneurs as "very special managers with rare aptitudes for generating continuing uniqueness." He observed that since an entrepreneurial act tends soon to be neutralized by market forces, entrepreneurs were those who could "create continuing monopolies by sustaining patterns of innovative combinations of resources to maintain disequilibrium."[12]

Another evolution in the concept was introduced by Arthur H. Cole, who established the Research Center for Entrepreneurial History at Harvard in 1948. Cole's entrepreneur was essentially an "organization builder," and his entrepreneurship was not limited to a single individual. Cole defined entrepreneurship as "the purposeful activity (including an integrated sequence of decisions) of an individual or group of associated individuals, undertaken to initiate, maintain, or aggrandize a profit-oriented business unit for the production or distribution of economic goods and services."[13].

Instead of limiting research to the proven path of internal management of individual American firms, the Center was to practice no unity of subject or method. In this regard, the field of entrepreneurial study would have almost unlimited boundaries. From this, Redlich distinguished between primary and derivative innovations, as well as subjective and objective ones and Jenks took a sociological approach believing that entrepreneurship tried to account not "for the performance of particular individuals" but rather "for the performance of similar functions by a considerable number of individuals."[14] Cochran added to this sociological approach and explored the relationships between social role and social sanctions in an effort to understand what an entrepreneur did and why he did it.[15]

Within the last twenty years, many scholars have taken the concept of entrepreneurship and fine-tuned it to deal with entrepreneurship within a corporation. In this "internal perspective," one finds different departments of a corporation performing the exact functions once reserved for the traditional entrepreneurial owner-operator, yet now without the extreme degree of personal risk. Chandler, for instance, attributes entrepreneuial functions to only the very top tier of executives who control capital allocations and long-range strategy. John Sawyer (1958) would expand that decision to argue that entrepreneurial behavior can be found in a whole range of functions from "the purely innovative to the purely routine," involving every decision which affects the allocation of resources under conditions where the outcome is not known.

Just as the concept of entrepreneurship has evolved to reflect the preeminence of the corporate world in economic affairs, so it will continue to evolve to embrace new realities. As the need to foster and promote entrepreneurship becomes more urgent, so does the need to understand what it is and how it operates in a variety of situations.

EXCERPTS FROM THE LITERATURE ON THE MEANING OF ENTREPRENEURSHIP

This section presents a compendium of definitions on entrepreneurs and entrepreneurship. Its strength is that it provides you with the author's actual words; its weakness, as with all excerpted material, is that the words are lifted from their broader context. The sources are noted, however, should you wish to investigate this broader context. The precise page(s) from where the excerpts are drawn are shown in parentheses at the end of each citation.

JEAN BAPTISTE SAY

1803

"(an entrepreneur) to succeed, he must have judgement, perserverance, and a knowledge of the world as well as of business. He must possess the art of superintendence and administration."

(Say, *A Treatise of Political Economy,* New York: Kelley, 1827, p. 295.)

1815

". . .as the agent who unites all means of production and who finds in the value of the products. . .the re-establishment of the entire capital he employs, and the value of the wages, the interest and the rent which he pays, as well as the profits belonging to himself."

(Say, *Catechism of Political Economy,* London: Sherwood, 1816, p. 28-29.)

RICHARD T. ELY AND RALPH H. HESS

1893

"In actual life the factors or agents of production are almost infinite in number, but to simplify the analysis of production the economist has grouped them in four categories or classes: *labor, land, capital,* and the *enterpriser* or *entrepreneur.* The last, a particularly elusive term, is applied to the ultimate owners of business enterprises, those who make the final decisions and assume the risks involved in such decisions. Corresponding to these four factors are the four basic *shares* in the distribution of the product: *wages, rent, interest,* and *profits.*" (p. 95)

"Economists have consequently resorted to the French language for a word to designate *the person or group of persons who assume the task and responsibility of combining the factors of production into a business organization and keeping this organization in operation.* They are called *entrepreneurs, or enterprisers.* The entrepreneur has been called a 'captain of industry,' for he commands the industrial forces, and upon him rests the responsibility for their success or failure." (p. 113).

"Briefly stated, the *entrepreneur* organizes and operates an enterprise for personal gain. He pays current contract prices for the materials consumed in the business, for the use of land, for the personal services he employs, and for the capital he requires. He contributes his own initiative, skill, and ingenuity in planning, organizing, and administering the enterprise. He also assumes the chance of loss and gain consequent to unforseen and uncontrollable circumstances. The net residue of the annual receipts of the enterprise, after all costs have been paid, he retains for himself." (p. 488)

(Ely and Hess, *Outlines of Economics,* New York: MacMillan, 1937, Sixth Edition.)

FREDERICK LAVINGTON

1922

"In modern times the entrepreneur assumes many forms. He may be a private business man, a partnership, a joint stock company, a cooperative society, a municipality or similar body."

(Lavington, *Trade Cycle: An Account of the Causes Producing Rhythmical Changes in the Activity of Business.* Vol. III. London: P.S. King, 1922, p. 19.)

JOSEPH SCHUMPETER

1934

". . .the function of entrepreneurs is to reform or revolutionize the pattern of production by exploiting an invention or, more generally, an untried technological possibility for producing a new commodity or producing an old one in a new way, by opening up a new source of supply of materials or a new outlet for products, by reorganizing an industry and so on."

"This function does not essentially consist in either inventing anything or otherwise altering the conditions which the enterprise exploits. It consists in getting things done."

(Schumpeter, *Can Capitalism Survive?,* New York: Harper and Row, 1950, p. 72.)

1934

". . .entrepreneurship, as defined, essentially, consists in doing things that are not generally done in the ordinary course of business routine, it is essentially a phenomenon that comes under the wider aspect of leadership." (p. 254)

"I have always emphasized that the entrepreneur is the man who gets new things done and not necessarily the man who invents." (p. 261)

"It has been emphasized above that when we speak of the entrepreneur we do not mean so much a physical person as we do a function, but even if we look at individuals who at least at some juncture in their lives fill the entrepreneurial function it should be added that these individuals do not form a social class." (p. 263)

"Finally, as has been often pointed out, the entrepreneurial function need not be embodied in a physical person and in particular in a single physical person. Every social environment has its own ways of filling the entrepreneurial function."

Richard V. Clemence, Editor, *Essays of J.A. Schumpeter,* "Change and the Entrepreneur," pp. 63-84, Addison-Wesley Press, 1951, p. 255.)

ARTHUR COLE

1959

". . .the purposeful activity (including an integrated sequence of decisions) of an individual or group of associated individuals, undertaken to initiate, maintain, or aggrandize a profit-oriented business unit for the production or distribution of economic goods and services." (p. 7)

"Although the word "entrepreneurship" will usually be used to indicate function or activity, occasionally I may use it to signify the commonality of entrepreneurs. By this I have in mind the aggregate of individuals performing that function or carrying on that activity in a given time and place, or even over considerable periods of time. . . ." (p. 9)

". . .decision-making is the critical or key operation in entrepreneurship, and even in singleman proprietorships the head of the enterprise rarely decides by himself, that is, under circumstances where the original suggestion or some later advice has not come from subordinates or staff. Effective administration is a necessary condition for innovation or other creative action by businessmen; and it is true that usually administration activity must also be shared by the individual entrepreneur." (p. 10)

". . .that entrepreneurship is interested in the economic and social significance of business procedures and institutions, whereas business administration must also give attention to their instrumental qualities." (p. 12)

"The entrepreneur looks toward an indefinite future, to a growth, a development, at least a continuation." (p. 14)

"Entrepreneurship, at least in all non-authoritarian societies, constitutes a bridge between society as a whole, especially the non-economic aspects of that society, and the profit-oriented institutions established to take advantage of its economic endowments and to satisfy, as best they can, its economic desires."

"What talent will be attracted into entrepreneurial activity, how well this talent will perform its function, and, to a considerable extent in modern societies, even how the national product will be shared -- all of these questions are determined by the combination of social and technical forces, most of them changing with more or less rapidity, and all having initial impingement upon, or receiving initial impetus from, the entrepreneurial actors." (p. 27-28)

(Cole, *Business Enterprise in its Social Setting,* Cambridge: Harvard University Press, 1959.)

DAVID McCLELLAND

1961

An entrepreneur was defined as "someone who exercises some control over the means of production and produces more than he can consume in order to sell (or exchange) it for individual (or household) income." (p. 65)

"Characteristics of entrepreneurship"

I. Entrepreneurial role behavior

    A. Moderate risk-taking as a function of skill not chance; decisive

    B. Energetic and/or novel instrumental activity

    C. Individual responsibility

    D. Knowledge of results of decisions

    E. Money as a measure of results

    F. Anticipation of future possibilities

    G. Organizational skills

II. Interest in entrepreneurial occupations as a function of their prestige and 'riskiness' (p. 207)

(McClelland, *The Achieving Society,* New York: MacMillan, 1961.)

ALFRED CHANDLER

1962

"The executives who actually allocate available resources are then the key men in any enterprise. Because of their critical role in the modern economy, they will be defined in this study as entrepreneurs. In contrast, those who coordinate, appraise, and plan within the means allocated to them will be termed managers. So *entrepreneurial* decisions and actions will refer to those which effect the allocation or reallocation of resources for the enterprise as a whole, and *operating* decisions and actions will refer to those which are carried out by using the resources already allocated." (p. 12)

"Their decisions may be made without forward planning or analysis but rather by meeting in an *ad hoc* way every new situation, problem, or crisis as it arises. They accept the goals of their enterprise as given or inherited." (p. 12)

Chandler, *Strategy and Structure: Chapters in the History of the American Industrial Enterprise,* Cambridge: MIT Press, 1961.)

HUGH AITKEN

1963

"To the extent that behavior in a business firm is organized (formally or informally), to that extent we have entrepreneurship; to the extent that it is disorganized, random or self-defeating, to that extent entrepreneurship is lacking. . . .The characteristics conventionally associated with entrepreneurship -- leadership, innovation, risk-bearing, and so on -- are so associated precisely because they are essential features of effective business organization."

(The Future of Entrepreneurial Research. *Explorations in Entrepreneurial History,* Second Series 1, p. 6.)

PETER F. DRUCKER

1964

"Resources, to produce results, must be allocated to opportunities rather than to problems. Needless to say, one cannot shrug off all problems, but they can and should be minimized."

"Economists talk about the maximization of profit in business. This, as countless critics have pointed out, is so vague a concept as to be meaningless. But 'maximization of opportunities' is a meaningful, indeed a precise, definition of the entrepreneurial job. It implies that effectiveness rather than efficiency is essential in business. The pertinent question is not how to do things right but how to find the right things to do, and to concentrate resources and efforts on them." (p. 6)

From *Managing for Results,* by Peter F. Drucker, New York: Harper and Row, 1964.

KIRK DRAHEIM

1966

". . .the active initiator of a new enterprise in the form of a new company. He plays a major role in starting the company and managing it, and usually has an important equity position in it."

(Draheim, Howell and Shapero, *The Development of a Potential Defense R&D Complex: A Study of Minneapolis-St. Paul,* Menlo Park, CA: Stanford Research Institute, 1966.)

WILLIAM BAUMOL

1968

"The entrepreneur (whether or not he is in fact also doubles as a manager) has a different function. It is his job to locate his new ideas and to put them into effect. He must lead, perhaps even inspire; he cannot allow things to get into a rut and for him today's practice is never good enough for tomorrow. In short, he is the Schumpeterian innovator and some more. He is the individual who exercises what in the business literature is called 'leadership.'"

(Baumol, "Entrepreneurship in Economic Theory," *American Economic Review,* May 1968, p. 65.)

ORVIS COLLINS AND DAVID G. MOORE

1970

"The independent entrepreneur is a man who has created out of nothing an ongoing enterprise." (85)

"Organization making, like an art, requires long and rigorous training. It also requires something more. It requires strong drive and well reinforced attitudes. This is true for men who create organizational extensions, but especially true for men who build organizations from scratch."

(Collins and Moore, *The Organization Makers,* New York: Appleton-Century-Crofts, 1970, p. 85.)

JOHN A. HORNADAY AND JOHN ABOUD

1971

"Compared to men in general, entrepreneurs are significantly higher on scales reflecting need for achievement, independence, and effectiveness of their leadership, and are low on scales reflecting emphasis on need for support." (p. 147)

..."the 'successful entrepreneur' was defined as a man or woman who *started* a business where there was none before". . . . (p. 143)

(Hornaday and Aboud, "Characteristics of Successful Entrepreneurs," *Personnel Psychology,* Volume 24, Number 2 - Summer 1971.)

PETER F. DRUCKER

1974

"...*an entrepreneur*...has to redirect resources from areas of low or diminishing results to areas of high or increasing results. He has to slough off yesterday and to render obsolete what already exists and is already known. He has to create tomorrow." (p. 45)

"The specific job of entrepreneurship in business enterprise is to make today's business capable of making the future, of making itself into a different business. It is the specific job of entrepreneurship in the going business to enable today's already existing — and especially today's already successful — business to remain existing and to remain successful in the future." (p. 47)

(Drucker, *Management, Tasks, Responsibilities, Practices,* New York Harper and Row, 1974).

JUSTIN G. LONGENECKER AND JOHN E. SCHOEN

1975

"The point is that entrepreneurs evaluate situations in terms that are meaningful to them, some of which are distinctly non-financial and which defy quantification, and then they act." (p. 28)

"The entrepreneur must have the autonomy to determine objectives and the time to search the environment and organization for opportunities. He must have the discretion to initiate and design projects. The entrepreneur must also be able to gain the confidence of key constituencies, commit resources, assess and decide between ventures, work outside normal channels, and control or supervise resources after their commitment."

(Longenecker and Schoen, "The Essence of Entrepreneurship," *Journal of Small Business Management,* Volume 13-N3, July 1975, p. 29)

ALBERT SHAPERO

1975

"In almost all of the definitions of entrepreneurship, there is agreement tht we are talking about a kind of behavior that includes: (1) initiative taking, (2) the organizing or reorganizing of social/economic mechanisms to turn resources and situations to practical account, (3) the acceptance of risk of failure. A major resource utilized by the entrepreneur, is himself...."

(Shapero, *Entrepreneurship and Economic Development,* Wisconsin: Project ISEED, LTD, The Center for Venture Management, Summer 1975, p. 187)

HARVEY LEIBENSTEIN

1978

"We may distinguish two broad types of entrepreneurial activity: at one pole there is routine entrepreneurship, which is really a type of management; and at the other end of the spectrum, we have Schumpeterian or 'innovational' entrepreneurship. By routine entrepreneurship we mean the activities involved in coordinating and carrying on a well-established, going concern in which the parts of the production function in use (and likely alternatives to current use) are well known for a firm which operates in well-established and clearly defined markets. By innovational entrepreneurship we mean the activities necessary to create (or carry on) an enterprise where not all the markets are well established or clearly defined and/or in which the relevant parts of the production function are not completely known. In both the routine and the innovative cases, the entrepreneur coordinates activities that involve different markets; he is an *intermarket* operator. But in the case of innovational entrepreneurship not all of the markets exist or operate perfectly and the entrepreneur, if he is to be successful, must fill in for the market deficiencies." (pp. 40-41)

"The entrepreneur is (1) a *gap filler* and (2) an *input completer.*" (p. 46)

(Leibenstein, *General X-Efficiency Theory and Economic Development,* New York: Oxford University Press, (1978).

KARL VESPER

1980

"The entrepreneur's role can be drawn in many forms and tends to appear different from different perspectives. To an economist an entrepreneur is one who brings resources, labor, materials, and other assets into combinations that make their value greater than before, and also one who introduces changes, innovations, and new order. To a psychologist, such a person is typically one driven by certian forces -- need to obtain or attain something, to experiment, to accomplish, or perhaps to escape authority of others. The unfavorably inclined politician may see an entrepreneur as one who is devious and hard to control, whereas a favorably inclined politician sees the same person as one who finds effective ways to get things done. To one businessman, the entrepreneur appears as a threat, an aggressive competitor, whereas to another businessman the same entrepreneur may be an ally, a source of supply, a customer, or someone good to invest in. To a communist philosopher, the entrepreneur may be a predator, one who usurps resources and exploits the labor of others. The same person is seen by a capitalist philosopher as one who creates wealth for others as well, who finds better ways to utilize resources and reduce waste, and who produces jobs others are glad to get."

(Vesper, *New Venture Strategies,* New Jersey: Prentice-Hall, 1980, p. 2)

NICHOLAS A.H. STACEY

1980

"Certainly at the outset of his career, the traditional entrepreneur's greatest gift is his ability to explore numerous avenues to ensure success, without becoming disheartened by failure along the way; one of his gifts is to cut his losses quickly, and another to pick himself up from the floor, dust himself down and try again."

(Stacey, *The Sociology of the Entrepreneur,* Canada: McMaster University, 1980.)

HANS SCHOLLHAMMER

1980

Regarding corporate entrepreneuring, there are five types...

"Administrative Entrepreneurship - This is the traditional R&D management approach. The development of new products or techniques or the improvement of existing ones is, in essence, perceived as a sequential, controllable, manageable process which involves the division of functional responsibilities between scientific-technical personnel (who are expected to use their expertise for the discovery of new knowledge, new products or techniques) and managers/administrators (who are expected to select viable domains of R&D activities, secure required resources and maintain an effective R&D organization)."

"Opportunistic Entrepreneurship - The corporate effort is directed toward scanning and surveillance of internal as well as external technological developments for the purpose of detecting and adopting promising innovative achievements. The emphasis is placed on the exploitation of perceived opportunities and their potential contribution to the company's growth and profit objectives. The involvement of a 'product champion' is generally an indication of an 'opportunistic' approach to internal entrepreneurship."

"Acquisitive Entrepreneurship - In this case internal entrepreneurship is exercised by means of acquiring other companies' technical capabilities in order to gain access to innovative technological developments which may provide a basis for accelerated growth, diversification, horizontal or vertical integration."

"Incubative Entrepreneurship - This approach to internal entrepreneurship stresses the formation of semi-autonomous units within the existing enterprise for the explicit purpose of initiating and nurturing new venture developments. These 'venture development units' as they are frequently referred to are thus intended as incubators for innovative, high-risk business endeavors and for providing an environment that is supportive of entrepreneurial efforts."

"Imitative Entrepreneurship - This approach stresses the replication or creative imitation of innovative technical achievements made by another firm (with appropriate modifications or refinements in case protected property rights are involved). An executive characterized this particular approach to internal entrepreneurship as 'learning from the innovator's heartaches and prospering by refinement.' In essence, it is innovative imitation and the internalization of externally made technological developments."

(Schollhammer, *Analysis and Assessment of Internal Corporate Entrepreneurship Strategies,* CA: Graduate School of Management, UCLA, 1980.)

GORDON BATY

1981

". . .neither innovative genius, nor hard work, not even luck is in itself a guarantee of corporate success. Assuming that all of these are present in the new venture in at least trace quantities, the missing catalytic element often seems to be what we might call the 'entrepreneurial state of mind.' It might be characterized as a degree of tough-mindedness that stops somewhere short of truculence; a confidence in one's intuitive as well as one's rational faculties, a capacity to think tactically on one's feet, as well as to plan strategically in the business school sense; an attitude which stresses timely action based on frequently inadequate information, ahead of prolonged fact-finding; a mental set stressing integration of many facts into action plans, rather than endless differentiation and analysis. It is an attitude that says, in short: 'I didn't just come to play the game -- *I came to win.*'"

"If winning, then, is to be our goal, how shall we define it? Allow me the following provisional definition: The entrepreneur shall have 'won' when he succeeds in bringing his firm to a position where, in order to continue the growth of sales and earnings a substantial infusion of new capital is required." (p. xi)

"Roughly defined, the entrepreneurial tasks involved the *setting up, planning* and *motivational* activities of the firm." (p. 178)

(Baty, *Entrepreneurship for the Eighties*, Virginia: Reston Publishing, 1981.)

THE CONCEPT OF ENTREPRENEURSHIP IN THE FUTURE

Entrepreneurship means many different things when the various definitions shown on the previous pages are considered individually. However, the definitions are not mutually exclusive and, when taken together, they reveal our expanding conception of entrepreneurship. Given this evolving and expanding nature of the concept, one is tempted to ask, what will entrepreneurship mean in the future?

Whatever developments occur, I cannot help but feel they will be influenced heavily by the growing and unprecedented acceptance of entrepreneurship. More than one observer has already spoken about the emergence during this decade of an entrepreneurial renaissance.[16] This prediction is accurate in the sense that it may reflect a "revival or rebirth" of increased entrepreneurial activity among independent entrepreneurs. Yet endorsement of entrepreneurial pursuits exists not only among independent practitioners but other groups as well who have resisted "entrepreneurism" in the past.

For example, entrepreneurship is being embraced officially by corporate executives of established larger organizations for the first time. Even Fortune 500 companies have come to realize that entrepreneurs play a critical role -- not just in the formation of new enterprises but in the growth and development of existing ones. This acceptance comes from the realization that the "professional managers" of the 1960s and 1970s have focused too much on efficiency concerns and problem solving as opposed to seeking new opportunities. Similarly, they have been overly concerned with shorter term issues compared to longer term effectiveness. While no less a commentator than Peter Drucker voiced these concerns during the mid-1960s, it is only recently that top corporate executives have begun to listen earnestly to the call for entrepreneurial managers.[17] Thus far the use of entrepreneurs in corporate settings to create new businesses has met with mixed results. My guess is that as entrepreneurs are used in new ways within corporate settings the concept of entrepreneurship itself will undergo some change.

The emergence of intellectual legitimacy for entrepreneurial studies within the academic community also represents a historical first. It is not a renaissance but a new beginning. The acceptance of entrepreneurship within the academic community is, of course, far from complete.[18] However, an intellectual bridge is being built which will help to fuel the institutionalization of entrepreneurship within future societies. Certain issues are becoming clearer here to scholars. Organizational size alone is not the critical issue. The critical issue is the presence or nonpresence of entrepreneurship in every organization. In and of itself "small is not beautiful."[19] Rather it is "entrepreneurship that is beautiful."

Why is entrepreneurship so attractive from an intellectual perspective? Why is it being accepted and legitimized not only in the world of commerce, but in the world of ideas? I believe the answer lies in the development of the concept itself which reflects our growing knowledge about the entrepreneurial process. And as this knowledge grows, so does our appreciation of the pervasive importance of the entrepreneurial function in many different sectors of society. But this importance is not true just of our own society, but of all societies throughout the course of human history.[20] Entrepreneurship is a kind of revolving constant which is present to some extent in all phases of economic and political growth. We know, for instance, that entrepreneurship functions in varying degrees in traditional societies as well as complex, modern ones . . . of its links to leadership, creativity, innovation, and change. And we have every reason to believe the extent of its existence plays a critical role in human and social development. Entrepreneurs brought mankind out of the Dark Ages. Entrepreneurs sparked the Industrial Revolution. They have defeated Marxism and will continue to do so. Stagnant, bureaucratic capitalism will be replaced increasingly by decentralized, socially responsive forms of entrepreneurial capitalism.

Where will this power come from? How will entrepreneurs transcend the most potent political and economic ideologies known to mankind? The answer becomes clearer with each passing day. Entrepreneurship is not only the core of the American Dream but potentially anyone's dream. Entrepreneurism is a World Dream of challenge, development, and independence that runs through the thread of history. It is a historical process that is still evolving. But it is also a human process experienced in a unique way by every entrepreneur that pursues an entrepreneurial career. It is the David Lockwoods of the world, proclaiming with pride and courage for all to hear, "I am an entrepreneur."

QUESTIONS FOR DISCUSSION

1) *Before* reading this chapter, write down your definition of a) entrepreneurship; b) who is an entrepreneur.

2) After reading this chapter, expand or amend your definitions if you have not done so previously.

3) Note what you feel are some common approaches to the definition of entrepreneurship.

4) What do you think entrepreneurship will mean in the future?

KEY READINGS

For those seeking more information on the history of entrepreneurship, I suggest:

Harold C. Livesay, "Entrepreneurial History," and Albro Martin, "Additional Aspects of Entrepreneurial History," in *Encyclopedia of Entrepreneurship,* edited by Kent, Sexton, Vesper, Prentice-Hall, 1982, pp 7-19.

Entrepreneurship from the social science perspective is treated by:

Peter Kilby "Hunting the Heffalump," *Entrepreneurship and Economic Development,* The Free Press, 1971, p. 1-40.

Other perspectives are provided by:

Edwin Harwood, "The Entrepreneurial Renaissance and Its Promoters," *Society,* March/April 1979, pp 27-31, and:

Albert Shapero, "Are Business Schools Teaching Business?" *Inc. Magazine,* January 1982, pp 13-14.

FOOTNOTES

[1]Israel M. Kirzner, *Perception, Opportunity, and Profit: Studies In the Theory of Entrepreneurship* (Chicago: The University of Chicago Press, 1979), p. 39.

[2]B.F. Hoselitz, "The Early History of Entrepreneurial Theory," *Explorations in Entrepreneurial History* 3, no. 4 (April 1951), p. 194 ff.

[3]William R. Sandberg and Charles W. Hofer, *A Strategic Management Perspective on the Determinants of New Venture Success* (Unpublished research paper), p. 3

[4]Israel M. Kirzner, *op. cit.,* p. 39.

[5]F. Redlich, "The Origins of the Concepts of 'Entrepreneur' and 'Creative Entrepreneur,'" *Explorations in Entrepreneurial History* 1, no. 2 (February 1949), p. 3 ff.

[6]Israel M. Kirzner, *op. cit., p. 38.*

[7]*Ibid.,* p. 40.

[8]J.B. Say, *Traite d'economie politique,* 6th ed. (Paris: Guillaumin, impression of 1876), pp. 84 n (cited by Cannan, *Review of Economic Theory,* p. 308).

[9]"Entrepreneur," *Encyclopedia Americana,* p. 478.

[10]Adolph Berle and Gardiner Means, *The Modern Corporation and Private Property* (New York: Harcourt Brace, 1967), Chapter VI.

[11]Schumpeter, quoted in Harbison & Meyers, *Management in the Industrial World,* McGraw Hill, 1959, p. 18.

[12]Daryl Mitton, "Defining Entrepreneurship -- One More Time," 27th World Congress on Small Business, Knoxville, 1982.

[13]Arthur Cole, *Business Enterprise in its Social Setting,* Cambridge: Harvard University Press, 1959, p. 7.

[14]F. Redlich, "Innovation in Business: A Systematic Presentation," *American Journal of Economics and Society,* 1950, pp. 289-91. Also,

Leland H. Jenks, "Approaches to Entrepreneurial Personality," *E.E.H.,* Winter, 1966, pp. 75-100.

[15]Research Center in Entrepreneurial History, Harvard University, *Change and the Entrepreneur: Postulates and Patterns for Entrepreneurial History* (Cambridge, 1949).

[16]See Edwin Harwood's "The Entrepreneurial Renaissance and its Promotors," *Society,* March/April, 1979, pp 27-31.

[17]See Peter F. Drucker, *Managing For Results,* New York, Harper and Row, 1964 pp 5-8. More recent declarations along the same theme are: Thomas J. Peters and Robert H. Waterman's *In Search of Excellence.* New York: Warner Books, 1983, and

Rosabeth Kanter's *The Change Makers: Innovation for Productivity in the American Corporation.* New York: Simon and Shuster, 1983.

[18]Albert Shapero notes some of the underlying barriers in his article, "Are Business Schools Teaching Business?" *Inc. Magazine,* January, 1982.

[19]The reference is to C. Shumaker's *Small is Beautiful.* London: Abacus, 1973.

[20]See Peter Kilby's, *Entrepreneurship and Economic Development,* New York: Free Press, 1981.

ON ENTREPRENEURSHIP, ITS MYTHS, AND ENTREPRENEURIAL PERSPECTIVE

The various definitions of entrepreneurship reproduced in the preceding chapter reflect the change and development of economic, social, and political life over the past two centuries. The definitions, taken together, encompass a vast breadth of human activity. For instance, entrepreneurship can mean routine as well as innovative activity. It can include the creation of an entity as well as its ongoing management and development as an enterprise. It can be done by one or more than one individual. It may be limited to one venture or many ventures. It may involve individuals working under the umbrella of an existing organization or those working independently or autonomously to create a new entity from scratch. It may occur for business or non-business purposes. It may erupt spontaneously or be carefully planned and managed. It may exist for long periods of time, evaporate all too quickly, or perhaps not soon enough.

But one thing is certain--as certain as we can be about nonphysical phenomena which cannot be measured precisely--while entrepreneurship remains elusive, it is an essential element of economic, social, and political life. Entrepreneurship may even be "the" essential element, for where it is lacking, we know that economic development, social progress, and political freedom are retarded or nonexistent.[1]

ENTREPRENEURSHIP IS THE PROCESS OF CREATING WEALTH

The importance of entrepreneurship exists for one simple reason, one that perhaps because of its simplicity, we tend to overlook: "entrepreneuring" is, and always will be, the crucial act in the creation of wealth. Successful entrepreneurship means nothing less than the creation of wealth. There can be no significant wealth nor major increase in the level of wealth without entrepreneurship.

How does one substantiate this claim? First, let us start with "big business." We know, for example, that every Fortune 500 company was started and developed by one or more entrepreneurs. These founders engineered the major advances over the years and were assisted by later generations of "corporate entrepreneurs," who were effectively "successors without portfolio."

Yet these founders and corporate entrepreneurs of large businesses represent no more than a small minority of all entrepreneurs and all businesses. It is rather the thousands upon thousands of entrepreneurs who have started, acquired, or franchised their own independent organizations that represent the bulwark of the American economy. We know they account for the lion's share of new jobs, a disproportionate share of new innovations, plus high shares of exports and taxes per every dollar of invested capital.[2]

All these contributions and much more make entrepreneurs our most precious resource. . . for in the end they determine, more than any other group or asset, the quantity and quality of other resources that are utilized to fuel our economy, generate productivity, and insulate our currency from other non-wealth creating activities. And whether these latter activities are for military expenditures to protect our freedoms, or welfare payments to protect the less fortunate, or cultural contributions to fund the arts, or any other "non-wealth" creating expenditure, the magnitude and growth of such expenditures are financed ultimately by entrepreneurs.

ENTREPRENEURSHIP DEFINED

> Entrepreneurship is the dynamic process of creating incremental wealth. This wealth is created by individuals who assume the major risks in terms of equity, time, and/or career commitment of providing value for some product or service. The product or service itself may or may not be new or unique but value must somehow be infused by the entrepreneur by securing and allocating the necessary skills and resources.

It is only through the ongoing process of infusing or creating value in a product or service that an activity becomes "entrepreneurial." It is, after all, what distinguishes entrepreneurs from investors, most managers, all extortionists, or others who reap some kind of profit or reward for their actions, legal or otherwise. To be an entrepreneur, one must provide honest value or be directly responsible for the value that is conveyed to the user of a product or service.

ECONOMIC ENTREPRENEURSHIP

I have defined entrepreneurship in very broad terms because the concept itself encompasses a wide range of activities. It is not our purpose, nor should it be, to exclude some of these functions from consideration. For example, some have viewed entrepreneurship and entrepreneurs--not incorrectly but more narrowly--as "organization makers."[3] Yet some "solo" entrepreneurs perform entrepreneurial acts without ever creating an organization *per se* and other entrepreneurs have the organization "made" or "created" for them by others. Of course, even a general introduction must draw a line somewhere and while we can discuss political entrepreneurs or social entrepreneurs (e.g., John Gardner, founder of Common Cause) within the boundaries of our definition, our focus is centered very definitely in the economic sphere. Our main concern then is economic entrepreneurship and the creation of economic value and economic wealth, but with the full realization that, at times, economic concerns unavoidably mingle with social and political issues.

THE NEED FOR AN ENTREPRENEURIAL PERSPECTIVE

An entrepreneurial perspective will help you to infuse economic value into the products and services you offer to your customers. In other words, it will help you to create wealth. In fact, an entrepreneurial perspective will allow you to determine how and what type of wealth you will attempt to produce as an entrepreneur. It will help you to define the kind of entrepreneur you want to be, can be, and even should be.

In my view, an entrepreneurial perspective is a critical component for helping you to improve your odds of experiencing entrepreneurial success. Can you be a successful entrepreneur without an entrepreneurial perspective? Yes you can. You might even become an entrepreneurial "failure" with it. Lady Luck does exist. But my belief is that armed with an entrepreneurial perspective, much more often than not, you will better realize your entrepreneurial aspirations and avoid the more serious pitfalls posed by an entrepreneurial career.

One purpose of this book is to help you understand the entrepreneurial process as it exists in many different guises and contexts so you can maximize your ability to create wealth. In this regard, my main objective is to help you to develop an entrepreneurial perspective which will improve your future capabilities as an entrepreneur. Should you decide against an entrepreneurial career, this perspective will at least improve your ability to understand and work with entrepreneurs in the future. But before proceeding any further, we need "to wipe the slate clean" by erasing some misconceptions about how effective entrepreneurs think and act. What follows are some specific myths and fallacies about entrepreneurs that can hinder or completely block your attempt to develop an entrepreneurial perspective.

THE MYTH THAT ENTREPRENEURS ARE DOERS, NOT THINKERS

All of us, of course, must decide whether we wish to operate on a principle of knowledge versus intuition and emotionally-based action when it comes to entrepreneurial pursuits. Our philosophic traditions favor a knowledge-based approach. Yet within the folklore of entrepreneurship, a tradition exists which essentially eschews a knowledge-based, thinking approach. Let me label these proponents the "Do-it" group. Their advice is essentially as follows:

> Don't think about it--at least for very long--just get out and
> do it. Entrepreneurs are doers, not thinkers.

They are only half right. And some entrepreneurs have experienced considerable success following their advice. Often we hear about them. They are vocal about their triumphs and often hard to ignore. Many more, however, have failed or experienced needless hardship early in their entrepreneurial careers when they leaped into a venture with little forethought. They are not vocal. We rarely hear from them but their experiences are very real. In fact, we know from interviews, case studies, and other research sources that entrepreneurs who have been effective over long time periods are not mindless doers nor gamblers willing to risk all on a hunch and a throw of the dice.[4]

They are thinkers, often very good thinkers, who carefully calculate their moves before deciding to act. An untold portion of the story is, in fact, how often they decide *not* to act after making substantial investigations of new venture possibilities.

But when the array of facts favors action, they do act. This combined ability to think, to assess accurately a particular situation, and to act at the right moment does separate entrepreneurs from many others who, given the same position, will not move ahead nor implement the decision to provide a product or service for others. These individuals, and others, may assist the entrepreneur in the creation of wealth. But without the entrepreneur, without the individual who is both thinker and doer, without a thoughtful mover, very little that is good will happen to a society.

THE "ENTREPRENEURS ARE BORN--NOT MADE" MYTH

A good deal of evidence now exists which reinforces the notion that entrepreneurial traits and tendencies are acquired characteristics or learned behavior.[5] A variant of the "entrepreneurs are born" myth is that entrepreneurship can not be taught or learned. In fact, it always has been taught and learned except that the educational delivery system has been an informal one, built around an entrepreneurial father, some other family member, the commercial orientation of a particular town or region, the conditioning dictates of religious belief, or the needs and traditions of particular cultural groups. The truth of the matter is that entrepreneurs are made, forged by learning and experience. No one denies that a certain level of intelligence, energy, etc., is required. But depending on the type of venture and the support of a local environment, the ranges of intellect or energy required appear to be quite pronounced.

One is much better off thinking of these genetic factors as necessary conditions rather than sufficient ones. After all, a great many highly intelligent and energetic people never become entrepreneurs. And we have every indication to believe they would be utter failures if they did. Worry less about the traits you were born with--you can't do much about them anyway. Concern yourself more with those characteristics which you can influence and we know are at least generally important for entrepreneurial success.

THE MYTH OF THE "PURE" OR "TRUE" OR "CLASSIC" ENTREPRENEUR

This view implicitly assumes more than one kind of entrepreneur exists but that some particular type is better and/or more representative of the "entrepreneurial function" than others. For example, some observers believe that the "true" entrepreneur is the one who innovates some new product or service that was unavailable before. They are "the elect" or chosen few as represented in the shaded portion of Figure 1. Others are even more restrictive. They feel that only a special subset of innovating entrepreneurs are the "pure" entrepreneurs that should concern us. Called "high-tech" entrepreneurs, these entrepreneurial bluebloods are, in practice, a difficult group to pin down simply because the concept of "high technology" has never been adequately defined. Who should be included or excluded is very debatable and probably unresolvable.

A quite different view of the true or classic entrepreneur is held by those who feel only those "who have pulled themselves up by their bootstraps" qualify for membership. A kind of reverse discrimination exists here: if you haven't been poor, you can't belong. Too many exceptions exist to take this view seriously.

A fourth perception of the classic entrepreneur applies only to those entrepreneurs who are always starting new ventures. I like to refer to these individuals as "roll-over entrepreneurs" because they are continually "rolling-over" into new ventures. Some are effective; others are not over the long term. But, whether successful or not, the critical assumption under this view is that the entrepreneurial process is contained by or limited to the start-up function. But where, in fact, should we draw the entrepreneurial line of demarcation separating venture initiation from "ongoing operations?" The latter implies some kind of steady state and the absence of strategic change--an environment better suited for professional managers or at least one that no longer requires an entrepreneur. I doubt such an environment exists, or will exist for any length of time, or even *should* exist. Many effective entrepreneurs have never started more than one venture during very long and distinguished *entrepreneurial* careers. They have continued to assume entrepreneurial risks, sometimes in the name of growth and at other times, to preserve the entrepreneurial environment and way of life they created. L.L. Bean is an excellent example. Starting in 1906, Mr. Bean maintained a smaller though highly profitable venture for over five decades because, as he put it, "I already eat three good meals a day and couldn't eat a fourth."[6]

Other notions of the "pure" entrepreneur exist. All are debatable but, even more important, all have limited usefulness for analyzing entrepreneurial situations.

Figure 1
Innovators and Entrepreneurs

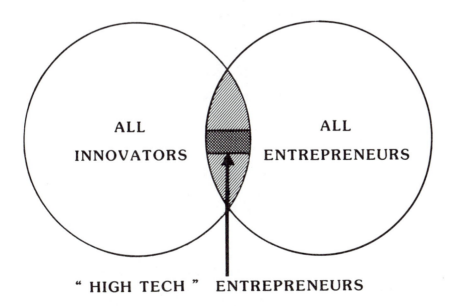

" HIGH TECH " ENTREPRENEURS

THE "ALL YOU NEED IS MONEY" MYTH

Some ventures invariably suffer, even fail, from undercapitalization and/or a lack of access to a plentiful source of inexpensive debt funds. Other ventures never start because a sufficient amount of debt or equity money is unavailable to prospective entrepreneurs. Nevertheless, in-depth scrutiny of specific cases indicates that money is used too often to explain a non-start or venture failure. However, its lack is generally a symptom of other fundamental problems or oversights, rather than a cause of them. I believe most successful entrepreneurs will agree that creativity and imagination *re* financial barriers are more important than "deep pockets" *per se*. The latter are nice and sometimes very necessary but they also represent an unimaginative and costly way out of difficulty when, in fact, a single, low-cost solution may exist. In fact, access to a ready supply of funds can be quite dangerous. The pitfalls of over-capitalization are just beginning to be appreciated by professionals in the field of entrepreneurial studies.[7] The dangers include salaries that are too large, outright embezzlement that proves to be too tempting, and the continued propping up or subsidizing of ventures that deserve to fail, or at least venture concept that should be changed.

And the longer I work with entrepreneurs and their ventures, the more I am struck by one simple fact: a great multiplicity of ways usually exists to put a venture together so that its startup and subsequent operation will have quite different cost structures and financial needs. Unfortunately, many entrepreneurs lock into one venture concept early in the pre-startup phase without considering variants that require less money.

THE "IGNORANCE IS BLISS" MYTH

The basic premise underlying this myth is lodged, to some extent, in all of us. For example, let's say you and I come up with a fantastic idea for a new business. After a round of cocktails, the idea no doubt looks even better. But the next day, the concept still seems great even after another hour or two of serious discussion. At this point, if no earlier, a little voice whispers within us and it says, "stop looking, stop examining--you'll only find negatives now. They always exist. Better not to know about them. They'll only stop you from starting the venture."

Unfortunately, this desire to stop analyzing is buttressed by folk wisdom spread by entrepreneurs--often younger ones (not chronologically but in terms of entrepreneurial experience) who claim all too loudly they would never have "done it" if they'd appreciated all the sacrifices, or identified all the negatives, or comprehended fully all they would need to do. Yet for every "folk hero," a thousand entrepreneurs or former entrepreneurs exist who wish they had looked harder--that they had grappled sooner with the negatives, and in the process discovered how to deal with them. Some of these ventures would not have been started, saving a great deal of subsequent heartache. But many others would still have been initiated, only on a stronger footing and with greater potential for success.

For, at the heart of the "ignorance is bliss" fallacy, is the misconception that a sound entrepreneurial venture has no negatives. In reality, no entrepreneurial venture, regardless of how good or timely the idea, is without them. Effective entrepreneurs do not play the ostrich. They identify the pros and the cons. Then they attempt to reduce or minimize the negatives. And they must have a feel, a perspective, for which negatives are fatal and which, despite the absence of ready solutions, are not mortal blows. Despite knowing the negatives, they are not stopped. Let us be up front here--at times, entrepreneurship takes considerable courage. It means proceeding when you know you haven't all the answers. Throughout this process, the danger of inaction by reason of overanalysis or "too much thinking," always exists. But few prospective entrepreneurs need fear this danger in my judgement. They are analogous to those few individuals who get severe reactions from penicillin. For most of us, the wonder drug means incredible benefits--the difference sometimes between life and death. So it is with a little more thought . . . even if it means discovering some camouflaged negatives.

THE "ENTREPRENEUR AS SOCIAL/ACADEMIC MISFIT" MYTH

Most myths have at least one kernel of truth and the myth that entrepreneurs tend mainly to be social and/or academic dropouts is no different. Some entrepreneurs do fit this profile. But so do some engineers, managers, salesmen, and scientists. My impression, based on a review of past studies plus my own work, is that the "misfit entrepreneur" has been overrated and blown all out of proportion. One can present evidence that entrepreneurs tend to be wanderers, low academic performers, individuals who can't hold down a job.[8] One can also present evidence that entrepreneurs are above-average performers in college, have strong family ties with a low incidence of divorce, and make considerable social contributions in terms of service to their communities.[9] Your particular findings depend mainly on sample size and the kinds of entrepreneurs being studied by a particular researcher. Earlier studies were limited in size (in terms of both the number and types of entrepreneurs studied plus the number of different geographic and demographic regions considered). These constraints plus other factors of study design account for what can be considered little more than random findings. Be suspicious of anyone who purports to have "the" profile of entrepreneurs. In fact, as we shall now discuss, there are many profiles.

THE MYTH OF "THE ENTREPRENEURIAL PROFILE"

Too many books on entrepreneurship do a tremendous disservice to prospective entrepreneurs. Invariably they start or contain some simple test or checklist which purports to tell you that you have or don't have the characteristics of an entrepreneur. In short, they hope to show you that you either fit the profile of an entrepreneur, or you don't.

In fact, there are a great many profiles because there are a great many different kinds of entrepreneurs. The range of types is very wide but the tests represent no more than a deceptive average, and probably the wrong average in most instances for you.

In a very real sense, the multiplicity of entrepreneurial types has confused and misled us simply because we have not recognized their various forms. We speak too often of entrepreneurs as if they were all lions or tigers. But they are probably as numerous and different as all the mammals of the animal kingdom. Of course, it's misleading to believe a cat is a lion or to identify and treat a tiger as a friendly dog. The consequences can be disastrous. Yet we do so everyday with entrepreneurs--and some of my fellow entrepreneurs are perhaps the worst offenders. Based on their singular experiences (an observation of "one" in statistical terms), they are too ready to advise one and all. But, what is sound advice for one entrepreneur can be death for another. With the best of intentions, others do even greater harm by putting their advice into print. Fortunately, a few have become serious students, drawing upon more than their personal experiences.[10] We can learn much from them.

Despite the potential for being misled, perhaps the true irony of the situation is that we can also learn from other entrepreneurs, if we are careful how we go about it. The Spanish have a saying that is appropriate here:

> En la tierra de los ciegos, el hombre que tiene un ojo es rey.
> (In the land of the blind, the man who has one eye is king.)

Entrepreneurs can help give you eyesight, especially when a one-on-one mentoring relationship develops. This type of relationship can prove particularly beneficial when you have joint interests in terms of similar business interests, similar goals, and perhaps even similar career interests. Practicing entrepreneurs often note, for instance, that the most instrumental person who helped them launch their entrepreneurial careers was another entrepreneur who was in a similar kind of business.[11]

But be wary of casual advice and be certain to size up who it is coming from. What do you have in common with XYZ entrepreneur, particularly in an industry and career sense? Are you moving along a similar entrepreneurial career pathway? Is this entrepreneur used to flying with ventures that can be characterized as single-engine aircraft? Or has he/she flown (over a short career) many different kinds of small planes. Perhaps the entrepreneur has only flown twin engine planes, or 747s, or F16s over most of his career. You are well advised to find out and make sure the advice and learning applies to your interests. Remember, in the wrong kind of plane, "one eye" can get you killed.

THE "ALL YOU NEED IS LUCK" MYTH

This belief sees entrepreneurial skill and knowledge as irrelevant or, at best, superfluous. What really counts is being at the right place at the right time.

One problem with this impression is that you can be at the right place at the right time and still lose. Furthermore, some individuals have an uncanny ability (or is it a skill?) to always be at the right place at the right time with the necessary capabilities to capitalize on the situation.

Still, chance and random events do exist and can affect us. With all the best intentions, you can also find yourself in the wrong place at the wrong time. Luck, whether good or bad, does influence our lives and careers.[12] The real issue is how to maximize good luck while minimizing its impact when it turns against us. In fact, this process is working when we describe someone as a person who "makes their luck." And to a large extent, an ability to make our luck detemines our effectiveness over the long haul.

But I do not mean to simply dismiss luck as something *potentially* under our control. The existence of imperfect knowledge makes such control impossible. When knowledge is exceptionally incomplete or imperfect and a venture is launched, the role of luck can become very pronounced. Under these conditions, risk is usually perceived as high, and so returns are potentially large. When they succeed, we tend to hear a great deal about such ventures. In fact, they garner a considerable share of newsprint and airtime. Eventually we also hear the entrepreneurs freely admit (or reluctantly confess) that a large measure of luck was involved. And so we tend to hear much about the role of luck in entrepreneurial ventures. But let's take another, closer look at luck and its breeding ground. . .imperfect knowledge.

While only recently discovered by economists, the existence of imperfect knowledge has long been appreciated intuitively by perceptive entrepreneurs and, I'm told, an occasional venture capitalist. Like most things in life, imperfect knowledge can work for or against you. The direction depends often on timing and circumstance. The "Columbus Syndrome" is a case in point.

We think of Columbus as an explorer and a mariner. Certainly he was, but he was also an entrepreneur. In fact, he was one of the first entrepreneurs recorded in history who raised significant venture capital to back his enterprise. His venture concept, as we all know, involved establishing inexpensive trade routes to the Far East by sailing. . .west. The up-front investment was huge. Fixed costs were high but the profit potential was also enormous. The latest and most sophisticated marine technology would be employed. Just the kind of situation that causes any self-respecting venture capitalist to salivate... high operating leverage coupled with a high-tech venture.

What we sometimes forget is that Columbus, no doubt armed with his business plan, was turned down by the first venture capitalist he visited, the Princes of Portugal. Undoubtedly, Columbus was extremely disappointed at the refusal since the Portuguese were acknowledged as the most experienced group for this particular industry. They had access to the latest navigational techniques and maps, all highly classified trade secrets, which Columbus thought might improve his venture's chances. But luck was with him. He was referred to another venture capitalist, the Spanish House of Isabel and Ferdinand, who decided to bankroll the venture. Based on their information, the concept seemed sound.

And that's what it's all about--information. The Portuguese, in fact, had more and better information than either Columbus or the Spanish House. The Portuguese used their cartographic knowledge, made what now seem simple calculations, and concluded that a western route to the Far East could not possibly be shorter and, therefore, they reasoned, probably not safer nor less expensive than their established route.

Of course, their knowledge was imperfect. No one knew of the great land masses and riches that existed to the west between Spain and Cathay. And so Spain reaped great wealth and assumed a position as the premier nation on earth because they had even less knowledge than the Princes of Portugal.

Should we then maximize "imperfect knowlege?" Such a posture, of course, makes no sense and belittles the skill of Columbus to reach the New World and return to report his discoveries. Luck was involved but at issue is whether the "Columbus Syndrome" is the exception or the rule. It must be the former, since we have no reason to believe that entrepreneurs have been excluded from the law of large numbers nor the law of averages. In fact, we have good reason to believe just the opposite. Fantastic luck derived from being at the right place at the right time exists, but it is in very rare supply. It is again the reason why effective entrepreneurs tend to be calculating types rather than gamblers. Columbus, after all, died a pauper in prison after many repeated failures. All of which proves it's very hard to hit the lottery *twice.*

THE MYTH OF "STRIKING IT RICH ON YOUR ORIGINAL VENTURE"

If the voyages of Columbus prove anything, it is the surprising existence and ubiquity of the "corridor principle." Columbus failed to achieve the goals of his original venture to reach the Far East. But his attempt led to new venture opportunities which he and other explorers pursued in later years. So it is with many entrepreneurs. A venture is planned and launched but the original concept does not bring the expected results. Yet the process of getting into business itself opens new horizons or "corridors" to unforeseen opportunities. In this sense, an entrepreneur travels along a venture pathway, off of which branch many corridors to new venture possibilities. To be sure, some entrepreneurs do succeed with a single venture and stick with it throughout their careers. But they appear to be a distinct minority, as we shall subsequently discuss. Most entrepreneurs pursue more than one venture during their entrepreneurial careers *and* a surprising number launch these other ventures within the early years of their careers.[13]

THE MYTH THAT "MOST VENTURES FAIL WITHIN FIVE YEARS"

I believe that it is important to start our study of entrepreneurship with some sense of reality about the likelihood of venture success. Currently, reality has been distorted to the point that nearly every other magazine or newspaper article on entrepreneurs mentions that some large percentage of all new businesses fail to survive each year and that the majority (anywhere from 63% to 80% depending on your source) fail within five years.

A good deal of the confusion stems from a misreading of statistics produced by Dun & Bradstreet. The misused numbers relate to venture failures only, where "failure" is defined as a company declaring or forced into bankruptcy. For example, "*of those companies who went bankrupt,* 8 out of 10 existed for five years or less." The limiting clause is crucial because business bankruptcies represent no more than a small percentage of:

a) all businesses in existence (estimated at 16,000,000 for 1982); and

b) all new businesses started annually (estimated at 400,000 to 500,000 per year).

For instance, the 1982 recession is witnessed a record number of bankruptcies, running at annual rate of over 20,000 companies. However, this represents only about 1% of the 2 million new ventures established over the last five year period.

A more sophisticated argument is that business bankruptcies actually reflect the number of ventures which are "discontinued" each year. But are these discontinued ventures really failures in a strict business sense? No one knows the exact magnitude of these discontinuances, but we do know they include:

a) companies sold that are discontinued legally but remained ongoing as another legal entity;

b) companies liquidated by owners after years of profit-making for any number of reasons (i.e., retirement, no successor, evaporation of the market, other better venture opportunities discovered, etc.)

c) companies that moved into the underground economy after their owners have listed them as discontinued; and

d) companies whose businesses were indeed insufficient to meet the initial or changing aspirations of their founders but which nevertheless terminated, leaving no debts behind them.

Certainly it is difficult to justify these discontinued ventures as failures in a business/economic sense. The waters, of course, become even murkier when we consider discontinuances and failure from both a philosophic and pragmatic perspective. Albert Shapero stated this position clearly and succinctly in a recent article:

> And is failure really failure? Many heroes of business failed at least once. Henry Ford failed twice. Maybe trying and failing is a better business education than going to a business school that has little concern with small business and entrepreneurship...
>
> Business failure isn't really a loss. The resources, human and material, are still there, though they've been redistributed. What people learn from business failure may even be a gain for society. The more people who try to start a new business, whether they succeed or not, the better off we all will be.
>
> We need more startups and more failures. We certainly need a better understanding of the numbers so that people, particularly the young, aren't discouraged before they get a chance to start.[14]

AN ENTREPRENEURIAL PERSPECTIVE DEFINED

Other myths exist about entrepreneurs and their activities. My purpose is not to discuss each one but to highlight those misconceptions which work against a view of entrepreneurship as a dynamic process. It is a view that sees entrepreneuring occuring often over substantial periods of time, a process that involves thought as well as action, a process that is influenced most often by a complex web of events rather than a single lucky event, a process that involves more than the start-up phase of a venture, a process that involves very possibly more than one venture, a process that may involve more than one entrepreneur, and a process in which the role of the entrepreneur is constantly changing.

Because entrepreneurship is a dynamic process, unique elements will always exist for each entrepreneur. Yet some commonalities also exist. An entrepreneurial perspective means being able to recognize both unique and common elements. What is relevant about your experience or the experience of other entrepreneurs to your present situation? Also, it means being able to see the short and long term implications of proposed action regarding a specific venture situation on your personal career as an entrepreneur in a particular place and at a particular time. Conceptually, the unit of analysis is *not* the proposed venture, nor the venture's environment, nor the entrepreneur at a particular point in time. The relevant unit of analysis is an individual's entrepreneurial career because many ventures, environments, and entrepreneurs are often associated with a particular individual's entrepreneurial career.

But I do not wish to mislead you. While an entrepreneurial perspective is organized partly around a career viewpoint, it is more than a career perspective. It entails an ability to assess several key areas along various dimensions and relate your assessments to your entrepreneurial career over the short and long terms. Because each entrepreneurial situation has unique and changing elements, entrepreneurs must assess their positions and determine appropriate action by:

1) identifying the relevant factors in three areas: i.e., the venture area, the human area, and the environmental area;

2) evaluating the various factors in each area along four lines of assessment: qualitative, quantitative, strategic, and ethical evaluation;

3) relating the implications of these evaluations to their particular entrepreneurial career.

This process is diagrammed in Figure 2.

I should stress that the assessment activities are interrelated and continuous activities over the life of any given venture. They are continuous--not in the formal sense of written analysis--but in the sense of ongoing thought and evaluation which may be formalized occasionally when such activity helps to clarify or crystalize thinking without compromising the need for secrecy or the element of surprise.

The assessment techniques are used to evaluate the people directly associated with a venture, the venture itself, and the various environments that impact the venture and its entrepreneur(s). In the past, entrepreneurs (as well as students of entrepreneurship) have limited themselves, in most instances unknowingly, to a venture-based, an entrepreneur-based, or an environment-based perspective of entrepreneurship. These three areas have presented the three principal traditions of thought about entrepreneurship. Let us examine each of these perspectives separately to see why a new entrepreneurial perspective is needed, one that incorporates elements from all three schools of thought, yet also goes beyond them to include a career perspective, supported by assessments along multiple dimensions.

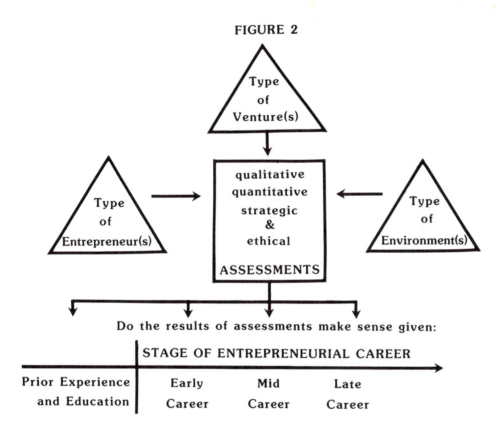

FIGURE 2

A VENTURE-BASED PERSPECTIVE

The Chinese have a saying, "failure is the threshold of success," and it applies most aptly to entrepreneurs. Most entrepreneurs report that they start or acquire more than one venture during the careers as entrepreneurs.[15] In-depth case studies also show that many have experienced one or more venture "failures" during their careers but often out of these failures emerge a new awareness, capability, and commitment to succeed as entrepreneurs. These experiences underscore the reason why a "venture perspective" has been and is terribly misleading: such orientations reveal only part, often no more than a snapshot, of what constitutes a full-length feature film. A venture perspective conditions prospective entrepreneurs to think, at best, no further than their initial venture and, more frequently, no further than the startup phase of their initial venture. The words of a retired entrepreneur who knew his share of venture failures and successes comes to mind here. He was fond of remarking in his inimitable way that, "any donkey can start a business. Keeping it going and making it succeed--not for a few years but over the long haul, or at least until you want to sell it--is what really counts." This orientation reflects partly what an entrepreneurial perspective is all about: selecting the right kind of venture opportunities, at the right time and place, to build the kind of career as an entrepreneur that is right for you. It also reflects a longer term view, one that goes beyond startup or "getting the doors open." Knowledge about initiating, maintaining, and discontinuing a venture is valuable indeed but it should be utilized with other information about the entrepreneurial process.

AN ENTREPRENEUR-BASED PERSPECTIVE

If a pure venture perspective is inadequate, perhaps we should focus on the entrepreneur. In fact, such focus represents the longest tradition of inquiry in entrepreneurship, one espoused by many entrepreneurs, professional psychologists, and most venture capitalists. The popular refrain among this latter group, is "I'm not so concerned with the venture *per se*. What I'm looking for is a quality entrepreneur. Given a preference, I'll always select an 'A' entrepreneur with a grade 'B' venture versus the other way around."

In the past, this orientation toward the 'A' entrepreneur has helped stimulate considerable research to identify and assess the traits and characteristics of such entrepreneurs. A few useful notions have emerged from this work but these efforts have not proven very productive for either the prospective or practicing entrepreneur, or for the venture capitalist for that matter.[16]

Why has an entrepreneur(or human) perspective been so unrewarding? The principal reason is that it is also based on a snapshot in time, even briefer than a venture perspective. For psychological tests are administered at very particular moments during the lives of individuals, often after they have become entrepreneurs. A useful and valid profile of entrepreneurial traits and characteristics requires a longitudinal approach, one that is probably impractical to research. Here tests would have to be administered throughout the lives of individuals, including non-entrepreneurs as a control group. Even if this feat were accomplished, careful distinctions would still need to be made between different generic types of entrepreneurs coupled with an ability to define what constitutes "success or failure" in a venture sense for each group--an impossible and irrelevant requirement as the venture "failures" of long-time, practicing entrepreneurs imply. Finally, the ability to execute a successful longitudinal study also implies the possession of a knowledge base that would avoid comparisons between the same kinds of entrepreneurs at different stages in their entrepreneurial careers. Inevitably, a longitudinal approach that focuses on the entrepreneur *per se* must assume a career perspective. It must also have meaning and application for individual entrepreneurs. And the operative questions for individual entrepreneurs are:

What traits, characteristics, and values can I influence over time? Which do I wish to influence? How much time and effort will it take to produce a desired change? And for what purpose? In other words, now or at any moment in time, do my traits, characteristics, and values relate well to a particular venture, in a particular environment?

Inevitably any assessment of yourself as entrepreneur cannot and should not occur in a vacuum. It must be integrated with and directed toward a particular venture and environment.

AN ENVIRONMENT-BASED PERSPECTIVE

Many economists, anthropologists, and sociologists have taken a very different view of entrepreneurship in the past. An explicit statement of their position, in effect, says:

> "It's neither the attributes of an entrepreneur nor his/her venture that cause the emergence of successful entrepreneurship. Rather, it is a complex and probably variable set of factors in an environment that detemines the number and type of successful entrepreneurs at any point in time."

As evidence, proponents of this view have shown why entrepreneurship exists or does not exist to some extent in certain places among certain groups.[17] More work is needed in this area, but the indications are that benefits will be macro in nature and, as such, of principal use to policy makers rather than entrepreneurs. Some spill-over benefits will be realized from this macro research on the environment, just as similar benefits have been gained from research focusing mainly on the entrepreneur or the venture. But my guess is they will be minor since they will lack a specificity of use for individual application. Each entrepreneurial situation is unique and, like hardy wildflowers, entrepreneurs often have a way of surviving and prospering in the harshest environments. I have little doubt that someday a history of entrepreneurship for the Soviet Union or The Peoples Republic of China will underscore once again the hardiness of the strain.

The uniqueness of each entrepreneurial decision underscores that, at the micro level of the individual entrepreneur, the operative question becomes: What constitutes a favorable versus unfavorable environment for me and my proposed venture at this particular time? Once again one must weave together or integrate human and venture factors with environmental conditions.

WHY STRATEGIC AND ETHICAL ASSESSMENT ARE NEEDED

A few words are needed at this juncture to explain why strategic assessment and ethical assessment have been considered separately from qualitative and quantitative analysis of human, venture, and environmental factors. The principal reasons are:

1. their very special importance to successful entrepreneurship over the long haul (i.e., in a career sense)

2. the failure by many prospective entrepreneurs as well as some practicing entrepreneurs to consider them.

REGARDING STRATEGIC ASSESSMENT

Entrepreneurs determine the direction, magnitude, and timing of resource allocation of an entire entity. Such entrepreneurial decisions are also, by definition, strategic decisions.[18] A plentiful supply of knowledge also exists which indicates that effective entrepreneurs are good strategists--at least in an intuitive sense. In fact, we probably all know at least one very successful entrepreneur who is, and freely admits to being, a lousy manager. Upon closer inspection, however, we'd probably discover that our entrepreneur is a weak manager in an "operating" sense. He manages poorly "through others," or has weak operating skills in finance, marketing, manufacturing, etc. What then accounts for this person's success as an entrepreneur? The chances are that he or she is quite capable of conceiving and executing a strong strategy--one that positions a company very favorably vis-a-vis its competition and provides considerable margin for error, which is to say the entrepreneur has the leeway to manage badly and still do very well.

Here the operative questions are: What constitutes a good venture strategy for me, given my entrepreneurial values and aspiration? How long does it take to develop a successful venture strategy? What are some of the classic strategies entrepreneurs have used in the past to insure their success--in both a venture and career sense? These important questions are addressed in a later chapter.

REGARDING ETHICAL ASSESSMENT

At first inclination, you may think an ethical perspective would be anathema to the development of effective entrepreneurial credentials. Deep down many of us believe that good entrepreneurs aren't ethical people. Why? Because we've been told many times that they are survivors; they are winners; they didn't come to lose; they're tough, cutthroat people who have a way of coming out on top. The supposition is that anyone who does entrepreneuring well can't possibly have clean hands.

Part of the confusion stems from bad press (i.e., good behavior rarely gets publicized), but part is also derived from a misconception that ethics and excellence are incompatible companions on an entrepreneurial career pathway. In fact, most entrepreneurs cannot survive long without both attributes.

Most successful entrepreneurs learn that their entrepreneurial capability is only as strong as their entrepreneurial reputation. Lose your reputation and you lose the other. Pursue unethical practices and eventually the odds are you will lose your reputation and your capability to pursue entrepreneurial activities. People simply won't trust you and trust is a keystone of entrepreneurial success. Your customers, suppliers, employees, bankers, lawyers, investors, etc.--all must trust you. Betray their trust and you will pay a price in terms of your entrepreneurial freedoms and latitude for future action.

Fortunately, most entrepreneurs, like most people, try to follow an ethical course. Sometimes they err in judgement. We all do, but to survive over the long haul, entrepreneurs generally require an ethical stature. Exceptions, of course, exist and if entrepreneurs have been more unethical at times than the general population, then perhaps it is because they have faced more and greater ethical problems. It is, after all, the difference between spectating and playing the game; and it is, perhaps, an unstated reason why entrepreneurs reap greater rewards: they take not only greater economic risks, but also greater ethical risks. For one thing is certain: entrepreneurs face ethical issues continually. Anyone who makes decisions about how resources are allocated, how products and services are delivered, will be placed inevitably in a position of trust. And trust spawns ethical issues and often ethical dilemmas.

The omnipresence of ethical concerns suggests that entrepreneurs should develop an awareness of and capability to deal personally with potential ethical transgressions. Also, we have evidence that the kinds of ethical issues you will confront differ both in type and intensity as you move through your entrepreneurial career. Developing an entrepreneurial perspective means developing an awareness of these ethical issues and a capability for practicing dealing with them throughout your entrepreneurial life. Ethical assessment is an acquired skill--one we will explore in greater detail later in this book.

QUESTIONS FOR DISCUSSION

1) Entrepreneurs are present and future oriented people. They are concerned with today and tomorrow--not yesterday. As such, history is *de facto* irrelevant to them and they will ignore it. Attempts to build an entrepreneurial perspective will fail insofar as they incorporate a historical view of entrepreneurship. Discuss.

2) What are some critical similarities and differences between an entrepreneurial career versus

a) a career as a manager?

b) a career as a lawyer (who never had his or her own practice)?

KEY READINGS

Gordon Baty, *Entrepreneurship for the Eighties,* Prentice-Hall, 1981.

David L. Birch, "Who Creates Jobs?" *The Public Interest,* Vol. 65, Fall 1981, pp. 3-14.

Orvis F. Collins and David G. Moore, *The Organizational Makers: A Behavioral Study of Independent Entrepreneurs,* Appleton-Century-Crofts, 1970.

David C. McClelland, *The Achieving Society,* Irvington Publishers, NY, 1976.

Albert Shapero, "Numbers That Lie," *Inc. Magazine,* May 1981, pp. 16-18.

Karl H. Vesper, *New Venture Strategies,* Prentice-Hall, 1980.

Edwin Zschau, "Statement of the Capital Formation Task Force before the House Committee on Ways and Means," March 7, 1978. Available from the *American Electronics Association.*

NOTES

[1] A great many citations are possible here. The relationship between economic development and entrepreneurship was postulated early by Joseph Schumpeter in *The Theory of Economic Development,* Cambridge, MA: Harvard University Press, 1934, and reaffirmed more recently by Albert Shapero in his article "Entrepreneurship: Key to Self-Renewing Economics," *Commentary,* April 1981, pp. 19-23. The ties between entrepreneurship and social and/or political development include Everett Hagen's classic "The Entrepreneur as Rebel Against Traditional Society," in *Human Organization,* Vol. 19, Winter, 1960-61, pp. 185-187; George Gilder's *Wealth and Poverty,* New York: Basic Books, Inc., 1981; John J. Carroll's excellent book on *The Filipino Manufacturing Entrepreneur: Agent and Product of Change,* Ithaca: Cornell University Press, 1965; and Stanley M. Davis', "Politics and Organizational Underdevelopment in Chile," which explores particularly the potentialities for entrepreneurial pursuits under conditions of political instability.

[2] See David L. Birch, "Who Creates Jobs?" *The Public Interest,* Vol. 65, Fall 1981, pp. 3-14 plus Dr. Edwin Zschau, *American Electronics Association Report,* Palo Alto, CA: AEA, 1979 regarding the contributions of smaller electronics firms in terms of jobs, taxes, and exports. Regarding innovations, see W.F. Mueller, in *The Rate and Direction of Inventive Activity: Economic and Social Factors,* R.R. Nelson, Ed., Princeton, NJ: Princeton University Press, 1962, pp. 323-360.

[3] Collins, Orvis F., and David G. Moore, *The Organization Makers: A Behavioral Study of Independent Entrepreneurs,* NY: Appleton-Century-Crofts, 1970. The need to narrow the definition of entrepreneurship for research purpose is quite understandable and necessary given the range of entrepreneurial types that exist. But the use of various definitions imposes a responsibility on authors to define the term for readers to be sure they know what a particular writer means when using the term.

[4] John A. Hornaday and John Aboud, "Characteristics of Successful Entrepreneurs," *Personnel Psychology,* Vol. 24, No. 2, Summer 1971.

[5] The seminal study in David C. McClelland's *The Achieving Society,* NY: Irvington Publishers, 1976.

Of shorter, more direct interest are his "Achievement Motivation Can Be Developed," *Harvard Business Review,* Nov./Dec. 1965; and "Business Drive and National Achievement," *Harvard Business Review,* pp. 99-112.

Also see Lawrence Lamont "What Entrepreneurs Learn From Experience," *Journal of Small Business Management,* Vol. 12, No. 4, October 1974.

[6] Harvard University, *L.L. Bean Incorporated,* Harvard Case Services, 366-013, Rev. 1970, Boston, MA: 1965, p. 10.

[7]See Richard Buskirk, "The Dangers of Overcapitalization in the Startup Stage," in *Frontiers of Entrepreneurship Research,* Vol. II, Babson Park, MA: Center for Entrepreneurial Studies, 1982.

[8]Collins, *op. cit.,* p. 50 which cites that 16 of 32 Michigan entrepreneurs who attended college had "dropped out."

[9]In an earlier study, Hornaday discovered that white male entrepreneurs that were considered successful had a very low divorce rate, much lower than the national average. See John A. Hornaday and Charles S. Bunker, "The Nature of the Entrepreneur," *Personnel Psychology,* Vol. 23, No. 1, pp. 47-54, Spring 1970. In a more recent study of Babson entrepreneurs, I discovered that some had better academic records on average than other Babson alumni in the same programs. Robert Ronstadt, *Entrepreneurial Careers: A Study of the Career Pathways Pursued by Babson Entrepreneurs,* an unpublished report, Board of Research: Babson College, 1981.

[10]The best of these books, in my opinion, is Gordon Baty's *Entrepreneurship for the Eighties,* Prentice Hall, 1981 which is an update of his earlier book, *Entrepreneurship: Playing to Win,* Reston, VA: Reston Publishing Co., 1974.

[11]Ronstadt, *Entrepreneurial Careers,* op. cit.

[12]*Fortune Magazine* recently published an interesting article which focused specifically on the role of luck in the careers of several businessmen. See "Luck and Careers" by Daniel Seligman, *Fortune,* November 16, 1981, pp. 60-72.

[13]Ronstadt, *Entrepreneurial Careers,* op. cit.

[14]Albert Shapero, "Numbers that Lie," *Inc. Magazine,* May 1981, pp. 16-18.

[15]Ronstadt, *Entrepreneurial Careers, op. cit.*

[16]Karl Vesper provides a fair critique of these efforts in his *New Venture Strategies,* Prentice Hall, 1980, pp. 9-11.

[17]Hagen, *op. cit.*

[18]The ties between resource allocation, strategic, and entrepreneurial decision-making are explored by Alfred D. Chandler, Jr., *Strategy and Structure: Chapters in the American Industrial Enterprise,* Cambridge, MA: The MIT Press, 1962.

EXISTING KNOWLEDGE ABOUT THE DECISION TO PURSUE AND TERMINATE ENTREPRENEURIAL ACTIVITIES

Not long ago I was approached by an undergraduate student who asked me if I were teaching a course this semester called "Starting New Adventures." I replied that, indeed I was and then noted that the course's title was actually, "Starting New Ventures."

At the time, I enjoyed both his Freudian slip and the obvious enthusiasm he displayed for the course. It's hard to ignore or forget old-fashioned, honest enthusiasm. But it wasn't until some time later when, upon reflection, I decided his course title wasn't half bad either. In fact, the more I thought about it, the more I grew to like it. For the term "adventure" has not only an exciting quality about it, but also a dynamic inference. One can "start a new venture" in a day. But for most of us, an adventure takes longer, spanning lengths of time during which exciting, sometimes dangerous things do happen. In short, an adventure has a process quality about it which, given sufficient time, has a starting point, a middle, and an end.

A fair amount of knowledge already exists about entrepreneurial "adventures"--both in terms of describing the process and the characteristics associated with this activity. A smaller but still healthy portion of this knowledge is even relevant to practicing entrepreneurs and we'd be unwise to ignore it. Yet, to date, this knowledge has been ignored or at least underutilized. The reason for this neglect is a very practical one. Knowledge about entrepreneurship comes to us from a great many sources, representing diverse disciplines, each with its own approach and terminology. Consequently, studies of entrepreneurship are often difficult to absorb and even harder to distill, label, categorize, and store for future use by practitioners when considering entrepreneurial problems and opportunities.

One way to organize these diverse materials is shown in *Exhibit 1*. This simple conceptual framework makes sense because nearly everything written on entrepreneurship falls into three "schools" or lines of inquiry. And each school or tradition has something to say either explicitly or implicitly about the decisions to begin, continue, and end an entrepreneurial career.*

What follows is a capsule view of each tradition...a view of what each school has to say about the decisions to start, continue and end an entrepreneurial career.

---

*The reader, however, should be alert to the fact that a few authors have produced individual works that cross more than one school of thought. Others have produced an article or book that falls into one school and then later produced additional work that represents another tradition.

Exhibit 1

ENTREPRENEURIAL CAREER DECISIONS: SOME EXPLANATIONS

School or Tradition	The Decision to Start Career	The Decision to Continue Career	The Decision to End Career
The People School	"The Right Stuff" Genetic Makeup Familial Incubation Psychological Displacement Educational Incubation	Psychological Factors Commitment to a Way of Life Shifting Goals and Entrepreneurial Teams	Personal Factors Diminishing Needs and Capabilities "The Wrong Stuff" Team or Partnership Breakup
The Environmental School	Cultural, Political and Economic Displacement Macro Factors and Positive Entrepreneurial Environments Industry Incubation Industry Life Cycles	Limited Options for Some Other Career Continuance of Displacement, Dependency, and/or Positive Macro Factors	Continuance of Displacement, Dependence, and/or Positive Macro Factors until Retirement. Discontinuance of above forces premature retirement or career exit.
The Venture School	Venture Opportunities Sources of Ideas Development of Concepts Implementation Requirements	Strategy and Degree of Success/Failure of Venture After Startup Venture Options and the Corridor Principle	Organizational Evolution Organizational Continuance and Succession Venture Failure and Career Path

THE PEOPLE SCHOOL AND THE DECISION TO PURSUE
AN ENTREPRENEURIAL CAREER

Tom Wolfe wrote a perceptive best seller in 1980 which examined the lives of America's leading test pilots and astronauts.[1] According to Mr. Wolfe, becoming a member of this select club meant possessing "the right stuff" - i.e., the proper mix of courage, coolness under stressful conditions, need for achievement, technical expertise, creativity, etc. While Mr. Wolfe wasn't talking about entrepreneurs, his position is similar to the basic thesis of "the people school" of entrepreneurship: a position which holds that a person has to have "the right stuff" to become a successful entrepreneur.

In earlier years differences of opinion existed within this school regarding the source of the proper ingredients - i.e., those traits and characteristics that produced an effective entrepreneur. For example, some observers like Roger Babson, the founder of Babson College and also a business entrepreneur, claimed that genetic inheritance was the prime determinant of the right stuff.[2] For Babson, the required intelligence, drive to achieve, energy, and necessary qualities of leadership were products mainly of ancestry and, to a considerble extent, were outside our control. While not denying the genetic factor, other studies supported the notion that the right parents produced "the right stuff." But here the proper parentage meant having a father or mother who was an entrepreneur. The appropriate DNA configuration might be necessary but the opportunity "to learn" first hand about entrepreneurial life was the pivotal factor.

Still other studies, notably those produced by David McClelland and various associates shifted the emphasis away from genes *per se* toward a view that many individuals could learn to acquire "the right stuff" - a critical component being the need to achieve.[3] Given sufficient time, achievement motivation could be developed and channeled into entrepreneurial pursuits. Similarly, other characteristics necessary to the entrepreneurial function could be developed and refined as the desire to achieve was nourished. Several researchers have investigated these characteristics and defined them variously as persistence, autonomy, courage, willingness to assume risk, creativity and/or more recently the "tolerance of ambiguity."[4]

How are these traits developed and then oriented toward an entrepreneurial goal? One explanation involves the notion of personal displacement...that is, an individual has a kind of personality and/or set of values that mades him or her unacceptable to social groups. This person inevitably fares badly in group situations and becomes in varying degrees a social dropout, a "displaced" person who can't complete school or can't hold a job. He or she is the classic loner, perhaps even a rebel, who nevertheless has a need to achieve and eventually creates an autonomous business to express this need.[5]

More recently we have witnessed work which relates entrepreneurial success to educational performance and attainment. First, let me say that certain kinds of educations coupled with particular social values, can inhibit a potential entrepreneur from launching an entrepreneurial career. Nowhere have these educational barriers been better documented than by John Hendrick in his short classic, "How I Overcame The Handicap of a College Education" which is reproduced later in this book.

But notwithstanding Hendrick's indictment of traditional Liberal Arts education, educational programs do exist which apparently support or help produce "the right stuff" as well as a positive entrepreneurial experience. Specifically, the studies of the link between education and entrepreneurship show the following:

1. entrepreneurs tend to be more educated than the general population;

2. entrepreneurs in high technology ventures are characterized by advanced education in engineering and the sciences;

3. many business administration programs which are designed to produce managers may inhibit entrepreneurial success.

In the past, entrepreneurial education has been confused with business training. In fact, entrepreneurial education within undergrduate business and MBA programs is just being developed. It will be many years before we know if entrepreneurial education fosters entrepreneurial success. In the meantime, some solace can be found in the observation that entrepreneurs claim they improve when it comes to starting second, third, etc. ventures. The same is probably true for learning how to better grow and harvest second, third, etc. ventures. Consequently, it seems reasonable to assume that specialized education focused specifically on these and other entrepreneurial issues will improve the entrepreneurial learning process. But only time and systematic study will provide the final answer. Until then, like most successful entrepreneurs, we must live with some uncertainty about the interplay between education, and entrepreneurship. In the absence of entrepreneurial education, all we can say is that the causal link between education and entrepreneurship can be both positive and negative, and when positive, causality is usually indirect at best--a kind of necessary condition but certainly not a sufficient one. For example, a considerable amount of evidence suggests that prolonged practical experience is a major precondition for entrepreneurial success. But often it is some form of education that opens the door to the technical, industrial, or avocational experiences which form the basis for a successful entrepreneurial career. At the same time, certain kinds of education, as Hendrick, Shapero, Merrill, and others have shown, can help to close the door on entrepreneurship forever.[6]

Two other variables seem to be part and parcel of the successful entrepreneurs's attitudinal baggage. One was discovered and explained several years ago by Harry Schrage who dubbed it "the veridical factor."[7] Acting veridically or having a veridical attitude means having a willingness to admit assumptions or unknowns and then a corresponding desire to discover the reality about these unknowns. It is the opposite of going on "gut instinct" or, more accurately, assuming you know the truth about a market, a product, a technology, or a potential associate, because of your personal feelings, opinions, beliefs, or experience. In short, veridical people admit it when they don't know something. Then, they proactively seek to discover the facts about what is unknown. This search for objective truth about unknown or fuzzy factors influencing venture success smacks of great veracity. Entrepreneurs are not usually considered as truth-seekers. Yet profiles of superior entrepreneurs reveal this veracious trait time and again, at least in terms of their desire to understand the forces affecting their ventures. Since few people understand the meaning of Schrage's original term, we will refer to the veridical factor as veracity factor (or veracious tendency) in subsequent discussion.

A second characteristic has become more visible with the emergence of the "professional MBA." A major complaint of employers about professional MBAs is their reluctance to solve problems or take advantage of opportunities with more than the resources under their immediate command or conveniently placed at their disposal. The process of thought of the professional MBA is:

1. What resources do I have at my disposal?

2. How can I use them optimally to find a solution?

The drawback of this mental set is that no good solution may exist given available resources and, rather than make waves, the professional MBA effectively gives up, gets transferred, or has the project assigned to someone else. By contrast, the entrepreneur (as well as the entrepreneurial manager) thinks and acts differently, both in a creative and "enterprising" sense. The process is more like the following:

1. What is a solution for this problem or opportunity?

2. What resources, skills, etc. do I need to implement the solution?

3. Now, can I get what's needed?

This distinctive "resource-seeking" thought process, along with other characteristics, attitudes, and world view color not only the beginning of an entrepreneurial "adventure" but the decision to continue and end the career. For example, the decision to continue an entrepreneurial career versus end it prematurely implies a psychological and behavioral bent that will "make it happen." Here, only a terminated *career* signifies "the wrong stuff," for true entrepreneurs will not let venture failure stop them. Ultimately, entrepreneurs with the right stuff will experience venture success (or at least survival) and such success will provide the needed psychological reinforcement and commitment to entrepreneurship as a way of life. It leads to "career anchors" and comments by entrepreneurs like, "I could never work for someone else."

Once this commitment develops, an entrepreneurial career ends only when physical decline dictates an end to the career or psychological needs radically shift. As we all know, many entrepreneurs die with their boots on after pursuing their careers as entrepreneurs for many years. Too often their ventures also die with them with no successor in sight. Others retire from the field, ostensibly because earlier needs for achievement, autonomy, and control decline while newer needs assume greater importance.

It seems a variety of explanations are at work producing the right stuff. But whether the right stuff is the product or mix of some genetic stamp, aggravated personal displacement, family role models, and/or positive educational exposure, the people school holds that prospective entrepreneurs will eventually and inevitably find a venture to start their entrepreneurial careers. And they will make these ventures succeed, if they are to succeed, by displaying great persistance, tenacity, creativity and willpower in the face of uncertainty. In doing so they exhibit not only courage but an attitude which psychologists and cultural anthropologists often describe as a "master of destiny" perception of the world. This perception of life says, "I will control what happens to me" or "I did not come to lose." It is a view which denies categorically the saying that "it is written" or "it is God's will." It is a world view which says, "I will write what happens to me and, for better or worse, the triumph or the tragedy, the success or failure, will be mine."

THE ENVIRONMENTAL SCHOOL AND THE DECISION TO PURSUE AN ENTREPRENEURIAL CAREER

The jump between the people school and the environmental school is a short but distinct one. The point of distinction is a focus on the group versus the individual. Members of the environmental school focus not only on the group but also the institutions, values, and mores that are produced by the group which, taken together, represent an identifiable sociopolitical environment.

For those who side with the environmentalists that "the group" is the primary causal factor of entrepreneurship, the dominating theory that explains the start of an entrepreneurial career concerns the notion of displacement. A critical component of this theory about the decision to start an entrepreneurial career is that, more often than not, those with "the right stuff" will not start an entrepreneurial venture unless other options are eliminated for them by others. Consequently, unless they are prevented or "displaced" by others from pursuing some other career, they will not opt for an entreprenurial career.

But there are several types of environment displacement and it pays to make the distinction between each type since each is associated with a different set of events that leads to the startup of an entrepreneurial venture and career. For instance, *cultural displacement* occurs when entire social groups are precluded from entering certain professions because of ethnic background, race, religion, and/or other practices associated with their cultural group. Members of these subcultural groups know that if they start some other career, they will be treated prejudiciously in terms of advancement and other rewards. We know, for example, that Chinese and Indian immigrants have experienced this kind of negative environment in many countries and their answer in many instances has been to start their own businesses. Anti-Semitic practices have forced Jews to turn to entrepreneurial pursuits down through the centuries.[8]Some women contend that women managers will turn increasingly to entrepreneurship as they confront similar kinds of prejudices that prevent advancement to the highest corridors of executive power.

Political displacement occurs when an environment becomes highly unstable over a period of time so that the free enterprise system cannot function or is not permitted to function. Such conditions can occur in authoritarian regimes of the right or left. They may occur on a national scale (Argentina, Chile, China) or at the level of your own town or county. But whatever the level, the political environment becomes unfriendly toward entrepreneurs because a) ideology identifies them as unnecessary villains; and/or b) political contacts become much more important than business/entrepreneurial acumen as a determinant of venture creation, continuity, and success.[9]

Economic displacement occurs when people lose their jobs for reasons which are largely outside their control. In this sense, economic recessions and depressions are often spawning grounds for new entrepreneurs. Invariably such entrepreneurs explain their entry into an entrepreneurial career along the following lines:

> "My company had to lay me off so I thought I might as well
> try to start my own business at this time."

But however phrased, the message is clear: If these individuals hadn't been displaced by economic events, they would not have launched an entrepreneurial career.

The existence of cultural, political, and/or economic displacement may lead to migrations across national borders as people seek a better life elsewhere. However, the opportunity to pursue professional careers or work with established organizations may be very difficult for the newcomers. Starting a business, in fact, may be the most viable option for these "cross cultural entrepreneurs." Based on their experiences in "the old country," they may see market gaps or product/service opportunities unrecognized by others in their new adopted lands. They may also know ways of doing things (process technology) which they can transfer in order to gain a competitive advantages.

Just as some environments (be they towns, states, or nations) drive out potential or existing entrepreneurs, others provide varying degrees of support and sustenance. Legal and economic policies can help to nurture certain kinds of entrepreneurs and make getting into business easier and less risky.

But the support for entrepreneurs may not always be direct. An economic and political environment that supports, for example, the birth and growth of new industries and technologies may create a training ground for new waves of entrepreneurs. A variety of studies have shown how prospective entrepreneurs in certain industries "incubate" in existing corporations, developing ideas, contacts, and support for their own entrepreneurial enterprises.[10]

In summary, it seems a combination of negative and positive forces must be at work in any environment in order to maximize the stock and flow of entrepreneurs into the economy. On the negative side, displacement barriers function which literally force individuals to consider entrepreneurial options. On the positive side, the number and quality of entrepreneurial options are maximized through a combination of social values, economic policies, and a political climate that fosters entrepreneurial life.

Under the environment scenario, the decision *to continue* an entrepreneurial career is explained by a continuation of displacement conditions in the environment. Other career options remain limited and existing entrepreneurs seldom face a better choice than to continue their entrepreneurial pursuits. As the entrepreneur moves into middle age and beyond, social barriers also emerge which inhibit shifts in careers. In many societies, employers become increasingly reluctant to hire older applicants. Also, a kind of social attitude develops frequently that suggests it is somehow wrong for someone who has been, in effect, a lead dancer to "step back" into the chorus line.

Of course, not all the forces are negative. Other positive forces are at work in the environment which keep entrepreneurs committed to their entrepreneurial careers. For example, as ventures develop, unwritten social contracts come into being which create mutual dependencies between entrepreneurs, their employees, and their local communities. For instance, a small town (or a bank in a town) may accord an entrepreneur preferential treatment because the latter accounts for a high share of the community's employment. In turn, the entrepreneur may reciprocate by pursuing what seem like (and may be) non-economic policies, e.g., maintaining a retail location downtown when he should move; keeping employees on the payroll when he shouldn't, etc.

Under the environmental scenario, the decisions to start and continue an entrepreneurial career are to a considerable extent outside the entrepreneur's control. Likewise the decision to end an entrepreneurial career anywhere short of retirement is similarly beyond the entrepreneur's power to control. Remember, we are talking here not just of venture termination but career change. For instance, the premature termination of an entrepreneurial career occurs according to the environmental school with the emergence of new displacement conditions that literally force existing entrepreneurs out of business and into other career pursuits. For instance, at state, national, and international levels, new policies or laws may suddenly contribute to business failures and thereby force entrepreneurs to reconsider their career options.

THE VENTURE SCHOOL AND THE DECISION TO PURSUE AN ENTREPRENEURIAL CAREER

The venture school is the youngest of the three lines of inquiry that to help us to understand the critical variables causing entrepreneurial success. For venture school proponents, the swing variables that cause the start of an entrepreneurial career involve the acts of discovering a viable venture opportunity, developing a venture opportunity into a workable venture concept, and then implementing or turning the concept into an operating business. The right (human) stuff or even the right environment are at best necessary conditions, not sufficient ones. Highly motivated, displaced individuals living in favorable entrepreneurial environments will *not* initiate a successful entrepreneurial career unless they find a viable venture opportunity and then are able to take the necessary steps regarding venture startup.

Neither is easy to do. For instance, evidence exists which suggests that finding a good venture opportunity is not simply a function of sitting down with one or two

Exhibit 2

REASONS GIVEN BY NONSTARTS FOR NOT STARTING A NEW VENTURE

Nonstart Reasons	Primary Reason		Secondary Reason		Primary and Secondary Reasons Added Together	
	#	%	#	%	#	%
1. Financial Considerations	52	54	10	15	62	39
2. Idea Not Good	17	18	5	8	22	14
3. Time Commitment	5	5	6	9	11	7
4. Family Considerations	5	5	21	32	26	16
5. Lack Industry Experience (e.g., No Good Site)	4	4	7	11	11	7
6. Local Constraints	3	1	1	1	4	2.4
7. Legal Concerns	0	0	5	8	5	3
8. Concerns About Competitors	0	0	3	5	3	2
9. Lack of Education	1	1	1	1	2	1.2
10. Personal Health	0	0	1	1	1	.6
11. Divorce	0	0	0	0	0	0
12. Other	9	9	5	8	14	9
	96	100%	65	100%	161	100%

Source: Robert Ronstadt, "The Decision *Not* to Start an Entrepreneurial Career," in *Frontiers for Entrepreneurial Research 1983.* Center of Entrepreneurial Studies: Babson College, 1983.

Exhibit 3

CONCEPTUAL MODEL:
A TEAM APPROACH TO NEW VENTURE INITIATION

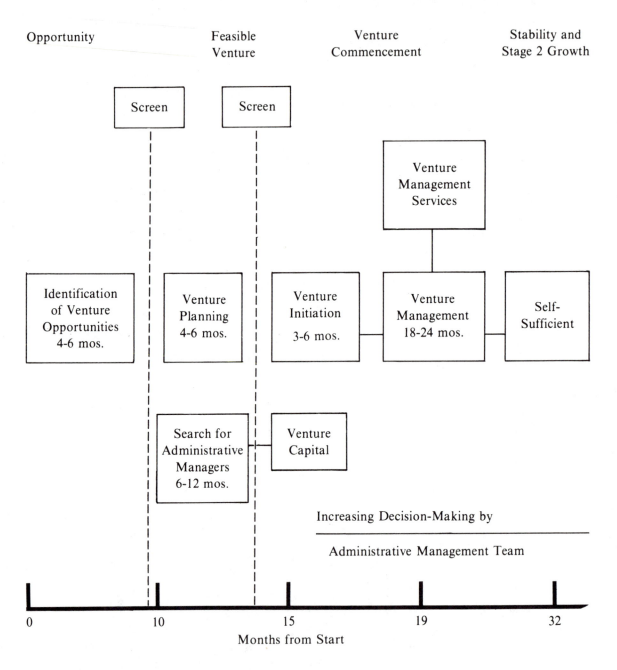

Source: William R. Osgood and William E. Wetzel, Jr., "A Systems Approach to Venture Initiation." *Business Horizons,* October, 1977.

acquaintances for an unstructured brainstorming session. Nor are you likely "to tap someone else's brain" for a truly workable idea. In this regard, one study revealed the following:

> One key finding was that instead of searching randomly, as many popularized books seem to suggest, the entrepreneur should closely examine his or her own education, work experience, and hobbies as idea sources. The large majority of entrepreneurs studied primarily used their own expertise rather than that of others.[11]

And once a venture opportunity is found, you may not have the capability to act upon it. For instance, closer scrutiny of the idea may reveal that you will need more startup capital than first thought; the particular location you need to make the venture viable may not be available; your spouse and other close family members may turn out to be dead set against the idea; a critical partner may decide against participating in the venture. The list of reasons preventing venture startup is no doubt a long one. The most prevalent reasons given by one group who seriously considered but did *not* start a new venture are shown in *Exhibit 2*.

For those who do launch a venture, various pre-startup steps will generally, but not always, be taken by entrepreneurs who subsequently realize a successful venture experience. There seems to be no set order to this pre-start sequence of events and the same steps are not taken by all or even most, entrepreneurs.[12] Consequently considerable difference exists among venture theorists about the usefulness of models which purport to provide a best way or better way to initiate a venture. At one extreme are proponents of a systematic or "systems approach" to new venture creation. *Exhibit 3* presents a conceptual model for one such approach which sees teams of "initiation specialists" starting businesses that are subsequently turned over to administrative managers. The gap between the venture school and the people school is perhaps at its widest here -- to the extent that the authors of this model see no inherent reason for the traditional entrepreneur.

> "An analysis of the process of new venture formation discloses no essential reason why the initiative must rest with the entrepreneur. We propose a pro-active business development model that shifts this initiative to a team of business initiation specialists who would have the active support of venture capitalists. The new organization could create ventures with sufficient market value (capitalized earning power) to recover all funds expended, including competitive returns for the time and risks involved."[13]

By contrast, others have suggested a systematic approach to venture creation which stresses careful assessment of the human component in combination with other venture factors. For example, one author suggests that the following conditions are needed for a successful launch of high growth businesses.

"Four ingredients emerged which characterize high potential, growth oriented ventures:

1. a talented lead entrepreneur with a balanced and compatible team;

2. a technically sound and marketable idea for a product or service;

3. thorough venture analysis leading to a complete business plan; and

4. appropriate equity and debt financing.[14]"

Still others place more emphasis on market assessment. The rationale is that a great deal can be wrong or go wrong with other startup factors but a venture will probably succeed if, for example, the customers are known and, even better, are presold. Guaranteed sales are the prescription for weak or untried entrepreneurs venturing in non-supportive environments under this scenario.

A related but different view places even greater importance on financial resources and planning. The theory here is that successful venture initiation is mainly a function of time. And enough time is mainly a function of "deep pockets." In other words, with enough money you can buy the time to make the necessary venture adjustments which will enable you to obtain or develop the right entrepreneurial team, find a sufficient market and customer base, or develop products with real commercial appeal.[15]

Finally, a number of venture startup proponents place little or no emphasis on any single function or area. Instead they argue that during the process of developing a business, it is important to examine one's policies, resources, skills, and plans for all the traditional areas of business activity. The result of this advice ranges from simple one-page lists of steps to very detailed guidelines for putting together a business plan that touches all the major bases.[16]

So much for getting started. Within the venture school, the earliest reasons explaining the decisions to continue as well as end an entrepreneurial career have been offered by people studying the business policy (or strategy formulation/implementation) process. The basic notion is that successful venture initiation eventually will face some kind of competition response. Product imitators will attack your market; new products/services will be innovated that become substitutes for your products or services; etc. Your chance to continue your venture and your entrepreneurial career rests mainly with your ability to devise a corporate strategy that will insulate or protect your business from competitive threats. A kind of Darwinian principle prevails here: only those with the strongest strategies survive while the strategically weak eventually perish.[17]

Of course, over the years various studies have been conducted which show the "reasons" for venture failure. Depending on the study, the main causes given are insufficient capitalization, insufficient management skills, and/or poor location.[18] Yet the student of strategy will argue, quite forcefully in my view, that these reasons are no more than symptoms of an inherently weak strategy, conceived by individuals with weak strategic skills, not only in terms of formulation but also execution. The supporting

Exhibit 4

The Distribution of Entrepreneurs

By Entrepreneurial Career Length and

the Number of Ventures

Number of Ventures	Entrepreneurial Career Length in Years As of 1981					
	0-1	**1-2**	**3-6**	**7-11**	**12-22**	**Over 23**
	#	#	#	#	#	#
Single	3	10	33	15	14	12
Sequential	1	3	13	12	5	8
Overlapping	0	4	20	16	19	16
Total 206	4	17	66	44	38	37
	%	%	%	%	%	%
Single	75.0	58.8	50.0	34.1	36.8	32.4
Sequential	25.0	17.6	19.7	27.3	13.2	21.6
Overlapping	.0	23.5	30.3	36.4	50.0	43.2
Total	100.0	100.0	100.0	100.0	100.0	100.0

Source: Robert Ronstadt, *Entrepreneurial Careers: A Study of Career Pathways Pursued By Babson Entrepreneurs*, unpublished manuscript, Board of Research, Babson College, 1982.

evidence, mainly in the form of detailed case histories, is extremely convincing in showing the central importance of the strategy concept for entrepreneurs.[19]

Unfortunately, a strong strategy and subsequent *venture* success do not insure the survival of the founder or lead entrepreneur in all instances. Exceptional venture success which results in large sales growth generally leads to increasing complex organizational structures and tasks.[20] The founder may discover that he or she does not possess the managerial capability or the inclination to manage a larger, more complex enterprise. There is, perhaps, no more classic illustration of this phenomenon in entrepreneurial history and education than the oft cited experience of Howard Head, the founder of Head Ski and later the Chairman of Prince Manufacturing which developed the revolutionary Prince tennis racket. In his own words:

> If I hadn't had the mistakes behind me at Head, Prince probably would have been a disaster. Yes, I was a lousy manager (while at Head Ski). I was the chief and everyone else was an Indian. Running a company like that, with 500 Indians, was too complicated for my way of thinking. There was no time for me to be entrepreneurial; it was too much of a strain. Prince moved along ten times more easily than Head. I was letting other people run the company. I could be a gadfly; they built the solid underpinnings of a good organization while I reserved myself for what I do best -- critical judgment."[21]

Howard Head's experience also highlights an experience shared by many entrepreneurs who leave a venture because it's too successful or even when it fails outright. Their venture exit does not automatically spell the end of an entrepreneurial career. There are often other ventures. The key is their ability once again to identify and take advantage of them.

Interestingly, the evidence available thus far indicates that *practicing* entrepreneurs have a higher capability and likelihood of identifying solid venture opportunities than prospective entrepreneurs. The concept of *the corridor principle* explains this capability which is based on access to information about new venture opportunites. Briefly stated, the "corridor principle" describes a phenomenon that often occurs *after* entrepreneurs have launched their initial venture. Once in business, entrepreneurs move along a particular venture pathway which allows them to see new opportunities that were not visible nor available to them before getting into business. In one sense, these new opportunities are "corridors" or pathways to new venture possibilities. An intriguing and vital aspect of this phenomenon is that often one or more of the corridors leads ultmately to the venture success that the entrepreneur sought, but did not find with his/her original venture.[22]

How quickly the corridor principle functions is represented partly by how rapidly entrepreneurs launch second and third ventures after starting their initial venture.

Exhibit 4 shows the involvement in multiple ventures for one group of entrepreneurs on both a sequential (one venture started only after an earlier venture was ended) as well as an overlapping basis.[23] The percentage distributions show, as one would expect, increasing relative numbers of entrepreneurs involved in some kind of multiple venture as the number of years of entrepreneurial experience increases. What is interesting is the speed of this involvement. Half of all the entrepreneurs in the study had experience with more than one venture within six years of starting their initial venture and the majority of these "multiple venture entrepreneurs" were operating more than one venture simultaneously (i.e., on an overlapping basis).

The implications of these findings for the decision to continue an entrepreneurial career can be painfully evident to the entrepreneur whose only (single) venture has failed. Many reasons may underlie the creation of multiple ventures. Yet whatever the reasons their successful existence offers an insurance or portfolio effect to entrepreneurs. As one entrepreneur explained, "No one likes having all their eggs in one basket." To which another replied, "Most entrepreneurs don't even like to have just one basket."

The ability then to continue an entrepreneurial career for venture theorists resides in each entrepreneur's capability to formulate an effective corporate strategy which fosters long term success of a single venture and/or an ability to spot and execute new opportunities which result in a stream of new ventures over an entrepreneur's career.

Under what conditions will an entrepreneur end his or her career? For those considering venture-related causes, the reasoning emanates from an entrepreneur's inability *or* unwillingness to discover and develop another venture opportunity coupled with a) the failure of the initial venture; b) a desire to discontinue the venture for any number of reasons; or c) a need to disassociate oneself from the original venture. No one knows the relative frequencies of these different conditions nor the underlying causes of career discontinuance. In the case of venture failure, no doubt the depletion of sufficient economic resources affects greatly the willingness or freedom of an entrepreneur to pursue another venture even though one or more opportunities may be identified. In other instances, there may simply be a paucity of good opportunities given the entrepreneur's industry, experience, and interests.

One final observation is necessary given information gained from case histories about entrepreneurs and their decision to cease entrepreneurial activities. It relates specifically to the inability of some entrepreneurs to end their careers. Where psychologists see strong willed entrepreneurs refusing adamantly to renounce control and retire, others see venture factors forcing entrepreneurs to hold onto the reins of control and leadership. Venture size seems important here. For example, some entrepreneurs are not able to exit from a venture because they have no successor and they have no successor simply because the venture is not large enough to sustain a successor prior to succession. Also, many smaller ventures may prove unprofitable to liquidate given the nature and value of their assets. For similar reasons, they may not be saleable on the open market. Some entrepreneurs are, in effect, locked into their ventures until they can no longer run them.

TOWARD INTEGRATING THE THREE SCHOOLS OF THOUGHT

It should be evident by now that each school of thought about entrepreneurship has value and offers important insights about entrepreneurs and their activities. There is also reasons to believe that a richer, more powerful understanding of the process of entrepreneurship will be forthcoming if we select and integrate the more important findings into a single analytic framework which can apply to differing entrepreneurial situations.

To some extent, we have stated this integration by examining knowledge about entrepreneurship within the unifying concept of a career. Certainly one does not usually think of entrepreneurship as a career. Yet if one envisions a career as a series of related positions, projects, or functions, then entrepreneurship is a career comprised of one or a series of ventures, in one or a series of environments, involving one or more entrepreneurs. How to evaluate the many combinations is part of the art of entrepreneuring.

DISCUSSION QUESTIONS

1. How can knowledge about the decisions to start, continue, and end an entrepreneurial career help:

    a) potential entrepreneurs?

    b) practicing entrepreneurs?

2. What are the advantages/disadvantages of focusing exclusively on people, environmental, or venture factors to explain entrepreneurial activities?

3. What variables do you think are the most helpful in explaining the decisions to start, continue, or end entrepreneurial activities? Why?

KEY READINGS

Stanley M. Davis, "Politics and Organizational Underdevelopment in Chile," *Comparative Management: Organizational and Cultural Perspectives,* Prentice-Hall, 1971, pp 188-209.

Merrill E. Douglass, "Relating Education to Entrepreneurial Success," *Business Horizons,* Vol. 19, No. 6, December 1976, pp 40-44.

Everett E. Hagen, "The Entrepreneur as Rebel Against Traditional Society," *Human Organization,* Vol. 19, Winter 1960-61, pp 185-7.

Harry Schrage, "The R & D Entrepreneur: Profile of Success," *Harvard Business Review,* November/December 1965, pp 8-21.

Albert Shapero, "The Displaced, Uncomfortable Entrepreneur," *Psychology Today,* November, 1975, pp 8-13.

Jeffry Timmons, "Careful Self-Analysis and Team Assessment Can Aid Entrepreneurs," *Harvard Business Review,* November/December 1979.

NOTES

[1] Wolfe, Tom, *The Right Stuff.* New York: Bantam Books, 1980.

[2] Babson, Roger W.,(1875-1967) *Action and Reaction: An Autobiography of Roger W. Babson,* Revised edition. New York: Harper, 1949.

[3] McClelland, David, *The Achieving Society,* New York: Irvington Publishers, Inc., 1976, particular the "New Introduction" to a landmark work originally published by O. Van Nostrand Co. Inc., 1961.

[4] A great many citations are possible here. Some representative work is Orvis F. Collins and David G. Moore, *The Organization Makers: A Behavioral Study of Independent Entrepreneurs,* New York: Appleton-Century-Crofts, 1970, based on their earlier work, *The Enterprising Man,* East Lansing, MI, Michigan State University, 1964.

Hornaday, John A. and John Aboud, "Characteristics of Successful Entrepreneurs," *Personnel Psychology,* Volume 24, No. 2, Summer, 1971.

Shapero, Albert, "The Displaced, Uncomfortable Entrepreneur," *Psychology Today, November 1975, pp 8-13.*

Schere, Jean Loup. *Tolerance of Ambiguity as a Discriminating Variable Between Entrepreneurs and Managers.* Unpublished Dissertation, University of Pennsylvania, available from University Microfilms International, Ann Arbor, MI, 1981

[5] Collins, and Moore, *op. cit.,* provide a lengthy description of this personality.

[6] Douglass, Merrill E., "Relating Education to Entrepreneurial Success," *Business Horizons,* Volume 19, No. 6, December 1976, pages 40-44, regarding education vis-a-vis the general population. See Albert Shapero's "The Process of Technical Company Formation in a Local Area," in *Technical Entrepreneurship*, eds. Arnold C. Cooper and John L. Komives, Milwaukee, WI, Center for Venture Management, 1972, p. 79, for the link between "high tech" ventures and education.

Merrill, *op. cit.* provides data which shows that *among practicing entrepreneurs* "business school graduates are not as successful as other college majors," p. 44. A more forceful argument against traditional management education is voiced by Albert Shapero in his article, "Are Business Schools Teaching Business?" *Inc. Magazine,* January 1983, pp. 13-14.

[7]Schrage, Harry, "The R & D Entrepreneur: Profile of Success," *Harvard Business Review,* December-November, 1965, pages 8-21.

[8]A landmark article here is: Everett E. Hagen's, "The Entrepreneur as Rebel Against Traditional Society," *Human Organization,* Volume 19, Winger 1960-61, pages 185-187; also see, Peter Kilby's, *Entrepreneurship and Economic Development,* New York: Free Press, 1971 for several other studies of this genre.

[9]See Stanley M. Davis' "Politics and Organizational Underdevelopment in Chile." *Latin America,* pages 188-209.

[10]See Arnold C. Cooper and John Komives, eds., *Technical Entrepreneurship,* Milwaukee, WI, Center for Venture Management, 1972 for a summary of this work.

[11]Vesper, Karl H., "New Venture Ideas: Do Not Overlook Experience Factor," *Harvard Business Review,* July-Aug., 1979, pp. 164-67.

[12]Vesper, Karl H. *New Venture Strategies.* Englewood Cliffs, NJ: Prentice-Hall, 1980.

[13]Osgood, William R. and William E. Wetzel, Jr., "A Systems Approach to Venture Initiation," *Business Horizons,* October, 1977.

[14]Timmons, Jeffry A., "New Venture Creation: Models and Methodologies," See also his "Careful Self-Analysis and Team Assessment Can Aid Entrepreneurs," *Harvard Business Review,* Nov/Dec, 1979.

[15]For example, see Clifford Baumback and Kenneth Lawyer, *How to Organize and Operate A Small Business,* 6th edition, Englewood Cliffs, NJ, 1979.

[16]For example, Tate, et al and Steinhoff present different lists of steps to take when starting a venture. Examples of detailed guidelines for business plans are provided by Haslett and Smollen as well as Kelley, Campanella, and McKiernan. The specific citations are: a) Curtis E. Tate, Jr., Leon C. Megginson, Charles R. Scott, Jr., and Lyle R. Trueblood, *Successful Small Business Management,* Revised Edition, Dallas, Texas: Business Publications, Inc., 1978; see particularly Chapter 6, "How to Establish Your New Business," pp 42-110. 2) Dan Steinhoff, *Small Business Management Fundamentals,* Third Edition, New York: McGraw Hill, 1982, pp 45-50. c) Leonard E. Smollen and Brian Haslett, "Preparing A Business Plan" in *Guide to Venture Capital Sources,* fifth edition, Stanley E. Pratt, ed. Wellesley Hills, MA, Capital Publishing Corporation, 1981, pp 50-60. d) Albert J. Kelley, Frank B. Campanella, and John McKiernan, *Venture Capital: A Guidebook for New Enterprises,* Chestnut Hill, MA, The Management Institute, School of Management, Boston College, 1973, pp 3-25.

[17]Some basic works in the field are Chandler, *op. cit.* and Kenneth Andrews, *The Concept of Corporate Strategy,* Homewood, IL: Dow Jones-Irwin, 1971; and David C.D. Rogers, *Essentials of Business Policy,* New York: Harper & Row, 1975.

[18]Management deficiencies are discussed in Clifford M. Baumback's *Guide to Entepreneurship,* Englewood Cliffs: NJ, Prentice-Hall, Inc. pp 36-40. Other weaknesses are described in H.N. Broom and Justin G. Longenecker's *Small Business Management,* 5th edition, Cincinnati, OH: Southwesten Publishing Co., 1979, pp 21-25.

[19]Some representative cases would be "The Tax Man, Inc.," "A.G. Brown and Son, Ltd." "Cartridge Television, Inc.," "Dansk Design, Ltd." and "National Franchise Management, Inc." all found in *Strategy and Organization: Text and Cases In General Management* by Hugo R. Uyterhoeven, *et. al.,* Homewood, IL: Richard D. Irwin, 1973.

[20]See Larry E. Greiner's "Evolution and Revolution as Organizations Grow," *Harvard Business Review,* July/August, 1972, pp. 37-46.

[21]Howard Head's remarks to Babson students on the occasion of his special visit, Fall, 1982.

[22]Other than the work cited below, I know of no systematic work on this important phenonenon. Karl Vesper speaks briefly of the relationship between "first and second ventures" in *New Venture Strategies, op. cit.* p. 82. Otherwise the literature is silent on the topic.

[23]Robert Ronstadt, *Entrepreneurial Careers: A Study of the Career Pathways Pursued by Babson Entrepreneurs,* unpublished manuscript, Board of Research, Babson College, 1982, pp 104-116.

QUALITATIVE ASSESSMENT OF NEW VENTURES, ENTREPRENEURIAL ENVIRONMENTS, AND ENTREPRENEURS

In this chapter the purpose of our qualitative assessment is to help you reach critical decisions which must be made about important entrepreneurial career issues. Such issues include the startup of a new venture, its continuance or termination; the decision to pursue your career with one or more entrepreneurial partners or sever these entrepreneurial relationships; the decision to pursue your career in a new environment whether this environment be a different community, state, region, etc., a different industry, or under substantially different macro economic and political conditions.

I should stress that we are talking about any issue that represents an important choice for your entrepreneurial career--one you will obviously want to think about before acting. This distinction is important so you will not be misled. Many other entrepreneurial decisions exist which require quick, sometimes instantaneous, response. The assessment approach and techniques discussed in this chapter may not apply to you under these action-intense situations. You simply won't have the time to produce a neat and orderly analysis. Nor should you produce one. Entrepreneurship involves varying degrees of messiness and chaos. It is part of the inevitable debris produced by the creative art itself--whether or not any Schumpeterian "destruction" takes place. For example, there are probably parts of the Sistine Chapel that were not painted "according to plan" but were created on a moment's inspiration. Michelangelo, I'm sure, was hardly concerned about staying neat, clean, and orderly as he lay stretched out on his back facing the ceiling. Still, much prior thought went into the project, and technique was important in the planning and execution of the project. So it is with entrepreneurial ventures. Just as there are times of nonanalytic action and decision making, there are other times when careful assessment is the order for the day.

For purposes of exposition, qualitative assessment is separated from quantitative assessment in this book. However, they are actually quite intertwined. Pushing a few numbers can only serve to improve your qualitative judgments in most instances. Furthermore, effective assessment should not be done in a vacuum. As a practical matter, it is not very helpful to evaluate the skills and resources of potential entrepreneurs without relating them to a potential venture. Similarly, the evaluation of entrepreneurial environments is practically useless unless your assessment is related to specific venture opportunties and particular entrepreneurs.

Procedurally, then, an effective evaluation of a key entrepreneurial issue means we may have to consider several assessments, each interrelated but with a principal focus on the venture, the entrepreneurial environment, or the entrepreneur(s). Of course, one can begin this assessment from any of these vantage points. The choice usually depends on the nature of the issue, e.g., for issues that are primarily venture-related, the starting point will be a venture assessment. For the rest of this chapter, we will assume the primary entrepreneurial issue is the emergence of a new venture opportunity.

Assuming the primary issue is starting a new venture, I recommend focusing on several key venture factors. The next step is to assess directly the quality of the entrepreneurial environment for the proposed venture. This assessment is followed by an evaluation of the entrepreneurial capabilities of the protagonist(s) to see if they are appropriate for the proposed venture under the given environmental conditions. Next I recommend that these three assessments be used as inputs for a strategic assessment and then an ethical evaluation of the overall venture.

Exhibit 1 diagrams the various assessment steps. In order to grasp this procedure, it is presented as a sequential process, and we are forced to discuss it accordingly for clarity's sake. Consequently, the format for this chapter follows the assessment steps identified in *Exhibit 1*. Yet, in reality, the assessment procedure is more circular than represented in *Exhibit 1* since it often makes sense to loop forward and backward when considering interrelationships between variables, relating observations about venture factors to environmental and human factors and vice versa. Again, we unavoidably confront the "messiness" of entrepreneurial decision making. The specific sequence itself is unimportant. What is important is that we follow a procedure that helps us to touch all the relevant bases and ask the right questions about the interplay of key variables. In fact, it is the interrelationships that are generally most insightful regarding a final recommendation to pursue or sidestep a new venture opportunity or any other decision about an entrepreneurial issue. Consequently, at various points throughout this chapter, I will pose questions which will force consideration of these interrelationships.

Finally, while *Exhibit 1* illustrates an analytic procedure, it does not tell us specifically what questions we should ask about each assessment area. Fortunately, our selection of questions does not have to be an arbitrary decision. The preceding survey about entrepreneurial activities provides considerable direction. Moreover, this survey suggests several ways to order our questions and analysis. If you reflect for a moment on this material, you will recall that it has one overriding purpose: to develop in you "a mental set" whereby you think about entrepreneurship as a dynamic process. This dynamic aspect should be applied to our assessment of new ventures. Specifically, our assessment approach must incorporate the element of time and the possibility of change in its framework. This emphasis on the temporal element will be intuitively obvious to practicing entrepreneurs who know that time is their scarcest and most precious resource. Whether and how time will be allocated for a potential venture determines its ultimate viability.

How then should we introduce the element of time?

Exhibit 1

A Sample Assessment
of a New Venture Opportunity

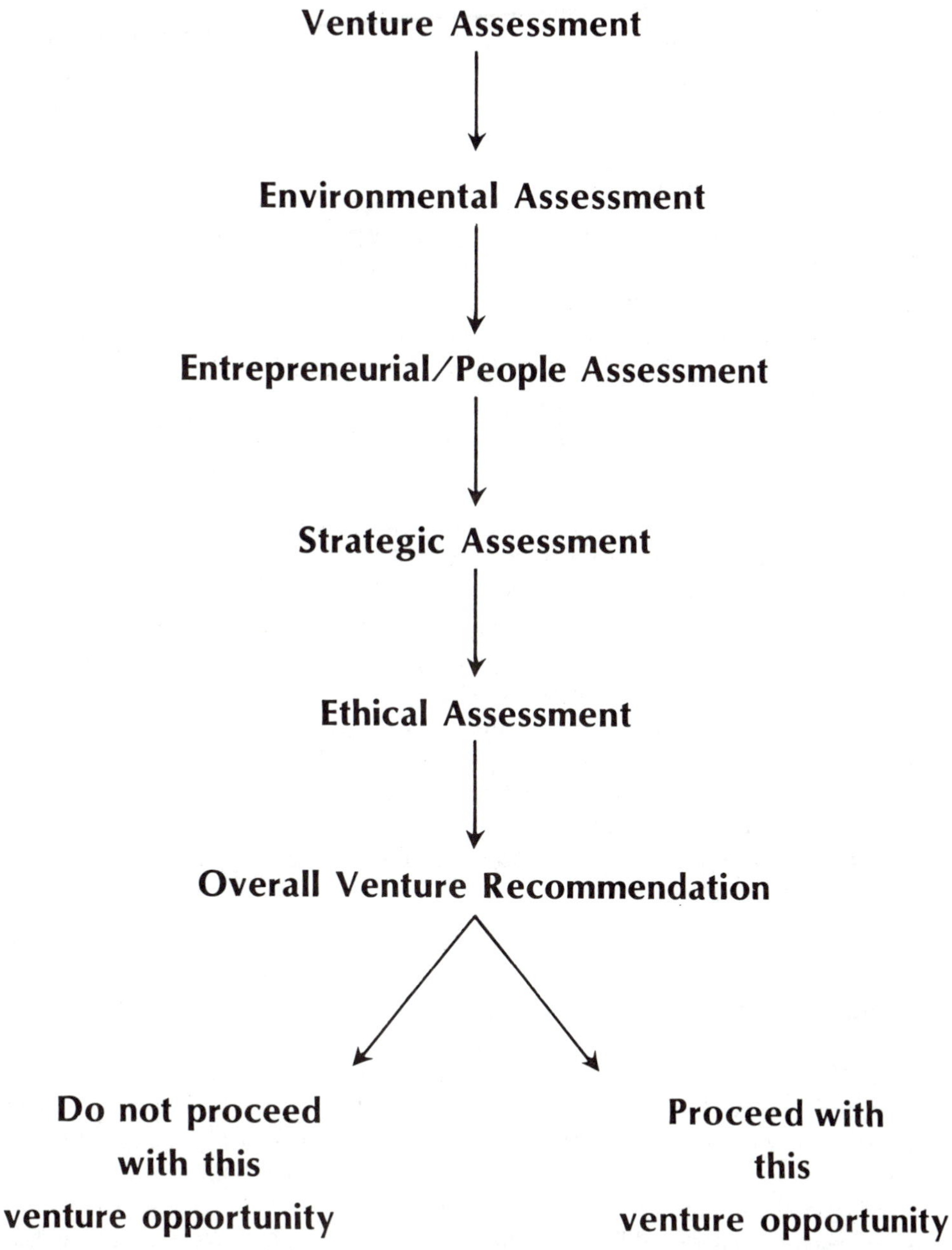

Venture Assessment

↓

Environmental Assessment

↓

Entrepreneurial/People Assessment

↓

Strategic Assessment

↓

Ethical Assessment

↓

Overall Venture Recommendation

**Do not proceed
with this
venture opportunity**   **Proceed with
this
venture opportunity**

A dynamic perspective was introduced earlier (Chapter Two, *Exhibit 2*) with the concept of an entrepreneurial career. How such careers unfold over time, and which pathways are preferable, will help us to put our assessment of entrepreneurs themselves into a dynamic context. However, for venture assessment, the venture process itself offers a better way to inject our assessment framework with a dynamic force.

I. ON VENTURE ASSESSMENT

All kinds of new ventures exist and, consequently, our evaluation of venture factors has one major objective: to identify or obtain a feel for the particular type of venture being considered for startup. This identification is possible by discovering the nature of certain venture characteristics and their relationship to the process of venture evolution. Let's start with the latter.

The process of venture evolution has at least three identifiable phases: a pre-startup phase, a startup phase, and a post-startup phase. By pre-startup, we mean the period that begins with an idea for a venture and ends when the doors are opened for business. The startup period commences with the initiation of sales activity and the delivery of products and/or services. It ends when the business is firmly established and beyond short-term threats of survival. The post-startup period lasts until the venture is terminated or the surviving organizational entity is no longer controlled by an entrepreneur and/or driven by an entrepreneurial spirit.

Various studies have focused on at least one of these phases, identifying other subprocesses or ways which ventures are started and developed over time. These studies all reinforce the fact that the three phases can vary considerably from one industry to another and one venture to another, even when similar ventures are in the same industry.[1] These time differences are caused by many factors, any one of which can affect the amount of time spent in the pre-startup, startup, or post-startup phases. And each phase may take literally a few minutes to many years. For example, one entrepreneur discovered a new venture possibility, already had the product available, and later that afternoon was making his first sale. By contrast, we are currently following another venture that has been in the pre-startup phase for over nine years. It is a large-scale venture involving the conversion of energy from geothermal sources. The basic research, process technology development, and testing have thus far resulted in an investment of over $20 million.

Similarly, the startup and post-startup phases can last for highly variable amounts of time. We often think of the startup period encompassing a few days or weeks or months. But in some cases it can go on for many years. The same possibility also exists regarding the post-startup phase. Generally we tend to look at the post-startup period as very long but it may, in fact, last only a short period of time. In some instances it may be impossible for an entrepreneur to predict with any sense of accuracy just how long this post-startup phase will be. Here we will be interested primarily in the pre-startup and startup periods. In other instances, we may be able to make some ballpark estimates about the post-startup period. We may know, for instance, that the entrepreneur plans to sell the venture as soon as it becomes established. In the absence of such plans, we may still be dealing with one or more entrepreneurs who have track records of moving on to new ventures after some period of time. In either event, we know that the continued existence of an entrepreneurial spirit is often tied to the continued association of the founder and/or entrepreneur who brought the venture through the startup phase. We also have evidence which suggests there are some key moments during the life of a venture when the lead entrepreneur is likely to leave the venture and/or terminate his or her entrepreneurial career.[2]

Fortunately, historical experience provides us with some good indications for the length of the pre-startup and startup periods. Also, we generally need no more than rough approximations to reach some interesting insights about the viability of a proposed venture. For example, the pre-startup phase for a small, traditional restaurant might be five to six months on average. This estimate may vary upward or downward depending on the prior experience of the owners and their knowledge of feasible locations. By contrast, the establishment of an unconventional restaurant may take anywhere from a year to several years to implement, especially when its concept is unique and/or it is being established on a size or scale previously untested or unknown by anyone else. Rocky Aoki's experience with Benihana is a case in point. Two years of work went into the pre-startup phase for the first Benihana unit which introduced a new kind of "Americanized" Japanese food to the United States, prepared unconventionally in front of the consumer.

Given this great variability in time, prospective entrepreneurs must identify the length of the pre-startup period and appreciate its implications. Will you have the appropriate skills and resources to move through the pre-startup phase? Most importantly, will you have the time to commit your own energies to the project during this period? Who else will you involve? And how will you involve them?

Your approximations of the time required to move through the three venture phases will change as you learn more about a given venture. But the extent of change will depend on your entrepreneurial experience with starting and operating new ventures. For example, the old rule of thumb about the pre-startup period is still pertinent to most prospective entrepreneurs with little or no prior entrepreneurial experience or training. As the saying goes, "figure whatever time you think it will take you to start a new venture, and then triple it."

Given this latitude, you may wonder if such time estimates have any use. The answer is "yes" for two reasons. First, your estimates will get better with practice. Second, even if they don't, you will still identify the rough order of magnitude under consideration. For instance, what we wish to know is whether a pre-startup period will take one week, one month, or one year of our time. It may turn out to be three weeks, three months, or three years respectively but even after considering the "triple it" rule, we will still have a useful approximation of the range of time involved.

Nevertheless, we can do better than a 300% error in our time estimates. Considerable improvement is possible and I expect the "triple it" rule exists simply because most prospective entrepreneurs do not know and/or do not consider explicitly how different venture, environmental, and people variables affect the element of time and the venture process.

The next step is to refine your assessment of the time to move through the venture process with information about the characteristics of the venture. Information from a variety of sources indicates that some critical venture characteristics are:[3]

1. the relative *uniqueness* of the venture;

2. the relative *investment size* at startup;

3. the expcted *growth of sales and/or profits* as the venture moves through its startup phase;

4. the *availability of products* during the pre-startup and startup phases; and

5. the *availability of customers* during the pre-startup and startup phases.

Obviously, these are *not* the only variables that may be important for a particular venture. The list can be expanded and you shouldn't hesitate to add variables you consider important. Let us now discuss each one regarding its relationship to the time process.

● *The time required to move through the pre-startup and startup periods increases as venture uniqueness increases.*

Of course, every new venture has unique elements; however, the range of uniqueness can be considerable, encompassing relatively routine ventures (another pizza parlor) to the relatively non-routine (companies producing biogenetic products). Aside from human and locational distinctions, what separates the routine from the non-routine venture is the amount of innovation required during pre-startup and thereafter. Generally speaking, how much innovation will be required to produce new products and services that haven't been produced before? This distinction also includes the need for new process technology to produce these services or products, as well as the need to service new market segments. Venture uniqueness is further distinguished by the length of time a non-routine venture will remain non-routine. For instance, will new products, new technology, and new markets be required on a continuing basis? Or will the venture be able to "settle down" after some startup period and utilize existing products, technologies, and markets with minor adjustments?

In extreme cases, the issue of uniqueness is obvious. Yet many new ventures get started without entrepreneurs appreciating the true uniqueness of their concept and hence its true impact on their time. Yet we know the amount of time required to define and develop a venture concept during the prestart period increases as uniqueness increases. Why? More is unknown and must be discovered about products, markets, and technologies before the venture can be ready for business. The acquisition of this knowledge takes time. The same is true for the startup period when new products and/or technology must be found for changing markets.

The following are some relevant assessment questions to ask about the entrepreneurial environment and the entrepreneurs involved with routine versus non-routine ventures:

1. What kinds of venture experience do the entrepreneurs have with routine ventures?...with non-routine ventures?

2. Are their skills particularly strong in the areas where the venture is non-routine? In terms of:

   a) new product development?

   b) the industry environment?

   c) the macro/political/economic environment?

3. For highly non-routine ventures, have they exhibited strong personal profiles regarding creativity, objectivity (veridical traits), and tolerance for ambiguous and unstructured situations?

• *The time required for the pre-start period increases as investment size increases. However, the time available for the startup phase decreases as investment size increases.*

The capital investment required to start a new venture can vary considerably in some industries--from under $100,000 to upwards of many millions. But in some industries only larger-scale startups are feasible. For example, one can start a smaller venture in the publishing industry which can grow into a larger venture or remain a smaller enterprise. By contrast, starting a new automobile company requires considerably more investment capital as John Z. DeLorean's recent attempt illustrates. Anyone attempting to crack major airline routes will also require a considerable up-front investment. New York Air is a case in point.

In fact, New York Air is a good example for this section since venture uniquesness *per se* was not a major factor in its startup. The product/services offered, the markets targeted, and the process technology (jumbo jets) were all routine in the sense they were not substantially different from those of other competitors. By far, the most distinguishing feature of the venture was its investment size which was related to the amount of capital equipment employed and the scope of operations. The size of the up-front investment meant a great deal of planning preceded actual operations...in fact, had to precede them given legal (regulatory), financial, marketing, scheduling, and other operating concerns. What is more, the complete venture system (all services) had to be ready the first day New York Air opened for business. A small, piecemeal startup was not possible which was another way of saying the smallest viable size of operations (minimum plant size) was quite large. Huge losses would occur if all elements of this operation did not come together like clockwork. But large profits were also possible early in the venture's life given the large amount of capital employed.*

---

*The concept of *operating* leverage, discussed in the next chapter, explains in quantitative terms why large profits or losses were possible outcomes.

Consequently, the startup period for such ventures tends to be relatively short. While many ventures can tolerate, even expect, several years of losses before turning a profit, it is unlikely that New York Air could have tolerated more than a few months "in the red" during its startup period. Remember, it is one thing to create a smaller or moderate-sized business and then grow it into a larger corporation. It's quite another cup of tea to start out relatively large the first day of operations. In these instances, a substantial investment must precede the startup period.

Consequently, a primary issue for any venture assessment is the extent and timing of investment funds needed to move through the venture process. Related questions about the environment and the venture's entrepreneurs are:

1. Will industry growth be sufficient to maintain breakeven sales to cover a high fixed cost structure during the startup period?

2. If not, is existing industry competition sufficiently weak to allow the capture of market share from direct competitors early in the startup period? or at a later date?

3. Do special allowances or support structures exist in the local or macro environment which will substantially reduce the payback period for such a large investment or otherwise help to protect the investment tax credits, etc.?

4. Do the principal entrepreneurs have access to substantial financial reserves to protect a large initial investment?

5. Do the entrepreneurs involved have the appropriate contacts to take advantage of various environmental opportunities?

6. Do the entrepreneurs involved have both industry and entre-preneurial track records which justify the financial risk of a large scale startup?

● *The time required to move through the pre-startup and startup periods increases as the expected growth rate of venture sales and profits increases.*

What is the growth pattern anticipated for venture sales and profits? Are sales and profits expected to grow slowly or level off shortly after startup? Are large profits expected at some point with only small or moderate sales growth? Another scenario is one that sees high sales growth and high profit growth or possibly limited initial profits, but *eventually* high profit growth over a multi-year period.

Exhibit 2 diagrams or classifies new ventures along a two-way continuum by their *expected* sales and profit growth. While many ways exist to classify new ventures, we have found that most entrepreneurs are comfortable classifying themselves into one of three categories along this continuum with a minimum amount of overlap.[4] These categories are defined below while *Exhibit 3* shows the actual distribution for 203 practicing entrepreneurs.

Exhibit 2

New Ventures Classified By Their
Expected Sales And Profit Growth

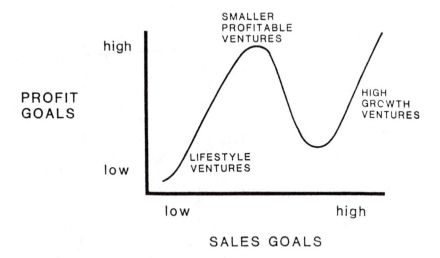

As *lifestyle ventures* where independence, autonomy, and control appear to be the primary driving forces. Neither large sales *nor* profits are deemed important beyond providing a sufficient and comfortable living for the entrepreneur.

As *smaller profitable ventures* where financial considerations play a more important role. Again, autonomy and control are important in the sense that the entrepreneur does not wish venture sales (and employees) to become so large that he or she must relinquish equity or ownership control and thus control over cash flow and profits which are hoped to be substantial.

As *high growth ventures* where significant sales and profit growth are expected to the extent that it *may* be possible to attract venture capital money and/or funds raised through public or private placements.

These distinctions are important because the time needed to move through the venture process varies for each kind of venture. While exceptions exist, we can generally say that:

For *lifestyle ventures,* the pre-startup period is often very short, characterized by easy entry with only modest planning efforts required. Similarly, the startup period can be relatively short before sales and profits plateau at a level sufficient for the venture to survive. Finally, the post-startup period is short relative to the other two kinds of ventures. While this period may last for many years, we know that lifestyle ventures tend to be started at a later age and perhaps more important, they tend not to survive the founder.[5]

For smaller profitable ventures, the prestartup period is generally somewhat longer (three months to a year). Various case studies also reveal that the startup period can be fairly long (from four to five years) before the venture is firmly established. Finally, the post-startup period for these kinds of ventures can be quite long, lasting beyond the founder's tenure since there are usually sufficient assets to attract and train one or more successors. Also, the relative smallness of the enterprise helps to maintain its entrepreneurial character.

For high-growth ventures, the pre-start period is relatively long, anywhere from one to three years or more. The startup period can be very fast; however, statisticians would say that there is considerable dispersion around the mean and if we take our cue from venture capitalists, these enterprises usually take seven to ten years to get on their feet. The post-startup period can also be highly variable. Once firmly established, the original founders may leave as bureaucratic malaise sets in; on the other hand, there are some glittering examples of high growth ventures that have maintained a vibrant entrepreneurial atmosphere for many years after becoming industry leaders.

It's important at this point to stress that we are looking at our assessment of the venture's sales and profit growth, not necessarily the entrepreneur's initial goals or expectations in this regard. There are, of course, several important questions to ask about the entrepreneurs and the environmental relationships associated with this venture factor. For instance:

1. Have the entrepreneurs asked what sales and profit growth will be?

2. Is their estimate consistent with yours? Are the entrepreneurs' goals in a sales/profit sense congruent with expected venture growth?

3. What will happen if more or less success is encountered in a profit/sales sense (i.e., a lifestyle venture encounters unforeseen sales and profits and evolves perhaps kicking

Exhibit 3

The Goals of 203 Entrepreneurs
When They Started Their Initial Ventures

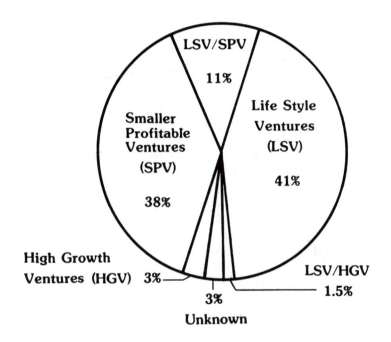

SOURCE: 1981 Survey of 203 Entrepreneurs by author

and screaming into a smaller profitable venture)? Will the lead entrepreneur be able to make the transition?

4. What if sales/profits are less than expected? Can the entrepreneur(s) downgrade their goals and aspirations?

5. Are there special support mechanisms in the local environment which will help secure the survival of a "marginal" lifestyle venture? ("Marginal" in a sales and profit sense.)

6. Will development or expansion of a smaller profitable venture invite competitive response from larger, stronger companies?

7. Do various macro economic factors support the launching of a high growth venture at this time?

• *The time required to move through the pre-startup and startup phases decreases with product availability.*

An essential condition for any venture is the need for something to sell. It may be a product or a service but, as we've seen with New York Air, it must be available for sale by the time the venture opens its doors to the public. This point may seem obvious yet it is surprising how often ventures fail to get started on time because of product delays. Do you have a product or service ready for sale?...not "in development," or "on its way from a supplier or subcontractor" but physically on hand? Larger scale startups can suffer greatly even from short delays in terms of getting their products and services on stream. Smaller scale projects or ventures may suffer just as intensely if the delay is long enough or customers become confused about the venture, its purpose, and image.

All other things held constant, the pre-startup phase will lengthen in direct proportion to the amount of time required to gain physical control of a product. The same statement applies to the startup period if new products and/or major product improvements will be required by changing customer needs and wants.

Pertinent assessment questions to ask about entrepreneurs and their environment in this regard are:

1. Do the entrepreneurs in question have the appropriate financial resources to obtain the necessary product or products in a timely manner?

2. If the products are not readily available, how will they be obtained? How much time will be required?

3. If products must be developed, do the entrepreneurs have the appropriate skills to manage the product innovation process?

4. What amount of resources must be committed before a product for sale actually exists?

5. What is the level of industry innovation regarding these products?

6. What effect specifically will innovation by others have on the lifecycle of your products?

• *The time required to move through the pre-startup and startup periods decreases as certainty about customer sales increases.*

If the venture's product is readily available before the venture is started, the risk of venture success is considerably lower than otherwise. Similarly, venture risk is affected by the availability and knowledge of customers for a venture prior to its startup. Perhaps the least risky situation is where customers are willing to pay you *in cash* for products or services to be delivered in the future (that is to say, before the venture is ever started). Any club or association that has a membership drive before opening its doors falls into this category. Slightly more risky are those customers you can identify who are willing to at least guarantee in writing that they will buy your products or services for some period of time as soon as they are available. These situations are not as uncommon as they may sound. An entrepreneur should be continually asking if there is some way to devise a venture concept so a way can be found to guarantee sales before startup.

At the other end of the risk continuum is the enterprise that gets started without knowing exactly who will buy its product. A critical question here is how long will it take you to determine who exactly are your customers, along with their buying habits?

There are indications that the relationship between time and customer knowledge is not always inverse nor linear. Generally speaking, the relationship is one where greater amounts of customer knowledge are associated with smaller amounts of time to move through the pre-startup and startup periods. However, expections occur when entrepreneurs feel that "all the market research in the world" will not conclusively prove that a market exists for their products. In short, when entrepreneurs feel that gathering information about the market will be so difficult, expensive, and inconclusive, they may ignore it altogether. In these instances, a severe lack of market knowledge may in fact accelerate the pre-startup period.

Of course, the decision to ignore the market is an extremely risky one. There are after all two fundamental criteria for entrepreneurial success. The first is having a customer who is willing to pay you a profitable price for a product or a service. The second is that you must physically possess and deliver this product or service. The farther a venture removes itself from certainty about these two rules, the greater its risk and the greater the time required to offset this risk as the venture moves through the pre-startup and startup periods.

Some assessment questions to ask about the entrepreneurs and the environmental conditions associated with this venture factor are:

> 1. Have they tried to presell their customers? Can the venture be conceived in such a way so that "customer certainty" is enhanced?
>
> 2. What steps can they take to increase customer certainty?
>
> 3. Do they have the skills and resources to take these steps?
>
> 4. Who specifically are the customers? What market segments are involved and how have other competitors and/or noncompetitors serviced these segments in the past?

SOME CONCLUDING OBSERVATIONS ABOUT VENTURE ASSESSMENT

Once information is obtained for these five venture factors, you will be in a position to begin estimating the time required to initiate the proposed venture and take it through the three venture phases. These estimates must then be translated into dollars. In short, you will be able to start making realistic projections of sales, margins, expenses, cash flows, required investment funds, breakevens, etc. for appropriate time periods given your time estimates.

Remember, as one moves through venture assessment, a picture should emerge which outlines a proposed venture. For example, we may see that the venture is a non-routine, large scale startup with high growth expectations, without readily available products or customers. To look favorably upon such a venture, one might expect to encounter very positive assessments of the entrepreneurs involved with this venture and the particular environmental setting of the venture. By contrast, a venture profile at the other end of the spectrum (routine, low upfront investment, lifestyle, readily available customers and products) might require a far less positive assessment regarding entrepreneurial and environmental inputs. Let us now turn our attention to one of these areas -- environmental assessment.

II. ON ENVIRONMENTAL ASSESSMENT

Environments change and so the assessment of an environment regarding its desirability for a particular entrepreneurial venture should be an ongoing activity. The current recession demonstrates the incredible impact that an economic environment can have on certain kinds of entrepreneurial activities, regardless of venture phase.

There are three kinds of environments that entrepreneurs need to assess for their support or non-support of entrepreneurial activities. The first is the local community environment where entrepreneurs locate their venture and possibly their primary residence.[6] The second is the industry environment of the venture. The third is the macro economic/political environment at both the state and national level (and in some cases the international level depending on the nature of the venture). As *Exhibit 4* shows, all three environments can be interrelated to some extent.

Exhibit 4
Key Environments for Entrepreneurs

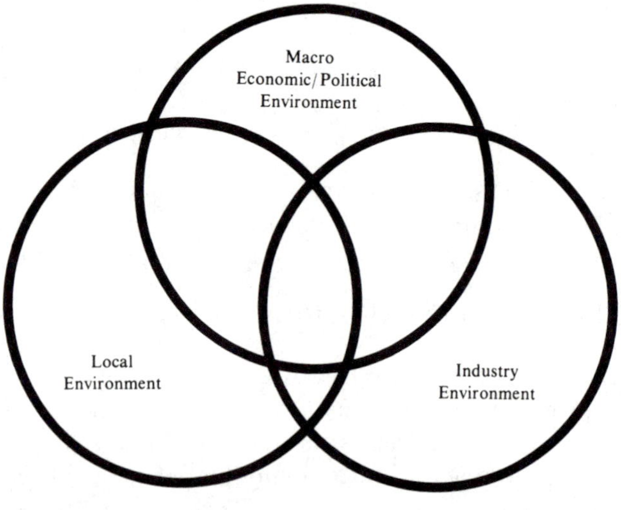

• *Assessing Local Community Environments*

At the community level, a critical factor is the size of your venture relative to other ventures in the community and the size of the community itself. In short, are you a big fish in a small pond or vice versa? Even if you are a small fish, the operative issue may be whether or not you are perceived as having the potential of becoming a more important force in the local business community.

At the local level, your relative importance is measured partly in terms of your venture's sales, employment, and/or payment of local taxes. Sales may not be just your sales but the sales you may produce indirectly for other businesses by bringing customers into the local community. Your sales level will also have an impact on your working capital needs and consequently, the amount of business you may be doing with local banks. Similarly, your use of local suppliers may have an impact on your working capital needs and consequently, the amount of business you may be doing with local banks. Similarly, your use of local suppliers may have an important impact on their businesses. The members of your local community may particularly appreciate the services that they receive from your business venture. Or they may particularly appreciate the image your business gives their community. Or you may be in the enviable position of accounting for a large percentage of a community's employment base. Or you may make meaningful contributions to property taxes and other taxes that help fund local community activities. The point, of course, is that you may have developed some support and allegiance from the local community because of your business activities. Extreme examples often make a better illustration of these observations. For example, the renowned mail order company, L.L. Bean of Freeport, Maine, has given to and received considerable support from its local community since the company's founding over 70 years ago. L.L. Bean has in a very real sense put Freeport on the map and helps to account considerably for the prosperity that town members have enjoyed over the years. The opposite kind of treatment was received recently from an entrepreneur who decided to open a retail outlet in Stoughton, Massachusetts. Local town members picketed, went to court, and succeeded in closing the business because of their objections to his products; pornographic magazines. Despite one's personal feelings about these materials, I should stress that this venture was a legal business. The local environment, however, made it a nonviable business.

A first cut at assessing the support of a local environment toward entrepreneurship can be achieved by simply appraising the extent of entrepreneurship in your particular area. For example, what type of entrepreneurs currently live in your area? How many? What kinds of ventures are most prevalent? What experience do the following have with entrepreneurs like you?

> Raw material suppliers
> Financial sources (local banks)
> Non-skilled employees
> Skilled employees
> Customers
> Government agency representatives

Sometimes familarity breeds contempt but generally the more experience these individuals have with entrepreneurs in your industry and/or technology, the easier will be your dealings with them.

Such analysis is the first step in determining if any possibility exists or could exist for exceptional support (or opposition) by various community groups. The following two exhibits illustrate two sets of conditions for the likelihood of community support. *Exhibit 5* relates the possible level of support given the community's reliance on an entrepreneur's venture and the entrepreneur's loyalty to the community, while *Exhibit 6* represents "David versus Goliath" syndrome. It is based on human behavior studies (equity theory) which essentially say, here is a nice young chap (David) who *deserves* to win--for any number of reasons. In David's case, it's his much smaller size compared to Goliath, as well as David's courage as he confronts his monstrous adversary who is simply too large, ugly, and awesome to identify with. The analogy, of course, breaks down somewhat since David never received any special help from his community with Goliath, though heaps of honors and privileges came his way later because, again, he "deserved" these rewards. The same can be true for entrepreneurs, particularly during times of crisis, if your community feels for any number of reasons that you deserve their special support. Such perceptions are also unavoidably intertwined with your community's ability to identify with you and/or your venture.

QUESTIONS FOR LOCAL ENVIRONMENTAL ASSESSMENT

Some assessment questions about entrepreneurs and their ventures vis-a-vis the local environment are:

1. How familiar is an entrepreneur with the community where his/her venture will be located?

2. How well known is this individual within the community?

3. Will the proposed venture make any special positive or negative impact within the community

    a) during the pre-startup period?
    b) during the startup period?
    c) during the post-startup period?

4. Are there any influential members of the community who will support or oppose the venture

    a) during the pre-startup period
    b) during the startup period?
    c) during the post-startup period?

5. Do the entrepreneur(s) have special skills in human relations with which to nurture key local contacts?

6. What action steps can be taken to strengthen local support and/or maximize local opportunities

    a) during the pre-startup period?
    b) during the startup period?
    c) during the post-startup period?

7. What action steps can be taken to reduce local opposition and/or minimize local problems

    a) during the pre-startup period?
    b) during the startup period?
    c) during the post-startup period?

• *Assessing Industry Environments**

Industry assessment poses two critical questions for every entrepreneur. The first question is what will be the intensity of competition facing you in your particular business given the present and likely future state of the industry? The second question is, given the nature of future competition, what is the likely industry life cycle for the products and markets of your venture? For example, we know from a variety of industries studied that new business developments in some industries have very fast or short growth periods before market saturation occurs and growth levels off. We also know it is generally easier to sell in growth markets than in stable ones. Competition almost inevitably becomes more intense as industry growth declines.[7]

The subjects of industry and market analysis are extensive and my purpose is not to review these topics in a few pages. Rather than a lengthy discussion of industry and market analysis, what I wish to do is provide you with a series of questions which I believe will help you to perform a better industry or market assessment. However, your application of these questions will not be effective if you forget what I believe is the key message of this section: good industry analysis made by and/or for entrepreneurs must relate to their prticular company and its problems and opportunities. A great industry analysis can be detailed, extensive, and informative but largely irrelevant if the analysis

---

*Portions of this section are reproduced with permission from Chapter Fifteen "Relevant Industry and Market Analysis" of my book, *The Art of Case Analysis,* Dover, MA: Lord Publishing, 1977 pp. 115-120.

Exhibit 5

ENVIRONMENTAL ASSESSMENT: THE LIKELIHOOD OF SPECIAL COMMUNITY SUPPORT

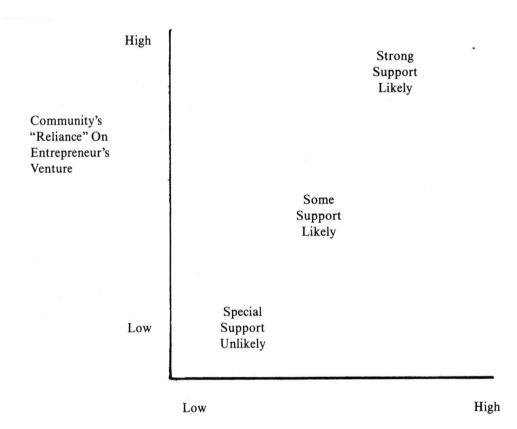

"Reliance" being defined as such things as:

- the % of total town employment accounted for by the venture
- the extent of debt or equity investment made in the venture by local banks or investors
- the extent to which the venture brings customers into the community for other businesses

Exhibit 6

ENVIRONMENTAL ASSESSMENT: THE LIKELIHOOD
OF SPECIAL COMMUNITY SUPPORT

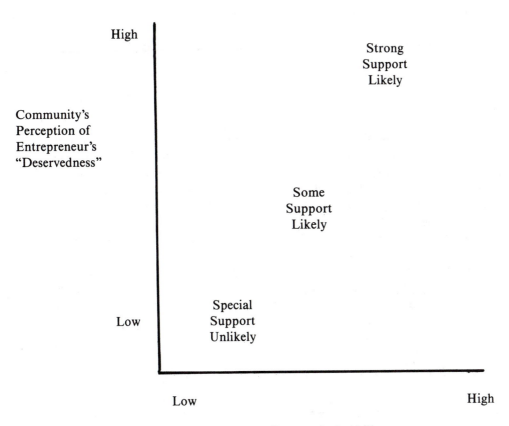

Community's
Perception of
Entrepreneur's
"Deservedness"

High

Strong
Support
Likely

Some
Support
Likely

Low

Special
Support
Unlikely

Low   High

Community's Ability to
Identify with You and/or Your Venture

does not have a reference point, e.g., the future competitiveness of a specific organization. Consequently the overriding question of you regading industry assessment is: how will industry trends and characteristics impact specifically on the venture you are proposing? Eight other questions will help you to answer this general inquiry.

1. *What is a relevant definition of the industry for our venture?*

In other words, who are the direct competitors or potentially direct competitors within a product-market-technology grouping that serves a basic function (e.g. transportation). I wish to stress the word "relevant" industry definition because changing circumstances (e.g., the strong possibility of radical innovation or the lack of it) may suggest a broader versus a narrower definition of the industry.

Many classic examples exist of business managers defining product/markets too narrowly (the buggywhip industry). Nevertheless, a great many businesses have been forced to sell out, merge, or liquidate because they defined (sometimes implicitly) their business too broadly. Consequently, you can rely on no pat formula to tell you what is the "relevant" industry. All we can say is that the relevant definition will change for particular firms over time. Equally important but less appreciated is the fact that the relevant definition of an industry may change for one or more firms in an industry but not for others. A healthy portion of the art and science of entrepreneurship is making good judgments about the impact of industry trends, product changes, and market shifts for a particular organization. Do changes in the industry indeed affect my company, my business, my strategy to the extent that I must change my conception of what is the relevant industry?

2. *How many companies are already in our industry and what characteristics do they have compared to our company?*

An analysis of the number, relative size, traditions, and cost structures of direct competitors in your industry can indicate the future severity of competition. A key question for you is to ask whether competition is likely to become more or less severe as the number and characteristics of competitors change over time in particular ways.

For instance, what will happen to the severity of competition if:

a) market growth increases rapidly?
b) direct competitors equalize in size?
c) one or two direct competitors become substantially larger in size?
d) product/service differentiation slows down?
e) values and aspirations of direct competitors become more diverse?

Other questions exist which affect the severity of industry competition. Try to identify and answer them. Initially, I suggest you pose simple questions with only one variable changing like those above. Once you grasp these simpler relationships, however, you must remember that real life situations are usually more complex. Three or four variables may be changing simultaneously and you must gather additional information to determine the net effect. For example, what will be the severity of competition if new entrants are increasing the total number of direct competitors in the industry while market size and growth are expanding rapidly and product differentiation is increasing.?

3. *How many suppliers service our industry, what are their characteristics, and what is their posture regarding our company?*

Basically, you want to determine the relative bargaining strength of your venture (versus other companies in your industry) with the companies that supply your industry with raw materials and component parts. Are you facing a supplier industry that is essentially a monopoly, an oligopoly, or is it characterized by a large number of firms? Do suppliers tend to favor or disfavor your company compared to other firms in your industry?

4. *How many buyers does our industry have, what are their characteristics, and their attitude regarding our specific company?*

The purpose of this set of questions is the same as for suppliers. You need to determine your relative bargaining power with buyers compared to other companies in your industry. First, you must ask who are the buyers? Are they end-users, distributors, representatives, other processors, or some combination of buyers? What kind of money (contribution dollars) do you make with each group or buyers? What influence will you have with each group of buyers in the future? What, most important, are their characteristics, existing needs, and future needs that your venture can possibly satisfy?

5. *How much "value added" is captured by suppliers, other companies in our industry, our company, versus buyers (i.e., distributors or other processors)?*

In a sense, value added analysis is an aggregated form of contribution analysis. In the latter, sales minus variable costs equals contribution dollars. However, data are not always available for all variable costs, while raw material purchases are often known, published across industry groups or easy to determine for individual ventures. Value added simply equals sales minus raw material costs. The purpose of the concept is to determine for comparative purposes how much "value is being added" to raw materials by different industry groups by their direct and indirect labor, capital (depreciation charge), and other overhead as inputs move through various stages of processing to final consumption by an end-user.

For our purposes, the value added concept is useful to see which group or groups have historically captured larger shares of value added. Usually, the profitability of a company is limited within some range by the amount of value it can add to a product or service. Finally, the concept is useful to determine the likelihood of forward or backward integration by companies associated with our industry, e.g., our suppliers, and/or our buyers. For example, the existence of low value added for one industry group may indicate easy entry by suppliers or buyers. Why? Because a supplier, for instance, may need to acquire little additional knowledge or skills (labor) or plant and equipment (capital) to produce the additional value added. The presence of high value added, however, often suggests the opposite. Considerable additional labor and/or capital are often needed to acquire the substantial new skills and resources that permit forward or backward integration.

6.*How has market size for particular industry products grown in the past, what is the present market size, and what is the potential market size in the foreseeable future?*

Industries are composed of products and markets which shift and change over time. Certain kinds of products are known to follow life cycles which move from birth and growth to maturity and decline. Indeed, industries often follow a life cycle when they are defined in terms of particular product/market technology groups (e.g., the internal combustion passenger automobile) as opposed to broad functional definitions (passenger transportion).

In practice, the determination of an industry position in its life cycle is no easy task. However, a look at the growth rate of market size in the past (in terms of sales and/or units sold) may provide a rough indication of future possibilities. Is the industry still growing rapidly, leveling off, or declining? What is the likelihood that new products and/or markets will be developed in the near future? Will these new product/market developments cause more rapid growth and attract new entrants, or will a modest new upswing in market growth occur with no significant change in the industry? Or will new product/market development simply result in a slight retardation of market decline with perhaps fewer firms leaving the industry than originally expected? Of course, the possibilities are more numerous than the few mentioned here, but that's what makes industry analysis an exciting and challenging affair.

7.*What impact will changes in the national and international economies have on our industry and our markets?*

Some businesses are more recession-resistant than other businesses. Others are more inflation-proof. In an age of "stagflation," some are both recession-resistant and inflation-proof. Conversely, businesses in some industries parallel closely the cyclical movements of the national economy. When the economy is up, business is good. When the economy is down, business suffers despite the presence of even the best managers.

For industry/market analysts, these different possible associations with the economy must be spelled out explicitly for two levels - the industry level and the company level. Both levels of analysis are necessary because the strategies, skills, and resources of individual companies often differ within an industry. An industry may indeed become violently ill when national or world economies become sick; but the sickness may not affect equally all firms in the industry. For instance, a severe recession may reduce demand and market growth for a particular industry while providing an opportunity for a smaller cost-efficient company to improve its market share position relative to other industry competitors. A superior job of industry/market analysis will determine these relative impacts within an industry for a particular company and its strategy.

8. *Finally, given our analysis of the preceding seven questions, what are the success criteria for this industry? Are these success criteria changing? What will they be in the future?*

Ask youself, who have been the winners and losers in this industry? Why have they been winners or losers? Will the emergence, resurgence, or decline of new product innovation, new process innovation, government regulations, consumer awareness groups, new market needs and tastes, and a host of other environmental changes cause a change in the success factors that made certain companies winners in the past?

QUESTIONS FOR INDUSTRY ENVIRONMENTAL ASSESSMENT

Finally, your answers to these eight industry questions will influence the kind of assessment questions you will pose about particular entrepreneur(s) and their ventures. For example:

1. Is the industry being defined in a way that favors the skills and resources of the entrepreneur(s) in question?

2. Is the industry being redefined in a way that favors the proposed location of the venture?

3. From a psychological perspective, can the entrepreneur(s) live with low or moderate industry growth?

4. From a capability standpoint, can the entrepreneur(s) manage a high-growth situation?...a low-growth situation?

5. Can the entrepreneur(s) manage a venture in an industry environment of intense competitive rivalry?

6. Are the proposed venture economics feasible if industry growth levels off sooner than anticipated?

• *Assessing Macro Political/Economic Environments*

There seems little doubt that action taken by the courts, different legislative bodies, and/or other government offices can have a tremendous impact on the decision to initiate a new venture or maintain an existing one. Furthermore, the process of shaping political and economic events is one that has not favored the entrepreneur, particularly the small business entrepreneur in the past--an unsettling situation for those who wish to control their destinies. Of course, the voice of "big business" has been heard in various arenas charged with setting macro policies. But even big business has stuggled to regain its preeminent position in this country's political and economic process since the Great Depression. The recent rise of PACs, "political action committees," in many larger corporations further emphasizes the importance big business ascribes to the political/economic process and the role it seeks to play. But whatever the outcome, there is little doubt that the 5,000 largest corporations in the United States have been vastly over-represented compared to smaller businesses in terms of policy affecting the political economy of the United States.[8] At the same time, the concerns of the more than 16,000,000 smaller and growing businesses in the United States have been vastly under-represented compared to their importance regarding job creation, R&D investment, the development of radical innovations, and the earning of foreign exchange through exports.[9]

Fortunately, attitudes toward smaller businesses and entrepreneurial startups (at least "high tech" startups) appear to be shifting favorably among political and economic decision makers as the evidence of their importance mounts.[10] Various associations have been created which help to develop and present the position of the smaller business entrepreneur. These include several regional associations which represent smaller businesses. National publications also exist which help to inform smaller business entrepreneurs about relevant issues. They, along with the national associations, are helping to alert entrepreneurs about new legislation and/or other activities afoot which affect their business operations.

Institutional encouragements, on the other hand, can go too far. From an environmental perspective, it seems that our involvement with entrepreneurship can neither be too easy nor too hard but must occupy a middle ground to flourish. For when entrepreneurship is made too easy, a variety of elements are lost which serve as motivators. Subsidized or synthetic entrepreneurship simply doesn't work. It has not worked in corporations where resources have been made too plentiful and the risks of ownership are removed. It has not worked among independent entrepreneurs where access to capital and other resources have been made too easy.[11] It is indeed one of the ironies of life, or at least of entrepreneurial life, that new venture roads usually lead nowhere when these highways are smoothly paved and the ride is too easy.

On the other hand, entrepreneurship cannot flourish when barriers to start and maintain a new business venture are too high. And society can erect many barriers. Often they appear under the banner of "the common good." For throughout history and across civilizations, tradeoffs have been made between individual versus communal rights. Here again, it seem entrepreneurs must occupy a middle ground in order to survive over the long haul. Certainly entrepreneurs can prosper greatly in environments where individual rights are championed to an extreme. However, history teaches us that inevitably a political economy that favors the individual without concern for the group invites devastating reaction to those very individual rights it sought to preserve. A society of robber barons in Newport mansions will not survive social reform or revolutionary upheaval. In either case, their wealth will be "redistributed," as social reactions to these inequities become polarized. Unfortunately the swing of the pendulum often goes too far during these periods of social reform. The rights of the group are placed so high they stifle all enterprising activity by individuals, especially those actively involving entrepreneurial pursuits.

QUESTIONS FOR MACRO ENVIRONMENT ASSESSMENT

There is no reason to presume this swing between individual versus social rights will cease. For entrepreneurs the critical assessment questions are:

1. What trends seem to be occuring regarding individual versus communal rights that impact upon my particular venture?

2. Are their any potential (likely) changes in state or federal laws that can alter significantly the way I start and operate my venture...e.g., changes in legal forms of organizing the venture; changes in regulatory laws; changes in disclosure requirements; etc..?

3. Will these changes be ongoing to the point that the lead entrepreneur should have a strong legal background, public relations capability, state and/or federal contacts, etc.?

4. What is the likely economic climate for ventures of this type over the next few years? How will interest rates, employment rates, and other economic variables affect the venture during the pre-startup, startup, and post-startup periods?

III. ON THE ASSESSMENT OF ENTREPRENEURS

The first rule of entrepreneurship is: there is always an exception. But what is the rule? And to what extent do you truly represent an exception? These questions constitute the core of human assessment and their answer requires great insight and truthfulness. Neither is easy--not only when assessing others but particularly when evaluating ourselves. What follows represents a means to make these difficult assessments somewhat easier or even possible by placing them into perspective, specifically an entrepreneurial career perspective.

Here our thesis is that at least four sets of factors should be considered in the context of the entrepreneurial career process when evaluating the entrepreneurs associated with a particular venture.[12] These factors are: (1) personal characteristics; (2) relevant experience; (3) initial goals; and (4) special skills and resources. Let me make a few general observations about the process of assessing entrepreneurs before discussing these variables.

First, if more than one entrepreneur is involved, it is necessary to assess each individual, and relate this assessment to your venture and environmental analysis.

Second, the need for careful self-assessment has been well-documented elsewhere.[13] However, I wish to stress that the issue is not whether a person is suited for entrepreneurial pursuits *per se* but what kind of venture, environmental, and other conditions make the most sense for an entrepreneurial commitment. For instance, a positive evaluation may be forthcoming for a twenty-year-old black female with little creative talent, weak veridical skills, and a poor tolerance for ambiguity *given* other human, venture, and environmental factors. Conversely, a negative evaluation may be proper for a thirty-five-year-old white male with exemplary creative capacity, a veridical profile, and an ability to live with unstructured, volatile situations *given* other human, venture, and environmental factors. What is true of the physical world is also true of social reality. All is relative; everything depends on context and our ability to comprehend the interplay of contingent factors. But like a unique configuration of chess figures, one must be ready to "read the board" and make a judgment regarding the next move.

A new assessment tool is being developed to help us determine what moves are appropriate. Like the venture process, this new tool evaluates human, venture and environmental factors over time in terms of the entrepreneurial career process. While research about this latter process is still underway, we will review what is known at this time since current findings already have significant implications for entrepreneurs.

PERSONAL CHARACTERISTICS: AGE AND THE ENTREPRENEURIAL CAREER PROCESS

In our search for the "rule" versus "the exception", let us begin with some relationships that exist between a critical personal characteristic--age--and the entrepreneurial career process. In fact, when evaluating entrepreneurs, there are six points about age and the entrepreneurial career process which should be kept in mind.[14]

> 1. *Entrepreneurial age is a critical variable which is not the same as chronological age.* There is every reason to assume from case studies that entrepreneurial experience (as represented by entrepreneurial age) is one of the best predictors of entrepreneurial success. At the same time, potential entrepreneurs enter or launch their entrepreneurial careers at widely different times and it is easy to confuse chronological age and quick venture success with entrepreneurial age and experience. Holding other factors equal, who would you bet your money on: a thirty-two-year-old successful entrepreneur with ten years experience in Industry X versus a thirty-eight-year-old executive with twenty years' experience in Industry X but no entrepreneurial experience? The former is ten years old in terms of entrepreneurial age. Entrepreneurially speaking, the latter has not yet been born.

> 2. *Most people initiate their careers between the ages of twenty-two and fifty-five.* Before and after these years, starting an entrepreneurial career is difficult, highly improbable, but not impossible. It is improbable at earlier

ages simply because most individuals are either not capable of starting or free to start an entrepreneurial career. It is improbable at later ages because of personal energy requirements as well as stronger needs for security and order versus other needs. An average age for the best time to start an entrepreneurial career is meaningless given the wide range that exists for launching an entrepreneurial career. Statistically speaking, there is a large standard deviation about the mean, one that is probably larger than for most other careers. The existence of considerable dispersion around the mean itself suggests that when one pursues an entrepreneurial career may be an important variable in explaining the variance in long-term success.

3. *Within this range of ages, milestone years exist when individual are more inclined to consider and start an entrepreneurial career.* The data in *Exhibit 7* show these years come in approximately five-year intervals (25, 30, 35, 40, 45, and 50) for practicing entrepreneurs. In-depth interviews with entrepreneurs reinforce this clustering around milestone years. Several entrepreneurs noted that the decision to start their initial ventures was preceded by a feeling that "it was now or never" as they approached these birthdays. As *Exhibit 7* shows, these milestone years were also experienced by those individuals who seriously considered but did *not* start an entrepreneurial career.

4. *Better ages exist to start an entrepreneurial career.* Available evidence indicates that, given appropriate training and preparation, earlier starts are better in a *career continuance sense* than later starts. It is important to emphasize that the unit of analysis is the entrepreneurial career since the incidence of venture failure may in fact be higher for earlier starts but entrepreneurial career continuance is also higher. This includes the likelihood of starting an entrepreneurial career as well as continuing it. For instance, we know those who seriously consider an entrepreneurial career but do not start one tend to be considerably older than practicing entrepreneurs when both groups are considering or actually starting their careers. Among those who do start and have ended their entrepreneurial careers, *Exhibit 8* shows the relationship between age and the duration of their entrepreneurial careers. I should note that there is a rationale for these relationships. The initiation of a venture at an earlier age often means, by necessity, a smaller startup. Less is at risk,

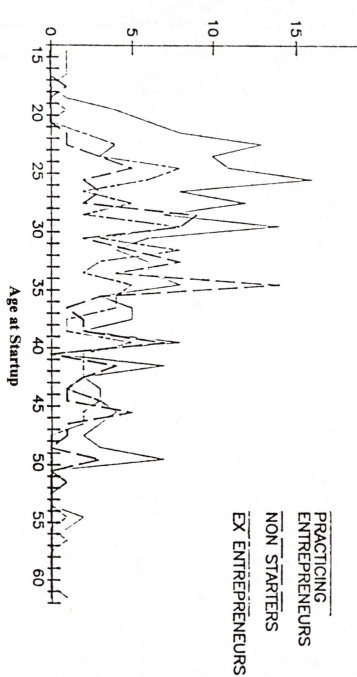

Exhibit 7

AGES OF ENTREPRENEURS AT STARTUP

Number in Age Category

Age at Startup

PRACTICING ENTREPRENEURS
NON STARTERS
EX ENTREPRENEURS

Source: "Ex-Entrepreneurs," *op. cit.*

Exhibit 8

The Duration of Entrepreneurial Careers for
Ex-Entrepreneurs* by the Age When Their First Venture Was Started

Age EC Started	Average Years Pursued EC Before Exiting	Number of Observations
Under 26	9.7	15
26-30	5.8	21
31-40	6.5	34
41-45	4.3	10
Over 45	2.3	7
		87
Under 31	7.4	36
Over 31	5.5	51
		87

* An ex-entrepreneur was defined as someone who had started an entrepreneurial career but was working for someone else by 1982.

Source: "Ex-Entrepreneurs," *op. cit.*

not only financially, but also along several other dimensions (family risk, psychological risk, etc.). If venture failure occurs, it results in either less loss (or a loss which is more absorbable) so that younger entrepreneurs are in a better position to start second or third ventures and remain in an entrepreneurial career mode compared to those considering a later career start. For this latter group, concerns for economic survival, family tranquility, and emotional stability apparently provide them with less leeway to continue with an entrepreneurial career in the face of a venture failure. The data in *Exhibit 9,* the first of their kind on ex-entrepreneurs and "serious nonstarters" (those who considered but did *not* start an entrepreneurial career) provides further support for this explanation.

5. *Some key years are associated with the entrepreneurial career process.* Available data on the decision to leave an entrepreneurial career indicate that the second, fifth/sixth, and tenth/eleventh years are critical points in the entrepreneurial career process. Essentially the first two years are the crises years and represent the career-entry period. Surviving the second year seems to raise the probabilities somewhat that one will last at least five-to-six years, which represents the early career period. Most individuals generally know enough about the viability of their ventures and entrepreneurial life to allow them at this juncture to make a decision whether or not to continue their entrepreneurial careers or shift to another career. To some extent, the same kind of thinking is going on during years ten and eleven which mark the mid-career point. However, exits from an entrepreneurial career at this time are less likely to be forced exits characterized by bankruptcy proceedings or business liquidations. Instead, the exit is characterized by a desire to harvest the business coupled with the desire to take on some other challenging responsibilities. However, if the decision is made to stay in an entrepreneurial career mode, the likelihood is quite strong that it will be for the long haul. Career exits then tend to reappear after twenty-years or more depending on how early in life the entrepreneurial career was initiated.

6. *Entrepreneurs pursue their entrepreneurial careers along three distinct pathways at significantly different average ages.* Each career pathway is defined partly by the number of years spent in other career activities before launching an entrepreneurial career and partly by the explicitness which

one goes about preparing for an entrepreneurial career. The first pathway is pursued by those individuals for whom entrepreneurship is an intended or actual first career. The second pathway is pursued by those individuals who explicitly pursue another career to prepare for an entrepreneurial career. The third pathway is pursued by those individuals who have *not* pursued some other career with an explicit plan for an entrepreneurial career but who ultimately consider and possibly start one.

For the "direct entrants" on pathway number one the pre-entrepreneurial career period is practically negligible (1 year) especially when one considers that the venture pre-startup period is part of this time for most of these individuals.[15] (see *Exhibit 10*) The pre-entrepreneurial period for those individuals explicitly planning an entrepreneurial career is 8 years versus approximately 11 years for those who do not explicitly choose a prior career to prepare themselves for an entrepreneurial career. As *Exhibit 11* shows, even among Babson entrepreneurs, most followed the last pathway. I think it's safe to assume that among the total population of entrepreneurs, the vast majority are found on this third pathway. However, it is precisely on this pathway that an even higher share of non-starts and career exits exist. Furthermore, the career exits occur fastest on this particular pathway, i.e., entrepreneurial career lengths are shortest—not just because individuals start these careers later but also because they end them sooner.[16]

OTHER PERSONAL CHARACTERISTICS AND THE ENTREPRENEURIAL CAREER PROCESS

Besides age, several other personal characteristics require our assessment. These include gender, race, creativity, veracity, resource seeking tendency, and ambiguity tolerance.

The first and second variables are dichotomous (you are or you aren't) and thus are easy to determine, although their implications for entrepreneurial success, are more difficult to judge given our knowledge about them. By contrast, the last three variables have known implications for entrepreneurial success, yet being continuous variables (i.e., a matter of degree), they are hard to assess--i.e., it is difficult to determine if individuals indeed possess them in sufficient quantities for particular ventures.

Exhibit 9

The Average Age Selected Groups Started or
Seriously Considered Starting an Entrepreneurial Career (EC)

	Serious Nonstarters (EC Not Started)	Practicing Entrepreneurs*	Early Exits Ex-Entrepreneurs (EC Under 7 Years)	Late Exits Ex-Entrepreneurs** (EC Over 7 Years)
Average Age Considered or Started EC	34.5	32.1	35.1	30.4
(Number of Observations)	(96)	(205)	(71)	(40)

* Many of these practicing entrepreneurs were still in the early phase of their entrepreneurial careers. Below are the average ages when practicing entrepreneurs started their careers when we distinguish between shorter versus longer careers:

**Some of these "late exit" entrepreneurs were retired and not working for someone else.

Among Practicing Entrepreneurs

EC Under 7 Years	EC Over 7 Years
34	30.7
(86)	(119)

Source: "Ex-Entrepreneurs," *op. cit.*

Exhibit 10
Entrepreneurial Career (EC) Pathways

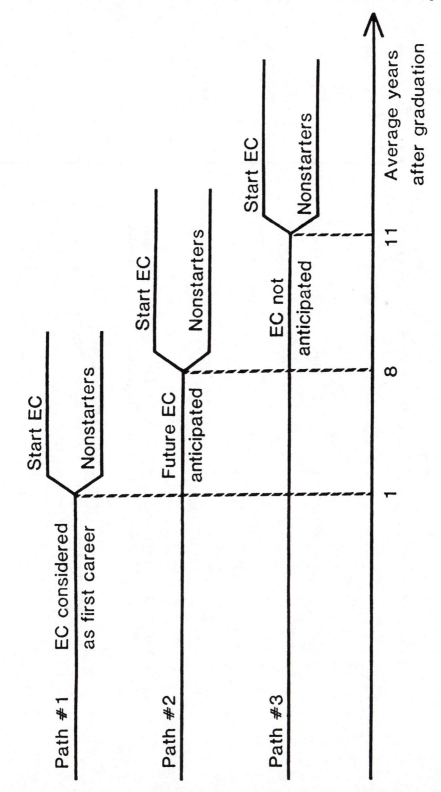

Exhibit 11

Entrepreneurial Career Pathways Pursued by Serious Nonstarters, Practicing Entrepreneurs, and Ex-Entrepreneurs (Number of Observations in Parentheses)

	Serious Nonstarters	Practicing Entrepreneurs	Early Exits* Ex-Entrepreneurs	Later Exits** Ex-Entrepreneurs
Direct Entrants Pathway #1	6% (6)	25% (38)	6% (4)	10% (4)
Explicit Planners Pathway #2	10% (9)	21% (32)	14% (10)	23% (9)
Nonexplicit Planners Pathway #3	84% (79)	55% (84)	80% (55)	67% (26)
TOTAL	100% (94)	100% (154)	100% (69)	100% (39)

*Under 7 Years
**Over 7 Years

Sources: Ronstadt, *Entrepreneurial Careers*, op. cit., "The Decision *Not* to Become an Entrepreneur," op. cit.; "Ex-Entrepreneurs," op. cit.

1. *GENDER*

The table below presents some similarities and differences between male versus female entrepreneurs. Fewer major differences have been identified than originally anticipated, though a few important distinctions have emerged.

SOME SIMILARITIES AND DIFFERENCES

Male Versus Female Entrepreneurs[17]

Personal Characteristics	Differences exist but are minor compared to nonentrepreneurs in general.
Experience	Most studies report females have more direct experience before starting their venture. Also, once they initiate a venture, they tend to spend less time (hours per week) running their businesses compared to male entrepreneurs.
Initial Goals	Females show an even greater tendency for life-style and smaller profitable ventures compared to male entrepreneurs.
Venture Factors	Studies show thus far a female concentration in smaller, more routine businesses which one study suggests is caused by environmental barriers. (see below)
Environmental Factors	There is a key difference here. Nearly all studies cite special problems with *sources of financing* and interacting with bankers and other financial intermediaries. Also, the distribution of female entrepreneurs by industry involvement shows a greater concentration in retail and service business compared to male entrepreneurs.

From an assessment standpoint, what represents a higher risk choice for a female entrepreneur? It seems the high-risk venture is one that:

      a. requires considerable operating time;
      b. requires strong financial contacts and interaction with financial intermediaries;
      c. must start as or become a high-growth entity to survive.

Generally these conditions exclude most non-routine and larger scale startups which probably accounts for the smaller involvement of female entrepreneurs in "non-traditional" and higher growth businesses. Of course, what has been true in the past does not mean it must be true in the future. While certain barriers have existed and will continue to exist to some degree, specific plans can be developed which address these potential problem areas should female entrepreneurs decide to start ventures where significant time, financial support, and sales growth are needed.

But if venture scaling-up via the corridor principle is instrumental in promoting more effective entrepreneurship, women entrepreneurs may be experiencing a further disadvantage in terms of the entrepreneurial career process. Specifically, the best evidence available thus far suggests very few women start entrepreneurial careers as first careers and an equally small share intentionally pursue another career explicitly to start an entrepreneurial career. In short, they appear to be starting their entrepreneurial careers later on average than male entrepreneurs with higher concentrations of female entrepreneurs on the non-anticipated pathway. And both conditions are associated with single-venture careers and shorter careers as entrepreneurs. In the future, more enterprising and longer entrepreneurial careers for women seem to be tied to new educational and career values which must be adopted at much earlier ages.

2. RACE

The issue of race (as well as ethnicity) is most complicated since numerous minority and non-minority groups are involved, each having very different experiences with entrepreneurship. Thus far more studies[18] seem to show that:

> 1. Minority entrepreneurs are more similar to non-minority entrepreneurs in terms of personal characteristics compared to the general population;

> 2. Like non-minority entrepreneurs, minority entrepreneurs tend to be better educated than the general population;

> 3. A key distinction among minority entrepreneurs is their freedom and ability to target their businesses toward "mainstream" or non-minority markets versus smaller minority "subeconomy" markets;

> 4. Minority entrepreneurs state they have encountered problems dealing with financial institution.

Like female entrepreneurs, ventures requiring large capitalization and large markets represent higher risk ventures for most minority entrepreneurs. Furthermore, more enterprising ventures often require "mainstream" customers which represents a particularly risky decision for minority entrepreneurs.

Once into entrepreneurship, moving beyond a lifestyle venture is difficult for many minority entrepreneurs. This fact partially explains why the total number of minorities entering entrepreneurship is itself small for most minority groups and an object of government concern.

3. CREATIVITY, VERACITY, RESOURCE-SEEKING, AND AMBIGUITY TOLERANCE

Our earlier discussions of "the right stuff" revealed numerous traits and characteristics which were helpful, even necessary, to launch a successful entrepreneurial career (courage, achievement motivation, locus of control, etc.). But what makes an effective entrepreneur once the first venture is underway? Strategic capabilities in thought and action seem to be especially required and, given their importance, they are discussed at length in the next section. However, four characteristics reinforce these strategic skills and minimal amounts of all four are needed which go beyond the average quantities found in the general population and the average manager.

The four characteristics are creativity, veracity (veridical tendency)*, resource-seeking, and ambiguity tolerance. For instance, even the smallest, simplest lifestyle venture requires a creative capability to identify and marshall scarce resources and produce viable products. Similarly, inevitable change causes unknowns to surface about products, markets, and other factors even in the most routine of ventures. Those with strong veracious tendencies admit that these unknowns exist and search for facts upon which to base their responses. And they are able to live with the ambiguity and uncertainty associated with not knowing until they discover what there is to discover about these unknown elements.

When will larger doses of creativity, veridical tendencies, and ambiguity tolerance be needed? Generally speaking, when the following considerations exist.

Conditions	Reason
the more non-routine a venture	... more is unknown about available resources, products, markets, and technology
the larger a venture becomes	... increasing size forces changes which must be solved in production, management, finance, and other functions
the more diversified a venture becomes	... increasing market and product complexities produce unknown conditions
the more unsettled or unfriendly a local, industry, or macro environment becomes	... more is unknown about the "right" way to start and run a venture

---

*The veridical concept is introduced at the beginning of Chapter Three. Veridical is defined broadly by Webster as "speaking the truth." It is used here to mean a strong tendency "to seek the truth about unknown elements." Entrepreneurs will often describe this activity as "keeping in touch" with customers, suppliers, new technology, etc. or "finding out what's really going on," as opposed to assuming what's going on.

A related question is when in their entrepreneurial careers prospective entrepreneurs should undertake ventures requiring large doses of creativity, veracity, resource-seeking needs, and ambiguity tolerance. Ideally speaking, I believe most of us will agree it should not be their first venture. But unless an entrepreneurial career has been nurtured and developed carefully, little or no option may be open to a prospective entrepreneur. Such pathways are fraught with risk. Success is certainly possible but the odds are not good--at least not as good as they could be.

RELEVANT EXPERIENCE AND THE ENTREPRENEURIAL CAREER PROCESS

The foregoing conditions suggest that a key question for our assessment of entrepreneurs is what constitutes relevant experience *given the type of venture being contemplated in a particular kind of environment.* In fact, there are four kinds of experience that can have a positive impact on entrepreneurial success. They are:

Educational experience.

Technical experience.

Industry experience.

Entrepreneurial experience.

Consequently, the more specific and operative questions become, "Do the entrepreneurs in question have the appropriate kinds and amounts of *relevant* educational experience, technical experience, industry experience, and entrepreneurial experience?"

1. *EDUCATIONAL EXPERIENCE*

Certain kinds of educational environments either retard or offer no particular help to entrepreneurial development and success. A principal culprit appears to be the traditional liberal arts education. In theory a liberal arts education should reinforce entrepreneurial proclivities. Such programs espouse development of thinking individuals with questioning and creative minds who are willing to explore new terrain in a logical fashion. Unfortunately, the gap between theory and reality is substantial. Too frequently, these programs foster conformity, which stifles creativity while maintaining highly structured environments, which works against the development of ambiguity tolerance. The end result is thought and behavior processes that refuse to admit ignorance, and social values that preclude "getting one's hands dirty" with entrepreneurial pursuits.[19]

Fortunately, there are some educational programs that have a beneficial impact on entrepreneurial development. So far as one needs a skill or some kind of specialized knowledge for entrepreneurial pursuits, then professional and scientific educations help to lay the groundwork for ventures requiring these knowledge foundations. For instance, few people can start high-tech ventures or other "educationally intensive" businesses without some form of specialized and/or advanced education. In fact, such educational experiences often provide the means for obtaining industry experience as well as technical know-how.

Business education can produce similar results--some useful skills in marketing, finance, etc., and easier access to obtaining industry exposure. Yet, like the liberal arts, business education and particularly MBA program can produce the opposite effect. The production of organizational men and women runs counter to entrepreneurial life, and the vast majority of business programs are not fashioned to develop entrepreneurial thought and action.

Yet students seek entrepreneurial education. New venture and small business courses are among the most heavily subscribed elective courses at most business schools. Does such exposure help? It will probably be another twenty years before we can tell conclusively given:

a) the newness of entrepreneurial education; and

b) the need to consider its impact from an entrepreneurial career
   viewpoint which in itself involves the passage of considerable
   time.

However, one study already indicates that, as expected, those taking entrepreneurship courses are considerably more likely to start an entrepreneurial career compared to other business school students.[20]

We can also assume they are more likely to pursue other activities to prepare themselves better for their entrepreneurial experience. After all, they have elected to take an entrepreneurship course and this election implies serious consideration of an entrepreneurship possibility. Consequently, they are more likely to start their entrepreneurial careers and start them sooner compared to students not interested in such courses. Such actions, as mentioned earlier, are associated with longer and apparently more effective careers in entrepreneurship.

2. TECHNICAL AND INDUSTRY EXPERIENCE

Both technical and industry experience can be obtained by working for others or through personal avocations and other experiences. For example, you may have a long-standing hobby or other avocation that generates the kind of experience that makes you technically informed and/or aware about industry developments. Similarly, you may have the possibility of learning about an industry and/or technical requirements of a particular business because your parents or some other family member or acquaintance has been involved with this industry. Here the term "technical know-how" is used in its broadest sense to include not only engineering and production know-how but also marketing and selling techniques.

For certain kinds of ventures, managerial experience may be as important as technical or industry experience. However, for the vast majority of entrepreneurs, managerial know-how may be the least important form of experience. It becomes relevant only when the venture becomes relatively large--not only in terms of the number of employees but particularly in terms of the number of employees who are also managers. Remember, most ventures require managing no more than one's own activities or the activities of a few part-time employees. Nearly all firms that get established end up having less than twenty employees; however, there is little doubt that managerial skills can be quite important for high growth ventures as well as smaller profitable ventures that involve managing multiple units where the size, complexity, and/or geographic diversity of the business requires the presence of other managers.

But managerial experience without relevant technical (product) and industry (market) experience can be illusory. For instance, we know a good number of individuals start ventures each year in areas where they have no direct experience in a technical and industry sense. Some of these are managers and, while their general business background may be helpful, they are clearly playing a risky game. For example, a larger share of non-starters and ex-entrepreneurs with shorter careers have *not had relevant work experience* in the area of their potential or actual venture compared to practicing entrepreneurs on the unanticipated career pathway (number 3) who have longer careers. What this suggests is that pathway number 3 can actually be split into two groups: (a) those who pursue some other career *without* explicit plans for an entrepreneurial career but who perhaps serendipitously find relevance between their prior career experience and their initial venture; and (b) those who pursue some other career without explicit plans for an entrepreneurial career and choose initial ventures that bear little or no relationship to their prior career experience.

3. *ENTREPRENEURIAL EXPERIENCE*

Entrepreneurs tell us it is generally easier to start a second, third, or a fourth venture than it is to start the first venture. This claim is quite reasonable and congruent with just about all human experience. The more you do something, the easier it generally becomes, assuming it holds your interest. One might also reasonably assume that the need for relevant entrepreneurial experience also increases as the magnitude of the venture increases along with its complexity. In these situations, teams of entrepreneurs are required. Such teams must be assessed not only for their educational, industry, and technical experience, but also for their combined and separate entrepreneurial experience. Specifically, who is providing the entrepreneurial component for the "entrepreneurial" team?

1. Does the lead entrepreneur have entrepreneurial experience?

2. What kind of venture experience?

3. Where are the "entrepreneurial" team members positioned in terms of their entrepreneurial careers? (Pre-career period? Entry period? etc.).

4. What entrepreneurial career pathways have they been following?

Entrepreneurial experience is not limited solely to venture experience but also an entrepreneur's experience working with other entrepreneurs. As anyone with partners will tell you, working harmoniously with a partner and/or other team members is a critical skill. Furthermore, it is a skill that must be enhanced with leadership capabilities. Most case studies and other work on entrepreneurial teams and partnerships suggest that, regardless of the number of entrepreneurs, there is a strong requirement for at least one entrepreneur who is the leader. More democratic/committee type approaches simply have not proven that effective. Again, Roger Babson's words are worth remembering:

> During a revival campaign in Gloucester, I remember D.L. Moody preaching a sermon on Noah. He began by saying that if God had left the building of the Ark to a committee, it (the human race) would have become extinct. Instead, continued evangelist Moody, God left the building of the Ark to one man named Noah, and held him responsible. Consequently, it was completed on time and the people were saved.*

One might suspect that Noah's children would also be good at building arks. The same association apparently exists for the sons and daughters of entrepreneurs. In a sense, entrepreneurial experience can be absorbed prior to starting an entrepreneurial career via role models. Here a strong correlation exists between role models, particularly *family role models* and entrepreneurial pathway. For instance, both non-starters and ex-entrepreneurs with shorter careers are congregated on the unanticipated career pathway, and they also have signfiicantly fewer fathers and mothers who are (or were) entrepreneurs compared to entrepreneurs on other pathways. The same is also true for practicing entrepreneurs on the unanticipated career (pathway number 3): they also have fewer parents who have entrepreneurial experience compared to entrepreneurs who are direct entrants (pathway number 1) or who have anticipated an entrepreneurial career (pathway number 2).

Finally, entrepreneurial experience itself exposes practicing entrepreneurs to other viable venture opportunities. In short, a critical relationship appears to exist between the entrepreneurial career process and the corridor principle.** Specifically entrepreneurs who are pursuing entrepreneurship as first careers or anticipated careers (pathways number 1 and 2) tend to start a higher number of ventures during their careers than entrepreneurs pursuing unanticipated careers (pathway number 3). We know these additional ventures are not being created later but earlier in the career for a high percentage of entrepreneurs; consequently, the great number of ventures is not caused simply by being in an entrepreneurial career mode longer.*** An opposite relationship

---

*Roger W. Babson, *Activated Reaction,* Harper & Row, New York, 1935, p. 93.

**Defined in the latter pages of Chapter Three.

***See Exhibit 4 in Chapter Three.

seems to exist: entrepreneurs pursuing entrepreneurship as first or anticipated careers are around longer because they are better able to move down "corridors of new venture opportunities" and actually start second, third, etc., new ventures. The data in *Exhibit 12* show the incidence of multiple venture formation on both a sequential and overlapping basis broken down by entrepreneurial career pathway.

INITIAL GOALS AND THE ENTREPRENEURIAL CAREER PROCESS

Approximately one out of every three entrepreneurs will radically change their goals during their entrepreneurial career.[21] This goal change is often voluntary for individuals whose initial goals are to create lifestyle ventures or smaller profitable ventures. A portion of these entrepreneurs create these ventures on what is effectively a preparatory basis, i.e., they are created to gain experience in order to prepare for larger, more enterprising undertakings later in the career.

From an assessment perspective, it pays to ask specifically what kind of lifestyle goals, smaller profitable goals, or high-growth goals each entrepreneur is pursuing. The *permanent* versus *preparatory* (or temporary) distinction applies to all three venture/goal categories. Another useful distinction for smaller profitable ventures is whether they are operated on a single unit or a multiple unit basis--the skills to run a multiple unit operation being more advanced and complicated. Similar kinds of distinctions can be made for high growth ventures in terms of skills and experience given the need for educational and technology-intensive skills for high-tech ventures, related skills for service ventures, and/or ventures that are geographically diversified on a national or multi-national basis.

Again, an appropriate question for assessment purposes is to ask how realistic, consistent, or congruent certain venture goals are with an entrepreneur's particular position in the entrepreneurial career process. Are these venture goals shared by other partners or entrepreneurial team members? Will someone need to alter their goals at some point--possibly scaling them upward or downward? For example, we know that *venture goals* for non-starters and ex-entrepreneurs with shorter careers tend to be higher than other entrepreneurs who have initiated ventures. Again the former are more prevalent on pathway number 3. Entrepreneurs who survive to experience longer careers on the unanticipated career (pathway number 3) actually tend to have very modest lifestyle venture goals.

SPECIAL SKILLS, RESOURCES, AND THE ENTREPRENEURIAL CAREER PROCESS

The need for sufficient time, special capabilities, the support of one's spouse and/or other family members are usually necessary conditions to start and continue an entrepreneurial career. The availability or strength of each of these factors, however, is also related to the kind of venture and environmental conditions. For instance, family support may be quite strong until you mention your real interest is in XYZ industry or you must move to another town or state to launch your new venture.

Exhibit 12

The Distribution of Practicing
Entrepreneurs by Career Path
and the Number of Ventures

All Practicing Entrepreneurs

Venture Number and Timing	All Regardless of Pathway		Path #1	Path #2	Path #3
Single Venture	%	43	38	46	47
Sequential Ventures	%	21	22	15	20
Overlapping Ventures	%	36	40	38	32
Total Number*	#	205	37	39	105

**Practicing Entrepreneurs for
More Than 6.5 Years**

	All Regardless of Pathway		Path #1	Path #2	Path #3
Single Venture	%	35	35	42	36
Sequential Ventures	%	21	13	11	24
Overlapping Ventures	%	44	52	47	40
Total Number*	#	117	23	19	58

*Total numbers for three pathways do not add up to total for "All Regardless of Pathway" because pathway data were not available in all instances.

Source: 1981 Survey of Babson Entrepreneurs by Author.

History also seems to indicate that it is the rare entrepreneur who can succeed over the long haul without sufficient resources to maintain ownership control. Entrepreneurial leadership generally means being able to make timely decisions versus the need to shape a consensus via time-consuming committee meetings. Equity control and ownership in this sense generally mean at least majority ownership. There are, of course, instances where entrepreneurs have renounced majority ownership and still maintained effective working control over their organizations. However, these seem to be the the exception rather than the rule. One temptation is to accept a minority equity position in order to ensure a larger scale and/or higher-growth venture. Generally speaking, entrepreneurs have found that accepting a minority position is a bad practice unless the venture has already moved through the startup phase and they have a way to maintain control (e.g., they personally own several key patents and/or trademarks; their personality is already identified-- especially by customers--with the venture; etc.). As a general rule, entrepreneurs are better off trying to start a smaller venture and maintaining full equity control in order to consolidate and develop their leadership position.

The kind of venture you choose to start and the environmental conditions under which you start it also influence one other resource variable which plays a critical role over your ability to move through the venture process as well as the entrepreneurial career process. This resource is quite simply your "contacts." At issue, is not only the number of contacts but their quality. For instance, one rarely starts a venture alone. Even the simplest, most routine lifestyle ventures require help from different sources. One needs good contacts to insure successful movement through the pre-startup, startup and post-startup periods. The quality of your contacts will depend on the extent they can help you across all venture phases with a particular type of venture you are starting or operating. For example, you may find that your contacts are appropriate to initiate a routine, smaller scale, lifestyle venture but inappropriate to initiate a non-routine, higher growth business; or your contacts may be very helpful during the pre-startup period but of little use thereafter.

As the data on family role models suggest, a potentially vital contact is a parent or close relative who is an entrepreneur. Those of us who are not blessed with this resource need to take special pains to develop a host of surrogate contacts and mentors who can lessen "the stings and arrows" of entrepreneurial life as well as improve our entrepreneurial opportunities. Of course, building contacts before launching your first venture is important. But it is probably just as important to select and structure your first venture so it will help you to maximize contacts, develop skills, and expand your entrepreneurial experience--since the first venture is seldom the last.

QUESTIONS FOR THE ASSESSMENT OF ENTREPRENEURS

The following questions may help you with the assessment of entrepreneurs given certain venture and environmental factors.

1. What is the capacity of the entrepreneur for thinking and acting creatively given the needs of the venture for low, moderate, or high creative inputs?

2. What capabilities does the lead entrepreneur have for thinking and acting in a veridical manner given uncertainties about the venture or the environment?

3. What capabilities does the lead entrepreneur have for finding and obtaining resources that are not readily under his/her control but will be needed during the life of the venture?

4. Given the type of venture and environment, is there a need for strong strategic capabilities both in terms of devising and implementing a competitive strategy? Does the entrepreneur in question have these capabilities?

5. What is the risk of venture failure and are the entrepreneurs (as well as their spouses and other relevant parties) psychologically ready and capable of bearing this risk?

6. Does the lead entrepreneur have the appropriate educational, technical, industry, and entrepreneurial experience for the proposed venture?

7. Do other entrepreneurs associated with the venture have relevant educational, technical, industry and entrepreneurial experience for the proposed venture?

8. Are the goals of the venture congruent with the goals of the various entrepreneurs involved in the venture in a profit and sales sense? If the venture is designed as a smaller profitable venture, do all the entrepreneurs share these goals or are some looking for high growth opportunities?

IV. ON STRATEGIC ASSESSMENT

Many successful entrepreneurs appear blessed with the ability to conceive and execute a forceful strategy. This quality does not mean they are necessarily good managers. The latter often require an administrative knack for detail, for tying up loose ends, and generally making certain that small but cumulatively important matters do not, as the saying goes, "fall between the cracks."

Good strategists are more concerned with effectiveness than with efficiency. Super strategists know not only the difference between doing something well versus doing the right thing but also which details promote effectiveness. By "effectiveness," we mean a concern for doing the right thing, or heading in the right direction, as opposed to doing something well (efficiently) so that costs are minimized. A great many examples can be dredged up to support this claim but the one I enjoy most is the observation of a government "efficiency" expert who had the opportunity to observe first-hand an entrepreneur's entrepreneur in a government position during the First World War.

> Mr. Roger Babson came to Washington early in 1918, and we had many talks. I had always been a careful analyst; and I had, in fact, some reputation for my closeness of analysis. Now I met a man of my own age who did not sit back and merely take lessons from me; instead, he contributed to my fundamental development. At first when he started to talk, it

seemed to me he was 'moseying around', but later I realized that while I was analyzing the details, he was looking at the picture as a whole, somewhat like a man who is standing on a mountain top. Many details might escape; but as to the direction in which we must go, his contribution was far more important than mine. In other words, while I had always been engaged in working out tactics, he was thinking about strategy.[22]

THE CONCEPT OF STRATEGY

A strategy for any entity is more than "how" to achieve some goal. Rather a strategy is a collection of objectives, policies and plans which, taken together, define the nature of an organization (what business am I in), determine its direction (where am I headed), and reveal a means of moving in a defined direction and obtaining certain goals (how will I get there).[23]

Sometimes the task of formulating and implementing strategy can be quite complex, particularly when organizations become very large and/or diversified in terms of the range of their activities. A great many elements in terms of objectives, policies, and plans must be woven together, sometimes spanning a great range of businesses. At other times, the elements that constitute a sound strategy may be few and relatively simple to comprehend, though not necessarily obvious nor explicit. In fact, a particular element of a strategy may be so crucial or powerful for some enterprises or business units that we can speak of "a strategic idea" that effectively makes a venture what it is. A less elegant and perhaps pejorative description is to call a "strategic idea" a gimmick. (Within Fortune 500 companies, gimmicks are referred to as strategic ideas). Despite the semantics, the power of the idea is sufficient to produce a good, perhaps even a superior strategy.

Finally, how does one identify a good business strategy? Actually, it is quite simple: a good strategy is one that produces substantial margins, net profits and cash flows over the long haul despite unforeseen adversities and despite the "less than efficient" management of operating, marketing, and financial tactics. And achieving good results for one or two years does not constitute the long haul. The inference here is that a good strategy must provide solid returns for many years, a critical distinction being that these returns will be earned despite inefficient operating management in any given year.

VENTURE STRATEGIES FOR ENTREPRENEURS

Many different ways exist to identify and discuss venture strategies. For example, a quantitative view might distinguish between venture strategies that produce high versus low operating leverages and/or strategies that make positive use of financial leverages.[24] Similarly, venture strategies can be described in terms of their industry implications and positions.[25]

Both these notions (relative positioning and relative leverage) can help us to visualize the different kinds of strategies that exist at the venture level. For instance, in terms of leverage, venture strategies can be identified to the extent that entrepreneurs "lever" their time or some unique element associated with a venture. In terms of positioning, venture strategies can be described to the extent that entrepreneurs "position" their ventures to take advantage of certain kinds of market growth or asset appreciation.

• Ventures That Leverage an Entrepreneur's Time

All human beings represent to some extent an investment in human capital. The larger and more specialized this investment, the more you want to be certain that the individuals involved utilize their time effectively and efficiently. Potential conflict exists, however, with the decision to start a new venture. During startup, entrepreneurs often need to spread their time over a great many different functions and areas. Limited resources fight against the principle of specialization. And so entrepreneurs who may be geniuses in product design or new market identification, find themselves preoccupied with personnel problems, financial matters, production schedules, and a host of other issues. This diffusion of efforts is unavoidable and necessary in most instances. However, it works against the concept of leverage and may inhibit the realization of a strong strategy.

• "For Fee" Versus "Oil Well" Strategies

One way to think about ventrure strategies is the extent to which an entrepreneur's time is leveraged. At one end of the spectrum, we have the situation where there is zero leverage--an entrepreneur provides a product or service for a specified fee by utilizing solely his/her time to produce the product or service. An example of this kind of "no leverage" or "for fee" strategy in the manufacturing sector would be a one-person job shop where the entrepreneur produces each customized product entirely through his own efforts and does the selling, billing, delivery, etc. In the service sector, a counterpart would be a one-office real estate operation where the entrepreneur/realtor carries out all the functions of the real estate process.

The oil well strategy represents the opposite extreme in terms of leveraging an entrepreneur's time. Here, an entrepreneur has specialized and/or concentrated his time so that the project or venture, once it begins producing, continues to make money long after the entrepreneur has ceased contributing his or her personal efforts. Besides the oil business, certain kinds of publishing businesses provide an example of the oil well principle. Considerable time may be spent developing, packaging, and targeting a particular book for a certain audience. But once the book is launched and reaches a stable sales pattern, the publisher can often move on to other projects while the book is managed by others and continues to accrue profits. Of course books, like oil wells and most other products, have variable life-spans. Some oil wells with deep reserves pump on for years. Others last only for a short period of time. Consequently, it becomes very important to have a good feel for the likely life cycle of a product and/or business.

To some extent, any venture can be converted to or move toward an oil well strategy. The task is to find ways to have the venture continue its operations while the entrepreneur retains all or partial ownership and yet removes himself to some degree from the venture. This removal can occur by leveraging other unique elements or altering the production process so it effectively leverages an entrepreneurs's investment in time and capital.

LEVERAGING UNIQUE ELEMENTS

Venture strategies are often constructed on four unique elements which, in a sense, serve as a fulcrum to lever an investment. These four elements are (1) unique markets, (2) unique people (special skills), (3) unique products, and (4) unique resources.

• Unique Markets: "Mountain Verses Mountain Gap" Strategies

Many entrepreneurs are extremely adept at identifying special market needs. There are at least two prevalent strategies for tapping unique markets. The first is to identify major growth markets which represent entirely new consumer or industrial markets, i.e., a whole new mountain to climb. Recent examples of two such markets are home video games and personal computers. Both markets were identified and attacked respectively by Nolan Bushnell's Atari and Steven Jobs' Apple Computer. A second kind of venture strategy is built on an ability to tap into smaller, specialized markets (i.e., the mountain gaps). Large markets attract competition, particularly larger companies, as Bushnell and Jobs have discovered. Smaller enterprises, however, are often able to dominate new smaller markets, particularly when the market's potential size and growth is limited. Such limited markets are also called interstice markets since they are often lodged between two larger markets (mountains). Interstice markets can be extremely profitable homes for entrepreneurs as long as they do *not* grow too fast or become too large, thus attracting competition from the companies servicing the larger adjacent markets. The so-called "alternative newspapers" of most major metropolitan areas represent examples of ventures that have been built on the interstice or "mountain gap" notion.

• Unique People and Skills; "Great Chef" Strategies

A great many ventures are built around strategies that utilize the unique skills of one or more individuals associated with a venture. The classic example is the restaurant whose patrons are attracted by the culinary skills of a famous chef. Such "great chef strategies" are viable because people are often willing to pay a premium for the certainty of consuming a great meal or at least one prepared by a renowned cook. Such special skills may include the ability to design and/or merchandise great dresses, computer software, appealing automobiles, or just about any other product or service.

There are some obvious drawbacks associated with the great chef strategy. First and foremost is the problem of controlling the unique person, especially when this individual is not the lead entrepreneur or even a partner in the venture. Many a great chef has left a prosperous restaurant to start his own operation. But even where control is feasible, or the lead entrepreneur represents the critical skill, difficulties often surface with growth and ultimately with succession. In short, the venture can survive only as long as the person with the unique or special skill is associated with it—a fact which makes selling or otherwise harvesting such businesses very difficult.

Finally, it is important to emphasize that these skills are unique only if they are unique *relative to the competition.* Possessing superlative financial or marketing skills, for example, does not necessarily mean they are unique if your direct competitors possess equivalent capabilities.

• Unique Products: "Better Widget" Strategies

Unique products may, of course, be associated with unique markets or they also may be associated with special skills. Product uniqueness may also vary from products embodying slight improvements to those that represent major new innovations. In either case, a venture may predicate its strategy on its ability to continue developing or acquiring new products as a means of garnering larger margins and profits.

However, some ventures may prosper over time simply because they can offer *a line* of products or services which is itself unique and difficult to duplicate. No single product may provide any significant advantage. It is the totality of products and services that constitutes the difference.

• Unique Resources: "Water Well" Strategies

Access to unique or scarce resources can also allow a venture to earn above-average margins and profits over the long term. This resource may take the form of land, labor, other raw materials, or capital sources. Examples of unique resources would be the following: (1) being able to identify and obtain a high-traffic retail site; (2) control of any scarce resource such as water rights or access to waterfront property that is in limited supply; (3) unlimited working capital or other sources of financing made available to you in unusual amounts or at preferential market rates; (4) an ability to attract and utilize labor at various skills levels at preferential rates; and (5) an access to inexpensive raw materials because of some location advantage.

• A Final Hope: Lever Appreciation Strategies

Over the years, entrepreneurs may utilize various leverage strategies to move or run their operations in a particular direction. Such movement creates profits...hopefully; however, some entrepreneurs do not realize significant returns until they decide to sell all or part of their business ventures. All too often, we hear entrepreneurs exclaim that they never made big money off their ventures until they finally sold the building where they were located or other assets long since written off. In short, it may prove profitable to run a marginal business as long as some or all of the key assets appreciate over time. These include intangible as well as tangible assets. Will a name or license possess considerable value on the open market in the future? In short, a bundle of assets may never be used effectively as a lever or a fulcrum to catapult operations into a zone of high returns. But the lever or fulcrum may grow in value even when it is not being used effectively to lever anything at all.

QUESTIONS FOR STRATEGIC ASSESSMENT

In terms of strategic assessment, the following questions should be asked about the venture.

1. Does the venture have a clear strategy which is based on some unique element? What is the unique element?

2. Does the lead entrepreneur have an appreciation for the importance of identifying a strong venture strategy either during the pre-startup or startup periods?

3. Does the lead entrepreneur have the ability to develop and execute a forceful strategy for the venture?

4. How will the lead entrepreneur's time be leveraged? Is such leverage necessary?

5. In the absence of a viable venture strategy, is it possible that some assets will still experience substantial appreciation?

6. If the venture shows signs of success, will competitive response be immediate (i.e., before the startup period is over)? Will such response force a change in strategy?

7. To what extent does the venture strategy insulate the business from recession? Inflation? Other environmental changes?

8. What kind of lifecycle is associated with the venture's key production or services?

V. ON ETHICAL ASSESSMENT

While difficult to prove, there is evidence indicating that a strong bond exists between ethics and excellence.[26] To truly excel, not just for a momentary period, but over an entire career, one must strive for ethical maturity. Yet such nurturing does not happen automatically or concurrently with the aging process. Instead, ethical maturity is something we learn and develop. It is learned from our own ethical confrontations as well as the ethical dilemmas of others which we may have the good fortune to observe and study firsthand. A similar bond also appears to exist between entrepreneurship, ethics, and excellence. I should stress that this view is *not* mine alone but the view of seasoned entrepreneurs. For example, one survey of entrepreneurs revealed the following:

> The most startling outcome dealt with the questions of ethics: 72% said ethics can and should be taught as part of the curriculum (only 20% said "no" and two respondents weren't sure). The most prominently cited reason was that ethical behavior is at the core of long-term business success, because it provides the glue that binds enduring successful business and personal relationships together. What's more, the responses reflected a serious and thoughtful awareness of the fragile but vital role of ethics in entrepreneurial attainment. Consider these comments:

"If the free enterprise system is to survive, the business schools better start paying attention to teaching ethics. They should know that business is built on trust, which depends upon honesty and sincerity. BS comes out quickly in a small company."

"Ethics should be addressed, considered and thoroughly examined; it should be an inherent part of each class and course. . .; instead of crusading with ethics it is much more effective to make high ethics an inherent part of business - and it is."

"It doesn't pay *not* to be ethical."[27]

Like environmental assessment, ethical assessment should be an ongoing entrepreneurial activity if real value and wealth are to be created through the entrepreneurial process. Each of us practices some form of ethical assessment and, while this process is largely informal and intuitive, I will suggest that it seldom begins with the consideration of major ethical transgressions. For most of us, our first ethical dilemma is not whether "to torch" the factory or "eliminate" one of our partners. Ethical confrontations usually start out on a much smaller plane, grow over time, and then in some instances escalate out of all control.

Using data drawn from published cases, films, and personal interviews, I have developed a number of observations or hypotheses about the propensity for ethical transgression by entrepreneurs. Although preliminary, a knowledge of and appreciation for the principal hypotheses may prove helpful to prospective and practicing entrepreneurs, enabling them to recognize and avoid those conditions and situations which may be conducive to major ethical transgressions. Actully, we have already suggested one:

Hypothesis Number 1: Various levels of ethical problems exist that confront entrepreneurs from "light" to "heavy" and the usual progression is from lighter to heavier ethical transgressions.

Others will now be presented as they relate primarily to venture, people, or environmental factors.

• Venture Related Hypotheses

Hypothesis Number 2: The propensity for ethical transgression increases during periods of venture crisis and/or venture failure.

Hypothesis Number 3: The propensity for ethical transgression increases in ventures that are highly overcapitalized or highly undercapitalized.

- **People Related Hypotheses**

Hypothesis Number 4: The lead entrepreneur's values will determine the level and incidence of ethical transgression. He or she can usually overpower partners or team members even when they realize wrongdoing is being proposed.

Hypothesis Number 5: The propensity for ethical transgression will increase if the lead entrepreneur is not capable psychologically and socially of cutting back on consumption whenever necessary. Such cutbacks include not only business perks and the usual trappings of a CEO, but also refer to the lead entrepreneur's personal life—e.g., the maintenance of a big home, expensive cars, private clubs, etc.

Hypothesis Number 6: Ethical transgressions will heighten in number and intensity as the lead entrepreneur gets older and sees fewer options if his or her business goes under or is threatened.

- **Environment Related Hypotheses**

Hypothesis Number 7: A higher propensity for ethical transgression exists in some industries because of accepted ways of doing business.

Hypothesis Number 8: It is easier to become increasingly involved in serious ethical problems when an industry has a reputation for accepting lighter or less serious transgressions.

Hypothesis Number 9: Younger high growth industries have a lower propensity for ethical transgression compared to older, highly competitive industries where the propensity for ethical transgression can be quite high.

More than one of the above conditions for ethical transgressions can occur at the same time. Consequently, one can hypothesize that the propensity to commit ethical transgressions will be most acute when there is a convergence of the above conditions.

In the end, of course, you must do just that: do good and avoid evil, since convincing philosophical argument exists that the good life, the contented life, the productive life will be characterized by doing good. Yet how to avoid evil is not easy for many entrepreneurs. Specific rules and a code of ethics must be developed by each entrepreneur, for at the end of your career it will have made no sense to have proceeded with a venture that compromised your ethics.

QUESTIONS FOR ETHICAL ASSESSMENT

1. What are the likely kinds of ethical problems posed by the venture under consideration?

2. Have you had experience dealing with these kinds of ethical dilemmas in the past?

3. What kinds of ethical transgressions are accepted

  a) in this industry?

  b) in this community, state, or country?

How will you deal with them?

4. Is there anyone associated with the venture whose ethics you question? How will you maintain your own ethical standards working with them? Can you?

5. When and under what conditions have you made mistakes in the past which you now feel tarnished or hurt your reputation? Are there any discernable trends or similarities about these events?

6. Can you look your son, daughter, spouse, or anyone else who really matters, square in the eyes and tell them everything you must do to make your venture a success? What would you leave out? Why?

DISCUSSION QUESTIONS FOR CHAPTER FOUR

1. What other *venture factors* (besides those mentioned in this chapter) do you feel are important when considering a new venture opportunity? What impact would they tend to have on the venture process?

2. What special environmental conditions (besides those mentioned in in this chapter) do you feel would produce:

  a) a favorable entrepreneurial environment?

  b) an unfavorable entrepreneurial environment?

3. How do you think a younger (under 30) first time entrepreneur should start

  a) his entrepreneurial career?

  b) her entrepreneurial career?

4. What entrepreneurial career path have you followed? Or intend to follow? Why?

5. What other human factors would you consider when evaluating the entrepreneurial capability of a

  a) potential entrepreneur?

  b) practicing entrepreneur?

6. Describe the cleverest (or most unusual, or most effective) venture strategy you've ever encountered or heard about.

7. Describe an ethical dilemma that you know someone has faced. How did they handle it? How do you think you would have handled it?

KEY READINGS

Larry E. Greiner, "Evolution and Revolution as Organizations Grow," *Harvard Business Review,* July/August 1972, pp. 37-46.

Modesto A. Maidique, "Entrepreneurs, Champions, and Technical Innovation," *Sloan Management Review,* Winter 1970, pp. 59-76.

Michael K. Porter, *Competitive Strategy: Techniques for Analyzing Industries and Competitors,* The Free Press, New York, 1980.

Robert Ronstadt, "Does Entrepreneurial Career Path Really Matter?" *Frontiers of Entrepreneurship Research,* Babson College, 1982, pp. 540-67.

Milton Stewart, "The Case for Smallness: Entrepreneurship, Conglomerates, and the Good Society," *Antitrust Law and Economic Review,* 1979, Vol. II (2), pp. 67-87.

FOOTNOTES

[1]See especially Larry Greiner's article, "Evolution and Revolution as Organizations Grow," *Harvard Business Review,* July-August, 1972, pp. 37-46.

[2]Ronstadt, Robert. *Entrepreneurial Careers: A Study of the Career Pathways Pursued by Babson Entrepreneurs,* Board of Research, Babson College: Wellesley, MA, 1982, pp. 32-39. Also, the same data are discussed in "Does Entrepreneurial Career Path Really Matter?" *Frontiers of Entrepreneurship Research 1982,* Center for Entrepreneurial Studies, Babson College: Wellesley, MA, 1982.

[3]The importance of products and customers is covered nicely in Karl Vesper's *New Venture Strategies*, Prentice Hall: Englewood Cliffs, NJ, 1980, pp. 98-114. The importance of venture uniqueness, investment size, and sales/profit growth is underscored by numerous case studies.

[4]Ronstadt, *Entrepreneurial Careers, op. cit.,* pp. 18-19. Both Wetzel and Vesper have used similar classifications. See the latter's *New Venture Strategies, op. cit.,* pp. 165-175.

[5]See my "Initial Venture Goals, Age, and the Decision to Start an Entrepreneurial Career," in *Proceedings 1983,* Academy of Management as well as the technical note on "Planning for Succession" in this book.

[6]One study shows that 63% of the entrepreneurs surveyed had their primary domiciles located in the same community as their ventures. *Entrepreneurial Careers, op. cit.,* p. 8.

[7]See Michael Porter's *Competitive Strategy: Techniques For Analyzing Industries and Competitors,* New York: The Free Press, 1980, which explores the relationship between competitive rivalry and various industry variables.

[8]See Milton Stewart's "The Case for Smallness: Entrepreneurship, Conglomerates and the Good Society," *Antitrust Law and Economic Review,* 1979, Vol. 11 (2), pp. 67-87.

[9]See Edwin V.W. Zschau's Statement of Capital Formation Task Force Before the House Committee on Ways and Means available from *American Electronics Association,* March 7, 1978. Also Modesto A. Maidique, "Entrepreneurs, Champions and Technological Innovation," *Sloan Management Review,* Winter 1980, pp. 59-76; and David Birch's article, "Who Creates Jobs?" *The Public Interest,* Fall 1981, pp. 3-14.

[10]See *Venture Magazine's* "Washington Discovers the Entrepreneur: A Special Report," January 1983, pp. 32-40.

[11]Norman Fast presents the bad news for corporate entrepreneuring in "A Visit to the New Venture Graveyard," *Research Management,* Vol. XXII, No. 2, March 1979, pp. 18-22. A more optimistic view is presented by Zenas Block in his "Can Corporate Venturing Succeed?" *The Journal of Business Strategy,* Fall 1982.

Regarding the independent entrepreneur, see Richard Buskirk's "The Dangers of Overcapitalization in the Startup Stage, in *Frontiers of Entrepreneurship Research 1981,* Center for Entrepreneurial Studies, Babson College, Wellesley, MA, pp. 425-429.

[12]The first part of Chapter Three presents numerous citations. For representative work regarding the importance of experience, see Vesper's article "New Venture Ideas: Do Not Overlook the Experience Factor", *Harvard Business Review,* July-Aug., 1979, pp. 164-167; regarding initial goals, see Ronstadt, "Initial Venture Goals, Age, and the Decision to Start an Entrepreneurial Career," *op. cit.*; regarding special skills and resources, see Harry Schrage, "The R&D Entrepreneur: Profile of Success," *Harvard Business Review,* Nov.-Dec., 1965, pp. 8-21.

[13]Timmons, Jeffry A. "Careful Self Analysis and Team Assessment Can Aid Entrepreneurs," *Harvard Business Review,* Nov.-Dec., 1979.

[14]The following six relationships are based on the data analyzed in several articles including my 1) "Initial Venture Goals, Age, And The Decision To Start An Entrepreneurial Career." *op. cit.;* 2) "Does Entrepreneurial Career Path Really Matter, *op. cit.;* 3) "The Decision *Not* To Become An Entrepreneur," *Frontiers of Entrepreneurship Research, 1983,* Center for Entrepreneurial Studies, Babson College, Wellesley, MA, 1983; and 4) "Ex-Entrepreneurs," forthcoming in *Frontiers of Entrepreneurship Research 1984,* Center for Entrepreneurial Studies, Babson College, Wellesley, MA, 1984.

[15]The data on average years comes from a survey described at greater length in "Does Entrepreneurial Career Path Really Matter," *op. cit.* The pre-entrepreneurial career period can be calculated using several benchmarks. For the figures cited here and in the

following paragraph, the benchmark was the date of graduation...i.e., the "Direct Entrants" started their entrepreneurial careers 1.3 years on average after graduating from college. This average included negative figures for those who initiated their entrepreneurial careers before graduating.

[16]Ronstadt, Entrepreneurial Careers, *op. cit.*, pp. 44-47 and "The Decision *Not* to Start an Entrepreneurial Career," *op. cit.*

[17]Regarding personal characteristics, see James F. DeCarlo and Paul R. Lyons, "The Emerging Female Entrepreneur: Who is She?," *Institute for Small Business*, Frostburg State College, MD., 1979. However, Sexton and Kent found little difference between 48 female entrepreneurs and 45 female executives--see Donald L. Sexton and Calvin A. Kent's "Female Executives and Entrepreneurs: A Preliminary Comparision," in *Frontiers of Entrepreneurship Research 1981, op. cit*, pp. 40-55; regarding experience, DeCarlo and Lyons report that the 122 female entrepreneurs surveyed had over 9 years of business experience of which 6.5 years were in the same line of business as their subsequent ventures, p. 5; regarding time, DeCarlo and Lyons report in "A Comparison of Selected Personal Characteristics of Minority and Non-Minority Female Entrepreneurs," *Institute for Small Business*, Frostburg State, MD, 1979, the female entrepreneurs work between 45 and 50 hours per week on average, considerably under the average for male entrepreneurs. "The Report on Women Business Owners" by Henry E. Binder, *American Management Association*, New York, 1978, offers some explanation for married female entrepreneurs, i.e., the need to balance family and business concerns, p. 216; regarding goals, Sexton and Kent, *op. cit.*, note that making big money is not a primary motivation. Binder's work, *op. cit.*, reveal that the size of these ventures is also small whether measured by employees or sales; regarding venture factors, see Robert D. Hisrich and Marie O'Brien's article "The Woman Entrepreneur as a Reflection of the Type of Business," in *Frontiers of Entrepreneurship Research 1982, op. cit.*, pp. 54-67, which compares women in "traditional" versus "nontraditional" businesses. The same study, along with several others already mentioned, note that women entrepreneurs experience particular difficulty with financing issues.

[18]See DeCarlo and Lyons' "A Comparison of Selected Personal Characteristics of Minority and Non-Minority Female Entrepreneurs," *op. cit.*, p. 3; also Eugene Gomolka's "Characteristics of Minority Entrepreneurs and Small Business Enterprises," *American Journal of Small Business*, Volume II, No. 1, July 1977, pp. 12-21, which shows a significant number of minority entrepreneurs tend to be college graduates. "Mainstream" versus "subeconomy" markets are discussed in Matthew C. Sonfield's "Aiming for the 'Mainstream' Market--The Key to Black Small Business Success?" *Journal of Small Business Management*, April 1979, pp. 33-35.

[19]The ties between creativity and nonconformity are explored at length by Clark Moustakas, *Creativity and Conformity*, New York: D. Van Nostrand Co., 1967. See also John Hendrick's classic "How I Overcame the Handicap of a College Education," Dover, MA, *Case Publishing*, 1982.

[20]Hornaday, John A. and Karl H. Vesper, "Alumni Perceptions of Entrepreneurship Courses After Six to Ten Years," in *Entrepreneurship Education 1981*, Donald S. Sexton and Philip M. Van Auken, eds., Center for Private Enterprise and Entrepreneurship, 1981, pp. 115-131.

[21]Ronstadt, *Entrepreneurial Careers, op. cit.,* pp. 68-75, discusses goal change in detail.

[22]Quoted from a letter by Mr. Ernest T. Gundlach, published in *Action and Reaction: An Autobiography of Roger Babson,* Revised Edition, Archives, Horn Library, Babson College, 1949, pp. 181-182.

[23]See David C.D. Rogers' *Essentials of Business Policy,* New York: Harper & Row, 1975, pp. 8-20.

[24]For an example of this approach see Herbert N. Woodward's article, "Management Strategies for Small Companies," *Harvard Business Review,* January/February, 1976, pp. 113-121.

[25]Michael Porter's previously cited book demonstrates this approach. See his *Competitive Strategy and Industry Analysis,* New York: The Free Press, 1982.

[26]The ties between business and excellence are developed by Thomas J. Peters and Robert Waterman, *In Search of Excellence,* New York: Harper & Row, 1983. These ideas are expanded by Mark Postin, the Director of the *Center for Private and Public Sector Ethics,* Arizona State University, Tempe, Arizona, in a series of Working Papers entitled "Ethics and the Art of Management," "The Integrating Role of Ethics in Effective Management," and "Why"--the unasked question that managers need to ask. Finally, the importance of ethics to entrepreneurs is voiced by many entrepreneurs. See "Entrepreneurship Educations in the 80's: What do Entrepreneurs Say?" by Jeffry A. Timmons and Howard H. Stevenson, Unpublished Research Paper: 75th Anniversary Colloquium Series, *Division of Research,* Harvard Business School, 1983, pp. 4-5.

[27]Timmons and Stevenson, *Ibid.*

5

QUANTITATIVE ASSESSMENT: NUMBERS FOR ENTREPRENEURS

I. THE NEED FOR A NUMBERS CAPABILITY

To what extent is a facility with numbers a required skill for most entrepreneurs? Opinions vary, but most teachers in the field agree that entrepreneurs should develop at least a minimum capability to apply (sometimes creatively) a few numerical techniques. I want to stress that we are talking about simple arithmetic--an ability to add, subtract, multiply, and divide numbers. No one, to my knowledge, claims entrepreneurs need to be quantitative whizzes. On the other hand, knowing how and when to use certain numerical techniques can save you both time and money -- two important assets for any entrepreneur. Time and again, both in discussions with entrepreneurs and in the classroom, I have participated in exciting and imaginative discussions of entrepreneurial ideas, and then have asked, "But will it work?" Only rarely can the "idea-people" quantify their venture visions adequately to get another perspective -- one that either supports or fails to support their qualitative judgments. In short, good quantitative assessment can help produce better qualitative-based decisions.

Since ventures vary widely, the need for "numbers sophistication" required by individual entrepreneurs varies widely as well. Some businesses require very little, next to nothing, in terms of a numbers capability. For example, a non-growth, one-person service business that operates on a cash-only basis may require little more than an ability to count properly and make change. In other instances an entrepreneur may have partners or team members who can handle those decisions which require numerical assessment. In certain kinds of lifestyle ventures, the need for quantitative ability may be quite low initially *and* as the ventures evolves over time. In others, a numbers capability may become more important, particularly if aspirations become more enterprising and move beyond "lifestyle" concerns.

For instance, smaller ventures with high profit aspirations that are run by a single entrepreneur invariably require a person with a fairly strong numbers capability in a few key areas -- a capability that certainly goes beyond an ability to read financial statements supplied periodically by an accountant. Interestingly, the need for strong quantitative skills *may* actually decline for a particular entrepreneur when venture goals involve high growth aspirations. The reason is that these ventures are seldom started and run by single entrepreneurs. High growth ventures usually mean venture teams, and in these situations one or more members of the entrepreneurial team generally must be very capable with various kinds of quantitative analysis. But some team members or partners may have other critical skills which do not necessarily include an affinity for creatively pushing numbers -- e.g., the super salesman or the inventive genius.

What I am suggesting is that a relationship exists between venture type, the number of entrepreneurs, and the need for a numbers capability. In fact, a good question to ask early on in the evaluation of a venture is: To what extent will a strong numbers capability be required by a particular entrepreneur over the life of a venture? And a second question, to follow immediately, is: what critical decisions in my venture should be mde using both qualitative and quantitative assessments?

WHICH NUMBER SKILLS ARE CRITICAL?

What are the number skills which you are most likely to need? They do not include the precise skills of the accountant, nor the abstract, complex skills of the mathematician or operations researcher, nor the applied statistical skills of the economist. Entrepreneurs need simple yet powerful skills to reinforce their visceral qualitative approaches to decisionmaking. These core skills revolve around an understanding of cash flow and techniques related to it. These include various types of projections, contribution margins, and cash break evens. Cash flow is central because the concept of "liquidity" is probably the most crucial issue for the future of a venture, since most ventures are not publicly traded companies where "profits" and growth in profits (earnings per share) become the critical criterion of value and success.

Decisions involving cash flow arise at every point of a venture's history, from inception to conclusion. For example, a great deal of time can be spent evaluating a venture's potential on a qualitative basis when the judicious use of a few numerical techniques can quickly tell us whether or not to proceed further in pursuing it. Again, a clear understanding of the venture's cost structure and cash flow requirements can indicate how an entrepreneur should be allocating precious time among competing tasks. Finally, some simple quantitative techniques can help to determine the value of a venture should we wish to disassociate ourselves from it.

Graphically, the decisions requiring numbers capability throughout the life of a venture are shown in *Exhibit 1*. I emphasize again that these techniques are not abstract exercises in pushing figures -- they are ways of saving you both time and money.

II. UNDERSTANDING CASH FLOW

DEFINITION

The concept of cash flow is quite straightforward. Certain decisions and events result in an increase of cash. The net result, for any given moment in time, is cash flow. Others cause a decrease in cash. Conceptually, there is nothing more to say about it. *Exhibit 2* shows some of the activities which cause an increase or decrease in cash.

PRACTICAL DIFFICULTIES

So much for the good news. While the concept of cash flow is very simple in principle,

Exhibit 1

NUMERICAL ANALYSIS CAN HELP WITH DECISION

startup & acquisition	To proceed with venture	Not to proceed. Spend time elsewhere
ongoing concern	Where to allocate scarce time & resources	Where not to allocate scarce time & resources
discontinuing venture	When & how to end venture	When & how not to end venture

Exhibit 2

THE CASH FLOW PROCESS

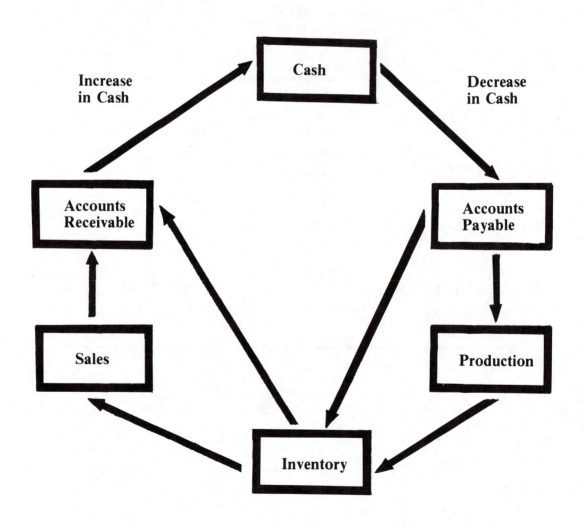

specific cash flows do not always appear as anticipated in practice. This misfortune occurs because future cash flows are sometimes hard to predict, especially in the case of a new venture when historical data – what actually happened over the last months or years -- are lacking as a guideline.

To aid the entrepreneur in cash flow prediction, I suggest three numerical techniques:

> . Cash, not accrual, accounting
>
> . Estimating historical cash flows
>
> . Projecting future cash flows.

Cash Accounting

The difference between accounting on a cash basis versus an accrual basis is illustrated in *Exhibit 3*. Accrual-based accounting was designed for big business, and as a recent article suggests, may be fatal to small ones:

> The accrual presentation...was designed to resolve the problem created by the various cycles in the flow of cash. By ignoring when cash actually flows, the accrual method provides a more orderly picture of profit. Profit, by the accrual calculation, is a mathematical concept. You can't get a bagful of profit. Cash, as owner-managers perceive it, is tangible. For the small business manager, who must worry about this week's payroll, profit is not cash and profit plus depreciation is not the available cash flow.[1]

Estimating Historical Cash Flows

There are two basic approaches:

1) Track or estimate the actual cash flows, noting each item that results in a cash *inflow* or a cash *outflow;*

2) Use proxy measures which estimate net cash flow for some period of time.

Let's examine the latter measures of cash flow since they can be expanded increasingly to approximate the first approach.

One of the fastest estimates of cash flow mentioned in the previous quote is simply to add depreciation to profits after taxes. This "quick and dirty" approximation can be expanded by including any other noncash expenses shown in the profit and loss statement. A critical assumption underlying this approximation is that the reporting period of the P&L statement (be it monthly, quarterly, or a yearly statement) is an appropriate time period over which to estimate cash flows. For example, the measure can be misleading if it is only available on a monthly or annual basis but cash flows must be

Exhibit 3

Accrual vs. Cash Accounting

	Sales (inflows)	**Expenses (outflows)**
Accrual Method	Accounted for when sale is made.	When expense is incurred.

ACCOUNTED FOR:

Cash Method	When cash is collected for a sale	When cash is paid for an expense

estimated on a weekly basis in order to insure the liquidity and survivability of the enterprise.

A second approximation of cash flow is to look at the flow of "funds" on a cash basis. Again, over a long enough period, the net changes in a sources and uses or funds flow statement will approximate cash flow. For example, *Exhibit 4* presents a list of sources and uses of funds and indicates a positive cash flow of $1 million (i.e., the amount by which total sources exceeds total uses).

A third and a much safer approach is to track actual cash flows over some relevant time period for your particular business. *Exhibit 5* summarizes this calculation. It lists some of the items that can result in a cash inflow or a cash outflow.

Projecting Future Cash Flows

A rough estimate of future cash flows can be a powerful and revealing aid to entrepreneurial decision making. This type of projection is especially useful when sales are increasing or decreasing rapidly. When sales change quickly, so do expenses. The key question for survival of a venture, however, is whether or not cash receipts are building up relatively faster than cash payments for expenses. The classic example of venture failure is the venture that grows so quickly that it produces a cash shortage that cannot be covered. Similarly, a sales decline can also produce a cash shortage if expenses and cash outflows are not reduced to offset the projected decline of cash receipts.

Projecting future cash flows is a relatively simple process. The first step is to determine what you feel is the relevant period for cash flow analysis (be it week, month, year, etc.). For instance, applicants for an SBA loan are asked to complete at least a monthly cash flow for twelve months. The specific format and guidelines are presented on the following pages. However, in some instances, a day by day projection of cash flow may be the proper time period (e.g., the first 20 or 30 days of a venture start-up). The second step is to calculate all cash inflows for this period, adding them to the existing cash balance. Then calculate all cash outflows for the same period and subtract them from total cash inflows to arrive at net cash flow for the period.

Any calculation, however, is only as good as the assumptions underlying it. My experience indicates that the critical assumptions regarding accurate cash flow projections are the following:

1) The time period chosen is correct or relevant to the particular venture situation;

2) The sales estimate for the time period is reasonable given what is known about the venture since this estimate will directly affect both cash inflows and outflows;

3) Both new and ongoing cash outflows are complete and accurate. If you are going to err, an underestimation on the cash inflow side is much more forgiving;

4) All other sources of financing remain the same or are replaced.

Exhibit 4

Funds Flow

Sources	Uses
Net Profit	Dividends
Depreciation	Net (+) In any asset except cash.
Net (−) Accounts Receivable	e.g. (+) fixed assets
Net (+) Loans	(+) inventories
(−) Taxes	(+) prepaids
(−) Payroll	Net (−) in any liability
(+) Stock	e.g. Net (−) A/P

Total Sources	**Total Uses**
$10,000,000	**$9,000,000**

Exhibit 5

Cash Flows

Cash Receipts	**versus**	Cash Disbursements
i.e.		i.e.
Cash In		Cash Out
+ Beginning Cash Balance		− Raw Materials Payments
+ Cash Sales Received		− Labor Payments
+ Credit Sales Collected		Other Expenses Paid:
+ Cash from Financing Received		− Taxes
		− Payroll
		− L/T Debt
		Etc.

A final warning about cash flow projections should be sounded. External events, over which the entrepreneur has no control, may upset the best-laid forecasts -- a shipping strike, a warehouse fire, the bankruptcy of a supplier. Of course, severe crises are often easy to read in terms of their cash flow impacts. Rather it is the host of smaller crises that are more difficult to assess. Most small businesses have no way of protecting themselves against these unforeseen events whether large or small except by resourcefulness with customers and creditors and possibly a good friend at the bank. While such occurrences cannot be included in a projected cash flow, entrepreneurs can determine quickly their impact on liquidity if a cash flow approach is employed. Can you ride out the storm without visiting that "friend" at the bank? Remember -- one can make only so many trips to the financing well and, in a very real sense, cash flow analysis tells us when to make the trip and also how much "liquidity" we need to draw from the well.

OTHER USEFUL PROJECTIONS

Two other types of financial projections are useful to assess not only profitability but also how resources are being allocated in a venture, and ultimately what cash flow needs will exist under different scenarios. The two are:

. Profit and Loss (P&L) projections

. Balance Sheet projections

First, some basic definitions and a few words of warning. A P&L (or Income Statement) records the revenues and expenses of a firm and the resulting profit or loss for a particular period of time at a particular date. The balance sheet gives a picture of the firm's accounting value on a particular date. However, both accounting devices arose from the needs of big business, big enough so that actual rates of change and growth were comparatively small over the accounting period. In small business, where sales, assets, inventories, and cash on hand fluctuate tremendously, the "point in time" look at your venture may be telling a very incomplete picture. As pointed out in the section on cash flow, a fixed asset won't help you meet your payroll, and your receivables may treble when you open tomorrow's mail. Nonetheless, all the line items represent aspects of your venture which you should be aware of -- and, even without historical information, be able to project.

Profit and Loss Pro Formas

> You can generate a projected profit and loss statement with nothing more than an estimate of future sales and a Profit and Loss Statement for the current period. The basic approach is to determine past expense loads (as a percent of sales) and project these expenses at their past percentage levels so they "vary" proportionately to the sales increase.
>
> If you have additional information about future production, sales, and other overhead charges, you may be able to determine if cost of goods and other operating expenses will

increase, decrease, or remain at their former levels as a percent of sales. The same estimates can be made for interest and other non-operating expenses. Will some "fixed" costs increase slightly, becoming semivariable? Will some variable costs increase in a non-linear fashion with sales?

Once you answer these questions and determine total expenses, the appropriate tax rate can be applied to obtain after tax profits.

Balance Sheet Pro Formas

The projection of a balance sheet also depends on knowing or estimating a sales forecast, plus applying ratio levels as they existed in the past. For example, assume next year's sales are forecasted to increase from $1,200,000 to $1,500,000 and that last year's balance sheet showed a cash balance of $66,667. Ratio analysis revealed cash turnover was twenty days in the past:

$$\frac{\$66.667}{\$1,200,000} \quad (360 \text{ DAYS}) = 20 \text{ DAYS}$$

If 20 days of cash are appropriate for the future, the cash balance for next year at the new level is:

$$\text{CASH} = \frac{\$1,500,000}{360 \text{ DAYS}} \quad (20 \text{ DAYS}) = \$83,334$$

The procedure for estimating accounts receivable, inventory, accounts payable, debt to equity, etc. is similar.

Since assets must equal total liabilities, you may select any one item on the balance sheet as a "plug" figure for your entry. Usually long-term debt or cash is used as the plug figure, because it indicates your cash or financing needs for a given projection.

CONTRIBUTION MARGINS

An important factor in a venture's cash flow is "the contribution" to fixed costs and profits generated by each sale of a product or service. Some costs remain fixed over some range of volumes while others "vary" with volume. Once these "varying" or variable costs are identified, they are subtracted from total sales and the remainder is the "contribution" to fixed costs and profits.

TOTAL SALES — VARIABLE COSTS = CONTRIBUTION TO FIXED COSTS AND PROFITS

MONTHLY CASH FLOW PROJECTION

INSTRUCTIONS ON REVERSE SIDE

NAME OF BUSINESS

ADDRESS

OWNER

TYPE OF BUSINESS

PREPARED BY

DATE

	Pre-Start-up Position		1		2		3		4		5		6		7		8		9		10		11		12		TOTAL Columns 1–12		
YEAR / MONTH	Estimate	Actual	Estimate	Actual	Estimate	Actual	Estimate	Actual	Estimate	Actual	Estimate	Actual	Estimate	Actual	Estimate	Actual	Estimate	Actual	Estimate	Actual	Estimate	Actual	Estimate	Actual	Estimate	Actual	
1. CASH ON HAND (Beginning of month)																											1.
2. CASH RECEIPTS (a) Cash Sales																											2. (a)
(b) Collections from Credit Accounts																											(b)
(c) Loan or Other Cash Injection (Specify)																											(c)
3. TOTAL CASH RECEIPTS (2a+2b+2c=3)																											3.
4. TOTAL CASH AVAILABLE (Before cash out) (1+3)																											4.
5. CASH PAID OUT (a) Purchases (Merchandise)																											5. (a)
(b) Gross Wages (Excludes withdrawals)																											(b)
(c) Payroll Expenses (Taxes, etc.)																											(c)
(d) Outside Services																											(d)
(e) Supplies (Office and operating)																											(e)
(f) Repairs and Maintenance																											(f)
(g) Advertising																											(g)
(h) Car, Delivery, and Travel																											(h)
(i) Accounting and Legal																											(i)
(j) Rent																											(j)
(k) Telephone																											(k)
(l) Utilities																											(l)
(m) Insurance																											(m)
(n) Taxes (Real estate, etc.)																											(n)
(o) Interest																											(o)
(p) Other Expenses (Specify each)																											(p)
(q) Miscellaneous (Unspecified)																											(q)
(r) Subtotal																											(r)
(t) Loan Principal Payment																											(t)
(u) Capital Purchases (Specify)																											(u)
(v) Other Start-up Costs																											(v)
(w) Reserve and/or Escrow (Specify)																											(w)
(x) Owner's Withdrawal																											(x)
6. TOTAL CASH PAID OUT (Total 5a thru 5w)																											6.
7. CASH POSITION (End of month) (4 minus 6)																											7.
ESSENTIAL OPERATING DATA (Non-cash flow information) A. Sales Volume (Dollars)																											A.
B. Accounts Receivable (End of month)																											B.
C. Bad Debt (End of month)																											C.
D. Inventory on Hand (End of month)																											D.
E. Accounts Payable (End of month)																											E.
F. Depreciation																											F.

SBA FORM 1100 (8-75) REF: SOP 60 10 1

Source: Small Business Administration, SBA Form 1100, United States Government, Washington, D.C.

GUIDELINES

GENERAL

Definition: A cash flow projection is a forecast of cash funds* a business anticipates receiving, on the one hand, and disbursing, on the other hand, throughout the course of a given span of time, and the anticipated cash position at specific times during the period being projected.

Objective: The purpose of preparing a cash flow projection is to determine deficiencies or excesses in cash from that necessary to operate the business during the time for which the projection is prepared. If deficiencies are revealed in the cash flow, financial plans must be altered either to provide more cash by, for example, more equity capital, loans, or increased selling prices of products, or to reduce expenditures including inventory, or allow less credit sales until a proper cash flow balance is obtained. If excesses of cash are revealed, it might indicate excessive borrowing or idle money that could be "put to work." The objective is to finally develop a plan which, if followed, will provide a well-managed flow of cash.

The Form: The cash flow projection form provides a systematic method of recording estimates of cash receipts and expenditures, which can be compared with actual receipts and expenditures as they become known—hence the two columns, Estimate and Actual. The entries listed on the form will not necessarily apply to every business, and some entries may not be included which would be pertinent to specific businesses. It is suggested, therefore, that the form be adapted to the particular business for which the projection is being made, with appropriate changes in the entries as may be required. Before the cash flow projection can be completed and pricing structure established, it is necessary to know or to estimate various important factors of the business, for example: What are the direct costs of the product or services per unit? What are the monthly or yearly costs of the operation? What is the sales price per unit of the product or service? Determine that the pricing structure provides this business with reasonable breakeven goals (including a reasonable net profit) when conservative sales goals are met. What are the available sources of cash, other than income from sales; for example, loans, equity capital, rent, or other sources?

Procedure: Most of the entries for the form are self-explanatory; however, the following suggestions are offered to simplify the procedure:

(A) Suggest even dollars be used rather than showing cents.

(B) If this is a new business, or an existing business undergoing significant changes or alterations, the cash flow part of the column marked "Pre-start-up Position" should be completed. (Fill in appropriate blanks only.) Costs involved here are, for example, rent, telephone, and utilities deposits before the business is actually open. Other items might be equipment purchases, alterations, the owner's cash injection, and cash from loans received before actual operations begin.

(C) Next fill in the pre-start-up position of the essential operating data (non-cash flow information), where applicable.

(D) Complete the form using the suggestions in the partial form below for each entry.

CHECKING

In order to insure that the figures are properly calculated and balanced, they must be checked. Several methods may be used, but the following four checks are suggested as a minimum:

CHECK #1: Item #1 (Beginning Cash on Hand—1st Month) plus Item #3 (Total Cash Receipts—Total Column) minus Item #6 (Total Cash Paid Out—Total Column) should be equal to Item #7 (Cash Position at End of 12th Month).

*Cash funds, for the purpose of this projection, are defined as cash, checks, or money order, paid out or received.

CHECK #2: Item A (Sales Volume—Total Column) plus Item B (Accounts Receivable—Pre-start-up Position) minus Item 2(a) (Cash Sales—Total Column) minus Item 2(b) (Accounts Receivable Collection—Total Column) minus Item C (Bad Debt—Total Column) should be equal to Item B (Accounts Receivable at End of 12th Month).

CHECK #3: The horizontal total of Item #6 (Total Cash Paid Out) is equal to the vertical total of all items under Item #5 5(a) through 5(w)) in the total column at the right of the form.

CHECK #4: The horizontal total of Item #3 (Total Cash Receipts) is equal to the vertical total of all items under #2 (2(a) through 2(c)) in the total column at the right of the form.

ANALYZE the correlation between the cash flow and the projected profit during the period in question. The estimated profit is the difference between the estimated change in assets and the estimated change in liabilities before such things as any owner withdrawal, appreciation of assets, change in investments, etc. (The change may be positive or negative.) This can be obtained as follows:

The **change in assets** before owner's withdrawal, appreciation of assets, change in investments, etc., can be computed by adding the following:

(1) Item #7 (Cash Position—End of Last Month) minus Item #1 (Cash on Hand at the Beginning of the First Month).

(2) Item #5 (t) (Capital Purchases—Total Column) minus Item F (depreciation—Total Column).

(3) Item B. (Accounts Receivable—End of 12th Month) minus Item B (Accounts Receivable—Pre-start-up Position).

(4) Item D. (Inventory on Hand—End of 12th Month) minus Item D (Inventory on Hand—Pre-start-up Position).

(5) Item #5 (w) (Owner's withdrawal—Total Column) or dividends, minus such things as an increase in investment.

(6) Item #5 (v) (Reserve and/or Escrow—Total Column).

The **change in liabilities** (before items noted in "change in assets") can be computed by adding the following:

(1) Item 2(c) (Loans—Total Column) minus 5(s) (Loan Principal Payment—Total Column).

(2) Item E (Accounts Payable—End of 12th Month) minus E (Accounts Payable—Pre-start-up Position).

ANALYSIS

A. The cash position at the end of each month should be adequate to meet the cash requirements for the following month. If too little cash, then additional cash will have to be injected or cash paid out must be reduced. If there is too much cash on hand, this money is not working for your business.

B. The cash flow projection, the profit and loss projection, the break-even analysis, and good cost control information are tools which, if used properly, will be useful in making decisions that can increase profits to insure success.

C. The projection becomes more useful when the estimated information can be compared with actual information as it develops. It is important to follow through and complete the actual columns as the information becomes available. Utilize the cash flow projection to assist in setting new goals and planning operations for more profit.

1. CASH ON HAND	
(Beginning of month)	Cash on hand same as (7), Cash Position Previous Month
2. CASH RECEIPTS	
(a) Cash Sales	All cash sales. Omit credit sales unless cash is actually received.
(b) Collections from Credit Accounts	Amount to be expected from all credit accounts.
(c) Loan or Other Cash injection	Indicate here all cash injections not shown in 2(a) or 2(b) above. See "A" of "Analysis"
3. TOTAL CASH RECEIPTS	
(2a+2b+2c=3)	Self-explanatory
4. TOTAL CASH AVAILABLE	
(Before cash out) (1+3)	Self-explanatory
5. CASH PAID OUT	
(a) Purchases (Merchandise)	Merchandise for resale or for use in product (paid for in current month)
(b) Gross Wages (Excludes withdrawals)	Base pay plus overtime (if any)
(c) Payroll Expenses (Taxes, etc.)	Include paid vacations, paid sick leave, health insurance, unemployment insurance, etc. (this might be 10 to 45% OF 5(b)
(d) Outside Services	This could include outside labor and/or material for specialized or overflow work, including subcontracting
(e) Supplies (Office and operating)	Items purchased for use in the business (not for resale)
(f) Repairs and Maintenance	Include periodic large expenditures such as painting or decorating
(g) Advertising	This amount should be adequate to maintain sales volume—include telephone book yellow page cost
(h) Car, Delivery, and Travel	If personal car is used, charge in this column—include parking
(i) Accounting and Legal	Outside services, including, for example, bookkeeping
(j) Rent	Real estate only (See 5(p) for other rentals)
(k) Telephone	Self-explanatory
(l) Utilities	Water, heat, light, and/or power
(m) Insurance	Coverages on business property and products e.g. fire, liability; also workman's compensation, fidelity, etc. Exclude "executive" life (include in "5W")
(n) Taxes (Real estate, etc.)	Plus inventory tax—sales tax—excise tax, if applicable
(o) Interest	Remember to add interest on loan as it is injected (See 2(c) above)
(p) Other Expenses (Specify each)	Unexpected expenditures may be included here as a safety factor
	Equipment expensed during the month should be included here (Non-capital equipment)
	When equipment is rented or leased, record payments here
(q) Miscellaneous (Unspecified)	Small expenditures for which separate accounts would not be practical
(r) Subtotal	This subtotal indicates cash out for operating costs
(s) Loan Principal Payment	Include payment on all loans, including vehicle and equipment purchases on time payment
(t) Capital Purchases (Specify)	Non-expensed (depreciable) expenditures such as equipment, building, vehicle purchases, and leasehold improvements
(u) Other Start-up Costs	Expenses incurred prior to first month position and paid for after the "start-up" position
(v) Reserve and/or Escrow (Specify)	Example: insurance, tax, or equipment escrow to reduce impact of large periodic payments
(w) Owner's Withdrawal	Should include payment for such things as owner's income tax, social security, health insurance, "executive" life insurance premiums, etc.
6. TOTAL CASH PAID OUT	
(Total 5 thru 5w)	Self-explanatory
7. CASH POSITION	
(End of month) (4-6)	Enter this amount in (1) Cash on Hand following month—See "A" of "Analysis"
ESSENTIAL OPERATING DATA	
(Non-cash flow information)	This is basic information necessary for proper planning and for proper cash flow projection. In conjunction with this data, the cash flow can be evolved and shown in the above form.
A. Sales Volume (Dollars)	This is a very important figure and should be estimated carefully, taking into account size of facility and employee output as well as realistic anticipated sales (Actual sales performed—not orders received)
B. Accounts Receivable (End of month)	Previous unpaid credit sales plus current month's credit sales, less amounts received current month (deduct "C" below)
C. Bad Debt (End of month)	Bad debts should be subtracted from "B" in the month anticipated
D. Inventory on Hand (End of month)	Last month's inventory plus merchandise received and/or manufactured current month minus amount sold current month
E. Accounts Payable (End of month)	Previous month's payable plus current month's payable minus amount paid during month
F. Depreciation	Established by your accountant, or value of all your equipment divided by useful life (in months) as allowed by Internal Revenue Service

SBA FORM 1100 (8-75)

Sometimes specific "units" of production exist and are identifiable for the products and services being produced. In these instances, "unit contribution" can be found simply by dividing total contribution by total unit output.

Why is it important to know the contribution for different products, services, or investment alternatives? The main reason is that it is possible to have high contribution products or services that provide low or no profit. Yet if one looks at profit alone, the temptation may rise to de-emphasize or even drop those products or services producing low or negative profits. Such action can inhibit a business from covering its total costs since some of these costs are fixed no matter what the business produces. In short, where contribution margins are high and/or where the absolute dollar amount of contribution is high, entrepreneurs have a better chance of "contributing" to the continued existence of their ventures.

Two numerical techniques useful for increasing contribution margins are:

. Pricing; and

. Cost control

Pricing. In my experience, many new entrepreneurs tend to price their goods or services too low; in fact they avoid what they believe to be "overpricing" like the plague, even when they claim their product or service is better than competitors. Many times, a calculation of what margin the product must contribute to justify its inclusion will tell you the MINIMUM amount you can sell it for before you even consider testing the market for price sensitivity. Perhaps, you will discover that this minimum price is far beyond the market's price tolerance -- but at least, you will find out in time to save yourself money.

Yet the willingness of some portion of the market to pay higher prices is often beyond our expectations. For instance, there is the story of one old, crusty entrepreneur whose soda bottling business flourished year after year. The entrepreneur in question had practically no formal education, hated numbers, and to top it all off, also wrote and spoke poor English, having migrated from Europe during his early adult years. But despite these disadvantages, he worked hard and prospered. In later years, he decided to sell his bottling business. In fact, he sold it twice, each time to highly trained MBAs. But each time, he was forced to repurchase it when they failed to make a go of it. Finally, he was asked why he was so successful when others educated in modern management techniques could not survive. His response was that his particular success was simply a matter of proper knowledge of his costs combined with a very thin markup. He explained, "You see, it's quite simple. Let's say my total costs are one cent. To this I add my profit of one cent. And there you have it -- a 1% markup." Often the latitude to price higher exists. Most fail to recognize this fact, but a few like the entrepreneur in this story err fortuitously in the right direction.

Controlling costs. In some businesses, there is a limit to what the customer will pay for a good or service -- despite the fact that the cost to the entrepreneur of producing that good or service continues to rise. In this case, the way to hold or increase margins is to cut costs.

An example of effective cost-cutting is the following, taken from an interview with Anthony Athanas, owner of Boston's famous Pier 4 Restaurant:

> I'm trying to keep my cost down, so I can give customers something to come here for. Otherwise, we're going to price ourselves out of the market. People say you can't price yourself out but I don't believe that... Working with people (employees), training them, teaching them, encouraging them to stay with you...to stay in the business. It's all part of controls. Our food costs here run around 39 or 40 percent. Labor costs are about 28 percent. You control turnover, you help stabilize your labor costs. Controls...
>
> Don't think you can solve your cost problems simply by adjusting menu prices. That's the last thing you want to do. Raising prices is very dangerous. I've had to do it...and still do it. (But) you're not going to get away with it forever. You tighten controls, you watch. For instance, our manager here watches the weather. If it's going to snow or rain he'll look at the history of what he's done in the past when it rained or snowed, so that right off the bat he'll know how to adjust his schedule for the week...Shop for bargains: chicken, fish, oysters. Balance your food costs with your labor costs. You don't have to get a 39 percent food cost for steak. You can sell it for 50 percent because your labor is low. You drop the steak on the broiler, turn it over, plate it. Run food and labor costs together.[2]

CALCULATING CASH BREAKEVENS

Finally, the cash-wise entrepreneur should learn to calculate breakeven points -- for single product businesses, or in more complicated cases, for multiple product businesses. This analysis is also based on distinguishing between fixed and variable costs. Once this dichotomy has been accomplished, breakeven analysis tells you how many units you must produce so that total revenues (net sales) will equal total costs. This point of equality is the breakeven point. *Exhibit 6* graphs this relationship.

Breakeven volume. In order to calculate the breakeven volume (BEV), you must know and divide total fixed costs (FC) for a particular product by its contribution per unit (CU). Another way of stating the same relationship is to divide fixed costs by the difference between unit sales price (SP) and unit variable costs (VC) for the product. The respective formulas are:

$$BEV = FC \div CU$$
$$BEV = FC \div SP - VC$$

In some situations, you may not know precisely the absolute amount of actual variable costs. However, you may be able to estimate what variable costs are as a percentage of total sales (e.g., from information given in historical P & L statements). For instance, suppose known fixed costs are approximately $400,000 for a given level of sales, let's say 100,000 units. Also you estimate that variable costs are about 70% of total sales. Since contribution sales = variable costs, the contribution margin in percentage terms is simply:

$$\text{Total Sales of } 100\% - 70\% = 30\%$$

Given this information one can solve for breakeven sales volume by dividing total fixed costs by the contribution margin expressed as a decimal. For example:

$$\text{BEV} = 400,000$$
$$1 - .70 = 400,000 \quad .30 = \$1,333,333$$

Basically, this breakeven calculation says an entrepreneur must realize more than $1,333,333 of sales to begin realizing a *profit*. Yet most entrepreneurs need to calculate the level of sales requied to realize a *cash* breakeven.

Cash Breakeven. To calculate a cash breakeven, you must determine which costs have *not* resulted in an actual cash outflow (e.g. depreciation). For instance, if depreciation in the above example were $20,000, the procedure would be to reduce fixed costs ($400,000) by $20,000. consequently, the cash breakeven would be some $67,000 less than the profit breakeven:

$$\text{BEV} = (\$400,000 - \$20,000) \quad .30 = \$1,266,666$$

Once you know breakeven sales volume, you can compare it with estimates of forecasted sales, total market size, your realistic share of the market, and/or your projected capacity of operations. Do you have sufficient production capacity to obtain breakeven volume? What will this capacity cost you in terms of additional investment in your venture? Is breakeven volume higher or lower than the share of market you can realistically hope to capture? Is the breakeven level of sales 40%, 60%, or 90% of forecasted sales? If 90%, how likely is it that you will realize breakeven?

Breakevens Under Multiple Assumptions. No discussion of calculating breakevens would be complete without a few warnings. First, fixed and variable expenses may not in reality follow the smooth or straight lines as shown in the following graph. Rapid sales growth may not be proportionate to goods shipped, especially in a new venture where initial growth may include:

> offering discounts, making contract deals, providing bonuses, and supplying potential customers with impressive quantities of free samples.[3]

Likewise, fixed expenses may not remain fixed for long, but may grow in steps, causing a variety of breakeven points to appear at different levels as the graph in *Exhibit 7* portrays.

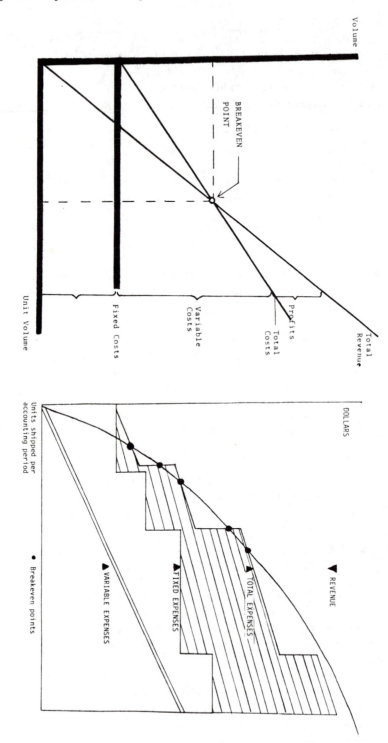

Exhibit 6

Breakeven Analysis

Exhibit 7

Break-even Graph for a New or Small Business

Source: Welsh and White, "A Small Business is Not a Little Big Business, *Harvard Business Review*, July/August, 1981.

Second, the relationship between fixed costs and variable costs may shift considerably over time. Such shifts are particularly possible and even probable for many new ventures. Here, fixed costs may be either inordinately low or high at startup depending on different circumstances. For instance, fixed costs may be kept low initially because demand is uncertain and/or the founders have limited investment capital. Variable costs are high because various activities are subcontracted with each sale. But as the business grows and proves itself, fixed overhead can be justified to handle inhouse what was previously a subcontracted variable cost. Conversely, it may be necessary (or perceived necessary) to initiate a new venture with considerable investment in fixed assets. Yet initially the productivity of these assets may be limited by several factors which keeps output and variable costs relatively low compared to fixed costs. Variable costs may increase substantially as output picks up with little or no change in fixed costs--and the increases in variable costs may or may not be directly proportional to sales growth.

In either of these cases, breakeven sales volume will shift considerably as the relationship changes in a new venture's cost structure,...i.e., the relationship between fixed and variable costs. Entrepreneurs should have a feel for the direction, magnitude, and timing of these changes in cost structure. The uncertainty and dynamics of the situation dictate multiple calculations under various conditions. Entrepreneurs may well be misled by their own calculations if they rely on one set of assumptions alone.

A technique to avoid this pitfall is sensitivity analysis,...i.e., how "sensitive" is your conclusion to a change in one or more of your assumptions. Sensitivity analysis can be used for many numerical calculations -- not just breakevens. But in this case, it means calculating the breakeven under a range of assumptions about key variables as they influence sales levels, fixed costs, and variable cost. Of course, the possible variations are often too numerous to count and, despite the advent of personal computers and spread sheet software which makes the longer, more detailed calculating far easier to do than in the past, you may want to limit your sensitivity analysis to a *worst, expected, best* scenario.

III. INTEGRATING CASH FLOW AND PROFITABILITY

It's difficult to understate the importance of real estate evaluation for most entrepreneurs. We've all heard of entrepreneurs who have created and run ventures that turned out to be marginal in an operating sense while the entrepreneur ended up doing very well because of the real estate investments made along the way to support the venture. However, another reason exists for understanding real estate numbers. It allows us to unite elements of cash flow to profitability. And understanding this unity, how cash flow and profitability are intertwined, requires an equal understanding of two critical concepts that relate not only to real estate investment but to all investment associated with a venture. These twin concepts are financial leverage and operating leverage.

Financial Leverage

Smart entrepreneurs, we are told, use other people's money to finance their ventures. Unfortunately a very limited and fixed amount of equity exists which can be used to attract funds, and many entrepreneurs quite understandably are loath to give up ownership for the privilege of using someone else's money. Smart entrepreneurs, we are told also, keep at least majority control.

This leaves debt as the other source of "other people's money." The greater the amount of debt you can obtain, the greater amount of assets you can control. Should one then seek unlimited debt? The answer is clearly "no" unless you have unlimited investment opportunities that can earn you continually more than the cost of debt. Since few, if any of us, will ever have access to unlimited debt, the practical question becomes: How much debt should we seek? The economic answer here does not change markedly from the earlier response, i.e., the amount of debt you employ must cost relatively less than the return it earns you when combined with your equity interest. The diagram on the next page presents the relationship. (*Exhibit 8*)

For example, if debt costs you 22%, then your return on investment must be greater than 22%. If your return is, in fact, lower, you will be experiencing negative financial leverage. Under these conditions, you would be better off making a smaller investment (if you could) using less debt at a lower price or using equity alone. Conversely, financial leverage is positive when you combine debt with equity to produce a greater return than you can achieve with equity alone after the cost of debt is included. When debt earns more than it costs, the surplus accrues to you and acts as a positive lever on your equity investment return. For example, assume you use all equity in one case and half debt - half equity in another. The total investment is $100,000 in both cases. Also you project a 15% return on your total investment regardless of the combination. The cost of debt now becomes the key variable. If it exceeds your cash flow return as a percentage of total investment, you will experience a lower return on equity compared to a straight equity investment. The following example demonstrates this negative effect when debt costs 20% as well as the positive effect on equity when debt costs 10%. (See *Exhibit 9*)

To create greater equity returns than the cost of debt, you must also generate a net cash flow which is greater as a percentage of total investment than the cost of debt. The preceding example also demonstrates this relationship. Once the cost of debt exceeds the total investment return, the return on equity declines below the "all equity" return.

Operating Leverage

The concept of "operating leverage" is a critical notion for business practitioners. Yet my experience is that very few entrepreneurs can explain the concept. Often it is confused with financial leverage. And some similarities exist. For instance both concepts are double edged swords: you can have both positive and negative leverage. Also, both concepts are relative notions. A company or investment can have high or low leverage only "in relation to" some other company or investment alternative. And both concepts use the idea of levering or increasing resources (debt in the case of financial leverage and fixed costs for operating leverage) to better accomplish some purpose.

High positive operating leverage simply means total profits increase at a faster rate than increases in sales volume once break-even volume is achieved, compared to a business with low operating leverage.

Exhibit 8

Financial Leverage

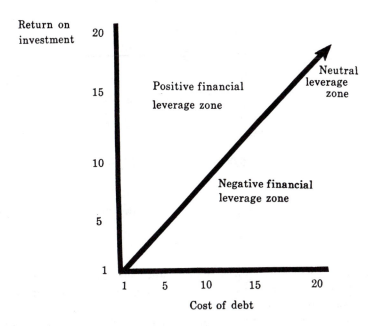

Assuming equal breakeven points, a business with relatively high fixed costs will have higher operating leverages compared to a high variable cost business. You can observe this relationship in the breakeven graph shown in *Exhibit 10*. The gaps (A) between the total revenue and total cost lines for the high fixed cost business have a wider angle of divergence above and below the equivalent breakeven points compared to the gaps (B) for the high variable cost business. Consequently, a 1% increase in volume beyond breakeven for both businesss may result, for example, in a 10% increase in profits for the high fixed cost business and only 2% for the high variable cost business. Another 1% volume increase may mean a 20% increase in profits for the high fixed cost business (double the original increase) versus a jump to 3% for the high variable cost business (or half the rate of increase as the high fixed cost business).

Since profit grows at a faster rate, the impact on investment returns can be very pronounced. In fact, it is these returns that are "levered" or grow faster in a business with higher operating leverage compared to one with lower operating leverage. The following chart (*Exhibit 11*) provides an example. It shows two businesses each doing $1 million in sales that experience the same increase in sales volume during their second and third years of operations. Both start with a 20% return on investment. The high variable cost business requires a lower investment ($500,000) because it has fewer fixed costs (represented as fixed assets on the balance sheet) associated with its startup and ongoing operations. The high fixed cost business requires a higher investment ($1,000,000) but is able to generate greater cash flow off an equivalent sales volume for an equivalent return.

Exhibit 9

An Example of Financial Leverage

	All equity	Half equity (debt 10%)	Half equity (debt 20%)
Equity	$100,000	$ 50,000	$ 50,000
Debt	0	50,000	50,000
Total investment	100,000	100,000	100,000
Return Cash Flow 15%	15,000	15,000	15,000
Cost of debt***	0	5,000	10,000
Net return	15,000	10,000	5,000
Return on equity	15%	20%	10%

***Tax has a positive impact on retainings since interest is a before tax expense. Essentially, the after tax cost of debt is lower depending on the percentage rate of taxes (e.g. taxes on 50% of the earnings would cut the cost of debt in half; taxes on 25% of earnings cuts the cost of debt by 25%, etc.). In the above example, the 10% and 20% costs of debt are assumed to be the effective after tax costs.

Exhibit 10
Operating leverages of two small businesses with equal breakeven points

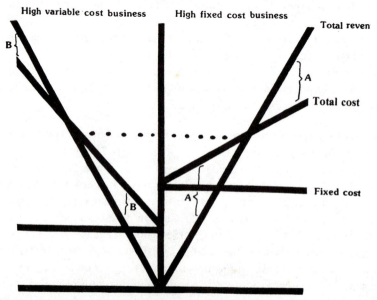

Profits also grow faster in the business with high fixed costs during the second and third years simply because a greater percentage of its total costs are fixed (i.e., do not increase) as sales volume increase.

But the same relationship holds for decreases below the breakeven point. Losses will increase at a faster rate for the business with high fixed/low variable costs. Consequently, businesses with high positive leverages also have high negative ones.

This existence of high operating leverages in high fixed/low variable cost businesses explains why executives in these businesses (e.g., large automobile or chemical producers) place great emphasis on marketing and sales activities. Great profits (and bonuses) or great losses (and the search for a new job) can occur with just small shifts in sales volume above or below breakeven points for businesses with high operating leverage.

However, I should note that once the condition of equal breakeven points is relaxed the relationship can change if the low fixed cost business also has relatively low variable costs. Consequently, *you should always determine what is the revenue/cost stucture for any organization.* The value of this exercise will be worth the effort since you will often discover where to allocate what is usually the scarcest resource for most entrepreneurs -- time.

A simple numerical example shows the relationship between time, profits, costs and revenues. First, consider the base situation on the following page where two companies have equal sales of $100,000. Both have different cost structures and both are just breaking even and show zero profits.

Exhibit 11

COST STRUCTURE AND FINANCIAL RETURNS

	High variable cost business			High fixed cost business		
Year	1	2	3	1	2	3
Volume	1,000	1,100	1,200	1,000	1,100	1,200
After tax cash flow	100	110	120	200	240	280
Investment	500	500	500	1,000	1,000	1,000
Return	20%	22%	24%	20%	24%	28%

BASE SITUATION

	High Variable Cost Business	High Fixed Cost Business
Sales	100,000	100,000
Variable Costs	80,000	20,000
Fixed Costs	20,000	80,000
Profits	0	0

Now let's suppose the management spends its time by making an all out marketing/sales effort. The effort pays off and results in a 10% growth in sales. However, variable costs also increase as volume expands. For simplicity's sake, we will assume variable costs increase proportionately with sales (i.e., also a 10% increase) while fixed costs remain fixed. Currently, sales have increased in $110,000 while variable costs are $80,000 or $20,000 plus 10% respectively. The new outcome is shown below.

10% SALES GROWTH

	High Variable Cost Business	High Fixed Cost Business
Sales	110,000	110,000
Variable Costs	88,000 [80,000 + (10% of 80,000)]	22,000 [80,000 + (10% of 20,000)]
Fixed Costs	20,000	20,000
Profits	2,000	8,000

The impact of sales growth for high fixed cost business now becomes evident. Profits have increased to $8,000 for our high fixed cost business or four times the profits realized by the high variable cost business.

However, let's look at one more example before you conclude that high fixed cost businesses always make better profits. Instead of a 10% sales growth, let's suppose our management decides to allocate its scarce time to a program designed to control and reduce raw materials and direct labor (e.g., variable costs). Again, management's efforts are successful and a 10% reduction in variable costs is realized by the new cost reduction program as shown below.

10% DECREASE IN VARIABLE COSTS

	High Variable Cost Business	High Fixed Cost Business
Sales	100,000	100,000
Variable Costs	72,000 [80,000 – (10% of 80,000)]	18,000 [80,000 – (10% of 20,000)]
Fixed Costs	20,000	20,000
Profits	8,000	2,000

Our cost reduction situation shows a much stronger profit performance for the high variable cost business, exactly the reverse of the sales growth situation. New profits for the high variable cost business are four times the high fixed cost business.

These few examples do not mean that entrepreneurs should ignore opportunities for sales growth in high variable cost businesses or cost reduction in high fixed cost businesses. They do provide, however, a simple means to determine priorities or relative allocations of time given opportunities for sales growth and cost savings for particular situations.

TRACKING CASH FLOW AND PROFITS: LESSONS FROM REAL ESTATE

Entrepreneurs who pursued their careers in the field of real estate have come to realize what many other entrepreneurs never discover. That is, one must find a simple way to track *both* profits and cash flow. For over the long haul entrepreneurs cannot afford to focus exclusively on either an income statement or cash flow statement as they are traditionally presented. The exhibit on the following page (*Exhibit 12*) presents a combined cash flow/income statement. It also preserves the distinctions between variable and fixed costs, which many traditional accounting statements fail to maintain.

A critical distinction in this statement is the calculation of taxes. Here taxes on profits allow the subtraction of noncash flow items (e.g. depreciation). However, the amount of depreciation taken is a function of the size of the project or the business which, in turn, is also a function of the amount of debt employed. Increasing debt means not only higher interest payments but larger assets and here the effects of both financial and operating leverages are felt on ultimate profitability.

Exhibit 12

THE CASH FLOW/INCOME STATEMENT

GROSS SALES

- Variable Costs
(discounts on sales, rental vacancies,
rental collection costs)

NET REVENUES

- Operating Costs
which are
Fixed Costs   (e.g. Insurance, Office rentals,
Salaries, Property taxes, Upkeep)

OPERATING CASH FLOW

Debt Repayments	+ Reserves shown on balance sheet
- Interest Outflows	- Interest paid
- Principal Outflows	- Depreciation taken

CASH FLOW BEFORE TAX	PROFIT BEFORE TAX
- Taxes	- Taxes
CASH FLOW AFTER TAX	PROFIT AFTER TAX

IV. EFFECTIVE ALTERNATIVE ANALYSIS:
DISCOUNTED CASH FLOW AND EITHER/OR DECISIONS

This note has stressed consistently the importance of cash flow for entrepreneurs. The choice between any either/or option is no different. At the quantitative level, the critical technique for entrepreneurs is *discounted cash flow.*

What impact will an investment decision make on net cash flows -- whether the decision is to make an item inhouse versus subcontract it, or to lease capital equipment versus buy the equipment outright?

Since liquidity is essential for entrepreneurs, the timing of cash flows has a definite cost or benefit on these kinds of decisions. A dollar received today is better or worth more than a dollar received the next day. Similarly, a dollar paid out today effectively costs more than a dollar paid at a later date. "Discounting" the cash flows by some cost of money factor equalizes cash flow streams for timing differences.

In the past, discounted cash flow has *not* been utilized greatly by entrepreneurs because the calculation was perceived difficult to compute. Simpler but less accurate techniques have been substituted (e.g., Return on Investment, Payback). However, inexpensive but sophisticated calculators and personal computers are changing and will continue to change this perception and use of discounted cash flow. While the technique is becoming easier to compute, a few important considerations remain which influence the applicability and accuracy of the calculation. For example, entrepreneurs must make a realistic assessment of:

1) the rate of return and/or cost of money that is relevant to their particular situation; and

2) how well they can actually track all the cash flows associated with each alternative.

Obviously the longer the time factor associated with a particular option, the more likely uncertain future events may alter a calculation significantly. Discounted cash flow, in short, may be a weak tool when long time periods are involved.

Two forms of discounted cash flow exist:

1) net present value; and

2) internal rate of return.

The net present value calculation assumes you know the appropriate return yield, or hurdle rate you need to earn on an investment. Given this rate, the net cash flows are "discounted back to the present." If the answer (i.e. the discounted dollars) is positive, then you can go ahead with the investment. If the alternative is also positive, you simply go with the option that produces the greatest amount of discounted dollars.

The internal rate of return calculation allows you to perform the same kind of analysis except the answer is expressed in percentage terms because the net present value is set to equal zero for each option. The calculation allows one the momentary luxury of *not* stipulating a hurdle rate. All other qualitative things being equal, one simply selects the investment option with the highest return. Still, you need to relate even the highest return to something else -- your real or alternative cost of money -- to determine if indeed the internal rate of return is high enough.

The basic formula for both calculations is shown below.

Net Present Value (NPV)

$$NPV = -\text{(initial investment)} + \frac{\text{Net cash flow for Period \#1}}{(1 + i)}$$

$$+ \frac{\text{net cash flow Period n}}{(1 + i)\, n}$$

where i = the required rate of return
n = the number of time periods

Internal Rate of Return (IRR)

$$IRR = NPV = 0 = \text{same as above}$$

V. EFFECTIVE ALTERNATIVE ANALYSIS: MULTIPLE POSSIBILITIES

In real life, the identification and ordering of alternatives in some systematic way is often more complicated than evaluating the alternatives themselves. I believe you should be aware of two methods that are particularly useful for analyzing different systems, processes, and alternatives that may confront entrepreneurs when considering a venture startup, major expansion or diversification of the business. Both methods involve diagramming techniques. The first is "Process Flow Diagramming." The quantitative technique associated with system or process flow diagramming is capacity analysis. The second diagramming technique is "Decision Tree Diagramming" and the associated quantitative technique is probability assessment.

Processing Flow Diagramming and Capacity Analysis

Process flow diagramming and capacity analysis are relevant tools for any venture that produces a product or a service whether the organization is involved in unit (job shop), batch, or continuous production.

The objective of process diagramming is to identify all inputs and trace the route taken by these inputs as they are converted into outputs. In short, the process flow is identified by noting each key "task", the "flows" between tasks, and "shortage or inventory points" throughout the process.

The key that makes process flow diagramming a powerful tool is the identification or calculation of some common unit of capacity for each task and storage point throughout the process.

The identification of bottleneck tasks is possible by comparing the capacities of all elements of the process. The task with the lowest capacity is the bottleneck or pacing element, and the final product cannot be produced eventually at a rate faster than the slowest element for very long.

This kind of process/capacity information allows an entrepreneur to evaluate different kinds of processes or systems for launching or continuing a venture. Specifically, he can judge different investment proposals by their impact on a bottleneck element (as well as disregard proposals that do not affect the bottleneck element, and such proposals often surface when careful process/capacity analysis is not done). With each increase in capacity, a different task or storage element may become the new bottleneck element.

Exhibit 13 provides a simple illustration. Because Task B is the slowest or pacing element, the rate of output of the process will eventually be 1000 parts per day. For instance, finished goods inventory will not build up past its capacity since final parts shipping is also operating at 1000 parts shipped/day. However, Work-in-Process (WIP) inventory will build up until its total capacity (10,000) parts is reached in 10 days (i.e., the difference between the in/out rate is 1000 parts in per day, so WIP will be up to 10,000 parts - by 1000 parts/day = 10 days).

At this point, Task A will be forced to reduce its output to 1000 parts per day. In turn, this lower rate of output will cause a build-up of raw materials inventory until its capacity is reached (also 10 days).

The operation of the process at 1000 parts per day may still not present a problem if inventory carrying charges are relatively small and the delivery rate can be reduced without loss of business. But what if the raw materials are "perishable" goods? What if inventory carrying costs are high? What would happen?

First, we would probably see long lines of vehicles waiting to make raw material deliveries. If we think of "raw materials" as customers entering the system, the result will be long lines of people waiting (if indeed they wait) to take advantage of your product or service. In more complicated organizations, the usual response is to increase raw materials inventory. This may be very expensive while only temporarily solving the delivery queuing problem. Without the benefit of careful process/capacity analysis, the wrong course of action is easy to recommend and accept.

Decision Tree Diagramming and Probability Assessment

Often, entrepreneurs are faced with decisions that are alternative or sequential in nature. For instance, if one decision path is followed, it gives rise to other possible decision alternatives, and so on.

Exhibit 13

Sample Process Flow Diagram & Capacity Analysis

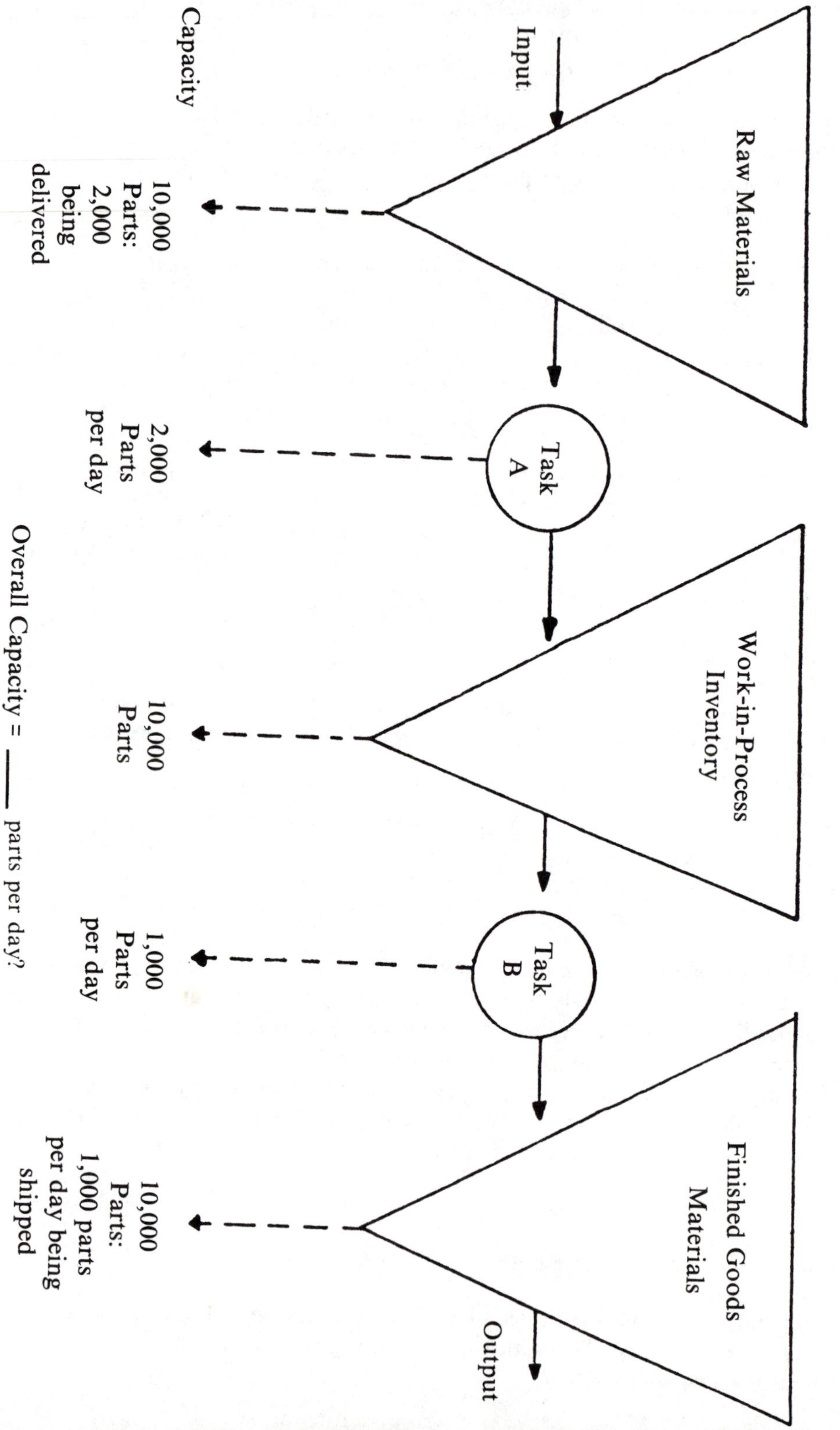

Input

Raw Materials

Capacity

10,000
Parts:
2,000
being
delivered

Task
A

2,000
Parts
per day

Work-in-Process
Inventory

10,000
Parts

Task
B

1,000
Parts
per day

Finished Goods
Materials

10,000
Parts:
1,000 parts
per day being
shipped

Output

Overall Capacity = _____ parts per day?

Generally, you can diagram these decision alternatives, and the events that make up each alternative. The resulting diagrams are called decision trees.

One benefit of constructing a decision tree is that the process of diagramming alone forces a decisionmaker to order his/her thoughts about the array of competing alternatives under consideration.

However, the purpose of decision diagramming is more than systematically arranging all the major alternatives and their component events. The technique also allows a decisionmaker to adjust outcomes by the probabilities of the events occurring. Consequently, you can calculate the net marginal or incremental benefits associated with each decision branch of the tree and, in a sense, "discount" these net benefits by the probability of occurrence.

The execution of the technique requires:

> 1) knowing or being able to assign probabilities for the various events;

> 2) adjusting (i.e., multiplying) cash flows associated with each group of alternative events by their probabilities, starting at the end points of the decision diagram and working backwards to the original decision fork;

> 3) calculating the expected value of event forks to serve as new end points as you work back toward the original alternatives.

Steps 2 and 3 are very mechanical. (*Exhibit 14* provides a sample problem, diagram, and calculations).

The key and usually difficult task in real life is determining the probabilities associated with each event. Yet a range of realistic estimates can often be made and many ingenious means have been devised to make them.

Two simple aids in this regard are worth mentioning:

First, if you know or think the probability of one event occurring is .6, then the probability of its alternative is simply (1-P) or a .4 chance of occurring.

Second, if you calculate the net benefit of one decision branch, you can calculate a break-even probability for another branch. This calculation states in effect what kind of probability you must assign to another alternative to produce the same break-even benefits as the known branch. You may then ask yourself if the break-even probability seems realistic to you.

Exhibit 14

Sample Decision Tree

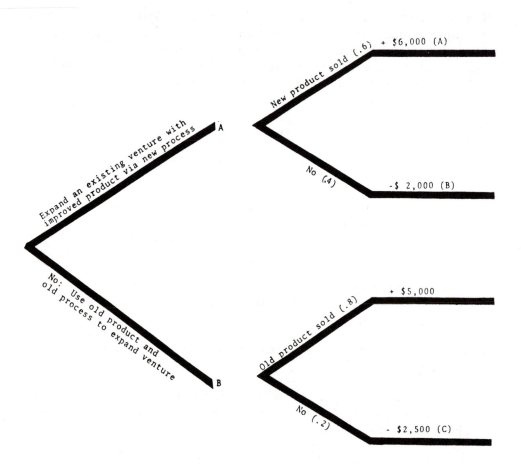

(A) Yields a higher contribution than old product because improvements allow higher sales price and lower production costs.

(B) New material inputs and process changes produce lower production costs than old process.

(C) A slight chance exists that a competitor may produce the improved product and sell it to our customer.

SAMPLE PROBLEM AND CALCULATION OF DECISION TREE PROBLEM

Situation: An entrepreneur must decide whether or not to produce a slightly improved product which requires a modified process for a one-time sale to each customer. Existing equipment can be used but must be rearranged to handle the use of a few new material inputs. Capital investment is zero.

The entrepreneur forecasts the outcomes (contribution dollars or relevant costs or losses) shown at the endpoints of the decision tree. From experience, the entrepreneur subjectively assigns the probabilities (in parentheses) for each of the four events.

Calculation: The entrepreneur calculates the expected value for decision points A & B:

Expected Value for
Improved Product: A = $6,000 (.6) + $-2000 (.4) = $2800.

Expected Value for
Old Product: B = $5,000 (.8) + $2500 (.2) = $3500.

Decision: Assuming there are no major qualitative considerations, our entrepreneur should stick with the old product/process since it has the higher expected value, $3500 vs. $2800 for the improved product.

VI. VALUING A BUSINESS: TECHNIQUES FOR BUYERS AND SELLERS

There are several measures that are used commonly to value a business. A number of different approaches also exist regarding how these measures are calculated. This section describes each of these measures and then presents a few different approaches or ways the calculations are made. I should emphasize that what follows focuses on "technical" or "economic" considerations regarding the valuation of an enterprise. Very often non-economic or non-technical factors can influence considerably the value of a business. Your job, as buyer or seller, is incomplete until you have identified and valued these non-economic factors.

Common Measures of Venture Value

Various values of a venture's worth are relevant under varying conditions and assumptions. These acquisition values are produced using three basic methods for evaluating a going concern: asset valuation, earnings (cash flow) valuation, and multiple (rule of thumb) methods.

Asset valuation is used frequently to present as many as three different values of an enterprise. These are: book value; adjusted book value; and liquidation value. The latter two values generally include assumptions about what will happen to assets if you acquire the business. Similarly, earnings valuations can be developed that assume major changes in the current operations of the venture once you have acquired it; or the valuation of earnings may assume no major changes, including no change in the existing ownership. This latter assumption can be very useful in negotiating, since it gives you an estimate of the future value of the venture to the present owners should they continue to own and operate their business.

Let us now define each of these measures of value and discuss some of the positive and negative attributes associated with each one.

Book Value

Book value is simply net assets (total assets minus total liabilities). Its principal attribute is that book value is usually an easy number to determine for most entrepreneurial ventures. However, some ventures (particularly lifestyle ventures) may have both assets and liabilities which have not been included on the venture's balance sheet. Nevertheless, book value does have some positive uses. It is not only a reference or departure point, but also a handy way to determine if there have been any major changes in the business and book value recently compared to earlier years. For example, substantial increases in book value for the latest year may indicate that the business is entering a growth phase or simply being "restructured" for sale purposes. Each buyer must ask: What has been the growth record in book value over the last five or ten years? Each seller must be prepared to explain this record.

Adjusted Book Value

Adjusted book value allows us to refine for obvious discrepancies (positive or negative) between stated book value versus actual or market value of an ongoing business. Such "adjustments" may include a downgrading of accounts receivables (either in terms of actual payment or the speed of payment) as well as downward or upward adjustments for inventory, plant and equipment, and real estate in order to better reflect their actual market values (versus historical cost values). Such adjustments may also include an increase in liabilities which you feel are understated and will be forced to inherit once you acquire the business in order to continue doing business with certain key creditors.

Liquidation Value

An important question to ask is: Should the business fail for some reason, will liquidation values represent a sizable downside risk vis-a-vis the price we expect to pay for the business? Practically speaking, liquidation values can range considerably depending on the severity of our assumptions. These depend partly on the amount of time available for liquidation. For example, will the amount of time available for liquidation be very short and hence disallow the opportunity to seek a reasonable offer for the business's assets which at least approach market value? The actual severity of our assumptions will also depend on the nature of the assets. For instance, are we dealing with a company that has no "real property" real estate? Also, is this an industry where other assets (inventory, office equipment, vehicles, etc.) often sell at a fraction of their "market value" regardless of the amount of time available for liquidation?

Future "Earnings" Assuming No Major Changes

Just as book value is a benchmark for asset valuation, so calculating the future stream of cash flow assuming no major changes in the business is a benchmark for earnings valuation. The objective here is to determine the value of ongoing operations to the present owners in terms of the discounted cash flows they can generate should they decide to keep the business. One can often use reported historical cash flows to put this valuation into context. However, at some point, you will have to make a reasonable estimate of the number of years you expect the present owners can continue to keep the business running. A second important step is the determination of an appropriate discount rate, one which reflects the risk to the owners of continuing a business. For example, you may determine that a sixty-year old entrepreneur in failing health can operate his business for no more than three or four years. Also, you may attribute a very high discount rate to the earnings he can generate during this period if you know he has no one who can take over the business should a further deterioration to his health force the liquidation of the business.

Future "Earnings" Streams Assuming Major Changes

The preceding valuation reflects the worth of the business to the present owners. This valuation reflects the worth of the business to you. Again, your purpose is to calculate the discounted cash flows which you believe will be generated by the changes you plan to make. Even if you plan to make no major changes, your presence alone represents a major change in most cases. For example, you may be younger and capable of operating the business over many more years than your predecessors. You may be willing to take less salary initially and, for any number of other reasons, your risk profile is different. Certainly, you must include the net cash flow effects should you decide to introduce new products, go after new markets, and otherwise expand your costs. Or perhaps you intend to slash costs in an attempt to pare the business down to its most profitable components.

Multiplier Methods

This method relies upon industry rules of thumb to estimate or approximate the value of the business. The multiple is simply a factor that is based on the historical experience of the industry regarding the sale of other companies. Depending on the industry's tradition, the multiple may be applied either to sales, gross profits (contribution), or net profits. A strong rationale can usually be generated for focusing on one of these numbers given industry practices and the accounting conventions that reflect these practices.

DISCUSSION QUESTIONS

1. Describe the concept of cash flow. Why is it so important to entrepreneurs?

2. What is the difference between financial and operating leverage?

3. What is the difference between a profit versus cash breakeven?

4. Why should entrepreneurs understand a venture's cost structure?

5. What factors would you consider when valuing

    a) a new startup venture?

    b) an existing venture?

KEY READINGS

David C. D. Rogers and Mimi Landis Rogers, *Numbers for Business Policy,* The Landis Press, Wayland, MA 01778, 1978.

Robert Ronstadt, *The Art of Case Analysis,* Lord Publishing, Dover, MA 02030, 1980, Part Three.

Timmons, Smollen, Dingee, *New Venture Creation: A Guide to Small Business Development,* Richard D. Irwin, Co., 1977.

John Welsh and David White, "A Small Business is Not a Little Big Business," *Harvard Business Review,* July/August, 1981.

FOOTNOTES

[1]Welsh and White, "A Small Business is Not a Little Big Business," Harvard Business Review, July/August, 1981.

[2]"Anthony Athanas: Impressions of a Master Craftsman," Stephen Michaelides, *Restaurant Hospitality,* May 1981, pp. 57 ff.

[3]Welsh and White, *op. cit.*

Part Two

CASES: INITIATING ENTREPRENEURIAL ACTIVITIES

Parts Two, Three, and Four

Entrepreneurial Experience, Role Models, and Case Analysis

Experience, we are often told, is the best teacher. No one can deny it. Most of us learn our best lessons from experience or, as my grandfather was fond of saying, "from the school of hard knocks." But such learning, while best, is clearly very expensive in time and effort. The cost of learning "the hard way" is particularly expensive for those acquiring entrepreneurial experience. Learning how to start and run a new venture may literally mean several years of your life. And experience, like everything else, does not occur in a vacuum. At issue is whether or not there are things we can do which will maximize the benefits of our entrepreneurial experiences as they occur, while limiting the costs. Perhaps even more fundamental is the choice of an appropriate entrepreneurial experience--one that is within our limits and will help us to develop as entrepreneurs over our careers.

One way to prepare for our entrepreneurial experiences is to select parents who are entrepreneurs. Of course, most of us have not been sufficiently foresighted to make this discriminating choice in heritage. Those individuals who are fortunate to have entrepreneurs for parents develop values, traits, and sometimes skills which lead to and enhance their later entrepreneurial experiences. Others, through chance or design, have developed a close acquaintanceship with other relatives or non-relatives who are entrepreneurs and who serve as role models. There seems little doubt now that such role models, whether they be the parental or nonparental variety, provide extremely helpful experience and confidence for those who are planning to start and pursue an entrepreneurial career.

To some extent, we believe a formal educational program in entrepreneurship can act as a partial surrogate and/or supplement to the informal education the "fortunate ones" receive from entrepreneurial parents. Such formal learning is particularly productive when we live vicariously the entrepreneurial experiences of others. Cases provide a cost effective way of obtaining this entrepreneurial experience. They are not as good as the real thing, but what they lose individually in quality of experience, they regain in quantity of experience over a much shorter time period. Within a semester or less, you will be exposed to a dozen or more real experiences that intersect a variety of entrepreneurial issues which would otherwise take a lifetime for an individual to experience.

From an educational standpoint, the question is how to maximize our learning when studying the case experiences of others. The answer is that each student must learn at least the rudiments of case analysis and discussion. It is not my purpose to provide such learning here. Space does not permit what has required a small book on a relatively complex subject.(For those wishing more information, see my book *The Art of Case Analysis,* Dover, MA.: Lord Publishing, Revised Edition, 1978.) I should note, however, that the cases in this book are not case *histories* but partial descriptions of one or more entrepreneurial situations and decisions. As such, the cases are an excellent way to learn about entrepreneurs, their ventures, and their environments, and also to develop the kind of decision-making tools that are relevant for entrepreneurs in unique, changing, and uncertain environments.

JOHN HENDRICK:

HOW I OVERCAME THE HANDICAP

OF A COLLEGE EDUCATION

When I graduated from Yale in 1937 with a degree in English literature, I was fortunate enough to be scooped up for a training course operated by one of our best known and most highly regarded industrial firms. At the age of 23, this represented to me a success of major proportions, and I went off happily to slay dragons. Now, at the age of 40, I can evaluate with a certain amount of perspective some effects of a college education.

The training course was great fun. Six of us trainees, Harvards, Yales and Princetons, traveled together for 18 months to a dozen different plants operated in as many states. Nice social connections always seemed to materialize, often sponsored by some friendly executive in our company. We were young, unmarried, on the loose, and the time went fast. Even some of the things we were learning about were intensely interesting. When this pleasant phase was completed, they split us up and I landed in one of the company's sales offices in Chicago -- in the Estimating Department. Three years later, my earning power had increased to $125.00 per month, and I had learned to add and subtract fairly well.

It must have been about this time that I sat down and wrote myself a long thoughtful letter. I ran across it the other day in some old papers, and it saddened me to recall how this boy had searched his soul trying to bring to light what was going on and where he was headed. He seemed to be most puzzled that the whispered insinuations from the early training days indicating that he was top executive material and might be President of the Corporation before too many years did not seem to be materializing. But then, patience, Rome was not built in a day. So the big job and big pay hadn't come through yet; all would be well. And still, there were those letters from the other boys in the training course indiscreetly advising that they too had been more or less promised the Presidency before long. Where was this leading?

Had the boy taken a closer look at his draft number before he wrote this plaintive question, he would have known the answer right away. Five years later he had gone from Apprentice Seaman to Lieutenant Commander, had commanded ships in both war areas, and could definitely add. He had also met a girl and married her. While in the Service, jobs weren't often discussed; the present simply floated between the past and the future. The war over, it was time to get a job -- probably the old job.

When I went to the General Office in Pittsburgh at company invitation, I was warmly received by the now Vice-President, whom I had known as a branch manager. This gentleman assured me that according to the law, nothing had changed. My job in the estimating department at Chicago was still waiting for me and best of all, my raises had been kept up while I was away in the Service for five years. I was now to get $250.00 per month, $10.00 less than they were offering new college graduates starting.

That's when I politely declined and went back to Philadelphia, to my wife and two year old girl, having seen the latter for the first time only three weeks before. And that's when I got thinking about things and began to argue with the other boys who were lying around and began to develop my own thoughts. As I argued and griped and recriminated and tried to get used to the idea of going to work, it gradually dawned on me that I no longer cared about the standing or prestige of the firm I was to be attached to. I was 32 years old now, and I had had the feel of responsibility and of doing something strictly on my own, and further, the wonderful satisfaction of having some of my wartime operations turn out well.

It was during this time and during these arguments that my feelings regarding college education as a handicap to personal progress evolved into a theory. I found myself explaining to anyone who would listen that when I had graduated from Yale I was being controlled by forces of prejudice, snobbery, social acceptance, rivalry, ambition, and they all stemmed from lack of information and understanding; my classmates had brought these forces to bear on me and I on them. Friends, neighbors and relatives had exerted a silent pressure on all of us unknowingly; and without realizing it, I had in those days yearned desperately to be associated with this or that giant industrial firm. There was not alternative if you were going into business.

These arguments now brought out another point which I was beginning to discern. Several boys I had grown up with or known in High School had their own businesses and seemed to be doing fine. Oh sure, there were those five years "wasted" in the Service, but that didn't account for everything because these boys had started their concerns well before the war. Where was I during the period when they were starting? Why, in the Estimating Department, of course, learning to add and subtract and waiting for the call! Was I dumb, lazy, incompetent? Well, maybe, but I couldn't see where Charlie Bianchi with his six cement mixer trucks and road building equipment was so much smarter. Anyway, he wasn't that smart in high school, and he hadn't had two nickels to rub together for capital. Now he was rapidly putting together a substantial contracting business and building himself a large house on the hill. The war? Yes, of course, but that still didn't quite explain Charlie and his growing operation and me lying around wondering -- not even knowing what I wanted to do.

It all came clear one night when I was arguing and describing how Charlie had not been able to go to college, but instead after working in a restaurant had bought a second-hand dump truck. That's when it dawned on me that BECAUSE I went to college I could NEVER buy a second-hand dump truck, not even a brand new one with someone else to drive it. When I ran across an old friend, I could not afford to explain that I was the owner of a dump truck. No, I was "with" the ABC Corporation. Not necessary to explain that they were the largest producers of this and that in the world. I was "with" them, and my friend was "with" someone just like them.

Recognition came fast then and the evidence piled up irrefutably. All of the boys I knew who had succeeded in making their own business were noncollege; none of my college mates, at least to my knowledge, had started anything. I was convinced that here lay the secret. But I was still bothered as to how Charlie Bianchi had suddenly become smart enough to make a thriving business out of nothing. During those trying weeks, I gradually became convinced that Charlie was no smarter than he had ever been. His main asset was that he was doing something, not just thinking about it or worrying about it.

I decided to kick all my pretensions in the face, lower my standard of living and make the big plunge on my own. Two weeks later, I went to work for the XYZ Corporation. This was not entirely my fault since they had offered me a job, and I had no more idea than the man in the moon what my own enterprise was to be. Also, my wife had intimated that we could not stay with her parents indefinitely.

This job lasted two years when it was brought to a halt by certain words and figures written on a pink slip. But I had learned something; I had learned what I could do, I was in better touch with industry and I knew in a general way where my interests lay. And now I had a son to consider.

While I was thinking things out, we ran out of money and I went to work for the largest corporation I had ever worked for. This pink slip did not take so long -- one year. In the next six months, I had eleven job offers and turned them all down. We moved to a poor street where we rented. I drew unemployment insurance because my wife was finding things difficult with the two children and no income. We gave up entertainment and our friends, and my wife with all her loyal support came close to giving me up. During this period, I made a feeble attempt to operate a sales promotion. It had to be put to bed before it got fairly started. We were not too far from cracking up.

Then I got an idea; a brand new idea. It required working with my hands and getting them dirty for the first time. A $5,000.00 loan financed it, and the first year, working alone in new surroundings near Boston I made $2,000.00. That was five years ago. Now we have a well-equipped shop which supports 33 people in our manufacturing type business. My income is very satisfactory, there are no debts of any description; my wife and I have been able to travel and enjoy ourselves and the tradition smashing idea is the sole source of our income.

Good you say? If you haven't had the experience, you just can't know how really good it is. And if you are the one who can't break through the social fences which have been set up by your college education, you probably never will know.

J. H. Hendrick
Wellesley, Mass.
1955

POST SCRIPT

What I wrote in 1955 seems even more true to me today. Of course, there never was any intention to prove that a college education is a "bad thing." Every kind of education is an asset, a "good thing" if integrated into the overall picture without allowing it to dominate other significant factors.

Sure, go to college by all means. Don't settle for less. But don't let your college education rule your life and exclude the excitement of enterprising your own private project.

ASSIGNMENT QUESTIONS

1. Why did Hendrick perceive his college education as a handicap to his entrepreneurial career?

2. When, in a person's life, is it easiest to start an entrepreneurial career?

3. What is the best type of preparation for an entrepreneurial career?

DAN FOSS

Dan Foss put the admissions application to a large Eastern business school back into its gray envelope, and rose to greet his visitor. His offices in Burlington, Vermont, were small and functional — two rooms, six desks, and assorted drafting boards, mechanical drawings and blueprints, textbooks and manuals — containing everything he needed to run his solar energy consulting firm. His visitor, a professor of environmental studies at a small midwestern college from which Foss had graduated in 1979, greeted his former pupil warmly.

"How's business, Dan?"

"$300,000 in gross sales our first year and we should double that this year."

The profesor blinked. "Can I mention those figures in my presentation at UVM this afternoon?"

"Please do. It's a pretty accurate indication of the demand for customized solar heating."

"Is customizing the secret for selling exotic energy?"

"It's no secret, it's the sales approach with the broadest customer base. The most effective way to sell solar, I think, is to do it customer by customer. I'm building a reputation for providing reliable equipment, designing a system appropriate for the user's need, and inspecting the system at regular intervals. You know I'm a crusader for alternative power sources, but I also have an entrepreneurial streak which reminds me that alternate energy is a growth industry and I should be a part of it."

"No one every said that a concern for the environment was anticapitalist, Dan. You've found a cause you believe in, a market niche, and a supply of customers — not bad for three years out of college. Now, where will you go from here?"

Dan glanced back at the admissions application. "That's what I wanted to talk to you about, Professor. But first I should tell you a bit more about this company.

"I started FosSUN two years ago with one partner and a loan for $25,000. Today, gross sales in the first nine months of fiscal '82 are $500,000; I have a third partner and a full-time staff of 12.

"My first concern is how to manage growth. Business is snowballing faster than I'd dared hope. I've already taken in one partner and am seriously talking to another, but I wish my plans for managing FosSUN were as solid as my ability to design and sell good solar systems, and they're not.

"My second concern is how to move this business into other fields of alternate energy. The opportunity is huge. For example, the photovoltaic cell is a solution in search of a problem. I've got some ideas for applications but they will require a fair amount of R&D. Right now we don't have R&D capabilities — no manpower, no equipment. Although everyone around is handy technically and learns quickly, we don't have high-tech expertise — and there's a big difference between selling solar heating and developing alternate energy applications.

"This brings me to the question of business school. The logical side of me says, you need management training. Take two years off and get it. But my entrepreneurial side says, look at the learning experience you've got right now. And do you know how I got to this point? Experience. I've started two other ventures."

"Other ventures? I'd never realized that."

Dan reached into the envelope and handed the professor a copy of his resume. (Dan's resume appears as Exhibit I.) "Neither did I when I was doing them," he admitted. "I started things I enjoyed doing and was good at instead of going right to college, selling and servicing motorcycles, and then classic cars. I learned a lot about how to build a technically-based small business; even my parents stopped bugging me about getting a college education when they saw how much money I was making. But after a couple of years, I decided to use the profits to get that education after all, and though they're all spent now it was an investment I'll never regret. I got turned on about the environment, and thanks to your practical approach I saw how I could make a real contribution to society. It was a quantum leap ahead of bikes and cars.

"Now I wonder if it isn't time to taken another leap, but the decision is much harder. I am building something big here, and I'm getting better all the time. This venture needs me, because I'm the only person who can make it fly. Plus that, my money is tied up in it. On the other hand, I don't have the managerial knowhow to do the future planning that must be done. What do you think I should do?"

EXHIBIT I

Daniel J. Foss

1205 N. Lakeview Avenue   Burlington, Vermont 05890   (802) 345-1999

EDUCATION

B.A., Political Science & Research Processes (Spring 1979)
St. Olaf's College—Danville, Illinois   Dean's Honor Roll (Fall 1979)

Special studies major emphasized application of creative thought processes and scientific analytical technique to research and problem solving. Studies included economics, computer, environment, political and communication skills. Worked under special research assignment to president of college.

Associates of Art (1973) Broward Community College — Fort Lauderdale, Florida

Studies included mechanical and architectural drafting, psychology, sociology, marketing, and speech.

Additional Studies (1974) NYIT Nova University — Fort Lauderdale, Florida

Studies included physics, statistics, communication, and interview techniques.

QUALIFICATIONS

Sales:	Accomplished in the sale of tangible and intangible products.
Sales Training:	Trained salespeople for dealers and manufacturers. Communicated successful sales and closing techniques and covered technical detail in an understandable manner by producing charts, graphics, diagrams, and models.
Marketing:	Developed and initiated marketing strategy at dealer/manufacturer level from market survey through product distribution.
Advertising:	Developed literature, brochures, logos, newspaper layouts, yellow pages ads, trade show displays, etc. Developed contacts capable of national and international response. Produced and expedited sophisticated questionnaires.
Management:	Extensive experience in organizing and managing small business with up to 12 employees. Handled intricate corporate, legal, banking, and accounting situations. Developed business plans, flow charts, and management strategy. Promoted communication techniques that max-

imized company harmony and efficiency. Work well with all personnel levels and encourage creativity.

Supervisory: Supervised over 50 solar energy installations including five complex space heating systems. Aspects covered included electrical, plumbing, carpentry, structural, and aesthetic consideration. Can adapt to many fields. Capable of coordinating and conducting highly detailed work.

Design: Can draw on over 15 years of mechanical and technical experience to develop unique, elegantly simple design solutions. Capable of creative design solutions. Have professional drafting and graphic arts experience. Developed owners operation and dealer installation manuals. Developed an intuitive understanding of material relationships from aesthetic, structural, and lifestyle standpoints through extensive work experience in a wide range of crafts and trades.

EXPERIENCE

FosSUN, Inc., 1205 N. Lakeview Avenue, Burlington, VT 05890
Owner   (1979-Present)
Type of Business: Solar consulting firm
Responsibilities: Render professional services on all aspects of active solar systems from business start-up, sales and design to installation. Expert on solar domestic hot water and active liquid-based solar space heating systems using water, silicone, oil, glycol, and Freon as transfer media. Directed a successful sales program, resulting in gross sales of $300,000 in their first year of business. Promoted and helped refine HELIOPHASE™, a passive, Freon-charged solar domestic hot water system for AB* Solar of Dover, NH. Developed a low-head, drain back system, as well as other storage innovations. Installed a high technology SUNMASTER™ evacuated tube space heating system.

Antique Classic Auto Restoration, Inc. (ACAR), Fort Lauderdale, FL
President   (1975-1977)
Type of Business: Sales and service of classic and special interest automobiles
Responsibilities: Most management and all marketing duties associated with the development of a technical multi-function small business.

Hoyt Motors, Inc., Fort Lauderdale, FL
Department Manager   (1973-1974)
Type of Business: Motorcycle and accessories sales and service
Responsibilities: Reorganization of a large accessories department to high profitability, management, marketing, stock, and sales.

Bankers Life and Casualty Company, Fort Lauderdale, FL
Life, Health, and Disability Insurance Agent (1972-1973)
Type of Business: Life, health, and disability insurance
Responsibilities: Insurance sales using targeted sales techniques; received several production awards.

Broward Community College Co-Op Program
Prior to 1972 I worked as an architectural draftsman on assignment by the college Co-Op program to G.R.A. Fishe-Consulting Engineer and E.L. Nezelic Construction Contractors.

ACTIVITIES AND INTERESTS

Instructor, Solar Domestic Hot Water Sales, FosSUN, Inc. (1980)
Board of Directors, New Hampshire Solar Energy Association (1979-1980)
Founder, *Think Tank Table*, St. Olaf's College (1978-Present)
Member, Senior Environmental Seminar, St. Olaf's College (1979)
Planner, Living Lightly Environmental Lifestyles Conference, St. Olaf's College (1978-1979)
County Campaign Coordinator for Senator Charles Percy (1978)
Feature and News Writer, College and High School Newspapers
Student Council Representative, College and High School
Former Member: DeMolay, 4H, Thespians

PERSONAL

Date of Birth: February 8, 1950

Have traveled extensively throughout United States, Mexico, and Europe. References available upon request.

ASSIGNMENT QUESTIONS

1. Should Foss decide to return to school at this point in his entrepreneurial career?

2. Looking at the problems with unexpected growth Foss is encountering in his solar venture, what additional help does he need to keep the company from choking on its own success? Education? Experience? Assistance?

3. Given Foss' entrepreneurial orientation, can you foresee any situation which he might in the future be able to handle more capably if he had an advanced degree?

BEN TRIPLET

On a fall afternoon in 1981, Ben Triplet was sitting in Professor John Stephens' office recounting the events which has led him to become an entrepreneur. As Ben talked, Stephens realized that he was hearing an unusually candid description of the intense personal commitment and sacrifice which Ben's career choice had required. Given Ben's comments, Stephens wondered aloud if Ben's wife, Karen, would mind commenting on his career from her point of view. Although Ben could not answer for his wife, he remarked that the venture had made a deep impact on their family life, and he believed she might want to share her experiences with others who were unsure about what such a career might entail.

Ben was talking to Professor Stephens because he was concerned -- not about the business itself, which after five years was prospering, but because of the dislocations within himself that starting and running the business had produced. He wondered if other entrepreneurs had faced similar personal crises. Was he at heart an entrepreneur, and would an entrepreneurial career, in the long run, fulfill his career needs? He described himself as a loner, driven by his own willpower, with a tremendous need to succeed and a desire to have his success acknowledged by others. He wanted to feel that he had "put it all together." Also, he considered himself a family man, who gave -- as well as gained -- enrichment from his wife and three children. However, he had not experienced the level of satisfaction from his job that he felt was appropriate and was not contributing to harmony at home. He felt flat and isolated - let down at the lack of excitement of having reached the "established" stage.

What were his options? He vowed, looking ahead, that he would never start another venture. At the same time, he resisted the idea, at this point, of returning to the status of an employee, regardless of the security such a move might imply. Had he reached an entrepreneurial threshhold of tolerance? What had gone wrong?

BACKGROUND: THE PRE-ENTREPRENEURIAL CAREER PERIOD

Ben Triplet was born in Massachusetts in 1937, the youngest of four children. His parents separated when he was four and Ben was sent to a nearby Catholic boarding school (grades 1-6) while his older sisters went to live in Maine. Since pocket money was scarce, Ben learned early to be resourceful: he collected and sold bottles and papers, and rented his bike to his fellow students at 5¢ a trip around the schoolyard. His mother worked, and Ben did not remember her having much time for him. Ben also did not remember enjoying school; he was a top student but grew to resent the institutional demands of a strict boarding school life.

At 16, Ben graduated from public school as a mediocre student and enrolled at the University of New Hampshire, intending to become a veterinarian. However, before the end of his sophomore year, he decided to leave secular college life and applied to a Catholic seminary. To meet the Latin requirement, he took intensive courses at Newman Prep and Boston College, became a good student again and was accepted at St. John's Seminary in 1956. But after a B.A. degree in 1958, he had a change of heart and realized that the priesthood was not his vocation. After working as a substitute teacher in Boston, he enlisted in the Marines, primarily he noted for the personal challenge.

After his tour of duty, Ben returned to the Boston area in the early 60's and concentrated on finding a challenging job. After considering a number of possibilities he accepted a position with a paper company, mainly because of its attractive sales training program which included classes at Lowell Tech one night a week. But when no territory was available at the completion of his training, Ben applied for, and accepted, a sales job in New York in the paper division of Continental Can Company. He remained there for four years. Although he believed his performance was more than adequate, he began to lose respect for the department since he disliked what he thought was an inordinate amount of "office politics."

By 1966, Ben's disenchantment was complete; he believed he had been passed over for a department position, and left to join the Scott Paper Company in Boston. Before leaving Continental, however, Ben had met and married (in 1964) Karen Johnson who had been a private secretary to one of Continental's top executives. When Karen and Ben returned to Boston, they were very happy. They both loved the Boston area and Karen was expecting their first child. Ben was also pleased with his new job. The department at Scott was lean, busy, and independent from corporate interference and politics.

But before long, Ben came to believe that he was potentially a better manager than some of his bosses. Consequently he decided to prepare himself for a career in management. His first step was to enroll in the evening MBA program at Babson College just outside of Boston. He also developed contacts at Eastern Paper, which was a division of Eastern Paper Specialty Co. and a client of Scott's. Ben sensed there might be more opportunity at Eastern in either management or sales compared to Scott. The manager of the Eastern's Paper Division left to start a new ventures division within the parent company and Ben was offered his job, which he accepted.

Ben described his new job during his meeting with Professor Stephens:

> Eastern was a third-generation family-owned company, and some management practices had gotten pretty slack. However, the division was successful for two reasons: it made quality products for specialty packaging; and due to

the complicated nature of the products and Eastern's impeccable reputation, the company enjoyed a virtual monopoly in that area.

The more I learned of the division's operations the more I could see that this was my opportunity to do something big. First, I decided to maximize profitability. For instance, I doubled the price of some specialty items and there wasn't even a ripple of protest from the customers.

For some items, I found a new supplier and decreased the cost by 50% while holding the price the same. I tripled the selling price of a type of tape, from $5 to $15. Profitability rose dramatically.

But the real reason I let Eastern take the risk of the price increase was that I had decided, someday, to go after the business myself.

The ideas about Ben's venture began to crystallize as his studies at Babson progressed, and he started to believe that some day he could successfully become his own boss. He took all the entrepreneurship-related courses he could find, and his enthusiasm grew. One professor corroborated his belief that he had the makings of an entrepreneurial "type". Another talked him out of the misapprehension that raising money ws the hardest part of starting a venture. A critical insight for Ben was the realization that the entrepreneur himself was the most important ingredient for success, compared to ideas for ventures which were "a dime a dozen." The Grade A man with the Grade B idea, according to one expert, was infinitely preferable to the converse. One class project required Ben to write a detailed business plan for starting his own venture, and he used the opportunity to refine the ideas for his paper company into objectives, balance sheets, P&L's, and cash flow charts. A course in Corporate Strategy helped him to clarify his own strategy and how best to proceed.

In 1972, Ben was still working on his MBA although his entrepreneurial course work was nearly completed. He still worked for Eastern -- though he had become thoroughly disenchanted with the paternalistic attitude of the company. This attitude enforced his determination about his own prospective venture. However, his wife, Karen did not agree. She called it "pie in the sky." The thought of Ben's being an entrepreneur ran contrary to her own hopes and expectations. Given her family upbringing, Karen believed in a steady job and money in the bank. She and Ben now had three small children, and she looked forward to purchasing their own house since Ben's schooling was nearly behind him. Eventually, she looked forward to going back to school herself.

It was a shock to them both when Ben was summarily fired from Eastern that summer, with only two weeks of severance pay. Partly because he needed to support his family, and partly because he believed he lacked experience in the area of managing a sales force, he went to work as National Sales Manager for New England Specialty Packing. Ben commented on this experience.

This was the one gap in my knowledge, learning how to

> handle other salesmen. The company was risk-oriented and new product-oriented. I set up rep groups who sold to department stores. I learned the whole of retailing and customer promotions. However, I had to travel a lot which I didn't like; it took me away from my family.

The strain of traveling and the entrepreneurial itch resulted in Ben's decision to submit the business plan for his new venture to his new employers, to explore the possibility of being an entrepreneur under their financial wing. They were delighted, and proposed that Ben become the general manager of a new division. However, Ben was advised by his friend and lawyer, Gil Pruitt, that New England was not doing him a favor. Ben recalled Gil's advice:

> You're not building anything for yourself. You're kidding yourself if you think they'll let you run it the way you want to. You've got the ideas. This concept about sending a direct mail promotion to suppliers is yours; you've got what it takes to make it go. There is no security in working for someone else.

Yet, as the summer of 1974 began, Ben was not ready to give up the security of being on a payroll. He could try his ideas without risking his savings. His children were old enough to let Karen return to school. For the time being, the arrangement was satisfactory -- even though Ben had to listen to his boss' admonishments to travel more and to back down on a decision he had made involving a supplier.

INITIATING THE ENTREPRENEURIAL CAREER

In retrospect, Ben could not point to one single factor which precipitated his decision to launch his own venture. There were a number of events: the travelling and the interference from his boss; the new security provided by the $20,000 inheritance from his father, who had died a few months earlier; the realization that he had never been asked to sign a non-compete contract with any of his employers; his belief that national economic conditions were favorable despite the paper shortage, for Ben knew that major paper companies set aside a portion of their budgets for new business, and he had the contacts to tap these resources. The clincher was that his friend and lawyer, Gil Pruitt, had reminded him that he was kidding himself with the objections he was raising against going on his own. Gil helped Ben to clarify his thinking. He could see what Ben wanted, as well as Ben's fearfulness.

In 1974, Ben formally incorporated his venture as Triplet Specialty Packaging Systems. He resigned from New England Specialty, taking one big customer with him and the promise of other orders to come. Karen was in a state of shock. She described her reactions:

> This was to be the time I was looking forward to for myself. I didn't know what Ben had in the back of his mind. My first reaction to Ben's venture was to reject it outright. I found it difficult to identify with a need that would require not only a commitment from Ben but from me as well. It went without

saying that our financial resources were integral to this commitment. The disposition of Ben's inheritance was an issue we had not yet resolved; we had discussed it only in general terms, because we had never had that much money before. For me, one important unfulfilled need was to have our own home; at this stage in our lives, I believed, we needed to take that step toward security. And there was the very large responsibility of three small children. This venture would mean starting all over at the bottom with all of the risks and many more responsibilities. But I knew in my heart that it had to be Ben's decision. Ultimately, that was the way it was resolved. He knew much better than I; he felt he could do it. He had to try.

Triplet Systems began operations from the Triplet's rented house, with Ben procuring orders and Karen doing the typing and bookkeeping. Within a few weeks, Ben had secured several large orders: one for $20,000, another for $40,000, with a total of $70,000 after the first month. At this point Ben, with a revised business plan based on the one he had prepared at Babson, applied for a business loan of $70,000 at the Shawmut Bank of Boston, which he learned was interested in backing start-ups. He obtained the loan without trouble.

THE EARLY YEARS

During the first year of his entrepreneurial career, Ben had energy to spare, buoyed by the excitement of being president of his own company. His salary was covered, and he showed a corporate profit of $70. Sales the first year were $185,000. The second year, however, Ben made a costly business decision against the advice of Gil Pruitt.

> I got on the bid list for a contract for the New York City hospitals. This was a contract that Eastern literally owned. I was the low bidder, and I got the contract. But it was the year of New York's fiscal crisis, and I was having trouble collecting -- although I'd been assured that they always paid within 30 days with a 2% discount. The job was too big for me. It paid my salary the second year but I really sweated it. And the worst part was the time I had to spend in those hospitals, when I should have been out developing new customers.

During the second year, Ben altered his lifestyle considerably. He gave up playing recreational hockey, his only physical outlet. He rationalized this, saying, "I just couldn't face another commitment which depended on me." In addition, he gave up all attempts at social life, even with his oldest friends.

This was Karen's reaction to the first years of Triplet Packaging:

> Ben wanted me to be involved right from the beginning, and I knew he needed my support. The office had to be at our home, because I had to meet the school bus -- and my family and my home are the most important parts of my life.

Ben wanted me to do the typing and bookkeeping. I am a good typist, but never had kept books; however, Ben wanted me to learn immediately. I became proficient. Ben has high expectations and I am a perfectionist myself. As a matter of fact, Ben now has three women doing the job I did.

The work itself was not unmanageable -- I did it while the children were in school and in the evenings -- but from the outset the venture became our whole lives. I couldn't get away from it or turn it off. I knew Ben's problems and I felt it was my job to spare him unnecessary pressures. Consequently, I took full charge of the children and the house. The children were involved in sports, dance, the usual, and I wanted to take them myself. In addition, I felt guilty about hiring cleaning help to do something I could do myself -- the line between luxury and necessity became blurry.

It was too much -- trying to keep everything running smoothly and helping with the venture. I could see Ben drawing more and more into himself, having less and less time for us. I was emotionally and physically exhausted. It was a difficult time.

In 1977, Ben moved his office out of the house and hired an inside person. After the setback with the New York hospital contract, he spent more time building the business. Thinking back, he said, "It took five years to establish a profitable ongoing customer base. I also began to rethink my own priorities; I was stretched too thin. A crucial issue was, 'When I'm vulnerable to competition, do I push inventory items or go after customers?' Ben resolved this question in favor of conserving his own energy. He promoted inventory items through direct mail and worked on increasing orders from existing customers. This decision resulted subsequently in steady growth for the company. Unfortunately it increased the administrative work which he disliked and reduced the selling time which he loved. "The bigger the business got the worse this administrative monster got. I rarely got to have any fun selling, marketing, creating new products, etc. The success of my earlier selling efforts were forcing me off the road and out of selling. I didn't know a way out of the trap."

At the end of the fourth year, Ben admitted that he was exhausted, and as the fifth year progressed he began to ask himself, "Is this a mid-life crisis? A burnout? Am I ever going to make it?" Physically, he experienced attacks of anxiety and shortness of breath. Even though his business was growing and prospering he found himself bored. Ben also remembered feeling like a machine. "I was on a treadmill. I felt irritable and moody even though the business was established. I couldn't understand why I didn't feel better." Sales were at $800,000 and profits were very good. "After five years I'll have it made. Well, we're making it but I don't feel any elation."

Karen remembered the period vividly.

I couldn't cope with any more problems and still be open to

the children. Ben was on his own so much; he could never turn off his business concerns. Conflict between us was a fact of life. Ben couldn't involve himself with the family even to the extent of reading Ben, Jr. a bedtime story. One weekend, Ben was waiting for a check to come in, to ease a critical cash flow problem. The tension level was extreme. His inability to disengage from the business even undermined our vacation time. For each of the first five years of this new venture, we took a one-week vacation at the Cape and Ben was on the telephone every day from the cottage.

In 1979, Karen made a critical decision and decided to stop working for the company in order to devote full-time to supervising the building of the Triplet's new home. They had enough money and Ben agreed that something had to be done to pull the family back together. It was not an easy decision for Karen, and she confessed that if Ben hadn't been able to hire a replacement, she never would have undertaken the project. She didn't know how to deal with the contractor and the workmen, and she didn't want to bother Ben. The situation caused her months of anxiety. Yet, she got the job done.

> Ben's business is not my thing. I don't relate to the product well enough; I don't know paper. I can run an office operationally, but I'm more people-oriented. I made up my mind that I wanted a house. And, by the time Ben, Jr. turned 18, I was going to go back to school.

During the sixth year of his entrepreneurial career, when Ben was 43, he was in a serious automobile accident and his hospitalization and convalescence lasted well over a month. This period of enforced rest gave him the opportunity to reflect on his priorities.

> I always had had an interior life and a feeling of the presence of God. But I had gotten away from the practice of meditating, and had lost touch with the center of myself. I was able to turn myself around. I spent more time with my family. I didn't stay up late. When I could return to work I spent the bulk of my time in solidifying the operation -- developing the discipline to do administrative work, developing staff procedures -- in finding ways to make the operation less dependent on me.

> I have to admit that I feel more rested, more patient, more sociable, more in touch with myself.

> If I grow to a sufficient size, maybe I'll sell, maybe I won't. If the business went down the tubes I'd never start another venture -- I would never repeat the last five years. At most, I'd consider acquiring another business. But if I had it to do again, I would -- I'm not sorry I did it. There are easier ways to make a living, but you have to try a lot of ways until you find one that suits you at a particular time in your life.

Karen also reflected on their experience of the last five years:

> I've learned a lot from Ben. Some day I might run my own business. I would encourage both boys to go into their own businesses. Independence and being your own boss are good. It's great not to be subject to corporate control. All three kids have worked for Ben, and we continue to be a closely-knit family. I feel very positive about the future. This has a lot to do with whom your married to. It's really a matter of exposure. My mother is in a state of shock every time Ben does something, but she knows that Ben has always provided well for me. I think I would like to work, but I know Ben would worry about any involvement that would take me away. He likes to know that I'm there. He needs a sense of security. Our home is the first home Ben has ever had. He would miss my not being at home.
>
> Although Ben has finally learned to relax, I'm not sure he's enjoying himself that much. He doesn't feel like a success yet; he doesn't have a good image of himself. But it's hard for him to give, to share -- maybe because of his lack of mothering when he was growing up. Also, Ben is a perfectionist and his definition of 'success' may be impossible for him to achieve.
>
> I know Gil cares for Ben, and has always given him advice which is in Ben's best interest. Gil believed Ben needed to be pushed to do what he needed to do, and Ben still feels he needs Gil to talk out his problems with. Gil has been a real friend to us both.
>
> Looking back, I know I made the right decision to support Ben and his venture. If I had said no he never would have been happy, and would have blamed me for holding him back. Now he knows he can do it. I feel good about him, and about me. I just wish he felt better about himself.

ASSIGNMENT QUESTIONS

1. Why doesn't Ben perceive that he is a success? What *is* success for Ben?

2. What effect has Ben's family, especially his wife, had on his entrepreneurial career?

3. What should he do in the future?

COPYPROOF PAPER

In mid-April, 1980, Ralph Barnes arrived at the moment of truth. After ten months of deliberations, meetings, and research, he had to decide whether or not to invest $12,000 in an inventor who claimed to be able to develop copyproof paper.

Risky investments were not new to Ralph, who liked exploring new opportunities when he was not teaching marketing at a large university in Boston. But never had he considered investing in anything before when his knowledge, involvement, and/or contacts did not play key roles. Now Ralph had the contract signed by the inventor, Jack Whetten, and his business partner, Albert Cameron. It only awaited Ralph's signature plus his check. Mr. Cameron had already phoned and was eager to start the venture. Ralph rethought the situation through once more. This time he had to come to a final decision.

BACKGROUND OF THE VENTURE

Late last April, one of Ralph's close friends asked him to meet with Al (Albert Cameron) who was job prospecting in the Boston area. The friend had met Al several times through a mutual friend. Al was experienced in promotion and advertising agency work and wanted to move out of the New York area. Ralph had been on Madison Avenue for ten years working for media and finally as an account executive on two General Foods brands at Ogilvy and Mather, Inc. Ralph ventured into education in 1968 and while teaching at a business school had met Al's friend. Such requests to talk with friends of friends, past students, or past business contacts was not unusual. So Ralph agreed to meet Al for dinner on his next trip to Boston.

Several weeks later over dinner, Ralph and Al discussed their backgrounds and Al's specific career interests. Ralph concluded that there were few opportunities in Al's lines of interest, but did come up with a person for him to contact. As the conversation shifted, Al mentioned how he did some promotional work on the speculation that if the new ventures worked he would get a "piece of the action" and/or a share of the first profits. He then enthusiastically detailed to Ralph his latest venture. It concerned an inventor named Jack Whetten whom Al had met while visiting his folks in Southern California. This chance meeting developed into a warm and trusting friendship. Jack had an engineering background, and at age 60, had a long string of design and invention credits in a wide range of fields from biomedical innovations to integrated social systems. Jack's latest efforts centered on designing a new concept in community living. However, Jack's latest projects needed funds. Al encouraged Jack to examine his numerous ideas and pick one to complete that had the broadest commercial appeal and dollar payout. Jack's idea for a way to treat paper so that it was copyproof emerged as the target project. Since both lacked the capital to secure the necessary equipment and to pay Jack's expenses while he concentrated on this project, they decided to seek an investor. After almost two years of looking, negotiating, and just missing, Al was wondering when and if this "sure winner" would ever get off the ground.

Ralph listened intently to this background data. It stirred a responsive chord of adventure and visions of potential profits. Al seemed to get more excited about reviving the idea, seeing Ralph's interest. And Ralph thought that $12,000 was not a lot of money. Al indicated that he and Jack would give up a one-third interest in the company they formed for this project. Ralph requested that more data be sent to him. If these data and his own research indicated a "go condition" he would contact Al to set up a meeting in California with Jack.

THE FOLLOW-UP

The next day Ralph got on the phone to a few of his friends in the investment community. They all agreed copyproof paper was a "gold mine" if Jack could do it, and $12,000 was a small stake to put up. They also voiced concerns that Ralph had had from the beginning of Al's enthusiastic comments the night before. If the concept were so good, the inventor so experienced, the payouts so great, why hadn't other individuals or one of the major paper companies themselves put up the small sum to launch it? Also, why had these giants of industry with all their resources not been able to develop the process? Finally, Ralph and his investment friends wondered why Al and Jack between them had not come up with the money themselves.

When the data arrived from Al, they indeed spelled a very large potential market for the process. Every major paper manufacturer and supplier said the same three things:

1) They had been working on such a project for years without success.

2) They would not fund the original research efforts of Jack.

3) Once a patentable process and a working prototype were ready, they would be very interested in negotiating a deal.

Ralph found that all those he queried shared his doubts, but also found a fascinating appeal for the project. However, each said he or she would not invest until there was some physical indiction of results. Meanwhile, Ralph continued to research the market potential of the idea. What he found made the project even more inviting, since its success would solve the following types of problems that daily plagued government and industry, costing billions of real and opportunity dollars yearly:

1) The federal government knew that frequently top secret design and diplomatic documents were photographed by and for sale to outside interests.

2) Private sector organizations had the same problem as trade secrets were frequently pirated away.

3) Book, magazine, and music publishers regularly lost sales as interested purchasers did not buy but merely photocopied the desired pages. Often one copy was purchased and numerous photocopies were made of it. In the education arena, non-authorized xeroxing was done on a daily basis without approval in spite of the copyright laws.

4) The Postal Service had long known that with rising stamp prices and the capacity for color photocopying, it was only a matter of time before people started illegally photocopying a sheet of stamps. The results represented quite a loss.

THE TWO MEETINGS

Armed with encouraging data about the market, Ralph had Al set up a meeting with Jack for early June 1979. The three met in the California home of Jack. Ralph had been told in advance to expect a simple, seven-room house on a small waterfront property in a lower middle income neighborhood. Jack had models of numerous projects mounted on the wall and on table tops. Seating was in heavy special modern chairs designed by Jack. Also, Jack had two young women who lived with him and assisted him in his work.

When Ralph and Al arrived, only the two women greeted him. Jack arrived in a few minutes with his very attractive Scandinavian girl friend. Ralph was impressed with Jack's friendly, articulate and energetic manner. He also noted that Jack left all the business details to Al. But for two hours, he electrified the room with his ideas on current, past, and future projects. He also pointed out how many of his best ideas had been stolen when he shared them. When asked about why others did not back him, he pointed out how conservative people were when it came to backing inventors. Jack detailed conceptually in very broad terms how the copyproof paper could be made. He was confident he could develop the process and be able to demonstrate it within four months. Ralph found it difficult not to get over enthusiastic.

Jack was a unique person, and very persuasive. Ralph had very little doubt that Jack could do what he said. He conveyed this enthusiasm to Jack and Al saying he would evaluate the project and contact them with a decision as soon as he had checked the legal details of the agreement for the project.

Ralph returned to Boston, unable to keep his mind off the project. Several weeks later, he found a business trip put him back in California. His wife accompanied him, as they planned to spend a few extra days vacationing. They "dropped in" on Jack after a quick phone call indicated he was at home. Jack was working on his own special design of an outdoor barbecue. One of the young women was finishing a model that represented a concept of helicopters. Jack was his usual charming self, and Ralph's wife came away very favorably impressed with him.

THE HOUR OF DECISION

When Ralph returned from California, the proposed contract from Al had arrived. He reviewed it, checked with two of his own lawyers. The contract in its final form made

Ralph a partner for an investment of $2,000 for a one-third interest in the company and $10,000 would be an unsecured loan at prevailing interest rates of 12% if repaid within a year, and 15% interest if repaid in whole or part thereafter. Jack had signed a performance contract with this company covering his best efforts and pledging priority to the copyproof paper project. Jack and Al would each have a one-third interest in the company.

As Ralph finished reviewing the final contract with the two signatures already on it, the phone rang. Al was on the other end, eager to know Ralph's decision. Ralph told Al he would call him back in two hours with his decision.

ASSIGNMENT QUESTIONS

Put yourself into Ralph Barnes' position. What would be your response to the following questions:

1. Today, personally, would you make this investment? (Assume that you have an extra $12,000.)

2. Estimate the payout potential of this investment.

3. What factors do you think Ralph should consider or factor into his decision?

4. Evaluate the contract terms. What changes, if any, would you recommend?

5. Overall, should Ralph make the investment? If your answer was "no", what factors would have to be different to make the answer "yes"?

THE BRIMMER STREET GARAGE:

Evaluating a New Venture Concept in Real Estate

Eliot Conviser, a young real estate developer, and his wife were finishing some egg rolls at the Golden Temple restaurant in downtown Boston in March 1979, when he spotted a familiar face at a nearby table. Wes Marins, a veteran broker in the real estate of Boston's downtown areas, had just paid his bill and was making his way over to the Convisers' table.

"What a coincidence, Eliot," Marins remarked. "You were on my list of people to call this week. Want to buy a garage?"

Although buying a garage was the farthest thing from Eliot's mind--he spcialized in residential condominium conversions in Boston's Beacon Hill and Back Bay neighborhoods--he was curious about the opportunity. "Sit down for a minute and tell me more."

"It's the Brimmer Street Garage," replied Marins, pausing to give his drink order to a passing waiter. "It will cost you $450,000 and it has 110 spaces. I think it might be a conversion."

Eliot Conviser had heard about the Brimmer Street Garage. He knew it was located in Boston's fashionable Beacon Hill area, that it had been recently declared a historic site, that it had been built sometime during the early 1900s for a company that manufactured carriages, and that it was later converted into a hack stable. Since 1944 the facility was used as the only contract-rental garage on "The Hill," notorious for its lack of parking space, and its list of tenants were as exclusive as any club in town. The property had been acquired in 1961 by Mr. Edward Bennett who charged uncomplaining clients $65-$100 a month per car. Parking was one privilege that even tight-fisted Bostonians were willing to pay for.

Eliot did a rapid calculation in his head: 110 spaces at say, $5,000 apiece, would be $550,000 right there. Anything more...?

"Sounds interesting, Wes," he replied casually, "but what's the catch?"

"No catch, Eliot. Ed Bennett tried to convert it to condos a few years back but the renters weren't interested. It's a pain in the neck for him to manage, and Ed's got better things to do with the money. If you're interested, give me a call this week."

"I'll do better than that, Wes. I'll meet you there tomorrow morning at 7:00, and I'll bring your check. If I like what I see, we can decide how to fill it out. And, speaking of checks--your drink is on me."

On the way back to their own car, parked on a dark side street at some distance from the restaurant, Eliot turned to his wife. "What do you think? Say the place is structurally sound and it will cost a maximum of $100,000 to put it into good shape. Say we treat it like any condominium property and bill it as a good investment as well as a good place to park. Say we charge $7,500 per unit. Why can't we be in the black from day one on?"

"I wonder why Ed couldn't convert the units himself," replied his wife, who participated actively in Mr. Conviser's business ventures.

"I wonder how much earnest money we can afford to put up," continued Eliot.

"I know the answer to that. No more than $25,000."

"Then that will be the amount I write on the check," said Eliot. "How would you like to be part owner of a garage?"

In the dark, he couldn't see the expression on her face.

BACKGROUND OF ELIOT CONVISER

Eliot Conviser grew up in the real estate/construction business. His grandfather, a Russian immigrant, founded the first Jewish carpenter's local in 1910. His uncle, trained as a lawyer, was a successful contractor all his life. His father, who had passed away the previous year, had built a legendary business by renovating and building theaters. During his career, he had supervised the reconstruction of over 200 venerable showhouses in the Northeast including the Shubert, the Colonial, and the Metropolitan Center in Boston.

Eliot received his education at Babson College located just outside of Boston, where he attended a four-year undergraduate business degree program. Eliot felt his education had provided him with a solid base of management and financial expertise to complement his hands-on experience in the construction industry. As a boy, he remembered going with his father to "file the necessary papers" at the Boston building department and getting various permits and licenses expedited. He realized early the importance of knowing how to cut through what seemed endless amounts of red tape--approval for everything from electrical wiring to plumbing permits, to elevator installations.

After graduating in 1960, Eliot immersed himself in work. He assisted his father with theater renovation and began investing, modestly, in downtown Boston houses suitable for restoration and then conversion to condominium properties. "On the side" he put together a line of Madras clothing accessories which he sold to retail outlets across the country. As it turned out, his sideline paid more than his full-time job. However, in 1965 he closed the door on his fashion career to devote all his time to real estate development.

Business became better and better for Eliot Conviser as he developed a reputation for quality work which was completed on or before the deadlines he negotiated. He was interested in three segments of the market: development of small tracts of land; residential condominium and commercial construction work; and income apartment management. He soon was active in all three of his targeted segments and, despite difficult economic conditions, his company Chestnut Development was turning a profit, thanks in part to Eliot's ability to sell the residential condominiums he had already converted.

"I had never thought of myself as a marketing man," he remarked, "but that's what you have to do to stay alive nowadays." He and his wife were working seven days a week, supported by an office staff of five.

FURTHER BACKGROUND ON THE BRIMMER STREET GARAGE

Aside from its historical significance, the Brimmer Street Garage provided the only safe and convenient indoor parking on Beacon Hill, a charming and historic community of old townhouses owned by socially and financially prominent Bostonians.* For the last 18 years, under the ownership of Ed Bennett, the Garage had been run by Bill (no one bothered with his last name), a personable fellow who knew all his "clients" by name, and provided special services such as obtaining gasoline during occasional shortages for a price. Many of the tenants were genuinely fond of Bill, and few ever batted an eye at the $100/month rental fee or the large bills for monthly gas. In addition to his clients, Bill had a number of "transient friends," who were happy to pay him by the day for the privilege of having a place to park. Bill kept the garage staffed 24 hours a day with a variety of friends and relatives, and the place--though far from pristine--was passably tidy. In short, the Brimmer Street Garage and its management were accepted as a kind of Beacon Hill institution.

In the mid-1970s Mr. Bennett, described by a friend as "a man who was nearly always too early or too late, but made a good living at it," hit upon the idea of converting the rental garage into a condominium arrangement--failing to turn a profit at pure garage management, conversion was a way out. He proposed that the clients buy their parking spaces outright and pay a nominal monthly maintenance fee. He made his intentions known in a letter to his 60-odd clients. His proposal was to sell the tenants their spaces at $6, $12, or $18 thousand apiece, depending on the layout of the spaces. (See floor plan in *Exhibit 2*.) Because of the layout, Mr. Bennett felt that he could not sell single units because there were no "easements" for the back one or two spaces when cars were parked in two or three solid rows. However, many of the tenants rented two or three spaces, so selling them as a single unit was possible.

The day after this letters were received by the Garage's tenants, his telephone rang off the hook. The clients were outraged. To have to pay as much as $18,000 in a lump sum for a service which now cost them $100 per car per month was unthinkable! Even to some of

---

*The nearby underground parking facility beneath the Boston Common was considered "unsafe overnight".-- *Exhibit 1* provides a map of the area.

Boston's finest financial minds, Ed's counter-arguments about equity interest and actual cost-savings in the long run were dismissed out of hand. Parking space was considered a rental item, and that was that. Mr. Bennett shrugged his shoulders and wrote another letter. "Out of respect for the tenants' wishes" the Brimmer Street Garage would remain a rental property and the matter was dropped. Subsequently, 6 months of effort produced 10-15 "contingent buyers" not enought for success. Suggestions to tenants about how well it was going were dismissed handily. Bennett had no poker face and belief in successful conversion and subsequent loss of rental space never tempted renters - they played better poker.

THE DECISION

Upon returning to his house in Brookline, Eliot Conviser went straight to his desk and began to make a list of all the considerations which would bear on the successful conversion of the Brimmer Street Garage to a condominium property. It was late when he set his alarm for the next morning.

A few minutes before seven, Eliot arrived at the Garage and watched as Bill greeted several early-rising clients whose cars were waiting for them at the entrance. Some minutes later Mr. Marins and Mr. Bennett arrived and together they made a thorough inspection of all three floors. Eliot's practiced eye took in every detail and he made notes along the way. The structure seemed sound. The elevator was balky. The lighting was dim on the second and third floors and non-existent in the stairwells. The sprinkler system looked inadequate and the water pressure in the lavatory was low. But above all, the place was dirty; years of grime, oil, and exhaust fumes caked the floors and walls.

An hour later, Eliot had completed the tour and received some additional information. On a yellow-lined pad, he estimated renovations costs as follows: rewiring, $20,000; elevator repair, $20,000; cleaning, painting, window replacement, $30,000; miscellaneous, $15,000--total, close to but less than $100,000. (See *Exhibit 3*.) He thought again about the risks involved, including the fact that he had never managed a garage, and he thought again about the potential profit. (See *Exhibit 4*.)* Finally, he thought about the $25,000 he and his wife had worked hard for and set aside for investment, and then he made up his mind.

---

*For the reader's convenience, *Exhibit 4* is reconstructed to show information actually drawn from several sources and points in time: some from Eliot's calculations the previous evening; some from information provided by Marins and Bennett that morning; and some from Eliot's observations on the tour.

ASSIGNMENT QUESTIONS

1. Should Eliot Conviser buy the Brimmer Street Garage? Why? Why not?

2. Assuming he buys it, should he convert it to a garage condominium? What else can he do with it?

3. Assuming he goes ahead with the concept of a garage condominium, what must he do to realize a successful conversion? Put together a detailed plan of action.

Exhibit 1

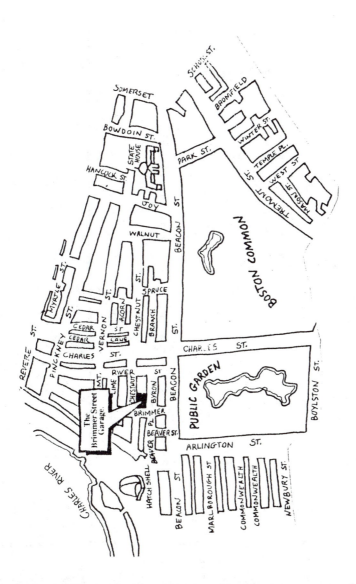

Exhibit 2

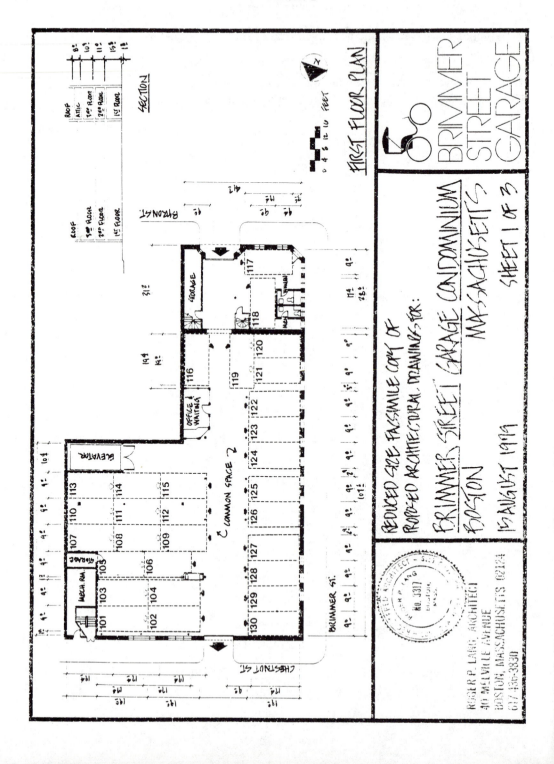

Exhibit 2

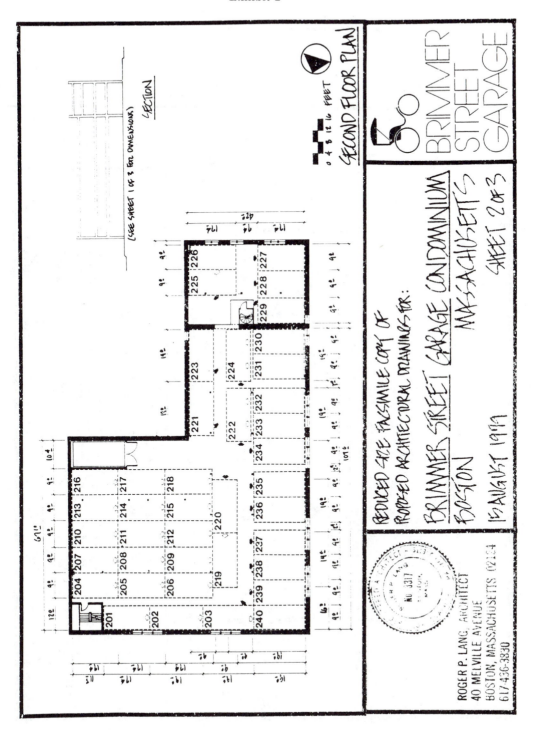

SECOND FLOOR PLAN

(SEE SHEET 1 OF 3 FOR DIMENSIONS)

SECTION

BRIMMER STREET GARAGE

BRIMMER STREET GARAGE CONDOMINIUM
MASSACHUSETTS
BOSTON
15 AUGUST 1979
SHEET 2 OF 3

REDUCED SIZE FACSIMILE COPY OF
RECORDED ARCHITECTURAL DRAWINGS FOR:

ROGER P. LANG, ARCHITECT
40 MELVILLE AVENUE
BOSTON, MASSACHUSETTS 02124
617/436-3330

Exhibit 2

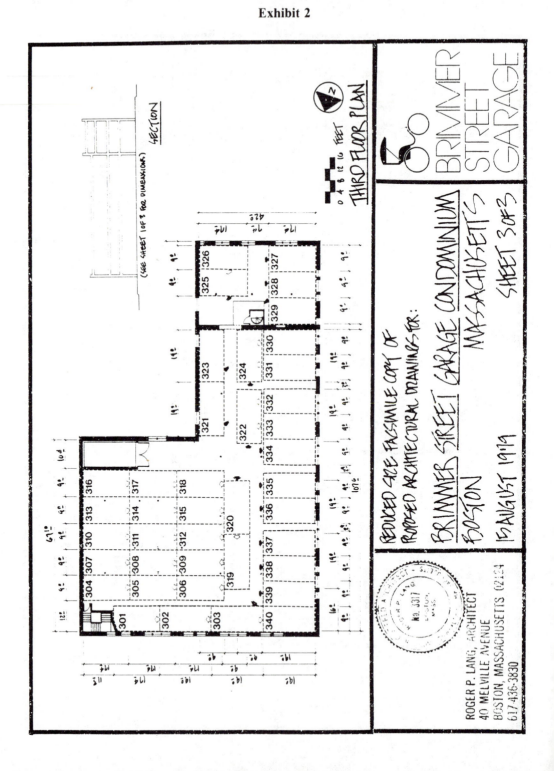

Exhibit 3

BRIMMER STREET GARAGE CONDOMINIUM

WORK NEEDED TO BE DONE

1. Roofing: Check and renew roof and flashing where necessary. Contractor's five (5) year warranty on the entire roof will be delivered to the Condominium Trust.

2. Heating: Renew all steam supply and return lines as necessary. Add five (5) new heater blowers throughout the garage. Repair or replace, as necessary, heating facilities in the office, lavatories, and storage areas.

3. Sprinklers: Repair sprinkler system so as to be fully operational and without leaks.

4. Fuel pumps: Install two (2) reconditioned gasoline pumps.

5. Lighting: Wash and relamp all fixtures. Install additional lighting in the pump area, hallways and office areas. Install emergency lighting in the hallways.

6. Communications: Install new two-way intercoms and telephone extensions to all floors.

7. Blacktopping: Repave or patch blacktopped areas where needed.

8. Painting and cleaning: Power wash and paint all walls and ceilings. Power wash all floors. Replace all broken glass. Stripe and identify all individual units.

9. Elevator: Fully inspect elevator and reactivate safety gates on every floor.

10. Garage doors: Install remote control door opening system.

11. Comfort facilities: Refurbish waiting room, lavatories and office.

12. Exterior: Repair exterior brick as needed, and repaint exterior sash and trim.

Exhibit 4
Brimmer Street Garage Condominium

Estimate of Annual Condominium Common Area Charges

ESTIMATED EXPENSES

Utilities (a)	$ 7,000.00
Garage Payroll (b)	42,000.00
Maintenance, Repairs & Garage Supplies (c)	1,800.00
Management (d)	7,200.00
Bookkeeping, Payroll & Office Supplies (e)	2,100.00
Insurance (f)	6,000.00
Elevator Maintenance (g)	1,500.00
Security (h)	720.00
Permits & Licenses (i)	140.00
Water/Sewer (j)	600.00
Trash Removal (k)	220.00
Legal & Accounting	1,000.00
Reserve for Contingencies, Improvements and Replacement	2,500.00

Total Estimated Expenses $72,780.00

ESTIMATED INCOME

Transient Parking Fees (1)	$22,000.00
Net Income from Sale of Gasoline (m)	3,000.00
Car Wash Fees (n)	4,000.00
Net Income from Sale of Miscellaneous Supplies, and Services, including Motor Oil, Transmission Fluid, Recharging Batteries.	1,000.00

Total Estimated Income   30,000.000

**Amount to be used to compute individual
unit net common area charge** $42,780.00

FOOTNOTES

(a) Utilities are comprised of electricity and oil for heating. The estimated expense for utilities shown above represents a 30% increase over the amount represented to me as having been expended for utilities in 1978 by the prior owner.

(b) The estimate for garage payroll, which includes employer's tax and insurance contributions, represents a 15% increase over the amount represented to me as having been expended for payroll in 1978 by the prior owners.

(c) The estimate for maintenance, repairs and supplies does not include the expenses to be paid by me in connection with the condominium conversion.

(d) Cost quoted by Pilgrim Parking, Inc., Boston, Massachusetts, for managing the garage under a self-extending one (1) year agreement, cancelable by either party on notice given at least sixty (60) days prior to the contract anniversary date.

(e) Includes $1,800,000 cost quoted by Pilgrim Parking, Inc. for bookkeeping services, plus $300.00 estimated annual amount for office supplies.

(f) The insurance premium as is currently quoted by an independent agent.

(g) Actual cost of $600.00 per year in accordance with existing annual contract with F.S. Payne Co., plus $900.00 estimated annual amount for parts and labor not covered by contract.

(h) Actual cost per existing annual contract with Burns Electronic Security Services, Inc.

(i) Estimated expense based upon amount represented to me as having been expended for permits and licenses in 1978 by the prior owners, including Garage Keepers' License, License to Store Gasoline and other Flammable Materials, Elevator Permit, and Fire Inspection Certificate.

(j) The estimate for water and sewer represents a 50% increase over the amount represented to me as having been expended for water and sewer in 1978 by the prior owners.

(k) Actual cost per existing contract with Charles Lee Disposal, Inc.

(l) Estimated income from transient parking fees is based on receipts of approximately $60.00 per day from transient parkers.

(m) Estimated net income from gasoline is based upon a $0.15 per gallon profit for 20,000 gallons per year.

(n) Estimated net income from car washes is based on two (2) washes per day.

WORLDPAPER

THE IDEA

Harry Hollins has the kind of quiet gaze and speech that inspires confidence. All 72 years of his experience stand behind his blue eyes. On a particular summer day in 1976, as he looked out to the ocean from the porch of his Maine cottage, he found himself saying to his wife, "There ought to be a newspaper for the world."

A graduate of Harvard College, Hollins spent 30 years with the New York brokerage firm now known as H.N. Whitney Groadby and Company. He was a partner when he left in 1961 to found the Institute for World Order. The Institute grew out of the World Federalists movement which Hollins had co-founded at an earlier date. He described the rationale behind the Institute for World Order in simple terms:

> A group of us saw that the arms race and cold war could not go on forever unchecked. Already the armament race was escalating into outer space. We have endeavored to set up what is really an educational foundation which attempts to train people to build the institutions which will promote international disarmament, world ecology and diplomacy. In this way, we will prepare ourselves for peaceful international cooperation. Our efforts have been varied, but we have, for example, given courses to some 500 university professors preparing them to teach courses on disarmament and world ecology to their students.

As he spoke to his wife, Harry Hollins began to think about the concept of a "world paper." His years of experience with the international community convinced him that some kind of publication was needed. But what precise form it should take was far from clear. Hollins wondered how he should proceed given his new idea.

Before reading further, list the specific steps you would take as Hollins regarding how he should proceed with his new idea.

THE TEAM

Harry Hollins' first step was to bring together a team to conduct a feasibility study. He explained the original purpose of WorldPaper to be the world's first completely international publication.

Hollins first approached John Cole, age 54, who was a newspaperman with 20 years of experience, the author of two books and numerous nationally-published articles. Cole was active with such organizations as the National Parks Advisory Council, the New England Regional Energy Council, the Maine State Natural Resources Council, and the Audubon Society. The regional newspaper he founded, *The Maine Times,* had won many awards for excellence including the national newspaper association's award--Best Weekly Newspaper in the United States. Cole had graduated from Yale in 1948 and after a tour with the Air Force had been a commercial fisherman for a time.

Hollins and Cole had become acquainted a few years earlier when Hollins had approached Cole in the hope that Cole would do a story about the new and malfunctioning lighthouse in the mouth of the Kennebunk River close to Hollins' summer cabin. Hollins felt that as a result of the story the Coast Guard was prompted to correct the situation.

In his own words, Cole was attracted to Hollins' idea because "it seemed like an interesting challenge and an idea that should be operable. The world has communications technologies way beyond what we are able to use. Given this technological resource, it made sense to attempt a paper for the global community which helped tie the world together and utilize technology that was available."

It was Cole who arranged the dinner at Boston's venerable Locke-Ober restaurant where Hollins and Cole got together with the two other members that formed the original team, Crocker Snow, Jr., and Mark Gerzon. Cole had known both Gerzon and Snow in the newspaper industry.

Crocker Snow, age 39, would become the Publisher of the new venture. But at the time of meeting he was National and Foreign News Editor of *The Boston Globe*. Previously, he had been the *Globe's* chief foreign correspondent (living in Tokyo), Assistant to the Publisher, and Assistant Managing Editor. In addition to winning a number of other awards in journalism, he had twice been a Pulitzer prize nominee. Snow was on "the inside track" at the *Globe* with a bright scenario for the future. His decision to leave was a shock to his employers. Snow's reasons for throwing in with WorldPaper revealed some of his motivation, "I knew that no matter how good I was or what position I eventually filled in a large organization like the *Globe,* I would never be more than a three percent difference. As publisher of WorldPaper, my input might make a major difference."

Mark Gerzon graduated from Harvard in 1970. While a student, he wrote a book on the sources of student dissent, *The Whole World is Watching* (Viking 1969), which received some national acclaim. Since 1970, Gerzon had made his living as a freelance writer working with *The New York Times, The Boston Globe,* the *University of Hawaii Press,* and the Carnegie Council. His work with Yale and the Carnegie Council led to a book called *A Childhood for Every Child* in which he analyzed the future impact of global developments on the well-being of future generations.

During the last part of 1977, Gerzon and Charles Everitt, who worked for Little, Brown Publishers, conducted the feasibility study and gathered background information for the formation of a world newspaper by consulting with journalists from all parts of the world. Fundamental issues dominated the agendas of these meetings. For example, how could such a newspaper best serve the global community? What form would the newspaper take--daily, weekly, monthly, quarterly? Who would publish it? Who would write for it? Who would own it? Who would read it? What costs would be associated with the editorial, production and distribution options available? Should it be foundation funded and a non-profit organization? Or could it be a profit venture and, if so, what would be the sources of revenue--advertising sales, subscription sales or what?

Gerzon commented about this period, "Everyone I talked to or met--primarily down in Washington--thought it was crazy and wouldn't work. The idea of a newspaper written by international journalists for a worldwide audience just seemed too far out."

Before reading further, evaluate the team Hollins has assembled. Do you feel he has proceeded properly?

THE CONCEPT EMERGES

During the fall of 1977, the feasibility team began to focus its investigations of the possibility of creating a "world paper" for the international community.

The first critical decision involved the form that WorldPaper would take. Hollins favored a newspaper with its own distribution system, e.g. individual subscribers around the world. Snow and Cole favored the form of a supplement to other major newspapers around the world. After considerable discussion, the decision was made to produce a supplement which was viewed the more feasible route. (*Exhibit 1* presents some background information on newspaper supplements.)

Many paid, underpaid, and non-paid consultants came, gave advice to the entrepreneurial team, and departed. Several key decisions which would form the cornerstones of future strategy were made during the winter months of 1977/78. WorldPaper would be a worldwide newsprint publication primarily distributed as a tabloid supplement in major quality dailies. It would deal with human affairs, geopolitics and international economics and be written for internationally-minded people. Initially, English language papers in key cities would be approached, but as rapidly as possible, WorldPaper would be translated into Spanish, French, and German and host papers in these languages would be sought. At this point, it was not clear just *how,* but it was decided that WorldPaper would attempt to be a viable business enterprise with a positive cash flow generated from advertising revenue.

VENTURE PHILOSOPHY

A fundamental view of the original team was that a "global community newspaper" could not be just another piece of Western journalism--another publication of the North owned by and written from the perspective of American multi-nationals. Rather, WorldPaper would try to be consistent with a trend which was evident to veteran internationalists. The North-South Dialogue required a vehicle which served the need for a two-way flow of communication. The less developed countries actually resented Yankee journalism and would not be attracted to yet another American enterprise; and the growing interdependency of the world suggested that developed countries needed to be more aware of the views of the less developed regions and vice versa. A need existed for a periodical which took a global view of global problems.

In other words, the editorial content of WorldPaper would be the work of outstanding Associate Editors from all corners of the world reporting from their regions on world issues. They would *not* be correspondents or stringers parachuted into specific locations to cover newsworthy events. Rather, these world-class journalists would be experienced resident writers who witnessd and participated in the struggles and achievements of their countries. WorldPaper would thereby offer "the voices of the world speaking for themselves."

During these formative months, Crocker Snow twice traveled around the world talking with journalists and publishers about the WorldPaper concept, approaching potential investors, and assembling a stable of Associate Editors (see *Exhibit 2*). The eleven Associate Editors received contracts and were paid a retainer of $5,000 for a year. They were attracted because their work would appear alongside that of other international journalists of stature. Their ideas would not be screened because of a political or cultural bias. Then, too, they would be read by a worldwide audience, not just a select group of foreign policy specialists.

PROPOSED EDITORIAL FEATURES

WorldPaper would have no editorial stand or slant per se but would represent different national and world region views. For instance, editorial features would revolve around a lead piece, jumping to the center spread called World Views which would compare or juxtapose different views of world issues or events. Another standing feature would be a guest journalist expressing his views on geo-politics on a page called, "One Voice." Crocker Snow would write a page called "World Diary." Also, "Letters" would be a standing feature.

OWNERSHIP

Given the editorial goals and policies of the proposed publication, the members of the entrepreneurial team were concerned about venture ownership. They felt strongly that the ultimate ownership of its capital should be international, with less than 50 percent of the capital coming from United States citizens.

CIRCULATION

The entrepreneurial team planned to have its supplement included in some of the most influential newspapers around the world. They realized that negotiating contracts with major newspapers scattered around the globe would not be easy. Fortunately, host paper development and relations were the special talents of Crocker Snow. These talents were vital because each prospective host newspaper would have its own set of variables and unique philosophical and editorial composition which would be affected by: regional or national political and legal constraints; the availability and cost of newsprint; the market's current business climate; pride of authorship and fear over a lack of editorial control; internal relationships between the editors and advertising departments--these were the most common variables which complicated host paper relations. Consequently, it would presently not be feasible to try to sell a standard contract to each one.

However, initial experience with possible host papers had begun to reveal a pattern by early 1978. WorldPaper had to be sold first to the editorial decision-maker. It was vital that this person be "turned on" to the WorldPaper concept and mission. If the editor wanted WorldPaper, then a hearing with the business decision-makers was in order. In this second stage, it was usually necessary to guide the general manager or advertising director to the conclusion that it was possible to cover the costs associated with publishing WorldPaper through advertising sales. Other selling points were the reader service and hence circulation value of WorldPaper and the promotional value of WorldPaper. WorldPaper was one more feature that could help a host paper in its own competitive environment. The "Avis" paper in many international markets might well be looking for a supplement which would give them an additional selling point.

COSTS AND REVENUES

Existing costs were based on the arrangement that the host papers paid the full production and distribution costs for a supplement provided by WorldPaper. Given cost differences around the world, these costs averaged five cents (U.S.) a copy for newsprint, ink, and presstime (or $5,000 an issue for a paper of 100,000 circulation). Each host paper would agree to print WorldPaper from a set of film negatives sent from Boston. The printed supplement would then be inserted by the host paper into its production run. In other words, WorldPaper provided the product--an editorial package with worldwide ads--at no cost to the host paper.

The host paper would cover its costs in two ways:

1. At their own rate, they would sell advertising for local distribution and retain all the revenue. WorldPaper designated three pages of each issue as "pull" pages. The editorial content on these pages could be dropped or re-edited by the host paper to accommodate local advertising space.

2. At the WorldPaper rate, the host paper advertising sales staff could sell advertising for regional or worldwide distribution. WorldPaper would pay the host paper a 15 percent sales commission for these ads, plus a percentage equal to the host paper's percentage of WorldPaper's total circulation. The agreement (below) summarizes these policies and provides an example of how both WorldPaper and host papers earned their revenue.

ADVERTISING AGREEMENT WITH HOST PAPERS

FOR LOCAL CIRCULATION ONLY:

The Host Paper may set the rates for and retain all revenue from such sales.

Space must be sold in full page units only.

Ads may be added to the WorldPaper package or substituted for editorial matter designated by WorldPaper at the rate of one ad for every eight page unit of WorldPaper.

FOR FULL WORLDPAPER CIRCULATION:

WorldPaper shall pay the Host Paper 15% of the net revenue *and* that percentage of the net revenue represented by its share of the total circulation of the ad.

All such ads must be sold at standard WorldPaper sizes and rates.

Ad copy must arrive in Boston 30 days before publication.

Purchase orders must come from international ad agencies directly to WorldPaper.

Example:

> A Host Paper whose circulation is 10% of WorldPaper's total sells a $10,000 ad worldwide. After receiving a purchase order from the ad agency, WorldPaper bills it $8,500 ($10,000 less the standard 15% commission). Upon receipt of payment, WorldPaper pays the Host Paper $1,275 (15% of the net revenue) *and* $850 (1/10 of the net revenue), or a total of $2,125.

N.B. After consultation with WorldPaper, a Host Paper may also sell regional ads.

For WorldPaper, estimated costs associated with the production of the negatives averaged $150 per set. Other costs would include an estimated $40,000 in monthly overhead which was made up of editorial retainers and purchases, a design firm retainer, payroll, office rent and supplies.

Other costs per issue would include:

Translations $3,500

Type Setting $4,000

Shipping $1,500

Travel and costs associated with advertising sales and host paper relations represented the most volatile expense category. The Publisher and Marketing Director were trying to work trades or barters with airlines and hotel chains to conserve operating capital. They relied on friends for a place to sleep whenever possible and were not shy about letting others pick up lunch tabs and taxi fares. As a result of his past travels, Crocker Snow had friends all over the world and he did not hesitate to drop in on them.

THE INITIAL OFFERING

In November, 1977, World Times, Inc. was incorporated in the state of Massachusetts as a Subchapter S corporation to publish a newspaper supplement called WorldPaper. After more than a year of concept definition, evaluation and organization building, the new venture's first supplement was published in January, 1979. The first WorldPaper was 32 pages long and appeared on four continents in two languages (English and Spanish). Five host papers distributed the supplement to a combined audience of over 1,000,000 readers. The host papers were: *The Boston Globe* (U.S.A.), *El Comercia* (Ecuador), *Hong Kong Standard, Melbourne Age* (Australia), *Minneapolis Tribune* (U.S.A.).

By April, 1979, a second edition of WorldPaper was published and carried by two additional newspapers: *El Tiempo* (Bogota, Colombia) and *Nairobi Times* (Kenya).

Several other newspapers had agreed to distribute WorldPaper in the near future. Approximately twenty newspapers (of the forty-five contacted) were seriously considering the addition of WorldPaper as a regular supplement.

Buoyed by their successes, the original founders of World Times, Inc. decided to issue a private placement in October, 1979, in order to raise additional growth funds and disseminate ownership of WorldPaper. *Exhibits 4, 5, and 6* summarized the financial situation of World Times, Inc. as of June, 1979, and were included in the prospectus announcing the private offering in October.

Essentially, World Times, Inc. sought to raise funds by offering 50 debentures for the principal amount of $24,000 each. There were initially fifteen investors and under the regulations for Subchapter S corporations in the United States, the first ten investors had to be U.S. citizens. The prospectus was registered with the Securities and Exchange Commission for the private placement of the debentures. Because the offering was a private placement, no underwriting was required. The 50 debentures were unsecured 8 percent, seven-year, convertible debentures due December 31, 1985. Interest was payable January 1 and July 1. (A working assumption of the Executive Board was that all debenture buyers would convert to 160 shares of common stock per debenture during a window period between 1/1/80 and 12/31/82.)

The following are excerpts from the October, 1979, prospectus.

Excerpt No. 1

Section IV

USE OF PROCEEDS

The net proceeds to the Company from the sale of debentures offered hereby are estimated at approximately $1,160,000 (if all the debentures are sold) after deduction of expenses incurred by the Company with respect to this offering. Expenses are projected to total $40,000, in the form of printing, legal, travel and related expenses. The net proceeds will be used as working capital for general business purposes; they have not been specifically allocated for any particular purposes.

The general working capital needs of the Company fall into five categories. These are, in order of magnitude: (a) advertising--advertising commissions and discounts; salaries and benefits for full-time advertising personnel, fees for representatives, and related expenses; (b) administrative and office needs--salaries and benefits for full-time personnel, legal and accounting fees, taxes, travel, telephone and postage, office rental, and related expenses; (c) production--salaries and benefits for full-time personnel, composition and production of master negatives, translation, air freight; (d) editorial--salaries and benefits for full-time personnel, Associate Editor fees, fees for articles and other editorial material, and related expenses; (e) interest on the debentures. Funds are also required to pay the expenses of this offering. The Company's expenses will increase in acordance with the increased frequency of publication of *WorldPaper*. Detailed information on the projected working capital needs of the Company is contained in Section X - "Projections of Expenses and Revenues."(Presented in the text of this case as "Excerpt No. 4").

The table (*Exhibit 3*) summarizes the projections of receipts, total disbursements, and annual and cumulative surpluses and deficits during 1979-82. The table also indicates the effect on the projected cumulative surplus or deficit (after factoring in present capital) (a) if it is assumed that only 19 debentures are sold, six in 1979 and the balance in 1980; and (b) if it is assumed that all the debentures are sold, six in 1979 and the balance in 1980. (In fact, the Company expects that any sales of debentures would occur primarily during 1979 and the first part of 1980. On the basis of discussions with stockholders, the Company believes that any short-term deficit in 1979 can be covered by loans from stockholders who will obtain personal tax benefits thereby under Subchapter S - see Section IXD - "Tax Status".)

Excerpt No. 2

C) Advertising

WorldPaper relies primarily on display and classified advertising for its revenue.

Display Advertising : The unique editorial and distributional approach of *WorldPaper* makes it an advertising medium which defies traditional media analysis. Present advertising efforts involve primarily those large international corporations whose financial resources, flexibility, and global marketing strategies make them likely candidates for buying space in *WorldPaper*.

Volume: Though there is no exact comparison with existing publications, *WorldPaper* has projected on the basis of its analysis of other similar publications what it believes to be a conservative initial volume of advertising sales. These projections indicate a range of three to six pages sold per issue in the first two years of publication.

Source: Display advertising is sold in three principal categories: 1) multinational corporations, including international financial institutions, banks, engineering and construction companies, and consulting firms; 2) government and tourist agencies; and 3) non-profit international organizations.

Advertisers have been advised that the Company anticipates a circulation base of 1,500,000 through 1979. Thus far, this goal has not been achieved; all advertisers are aware of the shortfall and have accepted the actual circulation base achieved. As an alternative to advertising in all host papers, advertisers have been offered the opportunity to select specific continental markets. Advertisers receive a significant frequency discount. Any circulation above the projected circulation base for the first four issues will be treated as a bonus for the advertisers by the Company.

Rate: In advertising terms, *WorldPaper* is positioned more as a magazine than as a newspaper. This is because of both its potential appeal to a select readership and its long life or lie-around value as a publication. Given its unconventional character, it is likely that its rate structure will be subject to change until publication has been underway more than a year and *WorldPaper*'s readership potential is better known. The initial advertising rate has been set at $10.00 cost-per-thousand issues distributed ("cpm") for a full page of advertising, or $10,000.00 per page for a base circulation of 1,000,000. This is higher than that of the host papers, but conservatively low in comparison to such international media as the *Economist, Newsweek International,* and *Asia Magazine.*

Advertising Representatives: In addition to direct solicitation by *WorldPaper* staff, an international network of advertising representatives is being assembled to sell advertising on a commission basis. The Company expects to reach agreements with such representatives before the end of 1979.

Excerpt No. 3

C) *Dividend Policy*

The Company has not paid any cash dividends to date and expects to retain any earnings in the foreseeable future for the anticipated needs of its business.

D) *Tax Status*

The Company has qualified as a "small business corporation" under Subchapter S, Section 1372(a) of the United States Internal Revenue Code, thereby avoiding taxation by the United States at the corporate level. Under this status, all net loss of the Company is being passed through to the stockholders and applied to their individual taxes in proportion to their shares of equity. In this situation, the Company has derived no deductions or other tax advantages from any losses. The Company expects to terminate its Subchapter S status on December 31, 1979, with the result that it will thereafter be treated as a taxable entity, retaining all losses thereafter incurred.

Excerpt No. 4

Section X

PROJECTIONS OF EXPENSES AND REVENUES

Attached as Exhibit 7 are tables representing the projected cash requirements for the Company for the period 1979-1982. The projections show a peak cumulative cash requirement at the end of 1980 of $1,068,000. The Company anticipates that operations will begin to produce substantial positive cash flow in the first half of 1981. The capital so far raised, $627,000, together with the $1,200,000 proceeds ($1,160,000 net proceeds) from this entire debenture offering, would cover the cash requirement of $1,068,000 and leave the Company with a contingency fund. If less than $456,000 worth of debentures is sold (19 debentures), the Company will experience a material deficit in 1980. On the basis of indications (not amounting to commitments) from banks with which the Company has a business relationship, the Company believes that it will have reasonable prospects of obtaining normal bank financing in 1980 (but there is no assurance that this will be the case) to cover any reasonable deficit, including any additional cash requirements because of errors in income or expense projections or because the sales of debentures do not take place as planned. (See Section I - "Risk Factors".)

The future expenses of *World Paper* are believed to be predictable with reasonable accuracy.

The revenue picture is less predictable because of a number of variables. These are:

Circulation

The total volume and character of the circulation of *World Paper* through the host newspapers directly affects the total revenue from advertising sales.

Advertising Rate

Rates charged advertisers vary widely among publications depending on their image and market. The projection of a $10.00 cpm (cost-per-thousand issues distributed) ad rate for *WorldPaper* is an average based on careful analysis of existing models worldwide. There is no exact precedent for such an international newspaper supplement; accordingly, the rate could go to $15.00 cpm or higher or drop to a lesser rate, depending on the nature and location of the host newspapers.

As an alternative to general circulation, the distribution of *WorldPaper* to a demographically selected and selective audience within the total circulation of a particular host newspaper would mean higher advertising rates. In order to reduce publication costs and increase advertising efficiency, many major metropolitan newspapers in the United States and Western Europe are currently developing special advertising and editorial supplements targeted to that segment of their total readership with the highest levels of income, education, and professional achievement. Some such supplements are distributed free as part of normal subscription rates; others only are available to a reader at addditional costs. *WorldPaper* is a likely publication for such demographic distribution. The effect would be to limit circulation, reducing a host newspaper's costs but increasing the unit value of the circulation, and thereby maintaining *WorldPaper's* projected advertising revenues.

Projections of advertising revenues assume that ads will be sold only the Company; it should be understood that any sales of ads by host papers will create additional revenue for the Company. Note that the revenue from pages of advertising may be slightly less than the cpm rate times projected circulation, since some ads in an issue of *WorldPaper* may be sold at a frequency discount, or as part of a series at a lower rate prevailing at an earlier date. Projections of income from classified advertising assume 5% of the gross billings to be uncollectible.

Advertising Ratio and Ad Pages

The ratio of advertising pages to editorial pages is an important variable. In daily newspapers in the United States, this ad ratio normally exceeds 50%. While projecting conservatively an average of about five to seven total advertising pages per issue in the first two years of publication (through 1980), *WorldPaper's* plan is for a 24-page publication in September and November, 1979, and for a 20-page publication thereafter. The advertising page ratio would thus run from 20 to 35 percent.

The unprecedented nature of *World Paper* as a publication makes definitive predictions of these variables impossible. A major change up or down in one or more of the variables would influence these figures considerably. The figures set forth in *Exhibit 7* are believed to represent a conservative projection. It must be emphasized, however, that investment in the debentures is highly speculative and that only persons who can sustain the total loss of their investment should consider investing.

The Company intends to furnish updated projections as often as material changes in the Company's financial situation require, and in any event no less often than every six months after the date of this Prospectus.

ASSIGNMENT QUESTIONS

1. Conceptually speaking, what are the strong/weak points of this venture?

2. What is the sales breakeven for this venture?

3. What changes in the venture concept do you recommend?

Exhibit 1

BACKGROUND ON NEWSPAPER SUPPLEMENTS

The newspaper supplements grew out of the "Sunday Supplement" tradition and first began to appear in daily newspapers as early as 1869. In the United States national supplements such as *Parade* Magazine reached mass circulation audiences of many million and offered advertisers color capabilities.

Host paper relations with the supplement were a key to the success of any supplement venture. In the 50s and 60s, supplements offered colored editorial features to the readers of the big city daily newspaper they did not normally receive. By the mid 1970s, a growing number of newspapers had their own special color supplements, like the *New York Times Sunday Magazine*, and they produced several special supplements on single subjects to attract special advertising categories.

Domestic and international practices in host paper relations varied widely. For instance, quite different contract terms often existed from one host paper to the next for a single supplement. Usually the independent supplement was delivered in bulk as a "pre-print." The host papers' only responsibility in such instances was to insert the supplement into the papers as they came off the press, either by machine or by hand. Sometimes the host paper paid on a per thousand basis for the right to carry the supplement. In other instances, the host paper charged a carrying fee which varied widely according to the size and weight of the supplement and the unique cost structure of the host paper. Costs were difficult to determine on both sides. The additional labor necessary for insertion was difficult to determine. Press time was also difficult to allocate. Postal rates and regulations also varied for different host papers in different countries. Consequently, considerable room existed for bargaining when two parties sat down to draw up a contract.

Exhibit 2

WORLDPAPER

ASSOCIATE EDITORS

Tarzie Vittachi
At Large

Yoshiko Sakurai
Northeast Asia

Mochtar Lubis
Southeast Asia

Arun Chacko
South Asia

Anthony Westell
North America

Carlos Rangel and
Sofia Imber
South America

Hilary Ng'weno
Sub-Sahara Africa

Silviu Brucan
Eastern Europe

Jacqueline Grapin
Western Europe

Associate Editors

Tarzie Vittachi is a contributing editor for *Newsweek International;* a correspondent for the BBC, the *Sunday Times*(London) and *The Economist*; and Chief, Public Information and NGO Office, United Nations Fund for Population Activities. He Began his journalistic career in 1950 as London Correspondent for the Associated Newspapers of Ceylon.

Mary Ellen Ayrton of Sydney, Australia, is a journalist. Her career includes four years with Australian Consolidated Press, working on a daily newspaper, a weekly current affairs journal, and *The Australian Women's Weekly.*

Silviu Brucan (East Europe) is now Professor of International Relations at the University of Bucharest, and for eleven years was editor of the Bucharest newspaper *Scintea* (circ. 1,600,000). He has been Ambassador from Rumania to the United States and to the United Nations.

Arun Chacko (South Asia) is Chief Reporter for *The Indian Press* in New Delhi, where he has worked since 1971. He has written a political column for *Onlooker*, a Bombay political fortnightly, and articles on development subjects for DepthNews India during 1975 and 1976. He was a Neiman Fellow at Harvard University in 1977-1978.

*Jacqueline Grapin (Western Europe),*a writer and financial editor for *Le Monde*, is also Editor-in-Chief of *Europa*, the economic supplement of *Le Monde, The Times, Die Welt* and *LaStampa*. Grapin is a graduate of the Institute d'Etudes Politiques of the Ecole in Paris where she is an Associate Professor.

Mochtar Lubis (Southeast Asia) is an Indonesian writer and editor, currently serving as editor of the Jakarta literary monthly *Horizon*. He founded the newspaper *Indonesia Raya* in December, 1941, coincident with independence from the Dutch. The newspaper was banned by Sukarno in 1956. *Indonesia Raya* reappeared in 1966 to be published until 1977. He is a member of the UNESCO Commission on the Third World News Agency.

Hilary Ng'Weno (Sub-Sahara Africa) is the editor, publisher and owner of several Kenyan publications, including the *Weekly Review*, a magazine devoted to national and international political, business and cultural affairs. Several years ago he helped to found *Joe* a satirical magazine on the follies of Kenyan society, and with his wife started a children's publication called *Rainbow*. Previously Ng'Weno had been editor-in-chief, at age 27, of Nairobi's largest daily paper, *The Daily Nation*. Early this year he founded his own Sunday newspaper, *The Nairobi Times*.

Carols Rangel and Sofia Imber (South America) are a husband and wife team based on Caracas, Venezuela. Together they edit a Venezuelan news magazine, *Autentico*, and host a morning television program, "Buenos Dias!". Carlos Rangel holds degrees from Bard College and New York University, and for a brief period was a university lecturer at Venezuela's Central University. He joined the Venezuelan Foreign Service in 1958, but left after several years to become a magazine editor. He is the author of *The Latin Americans*, published simultaneously in French, Spanish and English (Harcourt Brace Jovanovich, 1976). Sofia Imber is Director of the Museum of Contemporary Arts in Caracas and a columnist in *El Universal* (Caracas).

Yoshiko Sakurai (Japan) is Tokyo Bureau Chief of the Press Foundation of Asia. Educated at the University of Hawaii and a former correspondent for the *Christian Science Monitor*, Ms. Sakurai specializes in describing her region's cultures to non-Asians. Her writing has focused on Japan's role in world affairs.

Anthony Westell (North America) is an editorial page columnist for the *Toronto Star* and a Professor of Journalism at Carleton University in Ottawa. Mr. Westell has written for major papers and magazines in the United States. He is the author of two books: *Paradox: Trudeau as Prime Minister* (Prentice-Hall, 1972); and *The New Society* (McClelland and Stewart, 1977). He is the founding editor of the Carleton Journalism Review.

Exhibit 3
Effect of Sale of Debentures
on Capitalization

Projected Operating Results
(See Exhibit D)*

	1979	1980	1981	1982
Receipts	$120,000(1)	$713,000	$2,256,000	$3,826,000
Disbursements	552,000	1,010,000	1,751,000	2,153,000
Annual Surplus (Deficit)	(432,000)	(297,000)	505,000	1,673,000
Accumulated Surplus (Deficit) from Prior Periods	(339,000)	(771,000)	(1,068,000)	(563,000)
Cumulative Operating Surplus (Deficit)	(771,000)	(1,068,000)	(563,000)	(1,110,000)

Capitalization
A. Assuming Sale of 19 Debentures

	1979	1980	1981	1982
Capital Contributed in Prior Periods	627,000(2)	771,000	1,083,000	1,087,000
Capital from Sale of 6 Debentures in 1979 and 13 in 1980	144,000	312,000	-0-	-0-
Total	$771,000	$1,083,000	$1,083,000	$1,083,000
Net Worth After Sale of 19 Debentures	-0-	$15,000	$520,000	$2,193,000

B. Assuming Sale of 50 Debentures

	1979	1980	1981	1982
Capital Contributed in Prior Periods	627,000(2)	771,000	1,827,000	1,827,000
Capital from Sale of 6 Debentures in 1979 and 44 in 1980	144,000	1,056,000	-0-	-0-
Total	$771,000	$1,827,000	$1,827,000	$1,827,000
Net Worth After Sales of 50 Debentures	-0-	$759,000	$1,264,000	$2,937,000

(1) Includes actual revenues of first two issues in 1979.
(2) Includes $555,000 from sale of stock and $72,000 from sale of three debentures, all prior to June 10, 1979.

*Refers to Exhibits 4, 5, 6

Unaudited

Exhibit 4
World Times, Inc.
Balance Sheet
June 30, 1979

Cash

Checking	$ 30,266.93
Savings	6.57
Restricted	12,939.00
Petty	50.00
Accounts Receivable	
Display Ads	2,000.00
Classified Ads 752.52	
Furniture & Fixtures	5,971.35
Res Dep F&F	(463.35)
Organization Expense	1,672.00
Amortization	(392.00)
Deposits	450.00
Deferred Financing Costs	24,306.50
Total Assets	77,559.52
Deferred Income	895.24
Accounts Payable	17,379.58
Accrued Expenses	3,780.00
Accrued Taxes	113.24
Current Liabilities	22,168.06
Convertible Debentures	24,000.00
Common Stock	545,000.00
Deficit	(513,608.54)
Liabilities & Capital	77,559.52

Unaudited

Exhibit 5
World Times, Inc.
Income/Expense
Six Months Ended
June 30, 1979

Income:

Space Ads	$35,162.22
Classified	1,666.22
Coupon Ads	2,647.26
Sale of Papers	71.82
Subscriptions	743.35
Misc.	146.15
Sales Discount	(386.86)
Gross Income*	40,050.16

Mechanical & Distribution Expenses:

Typesetting	$ 5,876.45	
Typesetting (Spanish)	$ 8,295.51	
Translation to Spanish	3,643.40	
Negatives	1,191.18	
Negatives (Spanish)	746.40	
Newsprint	331.45	
Shipment of Negatives	412.47	
Designer	11,078.29	
Designer (Spanish)	1,872.00	
Freight	285.40	
Total		33,732.55

Editorial Expenses:

Salaries	$ 13,000.04	
Artwork & Photo	485.00	
Research	876.84	
Secretarial Services	288.00	
Associate Editor Fees	24,365.00	
Articles	925.00	
Copy Editing	692.00	
Travel	1,493.85	
Associate Editor Travel	1,815.58	
Total		43,941.31

*Net of representation and agency fees.

Unaudited

Exhibit 6
World Times, Inc.
Income/Expense
Six Months Ended
June 30, 1979
Continued

Advertising Expenses:

Salaries	$12,923.56	
Travel	4,622.43	
Promotion	8,663.96	
Classified	626.90	
Commissions	4,316.39	
Ad Representative	862.50	
Total		32,015.74

Administrative and General Expenses

Salaries	45,975.24	
Postage	2,538.07	
Office Rent	3,886.20	
Repairs	94.58	
Office Supplies	2,088.67	
Papers & Magazines	367.54	
Dues	25.00	
Photo Copies	1,096.18	
Travel	11,894.86	
Fees	441.25	
Secretarial Services	1,110.64	
Employment Agency Fees	1,614.00	
Audit & Legal	14,339.66	
Telephone & Telex	7,368.58	
Employee Benefits	3,886.44	
Payroll Taxes	5,880.01	
Interest	1,060.45	
Late Charges	117.54	
Corporate Insurance	676.07	
Miscellaneous	47.95	
Other Taxes	45.00	
Equipment Rental	131.25	
Total		104,685.21
Net Loss		174,424.65

Exhibit 7
Worldpaper
Projected Cash Requirements*

	First Year 4 Issues 1979	2nd Year 8 Issues 1980	3rd Year 12 Issues 1981	4th Year 12 Issues 1982
Cash Receipts				
Display Adv.	105,000	611,000	1,862,000	3,030,000
Mail Order Adv.	8,000	50,000	144,000	252,000
Classified Adv.	7,000	52,000	250,000	544,000
Total Cash Receipts $	120,000***	713,000	2,256,000	3,826,000
Cash Disbursements				
Offering Expense	20,000	20,000	---	---
Mech. & Distrib.	89,000	187,000	295,000	319,000
Editorial	114,000	163,000	251,000	305,000
Advertising Commissions	26,000	213,000	651,000	909,000
Other	69,000	125,000	160,000	181,000
General & Admin.	224,000	262,000	314,000	343,000
Interest Exp. 8% Sub. Conv. Deb.**	10,000	40,000	80,000	96,000
Total Disbursements $	552,000	1,010,000	1,751,000	2,153,000
Annual Excess (Deficit)	(432,000)	(297,000)	505,000	1,673,000
Cumulative Excess (Deficit)	(771,000)†	(1,068,000)	(563,000)	1,110,000

*	Totals have been rounded off to nearest thousand.
**	Assuming no conversion of debentures.
***	Includes actual revenues from first two issues in 1979.
†	Includes actual $339,000 cumulative deficit from 1977 and 1978 start-up period.

ENERGY PRODUCTS (A)

Ron Williams and Bill Shaw were facing a major decision about a new venture. Ron and Bill, both age 57, had just been through a grueling four months. What started as a simple idea -- the manufacturing and marketing of a log similar to "Duraflame" but functional in that it gave off heat -- had mushroomed into a time-consuming and costly proposal. Ron and Bill had to decide whether or not to leave their present positions and start a new business in the promising, although very risky, alternative home heating industry. The decision was further complicated by a lack of personal funds needed to get the product out of the planning stage and into the marketplace. Both men envisioned great things for their product, including national marketing within three years. Also, they both felt the business, if they entered it, must be successful by the time they reached 60.

RON WILLIAMS

Ron Williams was known as an affable and congenial person who had been a salesman all his adult life. Ron, who started in men's clothing, now sold computer equipment for a Massachusetts based company. Ron had been known to make boastful claims like, "I could sell sand to the Arabs!"

Even as regional sales manager for the small firm that he worked for, Ron still made sales calls. He earned roughly $45,000 per year, was married and had a son and a daughter. His daughter was attending a well-known private eastern university, and when she obtained her degree, she would be the first in Ron's family to have done so. Ron paid

© Michael J. Merenda and Audrey C. Savage, 1981.

This case was prepared by Michael J. Merenda, Assistant Professor in Business Administration, Whittemore School of Business and Economics and Audrey C. Savage, Project Director, Center for Industrial and Institutional Development, both of the University of New Hampshire, as the basis for class discussion rather than to illustrate either effective or ineffective handling of a business situation.

about 70% of his daughter's college expenses. Ron's son, Ron, Jr., was presently a private in the Army and stationed in South Carolina. Mrs. Williams, although she understood her husband's aspiration to have a "show of his own" was bit reluctant for him to leave his present position, especially since he only needed four more years before he would be fully vested in his company's pension plan.

BILL SHAW

Bill also had sales experience. Bill managed a small retail men's clothing store for ten years after graduation with an associate degree in retail merchandising from a community college. It was through this business venture that Bill and Ron met. They had been close friends for over twenty years.

Bill's business never really provided him with the lifestyle and income he desired. Although he said it was the greatest experience of his life, he still remembered when his checking account was overdrawn $3,000 with no money for the payroll due in a few days, and $20,000 of unwanted inventory on hand.

Bill eventually sold the business at a small loss and went to work for his brother, a successful businessman. Bill worked as Vice President for personnel in his brother's company, making about $40,000 per year, and was married with two married daughters.

Sam Shaw, Bill's brother, was entertaining a very attractive offer to sell his business. As part of the sale, the new owners wanted their own management people to run the business. Although Bill had built up several contacts over the years, he felt it was highly unlikely that at age 57 he would be able to land a similar position, especially since he wanted to stay in his native New Hampshire. If the deal went through, Bill stood to make about $20,000 from the shares he owned in his brother's company. The company had no pension plan.

THE IDEA

Ron and Bill had maintained their friendship over the years. On several occasions, they talked about going into business together, but it seemed that something always prevented it. In 1970, they considered opening a restaurant in Portsmouth, New Hampshire, but Ron's wife became seriously ill and had to spend several months in the hospital. Ron's medical plan covered only 80% of the cost, and as a result, the little bit of money he had saved went toward medical bills.

It was March of 1979 when Bill approached Ron with an idea. While sitting in front of his fireplace with an artificial log burning away, Bill was struck with the idea of making artificial logs available that could double the heat source. Bill believed that a market existed for the convenience purchase of fireplace logs that could be used as a secondary or emergency heat source in residential homes. Remembering his boyhood days of shoveling coal into his father's coal furnace, he thought that coal shaped into the form of logs would be an excellent substitute for artificial logs.

Ron agreed that the idea had potential. They felt that artificial logs were overpriced, left an unpleasant waxy smell in the house, had limited heating value, and faced little competition. Since the use of wood for heating was becoming more popular in the Northeast, they wondered if they could compete in this market.

Between the two of them, they could fund a preliminary engineering analysis of the feasibility of the coal log. Bill's neighbor was an engineering professor at the nearby university whose speciality was fossil fuels. Professor Ashton had been conducting research in alternative energy sources, specifically in coal, peat and other fossil fuels. Professor Ashton thought the idea had merit and would take on the project as a consultant for a fee of $5,000.

Ron and Bill finally thought they had what they were looking for. Their own business would soon be a reality! They figured they could raise the needed capital if Ashton's analysis indicated that the product was technically and economically feasible to produce. Ron was already visualizing a national distribution network for the log within two years. Bill also thought that they had to move quickly, for once they entered the market, others would copy their idea. They both felt the northern New England fireplace market was the market they should penetrate first.

ASSIGNMENT QUESTIONS

1) What factors should you consider in the formulation of strategy for a new business venture?

2) What motivates Williams and Shaw? Evaluate their probability for success. What does it take to be a successful entrepreneur? Comment on the goal of Williams and Shaw that the new venture be successful by the time they reach age 60.

3) What recommendations would you make to Williams and Shaw relative to proceeding with their product concept?

ENERGY PRODUCTS (B)

In early April, Ron Williams and Bill Shaw informally agreed to form a partnership, called Energy Products. Each would invest $3,000; all expenses and responsibility for the management of the partnership would be shared equally. Initially, both decided to stay with their present employers. Although not a formal delegation of responsibility, it was determined that Ron would handle all the marketing and sales, while Bill would concentrate on administration and manufacturing. All decisions would be made jointly and all financial obligations would be co-signed by each.

On April 15, they contracted with Professor Ashton for an engineering analysis. The report, costing $5,000, would assess the product's technical and economic feasibility. Both partners felt they were in a good position to line up potential investors if the report was favorable.

ENGINEERING ANALYSIS

On June 29, Bill received a report from Professor Ashton indicating that the making of coal logs, using anthracite coal bound together with a yet-to-be-determined binding material, was both technically feasible and economically competitive with cord wood. Ashton felt that the development of a retardant built into the coal log was technically possible and only presented minor problems. The retardant was necessary to prevent damage to wood stoves from the intense heat generated by coal. Ashton was enthusiastic about the benefits of the coal log and its potential to consumers--a realistic alternative to high energy bills. Ashton's conclusions were very encouraging; it was clear that he felt Ron and Bill had definitely locked onto a profitable and promising venture.

COST ESTIMATES

Ashton had prepared cost estimates for two different capacity plants (20,000 tons/year and 76,000 tons/year) to manufacture the coal logs. His estimates[1] showed that 20,000 tons and 76,000 tons per year of the product could be produced and marketed for $126 per ton, and $111 per ton, respectively. Table 1 shows that nine-tenths (.9) of a ton of coal provides the same BTU output as a cord of top quality hardwood. Analysis showed that to get the amount of thermal energy available in a ton of coal, the consumer would need to purchase 1.14 cords of wood. In its final form to consumers, Ashton estimated that a ton of coal logs would cost from $20 to $35 more than a ton of unprocessed coal.

Estimated capital investment for the 20,000 ton per year plant is $750,000 while the 76,000 ton/year plant required $2,000,000. Ashton recommended a market study to determine the best size plant (20,000 vs. 76,000 tons per year). The estimate assumed the bulk rail transport of buckwheat No. 4 coal from Pennsylvania to Dover, New Hampshire. (See *Exhibit 1* and *2*.

In addition to the cost/ton estimates, the engineering study reported on the advantages of anthracite logs over wood, the layout of a prototype manufacturing facility, and technical aspects of manufacturing anthracite logs.

DESIRABILITY OF ANTHRACITE COAL

Anthracite coal has long been used as an industrial and domestic fuel. While still used in some industrial markets in the United States, coal has been replaced for domestic heating by cheaper and cleaner sources of energy (oil and natural gas). With the national concern over energy and the increased costs of formerly inexpensive fuels, the demand for coal is expected to increase drastically.

It is estimated that the U.S. had 9,000 million tons of anthracite reserves. Prior to 1970, 20-30 million tons/year were mined, but as of 1978 only 6 to 7 million tons/year are mined. At present, the raw material can be purchased from mines in Pennsylvania. There is also some talk of possibly mining semianthracite coal in Rhode Island and Massachusetts.

According to Ashton, logs composed of compressed anthracite coal dust plus a binding material will possess the following product attributes:

• Depending on the binding material, the log may or may not be stored outdoors without a protective wrapping.

---

[1]The cost estimates included all material costs, manufacturing and administrative overhead, direct labor, depreciation, taxes and insurance, packaging costs, rent, sales and marketing, working capital, and a 40% return on investment before taxes.

• Even-sized anthracite logs will permit a more regular and thorough combustion in the firebox or furnace than will wood.

• Since anthracite coal has a low volatile matter content, logs made from it will produce much less smoke than wood.

• Unlike wood, anthracite coal will leave no deposits of creosote in the chimney.

• Anthracite coal logs will burn to a fine ash without clinkering.

• Heat losses in the stack gas are lower with coal logs because of the low moisture content of anthracite as compared with wood.

• Since anthracite coal burns more slowly than wood, a more uniform temperature at a longer duration can be maintained.

• Anthracite logs have a heating value greater than wood.

• Storage area for anthracite coal is less than that required for the amount of wood needed to get a comparable heat equivalency.

MANUFACTURING PROCESS

Manufacturing a coal log requires the following six steps:

1) crushing of coal to pass a 1/4 inch screen;
2) crushing or melting of the binding material;
3) drying or preheating of coal to remove excessive moisture;
4) mixing and kneading together of coal and binding material;
5) pressing of the mixture;
6) cooling and storage of finished logs.

TECHNICAL CONSIDERATIONS

The biggest question relative to the manufacture of anthracite coal logs is determining a suitable binding material. Three types of industrial binders are presently being used in similar processes:

• Matrix (petroleum asphalt, water gas pitch, coal tar pitch)
• Film (water, starch, sodium silicate)
• Chemical (lime, clay, kaolin)

Matrix type binders, while suitable for outdoor storage, give off smoke and an objectionable odor when burned. Film type binders such as starch are generally weaker than matrix or chemical binders, generally do not stand up to bulk handling, and cannot be stored outdoors. Chemical binders are either a derivative of matrix or film binders and thus possess the inherent weaknesses of each.

Table I
Amount of Other Fuels Equivalent to a
Cord of Air-Dry Wood

A Cord of Air-Dry Wood equals		Tons of Coal	Gallons of Fuel Oil	Therms of Natural Gas	Kilowatt Hours of Electricity
Hickory, Hop Hornbeam (ironwood), Black Locust, White Oak, Apple	=	0.9	146	174	3800
Beech, Sugar Maple, Red Oak, Yellow Birch, White Ash	=	0.8	133	160	3500
Gray and Paper Birch, Black Walnut, Black Cherry, Red Maple, Tamarack (Larch), Pitch Pine	=	0.7	114	136	3000
American Elm, Black and Green Ash, Sweet Gum, Silver and Bigleaf Maple, Red Cedar, Red Pine	=	0.6	103	123	2700
Poplar, Cottonwood, Black Willow, Aspen, Butternut, Hemlock, Spruce	=	0.5	86	102	2200
Basswood, White Pine, Balsam Fir, White Cedar	=	0.4	73	87	1900

Assumptions...

Wood: 1 cord = 128 cubic feet of wood and air or 80 cubic feet of solid wood at 20% moisture content. Net or low heating value of one pound of dry wood is 7,950 Btu Efficiency of the burning unit is 50%.

Coal: Heating value is 12,500 Btu per pound. Efficiency of the burning unit is 60%.

Fuel Oil: Heating value is 138,000 Btu per gallon burned at an efficiency of 65%.

Natural Gas: One therm = 100,000 Btu = 100 cu. ft. Efficiency of burning is 75%.

Electricity: One KWH = 3,412 Btu Efficiency is 100%.

Source: "Burning Wood," the Northeast Regional Agricultural Engineering Service, Ithaca, New York. 1978.

Without conducting any laboratory tests, Ashton suggested using a mixed binder with a starch base. Ashton felt that the manufacturing process would make the coal log resistant to air and water, and thus outdoor storage would not be a problem.

However, Ashton did caution that the quality of the coal log and its combustion characteristics had not yet been evaluated under actual conditions in wood stoves.

RECOMMENDATIONS

Although Ashton concluded the manufacture of coal logs made with a smokeless binder was an economic proposition and presented no technical difficulties, he recommended to Ron and Bill that they fund further studies:

1) To determine the optimal technical specifications for the product;

2) To determine the performance characteristics of the coal log by laboratory testing;

3) To undertake a market study to determine the optimal size manufacturing plant.

The additional engineering studies (recommendations 1 and 2) would cost approximately $15,000. The market study would cost an additional $9,000.

Ashton felt that if all three studies commenced immediately, the coal logs could be ready for the 1979-80 winter heating season. He suggested that Ron and Bill take two to three weeks to think through the recommendations, but cautioned them that any delay beyond this would seriously jeopardize the introduction of the log for the coming heating season.

ASSIGNMENT QUESTIONS

1) What information is necessary before Williams and Shaw can make a go/no go decision?

2) Comment on their goal of introducing the coal log for 1981-82 winter heating season.

3) Do you agree with Professor Ashton's final recommendations? Would you advise Williams and Shaw to invest another $24,000 into additional engineering and market studies?

Exhibit 1

Energy Products
Preliminary Cost Estimates

Plant Capacity (in tons)	20,000	76,000
Direct Labor	$172,800	$172,800
Burden	51,840	51,840
Supervision	35,000	50,000
Coal Dust	680,000	2,584,000
Binder	88,000	334,000
Freight	300,000	1,140,000
Packaging	200,000	760,000
Supplies	2,000	7,600
Utilities — Electricity	10,000	38,000
Drying	8,000	30,400
Maintenance	15,000	20,000
Rent	18,000	18,000
Depreciation	32,000	42,000
Taxes and Insurance	7,533	20,666
General and Administrative	79,650	358,708
Marketing	130,000	494,000
Distribution	400,000	1,520,000
Return on Investment (pretax 40%	301,333	826,666
Total Cost	$2,531,156	$8,468,680
Cost/Ton	$126.55	$111.43

Exhibit 2

Price of wood = $80 per cord (15% moisture)

Weight per cord = 1.5 tons

Net calorific value of wood dry basis $\quad = 8500 - (.54)(1100)$
$$= 7906 \text{ Btu/lb}$$

Net calorific value of wood wet basis $\quad = (7906)(.85)$
$$= 6720 \text{ Btu/lb}$$

Net calorific value of wet anthracite $\quad = (12,750)(.9)$
$$= 11,475$$

Cost of wood capable of supplying
thermal energy available in one ton of coal $= \left(\dfrac{80}{1.5} \right)\left(\dfrac{11,475}{6,720} \right) = \$91.07$ say $91

ENERGY PRODUCTS (C)

In mid-July, Ron Williams and Bill Shaw decided to proceed with the market study as recommended by Professor Ashton. To his consternation, they did not proceed simultaneously with his two technical recommendations to 1) perfect the product composition and manufacturing process; and 2) test the coal log in wood stoves.

Ron and Bill reasoned that, since they could not afford to support all three activities, they had to choose the most crucial task. Professor Ashton had indicated that he anticipated no technical difficulties in developing a suitable binder. Ron and Bill both felt that the size of the market for this product was a major uncertainty and needed to be ascertained before they committed further limited funds to the technical development of the product.

MARKET STUDY

At the recommendation of Professor Ashton and after considering a Boston consulting firm, the two partners contracted in late August with a team of consultants, Professors Claire LaRossa and Edgar Price, at the local university for a market feasibility study for their new venture. Since they did not want to rule out market entry for the 1979-80 heating season and they had already lost considerable time, Ron and Bill insisted that the results of this study be presented no later than November 1. Although pressed for time, the consultants felt that it was possible to prepare their findings and recommendations in two months. After several discussions with Bill, Ron and Ashton, Professors LaRossa and Price proceeded with their investigation which they described as follows:

> "A product concept exists to manufacture and market coal
> logs for residential heating. The objective of this study is to
> determine the market feasibility for this new product."

While the main focus of the study would involve definition and measurement of the potential market, pricing, promotion, distribution channels, and competition from other products, all parties agreed that a much broader strategic emphasis was more important than just a narrow market study.

After consultation with Bill and Ron, Professors LaRossa and Price postulated the following initial marketing assumptions:

- Product's primary use will be as a supplemental home heating fuel.
- Product is a prime substitute for wood.
- Product will be used in wood burning stoves and fireplaces.
- Product will be competitively priced with wood.
- Prime market segments will be in areas of the country where wood burning is most popular.
- The technical composition of the product is anthracite coal with a starch binder (used for cost projection purposes).

Over the next two months, Professors LaRossa and Price began gathering and analyzing industry data.

INDUSTRY DATA

As a first step, data were gathered on the potential consumers of the coal log. Assuming that a means of burning the product was a prerequisite to purchase, they sought data on numbers of wood stoves, coal stoves, multi-fuel stoves, and fireplaces currently in use in the U.S. (See *Exhibit 1* for some preliminary data.)

From the 1978 edition of *Woodstove Directory*, over 450 U.S. retail dealers in wood stoves, coal stoves, and fireplace inserts were identified. The U.S. Department of Energy[1] estimates that 1 million households currently use wood as the primary heat source, while 3 million households currently use wood as a secondary heat source. Projections for 1985 indicate that 10-15 million households will be using wood as a primary or secondary heat source. These projections appeared consistent with the numbers of woodstoves being absorbed in the U.S. market:

- 100,000 units in 1974[2]
- 750,000 units in 1977[2]
- 600,000 units in 1978[3]

In addition, data relative to wood and coal use in home heating and cooking was compiled from the Bureau of the Census for 1976.[4]

---

[1] *An Assessment of Proposed Federal Tax Credits for Residential Wood-burning Stoves,* study conducted by Booz-Allen-Hamilton, Inc. for Department of Energy, September, 1979.

[2] *Forbes,* November, 1978.

[3] *Sales & Marketing Management,* February 5, 1979.

[4] Census Bureau - Current Housing Reports, Series H-150 General Housing Characteristics 1976.

Houses using	1970	1976
Wood as heating fuel	794,000	912,000
Coal or coke as heating fuel	1,821,000	484,000
Wood as cooking fuel	405,000	208,000
Coal or coke as cooking fuel	157,000	18,000
Total houses	74,005,000	63,448,000

The consultants found several newspapers and periodicals were publishing articles on the increased use of wood and coal stoves by Americans seeking an alternative to the rising cost of energy. *Exhibit 2* includes an example of the type of articles being printed.

A growing concern about the environmental effects of wood and coal burning was also being voiced. An article dealing with the pollution aspect is shown in *Exhibit 3*.

Based on their preliminary analysis, the consultants concluded that good statistical data on woodstove and fireplace market size and use was inconclusive and definitely needed to be updated.

PRICE

The price sensitivity of consumers for the coal log was deemed an important item by the consultants. They felt that for pricing purposes, the market could be divided into two distinct segments. People who burn wood as an economy measure would probably not pay more per BTU for a coal log. But, because of the product's uniqueness over wood, the consultants anticipated that the coal log could sell at a higher price than an equivalent amount of wood in those markets that value novelty, convenience, security. Table 2 shows the price sensitivity of coal logs relative to pure coal and wood estimated by LaRossa and Price.

The consultants recognized that the cost benefit of a higher heating value of the coal log would have to be fully explained to the consumer, perhaps by comparing the BTU's available in this product vs. a cord of wood.

As the present trend for increased demand pushes the price of cord wood upward, the price for the coal log becomes much more competitive with wood. Cord wood availability and hence price differ from region to region. For instance, in Boston a cord of hardwood sells for $150 to $200, when available. One Cambridge, Massachusetts dealer will only sell its wood in bundles in 12 pieces (at $3.95). In Northern New England, the price of cord wood has tripled since 1973 from $30 to $90.

COMPETING PRODUCTS

There are two classes of competing products for the coal log: traditional raw fuels and the new processed fuel products. The consultants identified several competing new processed fuel products currently on the market. Table 3 contains comparative information on specific brands of competing products identified during the study.

According to LaRossa and Price it appeared that none of these products have achieved any significant market penetration.

Table 4 compares the prices of competing products on a cost per million BTU basis. It is apparent that the traditional raw fuels are priced as commodities, while the new processed fuels are priced as specialty products.

PRELIMINARY OBSERVATIONS

At a pre-arranged October first meeting with Ron and Bill, the consultants reported their progress in gathering data on the market. The consultants indicated the market for this product appeared promising, but cautioned that without a product sample, their findings would be tentative at best. Bill and Ron accepted this qualification since they were not prepared to invest any more capital into this project. The consultants agreed to continue their market analysis and present a formal report to Bill and Ron on November first.

ASSIGNMENT QUESTION

What recommendations would you make to Williams and Shaw? Why?

Exhibit 1
Selected Industry Data

Table I-A

Unit Shipments (thousands) by Manufacturers							
	1972	1973	1974	1975	1976	1977	1978
woodstoves	160	210	340	760	670	1,030	1,150
wood fired boilers & furnaces	NA	NA	NA	NA	NA	50	50
fireplaces*	NA	NA	NA	460	450	600	950

*Note: category probably includes only manufactured or fabricated units (e.g., Heatalator). May include damper units.

Table I-B

Projections of Airtight Stove Sales (thousands)							
1978	1979	1980	1981	1982	1983	1984	1985
239	267	297	327	355	394	414	443

Table I-C

Privately Owned One-Family Houses Completed in U.S. with:							
	1973 %	1973	1974	1975	1976	1977	1977 %
No fireplace	56%	672	482	419	430	493	39%
One fireplace	39%	471	405	403	542	688	55%
Two fireplaces	5%	54	52	54	62	78	6%
Total	100%	1197	940	875	1034	1258	100%

Table II
Price Sensitivity Matrix

	$150	$150-$175	$175-$200	$200
Cord wood selling at				
Coal log selling at $118/ton	No*	Maybe**	Yes***	Yes

	$90	$90-$100	$100-$150	$150
A ton of coal selling at				
Coal log selling at $118/ton	No	No	No	Maybe

*"No" indicates the product advantages do not compensate for price differential.
**"Maybe" indicates the product advantages may compensate for price differential.
***"Yes" indicates the product advantages do compensate for price differential.

Table III
Competing Product Information

	Composition	Price	Price/ Million Btu	Weight/ Dimension	Btu/pound
Product A	Densified Wood	a. $2.55 (4 log cs.) b.$3.65 (8 log cs.)	$25.50 $18.25	3lb. log 3" x 10"	6250
Product B	Coal	NA	NA	5lb. log 3" x 12"	12000
Product C	Lignite Coal	a. 18¼ lb. pack $2.80-$4.25 depending on location. b. 55 lb. pack $7.40 - $9.75.	$18.70 $18.00	18¼ lb. size pack of 16 briquettes 6⅛" x 15⅜"	9325
Product D	Cannel Coal	a. 20lb. pack $2.70 - $4.15 b. $4.10 - $7.15 (50 lb. pack)	$10.10 $6.10		13280

Table IV
Price Comparison of Competing Products

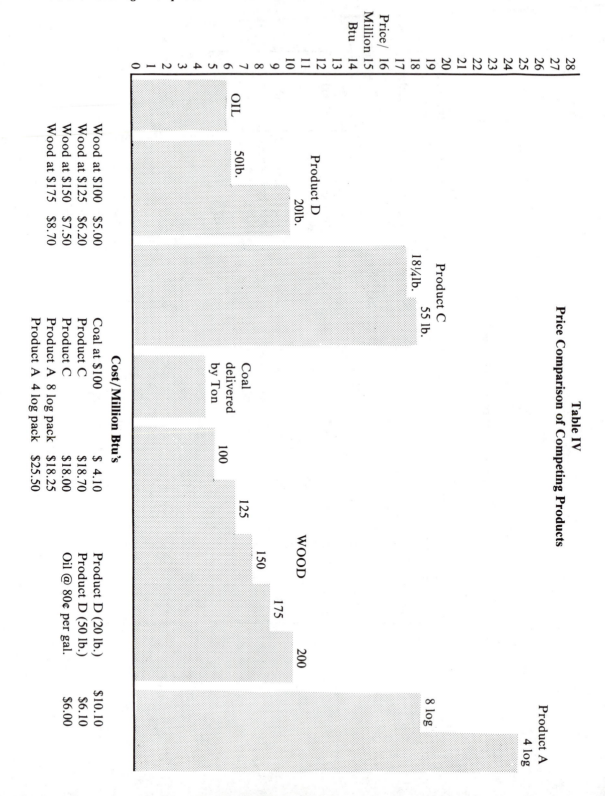

Price/
Million
Btu

28
27
26
25
24
23
22
21
20
19
18
17
16
15
14
13
12
11
10
9
8
7
6
5
4
3
2
1
0

OIL

Product D
50lb.
20lb.

Product C
18¼lb.
55 lb.

Coal
delivered
by Ton

100   125   150   175   200

WOOD

8 log

Product A
4 log

Cost/Million Btu's

Wood at $100	$5.00	Coal at $100	$ 4.10	Product D (20 lb.)	$10.10
Wood at $125	$6.20	Product C	$18.70	Product D (50 lb.)	$6.10
Wood at $150	$7.50	Product C	$18.00	Oil @ 80¢ per gal.	$6.00
Wood at $175	$8.70	Product A 8 log pack	$18.25		
		Product A 4 log pack	$25.50		

Exhibit 2

Hearth and home

Andrew Shapiro, president of the Wood Energy Institute in Camden, Me., ventured an "educated, not verified" guess last year that Americans had bought 750,000 wood-burning stoves in 1977 (FORBES, *Nov. 13, 1978*). That compared with fewer than 100,000 in 1974, one result of the Arab oil embargo and subsequent roaring surge in fuel prices. Americans, it seemed, were returning to the days of rural America, when most homes were heated—if at all—with wood.

Even enthusiasts like Shapiro, it turns out, were too modest. The U.S. Department of Energy commissioned Booz, Allen & Hamilton to generate some hard numbers to replace the industry's smoky statistics, and they are even more glowing than Andy Shapiro's guesses. (Not suprisingly, he agrees with them.) Combining a canvass of the army of stovemakers, federal reports and its own educated guesses, Booz, Allen told the DOE earlier this year that stove sales had passed the 1 million mark in 1977 and reached 1,150,000 in 1978.

The purpose of the DOE study was to determine whether burning wood would save enough on other fuels, particularly Arab-controlled oil, to justify giving tax credits to encourage use of the stoves of yesteryear. (The National Energy Act of 1978 did not specify stoves as eligible for credits but boosters on Capitol Hill insist that the Treasury already has at least an implicit power to grant them.)

The wood-burning cult apparently isn't waiting for tax credits (although stovemakers are praying for them as a sales booster). Carey Bohn, editor of the *Home Energy Digest & Woodburning Quarterly*, predicts stove sales of 1.5 million this year, primarily because of rising prices for heating oil. One million U.S. homes now use wood as a primary heat source, Bohn estimates, and another 3 million for supplementary heating. In chilly—and well-forested—states like New Hampshire, Vermont and Maine, the Institute's Shapiro says, surveys have shown that close to half of the homes burn wood and 20% rely entirely on it.

What of the future? David L. Hartman, who conducted the DOE study for Booz, Allen, ventures the personal opinion that sales of wood stoves will continue to be "strong but stable," probably between 1 million and 1.5 million a year. Part of the stability could come from the fact that wood-burners regard stoves more as part of their lifestyle than as a utility. *Blair & Ketchum's Country Journal*, a Vermont-based monthly, sampled its 200,000 subscribers and found that, among those with wood stoves, 88% said they would continue to use them even if dealers were giving away oil.

Stoves, of course, are only part of the wood-burning scene. The Booz, Allen report figured that home owners also had close to 1.5 million fireplaces, 650,000 of them the Christmas-card, built-in variety (which cost around $3,000), the same number of "zero clearance" types (inserted in a wall and costing $400 to $600, plus installation) and 150,000 freestanding fireplaces (running $250 to $500). And the Wood Energy Institute's Shapiro says the current hot item in the world of wood is the fireplace insert, a $250 to $750 glass- or steel-doored affair that turns a fireplace into a stove.

Exhibit 3

As Wood Fuel Gains For Heating Homes, So Does Pollution

* * *

Waterbury, Vt., Has Problem But Keeps On Using More 'Home-Grown Resources'

By LIZ ROMAN GALLESE

Staff Reporter of THE WALL STREET JOURNAL

WATERBURY, Vt.—At this time of year, this village of 2,500 is girding for the usual icy New England winter.

Storm windows and doors are mostly in place, and stacks of firewood lean against the neat frame houses. The stacks of wood are bigger than ever this year because the residents, who began reverting to firewood after the Arab oil embargo of 1973-74, have stepped up their wood burning with the ever-rising prices of fuel oil, which is the predominant home-heating fuel in New England.

Indeed, 17% of the homeowners in Waterbury consider wood to be their primary source of heat, according to data compiled by the state, and 40% heat at least partly with wood. Another 10% expect to turn to wood this season. The biggest institution and biggest employer in town is a state hospital —which burns wood.

Distinct Benefits

Reducing dependence on costly oil certainly has its benefits. William Anderson, a village trustee, is spending $300 this winter for a supply of logs that he split for fuel, whereas heating oil for the season would have cost about $1,500.

But wood also has a drawback, Waterbury is discovering: pollution. "Every time you open a stove, something comes out," Mr. Anderson laments. "A film forms on walls. Curtains and furniture get dirty."

Outdoors, it isn't any better. "You can see the clouds of smoke in the evenings," he says. As the smoke swirls from red-brick chimneys, a pungent odor fills the air.

Concern about wood-burning pollution is growing here and in many communities across the nation. But despite the recognition of the dangers, officials here and elsewhere believe that the high cost of oil and fears about its availability make the burning of more and more wood inevitable.

Scope of the Problem

Residential wood stoves "are like large, smoking cigarets," says John Cooper, a professor of the Oregon Graduate Center in Beaverton, Ore., who has studied the problem. "They are a significant source of air pollution."

Recent studies commissioned by the Environmental Protection Agency show that burning of wood emits far more particles suspected of causing cancer than burning of oil or natural gas and about as many particles as the burning of coal. Particles such as soot and ash also irritate the eyes and the nose. Moreover, burning of wood gives off far more carbon monoxide than the burning of oil or gas.

A lot of particles from wood fires make their way into the atmosphere, a study by Prof. Cooper showed. In a test of air quality on a winter day in Portland, Ore., 36% of the particles that could be inhaled came from wood burning, he says. That compares with about 5% to 10% from road dust, 8% from auto exhaust and 2% from oil burning. (Residents of the area don't burn coal.)

Students of wood energy explain that wood burns dirtier because it burns less efficiently. Only 80% of the material is converted in burning, compared with close to 100% of oil or gas. Much of the wood residue gathers in chimneys or blows out into the atmosphere.

This presents a particular problem for densely populated communities located in valleys, like Waterbury in the Green Mountains, because the warm polluted air can get trapped under a layer of colder air.

Lack of Regulation

"We're creating a tremendous monster," Mr. Cooper says. "We're encouraging the use of wood without knowing its impact on the environment."

Studies of pollution from wood burning are preliminary. But even stove makers see problems. "Stoves leave a lot to be desired" environmentally, says Duncan Syme, a vice president of Vermont Castings Inc., based in Randolph. "Sure, they don't pollute if you live alone on the North Pole."

The problem grows as more people burn wood for heat. About 1.2 million stoves will be sold this season, up eightfold from the 150,000 in 1973, prior to the Arab oil embargo, according to Wood Energy Resource Corp., a Camden, Maine, consulting firm. In northern New England, the region most committed, about 60% of the households now heat at least partly with wood, and 20% of those primarily use wood, up from 15% partial users and 2% primary users in 1973, the firm says.

Residential wood stoves, unlike commercial and industrial boilers of all types, aren't subject to state and federal pollution controls. A few communities have begun to crack down. In Missoula, Mont., the city-county health department requests that residents stop burning wood on days when air pollution reaches a certain level. Vail, Colo., forbids more than one wood or coal furnace or fireplace in new homes—but wood stoves are exempted. And the Tennessee Valley Authority which provides interest-free loans for stoves, recently ruled out loans to residents of areas that don't meet federal air-pollution standards.

But putting controls on existing stoves could be next to impossible. "How can you have control legally or mechanically over each person's stove?" says Tim Glidden, assistant program director of the resource policy center at Dartmouth College in Hanover, N. H. John Milliken, a project officer of the EPA unit studying pollution, says, "Can you imagine a Congressman proposing a ban on wood stoves" at a time when so many are turning to wood?

Probably no other state has as much potential for the pollution as Vermont, because it is burning so much wood. Heavily dependent on foreign oil and having little natural gas available as an alternative, the state is vulnerable to the soaring prices and dwindling supplies of oil. Almost two-thirds of the state's homes now use wood for at least some of their heat.

State officials, moreover, have been encouraging the use of wood by providing cut-rate prices on wood from state forests and turning to wood in some state facilities. Brendan Whittaker, secretary of the state's Agency of Environmental Conservation, says, "For Vermonters, wood is a declaration of independence. Wood is our oil. It is our home-grown resource."

But concern persists in such towns as Waterbury, which in fact is the subject of a study by the conservation agency. A test early this year showed that the number of particles in the air was far short of violating federal clean-air standards but high enough to prompt further study, especially because wood burning may be Waterbury's chief source of pollution. State officials currently are studying more air samples and measuring emissions from home chimneys.

For their part, residents of Waterbury know that pollution is a problem. Robert Winchell, village manager, says, "In early morning, the fog in the valley holds down the pollution so it can't drift away."

Edward Eldredge, a volunteer fireman who provides free chimney-cleaning services to residents, says dirty chimneys helped cause five chimney fires last year. "Requests for chimney-cleaning services are coming in so fast that we don't know if we can keep up with them," he says.

Emissions From Hospital

State officials also point out that the type of wood-burning industrial boiler that heats the state hospital in Waterbury emits four times as many particles as an oil boiler would, despite mechanical controls that filter out most of them before they hit the air. (Conversely, however, the wood-fired boiler emits far less sulfur dioxide than an oil-fired boiler, officials say.)

Although they recognize the problem, residents of Waterbury adamantly oppose controls on wood-burning stoves. Citing his large cost saving on switching to wood from oil, Mr. Anderson, the village trustee, says, "I'd rather pollute and live with the consequences." He adds, "My grandmother sat next to a wood stove for years, and she lived to be 84."

Patty Deal, a new homeowner, says, "What confuses me is that years ago, everyone heated with wood. Is there something different about it now?"

Environmental Outlook

Vermont has dealt sternly with environmental-type problems in the past: banning billboards, outlawing non-returnable bottles, passing a tough land-use law to discourage development. But, says Mr. Whittaker, the state conservation official, imposing wood-burning controls "would be a sticky wicket." He adds, "It's damned cold here, and we've got wood to burn. Anyone who talked about banning stoves would be crazy. You'd have a revolution."

Even environmentalists recognize the dilemma. "Environmentally, we're in an era when we can't have our cake and eat it, too," says Seward Weber, executive director of the Vermont Natural Resources Council, a leading environmental group in the state. "We have to accept trade-offs for energy." Besides, he adds, "It's tough to ban stoves when every damn household has one."

Offering some hope, officials say, is a new type of wood-burning furnace to replace oil burners. The "stick-wood furnace," as it is called by its developer, Richard Hill, a professor at the University of Maine, is currently being made by three firms. The furnace burns far more efficiently and cleanly than wood stoves, but, of course, it costs far more, too: $2,000 plus installation, against $350 to $800 for the stoves.

Reprinted with permission, *Wall Street Journal*, November 1979.

THE HONEY BEE BANKRUPTCY AUCTION

James Martin paced the floor of a small office at Honey Bee, Inc., an old and respected company in the juvenile products business, or at least it had been until the last few months. In a few minutes he would know what course his future would take. In late January 1979, Honey Bee had been forced into involuntary bankruptcy. Today, March 19, 1979, the bankruptcy auction had been held and Jim had submitted a bid for the entire company. Despite the sound advice given him by advisors and friends, the 32-year old CPA and MBA had been unprepared for the fierce bidding war just waged by over 400 competitors. If he were the successful bidder, Jim reflected, his entrepreneurial career would truly have been launched in the trenches of auction warfare.

EARLY BACKGROUND

James Martin was born in South Boston in 1947, one of several children in a close-knit, hard working family. Both parents encouraged Jim and his brother to get a good education including professional school beyond college, a privilege neither parent had ever enjoyed.

As a teenager, Jim worked part-time at Sears Roebuck where he began to demonstrate a dynamic and personable approach to business which was quickly recognized by both his peers and his superiors. He was also recognized by Miss Sheila Howland as "someone I would like to know better." She did, and Jim and Sheila were married in 1970, the same year Jim finished his undergraduate studies in accounting at Northeastern University in Boston.

While at Northeastern, Jim had met an older man who was to profoundly affect his future career, Milton DeVane. DeVane was a Harvard Law School graduate and a successful Boston lawyer. Mr. DeVane and his wife were childless, and perhaps because of this DeVane had developed a deep and continuing interest in helping promising young men to launch their business careers. Mrs. DeVane was a relative of Jim's and the DeVanes soon treated Jim like an adopted son. In addition to friendship and advice, Milton introduced Jim to a number of people in Boston's financial community, and in 1970--the year Jim graduated and was married--DeVane invited him to become a board member of a respected charity which he had served as a board member for many years: Children in Crisis, established to reach out to pre-teen youths who already had run up against the law.

THE 1970-1976 PERIOD

After graduation, Jim went to work for the accounting firm of Coopers and Lybrand. In 1971, he and Sheila had twins, and in 1973 they moved to Quincy, near South Boston, to be nearer to both sets of parents who still lived and worked in the area. Sheila Martin recalled this period, up to 1974, as especially lonely and difficult for her. Jim worked late hours, all four parents were away during the day, the Martins had only one car, and Sheila felt trapped at home with two babies. Though Jim performed brilliantly, he did not feel excited about a future as an accountant. These pressures and conflicts made the happy family life Jim and Sheila had hoped for difficult to achieve.

In 1974, Milton DeVane's guidance and personal recommendation led to Jim's application and acceptance at the Harvard Business School. The decision to apply was very much a last-minute one, since Jim had considered it an unaffordable luxury. But his acceptance was a cause for family rejoicing. For Jim's parents, it was the answer to their prayers.

To ease the financial burden of his education, Jim worked part-time in Milton DeVane's office doing consulting, financial planning, and preparing tax returns. It was through a mutual friend in his office that Jim, in his first year at the Business School, met Robert Dayton, a recent HBS graduate with a reputation as an effective promoter and entrepreneur with a marketing flair. The mutual friend was convinced that a Martin-Dayton team would be quite a combination.

He was correct; both the chemistry and the timing were right. Dayton needed a partner with financial expertise and business acumen to complement his marketing and promotional skills. When they first met, Dayton--in addition to his full-time executive position at Child Products Inc. (CPI)--was in the process of launching a venture with his then-partner, Brett Williams. Both Dayton and Williams had been very impressed with a product they had spotted at a European juvenile products show, a "Continental Stroller." It was a hot selling item in Europe mainly because it had a unique, easy-to-use construction that required no assembly by the customer. The Continental Stroller simply had to be pulled from the box and it was ready to use. Yet, because it was collapsible, the stroller required much less space for storage by both retailers and customers. Higher priced, the Continental Stroller appealed particularly to the high end of the stroller market, parents who were interested in "fashion goods" for their children. The stroller was manufactured in France by Capricorn Industries, a conglomerate which led that country in production of juvenile products. Williams and Dayton saw an opportunity to manufacture and distribute a version of the Continental Stroller in the U.S. (see Figure A)

Soon after their return, Dayton opened negotiations with a manufacturing acquaintance in Pittsburgh, Mr. Dino Carbone. The latter ran an injection molding business, Davis Plastics, which was a subsidiary of Tri-State Products. Mr. Carbone had built the sales of Davis Plastics to $12 million in four years, and assured Dayton that he had adequate capacity to produce 200 strollers a day.

During the negotiations, however, Dayton and Williams had an irrevocable falling out. Understandably, because of the great rapport that had developed between Jim Martin and Bob Dayton, it was not difficult for Dayton to sell Jim on participating in the venture to fill the void left by Williams' departure.

Both Sheila and Jim Martin were quite excited about this opportunity, considering their personal circumstances at the time. Bob and Jim decided to break down the operations of the new company along functional lines. Bob assumed responsibility for marketing, Dino took manufacturing, and Jim would have financial responsibility. The logistics, however, of implementing this venture when the principals were hundreds of miles apart and involved in other activities, presented some complications. Jim was still in school and still working in DeVane's office. Dayton was still an employee of CPI.

Sheila Martin remembered how hopeful they had been, but how she had become increasingly concerned about the wear and tear on Jim. The situation at home became incresingly chaotic when their third child was born. In addition, the venture was not progressing. Sheila related:

> There was a lot of activity with Bob but nothing was happening. He attempted to reassure Jim, telling him, "Just let me get started and I'll quit CPI." Jim was totally committed but Bob was not risking anything. He came from a family with money.

Sheila was truly concerned. She felt Jim might be in over his head and that he needed her more than ever. Jim was beginning to get disillusioned as well, and one Sunday before the start of his second year at the business school, he arranged to meet with Dayton. The future of the venture seemed to lie in Dayton's hands, but by the end of the meeting nothing had changed.

THE 1976-1978 PERIOD

After graduating from the business school in 1976, Jim almost decided to go with a large insurance company. Sheila realized that Jim was doing this for her -- that this wasn't his thing. After agonizing over his future, he reluctantly committed to sticking it out with Dayton. Although Sheila had some doubts about Bob Dayton, that maybe he was a phony or a con artist, she deferred to Jim's business judgment, to which she confessed some degree of awe. Despite his commitment to continue his association with Bob, the Martins and Daytons were not personal friends. According to Sheila, Bob Dayton did not like kids.

In the midst of these doubts and concerns, it became apparent that Carbone's company was in trouble. His deal with Dayton and Martin seriously compromised his subsidiary relationship with Tri-State Products. The deal, plus the high cost of the business, contributed to its bankruptcy in 1976 despite numerous trips to Pittsburgh on Jim's part to help Davis Plastics. According to Sheila, Jim felt very guilty for getting Mr. Carbone in over his head.

At the time, Martin and Dayton agreed to be partners in the stroller venture, they created a company called The Belmont Corporation. Although they agreed to be partners, no formal agreement was ever consummated that anticipated a potential split-up, separation, or buy-out. Unfortunately, their short-lived partnership was not without strain or conflict. Much to Jim's dismay and strong opposition, Dayton also became involved with an acquisition deal in Grand Rapids. According to Jim, Dayton negotiated a deal with the 77-year old owner of the Diamond Children's Products Company for a twenty-year payout of Diamond's earnings. Dayton could sell anything, Jim ruefully remembered. "My vehement opposition to the deal hinged on the fact that, with margins of 13-15%, there was little room to maneuver in a competitive business such as this, especially where the products could be made more cheaply in Taiwan."

In the spring of 1977, Jim and Bob decided to terminate their partnership. Bob Dayton admitted that Belmont Corporation was worth nothing and agreed to "walk away," leaving Jim with the company and a $25,000 note for Davis Plastics. Parting company was not a happy affair. Bad feelings spilled over from the Davis fiasco when Dayton charged that Jim had failed to assume responsibility. Finally, Jim and Dayton agreed to disagree, according to Sheila Martin, who was thoroughly disgusted with the entire relationship. The two young men went their separate ways. The Martins vividly recalled Dayton's final prophetic admonition to Jim: "Let's see which one of us is Roebuck."

Now, Jim had to do something about the $25,000 note for Davis Plastics. Following the advice of DeVane and others, he let Davis Products go bankrupt and then bought the assets form the bank. However, before the bank would grant title, Jim had to sign over the mortgage on his house. Milton DeVane also guaranteed the note.

Faced with significant interest and principal payments, Jim found himself rolling over the note every month. Liquidating for $25,000 was impossible. Jim ended with both assets: some inventory of for the "U.S. version" of the Continental Stroller and the $25,000 note for Davis.

Jim decided there was only one way to make the venture work and that was to go to Europe to see the people who made the Continental: Capricorn Industries. Jim had telexed Capricorn Industries, outlining in advance his proposals including a 2% royalty, which he felt was integral to the deal. He was told to come and negotiate the deal in person. It was a desperate gamble for the Martins. Neither of them had ever been to Europe, nor had ever dealt with Europeans in either a social or business relationship. And neither could speak a foreign language. But Jim still had his American Express Gold Card, a perk from his days in public accounting. In Jim's words, this would likely be their last fling before the roof fell in. They were very excited as they boarded Freddie Laker's initial flight to London in 1978 for the first vacation of their eight-year marriage.

When Jim and Sheila arrived at the Capricorn facility, they were met by Jean Sertot, one of Capricorn's top executives. However, he seemed totally unaware of what was going on and barely spoke English. Jim mistakenly assumed that Sertot was the inventor of the stroller; Sertot turned a deaf ear to any mention of negotiating. Jim felt that he was being stonewalled by Sertot and desperately wanted to plow through the small talk. But

Mr. Sertot was moving slowly and they literally walked through the day. Nothing was happening and the Martins could feel their anxiety rising with each passing hour.

In what was, according to Jim, an incredible stroke of luck, the Chairman of Capricorn Industries just happened to be in the factory that day. James Martin met Georges Deveraux and a rapport between the young American and the elderly Frenchman was instantaneous. Mr. Deveraux invited the Martins to his home in Brussels that very day. Within hours, Sheila and Jim found themselves being whisked to Brussels in Deveraux' Cadillac limousine. A maid greeted them at the door of the Deveraux mansion on Franklin Roosevelt Boulevard (Brussels' Embassy Row) and escorted them through an elegant hallway and into a magnificently decorated living room. This was hardly the kind of reception the Martins could ever had imagined when they boarded their flight to London two days earlier. Sheila Martin later said, "I literally had to pinch myself to make sure it was all happening."

As the conversation developed, Mr. Deveraux said he would like to have his son, Phillippe, meet Jim. Phillippe, whom Jim described as a young man in his early twenties, was one of three business students in his school in Brussels. He spoke little English but was capable of reading busines texts that were written in English. Mr. Deveraux' ambition for Phillippe was that he go to business school in the United States, preferably the Harvard Business School. Deveraux' position in the world of European business, as the head of an important conglomerate and the likely role Phillippe would assume in that scheme, necessitated the greater educational exposure, depth and contacts that a business school education in the United States implied. Mr. Deveraux discussed his concerns and ambitions at great length with Jim, at least as much as the language barrier would allow.

After several days in Brussels, Jim recalled, with some satisfaction, Georges Deveraux' assessment of him: "You have nothing behind you. I'm impressed by your incredible persistence. Your ideas are right on target." Georges also admired the fact that Jim was not a "straight-laced" individual. Georges confided in Jim that he had had some unpleasant dealings with Robert Dayton. Apparently, Mr. Dayton had tried to sell Davis Plastics (without Jim's knowledge) to Capricorn Industries when Davis was heading for bankruptcy. Georges said he did not trust Mr. Dayton, and was suspicious of his motives, and refused to make any deal with him.

Before leaving Brussels, Jim Martin did make a deal with Mr. Deveraux. Actually, the deal would be a test where Jim would have the opportunity to prove himself. A ship's container of strollers would be sent to the United States to be sold by Jim. If successful, he would acquire the rights to manufacture and distribute Capricorn's Continental stroller in the United States, with the purchase of a $10,000 license agreement.

Jim later commented, "Georges never forgot what it was not to have money. He could relate to me. The fact that we later looked out for Phillippe and that he stayed at our home increased Georges' appreciation."

THE HONEY BEE CONNECTION

Shortly after Jim returned from Europe in spring 1978, he received a call from Mr. Jared Kane, the president of Honey Bee. Mr. Kane was interested in distributing the Continental Stroller, and Jim saw this as another stroke of luck. Honey Bee, founded by Jared's father, Nathaniel, in 1918, had grown to be an industry leader with more than 400 employees at one point in its history. While the number of employees had fallen over the years, Honey Bee was still one of the more important and better known juvenile products companies in the United States.

Consequently, Jim entered negotiations with Jared Kane, and they were actually in the final stages of negotiating a contract to sell 75,000 strollers, a $2 million deal, when a serious setback occurred; Honey Bee filed for bankruptcy under Chapter XI. Since Kane had never mentioned that the company was in financial difficulty, Jim was taken entirely by surprise. He stood by as the Creditors Committee agreed on May 8 to a 50% writeoff. He watched as the workforce was pared to a handful of people, and saw the once solid reputation of the industry's leading company become severely compromised.

During the summer and fall of 1978, Jim, with Deveraux' approval at every turn, proposed a series of deals involving both the stroller distributorship and an offer to buy part of the company itself. One by one, Kane turned them down. Jim's final proposal, also rejected, was an offer to buy a good part of Honey Bee and to give the company a two-year exclusive sales agreement on the 75,000 Continental Strollers. Perhaps, Jim reflected later, Kane was unrealistically buoyed by the fact that Honey Bee's net worth had increased on paper by $200,000 after the execution of the Creditors Agreement. Perhaps, there were other reasons he would never know.

At least Jim still had the deal on the strollers with Capricorn. He moved his inventory from Pittsburgh to a friend's warehouse in Westboro, MA, borrowing $2,500 to ship the goods. The friend who owned the warehouse allowed Jim to use half of it in return for help Jim had given him several years earlier to start a new venture. (Jim's friend was 17 when he started his venture and a 7th grade dropout. His business venture, which started with seed money of $1,000, succeeded and was doing $2 million a year with the latest balance sheet showing $100,000 in retained earnings.)

By now, the dynamics of Jim's relationship with Jared had altered considerably. Earlier, Jim felt that Jared had treated him condescendingly, snubbing him and Sheila at a recent trade show. Now the balance of his power had shifted; Jared was making overtures to Jim, even if he wasn't accepting offers. In yet another attempt to resolve the issue, Jim demanded an audit. He uncovered some interesting information at Honey Bee. For example, he found that the company was tampering with employee withholding, had $8,000 of unshipped accounts receivable, $150,000 of unposted accounts payable, plus accounts receivable not posted for six months.

Finally, Jim was truly shocked when he learned that Kane didn't own the five-story building that housed Honey Bee's operations. Jim would later tell Mr. Deveraux: "The rent paid since 1918 could have bought the building many times over."

Jim had access to the offices and during the course of his numerous visits began to make friends. Gradually he won the respect and confidence of the employees. During one of his visits, Jim learned that Jared had purchased a new Lincoln Continental. The resentment that this caused was very apparent...One day, Jim casually asked, "Is there anything else I should know about?" His question was not in vain. Jim discovered that Kane was negotiating with other companies. This did not sit too well with Jim whose business philosophy was very simple: "You're either with me or against me."

Jared's behavior did not surprise Sheila. Describing Jared, she said:

> Jared is an insecure man who got in over his head. He knew
> it and tried to hide it. He was very patronizing to Jim. Jared
> even felt that he had to advise Jim how to dress when he was
> invited to Jared's country club. Jared was a phony. Mrs.
> Kane was the brains of the family. She spoke for Jared, and
> she had to protect him even though she acknowledged that
> Jared did some underhanded things.

Sheila Martin felt bad for them. But as far as Jim was now concerned, Jared Kane had removed himself irrevocably from any future considerations by his maneuvering.

In order to protect himself, Jim decided to go to a leading Boston bank for advice on acquisitions. He asked for the "work out guy" who gets the bad ones. He was directed to Bill Allen. Allen, who handled all the loans, gave Jim an education on bankruptcies, and advised him to buy Honey Bee at auction.

Jim also sought out a lawyer at Cable, Canty & Stassen who spent full time on bankruptcies. He convinced Jim to prepare carefully because, "There's no honor among men when it comes to bankruptcy auction. There are so many side deals going on."

His next stop was the Commonwealth Credit Corporation who held most of the paper on Honey Bee. Jim's proposal was simple. "I will take you out today with free and clear title to the assets." Commonwealth declined. Going to auction now seemed inevitable.

Georges Deveraux arrived shortly therefter to visit Jim at his home. Georges also visited Jared and subsequently invited the Kanes to visit Deveraux in Brussels where they eventually spent a couple of days together. Through the grapevine, Jim later learned that Jared talked about everything but the business during his stay with Deveraux.

EARLY 1979

By late January 1979, Honey Bee had been closed down totally; it was no longer a going concern. Jim had been collecting all the information about Honey Bee that he could lay his hands on: a monthly sales analysis by product for 1978 (see *Exhibit 1*); an analysis of total monthly sales for the 1975-1978 period (see *Exhibit 2*). With the help of his brother and his brother's partner, both principals of very successful retail enterprises, Jim projected a set of *pro forma* statements for Honey Bee for 1979. This information was all sent to Phillippe Deveraux who translated his father's business correspondence (see *Exhibit 3*).

The date of Jim's letter, February 26, coincided with the date of the financial letter from the bank, confirming Honey Bee's involuntary bankruptcy and announcing its intention to proceed to auction unless another more satisfactory resolution could be achieved(see *Exhibit 4*).

On the following Monday, Jim met with his lawyers to discuss the auction process and his strategy. They explained that the auction was a three-step procedure. The first step required bids on the entirety; the second step required bids on groupings of equipment; and the third step required bids on individual pieces. For Jim to be successful, his single bid would have to be larger than bids for the sum of the individual pieces or the groupings of equipment.

As he left his attorney's office, Mr. Martin wondered if there was anything else he could do before the March auction.

ASSIGNMENT QUESTIONS

1. What should Mr. Martin do prior to the auction?

2. What should he do at the auction? Be very specific.

3. What is the cost structure and breakeven for Honey Bee if Mr. Martin takes over?

4. Assuming he acquires Honey Bee, what advice will you give him? What action steps should he take?

   a) for the short term?

   b) for the long term?

Figure A

The Continental Stroller

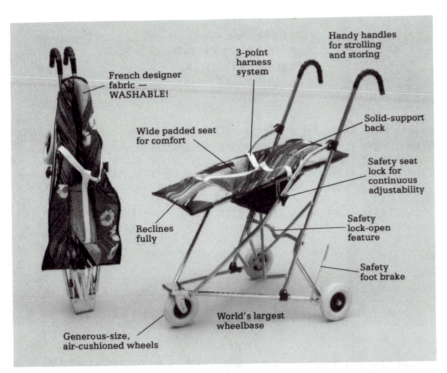

- Handy handles for strolling and storing
- 3-point harness system
- French designer fabric — WASHABLE!
- Wide padded seat for comfort
- Solid-support back
- Safety seat lock for continuous adjustability
- Reclines fully
- Safety lock-open feature
- Safety foot brake
- World's largest wheelbase
- Generous-size, air-cushioned wheels

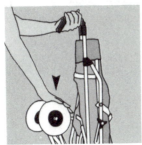

Holding handles, push rear wheels down.

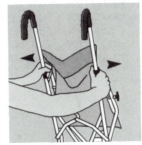

Pull frame open.

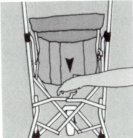

Lock firmly into place.

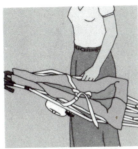

A snap to fold; lightweight.

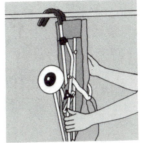

Hang where it's handiest for you.

Take it along! Easy to travel with.

Exhibit 1

Honey Bee, Inc.
Sales Analysis by Product
Year ended 12/31/78

Dollars

	Jan.	Feb.	Mar.	Apr.	May	June	July	Aug.	Sept.	Oct.	Nov.	Dec.	TOTAL
Mattresses	13,669	26,768	42,902	31,245	31,290	48,682	13,853	47,139	33,695	33,427	25,923	22,055	370,648
Pads	25,509	37,898	46,103	50,141	51,497	71,918	23,117	72,069	54,964	48,021	31,020	27,488	539,745
Car Seats	31,833	31,101	45,397	38,898	35,202	33,026	10,520	26,801	21,569	16,644	16,337	4,973	312,201
Scales	1,479	632	843	1,496	1,816	3,763	86	3,969	720	1,127	578	2,659	19,168
Potty Chairs	2,815	2,978	6,627	5,300	4,339	4,666	1,471	7,385	3,209	7,130	13,027	1,020	59,967
Walkers	2,852	2,915	9,301	11,115	13,070	7,335	9,236	9,995	14,060	8,833	5,519	4,450	98,681
Booster Chairs	1,964	3,302	8,691	10,147	7,387	6,645	5,639	7,673	6,456	2,528	6,818	4,782	72,032
Playpen-Vermont			7,718	14,391	15,602	2,976	554	730	6,514	1,245		527	50,257
Strollers-Capricorn						2,769		7,096	441	987	1,821	1,974	15,088
Playpen-Capricorn									4,861	941	804	412	7,018
Stroller Bag-Capricorn				1,515	1,815				15	14	900		4,259
	80,121	105,594	167,582	164,248	162,018	181,780	64,476	182,857	146,504	120,897	102,747	70,340	1,549,164

Units

	Jan.	Feb.	Mar.	Apr.	May	June	July	Aug.	Sept.	Oct.	Nov.	Dec.	TOTAL
Mattresses	1,263	2,453	4,538	2,960	2,771	4,402	1,479	4,307	3,248	3,050	2,563	1,958	34,992
Pads	6,990	9,852	12,432	14,082	13,621	19,399	6,847	18,655	14,771	11,912	8,100	7,118	143,779
Car Seats	2,022	1,982	2,761	2,118	1,850	1,668	623	1,301	1,150	858	903	269	17,451
Scales	201	84	116	197	242	491	60	922	164	223	412	356	3,468
Potty Chairs	488	498	1,176	891	725	800	253	1,270	548	1,228	1,943	171	9,991
Walkers	656	653	2,040	2,428	2,846	1,596	2,013	2,112	3,066	1,923	1,205	960	21,498
Booster Chairs	422	694	1,905	2,233	1,618	1,431	1,249	1,659	1,428	543	1,509	1,055	15,746
Playpen-Vermont			351	653	724	126	24	31	290	52		24	2,275
Strollers-Capricorn						113		287	18	40	70	79	607
Playpen-Capricorn									208	39	33	16	296
Stroller Bag-Capricorn				1,212	1,452				12	12	720		3,408

Exhibit 2

Honey Bee, Inc.
Analysis of Sales

	Orders				Shipments			
	1978	**1977**	**1976**	**1975**	**1978**	**1977**	**1976**	**1975**
January	80.5	166.3	133.5	197.7	80.1	168.9	105.7	88.0
February	115.7	210.2	136.9	169.8	105.3	161.3	134.4	150.5
March	210.1	210.0	209.5	183.8	168.1	242.9	192.5	151.4
April	190.7	203.4	171.2	201.1	164.3	200.0	185.0	223.1
May	136.0	202.8	114.7	205.1	162.4	178.6	170.8	211.9
June	93.0	168.0	132.9	118.1	64.8	72.1	69.8	107.2
July	97.1	122.5	113.2	118.0	64.8	72.1	69.8	107.2
August	138.5	157.0	136.5	144.9	185.5	182.0	140.3	144.7
September	128.7	135.4	126.0	140.1	150.3	134.0	132.6	171.5
October	116.3	173.1	109.5	137.6	125.0	126.5	122.4	153.4
November	86.1	126.5	100.3	101.3	105.7	150.1	120.2	98.3
December	62.5	180.1	162.5	87.9	70.3	165.7	80.9	68.4
	1455.2	2055.3	1646.7	1805.4	1563.3	1988.2	1600.8	1751.4

1979 Results

January Orders	113.9
January Shipments	48.5

Exhibit 3

THE HONEY BEE AUCTION

Letter to Phillippe Deveraux

From James Martin

February 26, 1979

Mr. Phillippe Deveraux
58 Franklin Roosevelt Avenue
Bruxelles 1050
BELGIUM

Dear Phillippe:

This has certainly been a learning experience for me. I can't get over the extent of the changes in the structure of the deal. Presently, Jared seems to have at last realized that we may be his only viable option open; yet, I am still not sure we can trust him. I will do my best to keep him in line. Today, the bank's attorney officially called default and now is in control of the assets. See attached letter. (Shown as *Exhibit 4*.)

Cable, Canty & Stassen will advise me on Monday or Tuesday on the specific strategy for bidding for the assets. The bank indicated a possible auction date of March 12, 1979. As of today, this is the position of Honey Bee, Inc.

Assets

Accounts Receivable - Actual	$83,000
Inventory - Guess	75,000
Fixed Assets (Fair Market Value $50,000++)	35,000
Total	$193,000

Liabilities

Bank Loan & Expenses of Bank - Guess	$110,000
Creditors Agreement - Actual	$138,000
Unsecured Creditors - Guess	100,000
Total	$348,000

I assumed a purchase price of $150,000 which, of course, will probably change. I further assumed an investment of $400,000 which, of course, is not a final figure. In this regard, I will defer to the judgment of our leaders on these important issues. I will need advice and counsel on the Belgium strategy of bidding.

I hope that this information will arrive on a timely basis for your review, but I am confident that we will have talked over the phone before this reaches you. I am very concerned that the more time passes, the greater the damage to Honey Bee and our ability to keep their customer base. I will talk with you about the marketing strategy which I feel will determine our eventual success or failure. In the meantime, I will immediately begin to market Capricorn separate from Honey Bee but there is considerable confusion over the Honey Bee issue in the marketplace. As you are aware, the buying season has already begun and Honey Bee has a sales backlog of $200,000. However, I feel we can only save $50,000 and even this assumes a quick and smooth closing.

My best regards to you and your family.

J. Martin

JM:cam

Enclosures

Honey Bee, Inc.
Pro-Forma Cash Flow & Balance Sheet Projections
1979
Exhibit 3A
(000's)

	Actual		PROJECTED									
	Jan.	Feb.	Mar.	April	May	June	July	Aug.	Sept.	Oct.	Nov.	Dec.
Beginning Cash			0	42.2	17.4	6.1	11.3	11.25	24.95	8.15	19.35	20.8
Add:												
Investment by Capricorn			400.0									
Bank Loan Proceeds				100.0	50.0	50.0			25.0			
Collection of Old Accounts Receivable			25.0	25.0								
Inventory Reduction												
Accounts Receivable Collections					100.0	150.0	200.0	225.0	150.0	200.0	200.0	175.0
Total			425.0	125.0	150.0	200.0	200.0	225.0	175.0	200.0	200.0	175.0
Deduct:												
Purchase of Equipment			25.0	25.0								
Increase in Inventory			150.0									
Purchase of Honey Bee Assets			150.0									
Bank Revolving Loan		CLOSED BY BANK						50.0				
C.G.S. – Material				56.0	84.0	112.0	125.0	84.0	112.0	112.0	98.0	98.0
– Labor			19.2	25.2	31.2	34.2	25.2	31.2	31.2	28.2	28.2	33.2
– Other			14.0	14.0	14.0	14.0	14.0	14.0	14.0	14.0	14.0	14.0
S.G.&A. – Salaries			14.6	14.6	14.6	14.6	14.6	14.6	14.6	14.6	14.6	14.6
– Commissions				5.0	7.5	10.0	11.25	7.5	10.0	10.0	8.75	8.75
– Other			10.0	10.0	10.0	10.0	10.0	10.0	10.0	10.0	10.0	10.0
Total			382.8	149.8	161.3	194.8	200.05	211.3	191.8	188.8	198.55	178.55
Current Assets:												
Ending Cash	.6		42.2	17.4	6.1	11.3	11.25	24.95	8.15	19.35	20.8	17.25
Inventory	113.6		200.0	200.0	200.0	200.0	200.0	200.0	200.0	200.0	200.0	200.0
Accounts Receivable	104.9		125.0	250.0	350.0	425.0	375.0	350.0	400.0	375.0	350.0	350.0
Other	17.4											
Total Current Assets	236.6		367.2	467.4	556.1	636.3	586.25	574.95	608.15	594.35	570.8	567.25
Other Assets	17.2											
Fixed Assets — Net	37.0		73.0	96.0	94.0	92.0	90.0	88.0	86.0	84.0	82.0	80.0
Total Assets	290.9		440.2	563.4	650.1	728.3	676.25	662.95	694.15	678.35	652.8	647.25

Current Liabilities:

Note Payable — Equipment	12.0										
Note Payable — Secured, Revolv.	88.7		100.0	150.0	200.0	200.0	150.0	175.0	175.0	150.0	150.0
Creditors Agreement	69.7										
Accounts Payable	84.0	61.0	91.5	122.0	136.25	91.5	122.0	122.0	106.75	106.75	96.25
Accrued Expenses	40.4										
Total current liabilities	294.9	61.0	191.5	272.0	336.25	291.5	272.0	297.0	281.75	256.75	246.25
Note Payable — Equipment	29.0										
Creditors Agreement	68.2										
Net Equity	(101.3)	379.2	371.9	378.1	392.05	384.75	390.95	397.15	396.6	396.06	401.0
Total Liab. & Equity	290.9	440.2	563.4	650.1	728.3	676.25	662.95	694.15	678.35	652.8	647.25
Working Capital	(58.3)	306.2	275.9	224.1	300.05	294.75	302.95	311.15	312.6	314.06	321.0

Exhibit 3B
Honey Bee, Inc.
Pro-Forma Projections — Monthly Income Statement
Year Ending December 31, 1979
(000's)

	March	April	May	June	July	Aug.	Sept.	Oct.	Nov.	Dec.	Total
Net Sales	100.0	150.0	200.0	225.0	150.0	200.0	200.0	175.0	175.0	175.0	1,750.0
Cost of Goods Sold	91.2	125.2	159.2	175.2	125.2	159.2	159.2	142.2	142.2	137.2	1,416.0
Gross Margin	8.8	24.8	40.8	49.8	24.8	40.8	40.8	32.8	32.8	37.8	334.0
Selling, General, and Administration	29.6	32.1	34.6	35.85	32.1	34.6	34.6	33.35	33.35	32.85	333.0
Operating Income/(Loss)	(20.8)	(7.3)	6.2	13.95	(7.3)	6.2	6.2	(.55)	(.55)	4.95	1.0
Cost of Goods Sold											
Material	56.0	84.0	112.0	125.0	84.0	112.0	112.0	98.0	98.0	88.0	969.0
Direct Labor	12.0	18.0	24.0	27.0	18.0	24.0	24.0	21.0	21.0	26.0	215.0
Final Expenses	14.0	14.0	14.0	14.0	14.0	14.0	14.0	14.0	14.0	14.0	140.0
Fixed Payroll	7.2	7.2	7.2	7.2	7.2	7.2	7.2	7.2	7.2	7.2	72.0
Depreciation	2.0	2.0	2.0	2.0	2.0	2.0	2.0	2.0	2.0	2.0	20.0
Total	91.2	125.2	159.2	175.2	125.2	159.2	159.2	142.2	142.2	137.2	1,416.0
Selling, General, and Administration											
Payroll — Administrative	7.2	7.2	7.2	7.2	7.2	7.2	7.2	7.2	7.2	7.2	72.0
Payroll — Marketing	7.4	7.4	7.4	7.4	7.4	7.4	7.4	7.4	7.4	7.4	74.0
Fixed Expenses	10.0	10.0	10.0	10.0	10.0	10.0	10.0	10.0	10.0	10.0	100.0
Commissions	5.0	7.5	10.0	11.25	7.5	10.0	10.0	8.75	8.75	8.25	87.0
Interest											
Total	29.6	32.1	34.6	35.85	32.1	34.6	34.6	33.35	33.35	32.85	333.0

Exhibit 4

THE HONEY BEE AUCTION

Letter to Honey Bee Creditors

From Bank's Attorneys and Counsellors-at-Law

February 26, 1979

To the Creditors of

HONEY BEE, INC.

As I previously advised, Honey Bee, Inc. has ceased operations. The principals of the company are attempting to find a buyer for all assets of the corporation, which presumably would yield a higher dollar return than the public auction sale. Since there are ongoing expenses, the finance company is making arrangements for a public auction sale, probably during the week of March 17th.

The prospects for a dividend for Trust Mortgage creditors diminishes with each passing day. If any creditor knows of any potential purchaser, I urge you to have them contact me.

I shall keep you informed of all progress.

Very truly yours,

Trust Mortgage

MERRILL ENTERPRISES, INC.:

A New Business Plan Proposal

In early August, 1977, David Merrill was waiting anxiously for the start of his meeting with the Capital Venture Group. He thought the next few hours would be crucial and could have a pronounced impact on his life. He expected that his meeting with the Group's four senior partners would be intense. But he believed he had done his homework. He had presented them with a comprehensive business plan, every detail of which he was familiar with. Let them fire away, he thought. He was ready for them.

THE BUSINESS PLAN

David Merrill's business plan had been prepared by him in collaboration with a private consultant, John Haskell Associates, Inc. The document began with a statement of purpose, followed by a table of contents. (Parts I and II of Mr. Merrill's business plan are reproduced in their entirety, along with selections from Part III. The original plan was 51 pages long.)

Table of Contents

*Not Included

STATEMENT OF PURPOSE

Merrill Enterprises, Inc., is seeking capital of approximately $400,000 to purchase an existing Class B or Class C FM radio station in the United States.

The acquired FM station will have tangible and intangible assets whose market value will be approximately $1 million. Merrill Enterprises will make an equity investment of $10,000, which together with other equity and debt financing, will be sufficient cash reserves, and provide adequate working capital to expand an existing market share in listeners and advertising revenues. These funds will finance the transition through an expansion phase which will allow the station to operate as an ongoing, highly profitable business entity.

PART I: THE BUSINESS

BUSINESS STRATEGY

The overall strategy of Merrill Enterprises is to identify and acquire an FM station that has the potential to be a first-class technical facility and does not compete directly with one or more stations owned by the large conglomerates that control a dominant share of the market.

Only stations that satisfy these two conditions will be possible acquisition candidates.*
The rationale for this acquisition policy is that billings (and ultimately profitability) are a
function of listenership and ratings which, in turn, are functions partly of coverage and
the ability of a station to be heard relative to its competitors. Consequently, a powerful
technical facility is a necessary condition of future growth in any given market.

For various reasons, an acquisition candidate may not have realized its full technical
and marketing capability. Merrill Enterprises will identify such stations and the changes
required to realize full potential. Upon successful acquisition, Merrill Enterprises will
implement these changes.

The market needed to sustain a technically powerful station must be a relatively large
one in order to achieve high profitability. However, the particular market cannot be
dominated by one (or a few) station(s) with access to substantial capital and managerial
resources. Capturing market share from such a competitor will prove to be both difficult
and risky as a long-term strategy.

KEY OBJECTIVES AND POLICIES

The key corporate objectives are to acquire and operate an FM station in the second
50's markets** which has the potential to produce:

1) Sales of approximately $2 million in five years (15% growth rate);

2) Operating profits of 50% of net revenues within five years of acquisition;

3) Profit before taxes of 15% of net revenues within five years of acquisition.

The principal policies are:

1. Acquisition Policy

Only stations with upside potential from technical and marketing changes will be
considered. Given available financial resources and future objectives, FM stations with
annual billings of approximately $400,000 to $500,000 will be possible candidates. At an
industry multiple of 2 to 2 1/2 times sales, the price range will be approximately $800,000
to $1,250,000 for an FM station with these billings.

---

*The acquisition candidates may also include: 1) stations that have both AM/FM
licenses and are being sold as a package; 2) AM stations that have a Construction Permit
to establish an FM station.

**Market size is determined by ratings of the American Research Bureau, on the basis of
net weekly circulation for the most recent year. The selling prices of FM stations in the
first 50's markets will be beyond our purchase capability.

2. Marketing Policy

Our marketing policy is to identify the market segments and programming which provides the optimum coverage given the geographic scope of our radio signal.

This policy may seem overly general to individuals who are unfamiliar with the radio broadcasting business. Nevertheless, the general nature of this policy is its strength in that it recognizes the unique situations of most radio stations. It is flexible in spirit and recognizes that pat marketing formulas generally do not work when applied "across the board."

3. Technical Facility Policy

Our policy is to create and maintain the best technical FM facility in terms of coverage and ability to be heard relative to local competition. This policy requires the acquisition of a Class B or Class C station.

NOTE: The FCC grants commercial licenses to three types of FM stations. Class A stations are licensed throughout the United States. However, they are low powered with a maximum of 3Kw of power. Both Class B and Class C stations are licensed in non-competing sections of the United States and have considerably higher power capabilities which provide them with a competititve edge.

4. Financial Policy

Our principal financial policy is to limit debt financing within acceptable boundaries to provide:

1) adequate cash flow for operations; and,
2) above average returns for equity investors.

The present market for FM stations is one which requires a buyer to have established lines of equity capital *before* entering negotiations for a specific site. FM stations with potential do not remain long enough on the market; consequently, prospective buyers must be capable of entering meaningful negotiations quickly and from a position of financial strength when an opportunity presents itself.

KEY SKILLS AND RESOURCES

Like prime beachfront property, a quality broadcasting property is a scarce commodity. One reason they are scarce is because the FCC limits the supply of all broadcasting stations. But within the existing supply of stations, the acquisition of a station with a high-quality potential is also affected by the ability of potential owners to:

1) find and identify a property with upside potential;
2) negotiate a sale at a favorable price and terms;
3) seek FCC licensing approval in an efficient and effective manner;
4) identify and implement the steps needed to realize the station's full potential.

Merrill Enterprises has the expertise to successfully realize the above requirements.

The principal skills possessed by Merrill Enterprises are the skills, capabilities, and experience embodied in its president, Mr. David Merrill.

The track record of Mr. Merrill speaks for itself (see Personal Resume in Section III). He has demonstrated a strong management capability with the special ability to turn marginal FM stations into much improved performers. While he has had numerous successes in his 20-year career in the radio business, his current position as General Manager of one of the top 100 stations in the United States has demonstrated particularly that he can handle even the bleakest of situations and is capable of taking proper and decisive action when required.

Overall, Mr. Merrill brings together several skills not usually found in a single person in the radio broadcast business. He has an above average knowledge of the technical aspects of broadcasting. He is one of the best FM marketing managers in the United States. He has numerous contacts throughout the industry which will provide a source of acquisition candidates and management/technical personnel. He has a working knowledge of FCC regulations and an established relationship with them. He has strong sales and sales management capability. Finally, he has developed the skills needed for general management.

Furthermore, Mr. Merrill is willing to relocate anywhere in the United States where a high potential FM radio station is discovered and acquired.

MANAGEMENT AND PERSONNEL

Mr. Merrill will be president and general manager of the acquired station.

Prior to takeover, he will staff the station with the best available personnel.

PERSONAL OBJECTIVES OF MR. DAVID MERRILL

Mr. Merrill's personal objectives are:

1) to apply his management experience and expertise in the FM radio business;
2) to obtain a majority equity position in an FM radio station in order to fully exercise his capabilities.

RELEVANT INDUSTRY TRENDS

A number of industry trends are emerging which are relevant to this investment proposal.

These trends include the following:

1) Several sources indicate that:

a) FM stations have performed well above average as a group, especially those stations employing a "beautiful music" format (see "FMs Continue to Show Strength in Latest Arbitron Sweep." Section III);

    b) FM stations have achieved their growth at the expense of AM radio stations (see "Cox Study." Section III).

    c) FM stations have achieved a position of strong positive cash flow which is expected to improve even further by 1981 ("Cox Study." Section III);

2) Market surveys indicates that radio listening habits are becoming more diverse. This trend suggests that creative marketing, including program definition, will become even more critical in the future. (See "Arbitron Radio Sweep Shows Listening Habits Diversifying." Section III).

3) The expectation is that independent FM stations in the top 125 markets will experience a sales growth of 25% - to - 30% in 1977. (See "Doherty Memo." Section III).

Excerpts from an FCC publication, "The Nature of American Broadcasting" present other trends relevant to this proposal. It is included in Section III.

PART II: FINANCIAL DATA

SOURCES AND APPLICATIONS OF FUNDS

The likelihood is that the search process for an FM station will uncover two kinds of potential acquisitions.

One kind is the FM station that has a facility with appropriate technical capability in place. The second kind is a station that does not have the appropriate facility but, for example, possesses a Construction Permit to establish the required plant and equipment. Our assumption is that the asking price for the former facility will be considerably higher than the station requiring incremental capital investment. Consequently, the application of funds will differ for these two kinds of acquisitions.

Exhibit 1 shows a sources and applications statement assuming no incremental investment in plant and equipment.

Exhibit 2 presents a similar statement assuming additional plant and equipment are required to achieve FM Class B or C status.

Professional and ethical considerations will require Mr. Merrill to inform his present employers that he intends to actively seek an FM station for purchase. He will probably have to relinquish his present position at the time he announces his intentions.

However, Mr. Merrill estimates that it will require between six to twelve months to locate, negotiate a purchase, and obtain FCC approval for the transfer of ownership. During this interim period, Mr. Merrill requires a salary that will allow him to meet his existing financial commitments. This salary is figured at an annual rate of $45,000.

BALANCE SHEET, P&L'S, AND CASH FLOW

The following exhibits demonstrate the potential of Merrill Enterprises to generate cash and profits.

Exhibit 3 shows a simple, opening balance sheet.

Exhibit 4 and 5 present a balance sheet and income statement for a potential acquisition XYZ, which is an "average" operation according to industry statistics.

Exhibit 6 shows the effect of acquiring XYZ on the balance sheet of Merrill Enterprises.

Exhibit 7 presents the consequences of retiring XYZ's debit immediately after acquisition.

Exhibits 8-12 provide income statements, cash flows, and balance sheets for Merrill Enterprises after one year of operations.

Exhibit 13 provides a five-year projection of income. One major assumption is that the company attains its five-year goal of reducing operating expenses to 50% of sales. A second assumption is that a 25% growth in sales is realized in year three from marketing changes instituted by Mr. Merrill during the previous two years.

Exhibit 1
Sources and Applications of Cash
(No Incremental P&E)

Sources

Mr. David Merrill	$ 10,000
Venture Capital	400,000
Bank Loan	800,000
Total	$1,210,000

Applications

Purchase Stock of Station	$1,050,000
Working Capital	100,000
Reserve for Contingencies	15,000
Pre-purchase salary for Mr. Merrill	45,000
Total	$1,210,000

Exhibit 2
Sources and Applications of Cash
(Incremental P&E Investment)

Sources

Mr. David Merrill	$ 10,000
Venture Capital	400,000
Bank Loan	800,000
Total	$1,210,000

Applications

Purchase Stock of Station	$800,000
Plant, Equipment & Renovations	250,000
Working Capital	100,000
Reserve for Contingencies	15,000
Pre-purchase salary for Mr. Merrill	45,000
Total	$1,210,000

Exhibit 3

Balance Sheet for September 1, 1977

Cash (Equity)	$ 410,000	Lt. Debt	$ 800,000
Cash (Bank loan)	800,000	Equity	410,000
Total Assets	$1,210,000	Total Liabilities	$1,210,000

Exhibit 4
Balance Sheet for December 31, 1977
of Acquisition Company X Y Z

Assets		Liabilities	
Cash	$ 6,889	Accounts Payable	$41,667
Accounts Receivable	76,444	Notes Payable	13,050
Prepaids	2,640	Accrued Expense	14,711
Deferred Reciprocal Expense	9,775	Deferred Reciprocal Revenue	17,322
Total Current	$95,748	Total Current	$86,750
Net P&E	200,000	Net Long-Term Debt	86,286
Net Goodwill	103,527	Total Equity	226,239
Total Assets	399,275	Total Liabilities and Equities	399,275

NOTES ON EXHIBIT 4

The figures in Exhibit 4 are derived from the operations of an actual station that is considered a representative example.

Cash -- Cash balances are traditionally low in the radio business. The equivalent of about 5.7 days is assumed in this example.

A/R -- Projected at about 63 days. 435,000/360/(63) x 76444.

Deferred -- Reciprocal Expenses and Revenues are trade accounts where radio advertising time is exchanged for goods and services. They are projected conservatively to show a net liability.

P&E -- Plant and equipment. Estimated by Mr. Merrill.

Goodwill -- Estimated from private source.

Accounts Payable -- Projected at 35 days off sales since information was not available for "purchases" nor "cost of goods sold."

Notes Payable -- The current portion of long-tem debt.

Exhibit 5
Income Statement for December 31
of Acquisition Company X Y Z

Sales	435,000	100%
Agency Commissions	52,519	–12
Net Sales	382,481	88
Operating Expenses	304,993	–70
(includes Depreciation)		
Operating Income	77,487	18
Other Expenses	12,487	– 3
(interest, amortization)		
PBT	65,000	15
Taxes	19,700	– 5
Net Profit	45,300	10
Depreciation	12,900	+ 3
Approximate Cash Flow	58,200	13

Notes for Exhibits 4 and 5 on the following page.

NOTES FOR EXHIBIT 5

Agency commissions, operating expenses, other expense, taxes, and depreciation in Exhibit 5 are derived from the operations of an actual station that is considered a representative example.

These calculations are supported by the National Association of Broadcasters (NAB) data which show that the average pre-tax profit of FM stations with sales in the $500,000 range is 14-15% of sales (See NAB, Radio Financial Report, 1976, p. 76).

Exhibit 6
Balance Sheet for January, 1978
Merrill Enterprises, Inc.

(Buys Station XYZ for $1,050,000 with net tangible assets of $122,712.)

Cash	$166,889	A/P	$41,667
	6,889	N/P	13,050
Accounts Receivable	76,444	Accrued Expense	14,711
Prepaids	2,640	D.R.R.	17,322
D.R. Expense	9,775		
Total Current	$255,748	Total Current	$86,750
P&E	200,000	L.T. Debt	86,286
		L.T. Debt	800,000
Goodwill	927,288		
		Total Liabilities	973,036
		Equity	410,000
Total Assets	1,383,036		1,383,036

NOTES FOR EXHIBIT 6

Net tangible assets = 122,712 = (from Exhibit 4)
(95,748 + 200,000) minus (86,750 + 86,286)

Cash = 160,000 = (1,210,000 - 1,050,000) + $6889 from cash account of acquired company.

All other current assets and liabilities from acquisition company.

P&E = Plant and equipment - from Exhibit 4.

Goodwill = difference between selling price (1,050,000) and net tangible assets (122,712).

Exhibit 7
Balance Sheet for January 2, 1978
Merrill Enterprises, Inc.

Given excess working capital position, assume Note Payable and respective long-term debt are retired immediately.

Cash	$ 67,553	A/P	$ 41,667
A/R	76,444	Accrueds	14,711
Prepaids	2,640	D.R.R.	17,322
D.R. Exp.	9,775		
Total Current	156,412		73,700
P&E	200,000	L.T.D.	800,000
Goodwill	927,288	Equity	410,000
Total Assets	1,283,700		1,283,700

NOTES FOR EXHIBIT 7

Cash balance of $166,889 reduced by 13,050 + 86,750 to $76,553.

Exhibit 8
Income Statement for December 31, 1978
Merrill Enterprises

Sales (15% growth assumed)	$500	100%
Agency Commissions	60	12
Net Sales	440	88
Depreciation	20	4
Operating Expenses	305	61
Operating Income	115	
Interest	45	
Amortization	45	
Pre-Tax Profit	25	5
Tax	6	1
Profit After Tax	18	4
Depreciation & Amortization	65	13
Cash Flow	84	17

NOTES FOR EXHIBIT 8

This pro forma is actually quite conservative since it reflects no significant reduction of costs which Mr. Merrill states is usually possible when taking over most FM properties. For instance, it is not unusual to find a station that is overstaffed. Still, we have projected operating expenses plus depreciation at 65% of sales. At the pre-acquisition sales level of $435,000, this is equivalent to 75% of sales. ($325,000/435,000) (100). Even under these conservative conditions, a profit after tax is realized plus a cash flow equivalent roughly to a 20% return on equity.

Exhibit 9
Cash Flow for 12 Months Ending December 31, 1978
Merrill Enterprises

Sales	$500,000
Cash Receipts (45-day lag)	437,500
Cash Outflows	
Operating Exp.	305,000
Debt Service	45,000
	350,000
Net Cash Flow	87,500

Exhibit 10
Changes in Balance Sheet Derived from 12 Months

P&L and Cash Flow Statements

Cash	+	87,500	A/P	plug + 64,044
A/R	+	62,500	Accrued + 1956 held at 12 days	
Plant & Equip.	–	20,000	D.R.R. — no change	
Goodwill	–	45,000	L.T.D. & Equity — no change	
Prepaids & D.R. Exp.		0	R.E. + 19,000	
Total		85,000	Total	+ 85,000

NOTES FOR EXHIBIT 10

Cash is derived from net cash flow of Exhibit 9 which is slightly higher but more accurate than rough cash flow shown in Exhibit 8.

Accounts Receivables is also derived from Exhibit 9 (sales $500,000 - cash receipts of $437,500).

Plant and equipment is depreciated straight line over ten years ($200,000/10) - $20,000.

Goodwill is amortized over 20 years. Actual figure is $46,364, but this was rounded to $45,000.

No change was assumed for prepaids, deferred reciprocal expenses and revenues, long-term debt, equity.

For conservatism, accrued expenses were held at a rate equivalent to 12 days of sales over 360/day year.

Exhibit 11
Balance Sheet for December 31, 1978
Merrill Enterprises

Cash	$ 155,053	A/P	105,711
A/R	138,944	Accrued	16,667
Prepaids	2,640	D.R.R.	17,322
D.R.E.	9,775		
Total Current	306,412		139,700
P&E	180,000	L.T.D.	800,000
Goodwill	882,288	Equity	410,000
		Ret. Earn.	19,000
	1,368,700		1,368,700

Exhibit 12
Balance Sheet for January 1, 1979
Merrill Enterprises

Cash Position Reduced to Retire 1/8th of L.T. Debt and Make Dividend
Payment to Preferred Stockholders

Cash	$ 36,053	A/P	105,711
A/R	138,944	Accrueds	16,667
Prepaids	2,640	D.R.R.	17,322
D.R.E.	9,775		
Total Current	187,412		139,700
P&E	180,000	L.T.D.	700,000
Goodwill	882,288	Equity	410,000
Total Assets	1,249,700		1,249,700

Notes for Exhibits 11 and 12 on following page.

NOTES FOR EXHIBIT 11

All balances are derived from Exhibit 7 and Exhibit 10. For instance, case of 155,053 in Exhibit 11 equals $875,000 (Exhibit 10) + $67,553 (Exhibit 11).

A/R	=	Accounts Receivable
P&E	=	Plant and Equipment
A/P	=	Accounts Payable
Accrued	=	Accrued Expenses
D.R.E.	=	Deferred Reciprocal Expenses
D.R.R.	=	Deferred Reciprocal Revenues
L.T.D.	=	Long-Term Debt

NOTES FOR EXHIBIT 12

Cash accounts reduced to adjust for principal payment of long-term debt ($100,000) and dividend payment ($19,000). Acid test or liquidity ratio still about 1:0.

Exhibit 13
Five-Year Income Projection

Growth Rate:	15%	15%	25%	15%	15%
End of Year:	1	2	3	4	5
Sales	500	575	719	827	951
Agency Commissions	60	69	86	99	114
Net Sales	440	506	633	728	837
Expenses					
Depreciation	20	20	20	20	20
Other Operating*	305	334	395	430	475
Operating Income	115	152	218	278	342
Other Expenses					
Interest	45	45	45	45	45
Amortization	45	45	45	45	45
Profit Pre-Tax	25	62	128	188	252
Taxes	6	18	50	79	109
Net Profit	19	44	78	109	143
Depre. & Amort.	65	65	65	65	65
Cash Flow	84	109	143	174	208
*As a % of Sales	61%	58%	55%	52%	50%

BREAKEVEN ANALYSIS

Radio broadcasting is a relatively high fixed cost business. The only variable cost element that changes month-to-month with sales is commissions. These commissions include payments to agency and internal sales personnel.

Consequently, the basic cost structure of the business is:

Sales	=	100%
Variable Costs	=	27%
Contribution		73%

Using a contribution margin of 73%, we can calculate a sales (profit) breakeven and a cash breakeven.

As noted in Exhibit 8, the percentage of agency commissions to total sales is 12%. The difference between 12% and 27% (total variable costs) represents commissions paid to representatives and manager overrides. This 15% amounts to $75,000 which is included in operating expenses of Exhibit 8. Once removed, total fixed costs are:

$340,000 = ($305,000 − 75,000) + 20,000 + 45,000 + 45,000

Consequently, "profit" breakeven is:

$$\$466,000 \ = \ \frac{\$340,000}{.73}$$

By removing non-cash expenses (depreciation and amortization of goodwill), a "cash" breakeven can be calculated as:

$$\$377,000 \ = \ \frac{\$340,000 - 20,000 - 45,000}{.73}$$

These breakevens represent respectively 93% and 75% of sales.

RISK ANALYSIS

Compared to most new venture investments, the risks associated with the proposed venture are considerably lower.

One reason for this lower risk is that the product (FM broadcasting) is a known and successful entity. Also, FM and FM/AM combinations appear to be entering the growth phase of their product life cycles and supplanting the more mature AM radio broadcasting.

A second reason for lower risk is that the entrepreneur in question is deeply familiar with the proposed business. He has direct management experience with the product, as opposed to someone with a new product but no experience managing a business built around the product.

A third reason is that the proposal calls for the acquisition of an on-going business, as opposed to a new startup. This will maximize Mr. Merrill's strengths as quickly as possible.

Fourth, a minimum amount of capital will be exposed before an FCC licensing decision is reached. The sum in question is approximately $20-25,000* for Mr. Merrill's salary during this interim period. Also, the estimated probability of denial is extremely low given the FCC's goals.

ASSIGNMENT QUESTIONS

1. What do you think of Merrill's venture?

2. How do you think the venture capitalists will react to Merrill's business plan? Which sections, if any, do you suppose they will wish to explore with him in greater depth?

3. As one of the venture capitalists, would you agree to fund Merrill's plan? Why or why not? If not, would you accept it with certain modifications? Specify.

---

*Assumes about a six-month period.

Part III
Supporting Documents
Appendix A

Personal Resume of
DAVID MERRILL

Married: 3 children
Age: 43
Health: Excellent

50 Lincoln Road
Weston, Massachusetts
(617) 235-1668

General Manager-Vice President WEZE Boston

1974 to
Present

Responsible for overall operation of station for last three years. During this time, turned the station around from huge loss of $250,000 to a breakeven situation. This past May was highest billing month since April, 1972. Major changes involved cutting operating expenses by $80,000 and changing format which increased billings by $100,000.

Vice President-General Manager WLKW Providence, Rhode Island

1970 -
1974

Responsible for daytime AM station. Also responsible for FM station with poor transmitter and program format. Identified hole in market for a professional stereo "beautiful music" station. Within 1½ years, ratings went from #7 to #1 in market. Billings increased from $275,000 to $788,000. After leaving WLKW, was retained by station as a consultant. WLKW has kept this format and has grown to $1.6 million by 1976/77.

General Sales Manager-WITH Baltimore, Maryland

1969 -
1970

Increased overall sales 25% within year. Obtained major league experience in competition with major stations, national sales, developed knowledge and contacts with major advertising agencies; developed more sophisticated skills in management of radio operations.

General Manager, WPST Trenton, New Jersey

1966 -
1969

Joined station when it was doing $35,000 and left it doing $200,000, of which $100,000 was personal billing. Hired and trained several salesmen. Position called for creative sales operation in general market area with 65 radio stations and 17 television stations. Developed one of the first restaurant guides for radio advertising. Station had no long-term advantage or reason for existence. Station has had little growth since 1969.

Sales Representative

1965 -
1966

Detail man for American Cyanamid - Lederle Labs. Developed sales and promotion skills. Was #2 man in 12-man district and #5 man in 36-man region within 1½ years. Left in order to get back into first love — broadcasting.

Program Director, KKIX Tucson, Arizona

1961 -
1965

Responsible for programming; developed programming market skills. Helped develop one of first good music stations in United States aimed at adult market — candlelight and sunlight unique music. This station served subsequently as model for some major stations in the United States, including WJIB, WLKW.

Announcer, KAIR and KTAN Tucson, Arizona

1957 -
1961

Broke into business as dee jay. Also going to college and running a drive-in theatre from 1956-1961. Responsible for all theatre receipts and operations.

Education

1961

B.S. in Business Administration, University of Arizona. Majored in Marketing.

1953 -
1956

Sergeant — United States Army, Fort Gordon, Georgia. Courses in communications, radio school at Southeastern Signal School. At end of course was made an instructor in radio communications. Served in this capacity for one year.

Transferred to West Point, instructor in communications and fire direction control of artillery.

Appendix B

THE NATURE OF AMERICAN BROADCASTING*

Broadcast stations are licensed to serve the public interest, convenience, and necessity. Because radio channels are limited and are a part of the public domain, it is important to entrust them to licensees with a sense of public responsibility. By law, each license must contain a statement that the licensee does not have any right to operate the station or use the frequency beyond the term of license. The maximum term of license is three years.

Under requirement of the Communciations Act, applicants must be legally, technically, and financially qualified, and they must show that their proposed operation would be in the public interest. They must be citizens of the United States. Corporations with alien officers or directors or with more than one-fifth of the capital stock controlled by foreign interests may not be licensed.

Licensees are expected to ascertain and meet the needs of their communities in programming. Applicants must show how community needs and interests have been detemined and how they will be met. The Commission periodically reviews station performance, usually in connection with the license renewal application, to determine whether the licensee has lived up to its obligations and the promises it made in obtaining permission to use the public airwaves.

The commission is forbidden by law from censoring programs. The Commissions Act, Section 326, states:

> "Nothing in this Act shall be understood or construed to give the Commission the power of censorship over the radio communications or signals transmitted by any radio station, and no regulations or condition shall be promulgated or fixed by the commission which shall interfere with the right of free speech by means of radio communications."

Although educational and other non-commercial stations share the airwaves, the American Broadcasting System, for the most part, is a commercial system. In this respect, it is supported by revenues from those who advertise goods or services to the audience. Advertising messages are presented as commercial "spot announcements" before, during and after.

ADVERTISING

The Commission does not regulate individual commercials. In considering applications for new stations, renewals and transfers, it does consider whether over-commercialization contrary to the public interest may be involved. Applicants proposing more than 18 minutes of commercials per hour must justify their policies to the commission. There is no commercial quota in FCC rules, but the 18 minute benchmark is part of the National Association of Broadcasters Radio Code.

*excerpts from *The ABC's of Radio and Television*, published by the FCC.

Under a cooperative arrangement with the Federal Trade Commission, which has jurisdiction over false and misleading advertising, the FCC notifies stations of broadcast advertising cited by the FTC so that they may take any necessary action against stations that are inconsistent with their obligation to operate in the public interest.

SALE OF TIME AND STATION MANAGEMENT

The Communications Act declares that broadcasting is not a common carrier operation. Unlike common carriers, brodcasters are not required to sell or to give time to all who seek to go on the air, nor are they subject to regulation of rates and business affairs. Because programming is primarily the responsibility of broadcast licensees, the commission does not ordinarily monitor individual programs or require the filing of scripts. However, stations are required to keep logs showing the programs presented and records of requests for political time.

The commission does not maintain surveillance of the day-to-day internal management of broadcast stations, or regulate time charges, profits, artists' salaries or employee relations. It licenses only stations and their transmitter operators, not announcers, disc jockeys or other personnel except where they are also employed as transmitter operators. Stations are required to keep technical and maintenance logs as well as program logs.

MONOPOLY

One of the Commission's foremost concerns is promotion of diversification in the broadcast media, avoiding monopoly or undue concentration of control. Commission rules prohibit the same person or group from operating more than one station in the same service (AM, FM or TV) in the same locality. They also limit to seven the number of stations in the same service that may be commonly owned in the nation as a whole (only five of any group of TV stations may be VHF). Acquisition of more than three TV stations (only two of which may be VHF) in the 50 largest TV markets is permitted only upon a compelling showing that it would be in the public interest. New licensees are now also prohibited from owning more than one full-time station (AM, FM or TV) in the same locality.

RADIO TECHNICAL OPERATIONS

Radio frequencies differ in characteristics, and each service is assigned to a frequency band to suit its needs.

The AM service occupies the band 535 kilocycles per second to 1605 kc/s. Radio waves travel with the same speed as light and are of different "frequencies" (cycles per second) and "wavelengths" (distance between points in successful cycles.) "Frequency" and "wavelength" vary inversely with each other. The latter term was formerly used generally to describe a particular radio wave and still is in some countries; but, in the United States, the use of "frequency" is much more common. The "medium" frequencies such as the AM band are usually referred to by their number of kilocycles (1000 cycles) per second; or for short "kilocycles." The higher frequencies are usually referred to by the number of megacycles (1000 kilocycles, or 1,000,000 cycles) per second (1000 megacycles) to describe the much higher frequencies now being used in many services, although not in broadcasting as such. The term "Hertz," as a synonym for cycle per second, has recently been agreed upon internationally and domestically along with its derivatives "kilohertz" and "megahertz", etc. AM stations are assigned at 10kc intervals beginning at 540 kc providing 107 frequencies.

FM broadcasting occupies the frequencies from 88 to 108 megahertz with 100 channels of 200 kilohertz width each, the lowest 20 of them reserved for educational use.

Although "AM" and "FM" are often used to refer to the standard broadcast and FM broadcast services, these terms more properly apply to the methods "amplitude modulation" and "frequency modulation" used to impress aural intelligence on the carrier wave. The "AM" principle is used not only in the standard broadcast service, but also in the picture portion of television and in the international "short-wave" service. The "FM" principle is used both in the FM broadcast service and in the sound portion of television.

AM AND FM SYSTEMS

Without being too technical, this is how a radio station technically works:

A person talks into a microphone as if it were a telephone. His voice sets up vibrations of various intensity and frequency. The lower the pitch, the slower the vibration. A cycle, or wavelength, is one complete performance of a vibration.

In the microphone these vibrations are converted into electrical impulses which are then greatly amplified at the transmitter before being put on the "carrier wave." The intensity and frequency of the carrier wave are constant. This wave, by itself, does not transmit music or speech, so it is varied to correspond with the fluctuations of the speech or music received at the microphone. This is called "modulation."

In Am broadcast the audio waves are impressed on the carrier wave in a manner to cause its amplitude (or power) to vary with the audio waves. The frequency of the carrier remains modulation (FM) the amplitude remains unchanged but the frequency is varied in a manner corresponding to the voice or music to be transmitted.

These modulated waves radiate from the antenna tower at approximately 186,000 miles per second (the speed of light). Some of them follow the contour of the ground and are called "groundwaves." Others dart upward and are called "skywaves." At night, the skywave portions of transmissions in the standard broadcast (AM) frequencies are reflected back to earth by electrical particles in the "ionosphere" portion of the atmosphere. This gives the listener a choice of more distant AM stations at night. Daytime reception is largely dependent upon groundwaves.

Radio waves may pass through buildings and other objects but are subject to absorption or interference. As in the case of ripples on water, radio vibrations weaken with distance. Seasonal disturbances and sunspot periods can throw them off their course and cause "freak" reception.

The modulated wave from the radio station is picked up by the home receiving antenna. In other words, the wave sets up in the receiving antenna a current having the same frequency characteristics as one transmitted. In the receiver the audio and carrier waves are separated by a device called a detector or demodulation. The carrier wave, no longer needed, is dissipated while the audio wave is relayed to the loud speaker where it is transformed back into the sound that is heard by the listener.

RELAY OF BROADCASTS

Simultaneous relay of broadcasting, including "networks" depends upon wire, radio connecting facilities (common carrier private). Most live-talent radio network programs are sent over telephone circuits, many across the continent, for re-broadcast. For local broadcasts, stations usually employ wire connections between studios and transmitters.

Broadcast programs can also be picked out of the air for re-broadcast. Because of its characteristics, TV cannot be sent over ordinary wire lines but depend upon coaxial cable or microwave relay. Both of these methods also handle AM and FM transmission as well as telephone and telegraph communication.

TRANSMITTING ANTENNAS

In the AM service, antenna height above ground is not usually a matter of much importance. The entire antenna structure acts as the antenna and usually varies in height with the frequency of the transmission. Few AM antennas exceed 1,000 feet in height and most are considerably less. By contrast, in FM and TV, where transmission follows "line of sight," service depends on the location of the receiver in relation to the transmitting antenna. Here, antenna height is extremely important. While FM and TV antennas themselves are short, they are often situated atop natural or man-made structures which give greater height, such as tall buildings, mountain tops, or tall antenna towers specifically built for this purpose. TV towers extend as much as 2,000 feet above ground and higher.

FM BROADCAST

Frequency modulation broadcast has several advantages over the older amplitude modulation method. FM has higher fidelity characteristics and is freer of static, fading and background overlapping of other stations' programs.

FM's greater tonal range capability is due primarily to the fact that it uses a wider channel than that employed for AM broadcast. Then, too, it occupies a higher portion of the radio spectrum where there is less static and other noises than at lower frequencies. FM receivers have this particular ability to suppress weaker stations and other interferences.

Since the frequencies on which FM operates do not ordinarily reflect back to earth from ionospheric layers (skywaves), it is possible for many scattered FM stations to use the same frequency without interference, night or day, unlike the AM band.

FM and AM broadcast do not interefere with each other since they are on widely separated bands. Because of the difference in their spectrum locations and the systems used, FM cannot be heard on AM receivers without special adapters. Likewise, AM broadcasts cannot be heard on sets made to receive only FM. However, combination sets receive both systems. Legislation has been proposed to require all radio sets to have both AM and FM capability, just as TV sets are required to receive both VHF and UHF channels.

FM ZONES AND CLASSES

In 1962, the commission revised its FM broadcast rules to divide the country into three zones (instead of the previous two). Zone l includes part or all of 18 northeastern states, plus the District of Columbia: Zone 1-A, is limited to Southern California, and Zone II includes the rest of the country.

Class A stations are low-powered with a maximum of 3 kw effective radiated power. The maximum power for Class B stations is 50 kw and for Class C, 100 kw.

Three classes of commercial FM stations (instead of the previous two) were created. Class A stations are assigned to all zones: Class B stations are assigned to Zone l and 1-A and Class C stations are assigned to Zone II.

An important factor in FM operation is the height of the antenna above surrounding terrain (see earlier section on Transmitting Antennas, line-of-sight transmission). Therefore, stations have maximum antenna heights in relation to power, 300 feet above average terrain for Class C. If the antenna height above average terrain is greater, power must be reduced commensurately. Minimum power requirements are also prescribed.

FM reception varies with location of the receiver in relation to the transmitting antenna. With maximum power and antenna height, good service extends about 15 miles for Class A stations, 33 miles for Class B, and 64 miles for Class C. The rule also includes minimum mileage separations between stations on the same or adjacent channels. This is to protect the service from interference.

In 1963, the commission adopted a table assigning commercial FM channels to states and communities. (This is similar to the TV table of channel assignments.) Nearly 3,000 FM channels were made to nearly 2,000 mainland communities. Assignments in Alaska, Hawaii, Puerto Rico, and the Virgin Islands were added in 1964.

FM stations owned jointly with AM stations in cities of more than 100,000 population may not duplicate AM programming for more than half the FM station's broadcast week.

The commission has said it believes that separate ownership of AM and FM stations is a desirable long-range goal.

Appendix C

Cox study sees big FM growth at AM's expense

By Alfred J. Jaffee
Major report on FM by broadcast group
finds that medium is
more profitable than
FCC figures show and
forecasts AM deficit
at start of next decade

*Television/Radio Age September 13, 1976. Reprinted with permission.

A picture of declining profitability in the radio industry starting late during this decade but with the FM sector gaining in financial strength and growing at the expense of AM is painted in a study released today (September 13, 1976) by Cox Broadcasting Corp.

A comprehensive, sophisticated analysis of FM, covering the past, present and future, the Cox study is not only extremely bullish on FM, but presents some surprising analyses about FM's past financial position. In a nutshell, what Cox nails down is this— that FM has been and is now more profitable than FCC figures indicate.

Furthermore, if Cox projections of FM's growth— financial and otherwise—are accepted as accurate, they are likely to have a major impact on broadcaster perceptions of FM's possibilities and on the dollar value of FM stations. Cox itself has five FM outlets.

Reflecting the bullish tone, in a "final note" to the study, Cox concludes that "after much delay...FM is now ready to approach its rightful place as a mature member of the broadcasting industry. In fact, in terms of growth over the next five years, FM radio will far exceed any other form of mass communications."

The study, which analyzes both AM and FM nationally and in the top 40 markets, is based on (1) analyses of past financial, programming and audience data, (2) computer projections using "advanced statistical forecasting techniques" and (3) "scores" of interviews with broadcasters, consultants, engineers, syndicators and ad agency buyers, including in-depth interviews of up to two hours with 50 individuals.

The study winds up with historical conclusions and a listing of 17 events "most likely to occur in the future." The latter, based on both the computer forecasts and judgmental predictions of experts, are:

"In the top 40 markets, FM's share of (radio) revenues could reach 28 per cent by 1978 and 37 per cent by 1981.

"For the total U.S., FM's share of revenues could grow to 26 per cent by 1978 and 36 per cent by 1981, vs. 15.5 per cent in 1974.

"FM revenues should grow at 22 per cent annually over the next five years, while AM revenues should grow at 4 per cent annually.

"FM expenses will grow at 20 per cent annually over the next five years, while AM expenses will grow at 6 per cent annually.

"For the total radio industry over the next five years, revenues will grow at 7.5 per cent annually, and expenses will grow at 9 per cent annually.

"Thus, FM stations as a group should continue to grow at a rapid pace into the 1980s. In fact, by 1981, the annual cash flow generated by all FM stations will be greater than the annual cash flow generated by all AM stations. FM stations will generate 26 per cent of total radio cash flow by 1978 and 51 per cent by 1981 vs. 10 per cent in 1974.

"In the top 40 markets, FM's share of listening will reach 49 per cent by 1978 and 56-60 per cent by 1981.

"For the total U.S., the FM audience should account for 42-44 per cent of all listening by 1978 and up to 50 per cent by 1981.

"The number of FM stations will grow from 2,806 in 1976 to 3,500 by 1981.

"The number of AM stations will stay relatively constant at 4,500-4,600 over the next five years.

"The cpm's charged by FM stations will rise to AM levels over the next few years. Some FM stations have already reached parity.

"The 30-second spot will eventually be the primary length of radio spots. As cpm's continue to rise over the next several years, more advertisers will move to 30-second spots.

"The inventory levels of AM and FM stations will continue to approach one another, with FM levels remaining below AM.

"Revenue share as a per cent of audience share of FM stations will continue to rise, but will not equal that of AM stations.

"There is overwhelming evidence to show that further specialization of programming, i.e,. further segmentation of the market, is occurring in radio. This will cause additional fragmentation of audience and revenue shares.

"In general, the FCC will not materially deregulate radio over the next few years.

"Superior AM facilities should show moderate growth over the next few years, while inferior AM facilities will experience little or no growth."

The Cox study starts off by tackling the problem of what it considers misleading FCC financial data. There is first the question of FM revenues. For 1974, the last year for which FCC radio financial figures are available, Cox lists the broadcast revenue figure for what the FCC calls "independent FM," but which is actually FM indies plus FMers associated with AMers, but which report separately. The revenue total for this group was $193.4 million.

The FCC, however, also lists a grand total figure for FM revenues, which includes also FM revenues reported by joint AM/FM operations for which no separate FM report was submitted to the Commission. In 1974, this additional FM revenue came to $54.8 million, making the grand total for FM $248.2 million (for more details on FCC reporting methods for FM, see *Radio profits dropped 23.6%, FM revenues zoomed up 25.5%, FCC 74 figures reveal. Television/Radio Age,* November 10, 1975).

However, as the Cox report points out, "No separate breakout of total FM expenses is listed, due to the fact that FM's reporting jointly with AM's are not required to divulge that data. In addition , in the case of many of these AM/FM combinations, no separate tally of joint expenses is kept—all expenses are joint ones." And, of course, no complete profit figure for FM is available.

Because of this reporting peculiarity, the FCC shows only the expenses of "independent FM." This came to $258.9 million in 1974, with a pre-tax loss of $10.7 million. Cox displays this along with FM revenues, expenses and pre-tax income of losses going back to 1964. In every year the pre-tax "income" for FM's was a loss, ranging from a low deficit of $200,000 in 1968 to a high deficit of $12 million in 1971.

So Cox decided to redefine terms to include the complete FM (and AM) financial picture. It also estimated the expenses of FM stations reporting jointly. And it added payments to owners to pre-tax income and added to after-tax income (assuming a corporate tax rate of about 50 per cent) depreciation and amortization to come up with a cash flow figure.

The Cox study had this to say about payments to owners (which excludes dividends and other payments from surplus):

"The amount of dollars classified as payments to owners in 1974 was $97.3 million for AM-FM, an incredibly large amount. (It was $10.6 million for FM alone.) These dollars are classified as expenses by the FCC rather than as pre-tax income, which is what they truly are in the majority of cases."

Finally, in underlining its case for the adjustment of FCC figures, the study points out that in 1974, 1480 FM stations reporting jointly with their AM sisters were included in the AM financial totals.

Having adjusted the method of classifying FM financial figures more or less to its satisfaction, Cox researchers then took a new "bottom-line" look at the FM dollar profile year-by-year from 1960 through 1974.

In the latter year, for example, FM showed an overall profit of $7 million, rather than a loss of $10.7 million. There was also a profit of $3.2 million in '74, compared with the FCC-reported loss of $10.8 million. While the previous years all showed Cox-calculated deficits, the biggest was $5.6 million in '71, about $10 million less than the FCC level.

Positive cash flow

Further, the Cox data show a positive cash flow for FM since 1964. "In other words," said the Cox report, "FM stations have been financially viable since the mid-1960s."

In 1974, the FM cash flow reached $16.8 million (after-tax profit of $3.5 million, plus $13.3 million for depreciation and amortization). This was 6.8 per cent

Pie charts from Cox Broadcasting study of FM contain both actual and estimated data. Projected data start in 1975 for top and middle line of the charts, start in 1978 for bottom line.

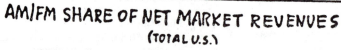

AM/FM SHARE OF NET MARKET REVENUES
(TOTAL U.S.)

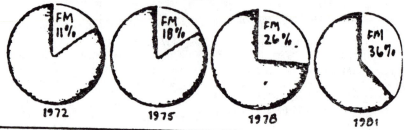

TOTAL RADIO INDUSTRY CASH FLOW
(INCOME AFTER TAXES PLUS DEPRECIATION & AMORTIZATION)

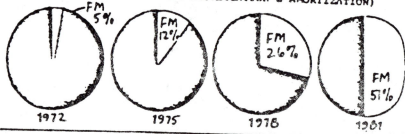

AM/FM SHARE OF AUDIENCE
(TOP 40 MARKETS)

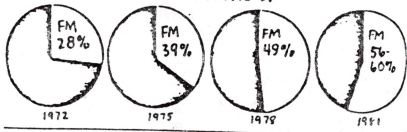

of revenues, also a peak. The FM cash flow began rising sharply in 1972, when it jumped from $3.6 million the year before to $7.8 million. In 1973, it jumped again to $12.8 million.

How important is cash flow compared with net income? Says Cox: "It would seem that most broadcasters are more concerned with cash flow than income. Only the *publicly-held* broadcasting companies (who certainly do not own the majority of AM or FM stations) would be primarily concerned with earnings due to their responsibility to their shareholders.

"To most other broadcasters, and to the public companies to some extent, it is the cash flow generated by the business that is the financial return on investment. It is the cash flow that allows for capital improvements so crucial to this industry. Especially in the case of FM stations, most of which are owned by closely-held corporations, private companies and/or individuals, the cash flow is the most important criterion of "bottom-line" performance."

And how does AM look in terms defined by Cox? A lot better. In 1974, pre tax income came to $174.4

million, compared to the FCC-reported $94.8 million. Yet, removing some of the FM revenues only reduced the AM total in '74 from $1,409.7 to $1,354.9 million.

"For the total U.S., FM's share of revenues could grow to 26 per cent by 1978 and 36 per cent by 1981, vs. 15.5 per cent in 1975. FM revenues should grow at 22 per cent annually over the next five years and AM at 4 percent."

Unlike FM, the AM cash flows have been running less than pre-tax profits, (though higher than the FCC-defined net figure). The 1974 cash flow for AM stations totaled $151.5 million. This was below the peak year of 1972, when cash flow was $164.4 million and pre-tax income $214.7 million in Cox' lexicon. As for cash flow as a per cent of revenues, the 1974 figure of 11.1 was the lowest since 1962.

The average AM station takes in a lot more money than the average FM station, of course. Cox figured out how much and it came to better than three times more in 1974. Using the total number of stations on the air as a base, Cox calculated the average revenue figure for 4,409 AM stations at $307,000 and for 2,547 FM stations at $97,000.

The broadcast company's researchers also updated these figures with estimates for last year and this. These show an overall radio revenue increase of 8.4 per cent for '75 and a 7.7 per cent for this year. Comparable figures for AM are 5.4 and 4.3 per cent and for FM, 25.1 and 23.4 per cent.

For the average station, revenues over the 1960-976 period were calculated as doubling for AM (whch probably represents little change in constant dollars), while they increased 10 times for FM stations. Noted the Cox report, "The tremendous growth in FM revenues has been due more to the ever-increasing net revenues per station than to the increse in the number of stations."

The moderate increase estimated for overall radio revenues this year (7.7 per cent) may be low. First, the estimate was made last spring and, second, Cox projections do not factor into the figures the historical peaks which show up every Presidential year.

Why FM has grown

In reviewing the history of FM, the Cox report does more than massage and analyze numbers. Among other subjects, it elicited opinions on why FM has grown so during the past 15-20 years.

There were seven different reasons given by at least 10 percent of the experts interviewed; some gave more than one reason.

Mentioned most often (58 per cent) was programming—"new," "different," "creative," "specialized," were among the terms used. Cox summed it up as "innovative" programming. The consensus of the experts was that FM took off after the FCC in the mid-60s required joint AM-FM operations to offer different programs at least 50 per cent of the time.

Second most common reason was FM sound quality (but not stereo capability). Half the experts cited this. Lower commercial load than AM was mentioned by 38 per cent. "Better" music got a 23 per cent score, though it was not always clear to Cox researchers whether "better" meant higher-caliber or more popular music. Promotion of FM was mentioned by 15 percent and this covered promotion by broadcasters and by outsiders such as the press and equipment manufacturers.

Two reasons were each mentioned by 13 percent of the experts—stereo capability and something Cox described as "consistency of format allowing more 'controlled' listening."

To get handle on just where FM has done well or not so well, Cox studied the top 40 markets in groups of 10, plus the rest of the country. The top 40, Cox pointed out, while containing only 15 per cent of all radio stations, accounted in 1974 for 44 percent of all radio revenues and 68 per cent of all radio pre-tax income.

A comparison of FM revenues and pre-tax profits in these market groups during 1969 and 1974 produced some surprising figures. The best financial performance during those years was turned in by FM in the smaller markets—those below the top 40. As a group, they lost $865,000 in '69. By '74, they were practically $6 million in the black.

How come? One theory cited by Cox was less competition, giving the station a larger probability of being sampled. At the same time, the fact that a large number were automated kept costs down and increased chances for profits.

The second biggest improvement among FM stations during the 1969-74 period was among the top 10 markets. They went from a pre-tax income figure of minus $2.2 million to $1.8 million in the black.

The theory in this case was that FM owners invested heavily in their top 10 market stations during the late '60s to build them up following the FCC's non-duplication rule. The profits of '74 were modest, however.

As for audiences, the FM share in the top 40 markets went from 10.5 in '67 to 38.5 last year, Cox pointed out in assembling Arbitron metro data. The top 10 markets still have a bigger share than the other market groups, but not by much.

Top 40 in FM

Top 40 share of revenues for FM went from 7 in '69 to 18 in '74. While this period is not idential to that used for audience shares, it can be seen that revenue share is staying below audience share.

Cox people indexed the relationship between FM audience and revenue shares (the latter divided by the former) to come up with a "sales efficiency" figure. Between '69 and '74 the sales efficiency index in the top 40 markets went from 37 to 53. All four market groups within the top 40 made essentially parallel gains, but the 11-20 market group did a little better than the other three market groups.

Three reasons were given for the better sales job: (1) With better ratings, stations can negotiate better. (2) Better salespeople. (3) Better ratings mean fewer FMs were being "given away" in combination sales.

Cox format analysis

In reviewing the current state of FM, Cox analyzed programming formats in the top 40 markets. Among 475 FM stations in those markets, the most common formats and percentage of stations carrying them last year were: beautiful music, 24.4 per cent; contemporary, 21.1 per cent, and MOR, 12.8 per cent. Among 600 AM stations the figures were: MOR, 26.2 per cent; contemporary, 17.3 per cent, and country, 16.2 per cent.

Tables from Cox Broadcasting FM study are computerized forecasts from FCC and other data. Revenues, expenses, pre-tax income are redefined by Cox, differ from FCC definitions. Table above shows AM and FM formats as of 1975. Top four formats make up the leading three for AM and FM separately in top 40 markets. Table below shows "sales efficiency" measure, which is revenue shares vs. AM divided by audience shares vs. AM. FM has been making progress here but still has a way to go—that is, where revenue share is equal to audience share, sales efficiency would be 100.

Cox people also probed into what characteristic were associated with the most successful FM stations—that is, successful in terms of attracting audience.

It appeared that the most successful FMers were indies. It was also found that the majority of the successful FMers were either indies or FMers with separate calls and formats from AM.

Among AM/FM combos only in the top 40 markets, there was some evidence that a greater per centage of these FMs is successful when Am is a daytime-only operation.

The future: AM and FM

While the Cox study deals with FM, the section that may get the greatest attention—and cause the greatest controversy—deals with projections of revenues and profits for AM.

The projections, also made for FM, give estimates for every year from 1975 through 1981. The small AM station revenue advances for last year and this had been noted and qualifications had been given.

AM revenue estimates for the succeeding years through '81 continue small and get smaller each year. From 1974 to 1981, the total revenue increase for the AM stations is estimated at about 25 per cent.

Meanwhile, pre-tax income for AM is seen as dropping sharply after 1975. The last Cox pre-tax income estimate based on FCC data (1974) was $174.4 million. The projection for '76 is $156.8 million. It then skids down to $21.6 million in 1980 and shows an actual deficit ($32.9 million) for '81.

AM cash flow is seen as holding steady for '75 and '76, but then drop off, sliding from $152.7 million this year to $82.8 million in '81.

Actually Cox doesn't think it will actually happen quite that way. Says the report: "These projections are based on (past) historical data and trends and are only valid if no major changes are made by AM operators in their method of doing business over the next six years. As AM owners continue to see their profits shrink in the future...(they) will probably change operating procedures by either lowering operating expenses to a more reasonable level and/or by pursuing additional revenues...with added vigor."

Happy FM projections

The report also made the point, in noting that projections do not have a built-in four-year cyclical trend, that "Due to the spectacular AM-FM performance expected in 1976, it may be 1977 or 1978 before our projected downward trend for AM profits becomes readily apparent."

As for FM, the projections will gladden any FM operator's heart. Pre-tax profits are estimated to increase more than 10 times over the '74 level by '81—from $7.0 to $78.9 million. During the same period, FM revenues will rise an estimated 277 per cent—climbing from $248.2 to $937.9 million.

Meanwhile, FM cash flow during the '74-'81 span is projected to increase more than four times, rising from $16.8 to $87.1 million.

Cox recognizes that these FM bottom-line projections may appear too optimistic. But it pointed out that FM cash flow has increased by a factor of eight over the past six years and adds: "This (future) quadrupling of cash flow generated by FMs is only predicted upon a very conservative increase in the FM cash flow margin over the present margin. The cash flow margin will increase to only 9 per cent from the current 6.8 per cent."

Combined projections

When the AM and FM bottom-line projections are combined the future looks like this:

Subject to previous qualifications, overall radio revenues from '74 to '81 will rise 64.8 per cent, while pre-tax profits will be cut 74.6 per cent, the latter dropping from $181.4 to $46.0 million. Cash flow will remain about level, but FM's share of cash flow will rise from 10 percent to about half.

Whatever actually happens, radio will be in for big changes during this decade. Cox' study will undoubtedly sharpen perceptions of this future and, by doing so, possibly alter it.

The 'bottom line': AM financial data, 1970-1981, actual and projections*

($ million)

Year	Net AM revenues	AM expenses	AM pre-tax income	AM net income	Add depreciation**	AM cash flow	Cash flow as a % of net revenues
1970	1,052.0	893.3	158.7	79.3	50.9	130.2	12.4
1971	1,143.0	969.2	173.8	86.9	53.8	140.7	12.3
1972	1,255.1	1,040.4	214.7	107.3	57.1	164.4	13.1
1973	1,303.6	1.109.4	194.2	97.1	60.4	157.5	12.1
1974	1,354.9	1,180.5	174.4	87.2	64.3	151.5	11.1
1975 est.	1,428.1	1,255.2	172.9	86.4	69.8	156.2	10.9
1976 est.	1,488.9	1,332.1	156.8	78.4	74.3	152.7	10.3
1977 est.	1,544.9	1,410.8	134.1	67.0	78.9	145.9	9.4
1978 est.	1,595.4	1,490.9	104.5	52.2	83.8	136.0	8.5
1979 est.	1,639.4	1,572.2	67.2	33.6	88.8	122.4	7.5
1980 est.	1,676.0	1,654.4	21.6	10.8	93.9	104.7	6.3
1981 est.	1,704.3	1,737.2	(32.9)	(16.5)	99.3	82.8	4.9

Assumption: Corporate tax rate at approximately 50%.
***Standard error of estimates: revenues, 18.6; expenses, 7.7; depreciation, 2.3**
****And amortization ( ) deficit**

The 'bottom line': FM financial data, 1970-1981, actual and projections*

($ million)

Year	Net FM revenues	FM expenses	FM pre-tax income	FM net income	Add: depreciation**	FM cash flow	Cash flow as a % of net revenues
1970	84.9	89.3	(4.4)	(2.2)	5.1	2.9	3.4
1971	115.0	120.6	(5.6)	(2.8)	6.4	3.6	3.1
1972	151.9	152.9	(1.0)	(0.5)	8.3	7.8	5.1
1973	198.3	195.1	3.2	1.6	11.2	12.8	6.5
1974	248.2	241.2	7.0	3.5	13.3	16.8	6.8
1975 est.	310.4	299.2	11.2	5.6	16.6	22.2	7.2
1976 est.	383.1	365.4	17.1	8.8	20.3	29.1	7.6
1977 est.	467.5	441.5	26.0	13.0	24.5	37.5	8.0
1978 est.	564.2	528.2	36.0	18.0	29.3	47.3	8.4
1979 est.	674.3	626.2	48.1	24.0	34.8	58.8	8.7
1980 est.	798.6	736.2	62.4	31.2	40.9	72.1	9.0
1981 est.	937.9	859.0	78.9	39.4	47.7	87.1	9.3

Assumption: Corporate tax rate at approximately 50%
***Standard error of estimates, 2.3; expenses, 1.4; depreciation, 0.2.**
****And amortization**

The relative importance of formats, top 40 markets

Format	Average # of stations/market	Format average audience share/market	Average audience share/station with format
MOR	5.5	23.2	4.2
Contemporary	5.1	21.9	4.3
Beautiful music	3.6	15.3	4.3
Country-western	3.5	9.2	2.6
Black	2.0	7.1	3.6
All-news	1.0	3.5	3.5
Progressive	1.2	3.4	2.8
Talk	0.5	2.6	5.2*
Oldies	0.8	1.9	2.4
Spanish	0.6	1.4	2.3
Classical	0.9	1.2	1.3
Religious	1.3	1.2	0.9
Other	1.1	0.7	0.6
Totals	26.9	92.6	3.4

Note: Totals may not add due to rounding.
If one dominant station in one market is included, figure drops to 4.0.

FM stations' sales efficiency

	1974			1972			1969		
	Rev. share	Aud. share	Sales eff.	Rev. share	Aud. share	Sales eff.	Rev. share	Aud. share	Sales eff.
Markets 1-10	20	38	53	15	32.5	46	8	21.5	37
Markets 11-20	17	32.5	52	12	26	46	5	16	31
Markets 21-30	18	35.5	51	12	28.5	42	7	19.5	36
Markets 31-40	17	29.5	58	12	24.5	49	6	15.5	39
Top 40 markets	18	34	53	13	28	46	7	18.5	38

GENENIX, INC.

Thomas Blanchard looked around the room at the four other members of the board of Genenix, Inc., and cleared his throat to break the ominous silence. It was December of 1980. The company had been incorporated just over a year and had gone public on the Denver stock exchange the following June to raise capital for applied research in biogenetics. Blanchard remembered the euphoria in this same room in August, 1980, after the initial offering of 4 million shares at $.50 had sold out within a week and the value per share had risen to $2.10. Since then, there had been bad news and good news. By October, the stock had fallen to $.60 a share, and today it stood at $.48. However, the company had eight projects in progress and one product ready for market.

Blanchard drew a deep breath. "Gentlemen, I believe that the field of biotechnology is one of virtually limitless potential. As to how we have positioned ourselves, I believe our venture has a sound concept. Furthermore, I believe we have a good management team. But I hear rumors that the investment community thinks we've stretched in too many ways too soon, and the price of our stock may reflect their concerns. Does anyone have any ideas?"

BACKGROUND

Thomas Blanchard was an entrepreneurial biochemist with proven expertise both in the laboratory and in the marketplace. In 1979, when he was research director of the Simmons Labs in Texas, he appeared on a local talk show where he was interviewed by Miguel Herrera, president of NewVen — a small firm specializing in the underwriting of "penny stock" issues. During the interview Blanchard spoke of his work in biogenetics, especially in the area of cell fusion, and of the endless range of applications he envisioned for the future. He estimated that commercial use of current investigations were no more than five years away. Soon after the interview, he was approached by three different groups of private investors who offered to back Blanchard if he would start his own company.

Blanchard, then in his early thirties, had already held several jobs of increasing responsibility in the field of applied biogenetics and was pleasantly surprised at the response. However, Blanchard thought starting his own company might create a conflict of interest with his employers at Simmons. But this problem was overcome when special agreements were negotiated to assure that Blanchard would maintain a consulting relationship with Simmons until his projects in process were completed, and that he would not further develop any of the projects in his own firm. These agreements were easy for both parties to sign because Blanchard had been gene-splicing at Simmons but intended to concentrate on gene fusion in his own firm.

Meanwhile, he began serious discussions with the private investors and settled quickly on Miguel Herrera and his scheme because he liked Herrera's entrepreneurial spirit and also felt some loyalty to Herrera for introducing him to a broader public. For his part, Herrera arranged to have Blanchard meet Arthur Finson, a wealthy Texas lawyer/promoter who had made a great deal of money in penny stocks, and the three of them put together a managing team of people known to Finson and Herrera through their professional contacts — Harold Dewey, a 26-year old marketing expert in the field of medical and health care products, and Frederick Farmer, 45, a former product manager in pharmaceuticals and presently a consultant in the field of health care.

The five men met frequently during the fall of 1979, redefining the market niche they hoped to fill and deciding on how to finance the venture. Their decision was to establish a contract research firm — to do R & D at universities and large companies who already had the facilities — and to finance it by going public, with no product and no revenue, as soon as the requirements for making a public stock offering could be fulfilled.

THE VENTURE CONCEPT

Genenix, Inc., "is conceived as a contract research firm. Research and development will be conducted on a contract basis by university and industrial laboratories, facilities which are already equipped, staffed, and highly specialized to do the work that is needed. Compare this approach to that of tackling the product development head on, and the cost in specialized people and equipment that would entail, and you begin to see the cost efficiency" of the Genenix approach.[1]

The market niche the company intended to fill was that of researching diagnostic agents — antibodies, hormones and enzymes — as opposed to therapies directly affecting the function of the human body. Two techniques would be employed:

---

[1]High Technology Investments, Vol. I, No. 8, June 1980.

- Cell fusion (hybridization), involving the joining of a malignant cell with a healthy cell whose normal function was the production of a specific antibody, and

- Tissue culturing, cloning cells which produce a specific antibody, hormone or enzyme as a natural byproduct of the cell's growth. (For a more complete explanation see Appendix A.)

Mr. Blanchard believed that researching diagnostic agents using these two techniques had several advantages. First, there was less competition. Most of the other biogenetic companies were concentrating on a third technique, gene-splicing, and in addition were working on medical agents rather than diagnostic substances. Second, diagnostic materials took less time to move through the approval process required by the Food and Drug Administration. If the products met certain criteria they could be classified as medical devices and clear the FDA in 90 days; if not, and they were classified as drugs, the testing and approval process could take years.[2]

Two other factors were critical to the concept of the venture. First was the timing of the public offering to raise R&D funds; the boom in biogenetic engineering had begun by late 1979, several companies had already gone public,[3] and several others were preparing to do so. Second was the physical location of the company; the principals believed that the Boston area was the most desirable because of the large medical community, the large number of university and research facilities in the area, and the proximity to Logan International Airport.

THE ENTREPRENEURIAL TEAM

As an experienced orchestrator of setting up new companies in the biogenetic field, Herrera was acutely aware of the necessity to put together a strong management team with experience in four key areas: management, technical expertise, familiarity with the industry, and marketing skills. This is how the team looked on paper:

THOMAS BLANCHARD, 34, President and Director

Mr. Blanchard obtained his Bachelor of Arts Degree in Biology/Chemistry from Boston University in 1967. Subsequently, Mr. Blanchard completed graduate studies at Princeton that did not lead to a degree. From 1971 to 1975, he was Director of Quality

---

[2]The three criteria for medical devices are:
- If the substance is not intended to affect the structure or any function of the human body.
- If it does not achieve its intended purposes through chemical action.
- If it is not dependent upon being metabolized for the achievement of its primary purpose.

[3]Bio-Response Inc.: October 1979.
Medical Monitors: 1980.

Control and the Director of Research and Development/Regulatory Affairs for Cambridge Nuclear Radiopharmaceutical Corporation. From 1975 until his association with the Company in November of 1979, Mr. Blanchard was Director of Research and Development/Regulatory Affairs for Simmons Laboratories, Inc. In this position, Mr. Blanchard was responsible for medical research and development as well as licensing of drug products in the United States and abroad with specific responsibilities for the preparation and completion of new drug applications (NDA), notices of claimed investigational exemption of new drugs (IND), drug master files (DMF) and product and establishment license applications to regulatory agencies on a federal, state, and local level.

From his past experience, Blanchard had developed three key skills:

- Management of research contracting to universities and commercial laboratories.

- Long-established contacts in the research community and the ability to gain cooperation from as well as to coordinate efforts among laboratories.

- Familiarity with successful strategies for the development of biotechnology. Blanchard believed that a program of wisely-directed research in several promising areas would produce commercially viable products before an intensive research campaign centered around a single brilliant idea.

HAROLD DEWEY, 28, Vice President and Director

Mr. Dewey attended Harvard University studying the natural sciences from 1973 to 1975 without obtaining a degree. Subsequently, he attended the School of the Boston Museum of Fine Arts concentrating in multi-media communications, without obtaining a degree. From 1975 until his association with the Company in November of 1979, Mr. Dewey acted as President and sole stockholder of Dewey and Company, Inc. The Company provided marketing services research and planning, public relations, new product introduction, packaging and national advertising campaigns with respect to medical and health care products.

FREDERICK FARMER, 47, Secretary-Treasurer and Director

Mr. Farmer received a Bachelor of Science degree in electrical engineering from the University of Colorado in 1953. Thereafter, he enrolled in post-graduate studies at the Massachusetts Institute of Technology without obtaining a degree. From 1954 until 1961, Mr. Farmer worked for his family-owned dairy business. In 1961, he co-founded and served as an officer for Electronic Medical Instruments, Inc., of Ft. Collins, Colorado. In 1963 when Electronic Medical Instruments, Inc., was acquired by Hewlett Packard Company, Mr. Farmer served as project engineer for its Loveland, Colorado office. From 1964 through 1966, Mr. Farmer was engaged as an independent consultant for NASA, the Federal Aviation Administration and the U.S. Army Advanced Projects Office in the field of research and evaluation of biomedical devices. In 1966 he joined Hoffman-LaRoche, Inc., where he became Assistant Director of Special Projects with responsibilities for diagnostic research, immunology, pharmaceutical projects, and acquisitions. Since 1978, when he terminated his employment with Hoffman-LaRoche, Inc., Mr. Farmer has served as a consultant with various firms in the field of health care. During his employment with Hoffman-LaRoche, Inc., and as an independent consultant, Mr. Farmer was not involved in cell fusion or tissue culture projects or procedures.

ARTHUR FINSON, 64

Retired Texas lawyer and financier. Primary source of Mr. Finson's wealth in his investment portfolio in the "penny stock" market in Denver.

MIGUEL HERRERA, 41

President, NewVen, a Denver-based investment company specializing in underwriting issues of start-up companies.

GOING PUBLIC AMONG BIOGENETIC VENTURES

In 1980, with interest rates approaching 20%, going public to raise capital for certain types of companies became a viable alternative to other traditional ways of raising money.[4] Although the associated costs might run as high as a fifth of the offering ($100,000 for an issue of $500,000 was not unusual),[5] entrepreneurs with ventures in oil and gas and certain high technologies, including biogenetics, found public offerings to be a good way to get started.

Genenix was but one of a number of biogenetic ventures to decide to go public to raise capital. Others included:

> • Bio-Response, Inc., went public in October 1979. The company was engaged in medical research and development. When it went public it had had neither earnings nor sales. 1,200,000 shares were sold at $2.50 per share.

> • Medical Monitors went public soon thereafter. This company producd electronic blood pressure monitoring devices. The company had previous earnings. 12,000,000 shares were sold at $.10 each.

---

[4]"The New Issues Boom," *Venture*, December 1980.

[5]*Venture*, July 1981, p. 12.

• Genetic Application Technologies, Inc., of Newport Beach, CA, also went public. It has been described as "founded by a couple of University of California microbiologists and a disbarred lawyer twice convicted of fraudulent stock activities."[6]

• Enzo Biochem, Inc., went public in September 1980. The company proposed to create enzyme production and purification. It resembled Genenix except that Enzo had generated sales to the managers of the public issue. 700,000 shares were sold at $6.25 a share.

• Genentech, Inc., captured the headlines when it went public. It was founded in 1975, and in fiscal 1980 generated revenues of $9 million and earnings of just $236,000. The company specializes in gene-splicing and "while the giant pharmaceutical and chemical companies debated the future of genetic engineering and its place of their industries, and other little companies explored a wide range of technologies, Genentech stuck to a five-year plan that plotted the slow, steady development of one potentially marketable hormone after another.[7] Genentech went public in October 1980. The initial offering at $35 a share raised over $36 million the day it was offered, and rose to $89 million a share the day the aftermarket opened.

• Cytox Corp. went public in January 1981. It had previous sales and earnings. 1,500,000 shares were sold at $2 each.

PREPARING TO GO PUBLIC

In accordance with the plan to go public to raise R&D funds, Herrera steered Genenix unerringly through the following sequence of events.

1. November 5, 1979. Genenix, Inc., is incorporated.

— 25,000,000 shares of stock, 1¢ ($.01) par value, are authorized.

— The following allocation of responsibilities are agreed to:

Mr. Blanchard, President and Director, will work full time.

Mr. Dewey, Vice President and Director, will work full time.

[6]*Inc.,* May 1981, p. 68.

[7]*Inc.,* May 1961, p. 62.

Mr. Farmer, Secretary/Treasurer and Director, will work 20% of the time.

Mr. Finson, as a Principal Stockholder, will work as necessary to introduce the Company to his associates in the financial world.

Mr. Herrera, as underwriter, will negotiate his remuneration independently.

2. November 29, 1979. Nine private investors buy 5,900,000 shares at par value.

	Principal stockholders:	
$12,500 in cash	Blanchard	9 %
	Dewey	4.5%
$46,500 in services rendered	Farmer	7.5%
	Finson	18 %

This placement raised more than 10% of the intended amount of the public offering.

3. Late December 1979. 1,350,000 additional shares are sold.

15¢ average price ($.149)
$201,000 raised

4. December 30, 1979. Two-year employment contract is signed by principals.

Blanchard's annual salary	$45,000
Dewey's annual salary	$35,000
Farmer's annual salary	$ 9,000

The contracts stipulated that should the employees fail to remain in the Company for a period of two years, Genenix would have the option of requiring the percentage of total shares issued to each employee equal to the percentage of the two years remaining at the termination of employment at the same price the shares were issued to the employee. ($.01)

5. January 1, 1980: financial status

7,250,000 shares sold
Book value of $260,000 less losses incurred during first two months of operations
3.5¢ ($.035) book value per share
January 1: office space rented in the Boston area

6. Public issue prepared: letter of intent drafted between Genenix and NewVen.

>   4,000,000 shares at $.50 per share
>   Minimum sale, 3,000,000 shares . . . if less, money will be returned to investors
>   Remuneration to Mr. Herrera: 10% of issue plus an undisclosed amount of warrants redeemable
>   at a future date for a predetermined price.

7. June 1980. Public offering is made

>   4 million shares sold out in a week
>   Book value diluted from $.50 to $.17
>   Stock worth $.135 a share.

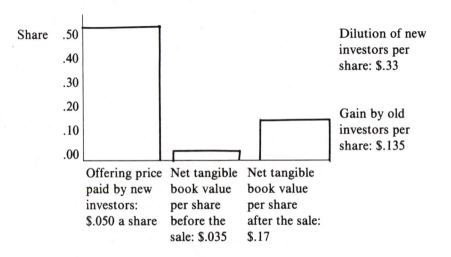

Dilution of new investors per share: $.33

Gain by old investors per share: $.135

Offering price paid by new investors: $.050 a share

Net tangible book value per share before the sale: $.035

Net tangible book value per share after the sale: $.17

The funds raised were to be allocated as follows over a two-year period:

a) Officers' salaries:

>   1) President - $45,000/year $90,000
>   2) Vice President - $35,000/year 70,000
>   3) Treasurer - $9,000/year 18,000

b) Employees' salaries:

>   An allocation of $45,000/year $91,000

c) General and Administrative expenses:

>   Including travel, business insurance, office expenses, entertainment, payroll taxes, professional expenses and other miscellaneous expenses - $64,500/year 129,000

d) Research and Development expenses:

To be allocated in accordance with
management during both years. 828,000

e) Marketing and promotional expenses 300,000

f) Reserve for working capital 184,000

Total Expenses During Period $1,710,000

The difference of $290,000 was spent in underwriter's commission
and other expenses in the issue such as accounting, legal, printing.

ACTIVITIES OF THE PRINCIPALS

Since the inception of Genenix in November 1979 the principal shareholders had
concentrated on two activities: generating interest in the financial community, and lining
up R&D contracts with biogenetic development laboratories. Mr. Blanchard was active
on both these fronts.

Herrera and Finson introduced Blanchard to a number of potential investors and
brokers, within the limits of the "due diligence" clause of discretionary promotion before
a company is brought public, and Blanchard's ability to project the concept of Genenix
impressed both veterans immensely. Blanchard developed a slide show, comparing the
potential of biogenetics to that of man's first step on the moon, and showed a depth of
understanding as to why the diagnostic market niche offered a favorable point of market
entry. "To say the least," Herrera commented, "the security analysts were very
impressed."

Blanchard and Dewey made a number of calls to professional acquaintances in
research labs across the nation, and were met with enthusiasm. Blanchard had compiled a
list of projects he believed were worthy of research, and a series of alternatives as to how
to use them for commercial gain. "Probably the fastest way to realize income is to license
the product to a manufacturing firm," he commented, "and then to let Mr. Dewey market
it, if he believes he can, or else to license a pharmaceutical company to market it. Of
course, the details will be contingent on the contract agreement we work out with
individual laboratories. It's much too early in our development to be making these types
of decisions." By June, Blanchard had negotiated several contracts.

Meanwhile, Mr. Farmer had been busy with cash flows and projections and had talked
up the concept of the diagnostics research company to his associates in the
pharmaceutical industry.

Herrera's time was entirely consumed with making the legal and financial
arrangements for which he, as principal underwiter, was responsible. After the letter of
intent was signed, he and his lawyer and accountant began to prepare the prospectus

required by the SEC, using the guidelines established for companies at the development stage.

Once he had his "red herring," Herrera, accompanied frequently by Blanchard and occasionally by Finson, began to solicit indications of interest from prospective investors without in any way trying to precondition the market, lest they be accused of "jumping the gun." On several occasions, Herrera hoped that Blanchard's infectious enthusiasm was not overstepping the bounds of the securities regulations.

The date of issue finally came in June 1980. Herrera transacted the sale of all 4,000,000 shares, and began work on the final prospectus, which by law had to be distributed to the stockholders within 90 days. In addition, he concentrated on maintaining the aftermarket for the newly-issued stock, since his fortunes were partially tied to the newly-public company.

In the six months between the public offering and the December board meeting where he stood now, Blanchard had been a human tornado. He had eight contracts in hand, and was overseeing the licensing of the first product to an overseas manufacturer. For each contract, he had three more in the wings, and only the constraints on his own time had prevented their completion. The overseas licensing negotiations had opened up an untapped market in western Europe which Blanchard was anxious to enter as soon as possible.

Dewey, finding Blanchard's style quite different from his own, had called on his own contacts to promote the concept of the contracts now in progress but felt the lack of something tangible to sell. Therefore, he had begun to work with Farmer on details of internal housekeeping, including an attempt to get Blanchard to set up an outside Board of Scientific Advisors in order to focus Genenix' projects more specifically. Blanchard supported the idea and expressed chagrin that he didn't have more time to assist them.

Finson had mixed emotions. On one hand, he knew that the performance of the stock was a reflection of the depressed market conditions in general more than a direct response to the operations of the company. On the other hand, he recalled the conventional wisdom of the successful penny stock investor — "All it seems that a company needs is an appealing concept with experienced management at the helm.[8] Was that, he wondered an accurate description of Genenix, Inc.?

ASSIGNMENT QUESTIONS

1. Did Genenix have a well-thought out venture concept? What specifically are the venture's strong and weak points?
2. Does Genenix have a good entrepreneurial team? Should it be reorganized or new people hired to give it more direction and expertise?
3. What are the pros and cons of a public offering in this instance?

---

[8] *Venture,* July 1980.

Appendix A

Excerpts from *Genetic Technology: A New Frontier,* Office of Technology Assessment, Westview Press, Boulder, Colorado, 1982. Pages 3-7. Reprinted with permission.

SUMMARY: ISSUES AND OPTIONS

The genetic alteration of plants, animals, and micro-organisms has been an important part of agriculture for centuries. It has also been an integral part of the alcoholic beverage industry since the invention of beer and wine; and for the past century, a mainstay of segments of the pharmaceutical and chemical industries.

However, only in the last 20 years have powerful new genetic technologies been developed that greatly increase the ability to manipulate the inherited characteristics of plants, animals, and micro-organisms. One consequence is the increasing reliance the pharmaceutical and chemical industries are placing on biotechnology. Micro-organisms are being used to manufacture substances that have previously been extracted from natural sources. Animal and plant breeders are using the new techniques to help clarify basic questions about biological functions, and to improve the speed and efficiency of the technologies they already use. Other industries--from food processing and pollution control to mining and oil recovery--are considering the use of genetic engineering to increase productivity and cut costs.

Genetic technologies will have a broad impact on the future. They may contribute to filling some of the most fundamental needs of mankind--from health care to supplies of food and energy. At the same time, they arouse concerns about their potential effects on the environment and the risks to health involved in basic and applied scientific research and development (R&D). Because genetic technologies are already being applied, it is appropriate to begin considering their potential consequences.

BIOTECHNOLOGY

Biotechnology--the use of living organisms or their components in industrial processes--is possible because micro-organisms naturally produce countless substances during their lives. Some of these substances have proved commercially valuable. A number of different industries have learned to use micro-organisms as natural factories, cultivating populations of the best producers under conditions designed to enhance their abilities.

Applied genetics can play a major role in improving the speed, efficiency, and productivity of these biological systems. It permits the manipulation, or engineering, of the micro-organisms' genetic material to produce the desired characteristics. Genetic engineering is not in itself an industry, but a technique used at the laboratory level that allows the researcher to modify the hereditary apparatus of the cell. The population of altered identical cells that grows from the first changed micro-organism is, in turn, used for various industrial processes.

The first major commercial effects of the application of genetic engineering will be in the pharmaceutical, chemical, and food processing industries. Potential commercial applications of value to the mining, oil recovery, and pollution control industries--which may desire to use manipulated micro-organisms in the open environment--are still somewhat speculative.

THE PHARMACEUTICAL INDUSTRY

Findings

The pharmaceutical industry has been the first to take advantage of the potentials of applied molecular genetics. Ultimately, it will probably benefit more than any other, with the largest percentage of its products depending on advances in genetic technologies. Already, micro-organisms have been engineered to produce human insulin, interferon, growth hormone, urokinase (for the treatment of blood clots), thymosin- 1 (for controlling the immune response), and somatostatin (a brain hormone).

The products most likely to be affected by genetic engineering in the next 10 to 20 years are nonprotein compounds like most antibiotics, and protein compounds such as enzymes and antibodies, and many hormones and vaccines. Improvements can be made both in the products and in the processes by which they are produced. Process costs may be lowered and even entirely new products developed.

The most advanced applications today are in the field of hormones. While certain hormones have already proved useful, the testing of others has been hindered by their scarcity and high cost. Of 48 human hormones that have been identified so far as possible candidates for production by genetically engineered micro-organisms, only 10 are used in current medical practice. The other 38 are not, partly because they have been available in such limited quantities that tests of their therapeutic value have not been possible.

Genetic technologies also open up new approaches for vaccine development for such intractable parasitic and viral diseases as amebic dysentery, trachoma, hepatitis, and malaria. At present, the vaccine most likely to be produced is for foot-and-mouth disease in animals. However, should any one of the vaccines for human diseases become available, the social, economic, and political consequences of a decrease in morbidity and mortality would be significant. Many of these diseases are particularly prevalent in less industrialized countries; the developments of vaccines for them may profoundly affect the lives of tens of millions of people.

For some pharmaceutical products, biotechnology will compete with chemical synthesis and extraction from human and animal organs. Assessing the relative worth of each method must be done on a case-by-case basis. But for other products, genetic engineering offers the only method known that can ensure a plentiful supply; in some instances, it has no competition.

By making a pharmaceutical available, genetic engineering may have two types of effects:

• Drugs that already have medical promise will be available in ample amounts for clinical testing. Interferon, for example, can be tested for its efficacy in cancer and viral therapy, and human growth hormone can be evaluated for its ability to heal wounds.

• Other pharmacologically active substances for which no apparent use now exists will be available in sufficient quantities and at low enough cost to enable researchers to explore new uses. As a result, the potential for totally new therapies exists. Regulatory proteins, for example, which are an entire class of molecules that control gene activity, are present in the body in only minute quantities. Now, for the first time, they can be recognized, isolated, characterized, and produced in quantity.

The mere availability of a pharmacologically active substance does not ensure its adoption in medical practice. Even if it is shown to have therapeutic usefulness, it may not succeed in the marketplace.

The difficulty in predicting the economic impact is exemplified by interferon. If it is found to be broadly effective against both viral diseases and cancers, sales would be in the tens of billions of dollars annually. If its clinical effectiveness is found to be only against one or two viruses, sales would be significantly lower.

At the very least, even if there are no immediate medical uses for compounds produced by genetic engineering, their indirect impact on medical research is assured. For the first time, almost any biological phenomenon of medical interest can be explored at the cellular level. These molecules are valuable tools for understanding the anatomy and functions of cells. The knowledge gained may lead to the development of new therapies or preventive measures for diseases.

THE NDC FRANCHISE

On a winter afternoon in early 1980, Alice Rogers had just finished reading the following short article:

> Following the shakeout of 1969 to 1970, when hundreds of companies floundered into bankruptcy, franchising had bounced back, settled down, matured, and grown. During the past three years, the failure rate of franchisors had further declined, averaging less than 4% a year. In 1978, a total of 30 franchisors operating 1,391 establishments failed. In contrast, according to Dun & Bradstreet, three out of every four conventional new businesses failed in a three-year period.
>
> "Franchising is healthy and growing stronger," said Andrew Kostechka, who headed franchise research for the U.S. Department of Commerce. "More companies are getting into franchising, and the odds of survival are greater in their favor because of the franchising concept," he said. Due to this healthy outlook, tighter government controls and tougher 'industry' standards, franchising continued as an attractive avenue for big business to expand. It was also a viable opportunity for the individual with a modest amount of capital to own a business."*

Alice Rogers recalled her recent graduation from Business School and the dilemma she now faced. Essentially, she was trying to find a way to balance her needs for fulfillment both in the home and in an as yet unspecified career. She thought the NDC franchise might be the answer.

---

*Reprinted from Success Unlimited, August 1979. Copyright 1979 by Success Unlimited, Inc., 401 N. Washbash Avenue, Chicago, IL 60611.

ALICE ROGERS: BACKGROUND

Alice Rogers was a woman in her late thirties, living in the Los Angeles area. She was happily married to a successful businessman and they had three children, all pre-teenagers.

Alice added the following information about herself:

> My pursuit of the MBA took five years of part-time schooling and was intended initially not only as an activity in and of itself but also to provide the security of an option to pursue a career. With graduation, however, I realized that being a 'domestic manager' was sufficiently time consuming to make it incompatible with a full-time management career. A full-time managerial position and its demands would introduce inevitable conflicts and tensions. Lacking compelling reasons to work, I discovered it was virtually impossible to make a 150% commitment to a full-time job on someone else's schedule.

> My instinct was that the entrepreneurial route was the answer. Although I had no specific ventures in mind, I felt that selling some kind of service rather than a product would be most compatible with my skills and interests. The fact that my husband was a successful entrepreneur also influenced my thinking.

> The fortunate happenstance that attracted me to the opportunities of owning a franchise was when I decided to shed some excess poundage. I discovered the diet counseling service was a business where I could apply, develop, and exploit my newly acquired business skills, in addition to operating a service I had personally experienced.

INITIAL EXPOSURE TO THE NDC CONCEPT

Alice's first contact with the Nutrition and Diet Council (NDC) was with Karen Davis, an attractive, articulate woman who was, according to Alice, a convincing case for the product and service she was selling. Alice had a slight acquaintance with Karen since they attended the same church with their respective families. Consequently, Alice did not find it difficult to make inquiries about her role in this enterprise.

> I had never been to a diet counseling service such as NDC. Instead of attending weekly group meetings, the dieter meets daily with the diet counselor on an individual basis to monitor the client's weight loss progress and to discuss any problems relevant to the diet and the dieter. It's more personal and more intensive in terms of the discipline of a

daily check-in than a weekly group diet program. The level
of motivation correlated very effectively with the frequency
of the visits. This type of program was also considerably
more expensive than the group-based program ($20-$30 a
week for the former as opposed to $3-$4 a week for the
latter). My initial impressions were extremely positive. I
liked the counselors and I liked the service they were
delivering.

Naturally, Alice was curious to know how Karen had decided to go the diet franchise
route. Karen stated that it was her husband's encouragement and insistence that led her
to buy a franchise rather than take an uninteresting, part-time selling job. She, too, had
had a weight problem and successfully lost the pounds through the very program she was
now marketing. She disclaimed any business judgment, insisting her husband was the
brains behind her very thriving venture.

Karen had purchased her franchise from NDC whose corporate headquarters were
located in San Francisco. Although very slow going initially, satisfied clients began
spreading the word of this unique approach to dieting on a one-to-one counseling basis.
Furthermore, the flexibility of scheduling appointments tapped a wider market of people
unable for whatever reason to attend weekly hour-long sessions.

Alice's own weight loss experience with the program reinforced Karen's claims. Alice
was impressed by her weight loss accomplishment and sensed that a large and still
untapped market existed in the Los Angeles area for NDC's services.

BACKGROUND ON NDC

NDC was founded by the Carter Smiths of San Francisco, California. Sara Smith had
experienced a weight problem for years. She finally focused on this experience to come
up with a well-rounded, nutritionally balanced diet which turned out be very successful
not only for herself but for her neighbors who sought her advice. She discovered that she
was very effective in counseling others. Eventually, sufficient interest was expressed in
what was truly becoming a service that her husband suggested that she market this diet.
How did you sell a diet? Their answer was franchising.

Carter Smith contributed the relevant experience since his own business was a
franchise. What they did was sell territorial rights and a distinctive product (the diet
capsule). Initially, the Smiths sold franchises for $2,000. Their feeling that individuals
would invest to own a franchise surpassed all their expectations as requests to purchase
these rights poured into their headquarters. A single important condition had to be met
before a candidate was accepted. The candidate had to lose weight on the program. Once
the negotiations were completed, intensive instruction and direction was provided at a
week-long training session held in San Francisco.

Ten years later, in 1980, the cost of the franchise was $14,000. For that fee, the
franchisee had exclusive rights to operate an NDC in his/her area. A guarantee buy-back
agreement was included. NDC provided advertising support, continued training by

correspondence and enough supplies to earn back the original investment. Franchisees paid a continuing licensing fee based on the number of dieters counseled. The fee was correlated with the amount of supplies they were using. Each dieter received 'free' one package of capsules daily. The franchisee paid for each package. What the dieter supposedly purchased was not the package but the service and the daily counseling. However, other products (vitamins, nutrition supplements, etc.) were available and sold to clients at their option.

By 1980, the Smiths had sold more than 1300 franchises throughout the country. Since 1975, the annual gross business of the franchise had grown by a factor of 12 to $25 million. Considering that the average NDC operator spent $250-$300 a month on advertising, national advertising was a healthy $3 million three years later. This figure did not include a quarter of a million in corporate advertising.

THE DECISION

Alice Rogers was ready to make one of the most important decisions of her life. It was a time of great anticipation and excitement for her.

> I learned in the course of my conversations with Karen that she had purchased additional franchises in the area for resale on a sub-franchise basis. Karen told me that she was deeply committed to the NDC concept. She found that the experience was personally so satisfying and rewarding that she decided to buy these additional franchises with the intention of selling them as sub-franchises. (90% of all NDC franchises were owned on this basis.) There was little question in my mind: I was a candidate for one of these.

Alice felt confident that she could take on such an enterprise given her educational training and financial resources. The fee for the sub-franchise was $10,000 compared to $14,000 for the original franchise. In exchange for this arrangement, the sub-franchisee agreed to buy supplies at a 60% markup from the franchisor (in this case Karen Davis). The first three months of advertising were assumed by the franchisor with an agreement by the franchisee to spend a minimum of $300 a month on advertising following the first quarter. The franchisor also agreed to foot the bill for the sub-franchisee to attend an intensive week-long training session at corporate headquarters. Needless to say, the success of the sub-franchisee correlated directly with that of the franchisor. So Karen's offer of every assistance had a double edge.

> The thought that I could satisfy my entrepreneurial goals so quickly and satisfactorily tuned me into her enthusiasm for the venture. Her support and desire to help encouraged me very much.

> Karen discussed with me at length her ideas for expanding

the business -- forging associations with local doctors and hospitals, writing a diet news column in a local magazine, appearing on radio and TV talk shows, running diet seminars, even sending brochures to women whose overweight pictures appeared in the local newspapers. She assured me I was the kind of person who would really make a go of it. After several meetings, she urged me to find an office so that I could be open for business within a couple of months. I ran a pro forma at different client levels based on the numbers she gave me verbally. (See *Exhibits 1 and 2.*) She indicated that she averaged around 60 clients a week at $20 a head. The client paid up front by cash or check. There were no accounts receivable. The $20 fee applied as long as the client was actually on the diet. However, a client could come in as often as was necessary on stabilization or maintenance to be weighed and counseled without paying so long as they had not gained weight. In effect, the NDC office saw many non-paying clients.

I judged the potential of the business to be very great. I had determined my own hurdle rate. If I could do no better than averaging 30 clients a week within a year, then the venture was not worth undertaking.

Having dieted for many years and given much thought to the subject of nutrition and dieting, I was convinced that fatness was a pervasive and recurring problem and that an effective diet service such as NDC could be marketed very effectively provided that the market was not saturated already with overlapping diet programs.

By 1980, losing weight was a national obsession, and the ever visible overweight American had become increasingly sophisticated and demanding when it came to weight loss programs. Eventually, I estimated that increasing numbers of potential customers would willingly pay to realize his/her weight objectives, despite the fact that their success rate for keeping weight off after a diet had been estimated at a mere 2%. Usually, most experienced dieters started out in group programs which basically were very sound. The pitfall for the chronic dieter was the so-called maintenance period which really signified for most dieters the end of dieting and a return to forme eating habits and then sooner or later to a new diet program. Many former 'group members' had become frustrated with the mickey mouse of group dynamics and were seeking out the more expensive one-on-one daily counseling. I now understand why people would pay so much for this kind of service.

The business was advertised by word of mouth and visual results since successful weight loss was perceived quickly by others. The other important aspect of the mix was the personnel operating the centers. They were and had to be physical symbols of the success of the program. Since they were catering essentially to a higher income market, the personnel had to relate to their clients on several levels. If these elements were missing, the business suffered accordingly. Rapport between the counselor and the client was integral to the success of the business.

Exhibit 1
Pro Forma P & L

	1	2	3	4	5	6	7	8	9	10	11	12	Year 1
Clients	15	30	30	30	30	30	30	30	30	30	30	30	
Sales	1935*	3870	3870	3870	3870	3870	3870	3870	3870	3870	3870	3870	44505
Products	605	1290	1290	1290	1290	1290	1290	1290	1290	1290	1290	1290	14835
Total Sales	2580	5160	5160	5160	5160	5160	5160	5160	5160	5160	5160	5160	59340
Expenses													
Wages	387	387	387	387	387	387	387	387	387	387	387	387	4644
Fringes	35	35	35	35	35	35	35	35	35	35	35	35	418
Products	610	1219	1219	1219	1219	1219	1219	1219	1219	1219	1219	1219	14019
Rent	450	450	450	450	450	450	450	450	450	450	450	450	5400
Advertise	0	0	0	400	400	400	400	400	400	400	400	400	3600
Telephone	70	70	70	70	70	70	70	70	70	70	70	70	840
Other	100	100	100	100	100	100	100	100	100	100	70	100	1200
Manager	1290	1290	1290	1290	1290	1290	1290	1290	1290	1290	1290	1290	15480
Total Expenses	2941	3551	3551	3951	3951	3951	3951	3951	3951	3951	3951	3951	45601
Profit	-361	1609	1209	1209	1209	1209	1209	1209	1209	1209	1209	1209	13739
Cum. Prof.	-361	1248	2857	4066	5275	6484	7693	8902	10112	11321	12530	13739	

Source: Alice Rogers' personal calculations @ 30 clients per year.

*15 clients x $30 x 4.3 weeks

$30 = new weekly rate used instead of $20 rate which was to be phased out.

Exhibit 2
Pro Forma P & L

	1	2	3	4	5	6	7	8	9	10	11	12	Year 1
Clients	15	32	35	37	40	42	45	47	50	52	55	57	
Sales	1935*	4128	4515	4773	5160	5418	5805	6063	6450	6708	7095	7353	65403
Products	645	1376	1505	1591	1720	1806	1935	2021	2150	2236	2365	2451	21801
Total Sales	2580	5504	6020	6364	6880	7224	7740	8084	8600	8944	9460	9804	87204
Expenses													
Wages	387	387	387	387	774	774	774	774	774	774	774	774	7740
Fringes	35	35	35	35	70	70	70	70	70	70	70	70	697
Products	610	1300	1422	1503	1625	1707	1829	1910	2032	2113	2235	2316	20602
Rent	450	450	450	450	450	450	450	450	450	450	450	450	5400
Advertise	0	0	0	400	400	400	400	400	400	400	400	400	3600
Telephone	70	70	70	70	70	70	70	70	70	70	70	70	840
Other	100	100	100	100	100	100	100	100	100	100	110	100	1200
Manager	1290	1290	1290	1290	1290	1290	1290	1290	1290	1290	1290	1290	15480
Total Expenses	2941	3632	3754	4235	4779	4860	4982	5064	5185	5267	5389	5470	55559
Profit	−361	1872	2266	2129	2101	2364	2758	3020	3415	3677	4071	4334	31645
Cum. Prof.	−361	1510	3776	5905	8006	10370	13127	16148	19563	23240	27311	31645	

Source: Alice Rogers' personal calculations @ progressive client levels.

ASSIGNMENT QUESTIONS

Suggested assignment questions are:

1. What is your evaluation of the NDC concept?

2. What is your evaluation of NDC's franchise terms from the perspective of the franchisee? From the perspective of the sub-franchisee?

3. Why is Alice considering this venture? What are the advantages/disadvantages of franchising?

4. How should Alice Rogers proceed if she decides to go ahead with NDC?

5. How should she proceed to find some other venture if she decides not to go ahead with NDC?

OMNIDENTIX SYSTEMS

Dateline: August 8, 1980: The Boston Globe

On a rainy Thursday the Mall in Medford was mobbed.
There were more than 50 fascinating shops at the mall, but
on this day things seemed different. The shoppers seemed
only mildly interested in the shoe stores, vaguely curious
about the jeans shops and practically indifferent to the
bookstore. On this day the real center of excitement was
down a newer wing of the mall, around the corner from the
Thom McAn store, across the hall from Weathervane. Next
to the tee-shirt shop were people lined up two and three deep
trying to get into a dentist's office.

The demonstration of public curiosity, as reported by one of Boston's leading
newspapers, was not exaggerated. It was newsworthy, however, because the excitement
was not caused by a celebrity or by the lure of free merchandise. Rather, it was opening
day for the first unit of the Omnidentix Systems dental care franchise chain. Dr. David A.
Pyner, D.D.S.P.C., who had been working with David Slater for nearly a year to launch
this new concept, remembers August 8 with a grin -- and a wince. "That was just the first
day," he recalled. "and we had no idea what was going to happen next. We just knew we
had a big tiger by the tail -- and now, we're still hanging on for all we're worth."

GRASPING THE IDEA

Dr. Pyner described the new approach to the distribution of dental care in these terms:

> I would define a retail dental center as a business using retail
> type management, promotion, and controls, located in a
> mall or other high traffic retail location.

The movement into retail dentistry began in 1977 when the U.S. Supreme Court
handed down a decision permitting dentists and certain other professions to advertise.
Since then dozens of clinics using modern promotion methods sprang up across the
nation, many claiming that they were providing treatments at prices up to 50 percent less
than their more orthodox counterparts in private practice.

Sears, Montgomery Ward, Two Guys, Time Square Stores, and Korvettes all jumped on the bandwagon by leasing space in their stores to dental clinics. Leasing was their only option since most state laws barred non-dentists from operating or owning dental clinics. Under lease conditions, the normal arrangement was for the lessor to take a percentage of sales.

According to Dr. Pyner, Omnidentix represented a rather radical departure from the new retail pattern. The key difference was that Omnidentix would be a franchise operation with a management team behind it that could boast some of the best brains in the business. David Slater, who took over his father-in-law's donut shop after Yale Law School and built it into the 350 unit nationally franchised Mr. Donut chain, held the title of Chairman of the Board. The Executive Vice President was Ronald Kupack, formerly of Benihana of Tokyo, the restaurant chain. Slater worked out of a converted carriage house on the grounds of his home in a West Boston suburb. The comfortable suite of offices was decorated lavishly with modern art and cool green furniture. Mr. Slater's views on business were reflected partly by his taste in art and vice versa. For example, in his office there was a stack of limited edition prints of Christo's Running Fence. Slater had commissioned these prints from Christo to use as perks at a franchising seminar he was holding. Christo was famous for his "project" and Slater offered his perspective.

> Christo says that if you do a work that hangs in a frame in a gallery, X number of people see that art in so many years. Let's call that a million people. One artist is involved. But when he puts up a project so many are involved and so much happens that say 20 million see it in a few weeks' time. He designs literally impossible tasks where hundreds of people are involved. To put up the Running Fence something like 17 hearings were held to cross hundreds of property deeds. To Christo, this process is art.

Mr. Slater also offered his perspective on the emergence of professional franchising.

> This is a new era of business. No one knows what they're doing really. But in the '80s the professions will move into franchising. Particularly the health care industry.

> In its initial stage, Omnidentix will share many similarities with opening a doughnut shop. A location must be market-researched and acquired, the store has to be designed and built, the equipment must be selected and supply sources including financing must be arranged. Although in this case the product is human care, the ever present quality control, customer service, and unit cleanliness must exist, whether it is doughnuts or dentistry.

> There is going to be a McDonald's, a Century 21, a Pearl Vision in this field, and we are out to be it.

HOW IT BEGAN

Dr. Pyner, the third member of the top management team, did not fit the image of a conventional dentist. Age 40, with stylishly long black hair, he often wore open-throated silk shirts and gold chains beneath his white lab coat. His interests centered around his family, tennis (he was an "A" player), his Porsche, and ski racing. Pyner talked about the early development of the idea.

> David Slater became a patient of mine when I had my practice in Wellesley, back in May of 1979. We became friends and tennis partners. One day in July he said to me, "Hey, we're going to be competitors, I'm going into the dental business." He was going down to New York to see a retail dentist who had contacted him about starting a franchise.
>
> I told him that sounded very interesting. I was tired of "wet finger" dentistry and was looking around for something else.
>
> He went to New York and when he came back he said, "The numbers are unbelievable but the guys are jerks." So, we decided to take a look at it together.

TAKING A LOOK

Even though his Wellesley practice was grossing more than $200,000 a year - and netting about $100,000 - while he averaged about 21 hours per week in the office, Pyner felt that the structure of the industry was changing rapidly and that someday he would be affected. For one thing, the industry had become overcrowded. This condition was due largely to a government program that enabled some 6,000 new dentists to graduate each year. Many dental schools, including leading schools like Tufts, had reduced their four-year program to three. On the positive side, research done by the Nexus Group, the Phoenix-based dental research organization, had revealed a hidden market: their studies showed that 50 percent of the population did not go regularly to dentists. Pyner was aware of the new overcrowding in his own field of endodontia (root canal specialist).

> I could see where the future of dentistry was going. As a specialist, I could see people moving into my field. I could see that we had to use modern merchandising techniques to get the 50 percent not going to dentists.

So Pyner and Slater took a ten-day trip visiting four or five cities in the U.S. and looking at a half dozen or so retail dental centers. After the trip they decided they could do it better. At this point, in August, the two men set aside one day a week to do some intense research. They met each week in Slater's carriage house office for the next three months to put numbers together and construct, on paper, a prototype office. The result of this work was "a black thing," that is, a five-year plan in a black cover which included complete pro formas - right down to staffing. It was enough of a document to get one of the most respected underwriting houses in the country to sign on the dotted line. The firm, Brown and Smith, Inc. with branch offices throughout the country, positioned itself as the oldest venture capital firms in the nation. (*Exhibit 1* presents financial projections and notes from the original five-year plan.)

BROWN AND SMITH, INC.

Actually, Pyner and Slater had spoken with two possible underwriters. The representative from Worldwide Capital met them wearing blue suede shoes and an open sport shirt, with a variety of gold chains mingling in the riot of black hair on his chest. The other possible firm was Brown and Smith and, given the evidence before them, Pyner and Slater selected Brown and Smith. According to Pyner,...

> ...the plan was to get an idea and at the same time to go
> public. David had gone public this way before.*

On November 2nd, Ted Autumn, Vice President of Corporate Finance from the Brown and Smith office in Cleveland, and S.E.C. attorney, Bob Johnson, came to Boston to meet with Pyner and Slater. Following two days of negotiations, on November 4th, the two entrepreneurs had a signed letter of intent from Brown and Smith to sell $1.4 million in stock. It was to be sold in units consisting of 20 shares of preferred stock at $950 per share and 500 shares of common stock at $2 per share. In other words, Brown and Smith undertook to raise a minimum of $1 million dollars by selling fifty $20,000 units of stock shares.

----

*David Slater was Chairman of his own corporation, Mutual Enterprises, which employed fifteen other people. Omnidentix ws incorporated under this firm as were ABC Mobile Brake and Community Group. In fact, one reason Slater liked the idea of retail dentistry was because of his investigations into law clinics. He concluded that the numbers in dentistry were much higher. Most people only need a lawyer a few times in their lives but they always need a dentist. He almost was drawn to the health industry because of his other interests.

Community Group was a chain of seven "half-way" houses providing sheltered workshops for the mentally retarded. The idea was to prepare these individuals for active participation in the community. Some 200 patients had been "mainstreamed" through Community Group Franchise Centers in two years. Slater believed strongly in the franchising model. At one point in his career he and two other investors bought "Tennis Lady." Slater forced them to buy him out 24 hours later when he discovered they wanted to develop a chain of company owned stores rather than franchise.

	Price To Offerees	Brown and Smith Sales Commissions	Net Proceeds to Omnidentix
Per Unit Total	$ 20,000	$ 2,000	$ 18,000
Minimum total to be sold	1,000,000	100,000	900,000
Maximum total to be sold	1,400,000	140,000	1,260,000

SOMETHING IN A NAME

The name Omnidentix was selected from a wide range of suggestions from the principals and their wives. "The Tooth Fairy" and "TLC" were among those weeded out. Slater talked about the name selection process.

> A name that's going to be a trade name has got to be unique, and as legally protectable as possible. Words like 'Family' and 'American' are out. My own feeling is that there is nothing better than to coin a word. It took us a couple of months to come up with Omnidentix. The thought was to coin a phrase using 'dental.' But whatever we thought up someone in the group didn't like it. I eventually came up with dentix and then started attaching prefixes and suffixes. Eventually we landed on Omni and the "d" then became a dentist's mirror in our advertising copy. The whole thing came together.

> You know how Zayre's got its name? The owners of the store are Jewish. The sons decided to go into the discount business and they took the idea to the old man - who had a heavy acent. When the sons told him their idea, he said "Zayer Good" (pronounced goot) which is yiddish for that's good. The point is you can't copy it.

> Mr. Donut was a lousy name. People pick these names because they're easy. However, you must actively protect your name or you lose exclusive right to it. So how far do you go? At Mr. Donut we sued 'Miss Donut,' 'Sir Donut,' and 'Mrs. Donut.'

CONTINUED RESEARCH: KOPACK COMES ON BOARD

At this point Slater brought his past assistant, Ron Kopack, up from Florida to offer him a job. Kopack was reported to have turned around Benihana and taken it out of trouble. Slater offered him a generous salary and a percentage of the parent company, and Kopack accepted the job and made arrangements to move his family up to New England in time to begin work on January 1st, 1980. He spent at least part of his time working on problems with the Mobile Brake Franchise while waiting for further development in Omnidentix. Kopack was an operations man and left much of the conceptual and start-up work to the other partners.

At this time (December 17, 1979) the company was formally organized under the laws of the Commonwealth of Massachusetts to "engage in the business of affiliating with dentists for turn-key retail dental centers."

For the next seven or eight months, the Omnidentix team spent over $100,000 in legal fees. Pyner commented about this period.

> Brown and Smith kept sending us shopping lists of things
> they needed in order to start selling. They were driving us
> nuts. They needed all kinds of legal opinions and
> information. For example, I think they required something
> like eight separate letters of opinion on the name. Each letter
> cost about $5,000 to $10,000 in legal research. All through
> this Ted Autumn kept saying, "It's a nine-and-a-half out of
> ten."

During the winter Brown and Smith required that Pyner sell his private practice. By spring, Dr. Pyner had spent $80,000 out-of-pocket on the project. Fortunately, he was able to finance his investment through a series of real estate transactions he had made in recent years. In January, Omnidentix also obtained a loan for $150,000 based on the personal equity provided by the three team members. Together, these funds formed the initial $300,000 capitalization of the corporation. "I was stretched as far as I could go," remarked Pyner. "In six months I had gone from a well-to-do suburban dentist to an over-extended partner in a high-risk franchise.

SITE LOCATIONS

The search for locations had been started back in October, 1979. A decision had been made to locate the prototype unit(s) in high-traffic malls, preferably of an up-scale nature. Pyner remarked:

> None of the decent malls wanted a dental clinic. Nobody
> wanted crying, the sound of the drill, and blood in their mall.

Slater stated that the three most important things in franchising - in retailing too - were location, location, and location. In an attempt to solve the location problem, which was becoming a major impediment to Omnidentix's progress, Pyner and Slater climbed into Slater's car to drive around. As Slater put it, "Let's drive around to all the Mr. Donuts in the area and see if we get some ideas." As they drove, Slater chatted about the trade secrets of site locations in franchising. Good sites were on the route home after work; they were on the far side of intersections--on the near side of intersections cars stopped at the light and blocked the entrance way; never locate on a hill; and with few exceptions, it was not good to locate on a divided highway. Slater relied heavily on traffic counts when studying a proposed site. He always counted the nearby church steeples to get a reading of the neighborhood's "community sense." He had found, for example, that the number of Catholic Churches was important.

The drive that day in October eventually took the two men to the highest volume Mr. Donut in New England, located in Wellington Circle in Medford. After passing it, they drove by a new mall under construction. The two anchors were under final construction and Pyner and Slater went in to look around. They found the construction trailer and the mall manager. The manager explained that they were sold out of retail space and, in any case, they didn't want a dentist. Pyner recounted what happened next.

> Just then this guy walks in and David says, 'Hi Steve.' It was Steve Winer, an old business associate of David's. Steve asked him what he was doing at this place and David told him about Omnidentix. David asked Steve what he was doing and Steve said 'I own this place.' The manager said right away, 'I told them we didn't have any units left.' And Steve said, 'Are you serious?' And we walked around the mall and picked out the best site. By the time we left we had a location and we had agreed on the money.

THE BUILDING PERMIT

As a next step, Pyner applied to the Medford City Council for a building permit for the Omnidentix unit, and to his consternation the application was rejected by the building inspector. Although Pyner intended to appeal the ruling before the Medford City Council, this would take several months -- and move the construction timetable from an early spring beginning to a date in May. If the Council overruled the building inspector's decision, Pyner would have to wait an additional 20 days to see if any objections were filed. If not, the Medford site would have to be abandoned and a new search initiated.

For Pyner, the City Council was a crucial test. Any further delays or even the loss of this mall site would call into question the viability of the Omnidentix concept.

The building inspector's position was that the land occupied by the mall was zoned for commerical and retail use, not medical use. Such was the "official" reason given for halting construction. But some of the developers of the mall felt that local dentists were applyng pressure through unofficial channels to have the Omnidentix building permit killed. Medford dentists were already concerned about the impact that the Harvard Community Health Center would have on their practices. The Harvard Community Health Center was already under construction and a dental clinic was included in the plans. The competitive environment would become tight, indeed, if both the dental clinic and Omnidentix entered the market.

THE OFFER FROM SEARS

In December, 1979, an interesting offer from Sears developed. Through his involvement with the YPO (Young Presidents Organization), Slater became acquainted with a Vice President of marketing from Sears. Sears was very interested in the concept but was experimenting already with its second group of dental clinics in California. The Sears concept was called Prodex.

From a YPO conference in Omaha, Slater found himself whisked away to Chicago where he and Pyner met in the tower with John Wurmlinger, Head of Concessions for Sears. Wurmlinger was very interested in a licensing agreement with Omnidentix, so Slater and Kopack went to look at the Prodex units in California. At the meeting in the tower, possible product testing sites in Sears' properties were selected in Philadelphia, South Florida, Houston, and Columbus. Slater and Kopack did not like what they saw in California. The Prodex units, in their view, occupied bad second floor locations away from the main traffic sections of the store. But Pyner was reluctant to pass up the Sears opportunity, especially because of the uncertainty surrounding the Medford site.

> I would not do it because I was seeing our difficulty in getting good locations. Montgomery Wards was doing it and I thought it looked good. But no matter how much we showed them (Sears) that their way was wrong, they would not budge.

In the end, Sears would not agree to the major changes the three Omnidentix executives felt would be necessary to create the kind of dental centers they envisioned. So the Omnidentix team decided to continue alone.

Slater believed that the selection of center locations, Omnidentix franchise purchasers, and membership affilitations had to be carefully restricted and controlled by Omnidentix Systems Inc. After a dental center was to be opened, he felt the relationship between the company and its members would be governed by an agreement. The key aspects of this agreement are presented in the "Notes" supporting *Exhibit 1.*

OUTSIDE RESEARCH

Support for the Omnidentix concept received additional support and was furthered by the results of market research completed in the early months of 1980. Omnidentix had commissioned a market survey from a specialist in medical marketing consulting. The objectives of this survey were to find how the market could be segmented, what people looked for in a dentist, what brought people into dentists' offices, and what kind of advertising would be most effective.

As Pyner eloquently put it:

> The old dentist's rule of, "pain brings 'em in and pain keeps 'em out" is a lot of baloney. What we found was it is a combination of many points.

Those points specifically were:

- convenience of time and location

- availability of services - the hours

- need for specialists

- the way the office looked, both the people and the layout

- the way the patient was treated, including what was said

Pyner continued.

Out of the survey came recommendations on how to follow through with what we had learned. We adopted the airline hostess model. Eventually I'd like to have a training school just like an airline school. We currently have plans for contests for diets and things like that to develop a family sense, modeling on what the Japanese have done.

In short, by March 1980 it seemed clear to the principals from the research and from trends in the industry that Omnidentix could be successful.

THE MODEL CENTER IS READY -- BUT IS MEDFORD?

By April, 1980, all the pieces for the Omnidentix concept were in place, save one -- approval by the Medford town fathers.

Physically, the first clinic was to be the embodiment of the future in American dentistry. It would have a polished, inviting "store front" walk-in foyer. The office would be equipped with a $28,000 computer to keep records and a white uniformed receptionist, trained along the lines of flight attendants, to calm nervous patients. An "open" concept would be utilized with a large 6-8 chair multi-specialty work area with common supply areas. See *Exhibit 2*. All equipment would be the most modern available. The physical appearance would be further customized with special wallpaper, red oak furnishings, and modern art designed to convey a contemporary image consistent with standards of high quality.

Price would be a major appeal of the Center which would provide treatment at up to 50 percent less than fees charged by the traditional private practice. Omnidentix rates would be displayed prominently in the reception area and would follow the schedule shown below.

COMPARE AND SAVE

Cleaning, x-rays, examination $29
Silver (amalgam) filling (per surface) $9
White (composite) filling (per surface) $12
Root canal (per root) $79
Partial denture (cast) $229
Full regular denture (upper or lower) $189
Full cosmetic denture (upper or lower) $239
Full crown or cap $249
Orthodontics (braces) (full 24-month case) $999
Ask about our other low prices.

Convenience would be a second important selling point. Complete with a laboratory, the Center would be open six days a week from 9:30 a.m. to 9:30 p.m. and geared for 20,000 patients a year at an average of five per hour. The 72-hour week would be twice as long as normal hours in the traditional dentist's office, which would mean lower overhead because the expensive equipment would get heavier use. Bulk buying of the equipment and supplies would also cut costs.

In order to capitalize on the uniqueness of Omnidentix, the promotional strategy had been carefully planned. Kopack commented as follows:

> Advertising represents an important part of the Omnidentix System, the purpose of which is to create a nationally identifiable image through the combined advertising purchasing power of a multi-unit chain. Each Dental Center will spend approximately $10,000 for its grand opening and $18,000 in annual ongoing advertising.

Since Omnidentix Systems could not own and operate a dental center under the state regulations, the Model Center, like the others to follow, had to be owned and operated by a licensed dentist. Thus, Omnidentix entered into an agreement with David Pyner. Under the terms of this agreement Dr. Pyner's separate corporation entered into a membership agreement with Omnidentix systems just as other affiliated members would in the future. Other terms stipulated were:

1) All furniture, fixtures and dental equipment were to be purchased by Omnidentix and leased to Pyner's Model Center.

2) Pyner had no personal liability to Omnidentix in connection with any of the obligations of the professional corporate membership controlled by him.

3) Omnidentix loaned $50,000 to Pyner to provide the funds for the internal cash investment necessary to commence operations.

4) Omnidentix held the right to exhibit the center to prospective members, representatives of financial institutions and to utilize the center and its staff in connection with advertising and publicity programs of Omnidentix.

5) The center and its staff would be used in connection with the training program to be operated by Omnidentix for new franchise buyers and their staffs.

6) The center would also be utilized to research, test and experiment with all facets of the Omnidentix System.

7) Pyner's salary would be payable by Omnidentix reduced by the net profits of the (his) dental center.

8) Pyner would remain as full-time President of Omnidentix Systems.

9) Pyner could not transfer the Center's Membership in Omnidentix Systems or sell interest in the professional corporate membership without the consent of the Omnidentix Board.

10) Upon termination of the membership for any reason, Omnidentix held the right to purchase any leasehold improvements, furniture, fixtures and equipment that may be owned by the center at the depreciated book value, deducting from the purchase price any sums as may then be owed to Omnidentix.

The Medford Mall contained approximately 250,000 square feet of covered space and had as its principal or anchor tenants Bradlees (a division of the Stop and Shop Companies) and Marshall's (a division of Melville Corp.). The lease Omnidentix signed with the trustees of the Mall was for about a 1500 square foot area constituting a single enclosed retail trading space. The lease called for a term of 15 years at an annual rate of $28,000 per year for the first 10 years and the same rent adjusted by the Consumer Price Index during the last 5 years. In no event could rent surpass $49,000 per year. Taxes, common area maintenance charges, and certain insurance charges were to be charged on a pro rata basis.

But the fate of the entire venture hung on opening and putting into operation the Medford unit. First, it would "prove" the viability of the concept. And second, it would serve as a training center for future Omnidentix franchises and staff. How ironic, reflected Pyner, that a year's work and hundreds of thousands of dollars hung on a decision over which the Omnidentix principals had no or very little control.

THE SUMMER OF '80

On April Fools Day Pyner appeared before the Medford City Council and stated his case with an admirable mixture of eloquence and humility. The next week the application was returned - APPROVED. With renewed energy, the team redoubled its activities to open the unit in August, and -- in light of the mandatory waiting period -- notified the contractors that work could commence on May first.

Two major problems had to be addressed: staffing and building design.

Pyner's initial approach to staffing was to prepare an ad for professional and support staff and run it on the sports page of the Boston *Globe*. Response came to a blind box number. The ad ran once. After one week, Pyner had received twenty responses from area dentists. By the end of the second week, he had received more than 150 resumes, confirming his strong suspicion that the market for dentists was overcrowded. Pyner interviewed what he felt were the top 25 candidates, hiring 10. Half of those he hired were older, experienced dentists looking for part-time hours to fill out their practices and half were younger dentists looking for full-time positions.

With respect to designing and building the first unit, the same architect who had designed the freestanding units for both Mr. Donut and Howard Johnson was retained to prepare the plans for the center. The plans for the model unit were then put out to bid. By bidding out the equipment rather than relying on suppliers, as was the standard practice among dentists*, Pyner figured that he saved some $25,000.

The interior of the Omnidentix center was designed to be sleek and modern. The long featureless reception desk, with the computer patient scheduling and billing system, resembled an airline reservation counter. The waiting room featured chrome framed prints by Matisse on the walls, large plants, a color TV, and special custom-designed "Omnidentix" wallpaper. (See *Exhibit 3* which shows a photo of the storefront.)

Inside, in the semi-open treatment areas, brightly colored dentist's chairs would ring a centralized arrangement of sinks, trays and dental paraphernalia used in common by the 13 dentists and 17 dental assistants. Dr. Pyner described the concept behind these plans:

> Our idea was to make the center as gorgeous a place as you could imagine. It's a dental center, not a "clinic." A clinic makes you think of tile floors and a sterile public institution run by some guy with beer on his breath who couldn't make it on the outside. A great deal of research and thought went into the appearance of the office.

Furthermore,

> We're hiring atttractive people who are capable, cool, and good with people.

Then Pyner talked about the stituation in May when his contractors were finally ready to begin construction.

> By this time everybody was mad at me because of the delays. The suppliers were angry, the contractors were upset, because we were now into their prime work periods. The equipment supplier tried to charge us interest on the equipment charges. A dentist would have paid that interest but we told him to stuff it and switched suppliers. At this time, I also started hiring the para-professionals.

During the months of May, June, and July, Omnidentix was heavy into construction of the model unit and the training of the staff. Toward the end of July, Pyner had several major problems on his hands. His office supervisor, who came over from his private practice, was supposed to be in charge of training the para-professional staff, except she was in the hospital. Also, the specially-designed logotype wallpaper was so poorly hung that it had to be torn off and reordered. Then, in the midst of construction, Service, Inc., sent out the word processing system which was to provide a computerized patient file. (At

---

*Normally, dental supply contractors assisted their dentist client by facilitating the leasing or buying of chairs and other equipment. Suppliers did this and obtained a commission from equipment manufacturers.

the touch of a key a patient's credit history, account status, insurance, and dental history appeared on the video terminal or hard copy printer.) It did not turn out to be the easiest day of the project.

> You've got to picture this. We are in the midst of construction with workmen and noise all around. It is the hottest day of the year. And here four or five of us are crowded around the terminal. Service, Inc., sent out a girl who had only four or five days of training herself along with somebody named "Brad" who saw the system for the first time yesterday. The training was totally inadequate. We still have problems that were fed into the machine at that time.

THE OPENING

The timing of Omnidentix's first promotion caused problems as well. Ron Kopack had found a clause in the mall lease obligating Omnidentix to spend $850 a year advertising in the Mall Flyer. The Flyer was to have total market coverage (TMC) of the 150,000 households in the mall's designated marketing area (DMA) eight times per year. He quickly renegotiated this term and obtained a standing reservation for the back page of the flyer/shopper for $800 per insertion.

The dental center was scheduled to open August 8. On July 29 The Flyer, containing the Omnidentix back page ad, hit the street and the phone came off the wall. Dr. Pyner, without his long-time office manager, with a new staff, a malfunctioning computer, and in the midst of training and decorating, was overwhelmed by the response. One consultant in the dental industry had forecasted 200-300 appointments a week for a new Omnidentix unit. Over 1200 appointments were made for the first week, and by the end of the week Omnidentix was book solid for a month. Pyner worked 18 hours a day, seven days a week, trying to get control of the situation. During the first week he doubled the staff.

> Everything went crazy. We had no control. I had put more stock in what the computer could do but, instead, it was an albatross. I had to forget the money and just handle the patients! One dentist on the staff said, "Hey, a friend of mine doesn't like where he is practicing and wants a job." I said, "He's hired." I hired him on the assumption that a dentist who's a friend of a good dentist is probably a good dentist.

It was hard to measure the actual amount of sales revenue because of misentries in the computer and uncollected insurance claims, but the revenue actually collected and recorded in August was considerably ahead of the forecast. (See next page)

Sales Weeks	Forecast	Actual	Variance %
1st	$ 15,000	$25,000	67%
2nd	$ 20,000	$ 40,000	100%
3rd	$ 25,000	$ 62,000	148%

Dr. Pyner's reaction?

> I was depressed. Everybody was mad at me. Here everything was successful beyond our wildest dreams and I was depressed. It's so hard to get the system to work properly.

David Pyner had completed the first important stage of a radically new business venture, but for perhaps the first time in his working career he had severe business pressures - contractors were mad over delays, suppliers were upset at being pushed around, and the problems of controlling runaway sales were overwhelming.

During the midst of all the confusion surrounding the initial period of operation on August 29, Dr. Pyner received a phone call from ABC Network News in New York. They wanted to bring a four-man crew up to do an interview. Pyner agreed and the segment they did subsequently played on Good Morning America and on the evening news. In the middle of the filming, Ted Autumn from Brown and Smith walked in on his way back from vacationing on the Cape to announce that he was leaving Brown and Smith. Although he was the only one at Brown and Smith actively on the account, he assured Omnidentix not to worry because "this thing is a 9 1/2 out of 10" even though no sales of stock had yet been made.

OPERATIONS SETTLE DOWN

By October, the operation of the model unit began to smooth out. Dr. Pyner described this time:

> We started to get our act together. At the end of October, I finally got around to getting in the insurance forms. There were thousands of dollars in insurance lying around which I didn't have time to collect before. Ron stepped in with business systems and got it running properly.

FINANCING FUTURE DEVELOPMENT

As fall wore on and winter began, Pyner and Slater found that the problems with Brown and Smith were beginning to act as a real constraint on the growth of Omnidentix Systems. Ted Autumn had really been the only person who knew anything about Omnidentix and no visible sales activities had taken place since his departure.

The private offering memorandum finally had been completed and dated August 12, 1980, after much controversy between Slater and Autumn over who should be responsible for what parts of its development and production. Sales efforts were to have begun as of that date but nothing was in fact sold. Because it was to be a private offering, registration with the SEC was unnecessary. The printing on the cover of the memorandum made the risk clear, however, to potential buyers.

> The units offered hereby have not been registered with the
> Securities and Exchange Commission under the Securities
> Act of 1933, as amended (the "Act") in reliance upon the
> exemption from such registration provided by Rule 146
> promulgated under the Act as well as other applicable
> exemptions. Accordingly, the units are being offered only to
> a limited number of sophisticated and experienced investors
> who have such knowledge and experience in financial and
> business matters that they are capable of evaluating the
> merits and risks of the investment or are able to bear the
> economic risk of the investment.

At this point, two months after the agreement had been signed, Pyner and Slater knew that a decision had to be made. The apparent options were limited. They could fire Brown and Smith and proceed with a private offering through another venture capital firm, or they could retain Brown and Smith and try to encourage them to sell the offering more vigorously. Still another possibility was to terminate the current relationship with Brown and Smith and explore the waters of a public offering.

FRANCHISE SALES

By the middle of 1981, Slater and Pyner had been successful in selling four Omnidentix franchises. Three had been sold to one dentist and one to another. Both purchasers had units under construction - one in Dartmouth, Mass., and the other on Cape Cod. In addition, Slater was confident that a third buyer had been located for Pyner's original model unit in Medford. A number of inquiries about franchising had also been received and a response letter and questionnaire had been developed to help screen potential franchisees.

In most interviews, Dr. Pyner would talk about the future of dentistry, and then Mr. Slater would talk about franchising. Some of Slater's ideas on the subject were summarized in an article in a trade magazine, *Franchising Today*.

> Professional franchisors and franchisees will not seek to
> create a "consumer image," but to develop an image of
> improved professionalism. Franchised medical clinics or
> legal offices will not compete with *red* bricks against *blue*
> bricks on their office facades or resort to gimmicks such as
> revolving stethoscopes or golden briefcases five stories
> above the street, but their increased efficiency, greater

service, and lowered fees. All will contribute to an enhancement of professional image, thereby proving to the world the wisdom of franchising in the professions.

When describing specifically the Omnidentix concept, Mr. Slater used a 35 mm slide presentation. Two of the slides on the carrousel described the relationship between the franchisor and franchisee. Both slides diagrammed what each party brought to the bargaining table.

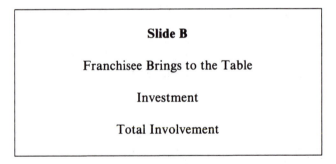

Slide A

Franchisor Brings to the Table

System
Know-How

Product Service   Franchise

Guidance

Slide B

Franchisee Brings to the Table

Investment

Total Involvement

Another slide showed the rather phenomenal growth (205%) of franchising over the past decade from $111 billion in 1970 to $338 billion in 1980.

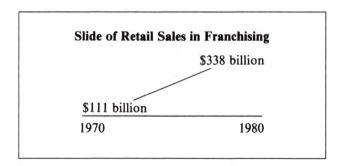

Slide of Retail Sales in Franchising

$338 billion

$111 billion

1970   1980

Slater went on to point out that one third to total retail sales in the United States were from franchise businesses - totally 15% of the nation's GNP. There were 488,000 franchise owners at last count. Furthermore, according to Dun and Bradstreet, 95% of all franchise units succeeded as businesses whereas 45% of all businesses failed. A study done by the University of Michigan found that initiative and drive were the two major components of business success. Following these points, the next slide in the presentation made the final arguments for franchising.

Why is Franchising Successful?

1. We do trial and error.
2. It's a process of duplication — improvements.

Regarding this second point, much of Dr. Pyner's time was being spent on the development of an operating manual for Omnidentix franchise buyers. The unique business problems asociated with the operation of a retail dental center went on, however. For example, a problem developed around how to do scheduling of staff. In fact, Pyner and Slater were having a "hassle" over the issue.

Slater styled a ratio of efficiency:

$$\frac{\textbf{Staff Salaries} \quad (\$)}{\textbf{Charges} \quad (\$ \text{ Volume})}$$

Slater felt that this ratio could be calculated easily using accounts receivables. But Pyner saw major difficulties judging the value and volume of work in progress in a dental practice. He argued that you simply don't have a way to attach a dollar figure to the work you've done in a single visit on a patient requiring multiple treatments.

> Take, for example, a $200 bridge. Today we make the impression and a week later the patient comes back in for the bridge. What are sales?

	Option A	Option B	Option C
Today	$100	$200	?
Week Later	$100	$ 0	?

> It may be that the second visit is easy. What is the best day to figure the sale and how do you develop a system for staffing against sales? How would you account for no-shows?

Slater attempted to explain what he was after.

> In every business you have to have controls - people controls. So we put in time clocks. If there are too many people on the staff, I'm going to lose money. On the other hand, if there aren't enough I'm going to go down in service. It's a risk to be taking and there are lots of factors to consider.
>
> The ratio appears to be about 17% of gross of staff dollars. A normal staff of 4 doctors being paid on a 40% commission (too high, at the next store we're going to cut it down to 30%), requires 4 assistants and 1 rover. Let's assume we're over-staffed. What can we do? We start a cleaning detail and start phoning to confirm appointments.
>
> It may be that the second visit is easy. What is the best day to figure the sale and how do you develop a system for staffing against sales? How would you account for no-shows?

Another question Slater was actively considering was whether or not to sue Brown and Smith. After the agreement had been signed, the underwriters had had sixty days to use their "best efforts" to sell the offerings. Slater stated that the only thing they did was mail the circular to 20 or 30 venture capital firms. The question was, did this solitary move constitute Brown's best efforts under law under the "reasonable man" concepts?

A good deal of time was being spent in the franchise sales efforts as well. And, because of the great interest in retail dentistry and Omnidentix, Pyner found himself being asked to give speeches regularly. With all this, he still spent about eight hours a week in private practice - doing root canals in the private office with lead-lined walls in the Medford Mall Model unit for $75 a job.

ASSIGNMENT QUESTIONS

1. From a systems analysis (process flow) perspective, what is similar/different about the Omnidentix operation compared to the business of a traditional dentist?

2. What are the implications for Omnidentix of these similarities/differences?

3. What is the profile of an ideal franchisee for this business from the franchisor's perspective?

4. What are the critical elements of the Omnidentix franchise from the franchisee's perspective?

5. What concerns should the Omnidentix team (Slater and Pyner) have about their venture at this time and what advice would you give them regarding these concerns?

Exhibit 1

Omnidentix Systems Corporation and Subsidiary
Projected Statements of Income
(000 Omitted)

	December 17, 1979 (Inception) to June 30, 1980 (Actual)*	1981	1982	1983	1984	1985
			Years ended June 30,			
Projected openings			4	10	25	40	50
Revenues:							
Initial franchise fees (Note B)	$ –		$200	$500	$1,250	$2,000	$2,500
Management services (Note C)	–		45	163	482	1,074	1,893
Real estate leases (Note D)	–		174	624	1,851	4,123	7,266
Commission on sale of equipment package (Note E)	–		34	113	281	450	563
Equipment lease (Note E)	–		34	33	34	33	34
Interest income (Note F)	–		136	109	57	122	217
	–		623	1,542	3,955	7,802	12,473
Cost and expenses:							
Expenses directly related to franchised dental centers (Note G)	–		116	307	910	2,015	3,545
Selling, general and administrative (see schedule)	(55)		555	628	899	1,122	1,305
Interest expense (Note I)	–		25	22	85	279	267
	(55)		696	957	1,894	3,416	5,117
Income (loss) before income taxes	(55)		(73)	585	2,061	4,386	7,356
Income taxes	–			170	1,051	2,237	3,752
Net income	$ (55)		$(73)	$ 415	$1,010	$2,149	$3,604

*See accountants' report and historical financial statements included elsewhere herein.
  The accompanying letter and notes and assumptions are an integral part of the projected financial statements.

Exhibit 1 (Cont.)

Omnidentix Systems Corporation and Subsidiary
Projected Schedule of Selling, General and Administrative Expenses
(000 Omitted)

	December 17, 1979 (Inception) to June 30, 1980		Years ended June 30,			
		1981	1982	1983	1984	1985
	(Actual)*					
Payroll	$ 14	$154	$303	$494	$648	$772
Payroll taxes	1	18	36	59	78	93
Start-up expenses**	1	125				
Advertising	2	85	50	50	50	50
Administrative charge — Mutual Enterprises		25	30	35	40	45
Professional fees	5	20	25	30	35	40
Auto	2	18	18	18	18	18
Occupancy costs	3	15	30	35	40	45
Travel	14	15	20	30	40	50
Publication — newsletter			15	18	20	23
Printing		10	10	10	10	10
Office supplies and expenses	4	10	13	15	18	18
Telephone	2	9	10	13	15	18
Life insurance		9	9	9	9	9
Depreciation and amortization (Note H)		2	4	5	5	5
Sundry and contingency	7	40	56	78	96	109
	$ 55	$555	$629	$899	$1,122	$1,305

*See accountants' report and historical financial statements included elsewhere herein.

**Includes development of promotional package, operating systems and forms and design costs.

The accompanying letter and notes and assumptions
are an integral part of the projected financial statements.

Exhibit 1 (Cont.)

Omnidentix Systems Corporation and Subsidiary
Projected Statements of Cash Flow
(000 Omitted)

	December 17, 1979 (Inception) to June 30, 1980 (Actual)*	Years ended June 30,				
		1981	1982	1983	1984	1985
Sources of cash:						
Net income (loss)	$ (55)	$ (73)	$ 415	$1,010	$2,149	$3,604
Depreciation and amortization		21	49	120	250	430
Proceeds from sale of common stock	150	1,225				
Proceeds of bank loans		150		600	900	
Payments of franchise fees receivable		17	50	119	266	485
Increase in franchise fee deposits		25	75	50	50	
Repayment of advance to Mutual Enterprises		21				
Repayment of advance to officer-stockholders		28				
Repayment of loan to affiliate			35			
Increase in accounts payable and accrued expenses	99					
Reduction in other assets		8				
	194	1,422	624	1,899	3,615	4,519
Application of cash:						
Equipment package — 1st dental center	70	20				
Loan to affiliate		35				
Leasehold improvements	28	272	720	1,590	2,610	2,880
Corporate office equipment	4	16				
Financed franchise fees		125	250	625	1,000	1,250
Payments on bank loans		10	22	29	31	228
Other assets	33					
Payments of accounts payable and accrued expenses	21	39				
Advance to Mutual Enterprises	28					
	184	517	992	2,244	3,641	4,468
Increase (decrease) in cash	$ 10	$ 905	$(368)	$(345)	$ (26)	$ 51
End of period cash balance	$ 10	$ 915	$ 547	$ 202	$ 176	$ 227

*See accountants' report and historical financial statements included elsewhere herein.

The accompanying letter and notes and assumptions
are an integral part of the projected financial statements.

Exhibit 1 (Cont.)

Omnidentix Systems Corporation and Subsidiary
Projected Balance Sheets
(000 Omitted)

	June 30,					
	1980	1981	1982	1983	1984	1985
	(Actual)*					
Assets						
Current assets:						
Cash	$ 10	$ 115	$ 147	$ 202	$ 176	$ 227
Certificates of deposit		800	400			
Current portion of franchise fees receivable		50	119	266	485	635
Due from Mutual Enterprises	21					
Due from officer-stockholders	28					
Advance to affiliate		35				
Total current assets	59	1,000	666	468	661	862
Property and equipment:						
Equipment	70	90	90	90	90	
Furniture and fixtures	4	20	20	20	20	20
Leasehold improvements	28	240	840	2,340	4,740	7,740
Construction in progress		60	180	270	480	360
	102	410	1,130	2,720	5,330	8,210
Accumulated depreciation and amortization		(21)	(70)	(190)	(440)	(870)
	102	389	1,060	2,530	4,890	7,340
Franchise fees receivable due after one year		58	189	548	1,063	1,678
Other assets	33					
	$ 194	$1,447	$1,915	$3,546	$6,614	$9,880

Exhibit 1 (Cont.)

Liabilities and Stockholders' Equity						
Accounts payable and accrued expenses	$ 99	$ 60	$ 60	$ 60	$ 60	$ 60
Notes payable — banks		140	118	689	1,558	1,220
Franchise fee deposits		25	100	150	200	200
	99	225	278	899	1,818	1,480
Stockholders' equity:						
Preference stock, no par value:						
Authorized — 2000 shares						
Issued and outstanding						
1980 — 150 shares	142					
1981-1985 — 1,550 shares		1,282	1,282	1,282	1,282	1,282
Common stock, no par value:						
Authorized—100,000 shares						
Issued and outstanding						
1980 — 52,500 shares	8					
1981-1985 — 91,875 shares		68	68	68	68	68
Retained earnings (deficit)	(55)	(128)	287	1,297	3,446	7,050
	95	1,222	1,637	2,647	4,796	8,400
	$ 194	$1,447	$1,915	$3,546	$6,614	$9,880

*See accountants' report and historical financial statements included elsewhere herein.

The accompanying letter and notes and assumptions
are an integral part of the projected financial statements.

Omnidentix Systems Corporation
8 Operatory Prototype
Projected Annual Statements of Income

Facility utilization	70%	80%	90%	100%
Revenue (Note II-B):				
General dentists	$374,400	$436,800	$499,200	$499,200
Specialists	172,800	172,800	216,000	259,200
Hygienists	40,000	60,000	60,000	80,000
Total revenue	587,200	669,600	775,200	838,400
Expenses:				
Professional services (Note II-B)	234,880	267,840	310,080	335,360
Staff salaries	69,940	83,980	97,500	107,120
Payroll taxes and fringes	9,092	10,917	12,675	13,926
Advertising	18,000	18,000	18,000	18,000
Collections	587	670	775	838
Computer costs	12,000	12,000	12,000	12,000
Dental supplies and materials	29,360	33,480	38,760	41,920
Health insurance	4,110	4,687	5,426	5,269
Insurance — other	1,000	1,000	1,000	1,000
Interest	2,500	2,500	2,500	2,500
Janitorial service	1,500	1,500	1,500	1,500
Licenses, permits and local taxes	500	500	500	500
Miscellaneous	2,349	2,678	3,101	3,354
Office supplies and postage	2,936	3,348	3,876	4,192
Patient amenities	1,174	1,339	1,550	1,677
Rent (Note I-D)	69,871	69,871	69,871	69,871
Repair and maintenance	1,000	1,000	1,000	1,000
Subscriptions — magazines	200	200	200	200
Telephone	2,500	2,500	2,500	2,500
Management service fee (Note I-C)	18,200	18,200	18,200	18,200
Uniforms and laundry	1,174	1,339	1,550	1,677
Utilities	5,000	5,000	5,000	5,000
Total expenses	487,873	542,549	607,564	647,604
Income before taxes*	$ 99,327	$127,051	$167,636	$190,796

*Exclusive of depreciation on equipment and amortization
of franchise fee (Note II-C).

The accompanying letter and notes and assumptions
are an integral part of the projected financial statements.

Exhibit 1 (Continued)

OMNIDENTIX SYSTEMS CORPORATION AND SUBSIDIARY

NOTES AND ASSUMPTIONS REGARDING THE PROJECTIONS

The projected financial statements are based on assumptions that have been provided by the management of Omnidentix Systems Corporation or its representatives. The assumptions disclosed herein are those that the management of Omnidentix Systems Corporation believe are significant to the projections or are key factors on which the financial results of the report depend. Some assumptions inevitably will not materialize and unanticipated events and circumstances may occur subsequent to June 9, 1980, the date of the projections. Therefore, the actual results achieved during the projected periods will vary from the projections and the variations may be material.

I. OMNIDENTIX SYSTEMS CORPORATION AND SUBSIDIARY

A. *General Assumptions Regarding the Projected Financial Data*

The Company is described in detail in the Private Placement Memorandum. The projections were prepared on the assumption that the maximum number of shares being offered are subscribed, that the underwriter immediately exercises its warrant to purchase 5% of the total shares of Common Stock to be outstanding immediately upon the completion of the Offering and that the expected timing would be achieved. Specifically, we assumed that the operation of the first franchise (to be owned by an affiliated entity - "affiliate") will commence on or about July 1, 1980 and that the offering of the shares will be consummated during August, 1980.

B. *Initial Franchise Fee*

There will be a franchise fee of $50,000 for each dental center, payable, except in the case of the affiliate, $25,000 prior to the opening of the center, and the balance monthly over a period of 60 months with 10% add-on interest ($625 per month). The affiliate will pay its franchise fee in 36 equal monthly installments of $2,000 including interest.

Franchise fees are recognized as income when both the Company and the franchisee have substantially performed their obligations under the franchise agreement relating to the initial fee. For purposes of these projections, income is being recognized at the time of opening of the dental centers.

C. *Management Service Charge*

Each franchisee will pay an annual fee of $18,200, payable $350 per week, for management services. Although this fee is subject to adjustment each year in accordance with increases in the Consumer Price Index, this has not been given effect to for purposes of these projections.

D.   Real Estate Leases

The Company will lease premises for each dental center and sub-lease to the franchisee. Leases will generally be for 15 year terms plus renewal options. Annual lease charges are calculated as follows:

Cost to company (average of 1,750 sq. ft. at $17/sq. ft.)	$30,000*
Additional rental charged to franchisee	17,500
Amortization of leasehold improvements**	
(cost of $60,000 plus 12½% mark-up	
amortized over 5 years at prime plus 5%-	
prime being estimated at 17% for purposes	
of this projection)	22,371
Annual lease charge to franchisee	$69,871

E.   Commission on Sale of Equipment Package and Equipment Financing

Each franchisee will purchase an equipment package, exclusive of data processing equipment, for which he will pay approximately $101,250 of which $11,250 will be a commission to the Company. The Company may finance the purchase of the equipment package by some of the franchisees.

The affiliate will lease its equipment from the Company. Rent for the first year will be $33,557.

F.   Interest Income

Interest income results primarily from the financing of one-half of the initial franchise fee and from the investment of available cash balances in short-term certificates of deposits or similar instruments.

---

*The Company was granted a three month waiver of rent under the terms of the lease for the first dental center.

**These projections have been prepared using the assumption that the Company will own and finance the acquisition of all leasehold improvements of th dental centers. It is quite possible that some franchisees will acquire their own leasehold improvements and finance their acquisition through financing arrangements made by the Company or themselves or that certain landlords will finance the construction of the leasehold improvements and adjust the lease terms accordingly.

G. *Expenses Directly Related to Franchised Dental Centers*

This item consists primarily of rent expense and amortization of leasehold improvements.

H. *Depreciation and Amortization*

Company owned furniture and equipment will have an estimated useful life of ten years. Their cost will be depreciated on the straight-line method. The cost of leasehold improvements will be amortized over the term of the related realty lease using the straight-line method.

I. *Interest Expense*

The Company has negotiated a $150,000, 66 month loan with a bank interest at a 10% add-on rate. The loan is payable interest only for the first 6 months and then interest and principal for the remaining 60 months at $3,750 per month.

During the third through fifth years, the Company will be required to borrow funds to finance its operations. For purposes of these projections, it is assumed that the Company will pay prime plus 2%, prime being estimated at 17%. The average borrowings are estmated as follows:

Year ended June 30,	
1983 (last six months only)	$ 700,000
1984	1,400,000
1985	1,400,000

J. *Loan to Affiliate*

Represents a working capital loan to the Company's affiliate. The loan is to bear interest at an annual rate of 18%.

II. EIGHT OPERATORY PROTOTYPE

A. *General Assumptions*

An eight operatory center will consist of 7 treatment rooms and one examination/x-ray room. The facility will be open six days per week for a total of 74 hours. Projections have been prepared upon 70%, 80%, 90% and 100% utilization.

B.   Revenues and Professional Services

All professional staff will be engaged as independent contractors and earn 40% of the gross revenues generated by their services. General dentists will generate revenues of $65 per hour, specialists $100 per hour and hygienists $20 per hour. The center will include a lab and the professionals will bear their own lab costs. It is assumed the lab will operate at a break-even.

C.   Depreciation, Amortization and Income Taxes

No provision for depreciation on equipment or amortization of the franchise fee have been reflected in the accompanying projected annual statements of income. The cost of the depreciable assets is $101,225 and the franchise fee is $50,000. Each franchisee will select useful lives and methods of depreciation and amortization based upon relevant facts and circumstances.

No provision for income taxes has been recorded since that calculation will depend upon the form of orgnization of the franchisee.

Exhibit 2

Layout of Medford Mall Unit

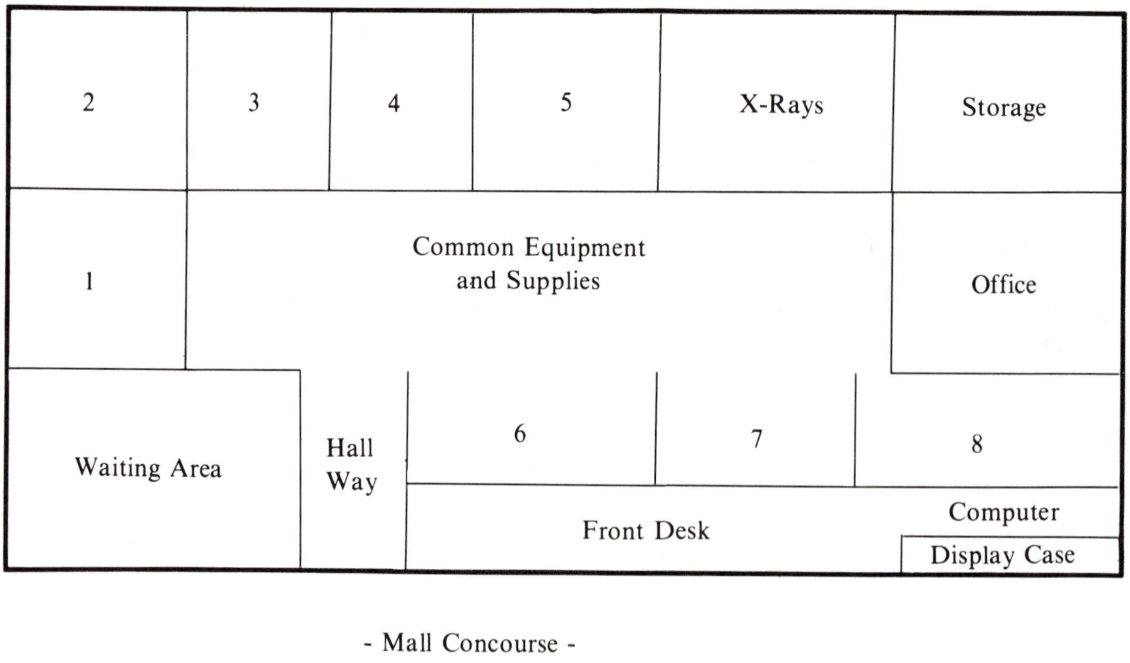

- Mall Concourse -

Exhibit 3

Part Three

REASSESSING, DEVELOPING AND NURTURING ENTREPRENEURIAL ACTIVITIES

THE COUNTRY SHOP PARTNERSHIP

During the spring of 1981, Tom Watson was wondering about what action he should take, if any, regarding the formalization of his four-year old partnership with Betsy Ames. Together, they had founded a retail outlet called The Country Shop that specialized in "American Country" (also called "primitive" or "Early American") furnishings. Typically, these pieces included furniture, pottery, textiles, and folk art created during the 1700 to 1850 period. More recently, they had also decided to offer their personal services as interior decorators.

BACKGROUND ON TOM WATSON

Tom Watson, age 23, had always been interested in antiques and knew that someday he would have his own shop.

During Tom's junior and senior years of high school, he attended art classes at Munson Gallery Museum, Farmington, CT., part-time. Tom started his first "business" at this time, selling antiques through direct mail orders. He advertised exclusively in *The Maine Antiques Digest*, a monthly trade publication. Although this venture was profitable, Tom found it extremely difficult to operate. Advertisements had to be submitted six weeks prior to printing. Often Tom could have sold the advertised item(s) before the mail orders arrived.

After leaving art school, Tom discontinued the mail order venture and took a job at Finlay's Inc.[1] where he was employed as a buyer for the garden department. He held this position for three years, the last year of which his responsibilities expanded to include the

---

[1] Finlay's Inc. was a specialty store dealing primarily in china, crystal, linens and other items for the home serving the greater Hartford area.

purchasing of china and crystal for the store. During this time, Tom continued to build an antique quilt collection (which he began during high school). Although he was happy with his job at Finlay's, Tom realized that his collection was becoming unmanageable and impractical. Too much of his money was invested in the quilts (he had nearly fifty of them).

In order to reduce his quilt collection, Tom joined an artisan's cooperative in Wolfeboro, New Hampshire. The atmosphere at the cooperative, with its many visiting craftsmen and dealers, exposed Tom to other primitive forms of art such as pottery, cupboards, and Early American Textiles. This exposure inspired Tom to start collecting new pieces of primitive art. As his product line expanded, Tom began to exhibit his new products at antique shows in addition to his quilt line at the cooperative. At these shows, Tom came into contact with many dealers. One in particular, Betsy Ames, shared a common interest in primitive antiques and the desire to open an antique shop one day.

BACKGROUND ON BETSY AMES

Betsy Ames, 25 years Tom's senior, had spent her life primarily being a wife and mother to two children. Her husband discouraged her from working, so she led for many years the typical life of a housewife. While much of her time was taken up domestically, she devoted some time to volunteer work for the Junior League of Hartford and various other clubs. She was also an avid tennis player. Betsy's marriage ended in divorce after a number of years, leaving her with the two children, but little in the way of furniture or other assets. Several years later, Bety married Dr. Henry Ames, a general practitioner affiliated with Hartford Memorial Hospital. Betsy chose to decorate her new home with Early American furnishings. As she added more pieces, her home decorating grew into a hobby, and Betsy became involved in antique shows in order to continuously upgrade her collection. After a period of time, she joined Tom in the shows, which they continued for two years, until the startup of their antique shop, Curiosities.

VENTURE STARTUP

When Tom and Betsy finalized their decision to open an antique shop, Tom took on the reponsibility of looking for a place to rent. The two had several specifications which they felt had to be met. First, they wanted to lease a shop with low rental expense located within a twenty-mile radius of their Farmington homes. Other restrictions included: they did not want to be located in a shopping center and they wanted a small shop, preferably in an old converted home (because it would have "character"). After six months of investigation, a Litchfield real estate agent informed Tom that a home was available which had been converted into a lawyer's office with an adjoining vacant room ideal for a shop. This old white clapboard house seemed to be just what Tom was looking for and the rent seemed reasonable, so he signed the lease. Tom showed Betsy the shop and she approved. The partners decided that Tom would control 70% of the business and Betsy the remaining 30%. Tom financed his portion with his cash savings and a loan from his parents. Betsy's portion was financed from profits derived at antique shows.

The two agreed on a rather unique partnership--each partner would buy his own goods with his own funds, but would integrate these goods in the shop. Tom's goods accounted for approximately 70% of the shop's floor space and Betsy's the rest of the shop, in accordance with their shares in the business. Both Tom and Betsy committed themselves to selling all of the goods--not simply their own, but the profit from any sales would revert back to the owner of the goods.

The shop opened on March 7, 1977 under the name of *Curiosities*. This name was chosen by Tom in part as a carryover from the New Hampshire cooperative, The Golden Past Gallery. The shop, specializing in American Country antique furnishings, featured such items as cupboards, pottery, and Early American textiles. Although there were several other antique shops in the area, the owners felt that competition from these shops was virtually non-existent because of their specialization in the American Country line of antiques. The owners did cite two shops: The Bayberry Shoppe, New Hartford, Connecticut, and The Antique Sampler, Plainville, Connecticut, as being competitors for the same market. However, the owners felt that their shop had an edge insofar as they offered a wider selection within the line and, in addition, a substantially lower markup than their competitors.

As a means of introducing themselves to the public, they chose to advertise in *The Litchfield Townsman,*[2] *The Maine Antique Digest*[3] and the Avon, Simsbury, Farmington edition of the *Town Crier*[4]. The advertisements brought in few Litchfield customers, but several from Avon, Simsbury, and Farmington.

In November, 1978, Tom's landlord made plans to enlarge his second story law office. Expansion necessitated enclosing the porch on the ground floor in order to extend the second story outward. With the expansion on the first floor, a bay window was added that would allow The Country Shop to acquire the street exposure that had been lacking up to this point. Tom and Betsy saw this addition as a chance to expand their own shop.

However, the additional floor space meant an increase in the rent payments. With the increased burden, Tom was no longer able to carry his share of the rent. Betsy agreed to increase her share to 50%. But before Betsy agreed to increase her share, she requested that they change the name of the shop from Curiosities to The Country Shop in order to better reflect the image they desired for the shop.

With the newly expanded shop came other changes as well. Now The Country Shop could feature more merchandise and utilize their large bay windows with interesting displays. The owners stated that they changed this window every seven to ten days and owned as many as a dozen pairs of curtains for it. New items were also emphasized by their visibility through the front window. They stated that many of their customers came window shopping each Sunday to see what was new and exciting in anticipation of the coming week.

----

[2] *The Litchfield Townsman* is a weekly local newspaper serving Litchfield, Ct.

[3] *The Maine Antiques Digest* is a monthly publication catering to the antique trade.

[4] *The Town Crier* is a weekly local newspaper serving the towns mentioned.

The owners took pride in getting to know their clientele and tried to give the shop an additional personal touch, as exemplified by their window and other displays and method of selling. The displays included fresh cut flowers, plants,homemade bread, gingerbread men, and fresh fruit--the effect of a "country" home. The owners' selling approach was decidedly "soft sell"--that is, they allowed their customers to browse for the first fifteen minutes or so that they were in the shop. The owners preferred not to have more than four people in the shop at any one time, so they could devote more time to each individual.

This personalized approach lent itself to developing a friendly relationship with their clientele. The owners made it a point to get to know their regular customers by name-- often remembering their birthdays with cards in the mail or having flowers delivered to their home. They also kept their eyes open for specific requested items when they were on buying expeditions. Both owners felt that these additional expenses were very beneficial to their business.

The decor of the shop lent itself to many questions about home decorating. Tom and Betsy often gave their customers ideas and suggestions for displaying their purchases in their homes. The owners hadn't given any serious thought to pursuing interior decorating until January, 1980, when they were invited to participate in the 1980 Decorator's Showhouse.[5] Of the five hundred professional decorators from across the country who were asked to submit bids,[6] Tom and Betsy were among the fortunate forty-six who were ultimately chosen to design a room. Decorator's Showhouse was a turning point for Tom and Betsy, for as many as 22,000 people visited the Showhouse and saw first-hand the bedroom that they had so skillfully decorated.

This exposure marked the beginning of their expansion into the interior decorating field and contributed to the business' breakeven in the spring of 1980. Competition in interior design was deemed negligible in the Litchfield area because customers interested in The Country Shop for interior design work would be attracted mainly due to the Shop's focus on American Country decor. Although The Country Shop's initial consultation fees were at par with their competitors ($100/hr.), a further competitive advantage was the lower follow-up offered (The Country Shop's $25/hr. vs. competitors' $50-$300/hr.) This aspect of the business slowly evolved to the point where they had decorated approximately eight private residences and were asked to refurbish a Guilford, Connecticut restaurant with a country theme.

---

[5] Decorator's Showhouse is an annual fund raising project sponsored by Junior Leagues in the United States.

[6] These bids are in the form of an essay (fifty words or less) explaining how one would decorate a given room. Each decorator may submit one bid for each of three different rooms.

The owners took pride in The Country Shop's rapid growth and loyal customer base. Mary Ellison Emmerling made note of the shop in her book, *American Country, A Style and Source Book*, which enjoyed great success since its publication in early 1980. The shop was featured via a two-page spread in the April issue of *Good Housekeeping* magazine and was scheduled to appear in either the June or July issue of *Better Homes and Gardens*. Both owners felt the shop's appearance in these national publications would increase their exposure and enhance their reputation even further.

With their business taking off, both in the shop and in the interior decorating area, Tom and Betsy began to question what direction they would take in the future.

THE NATURE OF THE PARTNERSHIP: A PERSPECTIVE BY TOM WATSON

When Betsy and I decided to go into business together, we didn't really give much thought to the structure of the partnership itself. Of course, we realized that a formal partnership agreement was important, but we had enough to worry about. Neither of us had ever started a business before, and looking back we've probably made many mistakes. Despite the fact that Betsy was 25 years older than I, we both had confidence that we'd make a great team. Not only did we both love primitive antiques, but we both had a creative streak in our blood.

Well, anyway, after spending about six months looking for a location for the shop, I finally found one with the help of a Litchfield real estate agent. Betsy was vacationing in Florida with her husband at that time and could not be reached. Even though I didn't have Betsy's "official" approval, I really fell in love with the shop and I just knew she'd love it too. Well, as it turned out, Betsy was pleased with my choice. Nevertheless, perhaps the location was our first mistake.

First of all, we found out that the town of Litchfield had a restriction that tied the size of sign a business could have to the expected sales volume. So, in our case, we would have a sign about 6"x24"--in other words, we might as well not have a sign. We were also really surprised and disappointed to find that we had hardly any customers from Litchfield! Worst of all, the stigma attached to Litchfield was unbelievable! Dealers assumed that just because we were located in little affluent Litchfield, that we'd have fantastic markups, so they wouldn't give us the standard dealer's discount (10%). Little did we know that our customers were not even from Litchfield. If Betsy and I had known about these problems, we might not have settled on the Litchfield location, but what the hell. You see, if we make it, we make it...

Anyway, back to the partnership. I really would have liked to have been sole owner, but unfortunately I was broke. I had some savings and was able to borrow some money from my parents, but even this would only have covered 70% of the money needed. Betsy didn't mind owning only 30%--she had plenty of money and instead of playing tennis and doing volunteer work, this would keep her occupied with her favorite hobby--buying and selling antiques.

I guess our agreement was kind of unique. We figured instead of buying the goods together and splitting the profit from the sales, as do most partners in the antique business, we'd try something different. Our plan would give us independence to choose our own goods. This way we wouldn't have to argue about our individual tastes or beliefs about what would sell. We wouldn't have to bicker about pricing strategies and we wouldn't have to worry about overdrawing a single checking acount when we're off in different directions buying. Of course, I was able to buy more, or larger pieces, for the shop than was Betsy because I had 70% of the floor space and she only had 30%.

After two years of operating like this, the rent was up. Hell, I'd put all the money I'd earned back into the business and I just couldn't afford the increase. I couldn't very well have borrowed money because I had no credit. I hated to give up control, but I asked Betsy if she'd be willing to put up another 20% and she agreed. Even though we operate on a 50/50 basis now, to tell you the truth, I usually have the final say.

By the way, we do have a third partner of sorts. Actually, this third partner is our joint checking account in the name of The Country Shop. It's not that we had a lot of extra cash, but we wanted to have an account where we could store money from consignment sales, which are currently running about 7% of our business. For example, we have a local man who makes reproductions of folk art decoys and fruit carvings. We also have a local woman who makes reproduction pierced lampshades and we have some women who make rag rugs for us. In addition, we no longer purchase antique mirrors, as we have a woman who supplies them for us to sell on a consignment basis.

We decided to draw on this account for only three reasons. One would be to purchase pieces for the shop that neither of us could afford as individuals. Another would be to purchase items for our displays such as fresh plants, fruit, new drapes for the bay window and the like. The final reason would be to purchase goods for Decorator's Showhouse 1981, if we're lucky enough to be chosen next year. Actually, I have taken small amounts of money from time to time for personal expense, but I'm getting no salary and I have to live. Betsy has a husband, but I can't keep borrowing money from my parents--it's enough that they still let me live at home.

Basically, Betsy and I are very happy with the way the business has grown. Of course, we haven't made a mint, but we did break even earlier this year--things are certainly looking up. We've been having great fun with interior decorating, too. It's really gotten off the ground since Showhouse, but it's very demanding of our time. As a result, we've hired a few "unofficial" employees to take care of the shop when we can't be there.

It's important that I mention that we wouldn't be where we are today without the help of both my brother-in-law and Betsy's daughter. You see, my brother-in-law, Bruce, helps us out by refinishing many of our cupboards, several of which are in pretty bad shape when we buy them. It's helpful to us to have someone so close by whose work we trust and whose prices are also quite reasonable. Plus, he really enjoys doing this. Betsy's daughter, Deborah, works as a photographer and, thanks to her, we appeared in the April issue of *Good Housekeeping*.

It's hard to believe we've come along as far as we have in just the three years since Betsy and I founded the business. Although there have been mistakes and disappointments along the way, they have been more than overshadowed by our "success," which seems to be growing by leaps and bounds every day now. Right now I'm concerned that this trend continue so we can realize all of the potential business that seems to be coming our way. The reason that this concerns me is that we have no formalized strategy for our continued growth and development as a business, nor do we have any written partnership agreement. At first, this didn't seem so important, as our time was so taken up by simply building our distribution channels, finding the best media for advertising, etc.--basically, just getting the business off the ground. But now it seems crucial that we do put this down in writing somehow.

I guess we should start thinking about the future, especially in light of Betsy's goals and my own. This business started out mainly as an expansion of a hobby for Betsy and remains so, but the problem is that the business has grown so that it requires an almost "permanent" commitment to see that it continues--*more* than the kind of commitment one devotes to a hobby, especially in terms of time. Also, in a few years Betsy's husband will be retiring. Betsy has made no secret about the fact that the two of them plan to retire to the farm in New Hampshire that they bought several years ago and have been refurbishing ever since. I can't help but wonder what will happen to the business when the day finally comes that she does leave.

For me, the starting of the business was more of trying to pursue a career in the antique field--one to which I devote the majority of my time and to which I'm willing to devote increasingly more time as various new opportunities arise. I see no end to the possibilities in the future and would like to pursue every avenue that becomes known to us, without the business getting out of hand. I have so many ideas! The problem is that I want to pursue them all.

I wouldn't mind concentrating more on interior decorating, but then again I don't want to give up our shop. I like the shop and wouldn't even mind just perfecting what we have. I also love the thought of opening another shop--or even a whole chain of Country Shops! Betsy and I have even talked about opening a shop in New Hampshire under the same name when it comes time for her husband to retire. That way, Betsy could run the shop up there and I could run the one in Litchfield. Actually, I wouldn't mind relocating to New Hampshire altogether--I always did like it there. We've also considered Avon, Connecticut, as a location. Or, we could stay right here in Litchfield and expand the shop--carrying a greater variety of antique pieces and also more in the way of fine quality folk art reproductions. If worse comes to worse, I guess I could always go back to Finlay's.

ASSIGNMENT QUESTIONS

1. Should Tom take any action regarding the four year old partnership? Why or why not?

2. What is unique about this partnership?

3. What are some potential areas of conflict between the partners?

4. Assuming they decide to develop a written partnership agreement, what should be included? excluded?

5. How could Tom enlist Betsy's agreement and participation to formalize their partnership?

LAUREL GROVE TENNIS CENTER

THE ENTREPRENEURIAL OPPORTUNITY

Until 1974, the weather in Laurel Grove, Tennessee, a quiet University town, limited the tennis season to eight months of the year because there were no indoor courts within a 75-mile radius of the city. Despite a growing interest in year-round tennis facilities, the county's Recreation Commission had not seriously considered the building of indoor courts to serve its population of 48,000 residents (30,000 permanent residents and 18,000 University students). The commission felt that such construction would receive more financial and popular support if it were undertaken by the University.

But when Brian Traylor, the University's 62 year old physics professor and part-time tennis coach, requested that indoor courts be added to the University's recently completed $12-million athletic complex, he received no encouragement. Since authorization of the complex, the Board of Regents had shifted its priorities to non-athletic campus construction. Furthermore, informal discussions with members of the Board convinced Traylor that indoor facilities would be viewed as an extravagance because the University presently maintained twenty outdoor courts for students, staff, and faculty.

After several months of investigation, Traylor decided that the best way to provide indoor courts would be to construct a privately-owned tennis complex.

Since Traylor was due to retire from the University in a few months, he decided to undertake the project himself as an alternative activity which could supplement his retirement income of $15,300 a year.

Before committing himself to the building of the courts, Traylor attempted to assess the city's need for such a facility. He based his estimates, in part, upon a survey of tennis facilities published in *Tennis* magazine. The magazine had estimated that at least 170 regular players were needed to support one court and that a population of 25,000 generally included about that many regular players. Traylor believed, however, that Laurel Grove could adequately support at least three courts, even though its population was far less than the 75,000 recommended in the article. He thought that Laurel Grove had more than its share of players because of the large number of residents he knew personally who had taken tennis lessons at the University, the local country clubs, and the County Recreation Commission Programs. He further reasoned that the number of regular players per court could be reduced from 170 to 155 because of the large number of women who would use the courts during the normally slack daytime hours.

Traylor already owned outright two acres of undeveloped land at the edge of town which would be suitable for the courts. As his own house was located on the property, placing the building there would make it convenient for him to supervise the operation of the facilities at all times. However, Traylor faced several delays before he could begin building the tennis center. A petition to eliminate a city right-of-way for the construction of a street through the property postponed issuance of the building permit for six weeks. Another six weeks was required for out-of-state office approval for utilities hook-up.

While waiting for the permits, Traylor sought the necessary financing. The survey in *Tennis* magazine had estimated that the average cost of an indoor tennis court would be $100,000, but Traylor's initial cash outlay would be less because he already owned the land. He was also able to reduce his required financing by deciding to purchase a prefabricated building and to contract only for its actual construction. (The more costly alternative would have been to authorize a contractor to purchase the necessary materials and to construct the building from a standard architectural design.) After several visits to local banks and meetings in nearby Middletown with representatives of the Small Business Administration, Traylor secured a nine percent, ten year SBA loan of $135,000 -- the amount required to construct two courts.

THE OPENING OF LAUREL GROVE TENNIS CENTER

A few months later, in January 1974, Traylor opened the Laurel Grove Tennis Center. It had two excellent indoor courts, though only the barest of additional facilities. On one side of the short hallway leading to the courts were two dressing rooms, each containing a wooden bench, five coat hooks for clothing, and a single shower, sink, and toilet. On the other side of the hallway was a small room serving as office and lounge. One office wall displayed a meager assortment of tennis clothing and equipment in lieu of an elaborate pro-shop.

Despite the spartan facilities, the tennis courts enjoyed immediate popularity due to the absence of competition and to Traylor's acquaintance with a very large number of local players. The rental rates for the courts were $7 per hour during the daytime and $9 per hour for evenings and on weekends. The rates were established based upon the results of a nationwide survey of tennis court rental fees. Traylor charged neither initiation nor annual membership fees, as were common in most private tennis centers. In fact, he offered a five percent discount to players who reserved courts on a regular basis.

Even the "pro-shop wall," as small as it was, received a lot of attention. Since it was intended only to provide a service to his regular customers, Traylor priced most items only slightly above their wholesale costs. Traylor would buy a tennis racket frame, for instance, for $20 and spend forty minutes stringing it with $1.50 worth of nylon cord. He would then sell the racket, complete for $30. An identical racket would sell for approximately $40 in local stores. As a result, the pro-shop acquired a favorable reputation throughout eastern Tennessee and North Carolina. Many customers would drive from nearby towns to shop at Laurel Grove, even when they were not able to reserve court time.

After being open for only a few weeks, the use rate neared 100 percent. The courts were open from 7:00 a.m. to midnight throughout the indoor tennis season of October to April, and the only unreserved times were the first and last hours of the day. In fact, operations were so successful that Traylor was able to make his SBA loan payments for the entire year from just the income obtained during the eight-month indoor tennis season. This payment schedule held true for each of the first three years of operations.

OPERATION OF THE CENTER

One reason Traylor was able to operate profitably was that the center had no paid employees. Despite keeping the center open 360 days a year for 17 hours a day, Traylor was adamant in his opposition to the expense of any employees. Although a tennis instructor was available on a regular basis, with the lessons arranged by the office, Traylor did not collect any portion of the instruction fees. Feeling justly compensated because the courts were rented, Traylor forfeited his "percentage" in order to avoid any possible complication of his tax calculations.

Occasionally, Mrs. Traylor worked at the center, and originally she was listed as the pro-shop manager. It became evident at the end of the first year's operation, however, that her inclusion as an official employee would result in additional income taxes of $800 to $1,000 per year. (The center was a proprietorship and its income tax was computed as a Schedule C attachment to Traylor's personal income tax return; filing a joint return, while at the same time listing Mrs. Traylor as an employee of the center, resulted in the additional required payment.)

Laurel Grove Tennis Center was profitable in each of its first three years of operation. Net income carried over from the Schedule C to Traylor's personal income tax form was approximately $11,000 each year. Traylor took this approach because he neither paid himself a salary nor deducted his implicit wages as a business expense in the business income statement. Instead, the income was retained and reinvested in the business.

In July 1974, just six months after the first two courts were opened, Traylor began making plans to add a third court. At first, he wanted to enlarge the original building to include the new court and thus save on heating costs. However, construction costs for the addition would have been high because the land on either side of the building was very steeply sloped. Instead, Traylor decided to construct a second building, attached to the first by a covered walkway. He added a small lounge area at the end of the walkway with a soft drink machine, a coffee maker, and a few lounge chairs. In order to pay for the new building, Traylor re-negotiated the bank loan to increase the amount from $135,000 to $183,000.

By reinvesting the profits of the next year's operations, Traylor was able to make a second major improvement. He had a door cut in the office wall that formerly constituted the pro-shop and added a 15' x 30' room adjacent to the office in order to expand the merchandise display area. Pro-shop sales were $50,000 in the first year of operations, $55,000 in the second, and $70,000 in the third. In each of the first three years, Traylor spent an amount nearly equal to pro-shop gross sales to replace and increase the merchandise inventory. By the end of 1976, what was left of the original wall, the new room, and a large part of Traylor's basement were filled with tennis rackets, clothing, and other assorted equipment. About half of this merchandise consisted of factory discontinued items which Traylor had been able to purchase at a very substantial savings. However, in order to take advantage of the savings, he was often forced to buy certain items in undesirably large lots, which resulted in a slow turnover of selected items.

In addition to increasing his inventory, Traylor felt forced to selectively increase his selling prices. Rather than using a predetemined markup percentage, Traylor set prices for each item based upon its apparent demand and the prices charged in local stores. However, the average item was tagged approximately 25 percent below the suggested retail price. Nevertheless, Traylor regretted having to make the increases, because he retained his original philosophy of viewing the pro-shop primarily as a service for his player customers.

THE SUMMER SEASON

The center functioned very much the same in the summer as it did during the busier winter months, despite the fact that the occupancy rate dropped to 30-50 percent of full capacity. Since outdoor tennis courts were readily available at a variety of locations throughout Laurel Grove, few residents appeared willing to pay the relatively high cost of playing indoors during warm weather.

As a result of the decreased demand for his courts, Traylor found it much easier to operate as a one-man business during his "off-season." For example, he was often able to shorten his operating hours either by opening the center in the late morning or by closing during the earlier evening hours when courts had not been reserved in advance. Also, because he did not choose to engage in advertising or promotional efforts, Traylor was relatively free to enjoy the summer months relaxing with his family or playing outdoor tennis with his friends.

While Traylor did not elect to promote his courts through media advertising, he did make two adjustments in light of the seasonal slump. The first was a reduction of all court rental rates to $6 per hour. The second was an informal contract which he has developed with the County Recreation Commission for six court rentals daily for a 10 week period. The Commission offered tennis lessons to county residents for a very nominal fee and used part of the revenues to pay Traylor $1,500 per summer for the use of his courts.

THE FUTURE

Traylor had no further plans for expansion. He believed that he had reached an optimal level of merchandise inventory and had as many courts as he needed and could adequately maintain.

Thus, Traylor intended to continue the existing operating strategy indefinitely. His decision stemmed in part from his belief that a minimum of six courts would be necessary in order to pay outside help and still preserve a reasonable return on his investment. However, the decision also reflected the fact that he felt comfortable with his present level of financial investment and absence of organizational complexity.

ASSIGNMENT QUESTIONS

1. What are the principal advantages and disadvantages of a "one person" operation?

2. What are Traylor's personal objectives for starting the tennis center?

3. How well are these objectives being satisfied?

4. How successful is Laurel Grove Tennis Center as a business venture?

5. What criteria do you think Traylor should use in assessing plans to revise his operation?

6. Given your criteria, what would you advise him to do?

MERCHANT OF CHINA, INC.

The following advertisement appeared in a local newspaper during July, 1980

Catalogue Venture

> Specialty catalogue needs Investor-Manager for immediate turn-around operation. Merchant of China, Inc., is entering its second year with a growing customer base, growing sales per catalogue (two catalogues to date), growing national recognition through advertising--and a temporary cash crunch. A challenging opportunity for operations-oriented strategic planner willing to invest.
> Contact Christopher Whitney, (714) 545-5872
> July 1980

Though the immediate future looked grim, Chris Whitney believed that his mail order company had a promising future if he could survive the next six months. Chris had raised $25,000 in the spring of 1979 to start his venture, after an initial testing period of nearly a year. Elements of his proposal appear in Appendix A. (For reference purposes, this Appendix has been divided into several exhibits). Under the new plan, Chris was aiming for the standard industry breakeven of gross sales twice the cost of the catalogue--for his next publication, scheduled to appear in October 1980. His first had returned 45¢ on a unit cost of 40¢, his second 55¢ on a unit cost of 30¢, and by the fifth quarter of business operations he had every reason to believe that his projected return of over 50¢ per 25¢ per unit would be accurate.

The chief difficulty at present was a lack of working capital. Chris had borrowed an additional $30,000 from a friend to pay for the second catalogue, but he was relying heavily on cash from incoming orders to cover outstanding bills to suppliers. At the moment, his payables were stretched to the limit and order fulfillment could no longer be delayed. He was $96,000 in arrears to customers and suppliers, threatened with legal action from both sources, and coping with an incipient ulcer and a frantic wife. He could not hope to generate enough cash internally to see his way through the present difficulties and pay for the printing of the next catalogue as well. But unless he could generate new catalogue sales, he would have no new sources of revenue. Chris Whitney needed help.

BACKGROUND

Chris Whitney was born in 1940 in San Bernardino, California, the only child of his conservative working-class parents. His father died unexpectedly when Chris was very young, and his mother moved soon afterwards to Los Angeles to be nearer her brother and his wife. Subsequently, Chris became very attached to his uncle, an entrepreneur who enjoyed the challenge and rewards of his self-made career. With his uncle's encouragement, Chris developed the art of selling door-to-door -- magazines, seeds, brushes -- and soon earned close to $100 a week which he invested in high growth stocks rather than opening a savings account as his mother would have preferred.

After graduating from parochial schools and East Los Angeles High, Chris went to work in the mail room of an insurance company, but he soon became bored and enlisted in the Army in September, 1959, for a 15-month stint. During his period he "rubbed elbows with college grads for the first time in my life," and after completing his service requirements he began the second phase of his formal education. He decided to become a chemical engineer because it paid well, and enrolled in Pasadena City College as a first step. In 1962 he transferred to a cooperative engineering program at the University of California at San Diego (UCSD).

While at UCSD, Chris began to question his choice of an engineering career, for his interests had turned recently toward writing--fiction and journalism--and he was thriving on his co-op job as reporter for a San Diego newspaper. As a project for his new dual major in engineering and English, he had the opportunity to interview his literary idol, Jack Kerouac, but came away disappointed. "I felt Kerouac was depressing, a victim of his own delusions."

With his dreams about being a bohemian novelist tarnished, Chris felt at loose ends and decided to take a year off to do manual labor and sort things out. The year proved a useful one; Chris graduated from USCD in 1967 and went to work for a local newspaper where he wrote political and business news as well as opinion columns. During this period, Chris also was a contributing editor to *New West* magazine and did some teaching at UCSD.

By 1976 Chris had become impatient with his newspaper job. He wanted managerial responsibility and his own column as well, but his bosses were uncooperative on both counts. Also, he had been unsuccessful in his bid to obtain a prestigious graduate fellowship.

Largely because of these setbacks, Chris decided to leave the paper to take a job in the city government as a consultant in public relations. Subsequently, in February 1977, he decided to strike out on his own as an independent public relations consultant. Relying on his skills as a writer and on his selling ability, he planned to find at least one large corporate client annually, and work for them on an annual retainer fee. However, client development was taking an unexpectedly long time; a year later several major corporations had signed on as clients, though the contracts were small.

Professionally, this is where Chris Whitney found himself in 1978. Fortunately, his personal life was more settled. In 1974 Chris had married Susan Evans. Subsequently, Susan had completed business school and was working in a small accounting firm. They had one child.

VENTURE CONCEPT

Public relations work was slow and so Chris began to think of other ways to increase his income which would utilize his writing and selling skills. Susan's mother ran a gift shop specializing in imported items as a profitable hobby. One day Chris accompanied her to a trade show, the industry's annual gift show. As he was walking through a trade show, the concept for Merchant of China was born. Chris explained:

> I responded very favorably to three areas of merchandising: Oriental, Nautical, and Early American. Since these areas interested me, I began asking people questions about the renewed interest in Oriental objects and the history and tradition of the China trade. By the time I left the trade show I had decided to investigate who might be selling merchandise along those lines.
>
> What I found out was that there seemed, to me at least, to be a very obvious niche in the marketplace for "specialty" Oriental wares based on the theme of the old China clipper trade. The only "specialist" I could find was Gump's in San Francisco. Since I didn't want the headache of a retail operation, I thought exclusively in terms of mail order. Again, Gump's catalogue was the only competition, but the more I investigated the more I realized they wouldn't be competitive. Their catalogue was used primarily to promote the store, not as a profit center in its own right. It's a "go-for-order" concept, unlike mail order which must "go for names" as well.
>
> Then I thought how my skills would fit the operation. I figured I could write really interesting copy about the objects in the catalogue, develop the whole romantic concept of trade between China and America in the 19th Century, and that I was a good salesman--I can get people to do things. I liked the name "Merchant of China" and decided the idea was worth pursuing.

DIRECT MAIL MARKETING - AN OVERVIEW*

Mail order has been an effective method of selling for many years, and the mail order catalogue is one technique for this type of marketing. Most people think "Sears" when the history of mail order catalogues is discussed, but beginning in the 19th Century a variety of other catalogues and flyers were sent to prospective customers through the mails, and a number of customers who liked the convenience, or the uniqueness of the product, or the price.

In the 1960's, the volume of direct mail sales and solicitation rose dramatically. Three principal factors were: the computer and its ability to print lists; the modernization of the U.S. Postal Service and the advent of zip codes; and the popularity of credit cards.

In the 1970's there was a boom of another sort--the "specialty" catalogue. Many of these catalogues were assembled by retail operations in order to expand their sales of selected merchandise to a specific audience, but the impetus unquestionably came from Roger Horchow, a successful buyer for Nieman-Marcus who introduced the concept of a catalogue "Collection"--a store without walls. Within several years he was doing millions of dollars of business.

Industry figures are difficult to compile because mail order sales frequently are made by non-mail-order business, which, however, included more than catalogue selling. A study in 1977 indicated that "collectibles" as a category of merchandise grossed a minimum of $1 billion through mail order sales. Another forecast showed the industry as a whole growing at an annual rate of 8 to 12 percent. Why? Convenience, the phone-option, the credit card, the increase of working women with more money and less time...though age and sex were not limiting factors in these "specialty" sales.

In recognition of the mail order boom, the Federal Trade Commission passed a series of regulatory measures in 1975. These included:

> . Merchandise must be received within 30 days unless otherwise specified.
> . If not, prompt refund must be made upon request.
> . After 60 days, a full refund must be made automatically.

The mail order business attracted hundreds of would-be entrepreneurs because of the low cost of entry (often no more than a few hundred dollars) and the promise of high returns. However, very few of these ventures began as "from scratch" catalogues; usually mail order was an extension of another proven venture, or of a media advertising effort.

———

*Information in this section is drawn mainly from:

"Direct Mail and Mail Order Handbook," Richard Hodgson, Dartnell Publishers, 1977.

"How to Start and Operate a Mail Order Business," Julian L. Simon, McGraw-Hill, 1981.

The classic success/failure story in the field was Kaleidoscope, a "specialty" catalogue conceived by a young woman with a flair for merchandising. Kaleidoscope started in a carriage house in 1974 with $5,000 capital. In 1978, the company reportedly grossed $20 million. In 1979, it filed for bankruptcy, leaving 19,000 angry customers with $850,000 of undelivered merchandise, and suppliers claiming over $2.3 million in unpaid invoices. The problem, said the critics in retrospect, was not the quality of the merchandise nor the lack of customers, but the internal management: lack of inventory control, cash flow analysis, payment schedules, and shipping procedures.

During these years, certain ratios became standard ways of measuring catalogue profitability. For example, 60% was accepted as the lowest possible markup per item, not including shipping. Generally, gross sales had to be twice the cost of printing the catalogue to achieve break-even. "Net Sales" for each catalogue item had to cover the cost per page (or per fraction of page) which it was allotted in the catalogue ("net sales" were gross sales less cost of goods and shipping).

INITIAL INVESTIGATION

Mr. Whitney knew he lacked experience in the mail order business and began at once to find out all he could:

> First of all, I started looking around at other catalogues. In order to sell gift merchandise you need a catalogue with a substantial amount of merchandise from which to select. It has to be done in color and it's an expensive product. I found that out right away by calling around to 50 people or so in the field. I also found out that advertising itself is a negative cash flow, but it is a necessary evil to develop new names.

> So I needed a catalogue and I needed lists of names. I figured I could choose the merchandise from trade magazines, and write the suppliers who seemed to be in the right lines. For the lists, I figured I could buy a few, and place a few ads. Then I could call other mail order people and make a deal on exchanging lists. It cut costs to deal directly with the mail order houses instead of using a broker, and swapping is cheaper than paying outright. So I started calling the guys, and got my name around.

STARTUP

In July 1979, Merchant of China was officially incorporated and, with the $25,000 he had raised, Mr. Whitney began work on the fall catalogue. He had planned to print a catalogue quarterly and he intended to start with a mailing of 100,000, increasing each mailing by an increment of 100,000 until he reached 400,000--by which time he projected break-even. He commented on the first catalogue:

> I got the first catalogue produced for $12,000. I jawboned my suppliers. It was a 24-page catalogue, digest size. Most people use a 32-page, full-size catalogue, which means my catalogue was about a third the size of the competition's. I knew this was bad, seriously bad, but it was all I could afford. I figured it would get us in and we could expand on it by making very tough decisions. Those decisions included stretching our payables and lagging with our fulfillment. We'd be taking it on both ends but I believed it was a sound decision.
>
> It took a lot of arm-wrestling with photographers, designers, color separators, printers--with everybody--but it got done, and virtually everyone in the industry who I've spoken to was amazed at my low production costs. It's a very nice looking catalogue.

The first catalogue appeared in October 1979, and at the end of two months had generated 45¢ on a unit expenditures of 40¢, somewhat lower than Mr. Whitney had hoped. Nonetheless, he hired an office manager, an order processor/bookkeeper and three part-time helpers to type and fill orders from the warehouse. Also, he had developed an inventory control system on cards and handwritten forms which enabled him to track a number of facts daily: which of the 12 rented catalogue mailing lists showed the highest rate of return, which purchases were in response to magazine advertisements, how much merchandise was presently in stock, and which items were the most popular.

THE SECOND CATALOGUE

After analyzing the sales of the first catalogue Mr. Whitney realized that his instinct for selecting desirable merchandise was not always reliable. Consequently, he hired a consultant who had worked as a buyer for "Kaleidoscope." Together they spent several days during the first part of November choosing a balance of high-price, high-margin items and easy to move merchandise such as mugs and ashtrays. Mr. Whitney planned to print 200,000 catalogues showing these products for mailing early in the spring of 1980.

After considerable hard work, the catalogue was in the mail in March 1980. Unfortunately, this was the same month that President Carter made his television address urging Americans to stop using their credit cards. Mr. Whitney figured that Carter's policy shift cost his company close to $100,000 in lost sales. He was not alone in his misery; reports from both retailers and mail order houses all indicated dismal sales in March and April. Chris Whitney explained what he did to try to offset the drop in sales:

> I took a very rapid action step. I wrote a letter that told people that we were giving them a 5% discount. I didn't know if a 5% discount would mean anything; I thought about a 25% discount but feared that would make things worse. So I decided that 5% was the right figure, which is about what the increase in bank handling charges would be for credit card customers. At first I was going to offer it only to credit card customers, but then I decided it wouldn't look good for check-paying customers, so I did it across the board. My letter pointed out that we were doing our patriotic duty by helping to implement Carter's anti-inflation plan.
>
> I also decided to cut the next catalogue in half, and send only 200,000 rather than the scheduled 400,000. My wife insisted on it, and it was a prudent decision, in view of our financial situation, but it diminished our chances of recouping our losses.

OPERATIONS: SPRING AND SUMMER 1980

Mr. Whitney described operations after the second catalogue had been mailed:

> The girl I hired for Customer Service really had her hands full. She was on the phone most of the day talking with customers who had questions, and most of them were pretty irate.
>
> Then I started getting hit from the other side. The suppliers and creditors began to call, and telephone messages began to pile up on my desk. "This call requires your immediate attention." I didn't call them back because I couldn't pay them. After a while I made a decision that I wouldn't return any calls. There were too many to possibly answer, so why be selective?
>
> That caused resentment and problems internally. The employees felt I didn't care. I could never really make them understand the problems, even though I had a chart up on the board so that everyone would know what the condition of the company was.
>
> The bookkeeper got very mad at me when one of her checks bounced. "Why are you yelling at me? You're the

bookkeeper," I said. But I know her problems were horrendous. The cash flow was really complex. There was money coming in daily in the form of personal checks and American Express and Master Charge payments. American Express sent a check payable to us -- a deposit would be made through American Express, and after 10 days to 2 weeks we would get a check. Master Charge was a bank transfer -- money would be transferred to our account but if a customer hadn't received his merchandise after several months he'd notify his bank that he wasn't going to pay for it. Then his bank would get the money back from my bank and would make a transfer out of my account into theirs. Things were really bad.

And yet, we had improved catalogue sales almost to the 2:1 ratio; 30¢ cost for 55¢ sales. I know that if we could figure out some way to get through one more round, we'd make it.

If I can get help in structuring a plan to turn this thing around, I'm sure other investors would fall into line, including the friend who invested the second round, "rescue" injection of $25,000.

ASSIGNMENT QUESTIONS

1. Would you take Chris Whitney up on his offer for a management and equity position in his venture, assuming of course you have the necessary funds for the investment? Why? Why not?

2. If not, under what conditions would you do so?

3. What would you recommend to Mr. Whitney?

APPENDIX A

**MERCHANT OF CHINA, INC.
FINANCING PROPOSAL
SUMMARY**

Merchant of China, Inc., operating from warehouse space in San Diego, has already obtained trademark protection of its name from the U.S. Department of Commerce. It will be the first mail order catalogue company in the country to develop an image for itself as a specialty outlet for high-quality antiques and reproductions from the Orient. The main thrust of the company will be to build an image of itself as a recreation of the Old East India Tea Company.

We feel this concept has the ability to attract attention as a focal point of several intersecting centers of interest currently developing in American society:

1. "Save Gas, Shop By Mail," is the central theme of a new advertising campaign currently being conducted by the U.S. Postal Service. It is a virtual certainty that this theme will be picked up by United Parcel as well and then played up by newspaper and magazine editors throughout the country. Our advertising will tie into the theme and we would expect to share in the benefits heavily through that tie-in and through our Public Relations efforts.

2. Antiques are rapidly becoming, with gold, among the most actively sought investment vehicles in the marketplace. We would carry perhaps 10 percent of our volume in affordable antiques ($50 range predominately, but going up all the way to $1,500...a concept that has already been successfully tested by Horchow and Shopping International).

3. Since the advent of our China diplomacy and the recognition of Mainland China, there has been a dramatic increase in demand for Oriental merchandise of all kinds.

4. In the aftermath of turmoil caused by Civil Rights, Drugs, Free Love, and the Vietnam War, Americans are turning to traditional values and a renewed respect for Free Enterprise. The tremendous appeal generated by "Roots" and "Proposition 13" are enough to convince us that a catalogue saluting the "Rugged Individualism" shown by the Early Clipper Captains with an editorial approach using short vignettes and homilies, together with high quality merchandise either from that era or vaguely reminiscent, will be passed around and used.

5. The spector of Recession is also apt to make more shoppers turn to mail order, since, in addition to gas savings, it is traditionally thought of as an economical way to shop.

THE MOC SUMMARY

Merchant of China, Inc., is seeking an initial capitalization of $25,000 through equity financing. Cash flow projections indicate that at this level, we will be in a solid position to conduct a growing, profitable enterprise. The current plan is to raise as much money as possible, however, by initially distributing shares on a basis of one percent for each thousand dollars invested. The shares will be increased in price as soon as the catalogue is in hand and again, of course, when the company hits turn-around. At the end of the first fiscal year, all unaccounted for shares will be distributed proportionately amongst the minority shareholders.

Our market research, conducted over the past year, points the way to which media will be most efficient and profitable for our very upscale customer profile. We anticipate that after our first year of business, our house customer list will be sought after and extremely valuable because of the high average purchase we have already achieved in the marketplace.

Analysis of the past performance leads us to expect a Return on Investment of just about 100 percent the first year (in terms of earnings). By the fifth year, earnings should represent a multiple return of 16 on investment, or $16,000 for each thousand dollars invested.

Applying a P/E factor of five to that number would give a value of $80,000 to each thousand dollars invested.

MANAGEMENT

The Merchant of China, Inc., will be headed by Christopher Whitney who conducted the market research for the initial phase of the company's development. Mr. Whitney will be assisted by a Merchandise Manager with long-term experience in mail order catalogue merchandising. Negotiations are currently under way with such a person.

In addition to the experience he has gained in conducting this one-year market research experiment, Mr. Whitney brings with him an understanding of media and markets gained through an extensive background in journalism and Public Relations Consulting.

After graduating from the University of California at San Diego in 1967, Mr. Whitney went to work for a San Diego newspaper. During his nine years with the organization he reported political and business news and wrote an opinion column. He also taught journalism courses at UCSD and was a contributing editor to *New West* magazine. In 1976 he left the newspaper to join the city administration as a Consultant in Public Relations. Since February 1977, he has been working as a private consultant to corporate and retail clients in Public Relations and Advertising.

Merchant of China, Inc., will gain directly from Mr. Whitney's credit relationships with publications like the *Los Angeles Times* and *The New Yorker*. The 15 percent agency discount will be immediately available to the Merchant of China through Mr. Whitney's formal recognition as an advertising agency by these publications. A two percent cash discount will also be available when the Merchant of China is in a position to take advantage of it. In addition to writing copy for the catalogue itself and the advertising copy, Mr. Whitney will work with editors in the field to develop a series of feature stories about the mail order industry and the Merchant of China's emerging role in it.

NATURE OF BUSINESS

The Merchant of China, Inc. will be the first mail order catalogue company in the country to carve out an image for itself as a specialty outlet of high-quality antiques and reproductions from the Orient. The main thrust of the company will be to build an image of itself as a recreation of The Old East India Tea Company. The concept will rely heavily on editorial content within the catalogue, again distinguishing itself from other companies in the field. Romance and history will be combined within the pages and through the sales promotions the company intends to generate.

This concept will also allow opening the line gradually to include early American as well as maritime-related items that would fit in a classically-designed, high-valuation home. Initial research through magazine advertising and brochure distribution already proves that there is a ready market for the concept and the merchandise. Merchant of China, Inc., will benefit immediately by taking the next step and bringing mail order economics into play, i.e., it will cost no more to produce the 32 page color catalogue, on a per unit basis, than it did to produce the test mailing piece.

COMPETITIVE STRATEGY

The Merchant of China, Inc., intends to carve itself a signficant share of the mail order furnishings market through simple product differentiation combined with an aggressive advertising and publicity campaign designed to achieve widespread name recognition on a short time span within the home furnishings buying public.

In addition to the appeal of the catalogue merchandising concept itself, which we feel has withstood the test of market research and analysis, we intend to generate a number of feature length magazine articles highlighting the historical aspects and motivation behind the concept. With the background of the company President, Christopher Whitney, we feel a reasonably sure chance of success with this goal which should heighten the appeal of the catalogue to potential buyers when they receive it in the mail.

Relations have already begun with manufacturers in the Orient and importing activities will proceed as soon as volume permits purchasing by the container load. Purchasing direct will achieve for us a minimum of 30 percent reduction in costs, half of which will be passed on to the customer in the form of lower, very competitive prices. Few catalogue companies are currently importing directly, Shopping International being a notable exception.

Once importing begins, The Merchant of China, Inc., will immediately begin wholesaling its line directly to interior decorators through direct mail. The line will *not* be offered to retailers. We, thus, expect to further our appeal as a distinguished provider of tasteful furnishings to the most discriminating homeowners in America. This marketing strategy will be maintained through our media buying and advertising layout and design. Only the most upscale magazines will be utilized for the most part (*Better Homes and Gardens* being the major exception, where we will accept a lower average order and a less discriminating customer for the potential it offers for low cost-per-inquiry volume) and the layout will be designed to connote elegance and exclusivity.

THE MARKET

The sales forecasts utilized in the Proforma are based on the experience achieved with our test brochure. The analysis of results from advertising in four national magazines indicate that the two most responsive audiences of the four are to be found among readers of *The New Yorker* and *House Beautiful* magazines. Future media campaigns will utilize this research and messages will be targeted at the customer profiles drawn from each of these magazines.

NEW YORKER

344 total inquiries, including direct sales
$2,898 total cost of advertising
for a cost per inquiry of $8.43
$4,542 total sales
for a sale per inquiry of $13.20

Dividing cost by gross profit, we find we only have to show a 6 percent improvement to break even. Since the catalogue will be in four-colors, with 32 pages and about 120 items, all displayed for the same per unit price ($.30) as the test brochure with its twenty items in black and white photography, the chances of success with *The New Yorker* seem rather fair.

HOUSE BEAUTIFUL

520 total inquiries, including direct sales
$1,107 total cost of advertising . for a cost per inquiry of
$2.13
$1,381 total sales .... for a sale per inquiry of $2.66

Dividing cost by gross profit, we find we only have to show a 34 percent improvement to break even.

HOUSE & GARDEN

180 total inquiries, including direct sales
$658 total cost of advertising for a cost per inquiry of $3.65
$752 total sales .... for a sale per inquiry of $4.18

Dividing cost by gross profits, we need a 46 percent improvement to break even.

SOUTHERN LIVING

313 total inquiries, including direct sales

$2,707 total cost of advertising   for a cost per inquiry of $8.65

$2,395 total sales . . . . for a sale per inquiry of $7.65

Dividing cost by gross profit, we find we need an 88 percent improvement to break even.

OVERALL

1,357 total inquiries, including direct sales

$7,370 total cost of advertising   for a cost per inquiry of $5.43

$9,070 total sales . . . . for a sale per inquiry of $6.68

Dividing cost by gross profit, we need a 35 percent improvement to break even.

The test brochure was mailed to 10,000 upscale catalogue buyers from two different lists rented for Camlier & Buckley and from Stratford House. Sales response avaraged 0.3 percent at an average order of $65. Mail order economics indicate the following:

The brochure cost $.30 per each to mail, or a total of $3,000 to the 10,000 prospects. With the gross margin of 60 percent, the brochure would have had to achieve sales of $5,000 to break even, or $250 for each of its twenty items.

In fact, the total sales achieved were $1,950, or $97.50 per item.

Obviously, break even for the *Brochure* would have taken a multiple improvement of 2.56, or 156 percent.

However, since the catalogue will cost the same, but contain about 120 items, the *Catalogue* still has to achieve the same $5,000 total sales, but with only about $42 sales from each item displayed. Therefore, if the catalogue does *43 percent as well* as the brochure ($42/97.50), it will break even.

One other fact remains to be stated in support of the conservative nature of our sales forecasts. We have not factored in expected sales from our own house list developed through the research and development stage of the business. These sales, of course, will come at the outset of the first months when they can be most useful.

Exhibit 1

MANAGEMENT AGREEMENT REGARDING COMPENSATION FOR DUTIES INVOLVED IN PROVIDING EXECUTIVE MANAGEMENT TO MERCHANT OF CHINA, INC., A COMPANY IN THE PROCESS OF BEING INCORPORATED UNDER CALIFORNIA LAW.

Agreement made in San Diego, California, in the month of June between Christopher Whitney, President, Merchant of China, Inc., residing in California, and _____, residing at _____.

Whereas, the First Party is engaged in providing executive management to Merchant of China; and

Whereas, the Second Party is a shareholder in Merchant of China; and

Whereas, both parties desire to stipulate what the compensation during the first year for executive management to Merchant of China, Inc., will be:

Now, therefore, it is mutually agreed as follows:

> 1. Christopher Whitney will hold the position of President of Merchant of China, Inc.
>
> 2. Compensation in salaries will be calculated on a monthly basis to equal five percent of total sales, not to exceed a total for the first year of $35,000.
>
> 3. Compensation in traditional benefits will be calculated on a monthly basis to equal seventy-five hundreths of one-percent (0.75%) of total sales, not to exceed a total for the first year of $5,250 or fifteen percent of the salaries.

dated, _____, San Diego, California.

Christopher Whitney_____
President
Merchant of China, Inc.

*Shareholder*_____

Exhibit 2

AGREEMENT TO OPEN ESCROW ACCOUNT FOR SHAREHOLDERS IN MERCHANT OF CHINA, INC., A COMPANY IN THE PROCESS OF BEING INCORPORATED UNDER CALIFORNIA LAW, SUCH ESCROW ACCOUNT TO BE USED AS A SOURCE OF WORKING CAPITAL FOR SAID CORPORATION UPON DEPOSIT OF A TOTAL OF $20,000 IN SHAREHOLDER FUNDS.

Agreement made in San Diego, California, in the month of June between Christopher Whitney, President, Merchant of China, Inc., residing in California and _____, residing at _____.

Whereas, the First Party is engaged in the business of selling Oriental household products through mail order catalogs; and

Whereas, the Second Party has submitted $_____ for an equity interest in Merchant of China, Inc., and

Whereas, the First Party desires the authority and ability to make certain financial commitments necessary in order to best be in a position to meet sales forecasts for the impending Christmas mail order buying season:

Now, therefore, it is mutually agreed, as follows:

1. That the First Party agrees not to commit any funds from the escrow account established to pool shareholder monies until a total deposit of such monies amounts to a minimum of $20,000.

2. That the Second Party agrees to accept a minimum of one percent shareholder interest in Merchant of China, Inc., upon its incorporation under California Law, and a maximum of two percent for each thousand dollars invested (or its equivalent in services to the corporation), the final distribution to be determined by the success of equity-raising efforts between the signing of this agreement and the close of the first fiscal year.

3. That the First Party agrees to accept a limitation of fifty-one percent shareholder interest in Merchant of China, Inc., and hold all unaccounted for shares of voting stock in the company's treasury until such time as they can be sold or distributed proportionately to all minority shareholders at the close of the first fiscal year.

dated, _____,San Diego, California.

Christopher Whitney_____
President
Merchant of China, Inc.

*Shareholder*_____

Exhibit 3

Merchant of China, Inc.
Statement of Income
to March 31, 1980

Net Sales	$15,481.82
Cost of Goods Sold	7,330.11
Gross Profit	$ 8,151.71
Operating Expenses	16,257.00
Operating Income	---------
Interest Income	---------
Income Before Income Taxes	$ (8,105.29)
Provision for Federal and State Income Taxes	---------
Net Income	$ (8,105.29)

Sales began May 1978.

Exhibit 4

Merchant of China, Inc.
Balance Sheet
to March 31, 1980

Assets		Equities	
Cash	$ 6,437.11*	Payables	$ 1,044.43
Inventory	7,307.03	Equity	21,485.00
Customer List	8,785.29		
Total	$22,529.43	**Total**	$22,529.43

*About $5,200 has been used for Administrative Salary.

Exhibit 5

Merchant of China, Inc.
Income Statement to December 31, 1978

	Receipts	Disbursements
May	$ 188.00	$2,050.42
June	329.00	1,693.63
July	294.75	671.61
August	356.65	1,399.68
September	320.15	1,399.77
October	1,409.97*	8,069.52
November	4,204.05	2,010.08
December	1,973.46	5,202.70
	9,077.03	22,497.41

First Quarter 1979

	Receipts	Disbursements
January	$ 2,370.38	$ 4,288.64
February	3,265.21	3,084.12
March	769.20	1,023.97
Total	$15,481.82	$30,894.14
Inventory	7,307.03	
Payables	608.00	
Net	(8,785.29)	

Net sales	$15,481.82
Cost of Goods Sold	7,330.11
Gross Margin	8,151.71
Net Loss	8,785.29

*The test brochure was printed and distributed in October.
Pre-October receipts were from earlier tests conducted on a smaller level.

Exhibit 6

Projected Cash Flow Year 1 Plus Start Up 2 Months

	Prestart A	Prestart B	Start 1	2	3	4	5
Cash Receipts			1,640	3,280	31,250	38,750	41,250
Cash from Debt & Equity	25,000						
Total Cash Receipts	25,000						
Operating Expenses: Payroll (Salaried)				1,000	1,500	1,500	2,500
Payroll (Hourly)				1,000	225	300	300
Payroll Taxes & Benefits				300	250	270	420
Ads & Promo				3,500	3,500	3,500	3,500
Printing			2,500			8,500	
Postage & Lists		2,850		3,800		5,400	2,600
Rent Travel & Entert.					500		
Telephone			250	250	250	300	300
Motor Vehicle Prof. Services	3,000	1,500		3,000	2,000		2,500
Corporate Ins.				200	200	200	200
Computer Services Production Supplies				1,000			500
Office Supplies				250			250
Freight Ins.			750			520	600
Cost of Goods			2,500		13,168		15,500
Capital Equipment Sub Total Other Expenses							
Legal & Accounting	500						
Interest Expense					100	100	100
Principal					200	200	200
Taxes Total Expenses	3,500	4,350	6,000	14,300	21,893	20,790	29,530
	21,500	(4,350)	(4,360)	(11,010)	9,357	17,960	11,720
Cum.	21,500	17,150	12,790	1,770	11,127	29,087	40,807

Exhibit 6 (Cont.)

6	7	8	9	10	11	12	Total
27,080	81,250	110,250	108,750	75,250	20,600	14,000	553,350
							25,000
							578,350
2,500	2,500	3,500	8,000	5,000	5,000	5,000	38,000
200	600	1,000	1,000	600	500	350	6,075
400	465	675	1,350	840	800	800	6,570
3,500	5,500	1,500	5,500	3,500	3,500	3,500	40,500
7,500	11,500	6,000	6,000	9,000			51,000
20,600	10,000	24,000		10,750			80,000
	500	500	500	500	500	500	3,000
500			1,000				2,000
150	250	250	250	250	200	200	2,900
						200	200
2,500							14,500
200	200	200	200	200	200	200	2,200
						2,500	2,500
	1,500			1,500	500		5,000
	250		250				1,000
450	1,365	1,800	1,800	1,250	350	250	9,195
16,500	27,332		80,430		77,280		232,710
						1,000	**1,500**
100	100	100	100	100	100	100	1,000
200	200	200	200	200	200	200	2,000
						10,000	10,000
55,300	62,262	39,725	106,580	33,690	89,130	24,800	511,850
(28,220)	18,988	70,525	2,170	41,560	(68,530)	(10,800)	66,500
12,587	31,575	102,100	104,270	145,830	77,300	66,500	

CRUMBLE STATION

On Monday, January 12, 1981, Mary Webb, president and owner of Crumble Station, the Cookie Stop, Inc., was gazing out her window at the falling snow. She was waiting for Joe Tilton, her accountant, to arrive with *pro formas* for a new retail site at Dock Square in Rockport, Massachusetts. As Mrs. Webb waited, the snow began to fall more quickly as she started to reflect on the history of her business.

Since December 1977, Mrs. Webb had been running her retail operation out of the old Sudbury train station (see *Exhibit 1*). Although she had chosen the location for its charm and quaint contrast to traditional bakeries, Mary Webb's operation had yet to turn a profit (see *Exhibits 2 & 3*). On the other hand, Crumble Station had more than kept her busy after her children had begun to leave home. In fact, she found herself spending as much as 80 hours a week trying to turn her small business into a viable, growing concern.

Located adjacent to Crumble Station, her baking facility had the capacity, according to Mary Webb, to more than triple cookie production. But as yet, that capacity had not been required. In December, 1979, she added a mail order cookie business, but it had not increased sales as expected. Also, for a short time, she had sold her cookies to wholesalers, only to find that product control and price had been lost in the process. Initially, Mary Webb's thoughts had been to manufacture only the highest quality cookies, work hard, and keep busy. Commenting about her products and business to a friend in 1977, she observed, "I believe, of course, because we produce only the highest quality cookies, that profits will follow. We are not a fast-food cookie shop."

But by January, 1981, the venture's idea still did not appear to be working. Mary Webb had yet to take a salary, and she knew she should seriously reconsider her options if she were going to remain in business. Perhaps she should try wholesaling again or maybe this time, franchising. Still another alternative was just to persist with the Sudbury retail outlet for another year. Amidst this uncertainty, she couldn't help feeling uneasy about the future.

At that moment, Joe Tilton arrived, greeting Crumble Station's president with a happy smile and some good news. "Here they are, Mary. You're really going to be pleased when you see these *pro formas*. The Rockport store is going to make that plant of yours hum." (See Exhibit 4)

PERSONAL HISTORY AND COMPANY BACKGROUND

Mary Colombosian grew up in Eastern Massachusetts as the youngest daughter of Armenian, immigrant parents. In 1929, determined to succeed in their new found homeland, the Colombosians started the Colombo Yogurt Company. As a child, Mary Colombosian helped her parents process, package, and deliver yogurt. After high school graduation, she attended a one year secretarial school. Mary worked as a secretary until 1957 when she married Douglas Webb. A year before their marriage, Doug Webb had started a lumber business in Saxonville, Massachusetts. For the next twenty years, the Webbs were both very busy with their mutual and individual endeavors. Doug spent sometimes as much as 80 hours a week in his lumber business, while his wife devoted her time and energy to volunteer work and their four children. Very active as a volunteer, Mary Webb often found herself organizing and running such activities as the Sudbury Cancer Crusade. During this period, Mrs. Webb's favorite pastime was baking homemade cookies with fanciful designs for her own children and their many friends. In 1978, the Webb's eldest son, Doug, left for college and their daughter, Pam, went off to a private school. At this point, Mrs. Webb realized her remaining two youngsters would soon be leaving home.

However, Mary Webb was neither ready nor willing to slow down her very active pace. She decided it was time she started her own business. After all, her parents and husband had done it; why couldn't she? Regarding her choice of business, Mrs. Webb explained, "After twenty years as a housewife, a woman's skills are in the kitchen." Consequently, during February, 1977, she incorporated under the name MCW Enterprises, Inc., with the Charter to "open a restaurant or other food-related concern." Initially, the new corporation was structured very simply, with Mrs. Webb serving as president, treasurer, and chairman of MCW's Board of Directors. An older sister, and the family lawyer, were MCW's only other voting members.

From the beginning, family and friends were a great help. Mary Webb's first idea was to open a small restaurant in Maynard, Massachusetts, where DEC (Digital Equipment Corporation) had extensive operations. Mrs. Webb and her supporters felt a sea of lunchtime clients would throng to an eating establishment. However, after numerous inquiries, Mary Webb could not find a location large enough to generate a profitable sales volume. At this point, she decided it was time to rethink her alternatives. For a few months, Mrs. Webb simply talked to her friends about business possibilities. Then one Saturday morning, over coffee and cookies, her brother-in-law challenged her to make a batch of cookies people would be willing to buy. Mary Webb accepted the challenge and, as he was leaving, she handed him the prototype of her product, chocolate chip cookies, artfully packaged in a plastic bag adorned with a bright red ribbon. By June, 1977, she changed the initial concept of her business to that of baking and selling the highest quality cookies.

THE SUDBURY STORE

During June of 1977, Mary Webb searched for an appropriate site for a cookie business. She felt three factors were particularly important in making this site location decision. Specifically, the site must:

1. be close to her home;

2. be located in a town whose inhabitants had a high disposable income;

3. be capable of supporting both a retail and manufacturing (baking) operation.

During September, 1977, after much discussion about "that cute little Sudbury train station" next to Doug Webb's own business, Mr. Webb leased the station and gave the lease to his wife as a birthday gift.

Mrs. Webb was elated with the gift and immediately attempted to secure financing for new equipment and leasehold improvements through local banks and the SBA. Unfortunately, these efforts were to no avail. Consequently, Mrs. Webb used $25,000 of personal funds to cover start-up costs, which included converting the dilapidated train station into an enchanting cookie shop. At the same time, she rented a 14 by 14 foot room on the second floor of the commercial building next door. She then remodeled this space into a bakery which met Sudbury's Board of Health specifictions and with the remaining funds she purchased baking equipment. Together, renovations cost $9,000, equipment purchases cost $15,000, and the final $1,000 was spent on miscellaneous expenses.

The first year after Mary Webb incorporated MCW Enterprises, to her surprise and unlike well known competitors, Famous Amos, Chipyard, etc., the business lost $11,500. During this period, her variable costs were 64% while competitors' variable costs averaged 51%. Still resolute, Mrs. Webb incorporated again in 1978, this time under Sub-Chapter S and was able to secure personal tax relief from potential future losses. And since 1978 Crumble Station had continued to show a loss. In 1979, losses totaled $4,300 and in 1980 they were $4,900.

Initially, Crumble Station opened its doors for business on December 7, 1977, just in time for the holidays. Its sign read, "Crumble Station, the Cookie Stop." Mr. Victor Mangan, a family friend and ad man, had coined the name late one fall day while looking at the train station. Thereafter, MCW Enterprises was known as Crumble Station. A week prior to opening, Mr. Mangan ran a full page ad for the grand opening in the Sudbury "Bentley's Calendar". That first day, Mrs. Webb closed early after selling all of her cookies: 6 dozen gingerbread men and 6 dozen Russian tea cakes for fifty cents apiece or $6.00 a dozen.

Within two months of opening, Mary Webb was given the option of renting a larger space just below her second floor plant. Space constraints and access difficulties already were apparent in the second story location. Although a second renovation was required to meet health specifications, Mrs. Webb moved her operations to the first floor during February, 1978. This move increased start-up costs to a total of $30,000.

By February, 1978, Crumble Station's product line had expanded to 24 different cookies. Sales volume had also increased to between 50 and 75 dozen cookies per day. Cookie prices ranged from $.35 to $.60 each (see *Exhibit 5* for a complete price chart).

The peak sales periods for the retail operation were lunchtime, Saturdays, and the week prior to a holiday. To differentiate her product, Mrs. Webb used only the highest quality, all-natural ingredients in recipes which she developed and tested herself. Doug Webb and the entire family were very helpful in these early R&D efforts. No cookie was sold until Mr. Webb also approved its taste, consistency and appearance. As each holiday passed, it became clear that Crumble Station sales rose and fell according to the holiday season. In an effort to please her customers, Mary broadened her offerings to include not only seasonal and specially decorated holiday cookies, but also holiday gifts. For example, at Christmas, she not only sold traditional gingerbread men, plain and decorated, but also Christmas cards; stuffed Snoopy(s) dressed in a train conductor's overalls and cap; small, colorful Christmas decorations; and red and green bowed baskets filled with cookies. All items including cookie tins and bell jars were marked with the train and gingerbread motif. For the summer she produced assortments of gifts, such as little girls' scarves, and a canvas tote bag with "Crumble Station" appearing in bold red letters. Later Mrs. Webb introduced a little white sand pail filled with tiny gingerbread men (see *Exhibit 6*) which complemented these accessories.

During December, 1979, mail order cookies were introduced using the theme, "Sweet News from Home." Developed in response to customer requests, Mrs. Webb printed brochures which emphasized the "Sweet News from Home" theme. She mailed these brochures to names on a mailing list of names that she purchased from Direct Marketing Concepts of Framingham, Massachusetts. The mailing list cost $500, the brochures $3,000, postage $300, and packaging supplies, $3,000. Not one order was received from that mailing. By 1981, mail orders accounted for about 2% of gross sales.

Mrs. Webb and Victor Mangan handled advertising. Together they developed the themes for magazine ads and local radio spots. The advertisements emphasized the products' high quality image as well as the shop's magical charm. Monthly, she advertised in the Sudbury Community Calendar. In an attempt to improve the mail order business, she advertised once in *Boston Magazine*. Although three inquiries were received, not one order was placed.

As of 1981, Mrs. Webb did not consider her wholesale experience a positive one. In one instance, cookies were sold wholesale to a novelty shop in Newton. Upon visiting the shop, Mrs. Webb discovered that the owner was using the cookies only as a display item to entice customers into the store. A "Marked Down" sign had been placed over the cookies.

OPERATIONS AND STAFF

Crumble Station's baking operations occupied 2,880 square feet of space in a spotless, 3,000 square foot open area. This space contained two large refrigerator/freezers, a 64-quart mixer, and two commercial size convection ovens. Functional sinks and counters were located on the side walls. Dry goods were stored on shelves against the back wall. The remaining 120 square feet accomodated cookie decorating tables, handmade cookie cutters, and space for retail sales.

During the summer, the train station was closed for the month of July due to decreased sales. Customers purchased cookies and gifts out of the front of the baking facility. From this sunny space, the customer watched cookies being made firsthand and smelled their delicious aroma.

Starting at six o'clock every morning, Jenny Somo baked the cookies needed for the day. She also updated inventory and shipment control sheets. About 10:00 A.M., Nancy Sullivan arrived to decorate the freshly-baked cookies and to satisfy special customer requests. As explained by the decorator, "Children's birthday parties are the most fun to do." The baker's day ended about 2:00 P.M.

During peak seasons, overtime was necessary but this had yet to exceed more than 20 hours per week for 2 to 3 weeks at a time.

The baker was paid a salary of $260/week and the decorator received $5.00 per hour. As Mrs. Webb explained, "With Jenny and Nancy working in the bakery, the baking operation runs very smoothly. Even if sales do triple, our present facilities can handle the increased production."

Besides the production staff, Barbara Mangan, Victor Mangan's wife, managed the Sudbury store. Mrs. Mangan supervised three part-time clerks who worked in the store for $5.00 per hour. Mrs. Mangan received $6.50 per hour. As noted earlier, Mrs. Webb had yet to receive a paycheck from the business.

THE ROCKPORT STORE

Mrs. Webb's growing dissatisfaction with the retail sales volume and poor consumer response to mail order led her to seriously consider the opening of a second retail outlet. To Mrs. Webb, the possibility of opening a second retail store, this time in Rockport, offered many opportunities.

She knew that Rockport's Bearskin Neck area (see *Exhibits 7, 8 & 9*) was a favorite tourist spot. When she contacted the Chamber of Commerce she found that during the summer, 600,000 daytrippers visited the little seacoast town to smell the sea air, get a glimpse of th sea, and view Motif No. l, a lobster shack made famous by the artist, James Wyeth. The Chamber of Commerce also explained that while these tourists strolled through the narrow and winding streets, they often stopped in at one of the many little shops to pick up an inexpensive trinket or grab a bite to eat. In the entire maze of over 200 shops, there was only one cookie shop, the Chipyard, and a strudel shop, The Edelweiss. The Rockport Police Department who regularly surveyed traffic flow, confirmed the 600,000 figure saying that the local population also increased in the summer from 6,000 to 20,000 residents.

After further investigation, Mrs. Webb found a two-story house that was for sale just behind Motif No. 1. The Webbs decided to seriously consider purchasing this house. However, they knew they would have to act quickly since such an attractive site would not remain on the market very long.

If Mrs. Webb decided to open a second outlet in Rockport, her daughter Pam had agreed to manage the operation during the summer while she was home from college. Pam and a college classmate would live in the second floor apartment rent free, and receive $40.00 per week. Possible store hours would extend from 10:00 a.m. to 10:00 p.m. daily. Mrs. Webb knew that if she started another Sub-Chapter S corporation through the Rockport store, additional tax write-offs might also be available.

THE DECISION

On receipt of the *pro formas*, Mrs. Webb figured she could increase her annual gross sales from $90,000 to $200,000 by the end of September, 1981. However, a few issues had to be worked out, such as the transportation of cookies from Sudbury to Rockport. But just maybe, she thought, a profit could be made with the increased sales volume.

ASSIGNMENT QUESTIONS

1. Evaluate the various *environments* which affect Crumble Station and Mrs. Webb, i.e., the industry, the geographic locations, etc.

2. Evaluate the Crumble Station *venture*, both qualitatively and quantitatively.

3. Evaluate Mrs. Webb as an entrepreneur.

4. Given your analysis, what advice would you give to Mrs. Webb?

Exhibit 1

**Crumble Station:
the Cookie Stop**

Exhibit 2
M.C.W. Enterprises, Inc.
D/B/A Crumble Station

Balance Sheet
December 31, 1980

Current Assets:		Current Liabilities:	
Cash	$ 9,945	A/P	$6,560
A/R	120	Notes Payable (Owners')	15,670
Inventory	4,475	Accrued Interest	6,030
Prepaid Expenses	2,035	Accrued Taxes	2,130
Total Current Assets	$16,575	Total Current Liabilities	$30,390
		Long Term Liabilities:	
		Stockholder Loans	$21,925
Fixed Assets:			
Machinery & Equipment	$16,070	Total Liabilities:	
Office Equipment	500	Stockholders' Equity	
Furniture	3,200	Common Stock	$10,000
Leasehold Improvement	9,350	Paid In Capital	8,000
Depreciation	(5,120)	Retained Earnings	(24,840)
Total Fixed Assets	$24,000	Net Income (Loss)	(4,900)
		Total Stockholders' Equity	($11,740)
Total Assets	**$40,575**	**Total Liabilities & Stockholders' Equity**	**$40,575**

Exhibit 3
M.C.W. Enterprises, Inc.
D/B/A Crumble Station
Union Avenue
Sudbury, MA 01776

Income Statement
For 12 Months Ended December 31, 1980

Gross Sales	$90,000	Expenses	
Retail Cookies	70,200	Operating Bakery	$21,150
Wholesale Cookies	4,590	Selling Expenses:	
Mail Order Cookies	1,800	Shop	28,800
Gifts	13,500	Gen. & Adm.	10,440
Gift Certificates	(90)		$60,390
	$90,000	Loss from Operations	($ 4,500)
Cost of Goods Sold		Other Income (Expense)	
Baking Materials	$13,770	Discounts taken	108
Supplies	990	Interest Income	24
Purchases-Gifts	3,150	Interest Expense	(532)
Direct Labor	16,200		$ 400
	$34,110	**Net Income (Loss)**	($ 4,900)
Gross Margin	$55,890		

Exhibit 4
Pro Forma Income Statement

Possible Rockport Store

	June, 1981		July, 1981	August, 1981
Gross Sales	$20,000	100%	$40,000	$50,000
Retail Cookies	16,000	80%	32,000	40,000
Mail Order	200	1%	400	500
Gifts	3,550	17.75%	7,100	8,875
Gift Certificates	250	1.25%	250	625
Total Sales	$20,000	100%	$40,000	$50,000
Cost of Sales				
Gifts	$ 400	2%	$ 800	$ 1,000
Cookies	8,800	44%	17,600	22,000
Total Cost of Sales	$ 9,200	46%	$18,400	$23,000
Gross Profit	$10,800	54%	$21,600	$27,000
Operating Expenses				
Bakery	$ 80	.4%	$ 160	$ 200
Selling Expenses				
Shop	1,240	6.2%	2,480	3,100
G & A	160	.8%	320	400
Total Expenses	$ 1,480	7.4%	$ 2,960	$ 3,700
Net Income	$ 9,320	46.6%	$18,640	$23,300

Exhibit 5

Sudbury Store					The Chipyard	Star Market	
Regular Cookies (Daily)	**Decorated Cookies**	**Cookie Brittle**	**Special Cookies**	**Gifts**		**Pepperidge Farm**	**Star's Own**
Chocolate Chip $.40 ea. 1¼ oz./ cookie ($5.13/lb)	Standard Train $1.25 ea.	Butterscotch $3.00/bag, $6.00/lb	At least 50 different recipes: For example: Passover cookies include:	Crumble Station: T-shirt: $9.50	Chocolate Chip Cookies $.85/Doz.	Chocolate Chip $2.85/lb.	Chocolate Chip $.91/lb
Ginger Crinkle $.40 ea.	Ginger Bread Boy Standard: $2.00 ea. Personalized: $2.50	Chocolate Chip Almont	O'Henry Fudge Bar	Tote Bag: $12.50 Scarf: $7.50		Gingerman Cookies $2.34/lb.	Ginger Snaps $1.29/lb.
Oatmeal/ Raisin $.40 ea.	Easter Egg $2.00 ea.		Chocolate Truffle	Goodie Bag: $14.50		Oatmeal Raisin $2.34/lb.	Oatmeal/ Raisin $.96/lb.
Golden Raisin $.40 ea.	50 types of seasonal hol- iday special occasion cookies including as news breaks, e.g., Pope's Crown, Red Sox, Bruins, Celtics, Happy Birthday Special Orders: if buy 3 doz. = $2.00/cookie with per- sonalization Also $.25 for each ribbon		Caramel Bar	Mexican Ceramic Easter Bun- nies: $3.00		Sugar Cookies Similar to decorated but without decoration $2.22/lb.	Chocolate Fudge Sandwich $1.39/lb.
Lemon Key $.40 ea.			Linzer Apri- cot Tort	Barretts: $2.00			
Double Fudge $.40 ea.			Peanut But- ter Penuchi	Paper Mache Dolls: $3.95		Peanut Butter $2.21/lb.	
Butterscotch $.40 ea.			Revel Bar				
Peanut Butter $.40 ea.			Almont Macaroon				
Peanut Blossoms $.60 ea. ($7.70/lb.)			Bittersweets				
Almond Macaroons $.60			Torts Raspberry Lemon Cheese Mocha				
Shortbread $.60							
Chocolate Surprise $.55 ea. ($7.05/lb.)							
Raspberry Tart $.75 ea. ($9.62/lb.)							
Almond Macaroon Apricot Tart $.75 ea.							
Hermit $.70 ea. ($8.57/lb.)							

Cookie Price Chart
(Prices as of January, 1981)
Crumble Station's Competitor Product/Price Chart

Exhibit 6

Front Cover of Folded Brochure

Exhibit 6

First Page of Open Brochure

Send your sweet message by mail, fresh from Crumble Station.

MERRY CHRISTMAS (or HAPPY HOLIDAYS)
Order now and your sweet Holiday Message gets baked and delivered just when the fun begins.
$18.50 Postage Paid

MESSAGE FROM THE HEART
Heart-shaped 2 pound chocolate chip cookie with your sweet message including: I love you turkey; Be my Valentine; You're a Big Sweetheart. State choice of message.
$18.50 Postage Paid

HAPPY BIRTHDAY
Give Giant-size sweetness on someone's special day. Two pound chocolate chip cookie is your big birthday wish! Name or message of your choice.
$18.50 Postage Paid.

HAPPY ANNIVERSARY
Right from your heart A 2 pound chocolate chip cookie for the two special people on their happy day.
$18.50 Postage Paid

GIFT CERTIFICATE
Let someone you like choose their own treats. Check-like gift Certificate sent in any amount with mail order brochure.

CRUMBLE STATION
THE COOKIE STOP

AT THE R R CROSSING, UNION AVENUE, SUDBURY, MASSACHUSETTS 01776   (617) 443-2132

Gift Certificate

_____ 19 __

With sweet regards to: _____

$ _____

_____ Dollars

Mary C. Webb
MARY C. WEBB, STATIONMASTER

From: _____

Exhibit 6

Second page Left-Hand Side of Open Brochure

Send your sweet message by mail, fresh from Crumble Station.

T-SHIRT
Red, Navy.
Ginger Brown print
on white 100% cotton
Children's: S-M-L-XL
Adult's: S-M-L-XL
CHILDREN'S $9.50
ADULTS $10.50
All Postage Paid
Packed with fresh
Gingerbread Super
Cookie.

GINGERBREAD PARTY PACK Six honey sweet
gingerbread persons ready to go to a party.
Choice of First name on either male or female
person cookie. With name $19.50. Without $16.50.
Canvas Tote Bag $4.00 extra. All Postage Paid.

TOTE BAG sturdy
natural color canvas
with strong red handles.
Design in red, black,
ginger brown. Just
right for Little
people school books
or big peoples'
everything bag.
Packed with fresh
baked gingerbread
girl $12.50
Postage Paid

CRUMBLE STATION SCARF Silver grey cotton
polyester "That's the Way the Cookie ... Crumble
Station" printed in red with dancing gingerbread motif. 22"x 22" also fun for party or
picnic napkins. Packed with
fresh-baked "personalized"
Gingerbread girl. $7.50
Postage Paid

STATIONMASTER'S COOKIE BAG Sent
to you in either a country calico
or striped reusable cotton bag all
tied together with a
bakers dough ginger
bread person.
Your choice of nine
delicious cookies. Choose
from (1 choice per bag) chocolate chip, chocolate,
oatmeal raisin, butterscotch, ginger crinkle,
or peanut butter. $10.50 Postage Paid

Exhibit 6

Third Page Right-Hand Side of Open Brochure

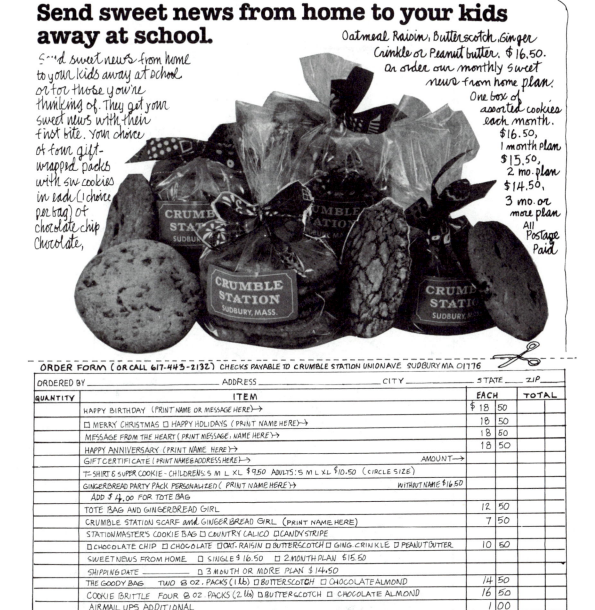

Send sweet news from home to your kids away at school.

Send sweet news from home to your kids away at school or for those you're thinking of. They get your sweet news with their first bite. Your choice of four gift-wrapped packs with six cookies in each (1 choice per bag) of chocolate chip chocolate,

Oatmeal Raisin, Butterscotch, Ginger Crinkle or Peanut butter. $16.50. Or order our monthly sweet news from home plan. One box of assorted cookies each month. $16.50, 1 month plan $15.50, 2 mo. plan $14.50, 3 mo. or more plan All Postage Paid

ORDER FORM (OR CALL 617-443-2132) CHECKS PAYABLE TO CRUMBLE STATION UNION AVE. SUDBURY MA 01776

ORDERED BY _____ ADDRESS _____ CITY _____ STATE ____ ZIP ____

QUANTITY	ITEM	EACH	TOTAL
	HAPPY BIRTHDAY (PRINT NAME OR MESSAGE HERE)→	$ 18 50	
	☐ MERRY CHRISTMAS ☐ HAPPY HOLIDAYS (PRINT NAME HERE)→	18 50	
	MESSAGE FROM THE HEART (PRINT MESSAGE, NAME HERE)→	18 50	
	HAPPY ANNIVERSARY (PRINT NAME HERE)→	18 50	
	GIFT CERTIFICATE (PRINT NAME & ADDRESS HERE)→ AMOUNT→		
	T-SHIRT & SUPER COOKIE - CHILDRENS: S M L XL $9.50 ADULTS: S M L XL $10.50 (CIRCLE SIZE)		
	GINGERBREAD PARTY PACK PERSONALIZED (PRINT NAME HERE)→ WITHOUT NAME $16.50		
	ADD $4.00 FOR TOTE BAG		
	TOTE BAG AND GINGERBREAD GIRL	12 50	
	CRUMBLE STATION SCARF and GINGERBREAD GIRL (PRINT NAME HERE)	7 50	
	STATIONMASTER'S COOKIE BAG ☐ COUNTRY CALICO ☐ CANDY STRIPE		
	☐ CHOCOLATE CHIP ☐ CHOCOLATE ☐ OAT. RAISIN ☐ BUTTERSCOTCH ☐ GING. CRINKLE ☐ PEANUT BUTTER	10 50	
	SWEET NEWS FROM HOME. ☐ SINGLE $16.50 ☐ 2 MONTH PLAN $15.50		
	SHIPPING DATE _____ ☐ 3 MONTH OR MORE PLAN $14.50		
	THE GOODY BAG TWO 8 OZ. PACKS (1 lb) ☐ BUTTERSCOTCH ☐ CHOCOLATE ALMOND	14 50	
	COOKIE BRITTLE FOUR 8 OZ. PACKS (2 lbs) ☐ BUTTERSCOTCH ☐ CHOCOLATE ALMOND	16 50	
	AIRMAIL UPS ADDITIONAL	1 00	
	GRAND TOTAL		

? TO: NAME _____ ADDRESS _____ CITY _____ STATE ____ ZIP ____

THANK YOU FOR USING SEPARATE PIECES OF PAPER FOR EXTRA MESSAGES OR EXTRA NAMES/ADDRESSES OF RECIPIENTS. ALL ORDERS SHIPPED VIA UNITED PARCEL SERVICE. GIFT CARD ENCLOSED WITH ALL ORDERS. STATE MESSAGE BELOW.

NOTE: CRUMBLE STATION COOKIES ARE BAKED WITH FRESH NATURAL INGREDIENTS INCLUDING PURE CREAMERY UNSALTED BUTTER AND UNBLEACHED FLOUR AND EACH COOKIE HAND-ROLLED AND CUT. SPECIAL KITCHEN RECIPES - ALL PURELY EXTRAVAGANT.

Exhibit 7
Map Showing Location of Rockport Store
Rockport, MA

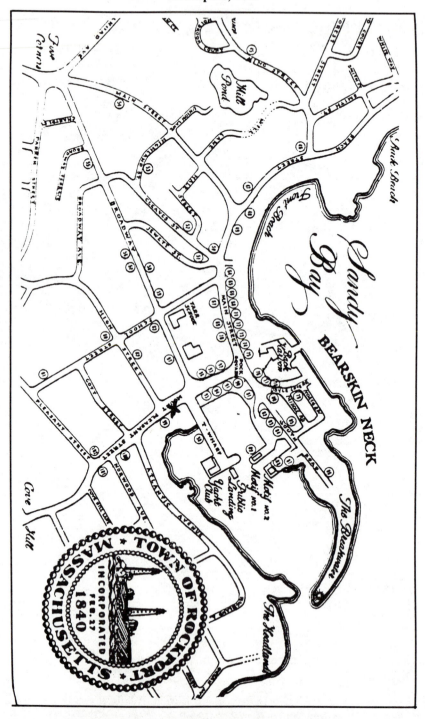

Exhibit 8
Demographic Data*

	Rockport, MA	Sudbury, MA
Population Density	803 People per square mile	999 People per square mile
Percentage of Total Population Under 18	30.4%	40-44.9%
Percentage of Total Population 65 or Older	18.2%	2.0-3.9%
Median Family Income	$10,000	$15,000
Family Income/ Educational Attainment	70.1% are high school graduates making $10,000 or over	85% or more are high school graduates making $15,000 or more
Percentage of Total Labor Force Employed in Blue Collar Occupations	46.1%	10%
Median Housing Value	$16,000	$25,000 or more
Percentage of Housing Units which are Owner-occupied	80.3%	90% or more

*Based on 1970 U.S. Census.

Exhibit 9

Motif No. 1

The Ice Cream Parlor

Entrance to Bearskin Neck Area

The Jelly Bean Shop

The Chipyard

APPENDIX A
NOTES ON THE COOKIE AND CRACKER INDUSTRY*

According to one expert, Carol Meres of Gorman publishing, *Bakery Production and Marketing,* "Generally, 75% of all consumers in the United States eat cookies and 10% of all persons who walk past a cookie shop stop in and buy cookies."

During 1980, there were approximately 15,000 retail bakeries in the United States. As explained by Carol Meres, "Today the cookie industry is where the donut industry was 10 years ago, the early growth stage."

Entry into the bakery products industry was relatively difficult compared to the retail cookie business due to the industry's highly technical nature. Opening a bakery required much knowledge. Use of yeast for breads, leavening agents and emulsifiers for cakes complicated the bakery production process. Also, many variables, (elevation, temperature, humidity, etc.), affected bakery products which increased risk and manufacturing costs.

Cookie production, on the other hand, was a comparatively easy business to enter. It was easier to learn about and control one product type, the cookie, and great technical expertise was not required because yeast, leavening agents, and emulsifiers were not used.

Chocolate Chip (1), Oatmeal Raisin (2) and Sugar Butter Cookies (3) were the industry's biggest sellers.

Major competitors in 1980 were:

- Famous Amos (a national franchise)

- Chipyard (a national franchise)

- Otis Spunkmeyers
  Old Tyme Cookies (a national franchise)

- Cookie Man

- Cookie Coach Company (a national franchise)

- David's Cookies

- That Cookie Place

All of these cookie shops were considered "fast food" cookie retailers.

Generally, according to George Kolov, a bakery products' wholesaler, retail cookie shops such as Famous Amos, Cookie Man and Chipyard were high markup businesses which earn profits within one year after opening.

*Written by Chris Kazo.

Cookie and Cracker Industry Profiles and Trends*

Cookies and Crackers: Trends and Projections 1975–81
(in millions of current dollars except as noted)

Item	1975	1976	1977	1978	1979*	1980*	Percent change 1979–80	1981*	Percent change 1980–81
Industry (SIC 2052)									
Value of shipments[1]	2,671	2,718	2,961	3,259	3,650	4,120	12.9	4,680	13.6
Value added	1,410	1,557	1,696	1,868	2,100	2,400	14.3	—	—
Value added per production worker-hour ($)	22.41	24.26	25.30	26.65	n.a.	n.a.	—	—	—
Total employment (000)	41.0	41.9	43.8	47.2	51.0	55.0	7.8	—	—
Production workers (000)	31.5	32.4	34.0	36.5	39.0	42.0	7.6	—	—
Average hourly earnings (Dec.–$)	5.07	5.47	5.76	6.19	6.68	*6.93	*10.2	—	—
Year-to-year percent change in average hourly earnings (Dec.–Dec.)	19.0	7.9	5.3	7.5	7.9	—	—	—	—
Capital expenditures	39.7	50.5	85.6	94.4	—	—	—	—	—
Product (SIC 2052)									
Value of shipments[4]	2,586	2,657	2,812	3,120	3,520	3,980	13	—	—
Year-to-year percent change in producers price index (Dec.–Dec.)	-.8	.6	18.2	1.7	8.1	*13.5	*	—	—
Trade									
Value of imports	52	54	59	78	82	85	2.4	—	—

[1] Value of all products and services sold by the cookies and crackers industry (SIC 2052).
[2] Estimated except for hourly earnings, price indexes, and 1979 trade data.
[3] Forecast.
[4] As of July 1980.
[5] July 1979 to July 1980.

* Value of shipments of cookies and crackers produced by all industries.
n.a. = not available.

Source: Bureau of the Census (industry and trade data), Bureau of Labor Statistics (hourly earnings and price indexes). Estimates and forecasts by the Bureau of Industrial Economics.

*This data is from the 1980 & 1981 editions of *U.S. Industrial Outlook*. SIC Code 2052, a manufacturer's code, is used. Although Code 5462 refers to companies which make and sell retail bakery products, there is no differentiation between bread and cookies, for example. Thus 5462 data is misleading. Consequently, per this writer's conversation with Diane Wilson, Office of Consumer Goods and Services Industries (202) 566-2202, Code 2052 is used because cookie data is more accurate.

1979 Profile

Cookies and Crackers

SIC Code: 2052

Value of shipments (million $)	3,506
Value added (million $)	2,050
Total employment (000)	48
Number of establishments, total (1977)	322
Number of establishments with 20 employees or more (1977)	171
Exports as a percent of product shipments . .	N.A.
Imports as a percent of apparent consumption [1]	2.3

Compound annual rate of change, 1974–79:

Value of product shipments [2]	8.5
Value of exports [2]	N.A.
Value of imports [2]	9.0
Total employment	4.3

Major producing States:
Pennsylvania, California, New York

[1] Imports divided by product shipments plus imports minus exports.
[2] Rates of change based on current dollars.
Source: Bureau of the Census; Bureau of Labor Statistics; Industry and Trade Administration (BDBD) estimates.

1980 Profile

Cookies and Crackers

SIC Code: 2052

Value of industry shipments (million $)	4,120
Value added (million $)	2,400
Total employment (000)	55
Number of establishments, total (1977)	324
Number of establishments with 20 employees or more (1977)	172
Exports as a percent of product shipments . . .	n.a.
Imports as a percent of apparent consumption [1]	2.1

Compound annual rate of change, 1975–80:

Value of product shipments [2]	9.1
Value of exports [2]	n.a.
Value of imports [2]	10.4
Total employment	6.1

Major producing states:
New York, California, Pennsylvania

[1] Imports divided by product shipments plus imports minus exports.
[2] Rates of change based on current dollars.
n.a. = not applicable.
Source: Bureau of the Census; Bureau of Labor Statistics; and Bureau of Industrial Economic estimates.

CENTURY OPTICS 21

(buzzzzz on office intercom)

Secretary: Phone call, Mrs. Todd. David Smith, line one.

Mrs. Todd: Who?

Secretary: Professor David Smith, Dean of Laurel College.

Mrs. Todd: Oh. Thanks, Chris . . . Good morning, David!

Smith: Hi, Pauline. Glad I was able to reach you. The president and dean enjoyed their meeting with you last week, and they'd like you to join them for lunch this Friday, tomorrow, to follow up on the discussion of a new Management Center at Laurel, as you recall . . .

Mrs. Todd: Yes . . .

Smith: Well, they want to firm up those plans. We hope you're free then for lunch — and still interested in bringing your management skills to Laurel College to build the new Center. Sorry this is such short notice.

Mrs. Todd: (PAUSE) . . . Well, Dave, I hear you, and I admit I'm intrigued by the challenge of establishing a Management Department *and* building a Management Center at Laurel. I'm also drawn by the opportunity to build something which will help women find careers in the business world. You know this would be a real career switch for *me* which would affect both my husband and family, and our company — I don't know how much . . .

(The phrase "How much" hangs in the air for a moment.)

Smith: Pauline, just between us, I think you can write your own ticket here. Blockmer is the Trustee behind this new move, conceptually *and* financially, which is why Joe and Ed feel a luncheon meeting with him would be appropriate, and most useful to you. You'd get a feeling for the environment in which you'd be working.

Mrs. Todd: Good point, and I do appreciate Mr. Blockmer's importance to the development of your Management Center. All right, let's see — I have an ad agency meeting and a performance review tomorrow morning. Can we set the time for 1:00 p.m.?

Smith: That's fine. We'll see you at 1:00 at the Faculty Club, President's Dining Room. Blockmer is a fascinating man with four daughters who have graduated from Laurel. You'll like his Texas charm. Remember that he is a little hard of hearing. Bye. . .

(Pauline put the phone down slowly, her emotions churning. She knew now that she was the "chosen one," that she would be offered the Chair of the new Management Department as well as a Directorship of the large, new Management Center at Laurel College. This would mean a combined salary of $60,000 — for as long as she clicked with Blockmer. She obviously had the votes of Joe, the president, and the all-male Search Committee.

(She felt a strong sense of pride. She would be the third woman department head at Laurel — and she didn't even have her Ph.D.! She wondered, "Do I really want this? What might it lead to in the academic community, especially *without* a Ph.D.? How long would the honeymoon last with an all male administration? Do I want the stress and politics of building a new department in a liberal arts college? What if Blockmer dies? What a challenge! — the chance to establish a program which could really put women on their feet professionally!"

(. . . and other questions: "How would Bill react to my leaving full-time work at Optics 21? Hasn't our marriage become stronger through sacrificing, struggling, sharing together? Who would take over marketing, trade shows, advertising, personnel, and the Treasurer's responsibilities? Would there be any time left for Optics 21? Should I continue at least to be a Director? . . . Yes, I've fought too hard and too long to divorce myself from our company now. How would this career change affect Jeff and Cathy and Ellen? Could I hire a housekeeper with that salary? Is there someone who could do that job without ruining the children?")

BACKGROUND

Bill and Pauline Todd started Century Optics 21 five years ago to introduce fiber-optics technology into various industrial and professional applications. Two fiber-optics experts helped them to get started but, after two years in which it became apparent that the company was orienting more and more toward specialized medical applications of fiber optics, the experts left. It had been two years of blind alleys and personality clashes between the experts and Bill, with Pauline as mediator, but now things were moving and the problems for the moment were reduced to those of production and cash flow. Pauline's and Bill's marketing and sales maneuvering with doctors, hospitals and HMO directors had begun to pay off and their products were beginning to be recognized as some of the best in the market. The company had begun to seek venture capital for its second-stage growth.

(buzzzz on office intercom)

Secretary: Mrs. Todd, it's Ellen on the phone, line two.

Mrs. Todd: Thanks, Chris. Yes, Ellen? Did you have a good day at school, sweetheart?

Ellen: (IN TEARS) Mommy, Jeff is picking on me. He told me it was three o'clock and I had to be on my bike and go to the dentist. And then he called me stupid out the window because I can't read the clock and it's only two fifteen.

Mrs. Todd: Ellen, dear, your brother is playing games again. Now calm down — no tears; I can't understand you when you cry on the phone. Has Jeff done his laundry?

Ellen: Jeff has done *his* but he won't help *me*. He knows I can't reach the dial. He teases me.

Mrs. Todd: Well, I'll talk with Jeff. Why don't you sit down and read in your clock book and learn all about telling time? Then Jeff can't fool you. You should leave in 30 minutes for the dentist. Now brush your teeth, ride your bike carefully, and be sure you stop at Stuart Street and cross with the light. Now put Jeff on the phone, please. I love you!

Ellen: Well, O.K. Please buy some more soda pop.

Mrs. Todd: I'll try to get more soda but there will not be time tonight. I have to speak tonight. Now get Jeff . . . (Pauline glanced at her "To Do" list,* thinking "If only we had the income to justify hiring a housekeeper!"

Jeff: Hi Mom. We had a neat science class today; we turned liquids into different colors and gases and back to liquids.

Mrs. Todd: I'm glad you like your science course, Jeff, but what are you doing to Ellen? Remember, she's only seven, and don't play games with her appointments.

Jeff: Okay, but she should learn to tell time herself. Mom are you coming to see our big soccer game Saturday? Oh, and can I have some new jeans? — I ripped mine today.

Mrs. Todd: I'll be at the game, but Dad left for Chicago this morning for the Medical Equipment Convention. He is on a panel Saturday and won't be home until Tuesday. Now, be a helpful brother and teach Ellen about time . . . ("Golly, I need a *wife*. I'm the one who ought to be helping Ellen learn to tell time.")

(buzzz on office intercom)

Secretary: Excuse me but Mr. James, President of Hospital Supplies, is on line two. Also, remember I need to retype your speech for tonight when you've made final corrections . . . And, Pauline, I *do* want to talk with you about my letter to you and Dave.

Mrs. Todd: Thank you Chris. Jeff, I have to go. Now, get your laundry and homework

---

*See *Exhibit 1.*

done. I'll be home at eleven. I have this speech tonight. Take something out of the freezer for dinner tonight for you and your two sisters. I love you. Thanks for being that good big brother. G'bye.

Pauline looked forward to arranging a meeting with Mr. James to complete a major order. She had met James through her election to the Finance Committee of Kaiser Medical Center. As the only woman on the committee, she had made important contacts with the financial and medical world which she enjoyed personally and found useful in developing business and signing up foundation support for Scott Day School, the most prestigious private, independent, secondary school on the Peninsula. Pauline had been elected as the second woman trustee a year ago after serving on Scott's Development Campaign Executive Committee, where she helped raise $25 million, the largest sum ever raised for an independent day secondary school.

TRAINING/CAREER

Pauline had gone east from Iowa to attend Miss Drake's Academy "for refinement, culture and preparation for Smith College." She grew both socially and intellectually at Miss Drake's and did indeed fulfill her own and her parents' goal of going on to Smith. After Smith, she earned an M.A. in History at Harvard and then studied in Europe to master French. She feared, not unreasonably, that adding a Ph.D. to her name might turn men off and leave her an old maid. But she had met Bill on a blind date while at Smith, and when she returned from Europe, he was there and waiting for her.

After the marriage, she followed Bill through three moves: from Des Moines to Philadelphia and Boston as Bill moved up the management ladder in aerospace engineering. The last move, eight years ago, had been to Los Altos, California, a suburb of San Francisco. In an effort to get out of aerospace, Bill accepted a position with Stanford University as a consultant in Technology Transfer. It seemed a good move; the job combined his R&D orientation from graduate work at Princeton with his management skills developed at M.I.T. (Master's in Management) and through work experience. By then, they had two children — Jeff in 1965 in Des Moines, Cathy in 1968 in Philadelphia. While in Los Altos, Pauline had decided to get an M.B.A. from Stanford. She graduated in 1973 and still remembers her final Corporate Strategy exam in May, with Ellen expected at any moment.

Two months after Ellen was born, Pauline received a call from the Chairman of Management at San Francisco State University. He asked her to accept the job of visiting lecturer in Marketing and Organization Behavior. She accepted, aware that all was not permanent for Bill at Stanford, aware that both she and Bill wanted to start their own business, aware that in the meantime the extra income would help bolster the family budget, and it met her need of a more flexible schedule which would give more time for the children.

After two years at S.F. State, Stanford University offered her a visiting professorship which she accepted. During this time, Bill and Pauline had founded their own company, Century Optics 21, in 1975 with five employees.

Bill owned 20% of the stock, was a Director, the President, and managed production, purchasing, engineering, and R & D. Pauline owned 30% of the stock, was a Director, the Treasurer and managed the office, order processing, shipping, personnel, stockholder relations, etc. They shared the marketing responsibilities, with Pauline handling the advertising. Bill's brother, an M.D. in nuclear medicine, owned 30% of the stock and served as a director. The rest of the stock was owned by family on both sides. Pauline and Bill worked seven days a week without vacations: Bill at Century Optics 21, Pauline dividing her time between her teaching commitment to Stanford and their company.

Now, at this juncture in her life, Optics 21 had 28 employees and sales had tripled, even quadrupled, since Pauline had stopped teaching at Stanford one year before. She was able to specialize in her strengths — Marketing and Personnel — and had delegated most of the Treasurer's function. She led seminars in Women Management Skills for Stanford and other Bay Area colleges. She liked the contact with developing women managers and the extra income (Bill and Pauline still were paying themselves minimum salaries to conserve cash.) The seminar groups and the new Bay Women's Club, for professional mid/upper management women executives, were her main source of female support. She was elected to membership in the Golden Gate Club — an exclusive businessmen's club which had decided finally to welcome female members. Being one of the first ten women elected to this club was meaningful to Pauline personally, and to Optics 21, and she had made valuable contacts among Club members. Indeed, it was probable that a Club luncheon meeting and discussion with President Joe Randolph of Laurel College led directly to her candidacy for the Chairmanship of the Management Department and consideration for the Directorship of Laurel's projected Management Center.

DECISIONS

Pauline hung up the phone from talking with Mr. James. Bill and she would make a presentation on the gynecological fiber optic instruments on Wednesday next week. Now to reading her In-Box mail.* She looked at her watch — two hours left before she must leave to get ready for the dinner and speech.

(Zzzap. . . . all the lights went out.)

ASSIGNMENT QUESTIONS

1. What decisions/actions must Pauline Todd make within the next 2 hours? In what order would you recommend that she make them and why?

2. Which decisions are the most crucial for the long-run health of Century Optics 21? Consider Pauline's In-Box items as well as her "To Do" List. Are these decisions doable in the context of Pauline's other rsponsibilities? If not, how could they be made so?

3. Using information drawn from the case, other cases you've had, or personal experiences with family members, draw up a list of "do's" and "don'ts" for husband/wife teams and/or other family members who are undertaking entrepreneurial ventures.

---

*See *Exhibit 2.*

Exhibit 1

To Do List

For Century Optics 21

1. Revise Personnel Policy
   - add new medical benefits
2. Call Jenkins re OEM project
3. Plan Advertising schedule for next 6 months
   - dates with Agency
   - budget
   - media
4. Arrange lunch meeting with Dr. Ryan and Dr. Sark
5. Hire new bookkeeper
   - ad in San Francisco Chronicle
   - ad in San Mateo Mercury
   - talk with CPA
6. Call Chuck Bragg - get landlord to put new carpet in office
7. Call Woodward - get $100,000 increased line of credit
8. Start investigation of software re computer for inventory control, accounts receivable, accounts payable
9. Review Accounts Receivable Aging
   - change or keep Collection Agency
10. Compare programs offered for financing by Ventures Unlimited Corp. and California Capital Resources - decision by Sept. 21

Personal

1. Get date to see Principal at Golden Gate School re referral of gifted Blacks or Mexican Americans for Scott Academy
2. Kaizer - check change of date re Financial Committee

For Family

1. Market
2. Jewelry repair pick-up
3. Sympathy note to McLeods
   - time, date of wake?
4. Cleaner's pick-up
5. Arrange carpool for soccer games
   - Jeff - Sat. at 2
   - Cathy - Sun. at 12
   - Ellen - Sat. at 9
6. Get Christmas card photo taken
7. Balance check book
8. Check on repair of garbage disposal at Sears, 598-8110 -Ron
9. Plan birthday party for Ellen; it's 3 months late; must be special!
10. Measure Ellen for gymnastic suit - get order with check mailed - due Friday Sept. 15
11. Sitter for Trade Show, Jan. 8-12
12. Send PSAT reservation with check for Jeff
13. Outgrown clothes to Church Rummage Sale by Sept. 16

3. Get well card for Miss Wickwire
4. Check dates for next 2 seminars for Management Women - conflict with trade shows in March and May?

In-Box Item #1

Memo

TO: Pauline

FROM: Garry (Finishing Shop Supervisor)

DATE: Thursday, September 14

FYI: RESPONSE NEEDED   ⟨ URGENT ⟩

The surface of the roller on the AEM grinding machine was gouged. Should we try to repair?

The deadline for shipping of the X518 parts which need to be ground on this machine is September 21.

Sorry to bother you with this but Bill is away.

In-Box Item #2

D. Riedler & Son Pty. Ltd.

Henley Beach Road, Torrensville, South Australia 1305
Postal Address: P.O. Box 57 Cowandilla, South Australia 1307
Telephone (08) 811 6758 Telex: AA98765; Code TX298A

17th August, 1981

Century Optics 21
2100 Light Avenue
San Mateo, California 94029
UNITED STATES OF AMERICA

Attention: Mr. William Todd

Dear Sir:

We refer to our telephone conversation held earlier this month relating to the lack of flatness in the face plates.

The 4″ units of the second shipment have all been repolished successfully without any breaking. A point of great concern to us is that the last shipment which we received all had a curve in them. We are currently in the process of resurfacing them to make them acceptable to our customers.

We have had to undertake a programme of 100% inspection before we release any of the small plates for sale. This is a procedure which we did not believe that we would have to undertake based on the trial shipment and a cost which we have not allowed for in our costings. Nevertheless we can sell them after we have corrected them.

Also of a major concern is the 16″ unit. The trial shipment all had straight edges and they were accepted extremely well. The subsequent shipments have had curved edges. As you know, the edge straightness has suffered badly with the change in production processes. Of the 16″ units we have tested there is a 0.016″ to 0.018″ curve along the edges. Because of the large curve we have started to get them returned as they are unsatisfactory.

We know that in most cases the curve should not cause too many problems particularly in the case of the small plates. The leaflets which come with each describes them as flat and straight edged. Our laws are so strict here, that if a product is described as being of a certain geometry, then it should be so.

Including the last shipment we have 70 which can be considered to have an excessive curve. In their present condition we do not feel comfortable about marketing them.

We fear that if we push these onto the market they may damage the name of Century Optics 21 and thus create problems when true face plates become available. What we both need is repeat business in a growing market rather than once only business in a declining market because of bad reputation.

Is there any possible way that we can correct the 16″ units? If they cannot be corrected we will have to be very careful where we sell them and will have to forego certain business until flat units can be received. As well as what we have in stock we can only assume that the 200 which are coming out via surface freight will have the same problem.

You have mentioned on the telephone that you were changing the tooling for the manufacture. Can you please advise us when "flat" plates will be available. If flatness cannot be achieved we would much prefer to purchase from production by the former process similar to the ones received in the trial shipment.

We wish to point out that more than anything we have been disappointed that the shipments subsequent to the trial shipment have not been of the same quality. We still believe that the product is a very good one and that it has a great potential. What we are experiencing at this stage are minor problems which we know can be overcome to our mutual benefit.

We feel that it is better to communicate that we have a problem rather than brush it under the carpet. We can only be controlled by our customers.

We look forward to hearing from you.

> Yours faithfully,
>
> D. RIELDER & SON PTY. LTD.
>
> DONALD RIELDER

In-Box Item #3

MEMO

(Note: This memo was handwritten in its original form)

TO: Mrs. Todd

FROM: Joe Bloom

DATE: 9-14-81

FYI   (RESPONSE NEEDED)   URGENT

Dear Mrs. Todd:

I'd feel better about my performance appraisal tomorrow if it were after lunch. Can the time be changed?

In-Box Item #4

POWARD TETERMAN & EISENBERG, S.C.

Attorneys At Law

700 North Water Street
Milwaukee, Wisconsin 53202
Area Code 414 819-6821

September 5, 1981

Mrs. Pauline Todd
Treasurer
Century Optics 21
2100 Light Avenue
San Mateo, CA 94029

Re: Century Optics 21 Vs: C.S.I. Corp.
Claim No. 2857266 for $12,500
(Invoices 6001, 6098, 6721)

Gentlemen:

Since our last report, a pre-trial conference has been scheduled for this matter for September 15, 1981, before Judge Raskin at the Waukesha County Courthouse. Although the Court requires clients to be present at the time of the pre-trial, I explained to the Court that client was in California and due to the shortness of time, that client would not be able to send a representative. The Court has assured us that this would be acceptable. However, we would appreciate client's advice as to what, if anything they would accept in the way of settlement, so that we at least have authority when we appear at the pre-trial conference.

Very truly yours,

POWARD, TETERMAN, EISENBERG, S.C.

ASolochek/rf

In-Box Item #5

BREWER & LORD

FOUNDED 1859

Insurance

40 Broad Street
San Francisco, California 94117
(415) 426-0830

September 1, 1981

Mrs. Pauline Todd
Century Optics 21
2100 Light Avenue
San Mateo, CA 94029

Dear Pauline:

As you are aware, the package policy is subject to audit based on actual payroll and sales. Please be sure that the enclosed, which shows figures for the 6-14-80/81 policy period, is accurate.

We should be in touch to go over international coverage soon due to your growing sales in Australia and Europe.

As ever,

S. Devereux Carter III

SDC/CM

Encs: Multi Peril Liability Policy

In-Box Item #6

Environmental Protection Agency
Northern California Office
San Francisco

September 11, 1981

Mr. William Todd
President
Century Optics 21
2100 Light Avenue
San Mateo, California 94029

Dear Mr. Todd:

On a recent inspection of the San Francisco Bay our inspectors found high levels of glass and abrasive effluents coming from your plant.

Mr. James Matthews, our chief inspector, will call on you on September 18, 1981 at 9 a.m. if that is convenient to discuss plans for Century Optics 21 compliance with the Clean Air and Water Act of 1971.

Sincerely,

David Williams

In-Box Item #7

MEMO

TO: Pauline

FROM: Marge (Supervisor of Packing and Shipping)

DATE: 9/12/81

(FYI)   RESPONSE NEEDED   URGENT

I think I should inform you that Joe Bloom's behavior was peculiar Monday and today after lunch. I think his problem of "smoking" at lunch time has returned. Some of the girls are afraid to work with him in the afternoons because he seems spaced out.

In-Box Item #8

September 14, 1981

Dear Bill and Pauline:

I have decided that I want to try working for a large company and have accepted a job at Intel Corporation to be trained on word processing machines. Intel will help pay for part of my college courses at night and I realize I should follow your advice to get a college degree if I want to go beyond a secretarial level.

I'm sorry to be resigning at this busy point but the training course starts on September 30 and I wanted to give you as much notice as possible. I'll do everything I can to help during the transition period. I think of you two as parents almost and appreciate all you've done to help me these past three years.

Sincerely,

Chris Young

Chris Young

In-Box Item #9

MEMO

TO: Pauline

FROM: Chris

FYI: RESPONSE NEEDED   URGENT

Final proof of new letterhead is in with telex added. Please approve.

Will be out of stationery next week so please check the proof today.

Thanks!

In-Box Item #10

MEMO

TO: Pauline

FROM: Fred Randell

DATE: September 14, 1981

FYI: RESPONSE NEEDED   URGENT

We do not have enough funds in the payroll account for this Friday. What do you want me to do? Need about $4,000.

Part Four

GROWTH, STRATEGY, SUCCESSION AND FINAL DISPOSITION OF ENTREPRENEURIAL ACTIVITIES

MEDICAL TECHNOLOGIES, INC.

On the morning of November 3, 1981, John Anderson, founder and CEO of Medical Technologies, Inc. (Med-Tech), located on the outskirts of Boston, was reviewing his agenda for the 10:00 A.M. Board of Directors meeting. The purpose for calling the directors to this meeting was to hear final arguments for and against the proposed acquisition of Simpson Hospital Supply Company (SHS) before he made his final decision on the matter.

Mr. Anderson knew that there would be substantial arguments for and against Med-Tech acquiring Simpson, but a final decision had to be made immediately as bids had to be submitted to Dupree Pharmaceutical, the divesting parent company, no later than the 12th of November. If the decision were to go ahead and try to acquire Simpson, then a competitive bid would have to be determined. Investigations revealed that Dupree would be receiving bids from numerous firms, including a bid submitted by the management of Simpson.

Dupree, a leader in the field of proprietary and ethical pharmaceuticals, had announced its intention to divest itself of SHS in early July. In the intervening months it had made available to interested bidders a complete dossier on the financial and marketing history of its Atlanta-based subsidiary, and a report on the company and the industry prepared by an outside consultant. In addition, Anderson and his Director of Corporate Development, Mayo Sheridan, had visited the company and met with the management on several occasions. Both the management and the board of Med-Tech had reviewed the findings thoroughly.

Anderson knew that determining a competitive bid would be no easy task; especially considering Med-Tech's own financial position, the lack of readily available funds, and the currently high prime interest rates offered by the banking industry.

HISTORY OF MED-TECH

Med-Tech was incorporated in 1974 by two physical chemists, John Anderson and Mayo Sheridan, to develop a line of disposable plastic medical products, design and build much of the equipment to manufacture those products in volume, and secure government approval to sell them in three rapidly growing product markets. These product/markets included systems for collecting, storing and administering blood, specialty intravenous products, and patient care disposables.

The chart below outlines the development process which took six years and approximately $13 million in order to initiate sales in the three product/market areas.

Exhibit 1

Development	Market Entry	Market Participation
1974	1980	

Design product

Design and fabricate tools, dies and molds

Design and fabricate certain production machinery and equipment

Design and construct pilot plant

Conduct pre-clinical portion of regulatory filings

File Investigational New Drug (IND) applications

Conduct clinical trials

File New Drug Applications (NDA)

Commence manufacturing and sale after FDA approval

Blood Products
$200 million market;
35% annual growth rate

Specialty Intravenous Products
$250 million market;
30% annual growth rate

Patient Care Disposables
$200 million market segment;
15% annual growth rate

Anderson and Sheridan were still in their 30's when they founded Med-Tech. However, they already had considerable experience in developing and distributing medical products before making the decision to start their own company. In the six years since 1974, they had assembled a team of over a dozen professionals with experience in every aspect of the developing enterprise: scientists, designers of equipment, and managers of production, marketing, and finance. The development period had gone relatively smoothly. Capital needs had been met. However, Med-Tech's management was impatient with the length of time required for FDA approval of their products. Partly because of the long pre-startup period, Anderson and Sheridan had committed themselves to a policy of acquisition, as well as development, to ensure future growth and earnings. In turn, this precipitated the decision to go to the public market for additional equity. Their initial offering was in January of 1981, and the stock was doing fairly well in over-the-counter trading.

During the past year, Anderson was interested specifically in acquiring state-of-the-arts technology and fast penetration into particular medical disposable markets. Consequently he had requested numerous medical supply companies to notify him if they desired to divest themselves of subsidiaries or product lines. Dupree responded to this inquiry when it announced its intended divestiture of SHS.

SIMPSON HOSPITAL SUPPLY COMPANY

SHS was founded in Atlanta in 1948 for the purposes of printing and distributing medical record forms. The forms were sold by telephone and mail order to small hospitals, nursing homes, clinics, and home care agencies throughout the Southeast.

All of top management, with the exception of the marketing manager, were native Atlantans who had been with the company since the early 1950's. The president had worked his way through the ranks, and was proud of his 25 years of service. Over that time, sales and earnings had grown slowly and steadily, and Dupree found it an attractive acquisition in 1973.

After 1973, Dupree added a broad line of patient care products to SHS's operations. The personal care supplies were distributed, as were the medical record forms, through telephone and mail order channels. Manufacturing of the product line was subcontracted to various suppliers, thus allowing SHS to concentrate exclusively its efforts toward distribution functions.

In 1979, SHS had hired a new marketing manager and subsequently made great strides in expanding its distribution. At this point, over half the sales were outside of the Southeast. Customers were serviced from two additional distribution points in Kansas City and Los Angeles.

By the end of fiscal 1980, SHS had registered sales revenues of $12 million and an after-tax operating profit of $1.2 million. Sales forecasts for the next two years indicated that sales would continue to increase by at least 7% annually. (Refer to *Exhibit 1* for SHS's balance sheet and income statements for selected years; *Exhibit 2* provides information about an appraisal of Simpson's fixed assets.) Nonetheless, in the spring of 1981, Dupree

Pharmaceutical decided to confine its future operations solely to the manufactuing and marketing of pharmaceuticals. Thus, Med-Tech and a number of other firms were notified of their intention to divest themselves of the Simpson Hospital Supply Company, which did not fit into Dupree's new scope of operatons.

SHS OPERATIONS

SHS's revenue was derived from two operational components. One revenue center involved the printing of medical and non-medical record forms, while the second component dealt with the distribution of printed medical forms and health supplies.

	Table A **Simpson Hospital Supply** 1980 Divisional Sales (1,000's)		
	Printing	**Distribution**	**Total Sales**
Sales	$2,755*	9,250	$12,005

As Table A indicates, printing operations constituted 23% of total sales for 1980. Broken down, the $2,755,000 sales figure included $2,023,000 to non-medical form dealers and $732,000 to Dupree Pharmaceuticals. As noted previously, an additional $2,411,000 in revenue was realized through sales via SHS distribution channels and was accounted for as distribution sales rather than printing revenue.

Medical forms printed by SHS were characteristically custom-run jobs and thus involved short and medium runs, typically averaging less than 20,000 forms per run. SHS supplied printed forms to regional business form dealers because it was unable to utilize all its printing capacity toward the printing of medical record forms.

Distribution of SHS printed medical record forms and health supplies contributed $9,250,000 or 77% of SHS total sales. Broken down, this figure included sales of $6,586,000 of printed medical record forms, $2,017,000 of medical supplies, and $648,000 of sundries.

---

*Printing revenues were actually $5,166, but $2,411 was accounted for in Distribution revenues, since SHS Printing acts as a supplier for SHS distribution function.

Examination of SHS's customers revealed that "distribution sales" were divided into the following categories:

Table B
SHS Distribution

Total Sales	$9,250,000	Sales Percentage:	100
Hospitals	4,369,000		47
Nursing Homes	3,422,000		37
Other (Clinics, Phys., Home Health Care)	1,459,000		16

Source: SHS

Small hospitals, under 200 beds, constituted SHS's primary customers for their printed medical forms. Other customers for their medical forms and health supplies were small and large "independent" nursing homes and clinics within their region of the country.

Market analysis by SHS's marketing manager revealed that SHS maintained a dominant share of the region's independent nursing home printed medical form business. The same analysis also showed SHS was extremely weak in servicing the ever-increasing number of nursing home chains in the area. Also, SHS's distribution of printed forms had not penetrated large hospitals, hospital chains, or hospitals outside a 400 mile radius of corporate headquarters.

PATIENT CARE PRODUCT DISTRIBUTION

Of SHS's 25,000 customer base, approximately 4,000 were known to be customers of the company's patient care product line. In 1980, through the efforts of an in-house staff of ten telephone sales representatives, sales revenues for this line exceeded $2.8 million. Equally impressive was the fact that even though SHS secured its entire product line from outside vendors, it was still able to obtain a 43.4% gross profit in the product line. Products marketed by SHS included such items as: arm slings, identification bands, urinary speciman containers, all-silicone foley catheters, leg bags, enema bags, instant ice packs, tongue depressors, surgical tape, and respiratory exercise devices. The majority of these products carried the identifying label of the institution which had ordered them -- in effect the products were "customized".

SHS had earned a reputation as the largest, quickest distributor of privately labeled disposable medical products in the industry. The company filled 97% of its orders within 24 hours. In order to do this, SHS maintained substantial inventories, pre-labeled by institution, for its more active accounts.

INDUSTRY FORECASTS

Analysis by industry experts in 1980 of future growth potential for the printing and distribution of medical record forms revealed that future earnings would be impacted by specific trends currently being experienced within both the printing and hospital care industries.

PRINTED MEDICAL FORM MARKET

In the printing sector, industry analysis indicated a continuing trend toward national concentration of printing manufacturing. For example, in 1972, the top 11 printing form companies accounted for 73% of the nation's printing business, but by 1976, this figure had increased to 77%. Local and regional printing firms were thus responsible for only 23% of market sales by 1976. Even regionally, consolidation of printing companies was seen as competition became more intense. Printing firms, in order to compete effectively, had to stress form management systems, reliable service, product quality, and most importantly, competitive pricing policies.

Although total sales for the printed form industry were approximately $2.2 billion in 1976, future growth rate projections were expected to be dramatically less than the 9% annual growth rate previously experienced by the industry. Contributing to deflated forecasts was the projected impact of computerized record keeping within health care institutions.

DISTRIBUTION OF MEDICAL FORMS MARKET

SHS as well as other distributors had noticed trends developing that would impact seriously their future earning potential, the distribution of the medical records forms. Within the hospital segments, there was a definite shrinkage in the number of hospitals under 200 beds. Instead the trend was toward expansion of existing facilities to meet increasing needs, rather than maintaining or establishing new smaller-sized local hospitals. It was also projected that by the mid-1980s, hospital chains would control over 30% of all hospital beds. With the adoption of chain operations, corporations running the facilities would stress standardization of medical record keeping. Thus, with large quantities of records required, chains would either opt for in-house printing or acquire forms from national printers who could accomodate large orders at discount prices.

"Chaining" of nursing home ownership was also seen to be increasing dramatically in the early 1980s. However, these chains were producing printed record forms in-house or acquiring from large distributors. Independent nursing homes still tended to utilize local or regional printers.

PATIENT CARE DISPOSABLE MARKET

In 1980, the disposable patient care market for all nursing care facilities was estimated to be $300 million with a projected annual growth rate of 15%. Sales for patient care products utilized primarily by nursing homes and home care operations were expected to increase dramatically with annual growth rates near 30%. Reasons for this increase were due primarily to: 1) "an increase in the over 65 age group of the population who consumed over 35% of the health care products and services, and 2) the cost containment pressures that were forcing hospitals to release patients sooner for continued care, either to nursing homes or to home directly."* Major distributors such as American Hospital Supply were concentrating on large hospital and large nursing home chains and their patient care needs. Thus, nursing home facilities and clinics were serviced by either smaller local or regional distribution.

MED-TECH'S POSITION

By 1980, Med-Tech had invested over $13 million into in-house research and development and product line acquisition. The company had also acquired specific products through a combination of stock exchanges, royalty payment agreements, licensing, and cash payment negotiations. Although Med-Tech was still running in the red in 1980 (see *Exhibits 3 and 4* for financial statements), the net sales figure for the year was up 79% over the 1979 figure. The dramatic increase in sales was due primarily to the marketing of eight new FDA approved products. (Marketing functions for Med-Tech were carried out through a network of sales representatives and independent dealers.)

Med-Tech executives, although concerned with high interest costs associated with R&D investment and acquisition financing, looked forward to the future with great optimism. Factors contributing to their optimistic outlook were items such as: the successful issuing of common stock for $6,376,000, utilization of low-cost facilities in Barbados, ever improving gross margins on all product lines, successful vertical integration, and experienced executive management. In addition, Med-Tech's product lines had been well accepted by their customers and with aggressive marketing methods, Med-Tech felt that they could become a quality second-source supplier in the highly concentrated disposable health care field.

Organizationally, Med-Tech had achieved its present position by structuring its operations around three divisions. Each division was responsible for one of Med-Tech's principal product/market areas.

THE LABORATORY PRODUCTS DIVISION

Utilizing internal research and development, coupled with acquisitions of various lines from major competitors, Med-Tech had become by 1980 a state-of-the-art manufacturer and marketer of a broad range of laboratory products. During 1980, sales dramatically increased in this sector by 300%, reaching $3.3 million by year end. This increase was due to the initial sale of both long-awaited FDA approved internally developed products and the sales from newly acquired product lines. Future sales would be dependent on keeping abreast of technological advancements, cost containment procedures toward manufacturing, and the ability to penetrate both domestic and the rapidly expanding international markets effectively.

---

*Med-Tech Market Analysis Reports

THE SPECIALTY INTRAVENOUS PRODUCTS

A second segment of Med-Tech's operations was focused toward intravenous products. In this segment, as in the Laboratory Products Division, product offerings were developed either in-house or through acquisition.

Products such as I.V. Prep Kits, anethesia extension sets, cut-down catheters, A-catheters, etc., were marketed by sales representatives and national hospital supply dealers. Sales for this sector for 1980 were $5 million, or a 150% increase over 1979 sales figures of $2 million.

THE PERSONAL CARE DISPOSABLE DIVISION

The third focus of Med-Tech's operations was penetration of the patient care disposable market. Attracted by growth projections of the market (15% annually), Med-Tech produced a broad range of patient care disposables for hospitals and nursing homes. The product line was broadened in January 1980 by the incorporation of various home care respiratory and urological products acquired from Wentworth Laboratories. Wtih the acquisition of the well-respected Wentworth label, Med-Tech management hoped to add prestige to its own line which was currently marketed through a network of independent sales representatives who, in turn, sold to regional and national dealers. The patient care disposable line contributed approximately $3.7 million to Med-Tech sales revenues in 1980.

Some of the patient care products being manufactured and marketed by Med-Tech are:

Arm Slings
Identification Bands
Urinary Speciman Containers
All-silicone Foley Catheters
Leg Bags
Enema Bags
Instant Ice Packs
Tongue Depressors
Surgical Tape
Respiratory Exercise Devices
Catheter Care Kits

Med-Tech executives anticipated that the patient care disposable line would increase its sales contributions due to the company's ability to offer quality line products at competitive prices in an expanding market.

BOARD OF DIRECTORS MEETING

As time approached for the start of the Board of Directors' meeting, John Anderson completed the review of his calculations and his list of pros and cons for the acquisition of SHS. Just as he finished, his executive assistant entered the office and told him that a recent communication from SHS had revealed that the management of SHS had stated collectively that if their bid was rejected by Dupree, they would all tender their resignations within two weeks of being acquired by any company.

On his way to the board meeting, John Anderson puzzled over his latest development. He thought: "If I go ahead with this acquisition and find a way to finance it, my incorporation of SHS into Med-Tech's operations will be complicated right from the beginning with management problems."

ASSIGNMENT QUESTIONS

Please read or review the note on Acquisition and Leverage Buyouts. Suggested questions are the following:

1. Should the acquisition of Simpson Hospital Supply Company be made? Why or why not?

2. Assume you plan to bid:

   a) What price would you bid?
   b) What other financial and nonfinancial terms would you include in your bid?

3. How should the acquisition be structured financally in order to insure long term success for Med-Tech?

Exhibit 1
Simpson Hospital Supply Company
Balance Sheet
(Dollars in $000 - Unaudited)

	Dec. 31, 1979	Dec. 31, 1980	June 31, 1981	Sept. 31, 1981
Assets				
Cash	$ 81	$ 480	$ 107	$ 275
Accounts Receivable	1,708	1,790	1,657	1,599
Inventories	3,079	3,133	3,724	3,264
Prepaid Expenses	19	20	10	10
Current Assets	$ 4,887	$ 5,423	$ 5,498	$ 5,148
Fixed Assets	1,824	1,807	2,059	2,044
Total Assets	$ 6,711	$ 7,230	$ 7,557	$ 7,129
Liabilities & Equity				
Accounts Payable	$ 318	$ 503	$ 420	$ 460
Other Current Liabilities	216	275	774[1]	955[1]
Capital Accounts:				
Common Stock	60	60	60	60
Capital in Excess of Par	1,010	1,010	1,010	1,010
Retained Earnings[2]	5,107	5,382	5,293	4,707
Total Capital Invested	$ 6,177	$ 6,452	$ 6,363	$ 5,777
Total Liabilities & Equity	$ 6,711	$ 7,230	$ 7,557	$ 7,192

1. Includes accrued federal income taxes of $530 and $759 in June and September balances, respectively. This account was transferred to parent company at year end in prior years.

2. Intercompany advances are combined with retained earnings as though dividends had been declared as of December 31, 1979 and 1980, June 30, 1981, and September 30, 1981. In August, 1981 the intercompany advances were collected and dividends declared to Dupree in an equal amount.

Exhibit 1
Simpson Hospital Supply Company
Income Statement
For the Periods Ending 1976-1981

	1976	1977	1978	1979	1980	Nine Months Ending Sept. 30, 1981
Sales	$ 8,228	$ 8,740	$ 9,503	$10,690	$12,006	$ 9,509
Cost of Sales	4,233	4,430	4,924	5,573	6,359	4,928
Gross Profit	$ 3,995	$ 4,310	$ 4,579	$ 5,117	$ 5,647	$ 4,581
Operating Expenses:						
Distribution Expense	$ 539	$ 543	$ 595	$ 648	$ 729	$ 1,129
Marketing	877	820	795	846	949	1,673
Administration	1,006	1,088	1,222	1,349	1,614	336
Corporate Allocations	115	115	-	92	191	116
Total:	$ 2,537	$ 2,566	$ 2,612	$ 2,935	$ 3,483	$ 3,254
Operating Earnings	$ 1,458	$ 1,744	$ 1,967	$ 2,182	$ 2,164	$ 1,327
Interest Income	3	49	115	170	241	366
Other Income/(Expense)	1	(7)	(5)	(1)	(9)	-
Earnings Before Tax:	$ 1,489	$ 1,786	$ 2,077	$ 2,351	$ 2,396	$ 1,693
Tax	721	835	993	1,135	1,127	791
Earnings:	$ 768	$ 951	$ 1,084	$ 1,216	$ 1,269	$ 902

Exhibit 2

Property Appraisal

Dupree Pharmaceutical

September 11, 1981

Mr. John Anderson
President
Medical Technologies, Inc.

Dear Mr. Anderson:

As an addendum to the Simpson Information Memorandum you received earlier, we are enclosing a summary of an appraisal of their plant, property and equipment which was conducted by American Appraisal Company. The appraisal indicates a fair market value for those assets of $4,562,000, as compared with a book value as of June 30, 1981 of $2,059,000. We trust this additional information will be helpful in your evaluation.

We will be contacting you shortly to determine your continued level of interest with regard to Simpson.

Regards,

Jeannette S. Sullivan

Exhibit 2
Summary of
Fair Market Value

Simpson Hospital Supply Co.
Properties
August 15, 1981

Land	235,000
Land Improvements	60,000
Building Construction and Services	2,470,000
Improvements to Leased Property	1,000
Machinery and Equipment	1,686,000
Office Furniture and Equipment	110,000
Grand Total	4,562,000

Exhibit 3
Medical Technologies, Inc.
Income Statement
For the fiscal years ending 1978-1980

Year ended December 31,	1978	1979	1980
Net Sales	$ 6,351,833	$ 6,738,730	$12,034,739
Costs and Expenses:			
Cost of Sales	5,542,559	5,369,729	8,688,189
Selling, General & Adminis. Expenses	1,828,107	2,179,152	3,201,107
Product and Development Expense	1,119,715	999,342	978,776
Other Development Expense	918,742	—	—
	$ 9,409,123	$ 8,548,223	$12,868,072
Operating Loss	$(3,057,290)	$(1,809,493)	$ (833,333)
Interest Expense Net	(279,221)	(448,936)	(884,956)
Minority Interest in Loss of Subsidiary	120,643	140,640	—
Loss Before Provision for Income Taxes	$(3,215,868)	$(2,117,789)	$(1,718,289)
Provision (Credit) for Income Taxes			
Federal	(144,000)	—	—
State	21,900	—	—
	$(3,093,768)	$(2,117,789)	$(1,718,289)
Deferred Dividends	$ 80,000	$ 194,500	$ 120,000
Weighted Average Number of Common Shares Outstanding During the Period	2,655,198	2,740,840	2,966,325
Net Loss Per Common Share (based on the weighted average number of shares outstanding during the period)	$(1.20)	$(.84)	$(.62)

Source: Medical Technologies Annual Report, 1980.

Exhibit 4
Medical Technologies, Inc.
Balance Sheet
For the fiscal years ending 1979-1980

Assets

December 31,	1979	1980
Current Assets:		
Cash	$ 636,714	$ 184,172
Marketable securities at cost which approximates market value	—	150,000
Receivable from sale of common stock	—	6,930,000
Trade accounts receivable, less allowance of $181,000 in 1980 and $120,000 in 1979	1,598,839	2,486,225
Inventories	2,888,022	3,618,250
Prepaid expenses	153,429	164,135
Total current assets	$ 5,277,004	$13,532,782
Investment in Commercial Paper, at cost which approximates market value	$ 450,000	$ 450,000
Deposits on Machinery and Equipment	$ 505,000	$ 859,181
Property, Plant and Equipment, at cost		
Land	$ 106,395	$ 106,395
Buildings, improvements and facilities	1,841,376	2,601,527
Machinery and equipment	2,576,506	3,304,618
	$ 4,524,277	$ 6,012,540
Less Accumulated depreciation	(1,074,371)	(1,405,152)
	$ 3,449,906	$ 4,607,388
Property and equipment, capitalized under lease agreements	—	2,726,174
Net property, plant and equipment	$ 3,449,906	$ 6,333,562
Other Assets		
Cost in excess of identifiable assets of acquired business, net	$ 99,591	$ 96,820
Patents, new drug applications & technology	194,404	1,044,080
Deferred financing cost	—	138,920
Total other assets	$ 293,995	$ 1,279,820
	$ 9,975,905	$22,455,345

Exhibit 4
Medical Technologies, Inc.
Balance Sheet
For the fiscal years ending 1979-1980

Liabilities and Stockholders' Investment

December 31,	1979	1980
Current Liabilities:		
Notes payable	$ 2,139,000	$ 1,085,986
Current maturities of long-term debt	325,874	666,854
Accounts payable	1,703,005	2,265,938
Accrued expenses:		
Payroll and related costs	117,261	285,297
Interest	131,360	328,608
Financing costs	—	421,930
Other	341,105	456,203
Dividends payable	96,250	160,000
Total current liabilities	$ 4,853,855	$ 5,670,816
Long-Term Debt, less current maturities:		
Promissory notes and mortgages	$ 2,700,472	$ 6,007,540
Capital lease obligations	—	1,670,107
	$ 2,700,472	$ 7,677,647
Deferred Revenue	$ 75,000	$ —
Stockholders' Investment		
$7.50 Convertible preferred stock, $1 par value (liquidation value of $3,000,000) -Authorized and outstanding –30,000 shares at December 31, 1979	$ 30,000	$ —
$8.00 Cumulative preferred stock, $.10 par value (liquidation value of $1,000,000) -Authorized and outstanding 10,000 shares at December 31, 1980 and 1979	1,000	1,000
Common stock, $.10 par value -Authorized - 10,000,000 shares in 1980 and 5,000,000 shares in 1979 Issued and outstanding - 5,075,068 shares at December 31, 1980 and 1,740,632 shares at December 31, 1979	274,063	507,507
Capital in excess of par value	10,031,047	18,426,196
Retained deficit	(7,989,532)	(9,827,821)
Total stockholders' investment	$ 2,346,578	$ 9,106,882
	$ 9,975,905	$22,455,345

Source: Medical Technologies, Inc., Annual Report, 1980.

GOLDEN SUNSETS, INC.

In March 1979 Thomas Gordy, President of Golden Sunsets, Inc., watched the sunset from his office in the Haight-Asbury district of San Francisco. He knew he would be up a good part of the night preparing for tomorrow's meeting with the firm's new owner, Terrence C. Burns. Mr. Burns was President of Prime Investment Corporation (PIC), a venture capital firm based in Atlanta, Georgia. Golden Sunsets had experienced cash flow problems from its inception. Although Mr. Burns had injected $250,000 at the time of the purchase early in 1978, the firm's working capital stood at ($97,537) at the end of February 1979. (See *Exhibit 1* for recent balance sheets.) Mr. Gordy felt that, despite dangerously low cash balances, the firm could begin to show a profit by mid 1979. As he was working on monthly projections for July-December 1979 (See *Exhibit 2* for January-June projections), Mr. Gordy was somewhat concerned that the February profit and loss statement (*Exhibit 3*) fell short of his projection. He wondered what recommendations he should make at tomorrow's meeting as well as what his future role with PIC might be.

COMPANY BACKGROUND

In 1970, Mr. Gordy and his partner, Rodney Jefferson, had the idea of custom printing the cover of a packet of cigarette paper as a specialty advertising item. Cigarette paper was familiar to "roll your own" cigarette smokers but was being increasingly identified as an item of "paraphernalia" used in marijuana smoking. At the time Mr. Gordy was selling a line of clothing to boutiques and so-called head shops in the Western United States. He reasoned that these retailers were a potential market for custom cigarette papers which could be imprinted with a store's name or logo and given away. Conversations with these retailers convinced him that there was a potential market and by May 1970 he had even received a few orders. Golden Sunsets was formally incorporated in August. Mr. Gordy recalled:

> What I did that summer was get a job at a printing shop, working for nothing because I didn't know anything about printing. I said to the printer, 'Look I'm really interested in learning about printing and I'll eventually give you business because I'm setting up a business that needs printing.' So I worked all summer until I knew how to get an order from

artwork into printed copy. By August we were ready to begin soliciting business. We ran an ad in *Rolling Stone**, their first ever for cigarette paper. The ad said something like 'Give away free cigarette paper to your customers with your name and logo imprinted.' It was something completely new and we got about 1,000 responses.

Over the summer, Mr. Gordy located a supplier of cigarette paper in Canada. The two partners pooled their resources and borrowed enough money to purchase $6,000 worth of paper, the supplier's minimum order. Problems immediately surfaced. Mr. Gordy said:

> We found that *that* paper wasn't really being accepted in the market because it wasn't wide enough and it was a thicker grade than people were used to using. Finally we knew we were getting nowhere with that paper so we returned it to the supplier and we got about $80 credit on it. So over a period of about four months we lost about $5800.

Early in 1972 Mr. Gordy and Mr. Jefferson negotiated a license agreement with the producers of an X-rated feature movie to produce "X-Rated-Papers." These papers were imprinted with twelve different scenes from the film and sales of the first printing were $25,000. Mr. Gordy said that, "X-Rated-Papers" were the first cigarette papers ever to be packaged in a 4 color leaflet. The partners attracted some additional investors, incorporated a separate company and reinvested everything they could with inventory, gearing for a second production run. Active production had been done by hand by the two partners and their friends but orders for the second printing of X-Rated-Papers soon exceeded their capacity.

The partners contracted production to the local Occupational Vocational Development Center for the Handicapped (OVDCH). Mr. Gordy remembered:

> It was Thanksgiving evening of 1972--I remember it was Thanksgiving because we were having a dinner and celebrating that we had finally gotten out of the doldrums and were actually turning the company into something. We had our custom business and X-Rated-Papers were beginning to take off. Anyhow, they had a fire over at the OVDCH warehouse and it burned everything including all of our inventory and, of course, the insurance company refused to pay off. So essentially we were out of business. That was a major bummer.

---

*A tabloid publication devoted to rock music.

Mr. Gordy said that Golden Sunsets was only able to survive because he was collecting unemployment at first and welfare later and was able to survive on $30 per week. Neither he nor Mr. Jefferson who had finished law school, took any salary for several years. After the demise of X-Rated-Papers, custom paper business continued to trickle in largely because of Mr. Jefferson's telephone sales efforts. The firm had some success during this period producing custom papers for rock groups notably The Dooby Brothers Band, Blood, Sweat and Tears, The Who, and Paul McCartney. Mr. Gordy said:

> Getting involved with those people was enough to convince
> us we were still making progress, even though we had just
> been burned out of business. You know if you're any kind of
> an entrepreneur, all you need is a thread of hope. You grab
> the thread and hope it turns into a string and then a rope.

In the early 1970s other firms introduced flavored and other novelty cigarette papers to the market. Mr. Gordy became convinced that his company needed such a national, branded product to survive. He began working on a process to mentholate cigarette paper. He felt that by providing cooler, flavored smoke, mentholated papers could revolutionize the industry.

Working closely with his Canadian paper supplier, he was able to complete the process in May of 1974. By August 1974 Mr. Gordy had developed the name "Coolit" and the product was ready to market. The firm, however, was seriously short of cash because of an ill-fated investment in another new product, "No Wind Paper." When a competitor successfully introduced an identical product, Golden Sunsets simply did not have the cash to produce and promote its own, according to Mr. Gordy.

Mr. Gordy described how Golden Sunsets was finally able to begin production of Coolit papers:

> I had my pilot's license which I had managed to get with my
> last $300 several years before so Jefferson and I rented an
> airplane and flew up to Canada to visit our supplier. We
> were dressed to kill--the whole works. Of course he gave us
> $15,000 credit just like that when we barely had $.15. The
> airplane was a fairly convincing act.

By incorporating a separate Coolit Company and attracting an additional investor, the firm was able to market the mentholated papers. Mr. Gordy felt that he wanted wider distribution than was available through specialty "head" shops and engaged what he termed "a major marketing firm in the tobacco industry" whose function was to secure distribution through large tobacco wholesalers and smaller local jobbers. During the first half of 1975, Coolit sales were $350,000. Mr. Gordy described the impact on the market:

> We made such an impact that it was getting our competitors
> uptight, especially Adams Apple, the distributor of Job
> papers. Adams Apple was doing $5-6 million a year in
> papers, pipes and other paraphernalia.

> They were threatened by our success with Coolit so they
> went to all the tobacco distributors they were in and
> announced their own menthol paper for September
> delivery. What they did was buy all of our paper back from
> the distributors and sold it off at one-half our lowest
> wholesale price. That was typical behavior in the industry in
> those days and it affected us quickly.

> We had no ready cash at the time we were expanding, buying
> inventory, making sure we had packaging and everybody
> geared up. They essentially cut off all our sales and left us
> with probably about $170,000 worth of liabilities and maybe
> $20,000 in inventory after we adjusted it downward. We
> immediately became illiquid and nobody was willing to
> provide us any evidence of their wrong doing. So we didn't
> even have a case against them.

The Coolit Company went into assignment for the benefit of creditors and the books
were not closed until June 1977, after intensive legal battles. Mr. Gordy said that the only
thing which saved Golden Sunsets, which was by then doing $10,000 to $15,000 a month
in custom paper sales, was an out-of-court settlement with Brown and Williamson
Tobacco. Brown and Williamson owned the trademark "Kool" and had been suing
Golden Sunsets for infringement. Golden Sunsets sold the name Coolit to Brown and
Williamson and was able to satisfy most of Coolit's creditors and stay in business.

Mr. Gordy said that Golden Sunsets then entered an era of "some stability" but
described a further encounter with Adams Apple:

> During this time we got a subcontracting job for a million
> booklets for $70,000 cash which sustained us for awhile. We
> had commitments for some further orders if we performed
> well on that first one. But after that order, Adams Apple
> *bought* the company that gave us the order so that was the
> end of that. They take the game so seriously that it distorts
> their perspective.

CHARISMA PAPERS

Mr. Gordy had approached Playboy and Penthouse magazines with proposals to
produce papers for them and had been flatly rejected. His attention turned to *Charisma*, a
pornographic magazine published by Wayne Davis. The magazine had a reputation for
publishing more controversial material than either Playboy or Penthouse. Mr. Gordy
said:

> I was at a friend's house thumbing through a copy of
> Charisma and I saw an ad for the Charisma Head Shop.
> They had pipes, bongs, cocaine paraphernalia but no
> papers. I said, 'This is it.' At that time the general public

thought that paraphernalia people and pornographers were the same type of scum-bags, anyway. So I knew we were in the ball park. I called them in December 1976 and asked, 'What is the Charisma Head Shop doing without Charisma cigarette papers?' They said, in effect, 'Good question. The Charisma Head Shop *shouldn't* be without Charisma papers. We'd like to order some.'

The initial order was for 500,000 booklets with a $40,000 cash advance and the first deliveries began in October 1977. Amid promises of a 7 million booklet order and Charisma plans to spend $3 million in advertising over three years, Mr. Gordy and Mr. Jefferson negotiated a loan arrangement with Mr. Cox. The loan was to be for $250,000 for both working capital and production equipment for the anticipated volume of Charisma sales. Mr. Gordy explained:

> The industry was in an interesting position at that point as far as production equipment and production time available and cigarette paper available. We felt that if a person was in the right place at the right time with enough money and the right equipment, he could really prosper. Well, we went for it.

> We started talking to another manufacturer. We flew jet planes around and wined and dined these guys. We made plans to buy their facilities. We entered into joint ventures, all because we couldn't have produced the Charisma papers on our own.

> Essentially our deal with Davis was a loan with a warrant, I think it's called. He was going to loan us $250,000 which we would pay back over five years. At the end of five years, he would have owned 50% of the company. We had the option to buy back 30% of his 50%--leaving him 20%--for a percentage of the profits at the end of five years. Those payments could be made over the next five years.

Mr. Gordy said that two factors combined to collapse the Charisma--Golden Sunsets partnership. First, he said, Mr. Cox insisted that the illustrations on th booklets be hard-core pornography (Mr. Davis had claimed 1st amendment protection for his publications). Mr. Gordy also said that in December 1977, "Davis flipped out." The result was, Mr. Gordy said, "that by February 1978 there was no money going back and forth between either of us. He had fired everybody in the organization that was a friend of ours--not because they were friends of ours but because he was totally paranoid at the time." Mr. Cox had set up a meeting in Washington for March 18, 1978 to discuss an outright purchase of Golden Sunsets. On March 16, 1978 Mr. Cox was attacked by unknown assailants in New York and left badly injured. Mr. Gordy said:

> That ended that. There we were with 1 million books of Charisma paper--not exactly the kind of stuff you can unload on Mom and Pop's corner store--in our warehouse. We were desperately short of cash. We were thinking, 'Hmm, we've pulled ourselves out of some heavy situations before but this time we might be in a little too deep.'

NEW OWNERSHIP

Upon the dissolution of The Golden Sunsets--Charisma partnership, Mr. Gordy approached Mr. Burns in desperation. Mr. Burns was interested in the future of the paraphernalia industry and offered essentially the same terms Mr. Cox had offered Mr. Gordy. Mr. Gordy explained:

> Terry had agreed to loan us money. So far it's been $200,000. In return, we agreed to consolidate Golden Sunsets with PIC. In order to consolidate, legally a company must have 80% of the other company's shares. So we gave him 80% of our shares.

> We can buy back a portion of those shares at what the book value was at the time of the transfer. That was a negative number. So in five years for $1 we can get back to 50/50 ownership.

> Beyond that we have the option to buy back 16% of the shares by paying him book value or not less than $2 million. That option begins 7 years from when the deal was signed and the money would be payable 20% down and the balance over five years at 2% over prime.

> Rod (Jefferson) and I think we have a good deal. It was a question of having 20% of something or 100% of nothing, really. Besides I don't think we'll ever try to buy him out. After all we saw Wayne Davis go from $100,000 per month in sales to $120 million in three years with Terry Burns and we'd like to see how far we can go.

THE INDUSTRY

At the turn of the century, brands of cigarette paper were identified with brands of roll-your-own tobacco. The most popular was Bull Durham. R.J. Reynolds introduced ready made Camel cigarettes in 1914 which hurt sales of both papers and loose tobacco. In France and Spain where world paper production was centered, ready made cigarettes were slower to spread and paper manufacture flourished. The Depression stimulated a boom in sales of imported Bull Durham papers and domestic Top and Bugler brands. In the post-Depression and especially World War II years, ready-made cigarettes became the standard American fare and cigarette paper sales fell sharply.

In the 1960s cigarette papers became identified with marijuana smoking and a distinct paraphernalia market also began to develop. Numerous companies began selling cigarette papers and manufacturing other paraphernalia. So-called head shops opened in large cities and near college campuses. As the paper market grew steadily, numerous product innovations appeared. Papers imprinted to resemble American Flags, Selective Service Cards, and $100 bills were marketed in 1970. Strawberry, banana, cherry and licorice flavored papers appeared about the same time.

The following list of cigarette paper sources appeared in *Dealer Magazine* in 1975:

Manufacturers:

Spain:	Papeleras Reunidas	- Bamba (flavors, Blanco y Negro, World.) Canada Goose
	Miguel y Costas	- Smoking Arroz, Smoking Hilo, Smoking Double Wide
	Jean	Roach
France:	Job	- Job Reefer Roller
	Abadie	- Abadie
England:	Rizla	- Rizla
Italy:	Modiano	- $100 Bill, Flag, Camouflage
Belgium:	Rizla	- Alfa, 2 in 1
U.S.:	American Tobacco	Bull Durham
	R.J. Reynolds	Top, OCB, Prince Albert
	Brown & Williamson	Bugler
	U.S. Tobacco	Zig Zag
	Coolit	Coolit

Importers:

Adams Apple	Job, Reefer Roller
Bamba Sales	Bamba, Big Bambu, Marfil, Blanco y Negro
Burey Karp	Rizla, Foy
Head Imports	One and 1/2, Bumbu (flavors)
Highway Imports	Joint, Joint Wides, $100 Bill, Flag
Ibis	Abadie, Smoking Arroz, Smoking Hilo, 2 in 1. Alfa
Robert Burton	E-Z Wider, Joker, Roach, Harvest

By 1979, the leading firms were U.S. Tobacco, Adams Apple and Robert Burton Associates. U.S. Tobacco's Zig Zag brand was by far the industry leader. The growth rate of Zig Zag sales had slowed to 10% annually from 1974 to 1977 from 25% annually from

1964 to 1974. Adams Apple imported Job brand papers from France and had cigarette paper sales of $15 million in 1977. That firm also imported and distributed various other paraphernalia. Total sales for 1977were $10.0 million. Robert Burton Associates had become an industry leader through the introduction of the E-Z Wider brand in 1971. This double width paper eliminated the need to stick two conventional papers together before rolling. Robert Burton Associates invested $10,000 in a shipment of double width paper in 1971 and by 1977 sales were $7 million and net income $400,000.

INDUSTRY PROBLEMS

The New York Times cited distribution as a key problem in the paraphernalia industry especially in the early days when the only retail outlets were "head" shops. This situation began to change in the early and mid 1970s as cigarette papers were introduced to and accepted by more conventional retailers such as record shops and convenience stores. Some mass marketers like K-Mart and even some Sears Stores began to sell cigarette papers. Industry sources pointed to the recent granting of a Universal Product Code designation to both Zig-Zag and E-Z Wider Brands as final proof of market acceptance.

The paraphernalia industry had been subject to numerous legal challenges as communities sought to ban the sale of "drug related items." The situation was serious enough that the Paraphernalia Trade Association had been formed to lobby on behalf of the industry and provide legal assistance. Mr. Gordy said that there were some legislative threats to the industry as a whole but that in general most legislation did not include cigarette papers. He felt that most "zealous defenders of public morality" were far more concerned with banning the sale of pipes, bongs, cocaine paraphernalia and the like than cigarette papers. He noted that successful anti-paraphernalia legislation merely prohibited sales to minors and did not extend to papers. He commented:

> We didn't see any pending legislation as a direct threat to us.
> Hell, we support banning paraphernalia sales to minors.
>
> Besides, we're not the guys who are turning everybody's
> children on to drugs. We're here because America said, 'Let
> us have implements to smoke marijuana.' We didn't say,
> 'Here's an implement. Now go and find some grass, kid.'

Mr. Gordy did feel that the availability of marijuana can affect his business. He said:

> I read about multimillion dollar pot busts, I know there's
> that much less on the market. That's *got* to hurt my business.
> Then there's the paraquat thing. When the news got out that
> the U.S. Government was sponsoring a program to poison
> Mexican pot to keep it off the U.S. market, the Mexican
> farmers didn't sit around and wait for their crops to die.
> They harvested right after the plants were sprayed. Smoking
> that contaminated pot can cause lung damage. So, when the
> news got out in 1978 that the government had in effect made
> pot smoking a capital crime, a lot of people got really scared.

The last part of 1978 was very bad for the paraphernalia industry.

INDUSTRY SIZE

By 1978, some estimates had retail cigarette paper sales as high as $200 million up from $50 million in 1972. Total 1978 paraphernalia sales were estimated as high as $400 million. Mr. Gordy felt that the paraphernalia industry could grow to $1.0 billion in 10 years or even more if marijuana were legalized. He said:

> Eventually it'll be legalized. Right now there's a lot of political opposition, but sometime they'll consider the economics of it. Time magazine said recently that the pot industry, if you take it all together, would be the third biggest company in the country behind Exxon and General Motors--something like $50 billion in sales. Imagine that-- $50 billion and not one penny taxed.

> You know Western Massachusetts, where my family lives, is great tobacco country. If pot is ever legalized, we'd like to have our own brand, Golden Sunsets, grown right on a family farm...

Mr. Gordy said that Golden Sunsets was currently "unbankable" largely due to the assignment of the Coolit Company. Prior to Coolit, Golden Sunsets had acquired "interleaving" equipment which folded and stacked papers to produce a "pop-up package." This equipment was the only such equipment in this country and probably in the world according to Mr. Gordy. Golden Sunsets paid for four interleaving machines by exchanging cigarette paper. Having acquired the equipment, Mr. Gordy approached the bank for a $50,000 loan to provide working capital to support Coolit. Mr. Gordy recalled:

> The equipment was worth $75,000 and we asked for $50,000 against it. Our bank said, 'That's a lot of money. It'll have to go to the Board of Directors.' The Board wanted to see financial statements, the first ones they had ever asked for.

> Not only did they find out that our balance sheet was absolutely terrible but also that we were already into them for $55,000, $35,000 of which was unsecured. Needless to say, they freaked out.

On the ensuing assignment, Mr. Gordy said that the company lost all bank support. He had been able to secure a $50,000 loan on the equipment but the lender "took a lien on everything--past, present and future." Mr. Gordy explained the current situation:

> Our balance sheet was still terrible when Burns came in! The money he loaned us went toward moving to our new

building, to pay for lack of production while we moved, to buy some new equipment for wired papers. Some of it went into payroll and a lot of it went to the IRS for old tax liabilities. We still owe them $100,000. In the early days, we'd negotiate, say, with the phone company to get an extension on a $200 bill. That was the current rap. Now, we're getting an extension on a $700 bill. It's the same rap. The same people. The same subject--just bigger numbers.

Now we're at a point where we still have payables that we have to deal with and cash flow problems. Two things hurt us recently. The last half of 1978 was terrible for the paraphernalia industry because of the paraquot scare. Also our wired papers started slowly because of legal hassles.

PENDING LITIGATION

At the same time the Charisma negotiations were taking place in 1977, Mr. Gordy was approached by Anthony Gillespie of Noclip Limited, a Boston firm. Mr. Gillespie had developed and patented a cigarette paper with a non-heat conductive wire attached to one end which could be used as a holder as the contents were smoked. Mr. Gordy felt that this was a major product innovation:

With good pot selling for $40 an ounce, people don't want to throw away their roaches. The wire lets the smoker smoke the entire joint. It makes the roach clip obsolete.

By late 1977, Mr. Gordy and Mr. Jefferson had negotiated licensing agreements with Mr. Gillespie whereby Golden Sunsets agreed to supply Noclip with cigarette paper, and to produce and market Noclip papers in the eastern U.S. Contracts were signed and Golden Sunsets introduced the new paper at a paraphernalia trade show in January 1978. The trade reception was enthusiastic but shortly after the show, Mr. Gordy's attorney, who had been investigating the patent, reported that it was probably invalid since a similar device for cigars had been patented in the 1890s. Mr. Gordy said:

We called Anthony and said, 'Look, the patent's no good. We have to move even faster than before. The only way to protect this product is in the marketplace.' Anthony said, 'Fine, but there are some areas of our contract I'd like to change, some loopholes to close.' Burns and I flew to Massachusetts to negotiate a new contract. We wrote off the old contract, but negotiations broke down. Finally, his attorney advised him to forget the whole deal. We weren't about to throw away the equipment we had bought or to kiss off the time we had spent, so in March 1978, we began producing our own version which we called Wired Papers. That's the situation. We're challenging his patent, he's suing

us and we're countersuing him. It will probably be a year
before it gets to trial.

Mr. Gordy felt that the litigation would keep other competitors from marketing their own wired cigarette papers but still was concerned about securing the Wired Paper market franchise.

PRODUCTION FACILITIES

Golden Sunsets had begun operations in the bedroom of Mr. Gordy's San Francisco apartment (about 80 square ft., he said). It had moved frequently and sometimes involuntarily until the present 17,000 square foot plant had been found.

In the early days production consisted of cutting the paper, which was delivered in bundles 50 sheets thick, using scissors. The cut bundles were then inserted into leaflets which were printed and cut by a local print shop. This completed the package. Mr. Gordy did the artwork and the color separations which the printer used in making his plates. He remembered selling the papers for $.05 per pack "because Bumbu was $.05 and so we thought we were competitive."

One of the firm's first purchases had been a small multi-lith printing press which was suitable for two and some three color printing. Mr. Gordy did the printing for several years. By 1979, Golden Sunsets had a complete print shop including three presses, two die cutting machines and two paper cutters. In addition, the company had complete composition and plate-making facilities.

The company had also acquired some sophisticated equipment for handling the cigarette paper itself. In addition to cutting equipment which replaced scissors, the firm had four interleaving machines. These machines folded and collated individual pieces of paper to produce the familiar 'pop-up' pack. These collated bundles were then inserted into the custom-imprinted leaflet.

Mr. Gordy had also developed special equipment to produce the wired papers. This equipment firmly attached a continuous strand of wire to a continuous roll of cigarette paper and then cut the paper into individual leaves. These leaves were packaged loose in an envelope, unlike the regular papers.

RECENT DEVELOPMENTS

Mr. Gordy felt that the company had made improvements in four areas since Mr. Burns had been involved: controls, sales, products and management.

Controls

Mr. Gordy felt that the company had no formal control systems or budgets before Mr. Burns. He said:

> What sounded good was what we used. We did what we

thought were cash flows but we were dealing with such uncertainties, nothing was predictable. Our technique was to tread water and wait for the next deal to come along.

Also our accounting was pretty weak. The only reliable financial statements we have are over the last several months. Terry has insisted on monthly statements. (See *Exhibit 4* for historical balance sheets.)

Mr. Gordy said the firm was developing a standard cost system. Work was not complete but Mr. Gordy estimated that a book of custom paper cost a total of $.10 to produce. This discovery led to a price increase. He explained:

One thing we've learned is that you didn't sell an item just to produce cash flow. We used to sell custom papers for as low as $.07 per pad. Now we won't sell for below $.15.

Sales

Mr. Gordy felt that the firm's sales efforts had not been effective because "we had just been looking for the next big deal." He explained some recent changes:

We used to have 20 manufacturer's representatives out there. But, we couldn't afford to pay them for awhile and also they just weren't effective. If a rep can't sell your product in about 10 seconds, he'll move on to the next one.

Now we have four of our own salesmen replacing the reps. They handle Wired Papers and sell to conventional stores. We also use a wholesaler who is our exclusive rep to the paraphernalia retailers.

We also have 45 advertising specialty companies to represent our custom papers.

We also have in-house people who are constantly making phone calls.

Mr. Gordy explained that a significant change under Mr. Burns had been the formation of a sales administration department, headed by his son. This department was responsible for developing information systems. Mr. Gordy said:

Originally we would have said to Jefferson, 'Go out to Michigan and sell papers.' Now we say, 'Let's go to Michigan and sell the following accounts who have done the following amounts of business with us in the past.'

Products

Mr. Gordy said that he had learned another lesson from Mr. Burns:

> Terry had taught us that you can't keep jumping around trying for new products. You've got to find a good one and make it work. The market is there. The industry is there. You just have to stick with it. We're concentrating now on our Wired Papers, customs and matchpapers which is a large pack of matches attached to a pack of rolling papers. (See *Exhibit 5* for projections of sales by product.)

The company had developed a new package for Wired Papers which allowed them to be dispensed from cigarette vending machines. Mr. Jefferson said that two factors favored the vending concept. First, he felt that vending machines were usually even more convenient than convenience stores. Secondly, he said that anonymity was important to some consumers and vending machines offered it.

A shortage of working capital had delayed the introduction of Vending Papers, as they were called internally, from February to March 1979. Mr. Gordy had just begun making sales calls by telephone. He described the initial response:

> I've been making cold calls to vending machine companies; this is the first time we've ever tried selling them and they haven't heard of me or my company. Roughly, 25% have shown at least some interest and that's pretty good for a new product.
>
> If we had the money I think vending machines could be moving $100 million worth of paper in five years. For now though, we're counting heavily on word of mouth advertising.

Mr. Gordy compared the gross profit to the vendor as follows:

	Cigarettes	**Vending Papers**
Selling Price	.75	.75
Cost of Goods	.33	.35
State Tax	.21	—
Location	.05	.05
Gross Profit	.16	.35

Management

Mr. Gordy said that he and Mr. Jefferson were learning management skills and building an organization under Mr. Burns' tutelage. (See below for organizational chart.) He explained:

> I graduated from UCLA in 1969 after 11 semesters with a degree in business. I started out in physics, then went to electrical, then mechanical engineering. Really, I was into finishing school in as long a period of time as I could with as little academic effort as possible.
>
> We were flower children, and we came along thinking that everybody in your company can really like you and will do their best because they like you. That worked for a while, but we found that it was pretty idealistic when you have 50 employees. We're learning techniques of managing people, and that it's OK to insist that people work even if they don't like to.

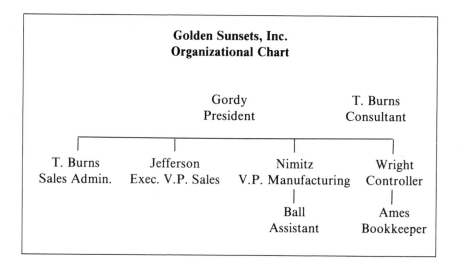

Golden Sunsets, Inc.
Organizational Chart

Gordy — President | T. Burns — Consultant

T. Burns	Jefferson	Nimitz	Wright
Sales Admin.	Exec. V.P. Sales	V.P. Manufacturing	Controller
		Ball	Ames
		Assistant	Bookkeeper

ASSIGNMENT QUESTIONS

Suggested questions for Golden Sunsets are:

1. Using the case information plus any other information you wish, project what you feel will be the major trends and opportunities in "the industry" over the next decade.

2. Evaluate the partners in terms of their entrepreneurial capabilities.

3. Develop the rudiments of a business plan that will turn Golden Sunsets around. Once you have defined this "turn around period", provide a *detailed cash-flow* for the Golden Sunsets operation over this time period.

Golden Sunsets, Inc.
Exhibit 1
Balance Sheets

	12/31/78	2/28/79
Current Assets:		
Cash	($ 302)	($ 8,368)
Accounts Receivable	139,787	219,756
Note Receivable	982	982
Inventory	180,495	139,843
Advances	563	505
Officer's Draw	42,840	49,560
Deposits	670	670
Prepaid Interest	2,360	2,360
Total Current Assets	$367,395	$405,308
Fixed Assets:		
Production Equipment	$159,386	$170,161
Office Equipment	7,556	7,585
Vehicles	18,480	18,480
Leasehold Improvements	18,260	18,400
Construction in Progress	2,261	2,299
Trademark	840	840
Accumulated Depreciation	(41,514)	(46,224)
Total Fixed Assets	$165,269	$171,541
Total Assets	$532,664	$576,849
Current Liabilities:		
Notes Payable	$ 15,235	$ 14,365
Accounts Payable	286,581	275,170
Accrued Payroll	10,074	18,778
Accrued Taxes	96,592	118,755
Rent Payable	—	2,800
Credit Due Customers	12,243	72,977
Total Current Liabilities	$420,725	$502,845
Long Term Debt:	$ 49,690	$ 49,690
Subordinated Debt:		
Recreation Incorporated	$ 76,750	$ 76,750
Prime Investments Corporation	217,076	231,263
Total Subordinated Debt:	$293,826	$308,013
Total Liabilities:	$764,241	$860,549
Owner's Equity:		
Common Stock	$ 64,513	$ 64,513
Retained Earnings	(296,090)	(348,212)
Total Owner's Equity:	($231,577)	($283,699)
Total Liabilities and Owner's Equity:	$532,664	$576,849

Golden Sunsets, Inc.
Exhibit 2
Projected Profit and Loss Statement 1979

	Jan.	Feb.	Mar.	Apr.	May	June
Sales:	$112,654	$165,987	$187,410	$198,090	$221,670	$260,850
Returns	(84,000)	(12,600)	(22,500)	—	—	—
Returns	(3,600)	(3,600)	—	—	—	—
Net Sales:	$ 25,054	$149,787	$164,910	$198,090	$221,670	$260,850
Cost of Sales:	$ 11,274	$ 67,409	$ 74,209	$ 89,141	$ 99,751	$117,383
Gross Profit:	$ 13,780	$ 82,378	$ 90,701	$108,949	$121,919	$143,467
Sales Expenses:						
Advertising	$ 6,000	$ 6,000	$ 6,000	$ 6,000	$ 6,000	$ 6,000
Brokers	1,240	2,820	3,575	3,690	3,761	4,410
Direct Sales	3,860	8,300	9,371	9,904	11,131	13,043
Samples and Promo.	3,000	3,000	3,000	3,000	3,000	3,000
Payroll	2,696	2,696	2,696	2,696	2,696	2,696
UPS	2,400	2,400	2,400	2,400	2,400	2,400
Total Sales Exp:	$ 19,196	$ 25,216	$ 27,042	$ 27,690	$ 28,988	$ 31,549
General & Admin.	$ 26,053	$ 26,052	$ 26,052	$ 26,052	$ 25,735	$ 25,735
Net Profit:	($ 31,469)	$ 31,110	$ 37,607	$ 55,207	$ 67,196	$ 86,183

Golden Sunsets, Inc.
Exhibit 3
Profit and Loss Statement

	Eight Months Ended 2/24/79	Seven Months Ended 1/27/79	Month of February 1979
Sales:	$996,019	$861,952	$135,066
Returns and Allowances	(241,920)	(193,702)	(48,218)
Discounts	(8,164)	(7,657)	(507)
Promotions	(82,090)	(81,390)	(699)
Net Sales:	$663,845	$579,203	$ 84,642
Cost of Goods Sold:	443,168	394,600	48,567
Gross Profit:	$220,677	$184,603	$ 36,075
Manufacturing Expense:			
Payroll	$ 9,447	$ 6,041	$ 3,406
Freight in	23,265	21,247	2,019
Repairs	9,770	9,508	203
Custodian	297	297	—
Depreciation	3,764	3,310	452
Manufacturing	(8)	(3)	(5)
Total Manufacturing:	$ 46,535	$ 40,400	$ 6,135
Sales Expense:			
Advertising	$ 99,059	$ 94,278	$ 4,781
Payroll	39,924	33,484	6,440
Commissions	12,569	12,251	319
Show Expense	9,308	9,170	138
T & E	33,151	32,671	481
Dues	254	252	—
Freight and Ret.	911	935	(24)
Samples	11,780	6,934	4,846
Total Sales:	$206,956	$189,975	$ 16,981
General and Administrative	$232,050	$210,291	$ 21,760
Net Income (Loss):	($264,864)	($256,063)	($ 8,801)

Golden Sunsets, Inc.
Exhibit 4
Balance Sheets

	6/30/76	12/31/77	6/30/78
Current Assets:			
Cash	$ 6,600	$ 25,129	($ 63,820)
Accounts Receivable	(18,452)	125,005	299,735
Inventory	10,139	88,748	233,846
Notes Receivable	—	—	983
Advances	360	—	300
Deposits	240	2,220	1,297
Due from Affiliate	3,013	—	—
Contractual Obligation Receivable*	—	172,512	—
Prepaid Expenses	—	26,569	2,360
Total Current Assets:	$ 1,900	$440,183	$474,701
Fixed Assets:			
Equipment	$ 4,884	$ 28,799**	$109,402
Office Equipment	—	1,560**	6,740
Vehicles	—	—	18,480
Leasehold Improvements	—	—	17,299
Trademark	—	840	840
Accumulated Depreciation	(486)		(26,611)
Total Fixed Assets:	$ 4,398	$ 31,199	$126,150
Total Assets:	$ 6,298	$471,382	$600,851
Current Liabilities:			
Accounts Payable	$24,466	$102,882	($110,610)
Notes Payable	27,272	8,598	95,155
Taxes Payable	2,045	—	100,804
Current Portion of Long-Term Debt	—	12,000	—
Accruals	2,183	1,450	15,890
Misc.	—	9,000	—
Total Current Liabilities:	$ 55,966	$133,930	$322,459
Long-Term Debt:	$10,685	$ 48,000	$ 24,249
Subordinated Debt:			
Recreation Incorporated	—	$288,000	$202,771
Prime Investments Corporation	—	—	132,696
Total Subordinated Debt:	—	$288,000	$335,467
Total Liabilities:	$ 66,651	$469,930	$682,175
Owner's Equity:			
Common Stock	$ 14,700	$61,220	$ 51,517
Retained Earnings	(75,053)	(59,768)	(132,841)
Total Owner's Equity:	($ 60,353)	$ 1,452	($ 81,324)
Total Liabilities and Owner's Equity:	$ 6,298	$471,382	$600,851

Golden Sunsets, Inc.
Exhibit 5
Sales Projections by Product 1979

January	106 cases of Wired	$ 48,000
	12 cases of Wired — Wholesaler (W)	4,500
	54 cases of Custom	21,600
	4 cases of Matchpapers	1,560
	7 cases of Tulsa Tops	1,548
		$ 77,208

February	180 cases of Wired	$ 72,000
	108 cases of Wired — (W)	40,500
	84 cases of Custom	33,600
	50 cases of Tulsa Tops	10,707
	12 cases of Vending	7,200
	6 cases of Matchpapers	1,980
		$165,987

March	240 cases of Wired	$ 96,000
	120 cases of Wired — (W)	45,000
	48 cases of Custom	21,600
	30 cases of Tulsa Tops	6,450
	24 cases of Vending	14,400
	12 cases of Matchpapers	3,960
		$187,410

April	300 cases of Wired	$120,000
	60 cases of Wired — (W)	22,500
	48 cases of Custom	21,600
	30 cases of Tulsa Tops	6,450
	24 cases of Vending	21,600
	12 cases of Matchpapers	5,940
		$198,090

May	180 cases of Wired	$120,000
	60 cases of Wired — (W)	22,500
	72 cases of Custom	36,000
	30 cases of Tulsa Tops	6,450
	48 cases of Vending	28,800
	24 cases of Matchpapers	7,920
		$221,670

June	360 cases of Wired	$144,000
	60 cases of Wired — (W)	22,500
	84 cases of Custom	42,000
	30 cases of Tulsa Tops	6,450
	60 cases of Vending	36,000
	30 cases of Matchpapers	9,900
		$260,850

Returns:	230 cases (W)*	
	50 cases other	

*Because of packaging change from 15 to 24 leaves per pack.
Note: There are 2,000 packs of papers to a case. This is standard.

COUPLES

In early September 1979, Frank Rance, General Manager of Couples, a resort exclusively for couples, in St. Mary, Jamaica, was considering what recommendations to make to John Issa, director of the resort. The Issa family, which owned Couples and numerous other enterprises in Jamaica was very concerned about maintaining the profitability of this almost two year old venture. The family also was considering expanding this unique resort concept into other areas of the Caribbean and the world. Besides refining basic operational procedures, Rance had several concerns to factor into his deliberations.

First, there was the long-term appeal of the couples-only concept. Next, there was the impact of competition from not only single unit resorts, but especially from experienced international multi-unit operations like Club Mediterranean (referred to as Club Med). Also, the impact on tourism of the economic trends of inflation and recession, especially in the United States and Canada, had to be assessed. If these factors on net were judged to be conducive to tourism, there remained the question of where to acquire or to build new sites, and any changes that should be made in merchandising and operating procedures of these new units. Rance knew his recommendations would be major factors in the Issa family's final decisions. Also, he had just one week to prepare them.

This case was written by Professor Rudolph Winston, Jr., of Babson College as a basis for class discussion rather than to illustrate either effective or ineffective handling of an entrepreneurial situation. The author acknowledges the financial support of Northeastern University which made this case possible.

OVERVIEW OF TOURISM

Generally, tourism worldwide has been increasing in recent years in terms of the total number of travelers and expenditures. U.S. citizens departing for foreign countries reflected this worldwide rise. In 1978, an estimated 23.5 million Americans traveled abroad, spending about $10.7 billion dollars. Compared to the previous year, this represented a 3% increase in travelers, and a 2.5% increase in dollars spent. An annual growth in personal income of 9% and spending a larger proportion (6.7%) on travel accounted for these increases. At the same time, the number of foreigners coming to the U.S. had increased at an even faster rate as shown by the decreasing deficit. In 1976, the number of Americans that traveled abroad exceeded the number of foreigners that came to the United States by 5.4 million. This deficit had been dropping steadily and was estimated at 3.4 million for 1978. Likewise, the travel dollar deficit for 1978 dropped to $2.6 billion, lowest recorded in the last eight years.

While in 1977, about one-half of all U.S. travelers' destinations was Canada, only 18% of total U.S. travel dollars were spent there due to shorter stays, use of automobile transportation, and low per capita expenditure. The situation was just the reverse in Mexico, which got only 12% of our total departures, but 25% of total U.S. foreign travel expenditures. The appeal of the floating peso, better air service, and more interest in tourism by the U.S. and Mexican governments explained the appeal of Mexico for U.S. travelers. Western Europe and the Mediterranean ranked after Mexico in popularity, followed by the Caribbean area (see *Exhibit 1*).

While the Caribbean has benefitted from the increased American travel, it lost share of market in terms of number of travelers. Due to the political unrest of the 70s, the Caribbean had lost not only share of market, but also experienced a decrease in number of travelers as well as expenditures. However, recent trends indicated more U.S., as well as foreign, travelers were discovering the area.

Data developed from various tour services indicated that there was a change taking place in the American tourist. While the new profile traits were noted of tourists with destinations overseas, judgment indicated they probably applied to the Caribbean tourists as well. These traits were in sharp contrast to traits of just a few years ago:

- Shorter stays of 2 weeks or less versus 3-4 weeks.

- More than one trip outside the country per year.

- Longer stay in one country.

- More culturally minded.

- More budget minded.

TOURISM IN JAMAICA

The tropical climate and varied but magnificent scenery have made Jamaica a popular tourist destination (for profile and map of Jamaica, see *Exhibits 2 and 3*). Since the late

1940s, the tour industry grew steadily and by 1978, tourism was the second largest source of foreign exchange behind alumina/bauxite. Over the past three decades, numerous resort areas were developed along the north coast and in and around Kingston, the island's capital. In these areas, luxury hotels, pension type inns, apartments, and fully-staffed villas were built to cater to the growing number of foreign travelers. The Jamaican Tourist Board, a government agency, spent in excess of $2 million (Jamaican*) annually to sustain the flow of foreigners and to encourage the development of new resort sites. Some of these new sites were government owned.

The Jamaican government was very concerned about its tourist dollars in light of the current economic problems confronting it at the start of 1979:

- A $110 million deficit budget for 1977/78.

- A foreign exchange shortage.

- High unemployment.

- Breakdown of confidence in the private sector.

- Immigration of skilled and managerial personnel.

These problems were caused and/or exacerbated by the following:

- 1970 oil prices were five times those of 1973.

- Undiversified export economy (70% Alumina/Bauxite).

- Exports' prices did not rise as fast as imports'
  prices.

- Recessions abroad.

- 40% decline in net tourism receipts since 1974.

- Net outflow of private capital.

Besides promoting tourism, the Jamaican government has taken a number of steps designed to strengthen the national economy. These included the following:

- Made an agreement with the International Monetary
  Fund to receive $250 million over the next
  three years.

- Secured credits from commercial banks,
  international organizations, and other
  countries.

---

*All dollar figures are Jamaican dollars unless otherwise noted. Prior to 1976, one Jamaican dollar equalled one U.S. dollar. After devaluation, one U.S. dollar equalled $1.66 Jamaican.

- Unified the exchange rate.

- Devalued currency.

- Limited bank credit expansion to public
  and private sectors.

- Increased taxes.

- Set up wage guidelines.

- Tightened import restrictions.

The government hoped that these steps would not only stabilize the economic situation but encourage foreign investment. Joint ventures to diversify Jamaica's exports were emphasized to improve foreign exchange earnings and alleviate domestic problems.

BACKGROUND OF COUPLES

Although Couples opened for business on January 20, 1978, the events leading up to the concept started in 1974. At that time, the Jamaican Government was interested in expanding tourism. Besides the extraction of bauxite, tourism was the major generator of foreign exchange. A potential resort site had been identified at Negril on the northwest coast. The seven miles of untouched beach had no industry and the areas surrounding it were also undeveloped. The government approached the Issa family and asked for a proposal of how they would develop the site. (See Map *Exhibit 3.*)

THE ISSA FAMILY

It was not surprising that the Issas were sought out to develop the Negril site. The family's ventures have touched every major aspect of business on the island.

Of Arab decent, the Issa family came to Jamaica in 1893 from Bethlehem led by their great grandfather who was a trader selling cloth. In 1946 the family bought a hotel in Kingston with the United Fruit Company. The Issas promptly broke with British colonial tradition by making the hotel the first to permit black Jamaicans as guests. This hotel did very well, and, in 1949 they built Tower Isle in an area so sparse that water had to be trucked in to mix cement. Since 1949, the family proceeded to purchase other hotels, as well as to establish foreign car dealerships, and the Hertz franchise. They also supplied equipment for the extraction of bauxite, the Island's primary natural resource.

John Issa's uncle was chairman of the Jamaican Tourist Board during the years that tourism prospered. Thus, as established business achievers, the Issas accepted the government's challenge to design, supervise construction, and manage the new resort. The Issas chose not to risk an equity investment, but received a fee for management services.

THE FORERUNNER OF COUPLES — STAGE 1

John Issa first examined the resort hotel market generally to see what was working and why. The Club Med concept immediately impressed him. It was the fastest growing international resort hotel chain in the world in terms of sales (1978--U.S. $358.5 million) and sites (87 in early 1979, plus 5 scheduled to open by the end of the year). These "Village Hotels" were positioned mainly for singles. Reservations were made in advance with guests paying for transportation and room. At the resort they paid additionally for drinks and for some activities. Recreational activities were numerous with trained staffers available to conduct scheduled classes geared to the guests' abilities. (For details on Club Med, see *Exhibit 4*.)

John Issa studied the Club Med formula, and noted that it had turned on a primary demand for foreign resort hotels. However, Club Med could not completely satisfy this demand for a variety of reasons. Among them there were high transportation costs to some of its sites, full bookings at peak seasons, and some aspects of the way Club Med resorts were run.

CLUB MED TRAITS AND THE ISSA RESPONSE

First there was the language problem. English-speaking and other non-French speaking guests had difficulty with the total French orientation in almost every aspect of the Club Med resorts, from promotional literature to menus. Next, there were beads used in place of money at the resort, with different colors representing different amounts. Guests often found they had too many of one color and not enough of another when purchasing an item or service. The decorum of the rooms was judged to be rather bare, no pictures on the walls and sparse furnishings. Activities were very structured at appointed times for groups, and meal hours were judged by some to be too short.

However, John Issa believed the basic Club Med format was a proven success. In spite of the weaknesses mentioned, almost 300,000 Americans, Canadians, and other non-French speaking tourists had signed up for the 1977-78 season. John Issa reasoned that if an alternative was offered, capturing the positives of Club Med and overcoming the negatives, there would be a profitable response. The result was the creation of Negril Beach Village, the Jamaican resort based on the theme of a "pressure-free holiday with simple but elegant service."

Negril differed from Club Med in several critical aspects besides location (no Club Med resort in Jamaica; the nearest ones were in Eleuthera in the Bahamas and in Acapulco, Mexico) and English-speaking orientation. The money problem of colored beads was solved by the use of shark teeth, each having the value of fifty cents ($0.50). Drinks and services were priced as multiples of this basic value assigned to the shark teeth. In addition, meal hours were longer and more flexible. Activities were informal, less structured, and peer pressure was judged to be less. Activities like horseback riding were offered free at Negril Village. The rooms were spruced up with pictures on the walls, extra furniture, radios, carpets, and central air conditioning, so that "people could stay in them, not just sleep in them." The Issas believed that these changes would attract North Americans and others, because guests would "be taken from the day-to-day cares of the world." To launch this new venture, John Issa hired Frank Rance to be the general manager in December of 1976.

BACKGROUND OF FRANK RANCE

Frank Rance was born 32 years ago, in Kingston, Jamaica, the third of five children. His father worked for a local tobacco company as a quality control supervisor. Rance, an above average student, completed high school and went to work for one year as a time keeper and cashier on a local sugar farm. In February, 1966 at age 19, he got a job as a checker and cashier at the Hilton International Hotel. He progressed well during his eight years with Hilton. In 1974 he became an auditor, a top position in financial control for the Jamaican Hilton. His potential had been identified during these 8 years and Hilton sent him to Montreal to its worldwide Career Development Institute to be trained in hotel management. The eight week program was soon to be followed by five trips to the Hilton Caribbean training center in Puerto Rico for additional training in hotel accounting, food and beverage operations, and general management.

In early 1975 Rance joined the Issa Hotels of Jamaica as Vice President of Administration and Sales for their Runaway Bay Hotel which was located 19 miles west of Ocho Ricos on the North Shore. While there Rance kept the hotel profitable, even though other resort hotels were failing and or losing money.[1] In late 1976 the Issas moved Rance to Negril Beach Village. This hotel was owned by the Jamaica Government, who contracted with the Issas for management services. Earlier the Issas had developed the idea for the hotel, but chose not to risk an investment in an equity position. The 4% of sales fee was judged by the Issas to be a better position to take given their other ventures.

At Negril Rance had introduced nude bathing to Jamaica. Although the practice was outlawed, he was permitted to do it because his hotel was successful. While Rance's first year at Negril had been judged excellent, other factors caused him to rethink his future. Even though the Issas had a contract for management services with the Jamaican government, a separate agreement had been made between Rance and the government to cover a bonus. Thus Rance was supposed to get a salary from the Issas, plus a bonus of 5% of the hotel's profits from the government. For the first year's operations this amounted to approximately a $50,000 bonus. The government *refused* to pay the bonus, with one official telling Rance, "...what would happen if the average Jamaican heard that you made over $50,000?" Rance left the Issas and Negril in late 1977 and became general manager of the Zemis Hotel in Nassau, Bahamas. He stayed there through May of 1978. During this period he formed Caribbean Hotel Consultants with an Englishman living in Jamaica. Also he commuted to Jamaica every two weeks to consult with the Issas on the development of the resort hotel that would come to be known as "Couples."

THE SUCCESS OF NEGRIL VILLAGE — STAGE 2

The results for the first year (1976-77) spelled success. Gross operating profit was $1.8 million Jamaican.* While gross revenues were $7.0 million, there was a net loss due to $1.0 million being written off because of the devaluation of the Jamaican dollar. More

---

[1]This hotel was sold by the Issas in 1977 after a bad 1976-77 winter season due to national unrest when Parliamentary elections were held.

*In late 1979, one U.S. dollar was worth $1.66 Jamaican.

noteworthy was the fact that a profitable gross margin and net profit was realized in July, a traditionally poor tourist month. For year one, Rance had targeted a $1.6 million net profit on gross sales of $6.4 million. This would represent a 25% net profit on sales compared to the Caribbean hotel average of 13% P.A.T. But management still considered the first year's results very good.

Besides the gratifying income statement, Rance and the Issas also noted the profile data on the guests. The profile extracted from the following findings proved quite interesting.

	Percent of all guests
Couples	53
Age group 22-32	65
Doctors	25
General Business Executives	42
Teachers, Engineers	15

They also noted that 89% of all reservations came from the United States. They interpreted this statistic as being proof that their desire to create an English speaking alternative was working. Other data indicated that word of mouth was a major factor in people's decisions to pick Negril Beach Village.

How Guests Heard of Resort	Percent of Guests
Travel Agent	56
Advertising (which was to trade only)	20
Personal friend	19

As these interesting data were being examined in late 1977, the Issas noted that two of their other hotels were losing money due to the unfavorable impact of the political unrest on the tourist trade. One of these hotels, The Runaway Bay, was acquired by the government and leased to a favored operator. But the Issas were determined to maintain the Tower Isle Hotel at St. Mary's as their flagship hotel. The question was how to make it viable again, while other hotels were failing.

THE BIRTH OF COUPLES - STAGE 3

While contemplating the problem of the Tower Isle Hotel, John Issa recalled the data generated by Negril Beach Village's first year. One statistic caught his attention particularly--more than half of Negril's guests were married or singles traveling as a couple.

A brainstorming session was held subsequently with three Canadians (one advertising consultant, a marketing VP, and a creative writer). They reviewed once more the Club Med model, and how they modified it for Negril. They searched behind the successful numbers and asked what could be done to improve upon Negril. More and more they focused upon the annoyances that couples usually had at resort hotels such as:

- Single guys making passes at wives
- Activities oriented more to single individuals
- The presence of children
- Hassling over payments for activities, services
- Check-in, check-out procedures.

It was then that they came to the question, "Why not a hotel especially set up for couples only?" They noted that four out of five adults lived as a couple, so they felt they were essentially catering to a mass market. Omitting children was judged not to be detrimental, because they were "Couples". Rance noted "Tower Isle was a beautiful lady in her time. It would have been rape to put the Couples concept onto the name. It was a brave step to change her name to Couples." The features of the resort were designed to overcome the negatives learned from the examination of Club Med and Negril. The tone of the resort was to be a place for people in love, who desired a simple hassle-free, but elegant vacation.

TURNING THE OLD LADY INTO SOMETHING NEW

Late in 1977, the transition of Tower Isle into Couples started. Structurally, a $1.2 million investment gave the old hotel a complete face lifting. The objective was to remove all traces of the former traditional operation, and create a relaxed tone and a relatively unstructured environment. Accordingly, the formal dining area was renovated completely. A more open, colorful style was created with tables for four, six, or ten people. This table arrangement encouraged open seating, and made it easy for guests to get to know each other. A piano bar was built next to the dining room. It stayed open from 11:00 P.M. until the last guest left, providing drinks, live music, and snacks. In addition, a large patio was built, which served as a dining area for breakfast and lunch, and an entertainment area with stage and dance floor for the evening. The entire patio area was open to the ocean breezes, yet protected from the sun and rain by a coconut thatch roof. Next to the patio area was a large swimming pool, with tables around it, plus sheltered activity coves where crafts, ping pong, and exercise equipment were available. The other structural change you would notice as soon as you arrived. Gone was the traditional black-tied doorman with long white socks and white hat. Also missing were the check in and check out facilities so common to every hotel. A desk with an attractive young lady behind it welcomed you. Finally, to create the new tone the personnel were encouraed to fraternize with the guests on a first name basis. Dress codes for guests as well as staff were relaxed...No ties or jacket, just casual sportswear was necessary for dinner. Bathing suits or shorts were the typical dress for breakfast or lunch on the patio.

Couples went one step further. The price guests paid for the trip would cover everything--transportation, room, board, all tips and activities. (See *Exhibit 5* for sample of all-inclusive rates. Also see *Exhibit 6* for net rates without transportation for various times of the year.) After their plane landed, a couple did not have to spend any money. Even transportation from the airport to Couples as well as the return trip were free. Guests paid only if they went shopping in local towns, or selected certain activities like scuba-diving, tours to nearby tourist attractions, or special boat cruises. The only necessary expenditure was a tourist tax of five dollars (U.S.) per person which was paid on departure at the airport. But cigarettes, liquor, meals--all you wanted of each,-- were covered by the basic one-time cost. Also noteworthy was the fact that there was a full day's complement of free activities like tennis, crafts, horseback riding, sailing, cycling, and live evening entertainers plus dancing and a piano bar. (See *Exhibit 7*, which was placed in each room to acquaint guests with services offered.)

Like Negril, the 131 rooms were large, well furnished, and the walls were decorated with pictures. Each had a set of sliding doors that opened onto a patio or terrace facing the mountains or the ocean. There were also four villas on the grounds, each of which could house two couples in separate bedrooms and bathrooms. The shared kitchen and living room made these villas ideal for two couples traveling together.

NEW PERSONNEL

In addition to these structural changes, John Issa released the entire staff of Tower Isle. This decision cost $330,000 because government regulations set strict guidelines for compensation of released workers. The released staffers were replaced by 182 new ones, seven of which were managers, 61 were supervisory, clerical, and activity coordinators, and the remaining 114 were hourly workers. The list below shows the number of hourly personnel by functional areas.

Distribution of Couples' Staff

Area	# Staffers
Stables	7
Water Sports	6
Kitchen (butcher, cooks, pot washers)	35
Maintenance	11
Housekeeping	23
Grounds	7
Bar	13
Sanitation	8
Bellhop	2
Store Room	2
Total of Hourly Workers	114

With the exception of most of the salaried staffers, all new hourly personnel had no hotel experience. About 85% of these persons had not been employed before, having just completed schooling and/or been unemployed - there being few jobs available on the island for unskilled workers.

For additional insight into personnel changeover, the casewriter interviewed Neville Hudson, Manager of Internal Support Departments, and Cargill Brown, the Resident Manager. Hudson pointed out that in the latter part of 1977, Couples went into the hills of the St. Mary area and put up posters which read, "If you want a job, come down to Couples." Over 700 people applied. Those judged the brightest were selected. They were trained for two weeks with some financial help from the Jamaican Tourism Development Company. The new employees were paid from the time they were hired. The service staffers averaged about $35-$55 per week. Most of the non-salaried personnel were 18-21 years old, with several over 25. A few had some high school, but most completed only primary school (9 years).

The salaried staffers often had to be recruited from other areas of the land. In order to attract the best ones, good salaries were offered, plus free housing across the street from the resort in small villas consisting of about four rooms plus bath.

PERSONNEL POLICIES AND BENEFITS

For this new staff, Couples initiated a number of innovative policies. While some resorts may have offered one or more of these benefits, none had the entire package that Couples offered:

- Payment while training.

- Staffers got all meals free while working.

- Free housing for staffers living far away or working odd hours, judged to be worth about $3,000 per year.

- 10% of gross revenues was distributed every 14 days to all staffers in equal shares with the exception of Rance, who reserved a yearly bonus based on profits. This revenue sharing averaged about $113 per person per week.

- To compensate for the currency devaluation, salaries were raised immediately to maintain buying power.

- Staffers were guaranteed year round employment, not just work during the peak season.

- Special awards of $100 or more were given for outstanding work. Most employees qualified for this bonus.

- All employees with potential were set to special training sessions on site. Management staffers were sent outside the country for training. At this time, the Chief Engineer and the Comptroller were attending a two-week seminar at Cornell University School of Hotel Management. Hudson was scheduled to go to this same seminar when they returned.

When Hudson and Brown were asked about problems with the personnel, they felt there were none of a serious nature. Absenteeism, which averaged about 1% per day, was considered the only difficulty with the staffers. Turnover was not a problem. In fact, the casewriter noted there were only a few new faces in June 1979 compared to December 1978 when he first visited Couples. Some of these new faces had come from Negril Beach Village where they had been activity coordinators. Rance, when asked about these new additions, said he told them, "Come on down. I know your work, I know you'll do good stuff." Commenting further on his dealings with staffers:

> I don't say that every worker is perfect in every sense, but while they're under my jurisdiction, they behave themselves and they don't want to let me down...I take the time to make certain that if I have to crack the whip, I crack it. And they listen. They leave wherever they are to work with Frank. At least (here) they know where they're going.

Rance also noted his preference for experienced staffers. "If you've had any experience abroad or in any other place, I'll hire you over someone without this background." The casewriter observed Rance's interaction with staffers and asked about it. "I don't believe in dominating. Guests should not see signs of management outside, but things should be working. I prefer to observe, then in my office give orders. I don't want guests to see me managing or more dressed than they are."

To reflect the attitude of employees and the atmosphere of the resort, Rance told the casewriter about one of the women in housekeeping. The young lady had been cleaning up this guest's room for several days, and knew his name was Ron. Ron was one of the travel agents Rance had invited to Couples. The young lady knocked several times, but got no response. Aware that the door was locked from the inside, she went outside to the bathroom window and called out several times, "Ron, are you all right?" Ron was awakened from his deep sleep and replied that he was fine. Later that day, Ron went to Rance's office and said how amazed he was that ..."she was genuinely concerned that I was O.K." Rance pointed out that he stressed to employees the need to be concerned and friendly with the guests.*

PROMOTING COUPLES

The promotional efforts for couples were modeled on the experiences of Negril Beach Village, and several other resorts. These resorts followed the theme of pleasure presented seductively but not sexually in their promotional literature. For example, Negril's posters featured the torso of a woman wearing a string of shark's teeth which hung between her

---

*The casewriter personally benefitted from this, when his luggage was delayed for two days. The staffers telephoned the airlines several times daily about it, as well as washed and ironed the clothes the casewriter was wearing. In addition, they got some personal effects and beachwear for the casewriter to wear. They never expected nor would accept any tip for these services, or any others rendered.

partially exposed breasts. The banner headline of the advertising was "Hedonism." Following Negril, in the fall of 1978, were Zemi in the Bahamas, Jamaica's Trelawny Beach, and the Dominican Republic Club Dominicus. Each picked some aspect of the sensual to stress. At Zemi, where apples were used for currency, the featured theme was "Edenism--the non-stop party in the Bahamas." Displays showed a big apple which looked like a female derriere (the bum come-on). Both Zemi's and Negril's marketing were executed by Toronto adman J. Alan Murphy. Trelawny Beach followed suit with "Ectacism," and Club Dominicus with "Sensualism". By the end of 1978, large tour operations were into this seductive theme running advertising, one of which read, "Club Med, Move Over! We've got Ectacism, Hedonism, and Edenism." The results indicated that vacationers were reponsive to this approach. Rance commented:

> At Zemi's and Negril, we used art to express the quality of the vacation being offered. There were too many ordinary vacations. The days of showing couples splashing in the water or lying on the beach are over.

THE LION'S ROAR

Murphy, Rance, and Issa agreed the sensual theme should be used for Couples. Rather than a word, they chose the symbol of two lions and the words, "Now the Couple Takes Its Rightful Place in the Sun." A Canadian artist, Heather Cooper, was commissioned to do the artwork. The finished product showed a male lion mounted from the rear atop a lioness with her full breasts showing. Like Negril's torso, no explicit sex or genitalia were shown. In spite of efforts to play down the sexual image, tourist agencies, the Jamaican Tour Board and others thought otherwise. Meanwhile, the fate of 10,000 posters costing $20,000, plus the plans for the lions to be Couples' logo to be featured on the brochure cover, were hanging in the balance. Rance pointed out in response that the lioness had a placid facial expression, that her tail was underneath her and therefore "there could be no penetration." He also mentioned that fact that the poster design "with breasts" had been awarded the New York Art Directors' Club gold medal for illustration.*

While the poster and logo remained intact, the brochure cover was changed. The lions were replaced with general views of the resort, which had to be photographed with live models while renovations were being done. However, the publicity about the dispute in the press and among the trade, created a lot of notoriety for Couples.

OTHER PROMOTIONAL EFFORTS

While the logo issue was being resolved, many travel agents were contacted personally.

———————

*In spite of winning the award, the Union Carbide people would not let the poster be hung in their exhibition of award winning posters. They did say if asked they would get it out of the closet for people.

From his prior affiliations, Rance was well known and respected. In fact, the Negril advertising all carried these final lines:

> If you would like to see before you send, give our "Chief" a
> call. He's Frank Rance, at 957-4200 in Jamaica. He'll
> probably tell you "Soon come, man."

He visited the large tour operators in Canada and the United States with a slide presentation:

> I visited one agency with 63 offices. If each office would give
> me one booking a week, that would cover over 45% of my
> capacity.

Rance also relied on his reputation, and judged tour agents' responses would be positive:

> Wherever Frank goes, that's where we'll send our people.
> We have confidence that all will go well or Frank will fix it.

While Negril had been presented to tour agents as an alternative to Club Med, Couples was presented to them as an "alternative to the alternative."

With the season already started and some negative images of Jamaica for tourism remaining, the January opening of Couples produced only 38 guests in the first week and 18% occupancy for the month. By the end of March, the occupancy rate had reached 30%. About this time, the decision was made to stress getting tour agents to visit Couples with their mates.* If they liked the experience, they would be more likely to recommend it to others. In June of 1978, Rance shifted from his consulting role to that of full-time general manager.

There were advertisements placed in trade magazines to reach tour agents. Although Couples placed no advertisments in consumer media, their tour operators did (See *Exhibit 8*). Ultimately, word of mouth recommendations of the tour agent and/or a friend who had been to Couples, was the major promotional technique. The tour operators received brochures to distribute to their agents who passed them out to potential guests. During the first year of operations, the tour packagers or representatives could sell as many rooms as they could, calling Couples to confirm the availability. In 1979 Couples started making allocations to tour operators, letting them do mailings to their agents and attending trade shows, which Couples used to do on its own. John Issa believed:

> ...Make the wholesaler sell, rather than perform a clerical
> function only.

---

*Tour agents normally got a 75% discount from the arilines, and a 20-50% off for accommodations. These discounts usually did not cover mates or children.

OPERATIONS

After Rance joined Couples in June 1978, and as more travel agents "came on down" to the resort, occupancy rates picked up. The flow of guests continued to increase until occupancy surpassed 100% in July 1979.* Advanced bookings indicated a full house for each of the off-season May-June and September-October periods. (See *Exhibit 9*). While occupancy rates, revenues and profits climbed, a number of operational problems surfaced during the first eighteen months that affected both management and the guests.

THE VIEWS OF THE GUESTS

The casewriter interviewed over thirty guests in June 1979 and a similar number in December of 1978. The following list was representative of the guests' positive and negative reactions to their stay at Couples.

Overall, most guests of all age groups liked the experience and intended to recommend it enthusiastically to relatives and friends. The lack of formality and structure, no money needed for purchases or tips, a wide range of free activities, friendly staffers, plenty of good food and liquor, live entertainment nightly, and room accommodations were judged by guests to be superior to the facilities offered by other resorts, particularly Club Med. One couple from Frankfort, Germany, liked Couples so much that they were just completing their second four-week stay within five months. They even invited any Couples staffers who came to Germany to stay in their home. Incidentally, this couple already had booked their next four-week stay for six months hence.

However, a few guests felt differently due to one or more of the following reasons:

- Faulty expectations

- High need for structure/formality

- Poor equipment maintenance

- Management problems

Some guests generously interpreted the brochures and/or descriptive comments by travel agents and friends. One couple expected breakfast to be served in their rooms on the terrace. Another had a friend that got travel bags and other handy travel items from their travel agent, yet they did not get these items when they booked the trip. Also, some guests booked ocean view rooms but found these had been oversold on arrival, and they had to take a mountain view room or a villa until an ocean view was vacated. A few guests complained about the lack of activities during rainy days. Others pointed out how

---

*Permitting travel agents to sell more than 100% was an acceptable practice due to cancellations and rescheduling by guests. When extra guests did arrive, they were placed in extra villas nearby and transported to the resort.

staffers often were not at their activity areas when guests needed them, but could be found at the bar or beach areas chatting with guests. A frequently voiced irritation was the lack of tennis pros to hit with or instruct guests. When the pros were found they seemed to enjoy playing with each other or with guests who were very good players. Also, the tennis courts had been painted with a high gloss paint that made footing difficult. There were not enough playing cards, tennis balls, ping pong balls, and the paddles needed replacing. There were also complaints about a significant amount of the activities equipment needing repairs (e.g., paddle boats, bicycles).

Everybody found fault with the transportation to and from the airport. The trip took an hour and a half or longer. The road was narrow, winding through small villages along the north shore. This trip was very tiring. Often, several stops were made to pick up or deposit guests at other resorts. Waiting for luggage to be untied from atop the van or unpiled from the rear did not help. There was also the waiting for planes in Miami (2 hours) and in Montego Bay, where some guests with later flights had to take the van with those who had earlier flights.

THE VIEWS OF MANAGEMENT

Interviews with John Issa, Rance and top managers indicated they were aware of these difficulties. While there was little that could be done about the transportation problems, the casewriter noted on his second trip that most of the equipment problems noted above had been solved. The reasons for the problems and the methods used to solve them were quite interesting.

The equipment problems were due to the management being unable to buy the spare parts or new items, even though the money was available. The Jamaican government had placed very strict limits on importation of any item by requiring all local buyers to have an import license. This was done to reverse the negative balance of payments and conserve foreign exchange. The procedures to import items were very involved and lengthy. Foreign sellers were discouraged by long waiting periods for payment after delivery. Sellers, therefore, when they did choose to deal with Jamaicans added on a significant factor in setting price to compensate for the administrative and cash flow problems. But management realized that the guests paid for a "hassle-free vacation," not problems with equipment. Hudson, the manager of internal support departments pointed out how difficult it was to get raw materials and supplies to maintain the resort. But he stated, "We don't believe in passing the buck. Somehow we'll get these things." He also commented that sometimes equipment was not available but some guests would hoard items like snorkel equipment. Management judged that tolerating the hoarding was a necessary trade-off to promote the friendly family atmosphere, which strict policing type controls would offset.

One way to secure some of the needed items was to have travel agents and other friends bring them when they visited. Foreigners and returning Jamaicans could bring such items duty free. The day of one interview, Rance had just returned from the U.S. with new ping pong paddles and balls, volley balls, and other sports equipment. When larger items were involved, such as replacing a unrepairable air-conditioning condenser, then the lengthy import process had to be started. The condenser took five months to get.

For some problems, Rance and the other staffers had to figure out other types of solutions. For instance, the tennis court had been painted originally with a durable enamel paint purchased locally. Once Rance realized that the court surface was slippery, he had a local painter make up the type paint that was needed. Rance expressed his approach to these operational problems:

> ...Don't throw up your hands and say you can't be bothered with Jamaica. Recognize there are problems and try to work around them... Keep them as low as possible... If you're going to stay here, make a living, work and get ahead, you've got to be creative... Stop griping, do something about it. Make things work. Otherwise, get out!

Overall, Issa and top management felt they were doing a good job. Issa commented to the casewriter:

> ...Guest satisfaction is extremely high. Things are not perfect. You can walk into any hotel and list two yellow pages of things that need doing... We are very conscious about keeping the product up to what is said about it.

THE RESULTS OF OPERATIONS

The first twelve months were almost break even, even though Couples ran at a loss for the first six months. Rance felt that this was considered in the trade as exceptional for a 131-room resort. He pointed out that operations figures alone showed a profit for the year (See *Exhibit 10 and 11*). But there were extraordinary start-up expenses such as the severence pay and the debt service costs that caused the loss. However, the exceptionally high occupancy levels maintained during June 1978 through May 1979 and bookings beyond this exceeding 100%, indicated a very profitable second year.

PRICING

At the start of 1979, prices were raised to cover inflationary trends. The rates paid by guests depended on the time of year and location of room. The highest rates were charged during late December through the first half of April. Medium rates covered the last part of April, July, August, November, and the first part of December. The lowest rates prevailed during the other early summer and fall periods. Within these seasons the ocean view rooms cost more than those with the mountain view. Overall, rates were based on a price for two people for a week's stay. While many guests stayed just one week, a significant number stayed for two weeks, and a few couples stayed longer. In addition to these rate schedules which applied to foreign and local guests, there were rates offered to locals for stays of a day or a weekend.

Rance commented on how important it was to read market conditions accurately by comparing pricing strategies of Negril Beach and Couples for the Summer of 1979.*

---

*The Issa family no longer managed Negril Beach Resort after 1978.

...Negril is priced now more than Club Med and Couples, and that's with no drinks included. Negril is caught in the marketplace. Demand is declining. People have a strong alternative which is Couples. Negril has managed to price themselves entirely out of the market. Negril felt too confident based on last year, so they figured the market could take high prices...They used medium prices in May and June. Couples went down in price during this low period. In terms of dollars Negril is not offering as much. Last year Couples considered doing what Negril did last summer. But we decided not to do this because Club Med did not. If Club Med with all their experience doesn't change to medium season rates in low season, why shouldn't we follow the people with 20 years experience.. No one has had 100% occupancy in the Caribbean before. The bottom line comes out extremely healthy.

Issa commented on the approach used in figuring prices:

...It's a matter of guesstimation because we are not experienced with all-inclusive packaging. The cost of serving free liquor is one of our trade secrets. We do not think in terms of percentages and traditional methods of control. We think in terms of dollar cost per person. It doesn't really matter where you allocate the reserve.

Based on the current schedule of prices, breakeven points could be reached with occupancy rates of 45% in high season, 65% in the medium season, and 75% during the low season. These breakeven points were approximations and assumed that travel agents got a 20% commission on rate charged.

Overall, Rance and Issa appeared satisfied with the financial state of Couples. They judged that mistakes and problems of other resorts had been avoided or solved by them. Couples had controlled their costs so that salaries and revenue sharing stayed about 48% of gross revenue. Many other resorts, even with seasonal lay-offs, ran this figure even higher due to management inefficiencies and low occupancy rates. During the spring and especially into the summer, Couples was one of the only three resorts on the island to turn a profit.

THE FUTURE

The casewriter asked John Issa and the key staffers what they saw as the problems and opportunities for Couples in the future. They were all confident about the viability of the concept, their current strategy and eventual expansion. They saw tourist dollars continuing to flow in and a gradual relaxation of import regulations. Hudson expressed his optimism:

...The concept of Couples is right, and that will make it a

> winner. Right now it's the most unique concept in Jamaica...
> The main contribution to our success is the staff.

Issa stressed the concept in terms of continuing to keep the product pure, not contracting tour groups or 3-4 day packages. When they tried this at Negril Beach as a favor to a tour operator during the slow season, it was a disaster. These people all stuck together and didn't meet others. Issa also pointed out that Couples believed its success was, and will continue to be, due to two factors that accounted for Negril Beach's failure in recent months. Namely, suitable management and "plowing back into the plant some of what you make to keep it fresh and crisp." In process were the building of more stables, a handball court, and a practice wall for tennis. Also, renovation of a fourth floor office and banquet room area will make room for 14 new rooms. These guest rooms will be completed by October 1979 and will pay for themselves by the end of the year. This fast payback was possible due to continued high occupancy rates. Demand for rooms had been so strong recently that Rance had to turn away more than half of those who wished to come. Interestingly, part of this strong demand was couples returning for a second stay.

But Issa and Rance both stressed the need to expand into other areas of the Caribbean. But this was not easy, said Issa.

> ...the Caribbean is doing so well that even the poorly run
> properties are making money.

Rance pointed out how difficult it was for start-up operations outside the Caribbean due to unions and competition. Those who tried have failed in Puerto Rico.

When asked about the merits of building a new Couples, Rance pointed out why it would cost too much.

> ...It cost $10 million to build Negril Village. At the time
> $1.00 U.S. equalled $1.00 Jamaican. Normally, it takes 5-10
> years for payback...By using low-rise building, no million
> dollar chandeliers, avoiding the Hyatt syndrome, then you
> could build from scratch and make it...But today, building
> costs are $50,000 (J) per room ($30,000 U.S.)...With cost of
> goods sold at 30% to 40%, and payroll with revenue sharing
> at 48%, not much left over for debt service and a profit.

Responding to a question about competition in the picture, Issa noted that:

> ...Many are trying to benefit from the concept. A resort in
> Puerto Rico spent a fortune to advertise to consumers and
> to the trade for two people in love. A tour director I know
> stopped by and observed two children at the bar. Now you
> have to make up your mind. Couples, on the other hand,
> made a total commitment...

Finally, on the last day of his second trip, the casewriter talked with Rance about Couples' future and his own:

> ...We're looking actively. I need that for my personal ambition. I would not like to know that we hit on such a beautiful concept and let it die after only one property. I want to see the concept developed in the Caribbean, for the Caribbean, and the holiday of the Caribbean. I want to see it that way...The holiday that people have been looking for all along.

Three months later, in September, Rance had to reflect on how best to formulate his recommendations for strategy to keep Couples viable and growing.

ASSIGNMENT QUESTIONS

Some questions that may help you are:

1. How do you evaluate the long term appeal of the Couples concept?

2. What factors in the Jamaican political and economic environment affect Rance's thinking and planning?

3. What do you think about the way Rance runs Couples now? What specific changes would you recommend?

   a. Handling of guests
   b. Handling personnel
   c. Problem solving

4. How is the resort doing financially now?

5. Evaluate the pricing.

6. Evaluate the promotional techniques.

7. Should Couples expand? If yes, When? Where? How?

8. What types of problems will Couples face in the future and how should they deal with them?

Note: Run the numbers for the effect on profits of your ideas.

Exhibit 1
Expenditures of U.S. Foreign Travelers, 1973-77
Millions of U.S. Dollars

	1973	1974	1975	1976	1977[2]
Total Expenses[1]	8,472	9,406	10,143	10,868	11,890
Transportation Fare Payments	2,946	3,426	3,726	4,012	4,444
Foreign-Flag Carriers	1,790	2,095	2,263	2,542	2,843
U.S.-Flag Carriers	1,156	1,331	1,463	1,470	1,601
Travel Payments in Foreign Countries	5,526	5,980	6,417	6,856	7,446
Canada	1,158	1,359	1,306	1,371	1,435
Mexico	1,264	1,475	1,637	1,723	1,911
Border Zone	715	904	1,047	1,007	1,125
Total Overseas Areas	3,104	3,146	3,474	3,762	4,100
Europe and Mediterranean[3]	1,993	1,802	1,918	2,150	2,365
Western Europe	1,800	1,600	1,709	1,885	2,065
United Kingdom	354	368	404	494	572
France	237	198	226	254	228
Italy	218	188	194	207	223
Switzerland	135	117	121	129	142
West Germany	170	153	174	195	212
Austria	77	61	65	70	68
Denmark	42	43	43	38	49
Sweden	27	32	29	37	41
Norway	33	31	44	40	36
Netherlands	63	47	60	58	57
Belgium-Luxembourg	25	31	39	35	35
Spain	201	138	135	117	146
Portugal	58	36	19	14	37
Ireland	45	47	55	83	96
Greece	88	84	73	90	97
Other Western Europe	27	26	28	24	26
Israel	100	95	57	118	140
Other[4]	93	107	152	147	160
Caribbean Area and Central America	570	685	787	784	821
Bermuda	80	110	118	133	132
Bahamas	136	151	161	168	162
Jamaica	109	122	118	109	95
Other British West Indies	95	87	103	125	149
Netherlands West Indies	55	60	97	102	[5]
Other West Indies & Cen. America	95	155	190	147	283
South America	132	209	242	232	257
Other Overseas Areas	409	450	527	596	657
Japan	123	102	131	145	149
Hong Kong	65	75	75	74	95
Australia-New Zealand	48	55	54	82	97
Other	173	218	267	295	316

[1]Cruise passenger fare payments included in transportation payments (predominantly foreign flag carriers).

[2]Unofficial U.S. estimates.

[3]Includes all European countries, Algeria, Cyprus, Egypt, Israel, Lebanon, Libya, Malta, Morocco, Syria, Tunisia and Turkey.

[4]Includes USSR.

[5]Not available separately; included in "Other West Indies and Central America."

Source: U.S. Department of Commerce, Bureau of Economic Analysis and United States Travel Service.

Exhibit 2

PROFILE OF JAMAICA

The Island of Jamaica, located in the West Indies in the Greater Antilles, had an estimated 1977 population of 2,109,400. While the cities of Kingston, the capital, and Montego Bay had the highest concentrations, the rest of the population was distributed throughout the island's 4,400 square miles. Jamaica was divided up into 14 parishes or regions. (Couples was in St. Ann Parish.)

Formally a British colony, Jamaica became independent on August 6, 1962 under Jamaican (Constitution) Order Council, 1962, made known by Her Majesty the Queen under the West Indies Act 1962 of the United Kingdom. Thus Jamaica was a dominion of the British Commonwealth. The English influences therefore remained not only in the language and culture, but in the government as well.

The Constitution provided for the appointment of a Governor General by the Queen and the establishment of a Parliament made up of Her Majesty, a Senate, and a House of Representatives. The Senate consisted of twenty-one senators, thirteen of which were appointed on advice of the Governor General and the eight remaining appointed on advice of the opposition. The President of the Senate and the Deputy President were elected from its members who were not ministers or Parliamentary secretaries. The House of Representatives was made up of forty-five to sixty elected members, with a Speaker and Deputy Speaker elected from the members who were not Parliamentary Secretaries. The entire Parliament lasted for five years, at which time appointments and elections were held. During the last elections in 1976, the disruptions and unrest spilled into the streets. Finally, a Declaration of a State of Emergency had to be declared.

Educationally, Jamaica had free public schools for children ages 6-15, in addition to government aided infant schools and departments for children ages 5-6. The seventy-eight institutions that were responsible for primary education in 1977 had an estimated 432,000 children. Secondary school (or what Americans call high school) was available only to those students who did very well in an entrance examination given at age 11. Top qualifiers were awarded free scholarships to either a public or private secondary school. As of 1974 Jamaica also had a University which was free to all qualifying nationals.

Source: The Caribbean Year Book, 1978/79, pp 297-311.

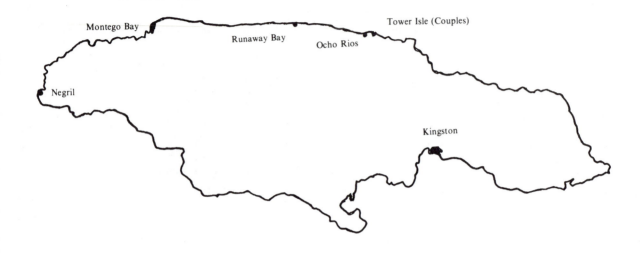

Montego Bay

Runaway Bay

Ocho Rios

Tower Isle (Couples)

Negril

Kingston

Exhibit 4

Club Med ads in France generally win prizes for the Club's two agencies, Synergie/K&E and Alice. These ads by Synergie/K&E cover the plethora of activities available at Club Med villages.

Equality-minded Club Med turns advisor to nations

Reprinted from AA/Europe January 29

BY CAROLYN PFAFF

Paris—Expansion is ever on the horizon for France's Club Mediterranee, the world's largest holiday club organizer which has transformed itself from the 4S'—sun, sand, sea and sex—into a promoter and adviser to foreign governments, particularly in the Third World.

This year alone, five new clubs will be inaugurated—one each in France, Egypt, Brazil, Malaysia and the Bahamas. The Club, too, will take over management of the Chateau Royal hotel in Noumea from the French airline, UTA.

The thrust of Club Med in the next decade, despite its strong orientation toward the underdeveloped world (that is where much of the world's sun, sea and sand is) will definitely be toward the big tourist spenders—the Americans and Germans.

Since opening its New York office in 1970, the club has continued to attract increasing U.S. interest to the point where Americans now make up the second most important national group at the club, after the French.

With a new village at Eleuthera in the Bahamas, and others planned or under construction in Mexico, Haiti and the Dominican Republic, the club feels it has only just begun to tap America's enormous tourist potential.

And recently it announced plans for the first invasion of U.S. home territory, a Club Med ski village at Copper Mountain west of Denver, Colorado. The club also is negotiating to set up yet another ski vacation resort near Breckenridge, Colorado. Already, Club Med is spending $2,600,000 in advertising annually in the States, and that for off-shore destinations. These new continental resorts should prove a great stimulant to the Club's U.S. ad spending, which currently equals about 3% of the turnover generated by the U.S. Club Med operation.

Club Med, which gives its 22 club offices autonomy in advertising, generally permits each office to spend up to 3% of annual turnover on advertising. However, this policy meets particularly with two exceptions: In Germany where the ad ante is now 6% of turnover; and France, where the club spends 0.84% of turnover.

Club Med holidays were handled by the Auto Club of Germany until the Club recently established its own office. The German ad spending is now $1,200,000 annually based on the 6% turnover. In France, where Club Med is such an institution, it only does *image de marque* advertising to keep its name before the public. Nonetheless, some $2,690,000 was spent on advertising in 1978 by agencies Alice and Synergie/Kenyon & Eckhardt. Small wonder that the club with a 1978 turnover of FF 1.5 billion ($358,500,000) and whose stock has quadrupled on the Paris Bourse since 1970, wields a big stick in the home country these days.

From the first tent village at Alcudia in 1950, the club has mushroomed into a multinational organization consisting of 87 clubs on five continents with backers as diverse as Baron Edmond de Rothschild, Fiat's Agnelli and American Express. In the 1977-78 season, 604,925 people representing 21 nations spent their holidays with the club. Of these, 306,832 were French and 86,910 American. But club devotees also came from as far afield as Australia (5,144), Japan (170) and South Africa (4,307). A surprising 2,792 were Turkish and a large contingent of 9,774 came from Israel.

Club Med's operation policies, to be sure, are geared to the Third World in both a businesss and philosophical sense. The club rents, but does not own its villages. In Egypt, for example, the Egyptian government has financed the construction of a 400-bed hotel complex on the Red Sea at Hougadah to be opened this spring. The club has agreed to rent and operate the hotel facilities at a guaranteed annual amount, indexed to the cost of living over a 15-year period.

In Mexico, the club operates its Playa Blanca village on behalf of a private consortium. But it is the Mexican government which invited the club to supervise the construction and operation of the new complex at Cancun, plus a chain of seven hotels at the location of Mexico's most famous archeological sites.

The Rumanian government has just signed for its second club-operated tourist resort. Haiti and the Dominican Republic have signed for their first. Liberia recently sent an SOS to Paris to help with a conference center it is building to welcome delegates to a Third World meeting in August. "They wanted us to run the hotel during the conference and then transform the center into a tourist operation. We had to say no," says director of international relations, Stefan Geissler.

Guinea, the next Third World host after Liberia, has already contacted the club. As for East-West relations, the club already operates villages successfully in Bulgaria, Rumania and Yugoslavia. However, they took a beating in both their Russian and Cuban ventures.

The Russian club at Sochi closed after two years. "It wasn't very attractive and we found that most visitors to Russia wanted to tour and not spend two weeks in a club hotel," admits Mr. Geissler.

The club went into Cuba two years ago but found that the "economy was just not ready for us." Mr. Geissler remembers two awful weeks when Club Med guests couldn't find a taxi or bus in all of Cuba because Third World countries were holding a conference down the road.

Not surprisingly, the club has already been in touch with China. "We are interested. They seem interested," says Mr. Geissler, refusing any further comment on the subject.

Nowadays, the club's formula has become somewhat legendary. It is known as a doctor fixit for every ailing holiday resort near and far, if only it will agree to accept the patient. For example, three years ago on the Spanish Costa Del Sol, when the real estate boom died overnight, Club Med agreed to rescue a monstrously ugly hotel in the hills behind Marbella.

"I didn't think we could make a go of it," says Stefan Geissler, "but after two years the hotel is booked almost solid." Why? Because the club installed a child care center, free of charge, open from 9 a.m. till 6 p.m. every day. We also arranged for a private beach, opened 12 tennis courts, organized scrabble and bridge tournaments, built a nightclub in the basement for teenagers before dinner and for adults after. This, together with all the Club Med's well-known touches made the difference. Over the years, many have tried to imitate the club's unique formula but up till now without success.

And the reason for this can be traced back to the almost missionary fervor that motivates management from the chairman, Gilbert Trigano, down to the youngest assistants, called GOs, (*gentils organisateurs*) in the club's villages. The club, as it was conceived by its founder, Gerald Blitz, a Belgian swimming champion, was an attempt to break with the old traditional class barriers of France in the aftermath of World War II.

The plan was to offer truly democratic vacations at the cheapest prices to everyone, regardless of class, creed or color, to help build healthier minds and bodies in a spirit of true fraternity and equality.

Gerald Blitz, with his visionary ideas, turned out to be a hopeless business man until he met up with Frenchman Gilbert Trigano. This year Mr. Trigano, at 58, was voted manager of the year by the readers of the leading French business magazine, *Le Nouvel Economiste.*

Exceptional business man he may be, but Mr. Trigano, member of the Resistance, ex-member of the Communist Party, also has his vision of society. And this is why the club has preserved to this day its very un-French formula of meals at communal tables of eight, money in the form of beads only, everyone on first name basis, and sports for all.

It also explains why the club has never taken advantage of many tempting merchandising possibilities that its wealth and position open up nearly every day.

For the first time last year, the club allowed four manufacturers to merchandise under their name. Sun Cream Products from L'Oreal, beach towels (Santens) suitcases (Besancon) and sunglasses (BK optic). These products already launched in France should start appearing on world markets this year.

But the club has announced that all profits from the enterprise will go into a special foundation, Club Med, to support humanitarian causes.

Even the club's latest venture into two nudist villages, called *les clubs natures,* turns out to be democratically motivated. "We feel that nudism is legitimate and those who wish to practice it should be allowed to do so in peace without being stared at and without paying prices three times over the norm," explains Mr. Geissler.

But so far the nudists have not responded to the Club Med call. Only 3,246 attended the two camps last year. This year ads will be placed in special publication and an attempt will be made to work through nudist groups.

Source: *Advertising Age,* February 12, 1979, p. S-16.

Exhibit 5

QUICK REFERENCE GUIDE

The holiday includes everything:
- Return flight from PHL/BOS/NY—Montego Bay
- Transfers/Baggage Handling
- Air conditioned Double Room w/Private Terrace
- Breakfast, Lunch/Dinner Daily
- All drinks with meals and at the bar
- All sports & equipment
- Nightly entertainment
- Hotel taxes, service charges/tips

PRICES PER PERSON PER WEEK—ALL INCLUSIVE

IT8JMIWWT2

SAT. DEPARTURES**	PHL/NY		BOSTON	
	Island View	Ocean View	Island View	Ocean View
NOV./DEC. 1-11	$559	$599	$639	$679
DECEMBER 16	691	731	726	766
DECEMBER 30	721	796	801	876
JAN./APR. 7, 14	679	754	759	834
FEB./MARCH	700	775	780	855
APRIL 21, 28	604	654	684	734
MAY/JUNE	554	604	634	684

NEW!

Villas for a Couple of Couples—private villas with 2 bedrooms, each with private bath, living room, kitchen, porch, free fully-stocked bar

Booking for 2 Couples required —$50 supplement per person over Ocean View

**Other dates available on request.
There are no Single or Triple Accommodations & no children. You must book as a couple.

NEGRIL BEACH VILLAGE

The trip includes:
- Roundtrip jet transportation to Montego Bay from PHL/BOS/NY
- Transfers/Baggage Handling
- Accommodations for 8 days/7 nights in modern air conditioned rooms
- 3 meals daily/free wine or Calico Jack Rum Punch served with lunch & dinner
- All sports & equipment
- Nightly entertainment & discotheque
- All taxes, tips/gratuities
- U.S. Departure Tax incl. (Jamaica Departure Tax. $5.50, not incl.)

DEPARTURE DATES/INCLUSIVE PRICES

IT8JMIWWT1

SAT. DEPARTURES**	PHILADELPHIA/NEW YORK	BOSTON
NOV./DEC. 1-11	$529	$599
DECEMBER 16	661	696
DECEMBER 30	716	796
JAN./APRIL 7, 14	674	754
FEB./MARCH	695	775
APRIL 21, 28/MAY/JUNE	614	694

**Other dates available on request.
No Single Supplement. All rates guaranteed share basis (double occupancy).

COMMISSIONS:
- **TO DEC. 11—12%**
- **DEC. 16-DEC. 31, 1979**
  11% up to 10 bookings
  12% (over 10 bookings retroactive)
  higher commissions with large volume

RESERVATIONS:
- **IN PA. CALL COLLECT 215-561-7788**
- **REST OF USA/TOLL FREE**
  1-800-523-2677

ASK ABOUT:
- Christmas Charters to Nassau/Jamaica
- Weekly departures to Trelawny Beach Club
- Atlantic City group departures

American Airlines
airJamaica

GLOBETROTTERS

121 S. 18th Street • Philadelphia, Pa. 19103 • (215)561-7788
24 Boylston Street • Cambridge, Ma. 02138 • (617)661-4550

Exhibit 6

AN ISSA HOTEL

RATES PER COUPLE PER ONE WEEK

FROM	TO	OCEAN VIEW	ISLAND VIEW
22/12/78	19/4/79	$1,150	$1,000
20/4/79	3/5/79	$ 950	$ 850
4/5/79	29/6/79	$ 850	$ 750
30/6/79	30/8/79	$ 950	$ 850
31/8/79	1/11/79	$ 850	$ 750
2/11/79	20/12/70	$ 950	$ 850

OUR COMMITMENTS

Our guests will have free use of all facilities. For the prices quoted above, we will provide accommodations, three superb meals a day including wine, all drinks available at our bars, room taxes. We will provide transport to and from the airport.

Included in our facilities are five tennis courts (three flood lit) with resident Pro., a stable of horses with instructress, beach, pool, sailing, pedalos, snorkeling, indoor games, tandem and single bicycles. Our guests will enjoy a complete programme of evening entertainment by our Resident Band and entertainers, and also, the delight of our Piano Bar which stays open until our last guest departs. Facilities are subject to change without notice.

OUR QUALIFICATIONS

As our name implies, we accept only COUPLES. *No children or singles.* We feel couples are any two people in love.

Gratuities are not permitted. Our rates are quoted in US Dollars and subject to change.

For further information contact your Travel Agent. Represented by Loews Representation International.

Tower Isle PO, Saint Mary, Jamaica
Telephone (809) 974 4271 Telex 7406 Couples Jamaica

Exhibit 7

COUPLES

Saint Mary, Jamaica

Tower Isle, P.O. Saint Mary, Jamaica Telephone (809) 974-4271
Telex: 7406 Couples Jamaica

Hello!

Welcome to Couples and Jamaica. We would like to take a little of your time to let you know about us.

WHAT YOU'RE GETTING FOR WHAT YOU PAID

Included in the price you have paid are, three meals a day, all drinks available at the bar, cigarettes for your personal needs, your accommodation and the use of all of our facilities.

THE "BANK"

The Bank located off the lobby will be open daily from 9 a.m. to 11 a.m. You will be able to cash your Travellers Cheques for such amounts as you may require and upon departure settle any incidental charges you may have incurred.

ACTIVITY CO-ORDINATORS

We have a staff of Co-ordinators who possess a working knowledge of all of the facilities that we have to offer. In addition, they will arrange and participate in a wide range of activities for you to enjoy. Feel free to let them know of any particular interests that you may have, so that where possible, they may endeavour to create similar activities for you to enjoy.

ACTIVITIES CENTRE

Couples Co-ordinators operate a centre, which is located off the lobby. You will find there any information you need about our sporting facilities and our daily activities, including our night time entertainment plans. You will also find there a stock of such games as Backgammon, Scrabble, Playing Cards and Chess, which are available for your use.

FOOD SERVICE

We feel that meal time should be a time to make new friends and renew acquaintances. At breakfast time you may take your choice of two locations. Our main breakfast will be served on the patio between the hours of 7:30 a.m. and 10 a.m. It is an informal buffet arrangement. For the late risers, we provide coffee and danish by the Tennis Courts between the hours of 9 a.m. and 11 a.m. Lunch is served on the Patio from 12:30 p.m. to 2:30 p.m. Dinner time is a special occasion for us. Our Dining Room is especially arranged to provide for meal service in a family style, when couples may dine at tables for fours, sixes and eights. You may dine with old friends or make new acquaintances, our staff will assist you in seating arrangements. Service will be provided from 7:30 p.m. until 10 p.m., and although the dress requirement is informal, we would appreciate a dress standard which is in keeping with the elegance of the dining room. On Wednesdays we provide a special barbeque dinner and beach party with service on the patio.

BAR SERVICE

Our main bar opens at 10:00 a.m. and continues to provide service until 2:00 a.m. Our Piano Bar opens at 11:00 p.m. each evening and continues to provide service until the last guest retires.

SHOPPING

Our Receptionists will sell you tickets at a minimal cost to do your shopping in the town of Ocho Rios, and they will also advise you of departure times.

TRANSPORTATION

Taxis or Car Rentals are available upon request and can be arranged through our Receptionists.

MEDICAL FACILITIES

Our staff includes a qualified nurse who can take care of minor illnesses, cuts, etc., also a limited supply of medicinal items are available. There is no charge for this service. Should the service of a Doctor be required the service must be paid for at the time of the visit.

ROOM SERVICE

Room Service will only be provided in the case of illness.

MAIL AND MESSAGES

Our Bell Desk located in the lobby will accumulate mail that has been forwarded to you and any telephone messages that arrive. You should check with them each day.

LAUNDRY

Our Housekeeping Department will be happy to arrange for your laundry to be done by an outside service company. There will be a charge for the provision of such service.

ELECTRICAL APPLIANCES

The electrical outlets located in our bedrooms are wired for 110 volts - 50 cycles.

TELEPHONE

This service is available but it is expensive because of high taxation. We suggest that you call collect if you must call overseas. Charges for calls that you make will be accumulated on an incidental account that must be settled at the Bank on departure.

SAFETY DEPOSIT BOXES

We provide Safety Deposit Boxes without charge for your use during your stay. Arrangements are made through the Receptionists.

Our aim is to make your stay with us an experience to remember and to this end if there is anything you are uncertain or unsettled about, please let me know.

Your host,

Frank

A DIVISION OF E.A. ISSA & BROS, LTD. 9-21 PRINCESS STREET, KINGSTON
DIRECTORS: A.E. Issa (Chairman, R.J. Issa, F.J. Issa, J.J. Issa, R.L.S. Morris, Secretary: Mrs. A.L. Nunes.

Exhibit 8

Introducing an amazing new holiday for couples only, where even the drinks are complimentary.

It's a racy world we live in. And with all the singles holidays around, it's going to get racier. This leaves a lot healthy, active couples out in the cold. But not at Couples. At Couples, we celebrate the couple: in fact, we admit no singles and no children. We give couples (two adults in love) the carefree time of their lives. You need no money at Couples. None. Everything is included: return airfare, accommodation, transfers, tips, taxes, three superb meals a day, all sports and entertainment. The price of the holiday also includes all wine and drinks at the bar. Even cigarettes are complimentary. This, of course, gives you a truly healthy commission. Couples in Saint Mary, Jamaica. A great value. For further information call:

Red & Blue Tours
Philadelphia
(215) 732-2800

Caribbean Vacation Center
Chicago
(312) 236-9390

Lotus Tours
New York
(212) 661-5040

Tour Tree International
Greenwich
(203) 661-4300

Globetrotters
Cambridge
(617) 4550 or 661-1818

Globtrotters
Philadelphia
(215) 561-7788

Travel Center Tours
Chicago
(312) 878-3141

Unitours (Canada) Ltd
Toronto
(416) 484-8000

COUPLES

Now. The couple takes its rightful place in the sun.

This ad prepared by
McLauchlan, Mohr, Massey Limited
Ad. No. U-CPL-1

Exhibit 9
Occupancy Rates

	1978	1979
January	3	90
February	25	104
March	30	96
April	34	91
May	41	110
June	45	105 (est.)
July		100 (est.)
August	79	100 (est.)
September	72	
October	82	
November	84	
December	80	
Total Year	53	

Exhibit 10

C O U P L E S

COMPARATIVE STATEMENT OF INCOME PROFIT OR (LOSS)

	MONTH OF MAY 1979					MONTHS ENDED MAY 31, 1979					
DEPARTMENTAL REVENUE	Budget 79	Actual 1979	%	Actual 1978	%	Budget 79 Amount	%	Actual 79	%	Actual 78 Amount	%
Rooms	102569	165047	24	57724	24	1070080	36	1100352	34	249947	39
Food	213150	346138	49	83236	49	1240477	42	1418560	44	224968	35
Beverage	106576	173635	25	60097	25	570052	19	656702	20	157741	24
Telephone	4752	8704	1	1143	1	26633	1	41487	1	8255	1
SubTotal	427046	693524	99	202200	99	2907242	98	3217106	99	638911	99
Miscellaneous Income	9914	33839	1	31211	1	53833	2	113880	1	47504	1
Total Gross Revenue	436960	727363	100	233411	100	2961125	100	3330986	100	686415	100
Cost of Sales											
Food	82242	109707	16	24388	16	447741	15	473796	14.7	75770	12
Beverage	24368	36020	6	8992	6	132664	5	159310	5.0	31606	5
Telephone	6216	9757	1	2578	1	33953	1	46535	1.3	13537	2
Total Cost of Sales	112826	155484	23	35898	23	614358	21	679641	21.0	120913	19
Payroll Related Expenses											
Rooms	16067	18655	2.5	11736	2.5	76062	2.5	81161	2.5	58052	9
Food	18115	23962	3.5	14500	3.5	85159	3.0	116127	3.6	72640	11
Beverage	11225	9864	1	1491	—	51225	1.7	51626	1.6	38288	6
Telephone	2019	2130	—			10048	.8	10505	.3	7054	2
Total Payroll & Related Expense	47426	54611	7	35506	7	222994	8.0	259419	8.0	176034	8
Provision-Operating Equipment											
Rooms	2096	3211	.6	2937	.6	10480	.3	33072	1.0	37339	6
Food	2400	15251	2.1	906	2.1	10250	.3	28555	.8	5078	.7
Beverage	300	2031	3	494	3	1500	.1	8003	.2	761	.3
Telephone											
Total Provisional-Operating Equip	4796	20493	3	4337	3	22730	.7	69630	2.0	43178	7
Other Expenses											
Rooms	17145	18126	3	18038	3	92579	3.0	81832	2.5	76353	12
Food	16231	11447	1	25320	1	88004	3.0	58983	1.8	77485	12
Beverage	20185	24968	3	26462	3	106948	3.3	120633	3.7	78264	12
Telephone	51	43	—	52	—	288	—	358	—	213	—
Total Other Expenses	53612	55484	2	69872	2	287819	8.3	261806	8.0	232315	36
Rooms.	218660	280022	40	145613	40	1147901	38.3	1270496	39.0	572440	90
Food	67261	124055	18	25013	18	890959	30.0	904287	28.0	78203	12
Beverage	94162	185771	27	18182	27	608823	21.0	741099	23.0	6005	1
Telephone	50497	100852	15	16370	15	277215	9.0	317135	0.0	6822	1
Subtotal	(3534)	(3226)	(1)	(2978)	(1)	(17656)	—	(15911)	—	(12549)	(2)
Miscellaneous Income	9914	33839	57	33211	57	53883	2.0	113880	60.0	66471	10
Gross Operating Income	218300	441291	60	87798	60	1813224	62.0	2060490	61.0	113975	12

Exhibit 10 (continued)

COUPLES

COMPARATIVE STATEMENT OF INCOME PROFIT OR (LOSS)

	MONTH OF MAY 1979					MONTHS ENDED MAY 31, 1979					
	Budget 79	Actual 1979	%	Actual 1978	%	Budget 79 Amount	%	Actual 79	%	Actual 78 Amount	%
Operating Income (Brought frwd)	218300	441291	60	87798	60	1813224	62	2060490	61	113975	17.0
Overhead Departments											
Payroll & Related Expenses											
Administrative & General	20511	30188	3.7	16508	3.0	97439	33	101515	3.0	76627	12.0
Sports	13347	12602	2.0	10502	2.0	64494	2.2	64205	2.0	47405	6.0
Advertising & Promotion											1.0
Heat, Light, Power & Water	3124	2419	.3	1103	.3	15232	.5	12560	.5	7533	1.0
Repair and Maintenance	6421	2910	1.0	5266	1.0	30218	1.0	39272	1.2	29548	50
Transportation	764	1016	-	667	-	3439		4293	.3	3217	-
Total Salaries and Wages	44167	54335	7.0	34048	7.0	210822	7.0	221845	7.0	164330	24.0
Other Expenses											
Administrative & General	14950	19349	3.0	10541	3.0	74741	2.5	92976	2.0	50413	7.0
Advertising & Promotion	27000	25020	3.5	119	3.5	132000	11.5	141293	4.5	80737	12.0
Repair & Maintenance	22923	44558	6.5	7829	6.5	116628	4.0	180346	5.4	45832	7.0
Heat, Light, Power & Water	32956	32309	4.5	15552	4.5	178064	6.0	130510	4.0	56335	8.0
Transportation	3889	9712	1.0	5023	1.0	19434	.7	40054	1.2	20952	3.0
Sports	2021	11109	1.5	1223	1.5	10035	.3	24049	.9	7235	1.0
Total Other Expenses	103739	142107	20	40287	20	530902	18.0	609228	18.0	261504	38.0
Total Overhead Departments	147609	196442	27	74335	27	741724	25.0	831073	25.0	425834	62.0
Gross Operating Profits/(Loss)	70394	244949	34	13463	34	1071500	36.0	1227417	36.5	311859	45.0
Rents Receivable	2150	3968		1450		11614	1.0	16993	.5	3133	3.0
Profit/(Loss) Sales of Assets		1230						4680			
Total G.O.P.	72544	250047	33	14913	33	1083114	37.0	1251090	37.0	308726	48.0
Other Deduc. frm GOP (pre-open ex)	6100	5000		16936		30500	1.0	25000	.7	16936	3.0
Special Accruals		20000						20000		1000	
Nonspecified	800	785	.1			4000		3928		3818	.5
Insurance	2700	4090	.5	4335		13500	5	19878	.5	13594	2.0
Interest	9000	9748	.8	5258		46000	1.5	49841	.2	20862	3.0
Total other Deductions	18600	39625	1.4	24515		94000	11.0	118647	3.0	56210	9.0
Profit/(Loss) Before Depreciation	53944	210424	31.6	<9602>		989114	22.0	1132443	34.0	<364936>	53.0
Depreciation-Plant/Machines	2660	2690	.5	2660		13300	.4	13450	.2	12000	1.5
Motor Vehicles	340	461	.3			1700		2405	.1	1304	
Leasehold Imprvmnts	-	5550	.8					2702	.3		
Total Depreciation	3000	8721	1.6	2660		15000	.5	43557	.4	13304	
Net Profit/(Loss)	50944	210203	30.0	<12202>		974114	32.0	1098886	33.0	<378204>	55.0
Credit Sales	351873	545447		182965		2368900		2425914		631206	
Occupancy %	75%	40%		41%		84%		89%		30%	
Room Rate per Guest	$17	$18.35		$17		$32				$25	
Moving Average Cost of Sales		20400		25837							
Moving Average Credit Sales		61836		86241							

Exhibit 11

COMPANY _____ Couples

RESULTS FOR ____ December 1978 AND THE PERIOD ENDED December 31, 1978

	CURRENT MONTH / CURRENT YEAR				YEAR TO DATE / CURRENT YEAR	
GAIN/(LOSS)	BUDGET	ACTUAL		ACTUAL	BUDGET	GAIN/(LOSS)
			Dept. Contributions/Profit			
2981	158434	161445	Rooms	700094	821748	(121654)
61061	58823	119884	Food	461302	426203	35099
20485	20853	41338	Beverages	182749	147489	35260
(869)	(3118)	(3987)	Telephone	(31506)	(126080)	5446
83658	234992	318650	TOTAL	1312639	1369380	(56741)
41672	8180	49852	Other Income	181551	96404	85147
125330	243172	368502	Gross Operating Inc.	1491490	1465784	28406
			Overhead Departments			
167	13939	13772	Sports	151511	122707	(28804)
(34718)	29715	64433	Admin. & General	369498	276893	(32605)
(14285)	18350	32635	Advtg. & Promotion	263847	247800	(16047)
(2679)	26694	29373	Heat, Light, Water	262412	230950	(31462)
(17410)	20057	37467	Repairs & Mtce.	245488	218928	(26560)
(8062)	2405	10467	Staff Housing	43338	30304	(14034)
(2608)	2298	4906	Transportation	55086	21575	(33611)
(79595)	113458	193053	TOTAL	1390578	1147555	(243023)
45735	129174	175449	House Profit/(Loss)	103612	318229	(214617)
863	1668	2531	Rents Receivable	18079	18806	(727)
46598	131382	177980	TOTAL	121691	337035	(215344)
			Other Expenses			
(173)	4100	4273	Pre-open Expenses	48605	24600	24005
−	−	−	Rent	1000		
1701	4000	2299	Taxes & Insurance	40533	46000	5467
(13110)	6000	19110	Interest	86547	62000	(24547)
(4923)	3000	7923	Depreciation	37914	31000	(6914)
−	−	−	Legal Expenses	6964	−	(6964)
(16505)	17100	33605	TOTAL	220843	163600	(57243)
30093	114282	144375	Net Profit/(Loss)	(99152)	173435	(272587)
			Statistics			
177219	382698	559917	Sales	3274688	3081539	193149
(8201)	66269	74470	Payroll	699551	688585	(10966)
48448	287024	335472	Credit Sales	2557516	2058272	499244
15	65	80	Occupancy %	53	58	(5)
9	38	39	Cost of Sales Food%	37	38	(1)
−	28	28	Cost of Sales Bev.%	27	24	(3)
(5)	34	29	Room Rate per Guest	20	23	(3)
(23869)	75694	99663	Cost of Sales $	728234	645983	(82251)

Moving Average Cost of Sales $ 61300
Moving Average Credit Sales $ 196459

AUTOEDIT CORPORATION:

SELLING OUT TO A LARGE CORPORATION

Stuart Dell replaced the crystal ball in his desk drawer and turned again to his well-worn copy of Machiavelli. He was about to begin a series of difficult negotiations which would determine if there was to be a future for Autoedit Corporation — and what, if any, role he would be playing in it. Now, in the fall of 1978, he found himself running the company with one hand and trying to sell it with the other. He had started, operated and sold several other businesses of his own — but he had never been in his present position, as a CEO and minority equity holder in someone else's venture. At this point, he and founder-owner William Warner were barely speaking to each other. Two entrepreneurs in the same venture, Dell reflected, were one too many.

October 15 was the date that Dell and his team would open negotiations with the Franklin Company, to try to work out an acquistion plan acceptable to both parties. Today was October 7 and Dell had still not resolved two big questions: What did he really want? and, What would he settle for?

BACKGROUND OF THE COMPANY

Autoedit Corporation was one of a series of companies started by William Warner, now in his 50's, described by his friends (when they were feeling friendly) as "the consummate entrepreneur". It had begun as Warner Medical Products in 1972 a vehicle for developing one of Warner's ideas — an optical scanner which could automatically read labels on Red Cross blood bags. Warner, who described himself as an inventor and designer, had seen a need for a fast and foolproof way to sort blood while working on a project designing hydraulic pumps for the Red Cross. Like other of his ideas, he first obtained a patent and then set up a Subchapter S corporation under which the device would be manufactured and sold.

Warner's entrepreneurial career followed a pattern. He had founded one very successful company, of which he was CEO and principal stockholder. From this financial base, he had started and spun off several smaller technological companies, using the Subchapter S status as a personal tax shield. In addition, he had invested in numerous technologically-based ventures. Here is his description:

> I like to start businesses, let them grow to $1 to $2 million in sales, and then get out from under them. I tend to lose interest in them once they start to run smoothly. When I start a business generally I get an idea for a product that is better than others on the market at that time and I try to build a business around that. Then later on when the business starts moving I try to hire people to handle the financial and operational aspects of it.

The five types of people Warner considered essential for an operating team were: a chief engineer, a manufacturing manager, a comptroller, a sales manager and a CEO. He had initiated this venture by hiring an engineer, Ernest Trout, a brilliant and dedicated electronics technician and a confirmed workaholic. In March of 1971 the two men, assisted by several other engineers hired by Trout, began to transform Warner's concept into reality. The concept of Warner's Optical Character Recognition system (OCR) was as follows: a printing element, consisting of standard letters and numbers on top and a special bar-code beneath each letter, would be produced. Then, an electronic scanning device capable of translating the bar-code under each letter into computer language would be developed. The result would be a label readable both by people and computers.

During this period, Warner also invited his friend and business adviser, Alfred Blatten, to become an outside Board member and to buy a small amount of stock ($5,000) in the company. Blatten agreed to this arrangement, as he had done in other of Warner's ventures.

By early 1972 the blood bag scanner was in production, and Warner brought in his son, Peter, to be head of manufacturing. Peter Warner had obtained an undergraduate degree in engineering in 1967, and was considered a hard worker and a "company man," as opposed to his entrepreneurial father. He chose to work for a straight salary without taking an equity position in the venture.

Warner now turned his mind toward sales, which, somewhat to his surprise, were not filling the company mailbox. He realized quickly that, although he had made the best product on the market to do the job of scanning bloodbags, there was virtually no demand for it. Consequently, he had Trout completely change the application from blood-bags to office word-processing. "I had looked around offices and saw all these people doing menial jobs, particularly hand-typing data into computers. I thought the reason they had to do all those jobs was because there was no inexpensive machine on the market that could do it for them. So we redirected the business with the goal of developing a low cost OCR machine." By mid-1972 the company had been renamed Warner Business Machines and Warner had committed a total of $750,000 to the newly-directed venture.

By spring 1973 a page-reader and typing element were in production, thanks to the heroic efforts of William and Peter Warner and Ernest Trout. Now, the senior Warner began to look both for markets and for venture capital. He hired two newly-graduated MBA's to assist with the latter job and contracted several marketing consultants for guidance in the former area. By the end of the summer it was evident that no progress was forthcoming on either front.

ENTER STUART DELL

In the fall of 1973 Stuart Dell was looking for a new venture. An entrepreneur with a Ph.D. in marketing, now in his early 40s, he had recently sold a venture he had started and nurtured to a large company for a comfortable profit. Since then he had reviewed and rejected close to 50 deals which had come to his attention. Dell ws introduced to Bill Warner through a mutual friend in the financial world, and was very interested by what he saw in Warner Business Machines. In December of 1973 he joined the company. Here is Dell's description:

> Warner's venture had great potential. He had already put a lot of money in and was prepared to put in more. I agreed to buy 25% of the stock and pay for it partly with cash and partly with a reduced salary. I came in as CEO with the job of getting the product finished and finding markets.

> (First) I needed to concentrate on finding a market. We had a parade of marketing consultants coming through but they all said different things. I finally decided that the graphic arts industry ws the best market.

> None of the regular business functions were in place when I got there. They were an engineering department without a company, sort of like a tail without a dog. I had to institute the financial controls. I also developed the literature including the service and operators manuals plus sales literature which showed product applications (see *Exhibit 1*). I then started hauling the prototype (bar-code type) around to trade shows. In March of 1974, we got an OEM contract for fifty machines from Photosett Industries as well as a couple of minor OEM contracts. Photosett manufactures photo-typesetting equipment.

> We began shipping the product in October of 1974 and became profitable at that time. Bill had agreed from the start that he would fund the company until it was profitable. He had put in $200,000 while I was there, which brought his total to around $950,000. All his accountants, lawyers, and tax people were telling him to get out of the business since he had already spent so much and it might go bankrupt.

> The second year, we were shipping for about seven months when we started to realize that we had made the classic

mistake, a very elegant solution to the wrong problem. Nobody wanted our product with the bar-code under each character even though we managed to sell some in the graphic arts industry."

We continued to ship to Photosett, but then their parent company bought a disaster and the whole company went belly up. Photosett canceled all orders. This was the beginning of the end. No OEMs could be found. Most people here were laid off. Bill was unwilling to put in more money. It was a time of bitterness but I was still optimistic and spent much time on the road and actually got a few new orders.

In October of 1975 I was paying about $15,000 per month out of my own pocket for the payroll and wasn't taking a salary. The company had reached the limit with the bank and I somehow negotiated a new line of credit. Bill wanted to dissolve the company, close the doors for two years, and open up with a new product. At this time, Ernest Trout figured out he could probably develop a machine to read characters directly. Trout worked day and night for five months and to his great credit, worked it out. Peter Warner left during this time for reasons of family harmony and health.

In January of 1976 we had a workable prototype that read the OCR-B type font. Bill and I negotiated a deal where we would cosign a bank note. I stayed on and ended up with about 50 percent of the business. Bill still owned the rights to the machine but I was able to use it by paying him royalties. This was a bleak time for me. I had been putting in five to fifteen thousand dollars every month and things were getting tight.

Finally to the unending credit of the engineers, we got the prototype into production. I developed new data sheets and literature and hit the road again. Now there was lots of interest. Word processing was arriving in 1976 and I realized this was the right market. We sold a few and shipped the first ones in May or June of 1976.

STRATEGIC RECONSIDERATIONS

In early fall, 1976, Dell was turning his considerable energies in two directions: marketing the new scanner, and raising venture capital. He successfully persuaded the Magnus Fund to invest $300,000 to be used for marketing and working capital, and then concentrated the marketing effort on what he considered to be the prime target — the OEM's. He based the strategy on the fact that it was the easiest market to reach, and one which was expanding so rapidly that even a small segment would mean a large piece of business for Autoedit. During 1977 he convinced the Magnus Fund to commit another $500,000 over the next two years. (The venture capital firm, in exchange, received 50% of Autoedit's stock; Dell and Warner each retained 25%.) However, before the end of the two years, in September, 1978, Dell was forced to reconsider his strategy.

> I thought we could sell the OCR on an OEM basis but we couldn't. Competition quickly sewed up some of the OEM's and the others saw us as a threat to their business — our OCR machine essentially eliminated the need for the end-user to have many word processing terminals.
>
> It became evident that we needed to go after the end user market. This would require a whole new sales strategy — more salesmen, a different type of literature, perhaps even a modification in machine design. In short, it was clear that we needed a lot more money.

But where was the money to come from? The capital necessary to build a direct field sales organization was beyond Warner or Dell. Warner was unwilling to go back to the Magnus Fund because his stock would be diluted into oblivion; he would have preferred to liquidate Autoedit. Dell, on the other hand, had a vested interest in having Autoedit survive; he calculated that he was "into" Autoedit for about $80,000 in cash, and had not drawn his $30,000 salary since January of 1977.

Blatten commented on this managerial log jam:

> After the first year, the relationship between Dell and Warner deteriorated radically. My role became that of mediator. I had to keep things from being too emotional. Although Dell's job was not primarily to raise capital, he was assuming that responsibility — and Dell was successful at convincing The Magnus Fund to invest $300,000, and then $500,000 more.
>
> You have great difficulty when one person owns a business and another runs it...Warner originally ran the whole thing; he put in the capital and he got the business going. Before this, he had never had a partner ... he's a tough businessman; he's the consummate Yankee trader and he's the type of guy who might go ahead with a deal even if it were not the nice thing to do. Overall, I think Warner's influence on the company was negative after Dell came in.
>
> Bill has the ideas and does them. He works very hard and is

very smart on all levels, but he's a solo player. He never should have been in business with someone else.

At Blatten's suggestion, the Board of Directors — Dell, the Chairman, Warner, Peter Warner (who remained on the board as Clerk, though he had no equity interest) and Blatten — met that month to discuss the options open to them if Autoedit were to remain in business. They could identify only three alternatives:

> — Try to find an additional investor or new venture capital firm. They perceived this option would be difficult to achieve because why should a new venture capital firm fund what might be seen as another venture capital firm's mistake?

> — Try to obtain notes allowing Dell to buy out Warner. This option would solve the problems between the principals, but it would still leave Dell with a nearly-bankrupt company.

> — Try to find a buyer.

The meeting broke up without any conclusions being reached, but Dell felt that he had been given carte blanche to "go out and see what you can do."

INITIAL STEPS

Dell did two things to initiate a possible sellout. First, he met privately with Alfred Blatten, to enlist his help in finding and screening possible buyers. Blatten contracted about a dozen companies he believed might be interested, by writing to the Corporate Development Office of each firm. Three firms exhibited a mild preliminary interest. At the same time, Dell took another tack. He decided to contact two firms that had previously expressed an interest in buying Autoedit. Before making any moves, however, he defined for himself what type of company would be a likely buyer. It would ideally be a company with an extensive service and marketing organization because these were the assets Autoedit lacked, but it might also be a diversified conglomerate with a lot of capital to pour into a promising division.

Of the two companies that had courted Autoedit in the past, the first, on the surface, seemed an unlikely suitor. LMI, Inc., of Dallas was really a leasing company — leasing and creating lease plans for computers. They had no service organization and a limited marketing structure. However, they were cash rich and wanted to diversify by buying equipment manufacturers. Earlier in the summer, LMI had approached Dell to ascertain his interest in selling the company so it seemed natural for Dell to contact them and say he was now prepared to entertain a proposal. He later commented,

> We really didn't want to get in bed with a leasing company, especially one without a service or marketing organization and eventually they backed out.

The other company that Dell contacted was Franklin Corporation, a large computer manufacturer. Franklin had been an early leader and had held the position of number two in the word processing industry. Recently its position had declined and many younger companies had surpassed it in sales of competitive lines. Taking his cue from Blatten, Dell first approached the Corporate Development Office.

I wasted almost a month talking with the Corporate Development Department at Franklin. An OCR was in their long range plan — for something like 1985. I tried to convince them that buying Autoedit would allow them to pull their time scale in and get a jump on the competition. But I ran up against an acute case of corporate inertia.

Acquisitions seem to be everybody's business and nobody's business. There was no established procedure at Franklin. They hadn't made an acquisition for over five years. It was a low priority on their board's agenda. And yet, it is only at the Board of Directors level that a decision can be made.

I finally concluded that the Corporate Development was not the right place to put my efforts. The position of Corporate Development Officer seems to be a chair held by a dropout, someone with no authority, no knowledge.

So I changed my approach; I went to the operating people who had a bottom line interest in what I was trying to sell. They seemed to be the best ones to carry my story to the head office.

I made a very cogent case to the operations head who was a customer of ours and a potential supplier, Harry Singer. He is a divisions manager for Facsimile and Word Processing. I opened his eyes to the existence of the OCR market and convinced him that if Franklin bought Autoedit it would be a bigger empire for him. Harry was very open-minded, and I never had to contend with the NIH factor. ("Not Invented Here.") He was the internal champion I needed.

Once Harry was convinced, he talked to top management. They seemed interested and that was my opening. I finally got a chance to present my case to the people who could make the decision, and they seemed receptive — if a good deal can be worked out. They will assign a guy on the Corporate Development staff to handle the negotiations with us. He has the reputation of being a troubleshooter — a hard negotiator but a nice guy. He represnts Franklin's philosophy that they should be able to buy a sick company cheap, and then spend their money to turn it around.

DELL'S POSITION: OCTOBER 7, 1978

At the same time that Dell was trying to structure a deal to perpetuate Autoedit he also had to keep the company running. He was finding it very difficult to be an effective manager.

> It was a problem to keep the venture going while I was trying to sell it. I couldn't afford to let things slip; the worse shape Autoedit was in, the poorer deal we'd be able to strike with Franklin or any other buyer. I had to keep up morale and keep banging on doors to promote the product. I know my own people felt uneasy, but I didn't know what to tell them. If several of my key people had asked me point-blank how secure their jobs would be in three months I wouldn't have had an encouraging answer, and luckily no one asked. Everything was unsettled. People kept trooping through to look at the operation and everyone knew something was going on.

> It is very difficult to sell a small company under any circumstances. A fragile equilibrium exists because of the natural fear of change. You go through a lot of psychological strain under these circumstances. You also don't want to lose your customers — rumors run wild on the street. The ones that confront you with it you can deal with, but those that don't, just disappear! Your dealers get nervous, too.

Dell had already decided on his negotiating team for next week's initial meeting — himself, Blatten and Blatten's lawyer — but he still faced a number of unresolved issues.

> I believe we're selling a company with a lot of potential, but I can't put a price tag on it. The operating results only tell part of the story (See *Exhibit II* and *III*). I am led to believe that Franklin wants a stock-for-assets deal, but I am going to need some cold cash, personally, very soon. I also have to answer some hard questions for myself:

> • First, do I want a guaranteed employment contract and a substantial salary as head of this new division, or do I want out altogether?

> • Second, how much in cash do I need — simply to cover my out-of-pocket expenditures during the last year?

> • Third, how much stock do I want in Franklin? How much faith do I have that, if the deal goes through, it's going to fly?

Finally, hanging heavy over my head is the time element; the longer we wait the harder Autoedit may be to sell. I may have to settle for less than we deserve in order to get a capital transfusion to keep the company alive.

I wonder what kind of a deal, if any, we are going to be able to strike with Franklin?

ASSIGNMENT QUESTIONS

Some suggested questions are:

1. What are the critical questions and issues confronting Mr. Dell?

2. What do you think he really wants?

3. As a minority stockholder, what do you think he should settle for?

4. Develop the price and the terms under which you believe Mr. Dell will sell Autoedit Corporation.

5. Given these terms, develop a negotiating strategy for the upcoming negotiations with Franklin Company.

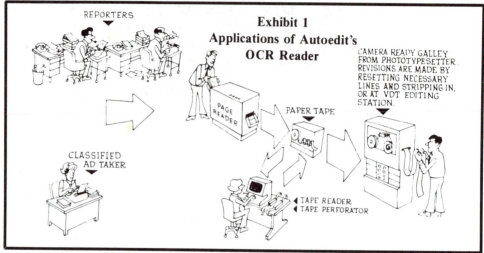

**Exhibit 1
Applications of Autoedit's
OCR Reader**

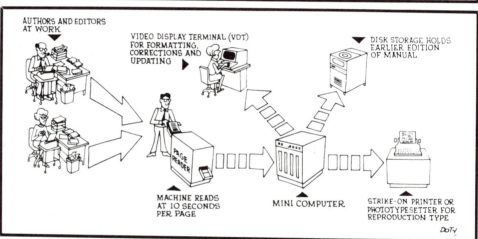

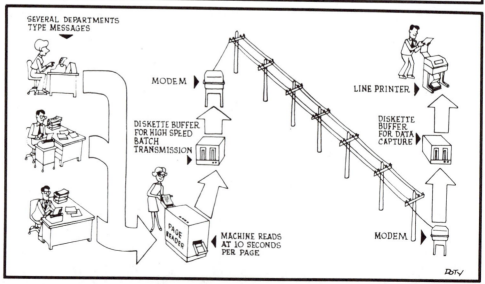

Exhibit II
Autoedit Corporation
Profit and Loss Statement
September 31, 1978

Description	Current Month	Cumulative to Date
Revenues	39,785	572,632
Cost of Sales		
Material	21,987	189,332
Direct Labor	4,318	35,799
Overhead Manufacturing	(29,201)	201,525
Purchase Variance	(131)	(645)
Tooling Amortization		
Cash Discounts	—	1,046
Total Cost of Sales	(3,027)	427,057
Gross Profit	42,812	145,575
Expenses		
Administrative	53,728	200,515
Marketing	19,608	163,967
Engineering	9,262	203,652
Interest	4,928	45,738
Royalty	3,398	32,673
Total Expenses	90,924	646,545
Profit Before Taxes	(48,112)	(500,970)
Provision for Income Tax		
Net Profit (Loss)		

Personnel: **22** Full Time   **3** Part Time

Exhibit III
Autoedit Corporation
Balance Sheet
September 31, 1978

	1978	1977
Assets		
Current Assets		
Cash	6,247	3,051
Accounts Receivable - Trade (Net)	185,669	203,294
Inventories	223,293	167,553
Prepaid Expenses & Other Current Assets	6,071	4,582
Total Current Assets	421,280	378,480
Fixed Assets		
Equipment	47,118	40,652
Less Reserve for Depreciation	(36,134)	(32,572)
Book Value	10,984	8,080
Deferred Financing Costs	25,040	25,040
Total Assets	457,304	411,600
Liabilities		
Current Liabilities		
Notes Payable - Bank	150,000	100,000
Accounts Payable - Trade	247,896	179,989
Accrued Expenses	27,556	
Total Current Liabilities	425,452	279,989
Long Term Debt		
Long Term Debt	500,000	100,000
Convertible Notes	305,000	305,000
Notes Payable - Stockholder	23,137	22,226
Net Worth		
Common Stock Issued & Outstanding	21,570	
Capital & Earned Surplus	(817,855)	
Net Worth	(796,285)	(295,615)
Total Liabilities	457,304	411,600

L.L. BEAN, INCORPORATED

Leon Arthur Gorman, a grandson of L.L. Bean and a vice president of the company, was wondering during the summer of 1965 if his grandfather's philosophy and methods of running the business could be transferred to new management, or whether there would have to be important changes to enable the company to continue its profitable growth in the future. Leon Gorman had recently made several recommendations that he thought would improve efficiency, cut costs, and increase sales but they had been turned down by the company's two top officers. His grandfather and his uncle felt since business was increasing there was no reason to risk upsetting people by making changes, even though the recommended changes might have merit.

Leon was told to wait for the day when he became president, and then he would be able to institute whatever changes he felt were needed. Although that day was certainly a few years away, he was still concerned about the company's future and decided to review the company's operations completely.

He commenced his study by rereading an article about his grandfather entitled "Mail Order Sportsman."[1]

---

[1] This article based on "The Discovery of L.L. Bean," by Arthur Bartlett, published in *The Saturday Evening Post* issue of December 14, 1946, subsequently appeared in 1964 as one of a series: "The Small Businessman in America," Regional Feature: IPS/Near East Branch. Reprinted by special permission of *The Saturday Evening Post,* 1946 by The Curtis Publishing Company.

This case was made possible by the cooperation of the L.L. Bean Company, Inc. of Freeport, Maine. It was prepared by Charles M. Leighton under the direction of Professor Frank L. Tucker as the basis for class discussion rather than to illustrate either effective or ineffective handling of an administrative situation. Reprinted by permission of the Harvard Business School.

In 1911, Leon Leonwood Bean dreamed up a new kind of shoe, and made it the foundation of a business. Now (1964) still active at the age of 92, Mr. Bean is running a company which sells goods at the rate of $3 million a year and growing. From his headquarters in the small town of Freeport, Maine, he sends out hundreds of boots, moccasins, shirts, jackets, hunting and camping gear, salt and fresh water fishing equipment - more than 400 items, all told - to sportsmen in all the states and territories, to Arctic explorers and Africa big-game hunters, and to residents of 50 foreign countries. And with good reason, each of his customers seems to share the illusion that L.L. Bean is a personal discovery and, very probably, a personal friend.

Mr. Bean started in the basement room of a Freeport clothing store. Now L.L. Bean, Incorporated, occupies a sprawling complex of buildings which dominate the business area of the little Maine community. But despite the growth, Mr. Bean's business methods and manners have remained those of a New England storekeeper, with a countryman's personal interest in each of his customers. His Yankee sense of thrift is so strong that he is almost as eager to save the customer money as to make money himself.

"We wish to call your attention to the fact that throwing away a pair of used Maine Hunting Shoes is about the same as throwing away a five-dollar bill," he warns in his catalog. Send them back, he says, and he'll rebuild them good as new. Or, "C.O.D. fees are very expensive for both customers and ourselves. We advise avoiding this service."

Greying and slightly thinner now, Mr. Bean remains a powerful, positive individual, and he continues to head the staff of two sons, two grandsons, and 140 employees. His joy in his work, and the success which compounds the joy, have been doubly assured by the fact that his passion for business has been closely rivaled, all his life, by his passion for hunting and fishing. His love for the out-of-doors, in fact, has been one of his valuable business assets. His more rugged hunting and camping days are over for the most part, but he remains an ardent fisherman. And to this day, every item he sells he himself has tested on a hunting or fishing trip, or has had tested by a trusted associate.

It was because his feet got tired on hunting trips, when he was a younger man, that he got the idea which founded his business. As an experiment one day, he left off his heavy hunter's boots, went into the Maine woods wearing a pair of shoe rubbers, over three pairs of stockings. These kept his feet warm, dry and comfortable, but he felt the need for support around the ankles. So he took the rubbers to Dennis Bibber, the local cobbler, and got him to sew leather tops on them. Mr. Bean found the leather topped rubbers personally satisfactory, had a few pairs made, and got the town's other hunters to try them. The reports were favorable, and he decided he had something to sell.

So he borrowed $400 and went into business. He got out a circular describing his shoes, and he mailed out the first 100 pairs to customers with a guarantee of absolute satisfaction. Within a matter of weeks the shoes began coming back, the tops torn away from the rubber. But L.L. negotiated another small loan, got together with the cobbler on the problem, and made good his guarantee. He has guaranteed the shoe ever since; and he has long since perfected it into an outstanding product. The guarantee has become, as originally intended, a good-will builder which costs little. The Maine Hunting Shoe remains, of all the items since added to the Bean line, the top seller.

One of the early items that L.L. Bean added, after the shoe, was naturally, stockings. Emma Toomey, up in Unity, Maine, had knitted him a pair and he liked them, so he arranged with her to knit some more, and put them in his circular. Before long, most of Emma's friends and neighbors were knitting for Bean, too, and they couldn't keep up with the demand. So L.L. had to add machine-knit socks and stockings to the hand-knit ones, but he still tried them out himself before he would offer them for sale. Even now, when his stocks ranges from Arch Support Moccasins to Zipper Duffle Bags, L.L. considers an item salable only if it is something he would choose for his own use.

About the time he was adding Emma Toomey's stockings, L.L. decided he had never owned a hunting coat with enough pockets in it, so he had one made with a total of seven, including a double back that made the most capacious pocket of all - plenty of storage space for shells, lunch, pipe, tobacco, license and game. Bean's jackets now are offered in many styles and fabrics for all hunting and outdoor sports.

As business increased and customers began to ask for other standard outdoor articles, Bean widened his offerings. If he decided that a sharpening stone was a handy thing to have on an outing - and if he could make a satisfactory deal to buy sharpening stones he liked - he included them in his catalog, and so with belts, pants, flashlights, decoys, knives, vacuum bottles, snowshoes, outdoor clothing and camping equipment of all descriptions. He even sells pipes and his own blend of smoking tobacco since, as he notes in his catalog, "most fishermen and hunters smoke."

Still, L.L. Bean sells only what he likes, and likes everything he sells and wants everyone to know it. The catalog may admit that an article is made by someone else (Bean manufactures many of the 400 odd articles listed in the book). But these articles, too, are unmistakably Bean's, since with one or two exceptions such as Hudson Bay Blankets, they are made to Bean's exact specifications.

Bean's factory at Freeport would drive an efficiency expert mad, but no ever-rolling production line could achieve Bean's individualistic results. Cutting tables, sewing machines and eyelet-punching machines are tucked in wherever they will fit; workers may be making duffle bags one day and game vests the next, and if L.L. has a new idea for a new type of pocket in the vest, he just goes and tells his workers what he wants.

The Bean building itself is as offhand and seemingly systemless as the production. When L.L. moved in, it was just a typical wooden small-town business block of two and a half stories, with the post office occupying the street floor. Piece by piece, as he needed more space during the years, he tacked additions on in nearly every direction. Altogether, he has 63,000 sq. ft. of floor space now, as compared to the 875 with which he started in the basement across the street. Stairways twist and turn through the building, which seems to be on at least a dozen different levels. Rooms full of machines merge inexplicably into rooms full of desks, and you have to go through both to get to Bean's little office on the third floor. The post office - Bean's is by far its biggest customer - was moved recently to a new building down the street, but a parcel post unit was left behind, and Bean's ongoing packages still are mailed on a moving belt which carries them from the shipping room to the postal unit below.[2]

Although 80% of his business is done by mail, Bean welcomes customers to the factory as he always has; he maintains a salesroom there, and it is his policy that Bean's is never closed. Twenty-four hours of the day, 365 days a year, people can - and do - call at Bean's to buy things they need for a camping, fishing or hunting trip. Recently, when the Maine legislature passed a law requiring business to close down on Sundays, the Freeport town meeting exercised its local option and voted 3 to 1 that Bean's be allowed to stay open on its regular seven-day basis, around the clock.

Regular salespeople take care of the customers, but L.L. frequently takes a hand if he happens to be passing through the salesroom. And he has an understanding with his employees that people who seem to be there primarily to get outdoors advice, or to swap yarns, shall be sent to him if he is there. He draws no distinction between ordinary hunters or fishermen and notables, but he sees his share of the latter. U.S. Supreme Court Justice Willliam O. Douglas and Mrs. Douglas are frequent visitors to the salesroom; General Matthew Ridgeway has been a Bean customer since he was a lieutenant-colonel. Actors Robert Montgomery and Myrna Loy, and baseball player Ted Williams (Mr. Bean is an ardent fan of the Boston Red Sox) come in to the salesroom regularly. Franchot Tone, the actor, telephones an order each fall from wherever he may be; Bing Crosby, mystery writer Earl Stanley Gardner, as well as golfer Sam Snead, order regularly by mail. So does the king of Afghanistan, and so do any number of diplomats and government officials overseas. One serious sportsman, although deaf and blind, has Bean's catalog translated into Braille.

Bean's reputation initially spread by word of mouth from one satisfied sportsman to another. This method is still his strongest asset. Over the years, however, he has increasingly promoted his name by extensively advertising his catalog in the leading sporting publications. And it is through Bean's catalog that most of his customers now discover him and become addicted to his services. It is a remarkable extension of his personality. L.L. Bean wrote every word of it himself for years, and although he now permits others to draft it, he invariably rewrites and revises so completely that their words become his. Wintering in Florida, as he and Mrs. Bean do each year, he still insists on seeing every one of the 100 catalog pages, and deadlines must be advanced 10 days to allow for his editing.

He himself becomes personally and unmistakably present on every page. "L.L. Bean wears them all year round," the catalog says of Bean's English Rib Wool Stocking; Bean's Pipe Holder, he notes, is "manufactured by use of elk tanned leather out of pieces too

---

[2]Editor's note: Some scenes from the L.L. Bean building are shown in Appendix A.

small for our Maine Hunting Shoe." Bean's Salt Water Rod and Reel is "the outfit used by Mr. and Mrs. L.L. Bean in Florida for sailfish and white marlin," and so on.

The catalog itself, although issued at the rate of 800,000 a year, is something of a collector's item. It is no unusual thing for Bean's (which thriftily does not accept collect calls) to get telephoned requests from as far as Texas, Oregon or California. The caller may be paying three or four dollars in toll just to obtain a free catalog by the first mail, or even to order, say a pair of Bean's Cold Proof Innersoles at $1.25.

Bean strews his wares through his catalog in the haphazard way of a country store. In one recent issue, there were jackets, trousers and shoes on the first page and scattered all through, with suspenders, duck calls, fishing lures, axes, maple syrup, soap and numbers of other items dropped in with equal casualness. Bean always tucks in plenty of good advice where it will fit. The current catalog has instructions on "How to Sharpen a Knife." Saving money and trouble for fresh-water fishermen, the catalog observes that "it is no longer necessary for you to experiment with dozens of flies to determine the few that will catch fish. We have made a survey of hundreds to determine how many we could eliminate. We have selected nine patterns that will give the proper flies for nearly all occasions."

Customers are encouraged to trade ideas with L.L. and his staff. Many suggested improvements for one product or another have been adopted. Bean sums up his success in a few words, "Sell good merchandise at a reasonable price; treat your customes like you would your friends; and the business will take care of itself."

In addition to the article, Mr. Gorman had accumulated a great deal of information about the company and its market opportunities. The following describes the situation as of mid-1965.

FINANCIAL DATA

1964 sales of $3 million and profits of $70,000 were at an all-time high for L.L. Bean, Incorporated. Their yearly sales, profits and financial statements are shown in *Exhibits 1* and *2*.

COMPANY ORGANIZATION

The company chairman, president and treasurer was the founder, Mr. Leon L. Bean. In 1965 he was 93 and his health permitted less activity in company affairs than he had formerly been used to. His secretary screened his mail and memos and sent to his home those that she deemed important enough for his consideration. However, he reviewed in detail all catalogs, advertisements, and price changes, which had to have his unqualified approval.

Second in command was Mr. Bean's son, L. Carl Bean, who was a vice president and assistant treasurer of the company; L. Carl Bean was born in 1901 and joined his father's company after he graduated from high school. His company activities concerned the personnel and production areas mostly. His wife was his secretary and they were both avid golfers. They had no children. Carl Bean spoke highly of Leon Gorman, his nephew. He felt Leon was more ambitious than he and enjoyed taking on as much responsibility as was given him. Carl Bean personally was content to keep the company as it was and he looked forward to retiring and acting as a part-time advisor.

Leon A. Gorman, born in 1934, was a grandson of the founder and a vice president of the company. He was a *cum laude* graduate of Bowdoin College, and spent three and a half years as a naval officer, and had worked for Filene's in Boston before joining the company as a clothing buyer in 1960. His present company responsibilities included purchasing, store and catalog sales, advertising, and assisting his uncle L. Carl Bean. His outside activities included being on the advisory board of the Depositor's Trust Company, one of Maine's largest banks, and being an officer of the Freeport Chamber of Commerce and Yarmouth Republican Town Committee.

Other family members in the company were L.L. Bean's other son, C. Warren Bean, assistant treasurer and clerk, and grandson John T. Gorman who was the receiving clerk.

The five family members plus the company controller, Mr. Hayes, and tackle buyer, Mr. Griffen, made up the board of directors. The board met infrequently and there were no plans for including outside people on the board. Except for L.L. Bean's office there were no private offices or conference rooms. There was no retirement age and the average age of the 136 employees was 62 years. The stock of the company was owned by the family with L.L. Bean being the major stockholder. Upon the death of any family stockholder the company had the option to buy back the company stock.

MARKET POTENTIAL

The three major customer classifications for L.L. Bean products had been fishermen, hunters, and campers. Although the company had tried to sell archery and ski equipment, their efforts had met with little success.

In 1961 according to Richard E. Snyder, economist for the National Sporting Goods Association, representative annual sales figures for the whole country were: firearms and supplies, $255 million; fishing equipment, $164 million; sleeping bags, $38 million; archery equipment, $28 million; and ski equipment, $17 million. According to *Hardware Age* magazine, "With the advent of more leisure time and disposable income the market potential for sporting goods has experienced an upward trend. One only has to look at the store space allocated by department stores such as Sears, or the space allocated in their mail order catalog to witness the ever widening scope of items for leisure and recreation." Also similar L.L. Bean mail order type catalogs, such as Eddie Bauer of Seattle, Thompson of Portland, Oregon, Gokey of St. Paul, Minnesota, and Corcoran of Stoughton, Massachusetts have entered this market.

Exhibit 3 estimates the number of U.S. fishermen and their growth in numbers compared to population growth. In 1945 there were 8.3 million buyers of fishing licenses, tags, and permits, compared to 24 million in 1963. This is an increase of 177% compared to a national population increase during this period of 30%.

According to a survey by *Outdoor Life* magazine, the average fisherman spends $9.33 for general equipment such as sleeping gear and clothing and $12.18 for fishing tackle each year. The survey also showed that one out of every three anglers is a female.

The Department of the Interior's Fish and Wildlife Service estimated in 1955 there were 11.8 million active hunters, in 1960 14.7 million, and in 1964 17.5 million active hunters. Eighty-three percent are small game hunters, 13% waterfowl hunters and 4% are big game hunters. One out of 15 hunters is a female.

With regard to the camping market, in 1964 11% of the total U.S. population or 19.8 million persons camped and another 9% would like to try camping, according to figures revealed by the Outdoor Recreation Resources Review Commission.

MARKETING

A breakdown of total sales shown in Exhibit 1 by product group would be: clothing, 43%; footwear, 33%; camping equipment, 12%; and sporting goods, 12%. Approximately 15% of sales were goods manufactured by L.L. Bean Company. The remaining items were purchased or produced to their specifications.

An advertising budget of approximately $50,000 with the objective of adding names to the mailing list was spent on advertisements in such magazines as *Sports Afield, Outdoor Life, Field and Stream, True,* and the *New Yorker.*

The mailing list of about 430,000 names received two catalogs of 100 pages each, one in February and one in August, and two 30-page circulars sent out in October and April. It cost approximately 25¢ to print and mail out a catalog. The address labels were typed by hand twice a year at the L.L. Bean factory. All catalogs and circulars were hand stuffed in the envelopes at the factory. A Chicago firm had quoted a much cheaper price for doing the labeling and stuffing on automatic machinery. However, their offer was turned down since it would have meant laying off about 25 women who now did this work and the envelope postmark would not have shown Freeport, Maine, but Chicago.

A catalog customer who sent in an order in excess of $2 once every three years was kept on the mailing list; otherwise the name was dropped from the list.[3] The mailing list was kept at the factory and on Leon Gorman's suggestion, a duplicate list was put in a fireproof bank vault.

The standard pricing procedure was to mark up all manufactured or purchased items 37 1/2%.

The factory store was kept open 24 hours a day every day of the year. Actually one of the main reasons for doing so was that L.L. Bean found it hard to find a night watchman who would stay in the building alone. So he decided to add another man to keep him

---

[3] In 1964, 170,000 catalog orders were shipped. Management anticipated sending out 960,000 catalogs in the fall of 1970.

company, turn on the store lights which lessen possibilities of theft and advertise the store as being open 24 hours a day for customer convenience. It turned out that their night sales more than covered the cost of the two sales-night watchman.

As can be seen in *Exhibit 1* the factory store sales showed a leveling off trend after the state express road bypassed Freeport, Maine. However, *Exhibit 4*, prepared by the L.L. Bean Company, shows how the parking lot which was Leon Gorman's suggestion has helped reverse this leveling of sales. Opening a store at the beginning of the Maine Turnpike at Kittery was also suggested. This was tabled in favor of keeping things as they were. It was also suggested that the store, located in the center of the third floor, be moved to the more attractive and accessible first floor street-front area leased by L.L. Bean to a drug store, but this, too, was tabled. The factory store was used by the firm's buyers as a place to test market an item before adding it to the catalog. The company did not have any two-, three-, or five-year plans that projected future sales.

PURCHASING

In 1965, clothing, shoes, tackle, hardware, and the factory store each had a separate buyer. There were few policy guidelines on make or buy decisions. Thus it was often true that an item was purchased on the outside merely because it was easier for the buyer to do it that way.

The buyers got many of their ideas from visiting salesmen and by going to trade shows. A buyer such as Mr. Griffen personally tried out most fishing and camping items before selecting what would be offered in the salesroom and catalog. There was no perpetual inventory control system. Each buyer gauged inventory needs by reviewing what was sold the previous year and by making visual inspections of the inventory on hand.

When asked what problems he foresaw in the future, Mr. Griffen felt the major problem was efficiency in operations. He felt greater efficiency was needed in the handling and shipping of orders. He felt there should be catalog numbers for each item. This would help packers in selecting items for shipment more quickly and in lessening their chances of making a mistake. Since catalog customers ordered by description, the packers had to be quite familiar with all the items. He also felt greater efficiency could be attained by putting the manufacturing operations on one floor and combining the stock rooms, rather than having them in separate rooms and buildings.

ACCOUNTING

According to Mr. Hayes, the controller, the accounting system was set up as if they were doing business with one item. There were no profit breakdowns by catalog sales vs. factory store sales, manufactured vs. purchased items, or by-products or product lines.

There were apt to be variances in the unit costs of manufactured items as a result of workers on an hourly wage producing at different speeds. Direct material costs were re-examined when invoices showed a variance greater than 5%. A standard overhead burden factor of 20% had always been charged to the manufacturing operations. This 20% charge included an allowance for catalog preparation costs, buyer salaries, etc.

Actually the 20% factory burden charge had not been verified for a number of years and it was not known how accurate it was. Storage costs and freight costs were not computed by product or product line but were all lumped together.

PRODUCTION

The factory consisted of a three-floor wooden building. The manufacturing operations were spread throughout this building as were the general offices and stock rooms.[4] There were 36 employees directly engaged in production work and their average age was around 60. Morris Hilton was the production superintendent and was in his late thirties. He felt there was a good employee attitude which was fostered by the older, and loyal employees. He preferred older employees as they were easier to work with. He said the younger people were often willing to work harder if they could earn more money and thus they preferred piece work rather than the standard hourly wage. Standards were generally set by the slow to medium worker and since everyone was on an hourly wage there was little motivation for employees to produce more than the standard. Mr. Hilton asked Carl Bean about the possibilities of putting in an incentive system but Carl Bean felt they should not change the present system. L.L. Bean's feeling were best summed up by his attitude of, "I would rather see an employee do a quality job than hurry, and anyway I eat three meals a day and couldn't eat a fourth." Mr. Hilton felt not having an incentive piece rate hurt the company in that older people, who wanted steady but less demanding work, were more apt to apply for openings than the younger, more ambitious applicants.

Mr. Hilton once approached L.L. Bean on another suggestion of putting the stitching room next to the cutting room for greater efficiency, but L.L. Bean pointed out that some people had been in the same spot for 30 to 40 years and would not like to be moved.

Job orders for items to be manufactured by the company were placed by the buyers, based on the buyer's estimates of sales requirements. Each week Hilton personally made a visual count of the inventory of major manufactured items to see if the number in stock was larger or smaller than the expected number. If there were significant deviations he discussed with the buyers the possible rescheduling of the job orders.

Hilton thought their own manufactured items gave more exclusiveness to their sales catalog and wondered if the company was becoming too dependent on purchase items. He felt, however, that the best policy is "to leave things alone when you are growing and making money."

FUTURE

The company in 1964 had had all-time high sales and profits and although the market potential for L.L. Bean products was still growing, Leon Gorman was concerned with certain aspects of the present condition and future prospects of the company. He felt that mail-order sales of their present product lines had not been exploited to the point of diminishing returns. After considering possible expansion through retail branches,

---

[4]See Appendix A.

concessions, and franchising, he stated, "Being originally shoemakers, I am inclined to think we should stick to our lasts and concentrate on the mail-order field which we know best...concentrating on hunting, fishing and camping...upgrading and improving an essentially static line."

Mr. Gorman thought the accounting system should be re-established on a basis that separated manufacturing and retailing, possibly through placing all production facilities in a wholly owned subsidiary. He hoped that eventually cost accounting would indicate individual item profitability. He felt that proper accounting would lead to controls on inventory, budget, shortage and overhead, and would assist in more logical organization and disposition of personnel and responsibility, as well as assist in a variety of management decisions. He thought there might be sufficient work necessary in modernizing the operations, from mailing list handling through production, to justify using a consulting firm. Mr. Gorman was also interested in sources for financing future growth and the possibility of bringing in professional outside help as a part of management and/or the board.

Even though he had recently been thwarted in making major changes, Mr. Gorman felt he should consider and list these and other changes that might have to be made in the future, arrange them by priority, and plan how they could best be phased into the company's operations.

ASSIGNMENT QUESTIONS

L.L. Bean is a company which has grown in the image of its founder Leon Bean. This is a wonderful opportunity to consider what has happened, why it has happened and what, if anything, should change when a new generation succeeds the founder.

1. Identify the strategy and objectives of L.L. Bean to date.

2. Identify the major values, traditions and policies.

3. Has L.L. Bean been successful? *Why?*

4. What are the concerns of Leon Gorman?

5. Why have Mr. Gorman's suggestions been rejected?

6. What changes would you want Mr. Gorman to consider for the future? Prepare a list of changes, assign priorities, and plan how the changes could best be phased into L.L. Bean.

7. How is succession being handled at L.L. Bean?

8. How should succession be handled?

Exhibit 1
L.L. Bean, Incorporated
Yearly Sales and Profits
(000)

Year	Factory Store Sales	Total Sales Store and Catalog	Total CGS	Total Expenses	Total PAT#
1964	$609	$3,103	1,938	1,050*	70
1963**	527	2,901	1,851	977	47
1962	456	2,539	1,593	868	42
1961	469	2,544	1,598	879	37
1960	433	2,233	1,408	743	42
1959	406				
1958	395				
1957	399				
1956	411				
1955***	494				
1954	471				
1953	456				
1952	399				
1951	381				
1950	345				

*The combined salary earned by the two top officers was in the high five figures.

**Factory store parking lot built in the spring of 1963.

***Opening of expressway which bypasses Freeport, Maine (location of factory store).

#Other income and taxes not shown.

Exhibit 2
L. L. Bean, Incorporated
Balance Sheets* 1960-1964

	Dec. 31, 1960	Dec. 31, 1961	Dec. 31, 1962	Dec. 31, 1963	Dec. 31, 1964
Cash & cert. of dep.	$ 429,856	$ 490,249	$ 471,002	$ 389,639	$ 580,516
Marketable securities	83,544	53,045	67,087	48,268	48,210
Notes receivable	1,000	750	—	—	—
Accounts receivable	11,009	15,176	14,374	23,068	27,387
Inventory	492,077	484,412	546,796	681,090	562,122
Other current assets	10,830	10,289	9,578	—	—
Total Current Assets	$1,028,316	$1,053,921	$1,108,837	$1,142,065	$1,218,235
Fixed assets	161,188	158,915	160,436	164,014	159,826
Investments	20,605	21,104	21,574	22,107	22,663
Prepaid-deferred	24,036	21,663	30,838	28,010	28,032
Notes payable def.	500	—	—	—	—
Intangibles (good will, mailing lists, trade marks)	150,000	150,000	150,000	150,000	150,000
Total Assets	$1,384,645	$1,405,603	$1,471,685	$1,506,196	$1,578,756
Accounts payable trade	99,809	80,111	98,267	106,433	111,813
Accounts payable other	31,322	25,312	31,300	9,368	7,720
Taxes	76,931	121,605	129,540	170,830	188,059
Federal income taxes	31,483	27,318	32,324	37,680	54,008
Due customers	20,742	24,904	43,690	29.696	25,408
Total Current Liabilities	$ 260,288	$ 279,250	$ 335,121	$ 354,007	$ 387,008
Common stock	259,700	259,700	390,750	390,750	390,850
Capital surplus	—	—	800	800	800
Earned surplus	864,659	866,653	745,014	760,196	800,198
Total Liabilities	$1,384,645	$1,405,603	$1,471,685	$1,506,196	$1,578,756
Net Working Capital	$ 768,028	$ 744,671	$ 773,716	$ 788,058	$ 831,227
Current Ratio	3.95	3.79	3.31	3.23	3.25
Tangible Net Worth	974,357	976,353	986,564	1,002,189	1,041,748

*The above fiscal financial statements are all based on audits by Ernst & Ernst, Accountants, Portland, Maine, or Lybrand, Ross Bros. & Montgomery, CPA's, Portland, Maine.

Exhibit 3
L. L. Bean, Incorporated

Estimate of Sports Fishing as Related to Population Growth*

	1955	1960	1976	2000
Total population	164,300,000	177,000,000	230,000,000	350,000,000
Percentage increase		7.7	30	98
Number of fishermen	20,800,000	25,300,000	37,500,000	63,000,000
Percentage increase		21.6	48	149
Percent of persons 12 years and up who fish	17.6	19.3	21	23
Fisherman days	397,400,000	465,700,000	750,000,000	1,300,000,000
Days per angler	19.1	18.4	20	20

*Outdoor Recreation in America known as the Rockefeller Report 1962,
U.S. Dept. of the Interior.

Exhibit 4
L. L. Bean, Incorporated

Value of Customer Parking Lot

1. Parking lot built in Spring 1963.

2. In 1963, Salesroom increased sales by 15.5% over 1962. In 1964 increase over 1963 was 14.7%.

3. Prior to parking lot, in 1962 Salesroom actually declined versus 1961 and 1961 increase over 1960 was only 8.6%.

4.
Salesroom gross in 1964	$604,923.00
Salesroom gross in 1963	$527,446.00
Increase	$ 77,477.00

   Increase was 14.7%. Our total increase was 7.6%; Salesroom sales at this rate of increase would have been $37,477.00 less than it actually was.

5. Federal Reserve Bank of Boston reports Maine's lodging and tourist figures in 1964 generally *below* 1963, partly because of World's Fair, but mostly due to adverse weather.

6. Salesroom was advertised in "Recreation Travel Guide" in 1964. Not in 1963. Of doubtful significance.

Appendix A

BLUE MOUNTAIN RESORTS LIMITED

In July 1975, Mr. George Weider, president of Blue Mountain Resorts Limited was preparing to meet with his Board of Directors and present plans for the future direction of the company.

Various projects were being considered in an effort to provide maximum utilization of the resort area. The construction of additional hotel accommodations, another triple chairlift, other recreational facilities, real estate development for chalets and condominiums and the development of convention facilities were among the possibilities that could be considered.

Management differed on the relative value of some of the projects but recognized that the time had come for a careful analysis to determine priorities for the planned undertakings. There were two projects, the added hotel accommodations and new triple chairlift, that appeared to have the higher degree of priority but each would require an investment of such magnitude that the company could only undertake one or the other, not both, within the time horizon currently being considered by Mr. George Weider. Gross revenues of the company had risen from just under half a million dollars in 1969 to about $1.2 million dollars in 1974 with net profit of $41,000 and $56,000 respectively.

BACKGROUND

Blue Mountain came into being as a ski resort in 1938 when a small group of club oriented, relatively wealthy ski enthusiasts from Toronto, Ontario founded the Toronto and Collingwood Ski Clubs. In 1941, Mr. Jozo Weider became the manager of the Toronto Ski Club and for the next 30 years directly controlled the growth and development of the whole Blue Mountain region.

Mr. Jozo Weider had left his job of managing a ski resort in Czechoslovakia in 1939 to come to Canada. While teaching skiing in Quebec, he heard about the Collingwood region and subsequently moved there, convinced that Blue Mountain had great potential for skiing. It was within easy driving distance of metropolitan Toronto, Ontario (95 miles) plus the fact that it had the second highest vertical drop (700 feet) in the region.

The difficulty of securing funds for the installation of lifts and the purchase of land hampered the growth of Blue Mountain in its early years. However, Mr. Weider did eventually manage to acquire 200 acres on the North area of the region and later obtained an additional 400 acres to the south. Most people thought the land was worthless. It was in fact totally inadequate for farming and consequently few people could conceive of it as a potential ski market.

Mr. Weider always had an interest in the arts and in keeping with his philosophy that ski resort operators had to diversify and make use of their hills and facilities the year round, he brought national ballet companies to Blue Mountain in the early years. To provide suitable facilities for them, he built a stage on the hill and a concert shell at the base. However, it was stated later that the market was apparently not ready for this class of performance, the projects weren't planned too carefully, the resort was insufficiently well known and "they were a failure."

The crafts were also an interest of Mr. Weider and he began a ceramic school with the assistance of a mold maker who had been a dishwasher in the kitchen clubhouses. Courses in the arts and crafts were given in the basement of one of the old buildings. At the same time, Mr. Weider broadened his own knowledge by reading books on the subjects and built the pottery operation into a major business — Blue Mountain Pottery Limited. The local availability of a durable flexible clay suitable for the pottery was, of course, an important ingredient to the success of the business. But pottery was in fact only a means to an end in that the sale of the pottery business in 1967 enabled Mr. Weider to devote his full energies and enthusiasm to the ski business.

OPERATIONS

Only in the decade since 1964 had skiing in the Collingwood region attained the mass marketing level requiring extensive investment in tows, snow making equipment and accommodations.

The first uphill improvement from the tow rope was a Poma lift, installed at the North area in 1956. Between 1968 and 1971, three $150,000 chairlifts were installed and the Base Lodge constructed at a cost of $200,000.

Snowmaking facilities became a necessity in order to provide the maximum utilization of the lifts day in and day out throughout the skiing season. Accordingly, snowmaking began in the mid-1960's and the system, completed in 1973 at a cost of approximately $600,000, represented the company's largest single investment. The snowmaking system was further expanded in the summer of 1975 with the aid of a $515,000 Ontario Development Corporation loan, part of which was used for a new triple chairlift. This chairlift was in operation during the winter of 1974-1975 and was capable of carrying 1,800 skiers per hour.

In mid-year 1975, there was a total of sixteen uphill facilities — six chairlifts, two T-bars, four Pomas, and four rope tows (*Exhibit 1*). Nearly ten miles of steel pipe were buried beneath the frost line to carry water from the twenty-five million gallon lake feeding twelve snow guns, capable of firing over one hundred gallons of water per minute. The system had the capacity to cover one hundred and twenty acres, sixty percent of all trails, with one foot of snow in less than a week or one acre with one foot of snow every two hours. The 20 trails were groomed by thirty pieces of equipment, including six $20,000 tracked Sno-cats.

Five restaurants were located on the property — the Base Lodge, the Hohenblick Cafe on top of the mountain, the Ski Barn, the Inn and the Toronto Ski Club — with a total seating capacity of over 1,000 people. The first four restaurants were operated through an arrangement with an outside caterer, while the Toronto Ski Club conducted its own food operations. The Blue Mountain Inn with 20 units and located at the foot of the mountain registered over 90 percent occupancy in the summertime. It featured an indoor heated pool, color T.V., licensed dining room and four tennis courts.

The Blue Mountain complex required approximately one hundred and fifty people in the winter excluding the fifty ski instructors and sixty volunteer ski patrollers who were employed in the Ernie McCulloch Ski School. The Blue Mountain people were engaged on the lifts, in grooming the hills, operating the snowmaking equipment, in the restaurants and the inn, in the nursery, the ski shop, in administation and for general maintenance and construction. All the repairs and installation of equipment were handled by Blue Mountain's own full time staff. Included among the workers were two welders, two carpenters and two grooming operators who served as bulldozer operators in the summer.

MARKETING

The slopes at Blue Mountain, like other facilities and accommodations, tended to be under-utilized during weekdays but crowded on weekends causing queues at the chairlift loading points.

The installation of a triple chairlift, for the 1974-1975 season, had done much to alleviate the waiting. On busy weekends the wait was currently seldom more than 15 minutes. The resort, however, still had the reputation of "being crowded."

Management now basically felt that in the winter they needed a little more cooperation from the weatherman and more midweek business. The snowmaking, begun in the 1960's, had gone a long way towards working with the weatherman. According to Mr. Gordon Canning, Vice President and General Manager, snowmaking probably added $200,000 in revenue for the 1974-1975 season. With regard to the midweek business, a trend had begun to become apparent with a greater use of facilities. "The midweek business has gone really well and we are concentrating on it," Mr. Canning reported. Blue Mountain served seven segments of the ski market, identified below in order of magnitude of revenue production in 1975.

Table 1
Relative Importance of Market Segments

Segment	Percent
Weekend Individuals	41
Season Pass Holders	18
Midweek Individuals	16
Special Seasonal Markets	15
Weekend Groups	6
Midweek Groups	3
Ski Week Packages	1
	100

WEEKEND INDIVIDUALS

Market studies showed that the skiers in this largest segment (41 percent) tended to be young, relatively affluent, single individuals and young couples, without families, under 35 years of age. Approximately 20 percent of these could be beginners or novices at any one time. A large number of the weekend individual skiers were said to be professional personnel or holding management level positions. To these skiers, services were considered to be as important as the hills. This meant therefore, continued pressure on Blue Mountain Management for more and better facilities, rental equipment and entertainment.

An increased demand was being experienced for rentals and lessons which in turn reflected a further need for more beginner facilities and services.

A major problem encountered with this and other segments of the market was related to snow reports. If there happened to be little or no snow in the southern part of the Province and the United States border points, the assumption was frequently made that there was no snow at Blue Mountain. It was crucial therefore, to dispense up-to-the-minute information on the real ski conditions. This information also had to reach into the United States since "much of the business comes from Ohio, Michigan, Illinois and Indiana. They are starting on three-day weekends," stated Mr. Canning. (*Exhibit 2*) It was equally important to provide "first class" facilities all around such as for food, washrooms, bars, lift operations and entertainment.

Management considered that its immediate objectives for this weekend market segment were to present the image of a "first class" resort, modern, swinging, to get the most accurate information to the skiing public and to improve the on-site facilities. A total of 75,600 weekend tickets were sold in 1970, dropping down to 36,500 in 1973 and rising to 72,300 in 1975. (*Exhibit 3*) A weekend ticket costs $8.00 per day in 1974-1975 and was expected to rise to $9.00 for the 1975-1976 season (*Exhibit 4*).

SEASON PASS HOLDERS

This second largest market segment (18 percent) represented essentially the "hard core" of family skiers who committed from $300 to $500 annually before the season started. Although the family aspect of the season pass represented over 70 percent of the total season pass tickets sold, a significant growth was experienced in the sale of the single season passes as the figures in Table 2 indicate.

The uphill capacity of Blue Mountain had been determined as 6,000 and according to an agreement with the Toronto Ski Club, whose members were all season pass holders, not to pre-sell more than one-third of the capacity, the limit for season passes would be 2,000.

While management fully recognized the importance of the weekend individuals, the season pass holder, as primarily the family skier, had to be regarded as the ambassador for the resort. To the extent that the resort wished to maintain this clientele, the feeling of a special privilege class ought to accrue to this segment, was the view expressed in the market study.

Table 2
Season Ticket Sales

	1975	1974	1973	1972	1971	1970
Family Number	1,054	1,097	737	751	746	621
Single Number	581	420	213	267	277	260
Total	1,635	1,517	950	1,018	1,023	881
Average Season Ticket Per Day, 20 Skiing Days	$6.07	6.12	5.27	4.42	4.26	3.95
Average Season Ticket Price	$121.40	122.40	105.37	88.41	85.11	79.00

MIDWEEK INDIVIDUALS

"The midweek market is very important. It has done really well. We are concentrating on it and are going to take advantage of it through marketing. We have looked at our weekends and it is going to be very difficult to squeeze anything more out of the weekends," commented Mr. Canning.

Although ranked third in terms of lift revenue, this category showed an 85 percent increase for the 1975 season compared with 1974 (*Exhibit 5*).

Market studies showed that a large proportion, probably 60 percent, of the midweek individual skiers were professional people and university students. " 'Goof-off' students appeared to have comprised the largest proportion of these skiers, primarily from Ontario points because 90% of the visits were of the single day variety."

Since these skiers were "one-day" trippers, the greatest single attraction was the snow conditions. Hence the importance of both the snowmaking equipment and also the accurate radio reporting in the major centers of population in southern Ontario mentioned previously.

It has been determined that many of these individuals listened to the rock stations, primarily CHUM-FM and CFTR-AM, so that snow conditions and other promotional information could be made available through these outlets.

Management held hopes that this market segment would continue to grow and the opportunities seen for midweek skiers were to capitalize on midweek holidays for high school students and university students with flexible schedules. The 'mini-ski-week,' whereby individuals skiing for three consecutive days get one dollar per day reduction on their lift tickets, was introduced in 1974 and had been well received by this market (*Exhibit 4*).

SPECIAL SEASONAL MARKETS

These markets have traditionally been the pre-season period. (i.e., early December), Christmas and the spring break in the Ontario school system in mid-March.

Pre-season skiing activities have been subject to the availability of snow and therefore could not be depended upon. With added snowmaking facilities an earlier start would be feasible with a corresponding added degree of dependability.

Special packages and groups sales in these three special market categories were envisaged as potential incentives to increasing the volume in forthcoming seasons.

Daily snow reports and saturation radio could be embarked upon if snow conditions warranted.

WEEKEND GROUPS

Group activities in Ontario centered on the various types of the numerous ski clubs, i.e., vagabond, university, high school or service clubs. Although the existence of these clubs was well known, management expressed the view that a problem existed with getting ski clubs to come to Blue Mountain more frequently than once a season which studies showed was generally the case. Opportunities were believed to be available for increasing revenue from this segment of the market by improving the frequency of visits by the exisiting groups and contacting new ones.

Nearby United States areas were heavily populated and had numerous ski clubs, but by the same token, the distance to Blue Mountain was great. Reaching these widespread groups in an efficient manner presented a major difficulty.

The organization of sales agents and travel agents with appropriate commission structure, generally 5 percent to 10 percent, was considered to be a means of reaching this market, together with promotional material.

Groups of 20 or more individuals were entitled to a 10 percent reduction in the price of lift tickets.

MIDWEEK GROUPS

Because of the one day feature, the skiers in this market segment were mainly from elementary and high schools, colleges and universities.

Among the major concerns encountered with servicing this group was the distance to Blue Mountain compared with competitive areas such as Barrie, Ontario and Mansfield, Ontario between 50 to 60 miles from Toronto (*Exhibit 2*). Other difficulties were in setting up a sales organization to reach this widespread market on an individual basis as well as providing adequate compensation for so doing while at the same time keeping the cost of the trip below $10.

Management believed this market could be increased with closer attention being paid to it by appointed sales agents concentrating on the schools, ski clubs and social clubs. For example, in Toronto, there was an increase in 1975-1976 to 12 professional days compared with 9 in previous years. Mr. Canning reported that "we have had 1200 students from North York by bus on February 14th and at least another 1200 who came up on their own on a Friday. That meant 2400 to 2500 from one schoolboard." Efforts had been made also to get students to Blue Mountain for educational visits through their physical education departments.

SKI WEEK PACKAGES

The principal market for this smallest lift revenue producing segment was thought to be the United States border cities.

One significant reason for this relatively small size was believed to be that if the experienced skier had a ski week planned he would prefer to go to the resorts in the Province of Quebec, the western regions of Canada or the United States or even to Europe.

The lack of promotional effort in the past directed to this market may have been a major factor contributing to the status of this market segment.

Summing up the marketing aspects of Blue Mountain ski operations, Mr. Canning said: "We know that we have rainouts and we know that we have days that are just not good for skiing, windy and cold, and we can advertise all we want but we know we just aren't going to get those 6,000 skiers here. So we dropped back our advertising budget to about $50,000 this year (1975) compared with nearly $80,000 in 1974." (*Exhibit 6*)

"Another opportunity for us is pre-Christmas, if the snow comes. Last year it didn't come but we still had $9,000 revenue through to January 1, 1975. If it does come though, we want to be there with some kind of promotion. We will begin making snow at the earliest opportunity, probably in November. We have to find a way to be ready in December. That is our number two opportunity."

"Our number one opportunity is our midweek. As for weekends, we have just got to try and maintain what we have got. It is better for us if we can lengthen the season at the beginning rather than at the end because people's interest begins to wane about the end of March."

"The 'over-crowded' image is indelibly imprinted on people's minds and we are trying to get over that by putting up a new cafeteria and improving the base facilities. We will take every opportunity we get to make them feel it is not so crowded. We have always tried to sell ski weeks but we don't have a hotel that holds 300 people which would justify having a band every night and a recreational director as some resorts do like Grey Rocks, in the Province of Quebec. Then you could put together a complete package that makes the ski school spin.

"Snow also does not stay as long naturally here as in some areas but we believe that with the snowmaking plant we now have, except for one or two weeks, they will be able to say that a good holiday is available at Blue Mountain. People are taking long weekends and that is something we are going to exploit. Accommodation is not really the problem, the right package is. The short midweek package and the long weekends will help us through. Accommodations built up one midweek lift revenue and we have already seen how it has come along.

"Our American market will continue to grow weekend and midweek. We have never spent very much money down there but we know the market is there. It would particularly help our midweek revenue. The Americans have a five to seven hour drive which means that they would be more likely to take three or four days off to come midweek. People do have the time off, if a person really wants to get away even with his family."

An integral facet of the ski marketing program was the Ernie McCullough Ski School. Invited by the late Jozo Weider to provide ski instruction, McCullough was a renowned Canadian skier, coach and instructor. His ski school in turn employed approximately 50 full-time instructors during the winter season. Originally called the Blue Mountain Ski School the name was changed in 1969 to its present format in order to capitalize on his name.

COMPETITIVE FACILITIES

Blue Mountain was the biggest resort in terms of ski facilities in the Central Ontario ski region. Its appeal was directed more to single individual skiers rather than to families and more so than any other resort in the area. "We don't even push for families." Accordingly, skiing at Blue Mountain was geared 65 percent to intermediate, 25 percent to beginners and 10 percent to expert skiers. It did face competition for skier patronage from other resorts.

The Talisman Ski Resort and Georgian Peaks Resort were approximately the same distance from the southern Ontario market. Facilities like Mansfield Skiways, Medonte Mountain, Moonstone Ski Resort, Snow Valley Resort, Horseshoe Valley, Hockley Hills were all situated close to Barrie, Ontario or at comparable distances from Toronto, Ontario. These latter areas could be reached by car from Toronto in approximately one hour while it took nearly two hours to drive to the Blue Mountain region.

The Talisman Ski Resort, 97 miles northeast of Toronto at Kimberley, Ontario offered three chairlifts, one T-bar, and one rope tow, a 600 foot vertical rise, daily fees of $5-$8 and a Resort Hotel and Beaver Lodge with dining-dancing and licensed lounge at the hill.

Georgian Peaks Resort located two miles west of Blue Mountain and 92 miles north of Toronto at Thornbury, Ontario, had the same lift facilities as the Talisman, a vertical rise of 820 feet and daily fees of $4-$8. The accommodation listed a day lodge with cafeteria and bar at the hill, dancing every Saturday evening and ski weeks in conjunction with a motel eight miles away. Motel and hotel accommodation was located in nearby Collingwood or Meaford and dormitory facilities were available for groups of 20 or more.

A press release in the summer of 1975 stated that Georgian Peaks was up for sale having suffered losses of about $180,000 in 1974-1975, $100,000 in 1973-1974 and $200,000 in the 1972-1973 season.

The ski facilities offered by the resorts to the south had slopes somewhat less, ranging from about 330 feet to 400 feet vertical drop, with daily rates varying from $5-$8 and most had snowmaking equipment. Their greatest advantage however, lay in their proximity to the southern Ontario populace, a fact well known and recognized by the management of Blue Mountain.

AFFILIATED ACTIVITIES

Greater utilization of the extensive and expensive facilities once the skiing season was over had presented serious problems for the management of Blue Mountain for many years. Every effort had been made to use as many as possible of the employees in the summer months to upgrade the facilities, e.g., craftsmen made all the chairs for the triple lift as well as the lift terminals, machinery and other equipment was overhauled, painted, repaired and general maintenance work undertaken. However, these activities did little to maximize the utilization of the physical plant. It was to this end and in keeping with the philosophy expressed earlier by the late Mr. Weider that saw the start of the summer music and also the real estate programs as an integral part of the resort area development.

Blue Mountain Summer School of the Arts

This school was founded in 1972 and was operated in conjunction with Georgian College in Barrie, Ontario. Enrollment in the summer of 1974 was 300 with participation in some 20 courses ranging from batik and ceramics, yoga and horsemanship to tennis and winemaking. The courses ran through June, July and August with fees from $10-45 per course.

Blue Mountain Summer School of Music and Dance

Georgian College, Barrie, Ontario and George Brown College, Toronto, Ontario participated in the opening of this school in 1974. Programs included orchestral and keyboard, band, vocal and music theatre, guitar and dance. Two hundred students enrolled in the period July 6 to August 16, 1975. Tuition with room and board ranged from $135-$160 per week.

Blue Mountain Summer School of Contemporary Music

Oriented towards a music festival, the program started in the summer of 1974, attracting 125 students ranging in ages from 11 to 65 years. The schedule for the 10 days,

June 22 to July 2, 1975, was designed to present most aspects of contemporary music — rock and roll, jazz and folk. Tuition with room and board cost $225 per student.

Blue Mountain Summer Chairlift

Opened initially in the summer of 1974 as a further means of utilizing facilities that would otherwise be idle in the summer, the chairlift carried 18,000 people at a rate of $1.50 for adults and $1.00 for children. Snacks were available at the top from the Skyline Cafe, known as the Hohenblick Cafe during the winter months.

Blue Mountain Central Reservation Service

This service connected 21 hotels and lodges in that region providing accommodation reservations to a total of 600 rooms. Deluxe hotel to dormitory facilities were available by telephone or writing to the central service.

Craigleith Development Limited

Over 400 acres of developmental land had been acquired by this company, owned by the Weider family interests. Lot sales had begun in 1969 at around $4,000 and by 1975 the latest sales were in the neighborhood of $20,000 each. The company expected to build 38 condominiums, to sell some of them, rent others and rent still others when the owners went away. By renting some of the accommodation, problems would be solved without requiring a large capital investment. There was a shopping centre and a restaurant nearby that would be expanded by Craigleith until it covered a 10-acre site.

PERSONNEL

Following the death of Mr. Jozo Weider in October 1971, his son George Weider became chairman of the Board of Directors and president of Blue Mountain Resorts Limited at the age of 31 (*Exhibit 6*). With planning one of his major responsibilities, nearly $1.5 million had been invested in plant and facilities in the expansion program undertaken within the past four years. Holding a Doctor of Philosophy degree, Mr. Weider was also a professor at an Ontario university.

Mr. Gordon Canning, (32), executive vice president and general manager engineered much of the expansion and development that had taken place since 1971. He obtained a Bachelor of Science degree from Queen's University, a Master's degree in Mathematics from the University of Waterloo and a Master of Business Administration from York University. He had worked previously with Imperial Oil Limited in the computer services department and in 1970 with the wholesale distributor of cross-country skis during which time his association began with Mr. Weider and Blue Mountain Resorts Limited. Mr. Canning was a brother-in-law of George Weider.

The other members of the Board of Directors were:

Dr. D. McGillivary   A physician and brother-in-law of Mr. George Weider.

Mr. J. W. Hetherington	President, Venturecan Limited, a marketing firm.
Mr. C. Trott	Business, Collingwood, Ontario.
Mr. W. Waters	Business, Collingwood, Ontario.

FINANCE

With the assistance of a number of friends, including the late Senator Peter Campbell, who became a partner, Mr. Jozo Weider gradually obtained control over the ski operation and built up Blue Mountain Resorts Limited. The sale in 1967 of Blue Mountain Pottery Limited provided much needed financial resources. These enabled Mr. Weider to concentrate on developing the ski facilities which had been his principal interest for a long time. Funds from the pottery business also enabled Mr. Weider to purchase the shares of the partnership held by Senator Campbell and to acquire 200 acres of land at the foot of the mountain. By 1975 the Weider family held 75 percent of the shares of Blue Mountain Resorts Limited, 8 percent were held by the Toronto Ski Club with the remaining 17 percent held by individuals, some of whom were employees of the company.

Since 1965 skiing capacity had tripled and revenues grown from $445,000 in 1969 to $1,137,000 at fiscal year end in October 1974 (Exhibits 7 to 11 contain the financial data.). Nearly 70 percent of the revenue in that year came from lift and season tickets compared with about 90 percent in 1969. This change reflected the broadened base of the operations that management had been planning in order to lessen its dependence on any one function. Further evidence of broadening activity can be seen by an examination of lift ticket sales in terms of revenue and numbers sold. In 1970 weekend and weekday tickets accounted for 61 percent and 10 percent respectively of tickets sold compared with 40 percent and 16 percent respectively by 1975 (Exhibits 3 and 5).

The bane of most ski resorts had always been the concentration of skiers on weekends, with lifts and accommodation relatively quiet during the week. The trend observed in the analysis of figures showed a greater proportion of midweek activity and was the basis of the comment by Mr. Gordon Canning that midweek business was "doing well now; we are concentrating on it and we know more about it."

Ski rates were competitive with surrounding locations at $8 per day for weekends and $6 per day for midweeks during the 1974-1975 season. They were expected to increase to $9 and $7 per day respectively for the 1975-1976 winter skiing. Reduced rates were available for half day skiing. The introduction in the 1973-1974 season of the mini-ski week where for three consecutive days midweek tickets were reduced one dollar per day proved to have been popular and showed signs of growing. Season ticket sales contributed nearly 9 percent of the lift revenues in 1970, compared with about 18 percent in 1975, reaching a peak at 24 percent during the 1974 season. There had been a steady growth in the actual number of these tickets sold in the past three years from 950 to 1,635 in the past season, mainly in terms of single tickets rather than for family usage.

While total revenues for the fiscal years 1969 to 1974 rose two and a half times, operating costs rose approximately three-fold (Exhibit 8). "Construction costs are heavy and the season is relatively short but did have a good year last year (1975) mostly because of snowmaking," reported Mr. Canning.

Over one million dollars had been spent for a snowmaking system, the first part of which was completed in 1973 and expanded further for the 1974-1975 season. Lift revenues had grown substantially on a comparable six month basis (Exhibit 11) and so had the sales of beverages, nearly doubling from $33,900 in 1974 to $63,000 in 1975.

Since 1973, the music school had provided a contribution to overhead through the rental of buildings, the food operations and accommodation facilities in the summer months. Mr. Canning stated, "We get some income from the rental of our properties and we rent to George Brown College which finances the summer school. We run the accommodation and food and should have $5,000 out of our share plus $8,000 rental fee for the use of our facilities as studios. That makes $13,000 and we will have spent $3,000 making the facilities suitable. This doesn't leave us very much but it could grow."

In addition to the summer school operations, the company had an arrangement with a food organization to manage and operate its four restaurants and also an arrangement with the Ernie McCullough Ski School. (See *Exhibit 12* for a description of summer activities in the Blue Mountain area)

THE FUTURE

Over the past five years in particular, a number of steps had been taken by management in the development of Blue Mountain Resorts. The Directors, however, held different opinions about the desirability of proceeding towards one or another of the alternatives that were available, recognizing that the financial resources of the company precluded their undertaking more than one major commitment at a time, certainly within the immediate future.

Mr. George Weider, president, and Mr. Gordon Canning summed up their views about the future operations of the company and the alternatives they had to deal with in the statements that follow:

> We are considering other means of increasing revenue and profits without necessarily undergoing a major feat of expansion. For instance, the midweek business had been increasing and this is a major factor of our marketing strategy. We are exploring other means in line with the resort's off-season activities.

> We have calculated the return on investment for a new cafeteria that we are just installing right now at a cost of $300,000. We need this in terms of sport facilities for the ski traffic. So if we double our capacity there is a great danger of over dependence on the one sport and we could face a diminishing return on our investment.

We haven't made the decision whether we should build another triple chairlift—we have already chosen the location—and add to the snowmaking or build a hotel and go into a twelve month operation. The hotel would probably do quite well in the winter time especially with the support facilities we have, the snowmaking especially, and the growth of the area. More people would come in midweek so there would be more fun. We would have a bar here and it would probably do quite well. Throughout the week, we would have a house band. Now that's the winter situation.

The next question is the summer. It is really easy to say 'why don't you guys do something in the summer.' So many people have said this to us in the past. It is also easy to say we should have the music school but maybe we should not have it. Maybe we should have had something else.

We do see a lot of opportunities. We have created traffic around here now through the music school and it is generating a little bit of income for us. It is making a little contribution and not really draining our resources.

The music school might be regarded as the basis from which a festival program could be developed similar to Stratford, Ontario. We see the Stratford and Kitchener hotels full as a result of the business going on at Stratford. If we could fill up all the hotels in Collingwood and hold people overnight, then we would benefit by this whole thing. Our hotel would be filled now (July) and we would be able to say that we had a strong second season which we don't have now.

So we have the winter which is reasonably solid for a hotel operation and summer which is coming along because we have created a business and something to hold people over with. Now we have to go into the other seasons with convention or conference business. We are in a good location for it but we would be taking on a risk.

We would build a large hotel with an investment of about $500,000. This is something that would have to be sold. The new triple chairlift has already paid for itself. If we install another chairlift we know we would get a return on our investment, although we could get a poor winter at anytime. But a good convention hotel will keep going, weather or not. But we would be going into a field that we know less well than running a chairlift. We know how to install chairlifts and how to run them. When we get into the hotel operation we are going to need a brand new sales effort and different thinking.

For example, Talisman Ski Resort at first would not rent out to conventions in the wintertime but then they got hit by bad winters and said, "Why not get in on a sure thing — let's take a convention if someone wants to come." You take a chance on not getting lift revenue. You get less lift revenue from a convention goer than you would from a person coming for a ski week because the latter is here to ski. But we would decide on how we could operate that when it happens. Probably if we added 30 or 40 rooms it would be at least $500,000 in added investment. We could make a go of it in conventions.

Take the music school. If George Brown stays with us we will succeed in establishing our festival. That will require added accommodation. In the convention business, we are getting into a field we know less well. This is the decision we have to make.

ASSIGNMENT QUESTIONS

1. What, if anything, strikes you as interesting about the way Blue Mountain was created and developed as an entrepreneurial venture? What can we learn from this experience?

2. What is the cost structure of this business (fixed versus variable)?

3. What markets should Blue Mountain Resorts attempt to reach? With what, products or services?

4. Evaluate in detail the two priority projects:

   a. added hotel accommodations
   b. a new triple chair lift

5. Which do you recommend? Why?

Exhibit 1

Ski Facilities

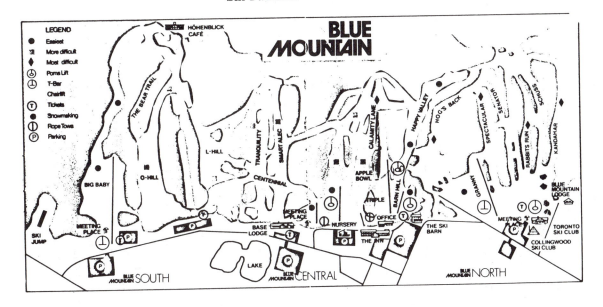

Exhibit 2

Geographic Location and Distances

Distance (by car) from:

Toronto	2 hours				
Buffalo	4 hours	Chicago	10 hours	Cleveland	7 hours
Detroit	5 hours	Rochester	5 hours	Toledo	6 hours

Exhibit 3
Blue Mountain Resorts Limited
Comparative Statement of Tickets Sold
16 Months Period Ending April 30th

	Number Sold					
	1975	1974	1973	1972	1971	1970
Weekend						
Day ticket	59,790	41,351	31,336	54,412	62,241	69,173
Half day	8,708	6,589	3,675	—	—	—
Red lift	3,844	3,188	1,536	2,400	4,397	6,501
Total weekend	72,342	51,128	36,547	56,812	66,638	75,674
Weekday						
Day ticket	35,225	20,994	19,748	19,007	19,427	15,129
Half day	6,785	4,217	2,291	1,385	1,123	823
Red lift	1,177	822	—	—	—	—
Rope tow	3,244	2,625	2,504	3,475	4,507	3,755
Single rides	—	—	—	10,140	13,240	11,301
Total weekday	46,431	28,658	24,543	34,007	38,297	31,008
Weekly						
Groups	468	379	242	490	737	472
Mini-Ski weeks	21,842	16,062	8,410	15,008	11,857	9,677
	2,259	978	—	—	—	—
Total tickets sold	143,342	97,205	69,742	106,317	117,529	116,831
Members	7,144	8,907	9,247	15,606	13,724	12,131
Non-members	136,198	88,298	60,495	90,711	103,805	104,700

Exhibit 4(A)

Ski Rates for 1974-75 Seasons

RATES FOR 1974-1975 SEASONS

LIFTS

Weekends & SCHOOL HOLIDAYS

All Lifts.	$ 8.00
Red Lifts.	$ 6.00
Rope Tow (any day).	$ 2.00
All Lifts Afternoon, after 1:30 p.m.	$ 5.00

Regular Weekdays

All Lifts, 3 or more operating.	$ 6.00
Red Lifts.	$ 4.00
All Lifts Afternoon, after 1:30 p.m.	$ 4.00
All Lifts Monday to Friday.	$25.00

Mini Ski Week

Any three or more consecutive days, $1.00 off regular rate per day. e.g. Monday, Tuesday, Wednesday & Thursday. . . . $20.00

INSTRUCTION

Group Lessons (1 hour).	$ 4.00
Group Lessons (2 hours).	$ 6.00
Children 12 and under (1 hour).	$ 3.00
Book of four 1 hour lessons.	$12.00
Private Lesson (1 hour).	$10.00
with two people. . . . . each	$ 7.50
with three people. . . . . each	$ 6.00
with Assistant Director.	$12.00
with Director.	$24.00
Ski Week (12 hours).	$25.00

Cross Country

Group Lesson (1 hour) minimum of 5 people.	$ 4.00
Group Lesson (2 hours) minimum of 5 people.	$ 6.00

RENTALS

Skis, Boots & Poles

Per day.	$ 7.00
Afternoon, after 1:00 p.m.	$ 3.50
Per Week (5 days).	$24.50
Cross Country per day.	$ 5.50
Cross Country Afternoon, after 1:00 p.m.	$ 3.50

N.B. Rental rates include breakage insurance but do not include 7% Provincial Sales Tax.

NURSERY

Full Day.	$ 4.00
Half Day.	$ 2.00

Only trained children 2 years and over accepted.
Open 9:00 a.m. to 12:00 noon and 1:00 p.m. to 4:30 p.m.

WEEKDAY SEASON PASS

Monday to Friday including Christmas & Spring Break. . . . $80.00

For information call 705-445-0231

ACCOMMODATION

BLUE MOUNTAIN INN - Winter

CAA & AAA approved, heated pool, 2 double beds, 4 piece bath and balcony in each unit. Licensed dining room.

WEEKENDS, CHRISTMAS & SPRING BREAK - PER DAY

Breakfast, Dinner & Lodging

Single.	$ 26.00
Two per room. . . . . each	$ 22.00
Three per room. each	$ 18.00
Four per room. . . . . each	$ 15.00
Children two years and under.	Free

SPECIAL MINI SKI WEEK PACKAGE - January 1st to 5th

Includes 4 nights accommodation, all meals, all lifts and 8 hours of lessons

Single.	$126.00
Two per room. . . . . each	$116.40
Three per room. each	$108.20
Four per room. . . . . each	$106.00
Children 12 years and under when sharing room with parent. . . . . each	$ 86.00

MINI SKI WEEKS

Mini Ski Weeks are available at several local motels throughout the 1974-1975 season (except Christmas). These packages include accommodation, lifts and breakfast. More information on request.

Accommodation rates do not include 7% Accommodation Tax or 10% Food Tax on dinners.

ALL RATES SUBJECT TO CHANGE WITHOUT NOTICE

SKI WEEKS:

		DECEMBER 1974				
SUN	MON	TUE	WED	THU	FRI	SAT
1	2	3	4	5	6	7
A 8	9	10	11	12	13	14
B 15	16	17	18	19	20	21
22	23	24	25	26	27	28
29	30	31				

		JANUARY 1975				
SUN	MON	TUE	WED	THU	FRI	SAT
			1	2	3	4
C 5	6	7	8	9	10	11
D 12	13	14	15	16	17	18
E 19	20	21	22	23	24	25
F 26	27	28	29	30	31	

		FEBRUARY 1975				
SUN	MON	TUE	WED	THU	FRI	SAT
						1
G 2	3	4	5	6	7	8
H 9	10	11	12	13	14	15
I 16	17	18	19	20	21	22
J 23	24	25	26	27	28	

		MARCH 1975				
SUN	MON	TUE	WED	THU	FRI	SAT
						1
K 2	3	4	5	6	7	8
L 9	10	11	12	13	14	15
	16	17	18	19	20	21	22
M 23/ 24/		25	26	27	28	29
N 30	31					

Exhibit 4(B)

Ski Rates for 1974-75 Seasons

SKI WEEK PACKAGES - Not available Christmas or Spring Break

#1 Includes 5 nights accommodation, all meals, all lifts and 12 hours of lessons. Awards night banquet, gluhwein and movie nights.

Single	$157.50
Two per room	each $147.50
Three per room	each $137.50
Four per room	each $132.50
Children 12 years and under when sharing room with parents	each $112.50

#2 Includes 5 nights accommodation, all meals, all lifts. Awards night banquet, gluhwein and movie nights.

Single	$135.00
Two per room	each $125.00
Three per room	each $115.00
Four per room	each $110.00
Children 12 years and under when sharing room with parents	each $ 90.00

#3 Includes 5 nights accommodation, 5 breakfasts, 1 dinner all lifts and 12 hours of lessons. Awards night banquet, gluhwein movie nights.

Single	$123.50
Two per room	each $113.50
Three per room	each $103.50
Four per room	each $ 98.50
Children 12 years and under when sharing room with parents	each $ 90.50

#4 Includes 5 nights accommodation, 5 breakfasts, 1 dinner, all lifts. Awards night banquet, gluhwein and movie nights.

Single	$101.00
Two per room	each $ 91.00
Three per room	each $ 81.00
Four per room	each $ 76.00
Children 12 years and under when sharing room with parents	each $ 68.30

N.B. Ski Weeks begin with dinner on Sunday evening between 6:00 and 8:00 p.m., check in time is 2:00 p.m. Ski Weeks end Friday after lunch, check out time 12:00 noon.

Accommodation rates do not include 7% Accommodation Tax or 10% Food Tax on dinners.

ALL RATES ARE SUBJECT TO CHANGE WITHOUT NOTICE

GROUP RATES FOR 1974-1975 SEASON

Blue Mountain offers special group lift, lesson and rental rates provided that:

(a) There are 20 or more in the group.
(b) You let us know in advance, in writing, the number of lift tickets, rentals and lessons required and when you will be here. In cases where rentals are required a list of height, weight, street shoe size, sex, age and name must be received by our office at least 10 days prior to the trip.
(c) One person comes in to the Administration Office to purchase all the tickets at once. Charges will not be accepted.

REGULAR GROUPS WEEKDAYS (Not School Holidays)

	Group Rate	Regular Rate
Lift	$5.00	$6.00
Alpine 1 hr. lesson (minimum 5 people)	$2.00	$4.00
Alpine 2 hr. lesson (minimum 5 people)	$3.00	$6.00
C.C. 1 hr. lesson (minimum 5 people)	$2.00	$4.00
C.C. 2 hr. lesson (minimum 5 people)	$3.00	$6.00
Alpine Rental (complete set)	$5.00	$7.00
C.C. Rental (complete set)	$4.00	$5.50

STUDENT GROUPS WEEKDAYS (Not School Holidays)

	Group Rate	Regular Rate
Lift	$3.50	$6.00
Alpine 1 hr. lesson (minimum 5 people)	$2.00	$4.00
Alpine 2 hr. lesson (minimum 5 people)	$3.00	$6.00
C.C. 1 hr. lesson (minimum 5 people)	$2.00	$4.00
C.C. 2 hr. lesson (minimum 5 people)	$3.00	$6.00
Alpine Rental (complete set)	$3.75	$7.00
C.C. Rental (complete set)	$3.00	$5.50

REGULAR OR STUDENT GROUPS WEEKENDS & HOLIDAYS

	Group Rate	Regular Rate
Lift	$7.20	$8.00

No reduction on rentals or lessons.

N.B. Above rental rates include .50c breakage insurance but do not include 7% Provincial Sales Tax.

GROUP ACCOMMODATION

The Blue Mountain Inn offers a maximum of 10 rooms to any one group on a weekend, based on at least four persons per room. The weekend package includes two nights accommodation, two breakfasts, lunch Saturday or Sunday, dinner Saturday evening and two days all lift tickets. The following per person rate is based on four or more persons per room. Weekend Package - $46.52 per person, tax included.

Exhibit 5
Blue Mountain Resorts Limited
Comparative Lift Ticket and Catering Sales Analysis
6 Month Periods Ending April 30th

	1975 $	1975 %	1974 $	1974 %	1973 $	1973 %	1972 $	1972 %	1971 $	1971 %	1970 $	1970 %
Weekend Tickets	$455,143	40.5	333,533	43.0	191,297	38.3	415,925	57.6	442,172	55.1	493,215	61.3
Weekend Groups	67,621	6.0	35,871	4.7	16,514	3.3	36,985	5.1	37,973	4.7	35,211	4.4
Weekday Tickets	176,907	15.7	95,597	12.3	53,996	10.7	73,956	10.3	76,138	9.4	82,637	10.3
Weekday Groups	34,591	3.1	25,853	3.3	15,883	3.2	28,398	3.9	19,760	2.5	16,678	2.0
Ski Weeks — Inn guests	5,342	0.5	4,147	0.5	3,960	0.8	5,940	0.8	7,280	0.1	4,670	0.6
Ski Weeks — Outsiders	5,918	0.5	3,706	0.5	1,795	0.0	4,825	0.1	5,580	0.1	4,895	0.6
Season passes	198,500	17.6	189,605	24.4	104,230	20.9	90,006	12.6	87,064	10.8	69,602	8.7
Xmas holiday	83,030	7.4	66,002	8.5	105,068	21.0	48,500	6.7	91,128	11.4	77,829	9.7
Spring holiday	84,023	7.5	12,923	1.7	9,129	1.8	20,784	2.9	33,476	4.2	19,440	2.4
Ski scene	—	—	—	—	—	—	—	—	2,214	0.3	—	—
Mini-Ski Weeks	13,198	1.2	8,594	1.1	—	—	—	—	—	—	—	—
Total lift sales	$1,124,273	100.0	775,831	100.0	501,872	100.0	725,319	100.0	802,785	100.0	804,147	100.0
Overall average daily ticket sale	$ 6.33		5.94		5.53		5.64		5.70		5.90	
Average daily ticket sale, excluding season tickets	6.50		6.06		5.70		5.97		6.08		6.28	
Average daily season pass ticket	6.07		6.12		5.27		4.42		4.26		3.95	
Average daily weekday season ticket	5.63		4.00		4.01		—		—		—	
Total catering sales	330,581		221,272		106,350		156,287		149,514		N.A.	
Average food and beverage consumption per daily skier visit	1.85		1.69		1.17		1.21		0.94		N.A.	

Source: Company records

Exhibit 6

Organization Chart

1975

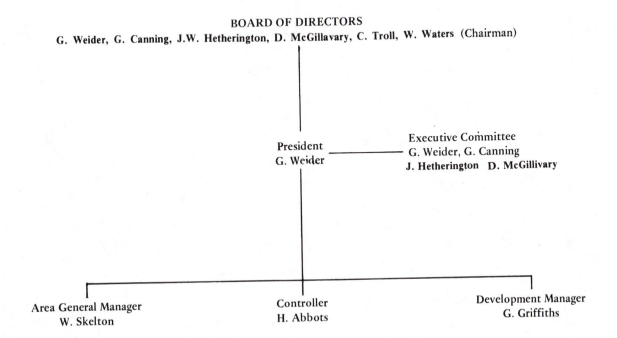

BOARD OF DIRECTORS
G. Weider, G. Canning, J.W. Hetherington, D. McGillavary, C. Troll, W. Waters (Chairman)

President
G. Weider

Executive Committee
G. Weider, G. Canning
J. Hetherington   D. McGillivary

Area General Manager
W. Skelton

Controller
H. Abbots

Development Manager
G. Griffiths

Affiliated Organizations

Ernie McCulloch Ski School
Blue Mountain Summer School of Music
Blue Mountain Summer School of the Arts
Blue Mountain Summer School of Music and Dance
Blue Mountain Summer School of Contemporary Music
Blue Mountain Central Reservation Service

Exhibit 7
Blue Mountain Resorts Limited
Balance Sheet
at October 31,

	1974	1973	1972	1971	1970	1969
Assets						
Current:						
Cash	0	9,397	1,930	9,403	10,962	1,039
Deposit receipts	10,179	0	0	0	0	0
Accounts receivable	11,603	8,660	63,262	52,924	36,108	20,692
Life Insurance proceeds receivable	0	0	0	200,000	0	0
Amount receivable from employees reshare purchase	0	0	0	941	0	0
Notes receivable	0	0	0	1,172	16,440	3,661
Income taxes receivable	32,290	54,200	0	0	0	0
Inventories, at cost which is not in excess of net realization value	32,138	18,225	14,938	15,754	13,942	0
Prepaid Expenses	14,404	12,854	5,041	5,291	2,256	5,862
Total Current	102,614	103,336	85,171	285,485	79,708	31,254
Investments, at cost:						
Mortgage receivable	2,200	2,700	9,200	10,200	0	0
Shares in golf club	6,375	6,375	6,375	0	0	0
Total Investments	8,575	9,075	15,575	10,200	0	0
Fixed, at cost:	2,761,257	2,423,709	1,950,017	1,508,709	1,320,585	1,119,128
Less, accumulated depreciation	928,335	808,120	695,644	601,137	518,111	439,493
Total Fixed	1,832,922	1,615,589	1,254,373	907,572	802,474	679,635
Other:						
Deferred financing expenses	0	0	0	0	1,232	2,463
Total Assets	1,944,111	1,728,000	1,355,119	1,203,257	883,414	713,352

Liabilities

Current:

	1974	1973	1972	1971	1970	1969
Bank overdraft	38,087	0	0	14,067	0	4,142
Bank load	50,000	110,000	150,000	125,000	0	50,000
Accounts payable and accrued liabilities	99,443	60,799	70,554	63,085	61,351	80,223
Note payable to affiliated company	0	0	67,046	0	0	75,000
Loans payable to shareholders	0	0	0	0	21,640	5,000
Mortgage payable to Industrial Development Bank	0	0	0	44,000	0	0
8% debentures, due June 30, 1971	0	0	0	0	100,000	0
Conditional sales agreement payable to Pomo-lift Industries Ltd.	5,165	0	0	9,000	0	0
Customers' deposits	0	9,926	325	0	0	0
Income taxes payable	0	0	40,208	57,250	139,334	5,450
Current portion of long-term liabilities	70,509	63,540	12,135	0	62,000	62,000
Total Current	263,204	244,265	340,268	312,402	384,325	281,815
Deferred income taxes	151,566	131,866	91,756	82,092	68,510	55,600
Long-term exclusive of current portion	605,300	484,410	47,950	0	53,000	215,000

Shareholders' Equity

Capital Stock

Authorized — 5% non-cumulative redeemable (at $26.25) preference shares, par value $25 each convertible into 25 common shares — common shares, no par value

(SEE NOTE BELOW)

Issued:						
Preference shares	$ 350	350	1,575	1,725	10,325	68,875
Common shares	295,774	295,774	294,399	294,399	201,064	53,750
	$ 296,124	296,124	296,124	296,124	211,389	122,625
Retained income	625,917	571,335	579,021	512,639	166,190	38,312
	$ 924,041	867,459	875,145	808,763	377,579	160,937
Total Shareholders' Equity	$ 944,111	1,728,000	1,355,119	1,203,257	883,414	713,352
Note: Number of authorized						
Preference	1,219	1,219	1,268	1,274	1,618	3,960
Common	239,525	239,525	238,300	238,150	229,550	171,000
Number of Shares Issued						
Preference	14	14	63	69	413	2,755
Common	156,550	156,550	155,325	155,175	129,660	53,050

Source: Company records

Exhibit 8

Income and Retained Income Statement				For the Year Ended October 31		
REVENUE	1974	1973	1972	1971	1970	1969
Lift and tow tickets	600,399	397,642	648,899	738,515	755,635	360,922
Season Tickets	189,605	104,230	90,006	87,064	69,602	39,529
Accomodation	41,809	35,744	0	32,412	44,906	27,331
Catering	238,775	113,656	0	0	0	0
Interest	7,039	3,137	6,673	5,240	7,748	5,389
Rentals	10,105	7,084	17,131	9,420	0	0
Tucker Snocat	8,138	9,055	31,703	4,121	0	0
Music School	21,124	0	0	0	0	0
Miscellaneous	20,159	3,700	1,349	15,846	3,725	11,868
Total revenue	1,137,153	674,248	795,761	892,618	881,616	445,039
EXPENSES						
Administrative and General	328,389	239,251	203,090	201,422	227,945	111,078
Lifts, hills, roads and snowmaking	225,494	169,689	246,271	221,329	220,503	133,116
Accommodation	26,639	19,652	0	18,552	31,043	28,288
Catering	211,728	102,088	0	0	0	0
Interest: — Short-term debt	1,545	10,331	5,526	5,840	11,613	12,502
Long-term debt	64,621	26,872	4,727	5,333	8,000	8,000
Rentals	1,172	1,686	8,316	0	0	1,931
Tucker Snocat	6,797	7,280	26,819	0	0	0
Ski instruction	0	0	0	0	0	9,070
Music School	32,338	0	0	0	0	0
Amortization of financial expense	0	0	0	1,232	1,232	1,232
	898,723	576,849	494,749	453,708	500,336	305,217
Income before depreciation and income taxes	238,430	97,399	301,012	438,910	381,280	139,822
Depreciation	154,768	112,475	94,508	84,037	80,126	63,902
Income (loss) before income taxes	83,662	(15,076)	206,504	354,873	301,154	75,920
Income taxes:						
Current payable (recoverable)	7,380	(47,500)	83,782	155,328	142,938	16,117
Deferred	19,700	40,110	9,644	13,582	12,910	18,450
	27,080	(7,390)	93,446	168,910	155,848	34,567
(A) Income before extraordinary item						
Extraordinary item: Life insurance proceeds	0	0	0	200,000	0	0
(B) Income before extraordinary item	0	0	0	185,963	145,306	0
Net income (loss) for the year	56,582	(7,686)	113,058	385,963	145,306	41,353
Balance of retained income at beginning of year	571,335	568,734	512,639	166,190	38,312	5,658
Adjustment of prior year's income taxes	0	10,287	0	0	0	0
As restated	571,335	579,021	512,639	166,190	38,312	5,658
Dividend on preference shares	0	0	(79)	(496)	(516)	(3,494)
Dividend on common shares	0	0	(46,597)	(39,018)	(16,912)	(5,205)
Balance of retained income at end of year	627,917	571,335	579,021	512,639	166,190	38,312
Earnings (loss) per share	0.36	(0.05)	(0.66)	0	0	0
Before extraordinary item	0	0	0	1.28	1.28	0.72
After extraordinary item	0	0	0	2.67	1.28	0

Exhibit 9
Blue Mountain Resorts Limited
Statement of Changes in Financial Position
For the Year Ended October 31

	1974	1973	1972	1971	1970	1969
Source of Working Capital:						
Operations —						
Net income (loss) for the year	56,582	(7,686)	113,058	385,963	145,306	41,353
Add — Expenses not requiring use of working capital —						
Depreciation	154,768	112,475	94,508	84,037	80,126	63,902
Amortization of deferred financing expenses	0	0	0	1,232	1,232	1,232
Increase in deferred income taxes	19,700	40,110	9,664	13,582	12,910	18,450
Common shares issued in payment of expense	0	0	0	560	5,151	1,000
Loss on disposal of fixed assets	322	0	0	0	0	0
	231,372	144,899	217,230	485,374	244,725	125,937
Long-term debt assumed, net of current portion	186,000	450,000	50,787	0	0	0
Sales of fixed assets — proceeds	90	950	0	8,435	2,121	4,548
Sale of common shares for cash	0	0	0	84,175	83,613	0
Reduction of mortgages receivable	500	6,500	1,000	0	0	0
Total Source	417,962	602,349	269,017	577,984	330,459	130,485

Use of Working Capital:

Assumption of mortgages receivable	0	0	10,200	0	0	0
Purchase of fixed assets	288,349	205,087	197,570	441,308	474,641	372,513
Purchase of Golf Club shares	0	0	0	6,375	0	0
Dividend on preference shares	3,494	516	496	79	0	0
Dividend on common shares	5,205	16,912	39,018	46,597	0	0
Reduction in long-term liabilities	17,000	162,000	53,000	2,838	13,540	65,110
Total Use	314,048	384,515	300,284	497,197	488,181	437,623
Net increase (decrease) in working capital	(183,563)	(54,056)	277,700	(228,180)	114,168	(19,661)
Working Capital (deficiency) at beginning of year	(66,998)	(250,561)	(304,617)	(26,917)	(255,097)	(140,929)
Working Capital (deficiency) at end of year	(250,561)	(304,617)	(26,917)	(255,097)	(140,929)	(160,590)
Current assets	31,254	79,708	285,485	85,171	103,336	102,614
Current liabilities	281,815	384,325	312,402	340,268	244,265	263,204
Working Capital (deficiency) at end of year	(250,561)	(304,617)	(26,917)	(255,097)	(140,929)	(160,590)

Exhibit 10
Blue Mountain Resorts Limited
Comparative Balance Sheet — Prepared Without Audit
6 Months Period Ending April 30th

	1975	1974	1973	1972	1971	1970
Assets						
Current Assets						
Cash on Hand	$ 516,470	$ 147,838	$ (117,800)	$ 1,408	$ 50,432	$ 8,480
Accounts Receivable	33,055	53,507	7,155	43,823	45,173	41,010
Other Receivables	231	223	11,895	86,968	226,308	226,630
Inventories	15,915	21,676	19,802	18,579	15,264	540
Prepaid Accounts	13,547	10,703	8,168	9,953	2,541	8,750
Work in Progress	429,016	29,992	200,353	27,330	40,438	22,250
Refundable Corp. Tax						1,790
Mortgage Receivable	2,200	2,700	3,200			
Accruals	152		339			
	$1,010,586	$ 266,639	$ 113,112	$ 188,061	$ 380,156	$ 309,450
Fixed (net)	$1,489,928	$1,594,771	$1,154,019	$ 931,092	$ 760,539	$ 683,120
Other Investments	6,375	6,375	6,375			
Total Assets	$2,506,889	$1,867,785	$1,293,507	$1,119,963	$1,140,695	$ 992,570
Liabilities						
Current	$ 51,762	$ 7,706	$ 118,031	$ 44,511	$ 56,117	$ 111,360
Long Term	676,401	484,410	44,939		184,000	246,000
Deferred Inc. Tax	151,566	131,866	91,756	82,092		
Shareholders' Equity	1,627,160	1,243,803	1,038,781	993,360	900,518	635,210
Total Liabilities	$2,506,889	$1,867,785	$1,293,507	$1,119,963	$1,140,695	$ 992,570

Exhibit 11
Blue Mountain Resorts Limited
Comparative Income Statement — Prepared Without Audit
Period Ending April 30th

	1975	1974	1973	1972	1971	1970
Gross Margin	$ 20,051	$ 17,180	$ 12,378	—	$ 15,995	$ 16,875
Lifts	902,119	598,988	335,421	557,612	628,545	646,605
Tennis Club	417	1,230	1,135	—	5	—
Machine Shop	999	23,256	(970)	(2,584)	236	—
Tucker Snocat	4,746	800	3,403	5,542	3,589	—
Rentals	769	7,584	5,326	4,966	1,706	—
Food	23,594	(7,675)	11,583	—	—	—
Beverages	63,008	33,902	3,773	—	—	—
Other Income	14,278	10,486	906	—	—	—
Total Gross Margin	$1,013,651	$ 685,751	$ 392,955	$ 556,526	$ 652,003	$ 667,762
Indirect Expense						
Commission	$ 126	—	—	—	—	—
Advertising	53,023	$ 77,085	$ 41,879	$ 30,855	$ 35,548	$ 28,413
Automobile	3,714	1,894	2,232	2,109	2,687	666
Bank Charges	183	(26)	368	192	597	652
Cash short-over	572	—	—	189	163	2,891
Depreciation	101,250	92,850	72,000	72,000	72,000	67,200
Directors Fees	325	125	425	225	419	1,250
Donations	775	1,150	1,860	2,245	585	3,980
Insurances	13,525	10,648	9,000	11,489	9,490	5,560
Interest Bank	26,570	28,049	4,378	2,013	82	606
Int. Debenture/Loan	—	—	1,256	—	4,000	4,000
Interest Mortgage	1,684	2,433	3,119	2,451	3,519	7,182
Licenses and Fees	1,430	436	35	1,042	41	554
Municipal Taxes	17,728	10,120	6,258	3,600	4,665	7,675
Membership Fees	1,855	1,516	1,941	373	545	—
Payroll-Office Expense	69,070	56,183	48,344	34,596	35,241	40,128
Postage	1,514	770	832	1,099	1,134	812
Professional Services	4,575	13,732	5,400	5,400	4,762	5,741
Repair and Maintenance	2,675	2,418	31	538	2	22
Sundry	5,977	2,855	9,523	3,986	2,481	3,771
Telephone	9,194	6,132	4,207	4,108	3,609	3,413
Travel	2,862	3,520	3,651	2,589	5,463	7,422
Utilities	2,582	2,672	974	1,335	1,498	153
Unallocated Payroll	—	(7,600)	1,317	(997)	(8,590)	(16,032)
Music Department	—	2,415	—	—	—	—
Interest O.D.C.	7,000	—	—	—	—	—
Total Indirect Expense	$ 327,643	$ 309,407	$ 219,030	$ 181,437	$ 179,948	$ 176,059
Net Income Before Taxes	$ 701,767	$ 376,344	$ 173,925	$ 375,089	$ 472,055	$ 491,703

Exhibit 12

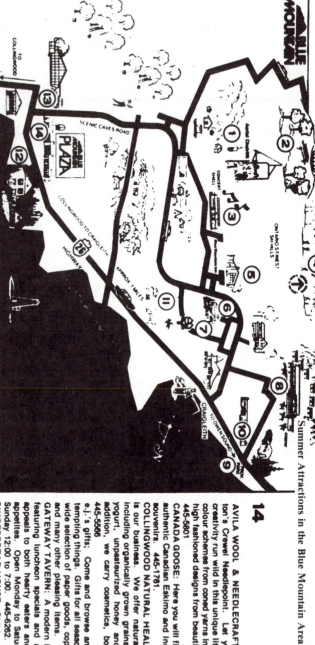

Summer Attractions in the Blue Mountain Area

Attractions in the Blue Mountain Area

1. **SUMMER CHAIRLIFT:** Get a lift this summer! Ride to the top of the mountain and enjoy a panoramic view of beautiful Georgian Bay.

2. **SKYLINE CAFE:** Once at the top of the mountain enjoy a delicious lunch in our rustic little cafe.

3. **CONCERT SHELL:** On most summer evenings students and faculty of the Blue Mountain Summer School of Music and Dance perform in public concerts at the outdoor Concert Shell or in the adjoining Base Lodge. There is no charge and everyone is welcome to attend. For concert schedule call 445-0231.

4. **BRUCE TRAIL:** This famous hiking trail runs from Niagara Falls to Tobermory.

5. **BLUE MOUNTAIN INN:** This summer the inn will be closed for the addition of a 200 seat dining facility.

6. **ARTIST'S STUDIO:** Robert G. Kemp, resident artist since 1981, invites you to view his many paintings done in the surrounding district. He's open every day from 9:00 a.m. to 9:00 p.m. and displays work in many media from oil to water colour. 446-2577.

7. **TYROLEAN VILLAGE:** Deluxe swiss chalets for rent weekly, monthly or seasonally. Ten tennis courts, tennis bubble, an outdoor heated pool, horses for hire, riding lessons, trail rides. Year round country comfort. Inquire locally at 445-1467 or in Toronto 534-8452.

8. **ARROWHEAD RANCH:** In July and August this is primarily a boy's and girl's camp with extremely high standards of riding, camping and swimming. Spring and Fall the ranch caters to organizations and individuals. Skiing groups are welcome in the Winter. 445-3987.

9. **CRAIGLEITH PARK:** All facilities for tenting, camper, trucks, trailers etc. Beach and playgrounds. 445-4467.

10. **PINE POTTERY:** This is one of the first potteries in the area and displays many traditional pieces as well as the more modern creations. 445-0049.

11. **CANADIANA PINE SHOP:** See an excellent selection of Canadian antiques, hand wovens and gifts. 445-5080.

12. **KAUFMAN HOUSE:** Here at Kaufman House you'll see twenty beautifully furnished and decorated rooms in Kaufman's lines of superb furniture, traditional, period and modern. 445-6000.

13. **BLUE MOUNTAIN POTTERY:** There's a factory sales outlet and an observation studio where you can watch skilled craftsmen making pottery. Open every day of the year. Plant tours for groups can be arranged by appointment. 445-3000.

14

AVILA WOOL & NEEDLECRAFT: Featuring Appleton's Crewel Needlepoint. Let your imagination and creativity run wild in this unique little shop. Blend your colour schemes from conned yarns inexpensively or create high fashioned designs from beautiful European Yarns.

CANADA GOOSE: Here you will find an art selection of authentic Canadian Eskimo and Indian crafts, gifts and souvenirs. 445-1761.

COLLINGWOOD NATURAL HEALTH FOODS: Health is our business. We offer natural, wholesome foods, including organically grown grains, dried fruit, balkan yogurt, unpasteurized honey and herbal teas. In addition, we carry cosmetics, books and vitamins. 445-5666.

e.j.'s gifts: Come and browse among a pot pourri of tempting things. Gifts for all seasons and occasions. A wide selection of paper goods, copper, brass, jewellery and many other pleasing items. 445-3845.

GATEWAY TAVERN: A modern licensed dining room featuring luncheon specials and a dinner menu that appeals to both hearty eaters and those with lighter appetites. Open Monday to Saturday 11:30 to 9:00. Sunday 12:00 to 7:00. 445-6262.

GINGERBREAD HOUSE: Children's fashions designed with creative imagination, perfect fit and great value for your little wonders. A broad selection for both boys and girls, from casual to dressy in infant to size 14. 445-5650.

HEN & CHICKENS: A fashion boutique catering to the contemporary woman. Lingerie, daytime and evening wear featuring Leonard, Ann Klein and Katja of Sweden in sizes 6 to 18. Please come in and browse. 445-3842.

LESSELS REAL ESTATE LIMITED: A local company fully licensed in all departments of real estate, employing only qualified personnel and specializing in the Township of Collingwood. 445-1991.

NOR MOS ARTS: Peruvian arts and crafts. Various special pieces of fine hand painted ceramics, wall hangings, leather and suede goods.

ROCQUE'S CARPET & COLOUR T.V.: A unique retailer of broadloom, stereo and colour T.V. Excellent selection of well displayed quality lines. Zenith authorized sales and service. Bargains on carpet remnants and cuttings. 445-5059.

UNITED PRODUCTS, INC.

Having just returned from lunch, Mr. George Brown, president of United Products, Inc., was sitting in his office thinking about his upcoming winter vacation where he and his family would be spending three weeks skiing on Europe's finest slopes. His daydreaming was interrupted by a telephone call from Mr. Hank Stevens, UPI's General Manager. Mr. Stevens wanted to know if their two o'clock meeting was still on. The meeting had been scheduled to review actions UPI could take in light of the currently depressed national economy. In addition, Mr. Brown was concerned about his accountant's report detailing results for the company's recently completed fiscal year. Although 1974 hadn't been a bad year, results were not as good as expected. This report along with the economic situation, was forcing Mr. Brown to re-evaluate alternative actions being considered for the future.

COMPANY HISTORY

United Products, Inc., established in 1941, was engaged in the sales and service of basic supply items for shipping and receiving, production and packaging, research and development, and office and warehouse departments. Mr. Brown's father, the founder of the company, recognized the tax advantages in establishing separate businesses rather than trying to operate the business through one large organization. Accordingly, over the years companies were created as business warranted and in some cases companies were either closed or sold off. By the mid-1960's, he had succeeded in structuring a chain of four related companies covering the geographic area from Chicago eastward.

In 1967, feeling it was time to step aside and turn over active control of the business to his sons, the elder Mr. Brown recapitalized the company and merged or sold off the separate companies. When the restructuring process was completed, he had set up two major companies. United Products, Inc. was to be run by his youngest son, George Brown, with its headquarters in Massachusetts, while his other son, Richard, was to operate United Products Southeast, Inc., headquartered in Florida.

Although the Brown brothers occasionally work together and are on each other's Board of Directors, the two companies operate on their own. As Mr. George Brown explained, "Since we are brothers, we often get together and discuss business, but the two are separate companies and each files its own tax return." This case only considers United Products, Inc. and the activities of Mr. George Brown.

During 1972, United Products moved into its new offices in Woburn, Massachusetts. From this location, it is believed the company is able to effectively serve its entire New England market area. "Our abilities and our desires to expand and improve our overall operation will be enhanced in the new specially designed structure containing our offices, repair facilities and warehouse," is the way in which Geroge Brown spoke about the new facilities. Concurrent with the recent move, the company segmented its over 3,500 different items carried to eight major product categories:

1) *Stapling Machines* including Wire Stitchers, Carton Stitchers, Nailers, Hammers, Tackers, Manual - Foot - Air - Electric.

2) *Staples* to fit almost all makes of equipment - all sizes - types - steel, bronze, monel, stainless steel, aluminum, brass, etc.

3) *Stenciling Equipment* and supplies, featuring Marsh Hand and Electric Machines, Stencil Brushes, Boards, Inks.

4) *Gummed Tape Machines*, Hand and Electric, featuring Marsh, Derby, Counterboy equipment.

5) *Industrial Tapes* by 3M, Mystik, Behr Manning, Dymo-specializing in strapping, masking, cellophane, electrical, cloth, nylon, waterproof tapes.

6) *Gluing Machines* - hand and electric

7) *Work Gloves* - cotton, leather, neoprene, nylon, rubber, asbestos, etc.

8) *Marking and Labeling Equipment.*

In a flyer mailed at the time of the move to the United Products' 6,000 accounts, the company talked about its growth in this fashion:

> Here we grow again - thanks to you - our many long-time valued customers...
>
> Time and Circumstances have decreed another United Products transPLANT - this time, to an unpolluted garden-type industrial area, ideally located for an ever-increasing list of our customers.
>
> Now, in the new 28,000-sq. ft. plant with enlarged offices and warehouse, we at United Products reach the peak of efficiency in offering our customers the combined benefits of

maximum inventories, accelerated deliveries, and better repair services.

By 1974, the company had grown to a point where sales were $3.5 million (double that of four years earlier) and employed 34 people. Results for 1973 compared to 1972 showed a sales increase of twenty-two per cent and a 40 percent increase in profits. Exhibit 1 contains selected financial figures for 1971, 1972, and 1973 in addition to the fiscal 1973 balance sheet.

COMPETITION

Mr. George Brown believes that UPI does not have clearly defined competition for its business. It is felt that since UPI carries over 3500 different items they have competition on parts of their business, but no one competes against their whole business:

> It is hard to get figures on competition since we compete with no one company directly. Different companies compete with various product lines but there is no one who competes across our full range of products.

On a regular basis, Mr. Brown receives *Dun & Bradstreet* Business Information Reports on specific firms with which he competes. Mr. Brown feels that since the competing firms are, like his own firm, privately held, the financial figures reported are easily manipulated and, therefore, are not sound enough to base plans on. Exhibit 2 contains comparative financial figures for two competing companies, and Exhibit 3 contains D&B's description of their operations along with two other firms operating in UPI's prime New England Market area.

MANAGEMENT PHILOSOPHY

When Mr. Brown took over UPI in 1967 at the age of 24, he set a personal goal of becoming financially secure and developing a highly profitable business. With the rapid growth of the company, he soon realized his goal of financial independence and in so doing began to lose interest in the company. "I became a rich person at age 28 and had few friends with equal wealth that were my age. The business no longer presented a challenge, and I was unhappy with the way things were going."

After taking a ten-month "mental vacation" from the business, George Brown felt he was ready to return to work. He had concluded that one way of proving himself to himself and satisfying his ego would be to make the company as profitable as possible. However, the amount of growth that UPI is able to realize is limited by the level of energy exerted by Mr. Brown. "The company can only grow at approximately 20 per cent per year, since this is the amount of energy I am willing to commit to the business."

Although Mr. Brown is only 31, he feels that his philosophical outlook is very conservative and he tends to operate the same as his 65-year-old father would. He has established several operating policies consistent with his philosophy that are constraining on the business.

I am very concerned about making UPI a nice place to work. I have to enjoy what I'm doing and have fun at it at the same time. I cannot make any more money since I'm putting away as much money as I can. The government won't allow me to make more money since I already take the maximum amount.

I like to feel comfortable, and if we grew too quickly it could get out of hand. I realize the business doesn't grow to its potential, but why should I put more into it? I have all the money I need. The company could grow, but why grow? Why is progress good? You have to pay for everything in life, and I'm not willing to work harder since I don't need the money.

Another thing, I am a scrupulously honest businessman and it is very hard to grow large if you're honest. There are many deals that I could get into that would make UPI a lot of money, but I'm too moral of a person to get involved and besides, I don't need the money.

To me, happiness is being satisfied with what you have. I've got my wife, children and health; why risk these for something I don't need. I don't have the desire to make money because I didn't come from a poor family; I'm not hungry.

Another thing - I have never liked the feeling of owing anything to anyone. If you can't afford to buy something, then don't. I don't like to borrow any money, and I don't like the company to borrow any. All of our bills are paid within 15 days. I suppose I've constrained the business as a result of this feeling, but it's my business. The company can only afford to pay for a 20 percent growth rate, so that's all we will grow.

ORGANIZATIONAL STRUCTURE

Upon his return to the company, George Brown realigned UPI's organizational structure as shown in Exhibit 4 (company does not have an organizational chart; this one is drawn from the researcher's notes).

We have to have it on a functional basis now. We are also trying something new for us by moving to the general manager concept. In the past when I was away, there was no one with complete authority; now my general manager is in charge in my absence.

In discussing the new structuring of the organization, Mr. Brown was quick to point out that the company has not established formalized job descriptions. "Job descriptions are not worth anything. My people wear too many hats, and, besides, we're too small to put it in writing." At present the company employs 34 people including Mr. Brown.

Mr. Brown is quick to point out tht he has never had a personnel problem. "All my people enjoy working here." He believes that "nobody should work for nothing" and has, therefore, established a personal goal of seeing to it that no one employed by UPI makes less thn $10,000 per year. Mr. Brown commented on his attitude toward his employees:

> The men might complain about the amount of responsibility placed on them, but I think it's good for them. It helps them develop to their potential. I'm a nice guy who is interested in all of my people. I feel a strong social obligation to my employees and have developed very close relationships with all of them. My door is always open to them no matter what the problem may be.

> I make it a policy never to yell at anyone in public, it's not good for morale. Maybe it's part of my conservative philosophy, but I want everyone to call me Mr. Brown, not George. I think it's good for people to have a Mr. Brown. Although I want to run a nice friendly business, I have learned that it's hard to be real friends with an employee. You can only go so far. Employers and employees cannot mix socially, it just doesn't work out over the long run.

> This is not your normal business. I am very approachable, I don't demand much, and I allow an easy open dialogue with my employees. Seldom do I take any punitive action. I'm just not a hard-driving tough guy...I'm an easy-going guy.

> It would take much of the enjoyment out of the business for me to come in here and run this place like a machine. (Researcher's note: When the researcher arrived at the plant one afternoon, he observed Mr. Brown running around the office deeply involved in a water fight with one of his office girls. By the way - he lost.).

> I find it hard to motivate the company's salesmen. Since we have so much trouble finding good capable men, I'm not likely to fire any that I have. This situation makes it hard for me to put pressure on them to produce.

> The bonus system, if you want to call it that, is I guess what you'd call very arbitrary. I have not set up specific sales

quotas, or targeted goals for my inside people, so as a result, I base my bonus decisions on my assessment of how well I feel an employee performed during the past year.

Recently, I've given some thought to selling the company. I could probably get around $3 or $4 million for it. If I did that, I'm not sure what I would do with my time. Besides my family and UPI, there is not much that I am interested in. A couple of years ago, when I took my extended vacation, I got bored and couldn't wait to get back to the company.

UPI'S PLANNING PROCESS

George Brown claims to be a firm believer in planning. "I find myself spending more and more time planning for the company. Currently, I'm averaging about 50 percent of my time and I see this increasing." As he described it, the planning process at United Products is really a very loose system. "We have no planned way as to how we do the planning."

Basically, the process is directed at ways of increasing the profitability of the company. I look at the salesmen's performance on a weekly and monthly basis, and use this information in the development of the plans.

Since we have a very informal planning process, we only forecast out one year at most. The company's plans are re-evaluated each month, and, if necessary, new plans are set. Only on rare occasions have we ever planned beyond one year.

However, I think the current economic and political situation may force us into developing plans that cover a two-year period.

Although goals are not formally developed and written down, Mr. Brown had identified objectives in three areas: sales, profits and organizational climate.

Specifically they are:

1) Increase sales volume of business by 20% per year;
2) Increase gross profit margin 1/2 to 1% per year; and,
3) Make UPI a friendly place to work.

Mr. Brown feels that the company has been able to grow at about 20% a year in the past and, therefore, should have no problems realizing that level in the future. In addition, he believes that sales growth is a necessary evil. "Those companies that don't grow are swallowed up by the competition, and besides, given the level of energy I'm willing to exert, I think 20% is a reasonable level of growth."

In the area of profits, the company actually sets no specific targeted figures other than saying they simply want an increase in the percentage of profits. Mr. Brown commented that:

> We do not set a goal because we would not have a way of measuring it. I have no way of knowing how much money I am making until the end of the year without considerable time and effort.

With respect to the third goal, Mr. Brown is concerned about the work-place environment and wants UPI to be a big happy family - and everyone employed to be happy.

In describing the planning process used at UPI, Mr. Brown emphasized the unstructured informal nature of the process.

> I am familiar with commonly accepted theory about planning systems, but I do not feel it is necessary for UPI to institute, in a formal manner, any of those I've read about. We perform many of the activities advocated in the planning models, but we do them in a relaxed, casual fashion. For example, I am a member of many organizations connected with my business and receive industry newsletters on a regular basis. In addition, I receive input from friends and business associates both inside and outside my line of business. Since we do not have a formal process, planning tends to be a continuous process at UPI.

When asked about UPI's strengths and weaknesses, Mr. Brown indicated the company has four areas of strength and one major weakness:

Strengths

1) The number of different products carried;
2) The quality of its employees, particularly salesmen;
3) No debt; and,
4) Purchasing capabilities.

Weaknesses

1) An inability to get and train new personnel -
   primarily in the sales function of the business.

The salesmen are not assigned a sales quota for the year but rather are evaluated based on Mr. Brown's assessment of the particular salesman's territory and initiative. He feels his salesmen make more than competitive salesmen. Several of the ten salesmen have earned as much as $40,000 in a single year. All salesmen are compensated on a straight commission basis - as shown below:

8% for first $180,000 sales
7% for next $60,000 sales
6% for next $60,000 and
5% for everything over $300,000

Mr. Brown is pleased with the sales success of his company and feels that UPI's greatest strength is its ability to "sell anything to anybody." However, the problem for UPI has been in finding good salesmen. "There just aren't any good salesmen around, and this is a problem because the salesmen are the lifeblood of our business."

INTERPERSONAL RELATIONSHIPS

Since Mr. Brown is concerned about the climate of the company, he has paid particular attention to the nature of the relationship within UPI. At the time of the company's reorganization, Hank Stevens was brought into the organization as general manager and assistant to the president. Over the past several years, Mr. Stevens' areas of responsibility have grown to the extent that they now comprise approximately 80 percent of the activities that were formerly done by Mr. Brown. As a result of this, George Brown sometimes finds himself with little to do and oftentimes works only five hours per day. As he describes it:

> Hank's management discretionary power has increased steadily since he has been here; partly as a result of the extent of responsibility I've placed on him and partly due to his aggressiveness. As it now stands, he makes almost all of the daily operating decisions for the company, leaving me with only the top management decisions. Let's be realistic, there just aren't that many top management decisions that have to be made here in the course of a day. A lot of the time, I walk around the plant checking on what other people are doing and, I guess, acting as a morale booster.

When asked about the management capabilities of Hank Stevens, Mr. Brown responded by saying, "Hank probably feels that he is working at a very fast pace, but when you evaluate the effectiveness of his actions, he is actually moving forward at what I would consider to be a very slow pace. However, everything else considered, Hank is the best of what is around. I guess if I could find a really good sales manager, I would add him to the company and relieve Hank of that area of responsibility."

MR. HANK STEVENS

Mr. Hank Stevens, 32, joined UPI at the time of the reorganization in 1970 after having graduated from a local university with a B.S. in Economics. As general manager, Mr. Stevens' responsibilities include planning, purchasing, sales management as well as involvement in other decisions that affect UPI policy. Mr. Stevens feels that he has been fortunate. "Ever since I came to UPI, I've reported to the president and in essence have had everyone else reporting to me."

When asked about the goals of UPI, Mr. Stevens responded that, "As I see it, we have goals in three major areas: profitability, sales level and personal relationships." In discussing his own personal goals, Hank explained that he hoped that the organization would grow and as a result he would be able to grow along with it.

Since Mr. Stevens works so closely with Mr. Brown, he has given considerable thought to his boss' business philosophy:

> I feel that George's business philosophy is unique. I guess the best way to describe it is to say that above all he is a businessman. Also, he has very high moral values and as a result of that he is extremely honest and would never cheat anybody. Actually, the company would probably look better financially if it was run by someone who didn't operate with the same values as George.

When asked about the salesforce at UPI, Mr. Stevens commented that "when a new salesman starts with the company, he does so with full salary. After a period of about two years we change him over to a commission basis." As has always been the case, UPI concentrates in sales efforts on large customers. Mr. Stevens noted that "on the average the company processes approximately 105 orders per day, with an average dollar value per order of roughly $132. It's not that we won't write small orders, we just don't solicit business from small accounts. It just makes more sense to concentrate on the larger accounts."

MR. JIM HANES

Mr. Hanes, age 24, has been with UPI for over six years and during that time has worked his way up from assistant service manager to his current position as the number-three man in the company functioning as the manager of purchasing and shipping. Jim is responsible for the front office, repair work and the warehouse. He feels that his reporting responsibility is approximately 60 percent to Mr. Stevens and 40 percent to Mr. Brown. "Since I have responsibility for all merchandise entering and leaving the company, I get involved with both Hank and George, and therefore, I guess I report to both of them."

In talking about where he would go from his present position, he explained that:

> I guess the next step is for me to become a salesman so that I can broaden my background and move up in the company. However, I am a little worried; I don't think the salemen in our company are given the right sales training. As the system works, a new man is assigned to work with an experienced salesman for about six weeks, after which time he is given his

own territory. Perhaps if our sales manager had more experience as a salesman, he would handle the training differently.

In commenting on his understanding of Mr. Brown's philosophy, Jim summed up his position by noting that, "George is a very open person. I think he is too honest for a businessman. He certainly gives his people responsibility. He gives you the ball and lets you run with it. I don't think enough planning is done at UPI. At most, it appears that we look ahead one year and even then, what plans are developed are kept very flexible."

UPI STRATEGY

When asked about the current strategy at UPI, Mr. Brown responded that "the company is presently a distributor in the industrial packaging equipment, shipping supplies, and heavy duty stapling equipment business. In the past when we've wanted to grow, we have done one or both of the following, either add new lines of merchandise or additional salesmen. For example, this past year I got the idea of what I call a contract sales department. It is a simple concept; I took one man, put him in an office with a telephone and a listing of the *Fortune* top 1000 companies and told him to call and get new business. You would be surprised at how easy it was to pick up new accounts."

Mr. Stevens looks at UPI as being in the distribution and shipping of packaging supplies business. "In order for UPI to reach the goals that have been set, we have to sell more products. That is, we can grow by doing the following:

1) Adding new salesmen;
2) Adding additional product lines;
3) Purchasing more effectively; and,
4) Undertaking more aggressive sales promotions."

Mr. Brown believes that UPI should try to maximize the profit on every item sold. To do this, the company tries to set its prices at a level which is approximately ten per cent above the competition. Mr. Brown explained his pricing philophy:

> I don't understand why people are afraid to raise prices. If you increase the price, you will pick up more business and make more money. That allows you to keep the volume low and still make more money. In addition, although the customer may pay more, he gets more. The higher price allows me to provide top notch service to all my customers.

Mr. Brown feels that UPI is an innovative company. "Until very recently we were always innovating with new products and new applications. Now, I think it's again time that we started to look for additional new and exciting products."

As a result of the stated strategy of UPI and Mr. Brown's conservative philosophy, it is widely recognized that the organization is larger than it has to be given the level of business. Mr. Brown explained the reasoning behind this condition. "I know the organization is bigger than it has to be. We could probably handle three times the present volume of business with our present staff and facility. I think it's because of my conservative attitude; I've always wanted the organization to stay a step ahead of what is really needed. I feel comfortable with a built-in backup system and, therefore, I am willing to pay for it."

In December, 1973, Mr. Brown had talked optimistically about the future. He felt that sales should reach the $6-7 million range by 1978. "Looked at in another way, we should be able to grow at 20-25 percent per year without any particular effort."

> I want to grow and, therefore, I am making a concerted effort. I am constantly looking for possible merger avenues or expansion possibilities. I do not want to expand geographically. I would rather control that market area we are in now. I recently sent a letter to all competitors in New England offering to buy them out. Believe it or not no one responded. I don't see any problems in the future. The history has been good, therefore, why won't it continue to happen? Growth is easy. All I have to do is pick up a new line, and I've automatically increased sales and profits. Basically, we are distributors, and we operate as middlemen between the manufacturers and users as shown:

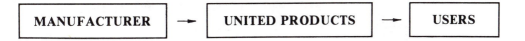

> In light of what has been happening in the environment, I feel that supply and demand will continue to be a problem. Therefore, I am giving serious thought to integrating vertically, i.e., become a manufacturer. This will guarantee our supply.*

> Actually, I don't want to do the manufacturing. I think it would be better if I bought the manufacturing equipment and then had someone else use it to make my products.

THE FUTURE

After reviewing with his accountant the results for the just-completed fiscal year, Mr. Brown was concerned about the nature of changes that should be made with respect to the actions taken by UPI in the future. "I know changes have to be made for next year as a result of this year, but I'm not sure what they should be." Mr. Brown continued:

> I think next year is going to be a real bad year. Prices will

---

*Refer to the Appendix which contains minutes of a United Products sales meeting held at the end of 1973.

probably fall like a rock from the levels they reached during
1974 and as a result those items that would have been
profitable for the company aren't going to be, and we have
much too large of an inventory as it is. It isn't easy to take
away customers from the competition. As a result of this, I
feel we have to step up our efforts to get new lines and new
accounts. Recently, I've given some thought to laying off
one or two people for economic reasons, but I'm not sure. I
will probably give raises to all employees even though it's
not a good business decision, but it's an ingrained part of my
business philosophy.

When asked if he had informed his employees of his concern about the future, Mr.
Brown referred to the minutes of a sales meeting that had been held in November 1974:

...Mr. Brown then presided at the meeting, and announced
that Al King had won the coveted award of "Salesman of the
Month." This was a "first" for our Al, and well deserved for
his outstanding sales results in October. Congratulations
and applauses were extended him by all present. The
balance of the meeting was then spent in a lengthy, detailed
discussion led by Mr. George Brown of the general, overall
picture of what the future portends in the sales area as a
result of the current inflationary, recessionary and complex
competitive conditions prevailing in the economy.

The gist of the entire discussion can be best summarized as follows:

1) Everyone present must recognize the real difficulties that lie ahead in these
precarious economic times.

2) The only steps available to the salesmen and to the company for survival during the
rough period ahead are as follows:

   a) Minimize contacts with existing accounts;
   b) Spend the majority of time developing new accounts
      on the less competitive products; and selling
      new products to established accounts.

3) Concentrate on and promote our new items.

4) Mr. Brown and inside management are making and will continue to make every
concentrated effort to find new products and new lines for the coming year.

In preparation for his meeting with Hank Stevens, Mr. Brown had prepared a list of
activities to which Hank should address himself while running UPI during George's
upcoming vacation. Mr. Brown believed that upon his return from Europe his activities

at UPI would be increasing as a result of the problems caused by the uncertain economic conditions. The first item on the list was a possible redefinition of UPI marketing strategy. Mr. Brown now believed that UPI would have to be much more liberal with respect to new products considered for sale. "I'm not saying we are going to get into the consumer goods business, but I think he will give consideration to the inclusion of consumer products requiring no service and at the same time capable of being sold with a high-profit-margin factor for the company."

As he sat at his desk thinking about possible change which he could make in UPI's planning process, Mr. Brown ws convinced that if he hadn't done some planning in the past, the situation would be more drastic than it was. Yet at the same time, he wasn't sure that if had a more structured and formalized planning process, UPI might be in a better position with which to face the troubled times that lay ahead.

ASSIGNMENT QUESTIONS

1) Why would you like/not like to work for Mr. Brown at UPI?

2) Why is it necessary for UPI to grow?

3) Are Mr. Brown's values constraining the future growth of UPI?

4) What kind of growth opportunities exist for Hank Stevens and Jim Hanes?

5) What do you think should be the role of the General Manager and Sales Manager at UPI?

6) What specific recommendations would you make to Mr. Brown? How would you convince him to accept them?

7) If you, rather than Mr. Brown, were running UPI, what would you do? In what ways would it differ from what you told Mr. Brown to do?

APPENDIX

UNITED PRODUCTS, INC.
Sales Meeting
December 5, 1973

Mr. Brown presided at the meeting. His opening remarks highlighted the extraordinary times our country and our company are going through as far as the general economy and the energy crisis are concerned, and the extraordinary effects of these unusual crises on people and businesses, including our company and our sources of supply.

He thanked all present for the many thoughtful, considered and excellent suggestions which they had offered in writing as to how best the salesmen and their company might handle the gasoline crisis without incurring an undue loss of sales and profits, and still maintain the high standards of service to which UNITED PRODUCTS' thousands of satisfied customers are accustomed.

The whole situation, according to Mr. Brown, boils down to a question of supply and prices. Mr. Brown reported that on his recent trip to the Orient, there were very few companies who wanted to sell their merchandise to us - rather, THEY WANTED TO BUY FROM US MANY OF THE ITEMS WE NORMALLY BUY FROM FOREIGN COMPANIES, i.e., carton-closing staples, tape, gloves, etc...and at inflated prices!!! The Tokyo, Japan, market is so great that they are using up everything they can produce - and the steel companies would rather make flat steel than the steel rods which are used for making staples. A very serious problem exists, as a result, in the carton-closing staple field not only in Japan, but also in Europe and America.

Mr. Brown advised that every year the company's costs of operating increase just as each individual's cost of living goes up and up yearly. Additional personnel, increased group and auto insurance premiums, increased Social Security payments, new office equipment and supplies, new catalogues, "Beeper system" for more salesmen - and all of these costs accumulate and result in large expenditures of money. Manufacturers cover their increased operating costs by pricing their products higher - but to date, UNITED PRODUCTS has never put into their prices the increased costs resulting from increased operating expenses. Last year, the 3% increase which the company needed then was put into effect by many of you. HOWEVER, in order for the company to realize that additional profit, this 3% price increase had to be put into effect ACROSS THE BOARD...all customers...all items!

Mr. Brown advised that UNITED PRODUCTS got LAMBASTED when all of the sources of supply started to increase their prices. When SPOTNAILS, for example, went up 10%, the salesmen only increased their prices 7%, etc. We did not get the 3% price increase ABOVE the manufacturers' price increase - and we needed it then, and need it even more NOW.

Eliminating the possibility of cutting commissions, there are three possible solutions for the problem of how to get this much needed and ABSOLUTELY IMPERATIVE additional 3% PRICE INCREASE ACROSS THE BOARD to cover the constantly growing operating costs for running a successful, progressive-minded and growing business whose high standards of service and performance are highly regarded by customers and sources of supply alike, namely:

a) a 3% increase on all items to all customers across the board.

b) a surcharge on all invoices or decrease in discounts allowed off LIST

c) a G.C.I. charge (Government Cost Increase) on all invoices.

Considerable discussion regarding these three possibilities resulted in the following conclusions concerning the best method for obtaining this special 3% ACROSS THE BOARD PRICE INCREASE, as follows:

a) A new PRICE BOOK should be issued with all new prices to reflect not only the manufacturers' new increased prices, but in addition the 3% UNITED PRODUCTS PRICE INCREASE. All of the salesmen agreed that it would be easier to effect the additional 3% price increase if the 3% was "Built in" on their price book sheets.

b) This new PRICE BOOK will be set up in such a way that prices will be stipulated according to quantity of item purchased...with no variances allowed. WITH NO EXCEPTIONS, the price of any item will depend on the quantity a customer buys.

c) Some items will continue to be handled on a discount basis — but lower discounts in order to ascertain that UNITED PRODUCTS is getting its 3% price increase.

d) Until these new PRICE BOOKS are issued, all salesmen were instructed to proceed IMMEDIATELY to effect these 3% price increases.

TEN NEW ACCOUNTS CONTEST

Seven of our ten salesmen won a calculator as a result of opening up ten new accounts each...a total of 70 NEW ACCOUNTS for our company!!! However, both Mr. Brown and Mr. Stevens confessed that the dollar volume amount stipulated in the contest had been set ridiculously low, as a "feeler" to determine the success and effectiveness of such a contest. All the salesmen voiced their approval of all of the contests offered to them — and agreed that they had enjoyed many excellent opportunities of increasing their personal exchecquers.

NEW CUSTOMER LETTERS

Mr. Brown again reminded all present that we have an excellent printed letter, which is available for sending to every new customer — and urged all to take advantage of this service by the office personnel by clearly indicating on their sales and order slips "NEW CUSTOMER." This procedure is but another step towards our goal of becoming more and more professional in our approach with our customers.

NEW CATALOGUES

Mr. Brown advised that by the first of the new year, hopefully, all our hard-cover catalogues with their new divider breakdowns will be ready for hand-delivering to large accounts. These catalogues cost the company over $5.00 and should only be distributed by hand to those customers who can and will make intelligent and effective use of them.

EXCESSIVE ISSUANCE OF CREDITS

As a result of a detailed study made by Mr. Brown of the nature and reasons for the ever-increasing number of credits being issued, he instructed all of the salesmen to follow these procedures when requesting the issuing of CREDITS:

a) Issue the CREDIT at the right time.

b) Do not sell an item where it is not needed.

c) NEVER PUT "NO COMMENT" for the reason why merchandise is being returned. EVERY CREDIT MUST HAVE A REASON FOR ITS ISSUANCE.

The ever-increasing number of credits being issued is extremely costly to the company: 1) new merchandise comes back 90 plus days after it has been billed, and frequently, if not always, is returned by the customer Freight Collect; 2) Credit 9-part forms, postage for mailing, extra work for both the bookkeeping and billing and order processing departments. More intelligent, considered and selective selling, plus greater care on the part of the order processing personnel, according to Mr. Brown, could easily eliminate a large percentage of these credits.

Exhibit 1
United Products, Inc.
Selected Financial Figures for UPI 1971-1973

	11-30-1971	11-30-1972	11-30-1973
Curr. Assets	$ 862,783	$ 689,024	$ 937,793
Curr. Liabilities	381,465	223,004	342,939
Other Assets	204,566	774,571	750,646
Worth	685,884	750,446	873,954
Sales			3,450,000

Following statement dated Nov. 30, 1973

Cash	$ 46,961	Accts Pay.	$320,795
Accts. Rec.	535,714	Notes Pay.	20,993
Mdse.	352,136		
Ppd. Ins., Int., Taxes	2,980		
	_____		_____
Current	937,793	Current	342,939
Fixt. & Equip.	42,891	R E	471,655
Motor Vehicles	49,037	**Capital Stock**	519,800
Real Estate	658,768	Surplus	354,154
	_____		_____
Total Assets	$1,688,486	Total	$1,688,486

Exhibit 2
United Products, Inc.
Financial Information on Selected Competitors

East Coast Supply Co., Inc. - Sales $1m.

	Fiscal 11-30-1971	Fiscal 11-30-1972	Fiscal 11-30-1973
Curr. Assets	$ 88,555	$ 132,354	$ 166,426
Curr. Liabilities	44,543	47,606	77,055
Other Assets	16,082	18,045	27,422
Worth	63,165	102,793	116,793

Statement dated December 31, 1973

Cash	$ 42,948	Accts Pay.	$ 41,668
Accts Rec.	86,123	Notes Pay.	27,588
Mdse.	34,882	Taxes	7,799
Prepaid	2,473		
Current	166,426	Current	77,055
Fixt. & Equip.	15,211	**Capital Stock**	10,000
Deposits	12,211	**Retained Earnings**	106,793
Total Assets	$193,848	Total	$193,848

Atlantic Paper Products, Inc. - Sales $6m.

	June 30, 1970	June 30, 1971	June 30, 1972
Curr. Assets	$101,241	$1,243,259	$1,484,450
Curr. Liabilities	574,855	502,572	1,120,036
Other Assets	93,755	101,974	107,001
Worth	403,646	439,677	471,415
Long Term Debt		402,094	

Exhibit 3
UNITED PRODUCTS, INC.
Descriptive Information on Selective Competitors

East Coast Supply Co., Inc.

Manufactures and distributes pressure sensitive tapes to industrial users throughout the New England area on 1/10 net 30 day terms. Thirty-four employeed including the officers, thirty-three here. LOCATION: Rents 15,000 square feet on first floor of two-story brick building in good repair. Premises are orderly. Non-seasonal business. Branches are located at 80 Olife Street, New Haven, Connecticut, and 86 Weybosssett Street, Providence, Rhode Island.

Atlantic Paper Products, Inc.

Wholesale paper products, pressure sensitive tapes, paper specialties, twines and other merchandise of this type. Sales to industrial accounts and commercial users on 1/10 net 30 day terms. There are about 1,000 accounts in Eastern Massachusetts and sales are fairly steady throughout the year. Employs 60 including officers. LOCATION: Rents 130,000 square feet of floor space in a six-story brick mill type building in a commercial area on a principal street. Premises orderly.

The Johnson Sales Co.

Wholesales shipping room supplies including staplings and packing devices, markers and stencil equipment. Sells to industrial and commercial accounts throughout the New England area. Seasons are steady. Terms are 1/10 net 30 days. Number of accounts not learned, 15 are employed including the owner. LOCATION: Rents the first floor of a two-story yellow brick building in good condition. Housekeeping is good.

Big City Staple Corp.

Wholesales industrial staples, with sales to 2000 industrial and commercial firms, sold on 1/10 net 30 day terms. Territory mainly New Jersey. Employs 10 including the officers. Seasons steady and competition active. LOCATION: Rents 5,000 square feet in one-story cinder block and brick structure in good condition, premises in neat order. Located on well-traveled street in a commercial area.

Exhibit 4
United Products, Inc.
Organization Chart - December, 1974

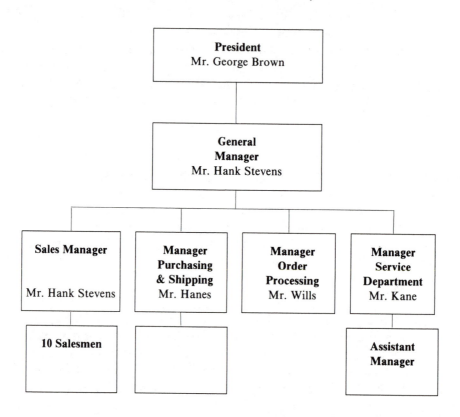

Part Five

TECHNICAL NOTES
FOR
ENTREPRENEURS

Part Five

Technical Notes for Entrepreneurs:

A General Introduction

These notes are intended to give entrepreneurs an overview of certain specialized bodies of information encountered during the life cycle of a venture. The notes are technical in the sense that they contain specific information about starting, operating, and ending a business venture. However, they do not constitute professional advice; nor should they be construed by the reader to represent professional opinion. This function lies entirely in the hands of lawyers, accountants, or other professionals whom you should consult regarding specific situations.

What then is the purpose of the notes? Their primary purpose is to make you conversant with professionals on issues of joint interest. As such, the notes are intended as an introductory overview of complex and changing subject matter. For example, legislative and administrative rules and regulations are constantly being revised. However, it is generally much easier to update new information as opposed to discovering it for the first time. In this sense, the technical notes serve as a benchmark or foundation upon which entrepreneurs and others can build a base of knowledge germane to entrepreneurial activities.

Another coequal purpose of the notes is to serve as background material for classroom discussions of particular case situations as well as other classroom activities and discussions. As such, let me reiterate that the notes are not intended to substitute for professional counsel and we cannot be responsible for their application to other specific situations.

A FINAL WORD ON THE USE OF THE NOTES

A unique feature of the technical notes is the use of examples that relate the technical information to concepts of entrepreneurship presented elsewhere in this book. However, many more conceptual relationships exist than are presented in the technical notes. My experience has been that students maximize their learning from the technical notes when they organize and relate this information to key entrepreneurship concepts.

LEGAL ISSUES

ABOUT LAWYERS, THEIR SELECTION, AND THEIR USE

WHY YOU NEED A LAWYER

Business is regulated by law, and all entrepreneurs, from pushcart vendors to founder/CEO's of budding multinational enterprises, must be aware of the legal rules and regulations which affect their particular businesses. Especially when starting a new business, entrepreneurs must be familiar with the legal constraints and protections relevant to a particular venture.

As an entrepreneur, you can do some self-education about the areas in which you will need legal assistance before hiring a lawyer. It will save you time - and money - if you know what you're looking for. The overview provided in the Legal Notes are designed to highlight some common legal problems which require different types of lawyers, and to indicate how and when changing legal issues during the life of a venture may dictate the type of legal specialist you will need.

Of course, a lawyer is an advisor and not the boss; you must make the final decisions. But the best decisions are those based on the best possible advice.

When Starting Up. In the very early stages of your venture, you may not know the types and numbers of legal specialists you will need; therefore, it is usually best to find a generalist who can serve as your primary source of legal counsel. If you define yourself as a "small businessman" then you should look for a lawyer experienced in small business start-ups. However, if your venture is a franchise, then you should seek a lawyer accustomed to assessing the contractual agreements associated with franchises. And if you are acquiring an existing company, your advice should come from a lawyer/accountant familiar with the legalities of acquisitions and real estate transactions, as well as one who understands and practices effective negotiating techniques.

At start-up, you will need a patent attorney if your venture involves a proprietary product. Also, you may wish to consult a tax lawyer if tax consequences will play an important part in the success of your venture. And even if taxes are not a primary concern, you may need a lawyer's help with the formal procedures of organizing an enterprise.

When Operating. Again, your needs will be dictated by your venture, but one common operating necessity is the execution of contracts. Contracts are ubiquitous; a General Partnership Agreement, employee non-compete contracts, bank loan forms, buy/sell agreements with customers and vendors, are but a few examples of important legal contracts. Another critical area in building your venture may be large-scale capital needs; especially if you plan to go public, or even if you are seeking venture capital funds, you will benefit from counsel experienced in these fields.

When Ending. If you have decided to sell your venture, or to merge it, a lawyer will help you design the terms that are most favorable to you -- in terms of payback over time, residual rights, and ongoing affiliation; mergers and acquisitions are a specialty of certain lawyers. And, finally, though one hopes not to need advice on bankruptcy, a lawyer experienced in bankruptcy proceedings can help you minimize your losses and perhaps even breathe new life into your venture. (See Note on Bankruptcy).

As you can see, there can be no single rule on how and when to use a lawyer. One good lawyer who is a general practitioner may be all you will ever need if the scope and complexity of your venture fits well within the understanding and capability of your counsel's practice. However, some ventures outgrow generalists, others need specialized counsel from the very beginning, and almost all ventures have different legal needs at different points during their lives. When, and how often, to pay the price for legal advice is your decision, one that you almost certainly will need to make more than once. Consequently, an awareness of the situations which often require consulting a lawyer will help you to decide wisely.

HOW TO CHOOSE A LAWYER

The conventional wisdom about how to choose a lawyer usually begins with two "don'ts" - not a family member and not a close friend. Lawyers themselves suggest shopping around for an individual or firm with proven experience in your particular situation.

Many first-time entrepreneurs have never dealt professionally with a lawyer before, and may feel apprehensive about what to ask and what to expect. Lawyers who deal with small businessmen are aware of this, and one offers the following advice:

> You are hiring a lawyer for his professional opinions about the legal aspects of your venture, not to run it for you. You are hiring him, not vice versa; you must have confidence and trust in this judgment, because you may be spending a good deal of time together. If you are dealing with a larger firm, you should ask to meet the junior partner who will be doing most of the work, to assure yourself that he/she has adequate experience and is a person with whom you can deal comfortably.

Seasoned entrepreneurs, or entrepreneurs leaving corporate life to start their own venture, will have had prior experience in how to use a lawyer, and the first-timer can benefit by talking to these people or by reading their suggestions which are frequently printed in business magazines.

Your choice of lawyers will ultimately depend on three factors: your type of venture, your personality and your bankroll.

Your Type of Venture. Aside from the functional areas of the law in which you will need advice, you should ask yourself a number of other questions: In terms of future expectations, what kind of venture do I have? And what kind of entrepreneurial career do I expect to pursue?

The following diagram may be a useful framework to use in organizing your thoughts.

	Profit	**Non-Profit**	**Routine***	**Non-Routine**
Life-style Ventures				
Smaller Profit-oriented Ventures				
High Growth Ventures				

Depending on where you put the X's, you have already defined some foreseeable future requirements for a lawyer. Non-profit organizations are chartered with laws of their own. High-growth venture often require substantial capital infusions and frequently imply a desire to go public. Consequently, a law firm with considerable experience in corporate affairs might be a wiser choice than a smaller, less experienced law partnership. On the other hand, a venture of limited size may be of such interest to a one- or two-person law firm that you might acquire a valuable partner by going to them for advice. Finally, if you are charting unknown waters, you may feel you need a lawyer with a reputation for creativity in helping to launch an extraordinary new concept.

---

*A working definition of a routine venture is one satisfying three conditions:

1. No radically new technology is used to produce your products or services;

2. Others produce the same or similar products or services;

3. Others sell their products/services to the same market segment. A non-routine venture would be one in which *any one* of the three conditions stated above does not exist.

Your Personality. In terms of myself and my venture, what type of lawyer will complement the image I need to project?

If you are your own best salesman but are no lawyer, you will be looking for someone with experience in your field and with whom you have good personal chemistry. If the venture initially involves raising substantial capital, a lawyer who is at ease with bankers, venture capital firms, and private benefactors will be a great asset. If your venture involves considerable hard-nosed negotiating, or dealing with labor unions, an aggressive and experienced person who doesn't mind slugging it out with the opposition will serve you best.

Your Bankroll. How much can I afford to pay?

A good lawyer is a good investment for an entrepreneur, and may even be a prerequisite for success. But good lawyers do cost money. How much? Address the issue directly from the outset; there may or may not be a charge for an initial consultation. Ask for the billing rates for the people who will be working with you, the estimated cost of research, searching titles, of filing necessary documents. Again, the conventional wisdom is to allow as much as you can afford for legal fees on your start-up cost schedule, and hire the best you can get for the money. Depending on the scope and type of your venture, you may find that you can't afford to start without necessary and costly legal advice, and these costs should be factored into your pro forma start-up calculations. Be honest with your lawyer about your own resources; you may be able to arrange a pay-back over time, or some other mutually acceptable compensation schedule, if you haven't the cash to pay for extensive but necessary pre-start up expenses.

WHERE TO LOOK

The most comprehensive directory of lawyers and law firms in the U.S. is published by Martindale and Hubbell, and is available in most libraries. Your local Bar Association can also serve as a reference service. But this approach is just a start. First, you can ask other entrepreneurs who have similar goals and types of ventures. Bankers, insurance brokers and others who regularly deal with entrepreneurs may also provide leads or have suggestions. Next, ask lawyers not seeking your business but familiar with the field (such as government or corporation lawyers and law professors.) Finally, the nearest Small Business Association office in your area may have compiled a list of lawyers with special interests in counselling smaller businesses.

A cautionary note: most persons who recommend a suitable lawyer will *not* be evaluating their suggestions using the criteria or the framework provided here. You must be certain that your particular situation is being considered in terms of your particular venture goals and career needs.

A CONCLUDING NOTE

Getting good legal advice and knowing how to use it can be critical to the smooth operation of many phases of your venture. To work effectively with a lawyer you must try to understand the legal issues yourself, you must trust him/her personally, you must ask questions when you have them, and you should accept cautionary advice as a rein, and not a deterrent, to your own enthusiasm. You should be comfortable, personally, with a lawyer -- and should be sure that your lawyer is comfortable with, and knowledgeable about, the scope and the uniqueness of your particular type of venture. Remember, the job of your lawyer is to help *you* do your best possible job in fulfilling your entrepreneurial goals.

LEGAL ISSUES

INTELLECTUAL PROPERTY PROTECTION

SOME KEY DEFINITIONS AND CONCEPTS

Does your venture involve a unique idea? If so, how do you plan to protect it? From the very beginning of your venture, you should be aware of the concept of intellectual property and the variety of protections provided by law. This note is intended as a general introduction to the topic.

The key to intellectual property protection is this: you cannot protect a pure idea, but if you can properly distill the idea into a form recognized by law you may be able to use it exclusively for a limited period of time. Whether it will be worth it to you in terms of time and expense is another question. Almost certainly you will need a lawyer (or an agent) who specializes in patent law and/or a lawyer skilled in writing protective employment contracts. Further, you will have to prepare and file a number of forms, and pay filing fees.*

Finally, the protection is remedial; to exercise it you will have to sue or be sued, resulting in substantial court costs and other penalties. Nonetheless, for certain ventures, success will be impossible without first-rate intellectual property protection.

First, let's look at some definitions for the most common forms of intellectual property protection.[1]

A *Patent* is an exclusive right to exclude others from manufacturing and selling something useful and novel which you have invented. The law recognizes three basic types of patents:

-Utility patents: for processes, machines, articles of manufacture and compositions of matter.

-Design patents: for original and unobvious designs for articles of manufacture.

---

*The following information pertains only to laws and regulations in the U.S. If you are considering filing a patent abroad you must follow the various procedures for each country; if you are filing here, you must be sure that a similar application from a foreign inventor is not already pending.

[1]A useful summary of these key considerations appears in Marc J. Lane's *Legal Handbook for Small Business,* AMACOM, 1977.

-Plant patents: for asexually reproduced plants excepting tubers and uncultivated plants.

A *Trade Secret* is any sort of confidential information you wish to maintain for the good of your business. Your right to protect *Trade Secrets* exists in each state's body of law that governs torts and contracts.

A *Copyright* protects literary and artistic property from unauthorized use or reproduction, and is granted by the Federal Patent Office, a branch of the Library of Congress.

A *Trademark* is a word, symbol, or device used to distinguish your product from others which may be superficially similar. Its value lies in its use. It is granted both at the federal and the state level.

The table shown on the next page provides a convenient summary of some key facts related to patents, trade secrets, copyrights, and trademarks. (Table I)

PATENTS

A patent is a contract between an inventor and the government. In exchange for the inventor's disclosure of his invention, the government promises him certain exclusionary rights for a limited period of time -- i.e., the rights "to exclude" others from making, using, or selling the invention. A patent is not a positive right to sell or license your invention, for reasons which will be discussed later. Neither is it a gift from the government, nor an invitation to monopoly. It is a contract. The concept was first written into law in the Federal Patent Act of 1790, with the intent to encourage "the useful arts" by granting some protection to an inventor of a tangible item in exchange for his willingness to disclose some information about it.

A few obvious examples of the three general types of patentable items will illustrate the definitions given earlier. A utility patent covers a *process* such as developing film; a *machine* such as a Cuisinart; an *article of manufacture* such as an aerosol spray device; and a *compostion of matter* such as nylon or the new biogenetic products. A design patent would cover a triple-gooseneck lamp or an impact-resistant car bumper. A plant patent could be obtained for a new variety of rose or a hybrid fruit tree. *The legal touchstone for these, and all patentable objects is that they be "useful" and "non-obvious."*

Here, the waters become murky -- especially when you consider that the safety pin was once patented. Though you, the inventor, are the only one who can obtain a patent, is your invention patentable? Generally you need expert advice from a patent lawyer with a background in engineering or design. Further, he should be familiar with your field and technology (mechanical, electrical, chemical, electronic, biogenetic).

Patents are issued by the U.S. Patent and Trademark Office (PTO), a branch of the Commerce Department, which has granted over a million patents since 1790. The PTO also administers two other programs: a *Disclosure Document Program,* where inventors

Table I
Intellectual Property Protection
Key Facts

	Utility Patent	Design Patent	Plant Patent	Trade Secret	Copyright	Trademark
What is Protected	Useful processes, machines, articles of manufacture, compositions of matter	Ornamental and novel designs for articles of manufacture	Asexually re-produced plants, excluding tubers and wild plants	Confidential information which gives your company a competitive edge	Works of art (writing, music, recordings, computer pro-grams) which are reduced to a fixed medium	Words, names, symbols — other marks distin-guishing one's goods from others
Sources of Protection	Granting of a patent by the U.S. Patent and Trademark Office	same	same	Employer-employee contracts. Employer-vendor con-tracts. State laws, mostly common law, on unfair competi-tion. No federal remedy.	Registration with the U.S. Copyright Office	Federal registra-tion by the Pat-ent and Trademark Office. State Registra-tion. Common law protection if used properly.
Where to Obtain Applica-tion and filing Fees (1979)	U.S. Depart-ment of Com-merce Patent and Trademark Office, Wash-ingD.C. 20231 (Patents are filed at the PTO ton, repository in Arlington, VA) Basic Fee: $65 Additional fees for copies.	See below.	Basic fees same as Utility Patent.		Register & Copyright Library of Congress, Washington, D.C. 20559 Fee $10	Federal: Patent and Trademark Office, Washing-ton, D.C. 20231 State: write the Secretary of State
Terms of Protection	17 years from date patent is issued.	3½ years — $10 7 years — $20 14 years — $30	17 years from date patent is issued.	Remedy varies from case to case.	Life of author, plus 50 years for works created after January 1, 1978	U.S. — 20 years from registration issuance; renewal every 20 years.

can file information prior to applying to a patent, to support their contention that they were "first" with the idea; and the *Defensive Publication Program,* for those inventors who do not want to obtain a patent but want to insure that no one else does either.[2]

The more the inventor knows about the procedure for obtaining a patent -- the patent search, and the preparation of the patent application -- the easier it will be for him to satisfy the PTO requirements. The patent search, in which the inventor is encouraged to

[2]David Burge, *Patent and Trademark Tactics and Practice,* John Wiley & Sons, 1980, p.6.

take an active part, can be conducted either at the PTO in Arlington, VA, or at a regional center. Here, the inventor can learn which patents already exist, along with the type and scope of the claims made for them. The patent application, a sample of which is included as *Exhibit 1,* contains the complete history and description of the invention, along with the claims made for its usefulness. The history should be documented with reference to a log kept by the inventor; the descriptions should include a general abstract and specific details; and the drawings must conform with the PTO specifications. The claims, the guts of the patent application, must strike a balance between the specific and the general, since they are the criteria by which infringement allegations will be judged. They cannot be so precise as to let others get around the idea (the diameters of screws which are not critical to the operation) nor so general that they obscure the uniqueness of the invention ("it threads needles"). When the application has been completed it is sent to the Patent Office, along with a basic filing fee and a surcharge for the number of claims made, and assigned to an examiner in the PTO.

After the application has been received, the status of the invention is Patent Pending. Though the application will be held in strictest confidence, the inventor must be watchful for the sudden appearance of inventions resembling his which are not patented. He may have grounds for a law suit to stop the potential competition.

After some months, office action will be taken regarding the application. The examiner assigned to the patent application may request additional information. He may want further clarification and he may disallow some of the claims. If, despite the inventor's responses, the patent is rejected, he may revise it and try once more. If it is accepted, he will receive a Notice of Allowance and a U.S. Patent Number. This affirms the validity of the patent for 17 years.

Once the invention is manufactured, the number should be displayed on the machine or container, and - if all goes according to plan - both the inventor and the venture will reap the commercial benefits. However, the patent is also an invitation to sue or be sued regarding questions of infringement or restraint of trade, proceedings in which your patent lawyer will be critical.

Finally, if patent rights are sold or licensed, the Patent Office must be notified immediately.

Some inventors and patent lawyers have adopted a rule of thumb as to when, and when not, to patent an invention - because not only is the process costly* but the court costs for infringement suits are even greater. Pragmatically, if you expect to realize less than $100,000 on the invention, the cost of patenting is not justified. At the other extreme, if you expect to realize huge profits from some invention, you may not be able to afford to protect your patent. If you have come up with a hot property, a large firm may use your invention regardless of your patents, figuring that the time and expense (to them) of

---

*At 1980 prices, the attorney's fee plus the cost of filing applications on a relatively straightforward invention will be at least $1,200.

fighting your claims in court are justifiable expenses compared to what they stand to gain.

Once you have been granted a patent, you may still need a license from a previous patent holder who has a claim on the basic subject matter your invention has improved. For example, if you invented a machine to thread needles *and* knot the thread, but a non-knotting needle threader was already in existence, you would have to obtain a license from the needle-threading patent holder in order to market your device. Under other conditions, you may be the one granting a license. For example, once you obtain a patent, another individual or company may wish to manufacture and sell your invention. And they may be in a much better position to do so than you are. Therefore, you may wish to sell your patent rights outright, or negotiate a licensing contract guaranteeing you a percent of the profits on your invention over the lifetime of the patent.

Now, suppose you're not the inventor, but an entrepreneur dealing with inventors. Suppose you hire an inventor to invent something useful to your venture on your time in your shop. Who gets the patent? To cover these contingencies, you (the employer) should require your employees to sign a carefully-drafted agreement prepared by your lawyer at the outset. In the former case, if litigation ensues, the court may give the employer the rights to the invention. In the latter case, the employer may be entitled to a "shopright", an implied license giving the employee the right to apply for a patent but allowing the employer to sell the product without paying royalties to the employee.

For a sample agreement of this sort, see Exhibit 2.[3]

TRADE SECRETS

A trade secret is difficult to define because it can apply to a wide range of information which a company wishes to protect. The standard definition derives from the Restatement of Torts (1939).

> ...any formula, patent, device or compilation of information used in one's business (which gives him an edge on the competition)....It may be a formula for a chemical compound, a process of manufacturing, treating or preserving materials, a pattern for a machine or other device, or a list of customers...Generally, it relates to the production of goods...It may, however, relate to the sale of goods...such as a code for determining discounts, rebates or other concessions in a price list or catalogue, or a list of specialized customers, or a method of bookkeeping...[4]

---

[3]William Hancock, *The Small Business Legal Advisor,* McGraw Hill, 1982, pp 214-6.
[4]Burge, *op. cit.,* p. 151.

Although some trade secrets are patentable, an entrepreneur may believe that the element of secrecy is more important than the element of protection offered by disclosing the product or process by obtaining a patent.

The concept of Trade Secrets stems from the doctrine of unfair competition and from contract law. Although trade secrets are not covered by federal law, a growing body of common law in each state offers protection; for this reason, it is important to consult an attorney who knows the law in the state in which you do business if protection of trade secrets is an important element of your venture.

Probably, the most effective method of protecting trade secrets from being leaked by employees is to require each employee to sign a Confidential Information Agreement, drafted by your lawyer, of the type shown in Exhibit 2. This agreement will protect your secrets both during the employee's time with you and after he leaves, and will serve as the instrument by which you can sue him if he violates it. A similar need to protect yourself against vendors leaking your secrets can be obtained by requiring vendors to sign a similar contract.

However, both these remedies are retaliatory in nature; legal suit can be brought only after the damage is done. Precautionary measures must be taken. Valuable information should be restricted to those who must know. Formulas and other non-patented secrets should be securely stored and unauthorized personnel should be prohibited from entering restricted areas.

COPYRIGHTS

If your venture is of a literary or artistic nature, if it involves publication or advertising, you should know something about copyright law. If not, this information may be only of tangential importance to you. Nonetheless, you may want to copyright company brochures and catalogues. Or you may wish to reproduce articles of interest for your employees and should be acquainted with both the concept and the mechanics of copyrighting.

Copyright protection is available for literary, artistic and informational creations. The Federal Copyright Law, recently revised in 1978, assigns to the creator the exclusive rights to reproduce, revise, distribute, perform or display the work -- but only if it is in a tangible medium of expression; copyrights protect the form of the work not the substance. Once granted, the copyright protection extends 50 years beyond the death of the creator for the benefit of his heirs.

The new law expands and extends the copyright concept to cover new technologies and contingencies in several important ways. One key change is the type of material covered by the law. In addition to "artistic" materials such as books and periodicals, dramatic and musical compositions, works of art, prints and photographs, sound recordings and choreographed works, protection is now extended to "fixed" works such as prose and poetry taped but not transcribed, dances and pantomines videotaped but not annotated on paper, and computer software, which is discussed in a subsequent section.*

A second revision extends the coverage of the copyright to 50 years beyond the death of the creator, and relaxes the requirements for how and where the copyright notice must appear on the material. In fact, copyright is implicit in common law, but in order to bring suit for infringement you must have a properly registered federal copyright. Proof of infringement is often difficult to establish since it must be proved that the act was deliberate. This requirement contrasts sharply with the requirement under patent law, where the fact and not the intent constitutes proof of infringement.

A third amplification of the new law deals with the reality of the copy machine and the concept of "fair use". In theory, the holder of a copyright must grant permission to reproduce the work before it can be copied; and a person wishing to reproduce a copyrighted work must first request permission to do so. But if a competitor duplicates your brochure to show his customer why he thinks his product is better, has he infringed your copyright? Or, if your venture is a franchised copy center, are you infringing a copyright if a teacher asks you to duplicate a magazine article for classroom use? Or, can you legally duplicate portions of a book on selling techniques to give to your salesmen? You may or may not be violating the copyright law in each of these cases since the law defines "fair use" in terms of motivation and whether the material will be used for profit and/or deprive the copyright holder of "fair" profit. You should be aware of situations tending toward possible infringement. If you aren't sure, consult an attorney. As the saying goes, ignorance of the law is no defense.

The registration procedure is relatively straightforward. First, the material must be reduced to a tangible form. Next, a copy of the work and an application form (see Exhibit 3) plus the appropriate fee must be deposited with the Copyright Office. When the copyright is granted, the owner must mark all copies of the work with "c" and the year it was granted.

COPYRIGHT PROTECTION FOR COMPUTER SOFTWARE PROGRAMS

Entrepreneurs should be aware that now software programs can be copyrighted. Previously, patents, copyrights, and trade secrets all had been used for protection, since the courts were unwilling to define the status of software. In 1980, the Computer Software Copyright Act was added to the Federal Code of Copyright Laws to clarify the situation. As defined by the law, "a 'computer program' is a set of statements or instructions to be used directly or indirectly in a computer to bring about certain results." Also as defined, a computer program applies only to the tangible product and not to the algorithms on which the program is based, which being "ideas" are not eligible for protection. Application may be made by either the author or the publisher. Owners of

---

*Traditionally, copyrights covered "artistic" works, whereas patents covered "utilitarian" items. The difference is reflected in the fact that copyrights are registered with the Library of Congress, whereas patents are granted by the Commerce Department.

copies of the programs are authorized to make copies for their own use without violating the act.

There are mixed reactions to the Software Copyright Amendment, but at least the legal status of this burgeoning industry is no longer in limbo.[5]

TRADEMARKS

A trademark is a handy means of identification -- a mark which one uses to distinguish his goods and services from those of others. The concept of trademark rights grew out of the doctrine of unfair competition, and was conceived as a means by which the owner of the trademark could prevent confusion in the minds of the public confronted with a variety of similar objects about which "brand" was his. Although trademarks are granted by the U.S. Patent and Trademark Office (as well as by state trademark offices), they are not patents and they are not patentable. Trademarks give the owner the rights to exclude others from using his mark; patents give owners the right to exclude others from making, using or selling his invention. Unlike patents (and copyrights), trademark rights do not end after a specific period of time. They are granted for a period of 20 years and can be extended indefinitely, as long as they remain in use.

You may wish to work with your patent attorney on the selection of a trademark, and to follow his advice about how to use it properly, since these two procedures are essential if you are to make the most of your trademark rights.

Trademarks may take the form of words, initials, numbers, slogans or distinctive symbols. Permissible trademarks fall into four general categories: *coined marks* (Kodak, Exxon) which offer a broad scope of protection against infringement; *arbitrary marks* (Shell Oil), which make an arbitrary association between a symbol and a product; *suggestive marks* (Arrid deodorant), which are usually limited by their nature to a single product or line of products; and *descriptive marks* (Ruberoid), which must gain consumer acceptance as a particular brand (in this case) of roofing material before it can be registered.[6]

Certain trademarks -- immoral matter, the U.S. flag, etc. -- are prohibited by law. Other types of trademarks may be disallowed: certain overused adjectives such as "hard" or "silky"; deceptive terms such as "european" soap for soap made in the U.S.; family names which could be used by another unrelated person with the same name; and geographical terms which could be used by anyone doing business in the same territory.[7]

The *concept of use* cannot be overemphasized, for it is in "using" a trademark, rather than registration of it, that the mark assumes its value. The more widely used, the more

---

[5]See *Datamation* Feb., 1981, "For Better or Worse," pp 49-50.

[6]Hamilton, Brook, Smith and Reynolds, "General Information On Trademarks," an unpublished note, Lexington, MA, 1981. Also see Burge, *op. cit.,*p. 115.

[7]Hamilton, *et al, op. cit.*

valuable it becomes, like "Xerox" or "Scotch" tape. The trademark must be used as an adjective -- "Scotch" brand tape, "Xerox" copy machine -- under the terms of the law. On some occasions, use as a generic noun (cellophane, aspirin) has resulted in the invalidation of the trademark.

Trademarks are granted both at federal and state levels. If your venture will be involved in interstate commerce, you should choose the federal registration since it gives more protection.

Federal registration recognizes five categories of trademarks: trademarks, service marks, collective marks, certification marks, and supplemental marks. To register your mark, you must file an application (including a black and white drawing with descriptions of the colors) and five specimens of the mark, to show that it is already in use. These data, plus the registration fee, should be deposited with the U.S. Patent and Trademark Office or a state office. After six years, a *Declaration of Use* should be filed with the PTO, and after 20 years you should file to renew your registration.

Once you receive your Certificate of Registration, you must display your trademark clearly, accompanied by the symbol "R". (A non-registered trademark should be accompanied by the letters TM or an asterisk with an explanatory footnote.) Any infringements should be reported to the Patent Office, and can be the basis of a law suit. You must also report the sale or licensing of your mark to the Patent Office.

THE PATENT AND TRADEMARK OFFICE PLANS FOR THE FUTURE

Flooded by increasing volumes of patent and trademark applications, the PTO has been unable to keep abreast of processing them. Happily, this state of affairs is about to be changed. The new efficiencies are described by Gerald J. Mossinghoff, Commissioner of Patents and Trademarks.[8]

Very real and pervasive problems plagued the Patent and Trademark Office at the end of the previous administration. The office was starved for funding. The number of patent examiners had been allowed to decline to a level lower than it had been in years. The backlog of more than 200,000 patent applications and 100,000 trademark applications was growing at an alarming rate of more than 25,000 cases each year. The time it took to get a patent—about 24 months—was increasing at the rate of about two months a year and the time to register a trademark was at an all-time high of about 25 months. The all-paper, 24 million-document file through which examiners must look when conducting a search was growing at a rate that would increase to 50

---

[8] *Enterprise,* National Association of Manufacturers, May 1983, pp. 4-5.

million documents by the turn of the century. Further, about 7 percent of that file was either missing or misfiled—a situation directly affecting the quality of the search and the issued patent. In short, the office was rapidly losing its ability to serve inventors and industry adequately.

Early in this administration, Secretary of Commerce Malcolm Baldrige made a firm commitment to improve the operations of the office through three major plans. The first of these is to reduce to 18 months by 1987 the average time it takes to get a patent. Currently we are on schedule. We have already hired more than 300 new patent examiners and will hire 500 more during the next three years. During the fiscal year, we will process nearly 100,000 patent applications, compared with 83,000 in FY 82. In FY 84 we plan to process almost 109,000 patent applications and will, for the first time in seven years, dispose of more applictions than we will receive.

The second plan—to reduce by 1985 the time on first action on trademarks to three months and the total disposal time to 13 months—is also on schedule. Pendency time for trademark applications is down to 22 months to disposal. As with patents, in FY 84 we will turn the corner on trademarks and dispose of more cases than are received.

The third major plan calls for a move toward a fully automated Patent and Trademark office in the 1990s. Here, we have already accomplished several important steps. All automation activities have been centralized under the newly created position of administrator for automation. In December, we delivered to Congress a comprehensive and detailed automation master plan. Under this plan, we will replace our vast collection of paper with computer-searchable data bases. This move will not only achieve 100 percent file integrity, but will also make patent documents available in useful form at our 38 patent despository libraries throughout the country.

We have now entered into cooperative patent automation agreements with the European Patent Office and the Japanese Patent Office.

Exhibit 1

United States Patent

Flint

KEY SETTABLE, PICK PROOF LOCK

Inventor: Orin Q. Flint, P.O. Box 536,
Linwood, Mass. 01525

Appl. No.: 787,307

Filed: Apr. 14, 1977

Int. Cl. E05B 25/00
U.S. Cl. 70/383
Field of Search 70/383, 382, 337, 340,
    70/341, 342, 343

References Cited

U.S PATENT DOCUMENTS

2,112,007 4/1938 Swanson 70/340

Primary Examiner--Robert L. Wolfe

Abstract

A lock comprises separate key plug, lock plug and memory storage of a key image inserted in the key plug and transfer of the stored image to the lock plug for testing of the image at a site removed from the key plug. The key image memory and transfer mechanism comprises multiple chips offering a flexibility for key changes by any inserted key when the key plug and lock plug are in "unlocked" position. The memory is changed to the new key image. Testing is accomplished after lost motion rotation of the key plug to preclude manipulation of lock pins in the lock plug during testing of the key image (i.e., torquing of the lock plug).

5 Claims, 22 Drawing Figures

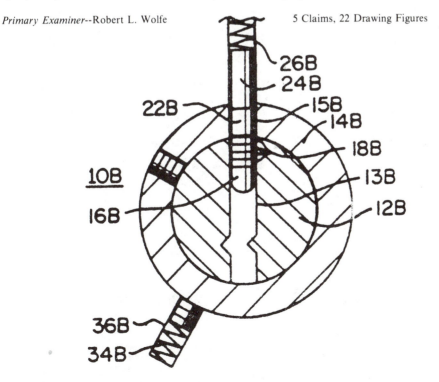

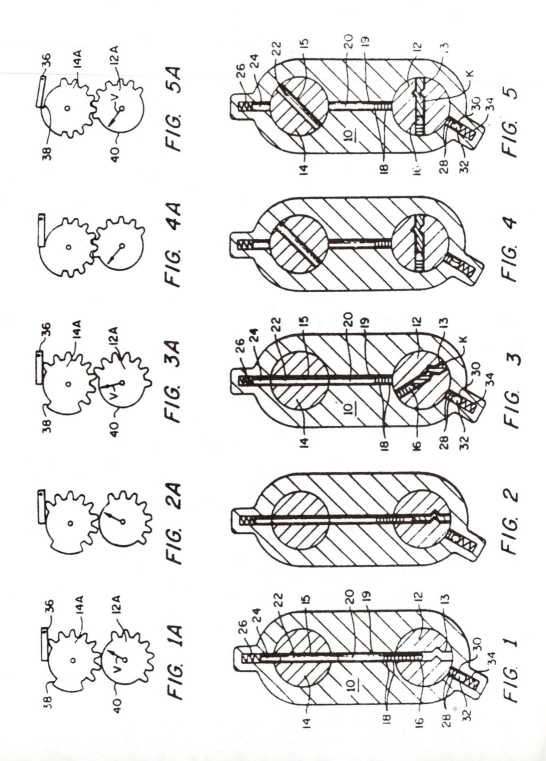

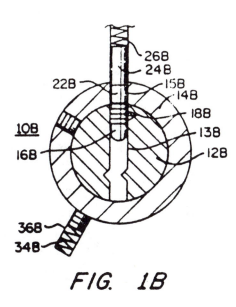

FIG. 1B

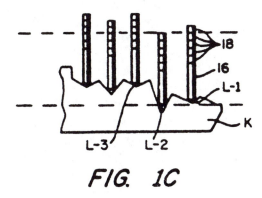

FIG. 1C

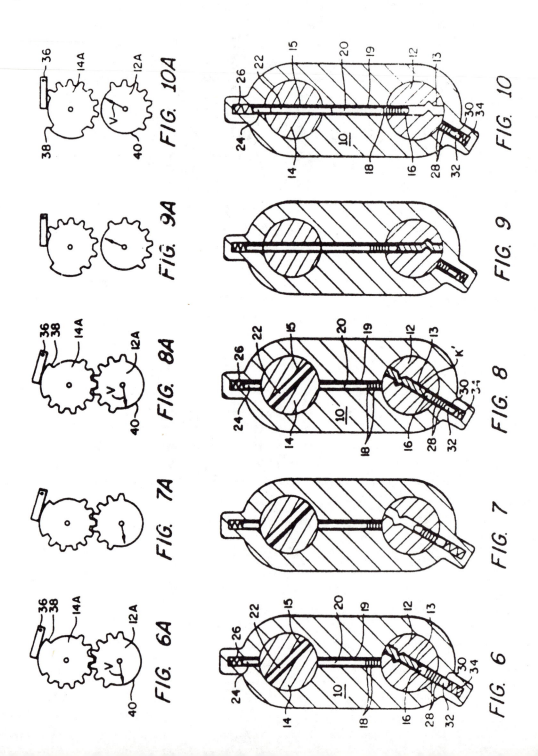

FIG. 10A

FIG. 10

FIG. 9A

FIG. 9

FIG. 8A

FIG. 8

FIG. 7A

FIG. 7

FIG. 6A

FIG. 6

Key Settable, Pick Proof Lock

Background of the Invention

The present invention relates to a new type of pin tumbler lock and is particularly characterized by the unusual operating features of being pick-proof and key changeable. That is, the keying of the lock may be changed simply by inserting the new key under specified conditions. No lock disassembly is required.

Conventional pin tumbler locks can be picked because the pins may be aligned one at a time in a serial fashion, although the intention is that all pins must be aligned simultaneously to open the lock.

It is a further object of the invention to provide user key change capability without disassembly consistent with the preceding object.

It is a further object of the invention that serial pin setting cannot be accomplished consistent with one or both of the preceding objects.

Summary of the Invention

In accordance with the invention, a lock is provided with the following operating mode, contrasted with prior art, for pick-proof protection and key change capability without disassembly. A key is inserted and the configuration of the key is 'memorized'. The memorized configuration is then 'tested'. At the time the key configuration is tested, there is no access to the lock pins, or memory and hence, they cannot be manipulated in a trial and error fashion.

The lock memory is provided in the following way: First, consider a prior art master keyed pin tumbler lock. Two keys can open the lock because there are two sets of cleavage lines (between lock pin segments). (Actually, 2^n different keys, where n is the number of split pins, can be made which will open the lock). Now introduce another set of cleavage lines so that the lock is keyed for two master keys and a service key. This lock could be opened by 3^n keys. In accordance with the present invention, continue this subdivision process until all properly cut (i.e. turnable through the last motion zone) keys will open the lock. The usual longer lock pins have now been replaced by stacks of pins. When any key is inserted and rotated, the number of pins trapped in the plug in each column is a negative representation of the key, while the number of pins remaining behind in the cylinder is a positive representation of the key. Thus a representation of the key is stored in the cylinder when the key and plug are rotated and access to the pins in the cylinder is not available from the outside.

In the present invention, the stored representation of the key configuration is tested by a separate lock plug interconnected to the key plug. In one preferred embodiment the key plug and lock plug have parallel or slightly converging axes and the pin tumbler holds

extend from the key plug through the cylinder to the lock plug (and through the lock plug into the cylinder again where the pin springs are located). An interlock prevents the lock plug from being turned unless the key plug is first rotated. Alternatively, the lock plug may be turned by an interconnecting means from the key plug. In another preferred embodiment, the lock plug is concentric with the key plug, i.e., the lock 'plug' is a sleeve. In all cases, the 'memorized' configuration acts like a 'key', which sets the pins in the lock plug.

The key change feature is as follows: Assume the proper key has been inserted in the lock described above and the key plug rotated. The cleavage lines for the lock plug are properly aligned so that the lock plug may be rotated. Each column in the key plug contains a sufficient number of small pins so that the key plus the split pins fill up the columns in the plug. A different key would require, in general, a different number of pin segments to fill up each column in the plug. To change the keying, there is provided in accordance with the invention, a set of key relief holes, pin segments, and springs. The key plug, is further rotated so as to align the pin holes in the plug with the key relief holes in the cylinder. The key may then be removed. The springs in the key relief holes force columns of pin segments into the plug. Then a new key is inserted forcing back into the key relief holes, in general, a different number of split pins. The key and plug are not rotated back to the operating position. The lock is now keyed to the new key.

Access to the key change position may be controlled by a master key or by other means. For instance, in the extreme, the ability to change keys may exist only at the factory. The lock, as far as the user is concerned, is an ordinary, although pick-proof, lock. An advantage of this approach is that all locks could be made part-for-part identical and keyed by merely inserting a key. The lock sets itself to the first key inserted.

In a hotel application, lock changing ability may be under control of a master key used by the bellhop who resets the lock for each new room occupant. Since the number of times a lock will be used by an average room occupant is small, disposable plastic keys might be used. The keys could be picked at random from a large collection of pre-cut keys.

Some advantages of the invention include use of standard lock parts and keys. The keys may be standard and may be reproduced on standard key copying equipment. The key plug, driver pins, small pins, and springs, may all be standard. The cylinder or main frame has standard tolerance requirements.

The lock may be 'hybrid'; that is, some of the pin

channels may work according to the principles of the present invention, while the other channels operate in the other manner. Ordinary master keying may be used in lieu of or in addition to key changing as indicated above.

Other objects, features and advantages of the invention will be apparent from the following detailed description of preferred embodiments thereof, taken in connection with the accompanying drawing, in which:

Brief Description of the Drawing

FIGS 1-10 are diagrammatic, cross section views of lock apparatus, with FIGS. 1A-10A being diagrams of related gearing, in accordance with a first preferred embodiment of the invention and FIGS 1B-1C show a second preferred embodiment.

Detailed Description of Preferred Embodiments

FIGS. 1-4, together with FIGS. 1A-4A, show a preferred embodiment of the lock of the invention at different stages of locking and FIGS. 5-10, together with FIGS. 5A-10A, show lock changing therefor. The structure of this embodiment comprises a lock body 10,

means forming a movable key plug with a locking channel,

means defining at least one key chip movably mounted within said locking channel for resting on a land of a key inserted into said channel,

means defining a movable lock plug with a channel therein,

means defining surrounding lock body structure containing said key plug and lock plug.

means forming a lock pin movably arranged within said lock plug channel and being movable between a first position extending partly out of said lock plug channel and engaging the body to lock the lock plug and a second position wholly within the channel to unlock the lock plug.

first means-for-interconnecting the key chips with the locking channel such that when the chip or chips is moved to a predetermined height by a predetermined key land height, then the chip or chips in turn act through said first means-for-interconnecting to allow movement of the lock pin from locking to unlocking position,

means for interconnecting the lock plug to a latch so that unlocking the lock plug and moving it in turn releases the latch and means for moving the lock plug when unlocked,

lost motion interconnection means between said plugs allowing initial key plug movement to separate chips in said body channel from chips in said key plug channel before lock plug movement can be attempted

to test the control key image of chips stacked in the body channel, the chips having a control key image that works in response to correct service key insertion in the key plug,

means in said lock body structure for storing chips, and,

second means-for-interconnecting said storage means and key plug channel for chip transfer to change to lock setting,

said second means-for-interconnecting being operable by a present correct service key and accommodatable to a new service key to effect such chip transfer.

Exhibit 2

Employee Invention and Confidential
Information Agreement*

(The Company Name)
XYZ, Inc.

XYZ's special competence in its various fields of endeavor is the secret of its growth, and provides the source of both career opportunities and security for employees throughout the company. Career opportunities of XYZ people have been a Company tradition not only because of the generally high competence of XYZ personnel, but also because of Company growth. Such growth depends to a significant degree on the Company's possession of proprietary information—not generally known to others—more and better information than others have about research, development, production, marketing and management in XYZ's chosen fields.

To obtain such information and use it successfully, XYZ spends considerable sums of money in research and product development, product improvements, the development of marketing methods, and service to its customers. Many XYZ people make major contributions. This results in a pool of information which enables XYZ to conduct its business with unusual success, and thus with unusual potential for its employees. However, this potential exists only as long as this information is retained proprietary within XYZ. Once generally known, this information gives no advantages to XYZ, its employees or its stockholders.

In effect, all XYZ employees have a common interest and responsibility in seeing that no one employee accidentally or intentionally siphons off or distributes to non-XYZ people any part of this pool of information.

To help protect you, all other employees and the Company against such a possibility, this Employee Agreement has been prepared for your signature and the Company's so that we have a common understanding concerning our mutual responsibilities in this connection. Please read it carefully so that you may understand its importance.

Employee's Last Name

First Name   **Initial**

Inventions

1. I will promptly disclose in writing to the Company all inventions, discoveries, developments, improvements, and innovations (herein called "inventions") whether patentable or not, conceived or made by me, either solely or in concert with others during the period of my employment with the Company, including, but not limited to, any period prior to the date of this agreement, whether or not made or conceived during working hours which,

(a) relate in any manner to the existing or contemplated business or research activities or the Company, or
(b) are suggested by or result from my work at the Company, or
(c) result from the use of the Company's time, materials, or facilties and that all such inventions shall be the exclusive property of the Company.

---

*NOTE: This form covers *both inventions* and *confidential information*. The drafter can divide these into separate forms if it is thought appropriate. If the agreement is not signed at initial employment, be sure it is supported by consideration.

2. I hereby assign to the Company my entire right, title and interest to all such inventions which are the property of the company under the provisions of paragraph 1 of this Agreement and to all unpatented inventions which I now own except those specifically described in a statement which has been separately executed by a duty authorized officer of the Company and myself and attached hereto and I will, at the Company's request and expense, execute specific assignments to any such invention and execute, acknowledge and deliver such other documents and take such further action as may be considered necessary by the Company at any time during or subsequent to the period of my employment with the Company to obtain and defend letters patent in any and all countries and to vest title in such inventions in the Company or its assigns.

3. I agree that any invention disclosed by me to a third person or described in a patent application filed by me or in my behalf within six months following the period of my employment with the Company shall be presumed to have been conceived or made by me during the period of my employment with the Company unless proved to have been conceived and made by me following the termination of employment with the Company.

Confidentiality

1. I will not during or at any time after the termination of my employment with the Company use for myself or others or divulge or convey to others any secret or confidential information, knowledge or data of the Company or that of third parties obtained by me during the period of my employment with the Company and such information, knowledge or data includes but is not limited to secret or confidential matters.

(a) of a technical nature such as but not limited to methods, know-how, formulae, compositions, processes, discoveries, machines, inventions, computer programs and similar items or research projects.
(b) of a business nature such as but not limited to information about cost, purchasing, profits, market, sales or lists of customers, and
(c) pertaining to future developments such as but not limited to research and development or future marketing or merchandising.

2. Upon termination of my employment with the Company, or at any other time at the Company's request, I agree to deliver promptly to the Company all drawings, blueprints, manuals, letters, notes, notebooks, reports, sketches, formulae, computer programs and similar items, memoranda, customer's lists and all other materials and all copies thereof relating in any way to the Company's business and in any way obtained by me during the period of my employment with the Company which are in my possession or under my control.

I further agree that I will not make or retain any copies of any of the foregoing and will so represent to the Company upon termination of my employment.

3. The Company may notify anyone employing me or evidencing an intention to employ me as to the existence and provisions of this Agreement.

4. The invalidity or unenforceability of any provision of this Agreement as applied to a particular occurrence or circumstance or otherwise shall not affect the validity and enforceability or applicability of any other provision of this Agreement.

5. This Agreement shall inure to the benefit of and may be enforced by the Company, its successors or assigns and shall be binding upon me, my executors, administrators, legatees, distributees and other successors in interest and may not be changed in whole or in part except in a writing signed by a duty authorized officer of the Company and myself.

I agree to comply with and do all things necessary for the Company to comply with provisions of contracts between it and any agency of the United States Government or contractors thereof. This includes but is not limited to all provisions relating to invention rights or to the safeguarding or information pertaining to the defense of the United States of America.

Exhibit 3

FORM TX

UNITED STATES COPYRIGHT OFFICE
LIBRARY OF CONGRESS
WASHINGTON, D.C. 20559

APPLICATION
FOR
COPYRIGHT
REGISTRATION
for a
Nondramatic Literary Work

HOW TO APPLY FOR COPYRIGHT REGISTRATION:

- *First:* Read the information on this page to make sure Form TX is the correct application for your work.

- *Second:* Open out the form by lifting on the left. Read through the detailed instructions before starting to complete the form.

- *Third:* Complete spaces 1-4 of the application, then turn the entire form over and, after reading the instructions for spaces 5-11, complete the rest of your application. Use typewriter or print in dark ink. Be sure to sign the form at space 10.

- *Fourth:* Detach your completed application from these instructions and send it with the necessary deposit of the work (see below) to: Register of Copyrights, Library of Congress, Washington, D.C. 20559. Unless you have a Deposit Account in the Copyright Office, your application and deposit must be accompanied by a check or money order for $10, payable to: *Register of Copyrights.*

WHEN TO USE FORM TX: Form TX is the appropriate application to use for copyright registration covering nondramatic literary works, whether published or unpublished.

WHAT IS A "NONDRAMATIC LITERARY WORK"? The category of "nondramatic literary works" (Class TX) is very broad. Except for dramatic works and certain kinds of audiovisual works, Class TX includes all types of works written in words (or other verbal or numerical symbols). A few of the many examples of "nondramatic literary works" include fiction, nonfiction, poetry, periodicals, textbooks, reference works, directories, catalogs, advertising copy, and compilations of information.

DEPOSIT TO ACCOMPANY APPLICATION: An application for copyright registration must be accompanied by a deposit representing the entire work for which registration is to be made. The following are the general deposit requirements as set forth in the statute:

Unpublished work: Deposit one complete copy (or phonorecord).

Published work: Deposit two complete copies (or phonorecords) of the best edition.

Work first published outside the United States: Deposit one complete copy (or phonorecord) of the first foreign edition.

Contribution to a collective work: Deposit one complete copy (or phonorecord) of the best edition of the collective work.

These general deposit requirements may vary in particular situations. For further information about copyright deposit, write for Circular R7.

THE COPYRIGHT NOTICE: For published works, the law provides that a copyright notice in a specified form "shall be placed on all publicly distributed copies from which the work can be visually perceived." Use of the copyright notice is the responsibility of the copyright owner and does not require advance permission from the Copyright Office. The required form of the notice for copies generally consists of three elements: (1) the symbol "©", or the word "Copyright", or the abbreviation "Copr."; (2) the year of first publication; and (3) the name of the owner of copyright. For example: "© 1978 Constance Porter". The notice is to be affixed to the copies "in such manner and location as to give reasonable notice of the claim of copyright." Unlike the law in effect before 1978, the new copyright statute provides procedures for correcting errors in the copyright notice, and even for curing the omission of the notice. However, a failure to comply with the notice requirements may still result in the loss of some copyright protection and, unless corrected within five years, in the complete loss of copyright. For further information about the copyright notice and the procedures for correcting errors or omissions, write for Circular R3.

DURATION OF COPYRIGHT: For works that were created after the effective date of the new statute (January 1, 1978), the basic copyright term will be the life of the author and fifty years after the author's death. For works made for hire, and for certain anonymous and pseudonymous works, the duration of copyright will be 75 years from publication or 100 years from creation, whichever is shorter. These same terms of copyright will generally apply to works that had been created before 1978 but had not been published or copyrighted before that date. For further information about the duration of copyright, including the terms of copyrights already in existence before 1978, write for Circular R15a.

FORM TX

UNITED STATES COPYRIGHT OFFICE

REGISTRATION NUMBER
TX   TXU

EFFECTIVE DATE OF REGISTRATION
. . . .
Month   Day   Year

DO NOT WRITE ABOVE THIS LINE. IF YOU NEED MORE SPACE, USE CONTINUATION SHEET

① Title

TITLE OF THIS WORK:

PREVIOUS OR ALTERNATIVE TITLES:

If a periodical or serial give: Vol. . . . . . . No. . . . . . . Issue Date . . . .

PUBLICATION AS A CONTRIBUTION: (If this work was published as a contribution to a periodical, serial, or collection, give information about the collective work in which the contribution appeared.)

Title of Collective Work: . . . . Vol. . . . . . No. . . . . . . Date . . . . Pages. . . . .

② Author(s)

IMPORTANT: Under the law, the "author" of a "work made for hire" is generally the employer, not the employee (see instructions). If any part of this work was "made for hire" check "Yes" in the space provided, give the employer (or other person for whom the work was prepared) as "Author" of that part, and leave the space for dates blank.

1

NAME OF AUTHOR:

Was this author's contribution to the work a "work made for hire"?   Yes. . . . . .   No. . . . . .

DATES OF BIRTH AND DEATH:
Born . . . .   Died . . . .
(Year)   (Year)

AUTHOR'S NATIONALITY OR DOMICILE:
Citizen of . . . . } or { Domiciled in . . . .
(Name of Country)   (Name of Country)

AUTHOR OF: (Briefly describe nature of this author's contribution)

WAS THIS AUTHOR'S CONTRIBUTION TO THE WORK:
Anonymous?   Yes. . . . . .   No. . . . . .
Pseudonymous?   Yes. . . . . .   No. . . . . .
If the answer to either of these questions is "Yes, see detailed instructions attached.

2

NAME OF AUTHOR:

Was this author's contribution to the work a "work made for hire"?   Yes. . . . . .   No. . . . . .

DATES OF BIRTH AND DEATH:
Born . . . .   Died . . . .
(Year)   (Year)

AUTHOR'S NATIONALITY OR DOMICILE:
Citizen of . . . . } or { Domiciled in . . . .
(Name of Country)   (Name of Country)

AUTHOR OF: (Briefly describe nature of this author's contribution)

WAS THIS AUTHOR'S CONTRIBUTION TO THE WORK:
Anonymous?   Yes. . . . . .   No. . . . . .
Pseudonymous?   Yes. . . . . .   No. . . . . .
If the answer to either of these questions is "Yes, see detailed instructions attached.

3

NAME OF AUTHOR:

Was this author's contribution to the work a "work made for hire"?   Yes. . . . . .   No. . . . . .

DATES OF BIRTH AND DEATH:
Born . . . .   Died . . . .
(Year)   (Year)

AUTHOR'S NATIONALITY OR DOMICILE:
Citizen of . . . . } or { Domiciled in . . . .
(Name of Country)   (Name of Country)

AUTHOR OF: (Briefly describe nature of this author's contribution)

WAS THIS AUTHOR'S CONTRIBUTION TO THE WORK:
Anonymous?   Yes. . . . . .   No. . . . . .
Pseudonymous?   Yes. . . . . .   No. . . . . .
If the answer to either of these questions is "Yes, see detailed instructions attached.

③ Creation and Publication

YEAR IN WHICH CREATION OF THIS WORK WAS COMPLETED:

Year. . . . .
(This information must be given in all cases.)

DATE AND NATION OF FIRST PUBLICATION:

Date. . . . .
(Month)   (Day)   (Year)

Nation . . . .
(Name of Country)
(Complete this block ONLY if this work has been published.)

④ Claimant(s)

NAME(S) AND ADDRESS(ES) OF COPYRIGHT CLAIMANT(S):

TRANSFER: (If the copyright claimant(s) named here in space 4 are different from the author(s) named in space 2, give a brief statement of how the claimant(s) obtained ownership of the copyright.)

- *Complete all applicable spaces (numbers 5-11) on the reverse side of this page*
- *Follow detailed instructions attached*
- *Sign the form at line 10*

DO NOT WRITE HERE
Page 1 of . . . . pages

HOW TO FILL OUT FORM TX
Specific Instructions for Spaces 1-4

> - The line-by-line instructions on this page are keyed to the spaces on the first page of Form TX, printed opposite.
> - Please read through these instructions before you start filling out your application, and refer to the specific instructions for each space as you go along.

SPACE 1: TITLE

- *Title of this Work:* Every work submitted for copyright registration must be given a title that is capable of identifying that particular work. If the copies or phonorecords of the work bear a title (or an identifying phrase that could serve as a title), transcribe its wording completely and exactly on the application. Remember that indexing of the registration and future identification of the work will depend on the information you give here.

- *Periodical or Serial Issue:* Periodicals and other serials are publications issued at intervals under a general title, such as newspapers, magazines, journals, newsletters, and annuals. If the work being registered is an entire issue of a periodical or serial, give the over-all title of the periodical or serial in the space headed "Title of this Work," and add the specific information about the issue in

the spaces provided. If the work being registered is a contribution to a periodical or serial issue, follow the instructions for "Publication as a Contribution."

- *Previous or Alternative Titles:* Complete this space if there are any additional titles for the work under which someone searching for the registration might be likely to look, or under which a document pertaining to the work might be recorded.

- *Publication as a Contribution:* If the work being registered has been published as a contribution to a periodical, serial, or collection, give the title of the contribution in the space headed "Title of this Work." Then, in the line headed "Publication as a Contribution," give information about the larger work in which the contribution appeared.

SPACE 2: AUTHORS

- *General Instructions:* First decide, after reading these instructions, who are the "authors" of this work for copyright purposes. Then, unless the work is a "collective work" (see below), give the requested information about every "author" who contributed any appreciable amount of copyrightable matter to this version of the work. If you need further space, use the attached Continuation Sheet and, if necessary, request additional Continuation Sheets (Form TX/Con).

- *Who Is the "Author"?* Unless the work was "made for hire," the individual who actually created the work is its "author." In the case of a work made for hire, the statute provides that "the employer or other person for whom the work was prepared is considered the author."

- *What is a "Work Made for Hire"?* A "work made for hire" is defined as: (1) "a work prepared by an employee within the scope of his or her employment"; or (2) "a work specially ordered or commissioned" for certain uses specified in the statute, but only if there is a written agreement to consider it a "work made for hire."

- *Collective Work:* In the case of a collective work, such as a periodical issue, anthology, collection of essays, or encyclopedia, it is sufficient to give information about the author of the collective work as a whole.

- *Author's Identity Not Revealed:* If an author's contribution is "anonymous" or "pseudonymous," it is not necessary to give the name and dates for that author. However, the citizenship and domicile of the author **must** be given in all cases, and information about the nature of that author's contribution to the work should be included if possible.

- *Name of Author:* The fullest form of the author's name should be given. If

you have checked "Yes" to indicate that the work was "made for hire," give the full legal name of the employer (or other person for whom the work was prepared). You may also include the name of the employee (for example, "Elster Publishing Co., employer for hire of John Ferguson"). If the work is "anonymous" you may: (1) leave the line blank, or (2) state "Anonymous" in the line. or (3) reveal the author's identity. If the work is "pseudonymous" you may (1) leave the line blank, or (2) give the pseudonym and identify it as such (for example: "Huntley Haverstock, pseudonym"), or (3) reveal the author's name, making clear which is the real name and which is the pseudonym (for example, "Judith Barton, whose pseudonym is Madeleine Elster").

- *Dates of Birth and Death:* If the author is dead, the statute requires that the year of death be included in the application unless the work is anonymous or pseudonymous. The author's birth date is optional, but is useful as a form of identification. Leave this space blank if the author's contribution was a "work made for hire."

- *"Anonymous" or "Pseudonymous" Work:* An author's contribution to a work is "anonymous" if that author is not identified on the copies or phonorecords of the work. An author's contribution to a work is "pseudonymous" if that author is identified on the copies or phonorecords under a fictitious name.

- *Author's Nationality or Domicile:* Give the country of which the author is a citizen, or the country in which the author is domiciled. The statute requires that either nationality or domicile be given in all cases.

- *Nature of Authorship:* After the words "Author of" give a brief general statement of the nature of this particular author's contribution to the work. Examples: "Entire text"; "Co-author of entire text"; "Chapters 11-14"; "Editorial revisions"; "Compilation and English translation"; "Illustrations."

SPACE 3: CREATION AND PUBLICATION

- *General Instructions:* Do not confuse "creation" with "publication." Every application for copyright registration must state "the year in which creation of the work was completed." Give the date and nation of first publication only if the work has been published.

- *Creation:* Under the statute, a work is "created" when it is fixed in a copy or phonorecord for the first time. Where a work has been prepared over a period of time, the part of the work existing in fixed form on a particular date constitutes the created work on that date. The date you give here should be the year in which the author completed the particular version for which registration

is now being sought, even if other versions exist or if further changes or additions are planned.

- *Publication:* The statute defines "publication" as "the distribution of copies or phonorecords of a work to the public by sale or other transfer of ownership, or by rental, lease, or lending"; a work is also "published" if there has been an "offering to distribute copies or phonorecords to a group of persons for purposes of further distribution, public performance, or public display." Give the full date (month, day, year) when, and the country where, publication first occurred. If first publication took place simultaneously in the United States and other countries, it is sufficient to state "U.S.A."

SPACE 4: CLAIMANT(S)

- *Name(s) and Address(es) of Copyright Claimant(s):* Give the name(s) address(es) of the copyright claimant(s) in this work. The statute provides that copyright in a work belongs initially to the author of the work (including, in the case of a work made for hire, the employer or other person for whom the work was prepared). The copyright claimant is either the author of the work or a person or organization that has obtained ownership of the copyright initially belonging to the author.

- *Transfer:* The statute provides that, if the copyright claimant is not the author, the application for registration must contain "a brief statement of how the claimant obtained ownership of the copyright." If any copyright claimant named in space 4 is not an author named in space 2, give a brief. general statement summarizing the means by which that claimant obtained ownership of the copyright.

LEGAL ISSUES

FORMS OF ORGANIZING THE ENTERPRISE

INTRODUCTION: SOME BASIC OPTIONS

The way you choose to structure your enterprise depends on two things: your needs, and the purpose and goals of the enterprise itself. Choosing a structure is a critical decision which must often be made in the pre-start-up phase, It will require you to establish priorities among matters vital to the success or your venture:

- Initial costs
- Liability and accountability
- Degree of managerial autonomy
- Continuity of management
- Ability to raise capital
- Taxes.*

Further, you will have to weigh some intangibles:

- The attitude of suppliers toward non-profit organizations vs. profit-making ones
- The image and reputation you wish to impress on prospective customers or clients.

At the most general level, your choice involves two decisions:

1. Either Profit or Non-profit Venture; and,
2. Either Corporate or Non-corporate Venture

---

*Appendix A provides some tax information of general interest to entrepreneurs.

Schematically, it looks like this:

	Non-corporate	**Corporate**
Non-profit	Unincorporated Association ———— Charitable trust or foundation	"Regular"
Profit	Sole Proprietorship ———— Partnership	"Regular" ———— Sub-S

The variations on these main forms boggle the mind, as you can see for yourself by counting the sub-headings in Black's Law Dictionary under "partnership," "foundation," and "corporation." Each variation is an attempt to package the best of everything to suit a particular enterprise, which should be your goal too.

In a few instances, you may be able to establish your venture without the help of a lawyer. Other situations may require the immediate and frequent advice of a lawyer, and even a change in form as your venture gets under way.

This note is intended to introduce you to the territory.

Exhibits 1, 2 and *3* present the information in summary form.

NON-PROFIT VENTURES

"This venture isn't going to make money for a couple of years, so I guess I'll start it as a non-profit corporation."

"If I start a non-profit venture, I won't have to pay taxes."

"Why should anyone who wants to make a profit start a non-profit venture?"

These are but three of the many misconceptions surrounding non-profit ventures. As one expert in non-profit organizations notes, "Never is it the object of a non-profit organization to operate non-profitably. Rather, the point is not to translate its profit into monetary gain for its members or managers *except* as reasonable salaries paid for services actually rendered."[1]

———

[1] Lane, Marc, *A Legal Handbook for Non-Profit Organizations*, AMACOM, New York, 1980, p. 1.

Traditionally, non-profit organizations exist to provide services for a particular group of people with a specific need. As an incentive to and in recognition for providing these services, federal, state, and municipal governments grant the qualified organization a number of cost-saving privileges. These include tangible benefits, such as:

-Special postal rates
-Full or partial real estate and income tax exemptions
-The privilege of soliciting contributions and bequests
-Tax deductibility to the donor as an incentive for giving
-Exemption from mandatory contributions to certain unemployment funds.

Intangible benefits include, for example, the "goodwill" accorded by the public to certain charitable endeavors.[2] However, the possibilities for non-profit ventures go well beyond the traditional concept of "charitable;" they fall into a number of categories:

-Charitable: health, religion, education, civic concerns
-Cultural: museums, orchestras, theater companies
-Social: clubs, fraternal orders
-Trade associations: Chambers of Commerce, labor unions
-Political: party organizations, political action committees
-Government: government and municipal organizations (however, these are usually operated by a special set of government regulations).

Even these general categories are not inclusive. Any of the following ventures might qualify as non-profit:

-A student-operated laundry run for the benefit of college students and employees
-A store selling products made by the handicapped
-A jitney service for senior citizens
-A day-care center run for the employees of a "for profit" company
-A food cooperative
-A neighborhood economic development corporation
-A public service law firm.

The criteria for defining non-profit organizations are becoming less applicable to what they do and more to what they do *with their profits*. If the profits, excepting "reasonable" salaries of services rendered and "reasonable" overhead, are ploughed back into the venture, and if the venture can be said to benefit a particular segment of society, then the venture may be able to enjoy the benefits of non-profit status.

SOME ALTERNATIVES

If you and your lawyer agree that your enterprise could qualify as non-profit, you can choose from a variety of forms of organization. Three of the most common are described below.

---

[2]Ibid. pp 2-3.

Unincorporated Associations

These include sports and social clubs, civic societies, political committees, and trade associations. The term "Unincorporated Association" is hard to define precisely, since it is a collection of individuals rather than a partnership or a corporation--and its rights and responsibilities under law differ from state to state. However, in all cases, it must describe its purpose and structure in Articles of Association, a Constitution and Bylaws, and in many states these documents must be filed with the Secretary of State.

Unincorporated Associations have great freedom to define their mission and may limit membership to people or corporations of their choice. For this reason, social clubs and various types of homeowners' associations find this alternative very attractive. However, state legislatures are looking hard at these hitherto nebulously circumscribed associations, and a lawyer familiar with the changes likely to occur should be consulted at the outset.

Charitable Trusts and Foundations

A charitable trust is an arrangement where assets are deeded by a donor to the custody of a trustee, who distributes the assets to benefit the public or some class of it. A private operating foundation is a more restricted form of charitable trust for the purpose of allowing private donors, through a board of directors, to distribute money to certain endeavors to benefit the public. Their existence and effectiveness depends entirely on a written Trust Instrument which should be drawn by a reputable trust lawyer.

The entrepreneur may be curious about these forms of organization because they have received so much notoriety. As conceived, both trusts and foundations were intended to give tax benefits to wealthy individuals who wished to distribute a portion of their income toward certain projects of interest to them and of benefit to the commonwealth--medical research, art museums, whatever. However, certain business corporations found that they could gain tax-exempt advantages and much favorable publicity by setting up their own foundations, frequently for research on their products, and thus gained an unfair edge on their fully-taxed competition. Today, foundations are closely scrutinized, and a heavy tax penalty is assessed against both the foundation and its manager if there is any evidence of self-dealing, undistributed income, excess holdings, injudicious investments or improper expenditures.

Non-Profit Corporations

The non-profit corporation is becoming the most popular form of organization for non-profit enterprises. As a corporation, it is a separate legal entity with limited liability and an ongoing life of its own. It can negotiate contracts, deal in property, raise money, and sue and be sued. The advantages of the corporate form are discussed in greater length in the following section on profit-making corporations; here, it should be mentioned that the formal procedure of incorporation differs from state to state, and may fall under one of several jurisdictions depending on its purpose (education, religion, social welfare). Again, state legislators are working toward a more uniform treatment of non-profit corporations, to more clearly define the structure and the laws governing their insurance and indemnity protection; and if this trend continues, it promises to be the most efficient and sophisticated way to organize a non-profit business.

The granting of a non-profit charter does not automatically make the organization tax-exempt. On the contrary, a separate form must be filed both with the IRS and the state. Since tax-exemption is a potentially inviting loophole, this application must be carefully written with the assistance of a lawyer.

If you believe that your venture is a potential candidate for non-profit status, by all means see a lawyer with experience in this field-- because the laws and the courts are moving at different rates in different states, and any of the examples above might rate a potential "yes." Several states have a Not-for-Profit Corporation Law allowing certain businesses to mix profit and non-profit activities, and this concept is gaining acceptance too.

Naturally, non-profit status carries its own burdens. It is an open invitation to scrutiny by both government officials and the general public. Even the appearance of excessive profitability must be avoided. If a "not-for-profit" entrepreneur makes an unexpected profit, he cannot increase his own salary dramatically but must use the money to further the stated purpose of the venture. Nor is a non-profit organization immune from anti-discrimination suits brought by rejected applicants. Nonetheless, if you and your lawyer agree that your venture in purpose and in form should be non-profit, you stand to make a handsome salary, including fringe benefits, and to provide a valuable service to society as well. More importantly, a non-profit status may be the best or only way to make the venture succeed.

FOR-PROFIT VENTURES

If you have decided that the purpose of your venture is chiefly to make money for yourself, your partners, and your investors, you have a choice between three basic forms of organization--and a number of variations. Your choice will be guided by your own priorities, mentioned in the Introduction.

Sole Proprietorships

"A sole proprietor is simply a person who independently conducts an unincorporated business for profit."[3] Sole proprietorships are quick and inexpensive ways to start a new venture since this form of organization requires no formalities other than complying with the laws affecting local licensing and registration of the name of the business (Doing Business As). In addition, you are the only and undisputed boss and the profits are all yours.

However, there is a price for this ease and independence. You are personally liable for all business debts and failures, without limit. You are also taxed at the higher personal

---

[3]Lane, Marc, *A Legal Handbook for Small Business*, p. 20.

rate on all profits, and should you become ill or incapacitated, your cutomers and creditors have no assurance that you will be able to meet your obligations, which may limit your ability to attract them initially.

Partnerships

Some new ventures decide to begin as General Partnerships, a group of two or more people recognized as a legal entity for certain transactions involving loans and real estate, among others, and as a tax-reporting BUT NOT A TAX-PAYING entity by the IRS. In some ways, a general partnership is like an expanded sole proprietorship. There are no statutory filing requirements, and each partner has unlimited liability should the enterprise fail or be sued. (However, in both instances insurance is one means of protection.) A general partnership allows an individual more flexibility than if he were doing business alone--administrative responsibilities can be allocated, decision making can be shared, and, if provided for, profits can be spread among the partners evenly so that each pays an equal amount of personal income tax on his share.

It is, of course, possible to do business as a partnership without drawing up a formal agreement -- although, as the business grows, "getting things down on paper" will prevent certain potentially damaging misunderstandings: profit (or loss) sharing, liquidation if one partner withdraws, general areas of responsibility, etc.

One of the most critical elements in a successful partnership are the partners themselves: do they have complementary strengths and unity of purpose? Much has been written on the importance of choosing the right partner, though opinions differ as to what is "right."[4]

Another critical element for success is drafting a Partnership Agreement. This is an internal document, which should be drafted with the help of a lawyer, and need not be disclosed to anyone except the partners who sign it. The agreement should distill into writing the policies and rules which will govern its operation: the name and nature of the partnership and of the partners; the duration of the partnership; if its purpose if limited; the rights and duties of each partner; the price of a partnership; a formula for dividing the profits; and provisions under which partners may withdraw and new partners be admitted, since a partnership is technically dissolved at the death or withdrawal of any partner unless otherwise stipulated.

Depending on the size and purpose of the partnership, this document may be very informal or it may run for pages. It may be a cornerstone of the entreprise, or it may evolve only as the enterprise evolves. In either case, the agreement constitutes a binding contract, and if you are not familiar with contract law you should find a lawyer who is familiar with this body of law as it applies to business activities.

---

[4]For example, see Karl Vesper, *New Venture Strategies,* Prentice Hall, New Jersey, 1980; Joseph Mancuso, *Fun and Guts: The Entrepreneur's Philosophy,* Addison Wesley, Reading, MA, 1973; Melvin Wallace's *Partners in Business,* Enterprise Publishing, Inc., Wilmington, Delaware, 1981, Chapters I & II, pp 1-18.

As in any alternative, the general partnership has drawbacks. Each partner is personally liable without limit not only for his role in the business but also for the sins and omissions of other partners. A partnership also has as many bosses as partners, unless otherwise stipulated. Because of its potential vulnerability and decentralized decision making, it may not inspire faith in prospective investors if raising capital is of importance. Finally, for the individual partner, his profits are taxed to him at the higher rate of personal income; although the partnership reports profits, it is a conduit for the monies themselves, and the partners are taxed on the income as soon as it is reported, regardless of whether or not it has been distributed to them.

Variations of the partnership form have been devised to better suit certain types of ventures. Some of these are listed below:

a. *Limited Partnership* - A limited partnership is comprised of a general partner (or partners) who actively manage the business and are personally liable for its debts, and a number of partners who are strictly financial backers. These "limited" partners are liable only for the amount of money they contribute and have no management responsibility (nor can they have such responsibility). A limited partnership is useful as a tax shelter for real estate, oil, and gas deals.

The creation of a limited partnership is strictly governed by law and must adhere to the Uniform Limited Partnership Act in most states. Two of the most important requirements are the disclosure of the names of all the partners, and the proviso that a limited partner will lose his limited liability if he engages in an active managment role.

b. *Silent Partner* - A silent partner is like an informal limited partner--a financial backer, who may contribute time and services but only after the regular working day and who wishes to remain anonymous to the public. A document drawn up for a silent partnership defines the terms of the partner's liability and the percentage of the profits he will be allowed to share.

c. *Joint Stock Company* - Historically, Joint Stock Companies were a popular form of organization, both here and abroad (The Dutch East India Company, the Hudson Bay Company). They were relatively easy to establish, requiring only Articles of Agreement among the individuals who put up cash in return for shares of the company: the shares were transferrable, the company was managed by an elected board of directors, and it was not subject to public scrutiny. It represented a hybrid between a corporation and a general partnership. However, as corporation law evolved, Joint Stock Companies have been treated more like corporations, including "double" taxation, with the exception of the limited liability privilege; consequently, they are no longer popular. Joint Stock Companies are a good example of how a particular form of organization, designed to meet a particular need, can become obsolete as regulatory agencies search for loopholes and changes in corporation law present more attractive alternatives.

d. *Real Estate Investment Trusts* - A REIT is an unincorporated trust or association managed by one or more trustees for the benefit of 100 or more beneficiaries. The REIT must derive at least 75% of its revenues from income on real property--rents, mortgages, purchase and sale of land. The beneficiaries must receive at leat 90% of the trust's income. If these and other[5] obligations are met, the Revenue Code now allows REIT beneficiaries to be taxed individually on the income from this source, thus avoiding capital gains tax. A REIT has some of the virtues of a corporation--continuity, free transferability of interests--while maintaining the greater degree of privacy of a partnership. It was a popular tax shield in the 1970s.

INCORPORATION

A corporation differs from a proprietorship or partnership because it is a legal entity existing independently of its members, an "artificial person" in the eyes of the law. Because of the unique legal status of a corporation, there are a number of laws regulating its operations with several important consequences for entrepreneurs. High on the list of desirable qualities is the "limited liability" which accompanies the concept of a separate entity; the corporation is responsible only for its own debts, and individual shareholders may not be sued. In addition, corporate profits are taxed at lower rates, corporate employees are entitled to Workmen's Compensation and certain retirement benefits not available to the self-employed, a corporation exists in perpetuity regardless of the change in shareholders, and the management, by statute, is centralized in an elected board of directors. The latter two considerations make it by far the most attractive alternative for raising capital.

One aspect of incorporation which the entrepreneur will want to consider carefully is "double taxation." In essence, the IRS collects twice: once from the income of the corporation itself and again from the individuals who receive income from the corporation. The corporate tax is lower in percentage, and it has been argued that "double taxation" can still have the incorporator's money[6]; nonetheless, this distinguishes it from a partnership form, where income is taxed only once, albeit at the higher personal income rate. Other negative aspects are: the greater initial expense; the great amount of paperwork needed to satisfy numerous federal and state laws governing corporations; and potential constraints upon the entrepreneur who wants to be his own boss, since corporate members elect a board of trustees who set policy to be implemented by the corporation's officers.

A listing of the formal steps needed to comply with corporation regulation may give you a clearer idea of what is involved. The procedure is available in more detail in a number of handbooks for entrepreneurs.

1. Apply to the IRS for a Corporate Taxpayer Identification Number.

2. File a Certificate of Incorporation with the Secretary of the State in which you plan to incorporate. Forms can be purchased at a commercial stationer, but since procedures

---

[5]Rohrlich, Chester, *Organizing Corporate and Other Business Enterprises,* Matthew Bender, New York, 1975 and supplements to 1980, no. 2, p. 51.

[6]McQuown, Judith, *Inc. Yourself,* McMillan Publishing Co., New York, 1980.

and expenses vary widely from state to state, check first with your state authorities. Generally, you must state the name of the corporation, the purpose, the location of the headquarters, the amount of stock you wish to issue, and the termination of your fiscal year. If you issue par-value stock, you must have the cash in your treasury to back it up; no-par value stock means that, at the outset, no stockholder investment is necessary.

3. Once you have filed, order a set of corporate records (a loose-leaf-ledger will do) and a corporate seal. With these, and your IRS Identification Number, you can now open a corporate bank account.

4. Hold a stockholder's meeting to elect directors. The directors then elect the corporate officers responsible for the company's operation. They also adopt bylaws (rules of internal management) and approve the issuance of the stock. By law, corporations require that the directors convene one meeting annually and the minutes must be a matter of record.

A lawyer can walk you through the incorporation process, for a fee, and--depending on the nature of your venture--he may suggest that you incorporate in Delaware because of its permissive corporate laws.[7] Once you are a corporation, you must keep careful financial records and file certain forms annually with the IRS and with your state tax authorities.

After considering the objectives of your venture, especially with regard to liability, raising capital, and taxation, you may conclude that a general corporation, or one of the variations listed below, is the most practical way to organize your business.

a. Incorporating Yourself - If you have, until now, been a sole proprietor, there is a strong argument for incorporating yourself to take advantage of certain corporate privileges.[8] These include: limited liability; eligibility for Workman's Compensation, and certain medical deductions; a "double tax" structure which may end up saving you money; and a higher limit on the amount you can contribute to a Keogh or similar retirement plan. *Inc. Yourself,* by Judith McQuown, is a how-to-book, and includes the cost and requirements in each of the fifty states for incorporation.

b. Professional Corporations - Until recently, most professional organizations were partnerships, such as law firms, but now the professional corporation as a legal business entity is recognized in all fifty states. The critical requirement is that every member of the corporation be a licensed professional. But if this requirement is met, and if the proper steps for incorporation are followed, the professionals can enjoy the limited liability, tax, medical, and pension benefits available to corporations.

c. Closely-Held Corporations - Although formally classed as a corporation, a closely-held corporation is functionally more like a partnership. One generally-accepted

---

[7]Lane, *A Legal Handbook for Small Businesses,* p. 29.

[8]McQuown, *op. cit.*

definition is "a corporation wherein all the outstanding stock (there being no publicly held securities of any other class) is owned by the persons (or members of their immediate families) who are active in the management and conduct of the business."[9] In other words, the closely-held corporation provides the liability protection and other benefits of incorporation to a business run by its stockholders, thus enjoying the lack of public scrutiny associated with partnerships.

Until 1960, neither statutory law nor judicial opinion attempted to make clear distinctions between the "close" corporation and the general corporation, since closely-held corporations kept a low profile--attracting public notice only in the case of internal disagreement about buy-outs or external pressure to let an outsider buy in. However, both bodies are now recognizing that the distinction needs to be made. Rules for incorporating "close" corporations are becoming more flexible; but on the other hand, restrictions on transferability of stock are being monitored more closely. Some states prohibit the stock from being publicly traded as a way of raising capital, and other states limit the number of shareholders. The attempt to balance the privacy of a partnership with the advantages of incorporation is difficult, and if you choose this option you will need a lawyer familiar with the latest laws affecting closely-held corporations in your state.

d. Subchapter S Corporations - Today, in 1984, Subchapter S corporations are history; the change in tax laws has redefined them, and they are now called S corporations.

> Subchapter S Corporations were introduced in 1958 as a result of the Small Business Tax Reform Act, allowing a small business to "choose the form of organization it preferred without undue regard for tax consequences."[10] To qualify, this entity had to be limited to 25 stockholders and one class of stock, at least 80% of its gross receipts had to be earned within the country, no more than 20% could be earned from passive income investments, and the company coult not be a subsidiary of another corporation.

> If qualified, a Subchapter S Corporation paid neither a federal income tax nor a penalty for accumulated earnings at the corporation level (although an informational return had to be filed); rather, it was taxed as a partnership for the benefit of its stockholders, with profits considered as ordinary income. Losses were deductible by individuals, and could be carried forward or backward to offset other gains; this advantage was attractive to potential investors if the venture was projected to lose money in the first several

---

[9]Rohrlich, Chester, *op. cit.* no. 2, p. 21.
[10]Rohrlich, Chester, *op. cit.* no. 3, p. 59 and 70.

years. When the venture became profitable, the
shareholders could vote to terminate the "Sub S" status and
become taxed as a general corporation.

S Corporations - The principal differences in the S Corporation regulations are in the
treatment of:

- losses, capital gains and credits (requirements have been relaxed)
- passive income limits on interest, rents, royalties (no limit on new S Corporations, a
  higher limit on former Subchapter S Corporations)
- number of shareholders (35, as opposed to 25)
- administration (timing no longer determines when a distribution is taxable, unless
  amounts are distributed in excess of basis)
- penalties (the inadvertent termination of the S-status can be worked out with the IRS,
  rather than serving as cause for a fine).

Further, explanation was provided in a recent article:[11]

> To elect S-corporation status, an eligible corporation must
> file Form 2553 with the IRS. On that form, shareholders
> unanimously consent to the election during the first two
> months and 15 days of the taxable year, since, in most
> circumstances, an S corporation is restricted to the use of a
> calendar year. Any shareholder owning stock during the
> year prior to the date of the election must also consent to this
> form of organization.
>
> If you previously terminated a Subchapter-S corporation,
> you can still elect S-corporation status. Under the old law, a
> five-year waiting period was required. The new law also
> imposes a five-year waiting period, except where
> termination occurred, under the old law. If you qualify, you
> can elect S-corporation status for 1984, even if Sub-S status
> was terminated as late as 1982.

However, the author cautions:

> Before deciding to choose an S corporation as your form of
> business, consult a tax attorney or accountant. In particular,
> ask if your state recognizes S corporations. Some states treat
> S corporations like regular corporations, which means that
> your company would be exempt from the federal corporate
> income tax but not the state income tax.[12]

---

[11]"Taking the S-Corporation Route to Tax Savings," *Inc. Magazine,* December, 1983, p.
164.

[12]Ibid.

SPECIAL ADVANTAGES FOR SMALL BUSINESS

Small business lobbies both in Washington and in the state capitals have been actively proposing new ways to "give the little guy a break" and to encourage the American entrepreneurial spirit. New laws affecting various aspects of business continue to be modified to recognize the special needs of a smaller business, and a few of these are listed below:

a. 1244 Stock - This option provides a tax shelter for shareholders, enabling those who sell at a loss to treat the loss as an ordinary loss, rather than as a more costly capital loss. 1244 status must be recorded before any stock is issued.

b. New Regulation Laws (1980) - The Regulatory Flexibility Act orders all government agencies to consider the impact of proposed regulations on small business and to adjust them when possible. In addition, courts can direct federal agencies to reimburse small businesses for the legal fees incurred when they sue and win.[13]

c. New Investment Laws (1980) - Congress raised from $2 million to $5 million the ceiling on "detailed" registration and reporting of data on stock offerings, to allow the small business less paperwork encumbrance. It also loosened the regulations on venture capital firms, and allowed certain qualifying banks to certify applications for SBA loan guarantees, rather than vesting this power exclusively in the SBA.[14]

CONCLUSION

In choosing a form for your venture, the overriding concern should be that the form enhances the objectives and goals you have set for it. In most instances, the advice and assistance of a lawyer will be helpful, but in every instance you will be able to use a lawyer more effectively if you familiarize yourself with the alternatives available. A lawyer can and will offer advice--but it is you who must assume the challenge and responsibility of running your venture.

The legal options available to organize and operate a venture can be viewed as tiresome subject matter for entrepreneurs which impose constraints on time and freedom of action ...or they can be viewed as a creative opportunity to customize a legal structure ideally suited to foster a successful entrepreneurial experience.

---

[13] *Business Week,* Nov. 3, 1980, p. 100.

[14] *Business Week, op. cit.*

APPENDIX A

TAX INFORMATION FOR ENTREPRENEURS

A LOOK AT THE 1981 ECONOMIC RECOVERY TAX ACT*

INTRODUCTION AND DESCRIPTION PROVISIONS

In August, 1981, President Reagan signed into law the Economic Recovery Tax Act (ERTA), a stupendous set of tax cuts totaling $750 billion -- roughly equivalent to the combined earnings of the 25 largest U.S. corporations. The purpose of this new economic legislation was to return to American citizens more cash -- to spend, to save, and to invest -- as a way to increase productivity and generate jobs.

The changes in the tax law fall into two major areas: business and individual, including both personal income tax and estate and gift taxes. As an entrepreneur, your business and personal affairs are necessarily intertwined -- the more you can save on your personal taxes, the more you can invest in your business -- so it is imperative that you be familiar with the tax impact in both areas.

Some key provisions of ERTA of benefit to entrepreneurs are listed below. Each is then described briefly. All the provisions are beneficial to the business community as a whole; however, certain ones will be especially helpful to particular types of ventures.

A word of caution. This note is being written when the ink is barely dry on the new legislation; consequently, the IRS has not yet issued regulations or rulings, so plan on a lengthy consultation with your tax advisor before using ERTA as a basis for future financial planning. For good reason, the law has been dubbed "The Full Employment for Lawyers and Accountants Act."

-----

*The information for part of this note was drawn from several sources; however, the following were particularly useful:

Irving Blackman, "Overview of Economic Recovery Tax Act" and "Biggest Tax Cut in History," *National Petroleum News,* October, 1981. pp. 74ff, 102.

Roger Lopata, "The Tax Package: What it Does, What it Doesn't," *Iron Age,* September 7, 1981, p. 45.

William G. Flanagan, "Tax Planning: Don't Dawdle," *Forbes,* October 12, 1981. p. 199.

"New Tax Law Defines New Area of Small-Business Opportunity", *NFIB Mandate,* No. 437, Vol. 39, No. 6. p. 1.

KEY AREAS AFFECTED BY 1981 ECONOMIC RECOVERY TAX ACT

NEW BUSINESS AND CORPORATION TAX LAWS

- Depreciation
- Investment Tax Credit
- Inventory Reform
- Corporate Tax Reduction
- Leasing
- First Year Writeoffs (for startups)
- Writeoffs for rehabilitating old buildings
- Sub-S Regulations
- R & D Allowance

NEW INDIVIDUAL TAX LAWS

Personal Income Tax Changes:
- Individual rate reductions
- Indexing
- Incentive stock options
- IRA ceiling lifted
- S & L tax exemptions

Estate and Gift Tax Changes:

- Increased estate tax exemption
- Increased marital deduction
- Increased gift tax exclusion

CHANGES IN THE BUSINESS AND CORPORATE TAX LAWS

General Summary: The new business and corporate tax laws give the biggest advantage to:

- large, established capital-intensive companies, and
- large-scale startups.

These enterprises can take advantage of rapid depreciation for large capital expenditures, special leasing provisions, and investment tax credits. For smaller, labor-intensive businesses, tax savings will not be as dramatic -- though the decreased corporate income tax (where applicable), the revised Sub-S law, and the simplified depreciation system will undoubtedly help.

Depreciation

To encourage capital expenditures, depreciation schedules have been accelerated and simplified. The new law eliminates the "useful life" concept and replaces it with four well-defined recovery periods:

- 3 years: automobiles, light trucks, R&D equipment
- 5 years: everything else (except real property) -- from computers and heavy machinery to desks and typewriters.
- 10 years: special types of property, such as public utility property, theme parks, and mobile homes.
- 15 years: real estate and buildings

Investment Tax Credit

Complementing the new depreciation schedule, tax credits for capital expenditure have also been simplified and increased.

- A tax credit of 6% is allowed for equipment with a three-year life; 10% is allowed for anything with a longer life.
- The $100,000 limit on used property eligible for the investment credit has been increased to:

> $125,000 until 1981;
> $150,000 thereafter.

- If property is sold before its depreciable limit, a 2% tax credit is allowed.
- The investment credit carry-over period is extended from 7 years to 15 years.

Inventory Reform

LIFO inventory accounting (Last In First Out) offers considerable savings in an inflationary economy, but many small businesses find that the first-year tax bite associated with changing to this method is unbearable. The new laws will make this conversion simpler and less costly.

Provisions include: one pool; easier indexing; and a 3-year period over which to spread income pick-up caused by the prior methods of accounting.
Starts: 1982.

Corporate Tax Reductions

The tax rate has been cut for the two lowest brackets.

Taxable Income	1981	1982	1983 and thereafter
First $25,000	17%	16%	15%
Next $25,000	20%	19%	18%
Over $50,000		No Change	
Next $25,000	30%	30%	30%
Next $25,000	40%	40%	40%
Everything over $100,000	46%	46%	46%

Capital Gains Tax Reduction

For all capital gains (investments held longer than a year), the first 60% remains tax free. Tax on the remainder has been lowered from 28% to 20%. This law implies to both corporate and personal capital gains.

Leasing

The new law will enable many more businesses to qualify as lessees of costly equipment, allowing them to modernize worn-out or obsolescent production facilities and increase production at considerably less cost than before.

* Lessors will have to pay for only 10% of the cost of the equipment (down from 20%); the remainder can be financed.
* Some of the tax benefits held by the lessor (depreciation, investment tax credits) may now be passed to the lessee.
* Lessor and lessee may agree upon a buying price at the outset, instead of at the conclusion of the lease. This offers the lessee a hedge against inflation.

First-year Writeoffs

Especially helpful for small business, the new law will enable up to $10,000 per year of certain types of property to be expensed, rather than depreciated. This should ease the burden for start-ups requiring substantial capital investment.

1982: $5,000 limit
1983: $10,000 limit to be phased in over 1983-87 period.

Rehabilitating Old Buildings

A 15% tax credit will be allowed for rehabilitating buildings more than 30 years old.

R&D Tax Credits

An R&D tax credit for 25% has been provided. However, it applies only to increased expenditures over a three-year period, and is not scheduled to take effect until 1986.

CHANGES IN THE PERSONAL TAX LAWS

General Summary: For entrepreneurs in smaller business ventures, the changes in the personal tax laws (rather than those in the area of business) are the most welcome. Individual rate cuts and estate tax reforms were heartily endorsed by the NFIB (National Federation of Independent Businesses) since

* individual rate cuts provide businessmen with more of their own money to invest in their businesses, and

* estate tax reform promises virtually to eliminate estate taxes, allowing entrepreneurs to leave the estate tax-free to their spouses, and, with some planning, tax free to their heirs.

The reduction of personal income tax is also expected to increase the capital pool available to entrepreneurs searching for outside funding.

Personal Tax Changes

Individual Rate Reductions

A cumulative 23% rate reduction is scheduled over a three-year period:

1981	1¼%
1982	10%
1983	19%
1984	23%

Starting in 1982, the top bracket will be 50%.

Indexing

In theory, this system will eliminate "bracket creep" due to inflation. Personal tax rates, personal exemptions, and the zero-bracket rate will be pegged to indexes that reflect inflation. Indexing is expected to start in 1985.

Incentive Stock Options

This alternative makes stock option plans more attractive. An executive will be able to exercise up to $100,000 a year in options without paying capital gains tax. The options will be deferred until the stock is sold.

IRA Ceiling Lifted

The upper limit of tax-free annual contributions to an IRA account has been raised to $2,000 for an individual: $1,750 for a spousal account.

S&L Tax Exemptions

This is an experiment to encourage saving. Tax-exempt income will be permitted from savings and loan certificates up to $2,000 a year.

Estate and Gift Tax Reform

Estate Tax

The amount of the exemption will increase and the maximum tax rate will decrease as follows over the next six years:

Year	Exempt from Tax	Maximum rate
1982	$225,000	65%
1983	$275,000	60%
1984	$325,000	55%
1985	$400,000	50%
1986	$500,000	50%
1987	$600,000	50%

Marital Deduction

The marital deduction is now unlimited. This means that you may leave your estate to your spouse tax-free. This will solve estate tax problems for many small business people. However, the surviving spouse will have to do some estate planning in order to avoid presenting heirs with a tax burden. To illustrate, see the next section on Gift Tax Exclusion.

Gift Tax Exclusion

The gift tax exclusion has been increased from $3,000 to $10,000 per year, a substantial benefit. A donor may now give up to $10,000 to any number of recipients without incurring a taxable gift or a gift tax liability.

For estate tax purposes, a husband and wife can now give each of their heirs up to $20,000 a year (jointly) over a period of years, until their estate has been transferred to their heirs tax-free. Tax planner Irving Blackman gives the following illustration:

> John Jones is married and has five grandchildren. He hates to pay taxes. Starting in 1982 he gives $20,000 to each grandchild (or total annual gifts of $100,000) and continues the practice for eight years. John dies on Jan. 1, 1990, leaving an estate of $1.2 million to his wife. The combined gift and estate tax to John on the $2 million ($800,000 in gifts and $1.2 million estate) is zero.[1]

For the purposes of extraordinary expenses, such as tuition and medical costs, the donor of these payments may claim an unlimited exclusion for up to the $10,000 limit.

Exhibit 1
Forms of Organization
Non-Profit

	Charitable Trusts	Private Operating Foundations	Non-Profit Corporations
Initial Organization Requirements and Costs	Trust agreement must be drafted by lawyer and be sanctioned by the IRS.	Must meet a complex set of qualifications regarding assets, endowment support; must file with the IRS; must report periodically.	Formal articles of incorporation are prepared by an attorney and executed in state where corporation will operate; internal bylaws are prepared with help of attorney; fees and regulations vary.

---

[1] Irving Blackman, *op. cit.* p. 74 & 102.

Exhibit 1 (Continued)

	Charitable Trusts	Private Operating Foundations	Non-Profit Corporations
Liability of Owners	A trustee acts as an individual, and can be held liable for failure to manage the trust prudently.	Manager may be personally liable for violating IRS laws.	Liability of directors usually limited to assets of corporation of annual report is filed; however, directors as a body may be found personally liable, and an increasing number carry liability insurance.
Continuity	Perpetual, unless terminated by trustees	Perpetual, unless otherwise specified	Continuity provided by corporate member elected Board of Directors; death or departure of corporate members or officers does not affect entity.
Transferability of Interests	Trustees may be appointed by the benefactor or resign without impairing the activity of the trust.	Not an issue.	Voting rights granted only to members of the corporation.
Management	Trustees have full authority to act as a fiduciary for the trustee. They must make periodic reports to the state's attorny general — usually annually.	Manager does not answer to a constituency for his actions — he only must abide by the law.	Management in hands of Board of Directors, elected by the corporate membership. Duties and reponsibilities described in by-laws. Directors answerable to corporate membership.
Attractiveness for Raising Capital	The trust is a repository for capital, not a fund-raising entity	Not an issue.	For fund-raising, both the elementary purpose of the corporation and the tax-deductible status of the gift are attractive to potential donors.
Taxes	Taxable entity, unless granted non-exempt status by IRS.	Tax-exempt.	Tax-exempt, if tax-exempt application is approved by IRS.

Exhibit 2

Forms of Organization
Profit

	Sole Proprietorship	General Partnerships	Limited Partnerships
Initial Organization Requirements and Costs	Minimal expenses; no formal filing fees except for special licenses.	No formal filing fee; partnership agreement, drafted by attorney, advisable.	Statutory requirements stated in uniform Limited Partnership Act in most states; legal costs associated with preparing contracts.
Liability of Owners	Unlimited personal liability.	Unlimited personal liability.	Limited partners liable for amount invested; general partners, unlimited personal liability.
Continuity	None — entity dissolved at death of sole proprietor.	None — unless provision is made in general partnership agreement.	Limited partners do not affect continuity; death or departure of general partners may dissolve partnership unless otherwise provided in partnership agreement.
Transferability of Interests	Entitled to sell or transfer interests.	Consent of all partners required.	Limited partners can sell interest at will; general partners can sell or transfer interest with consent of other general partners.
Management	"Own Boss".	All partners have a voice; procedure is provided in partnership agreement.	Limited partners prohibited from managing; general partners manage according to terms of agreement.
Attractiveness for Raising Capital	Depends entirely on capability of entrepreneur and attractiveness of venture.	Depends entirely on capability of partners and attractiveness of venture.	Limited liability (downside) and unlimited upside make limited partnerships attractive to potential investors.
Taxes	Income tax — personal tax rate; entity is non-taxable conduit.	Income tax — personal tax rate; entity is non-taxable conduit.	Entity is a non-taxable conduit; limited partners may be able to use investment as tax shelter for loss; income may be taxed as capital gain or ordinary income.

Exhibit 3

**Forms of Organization
Profit**

	Corporations	"Sub-S" Corporations
Initial Organization Requirements and Costs	Formal application and filing fee required in state where business is incorporated; more expensive and time-consuming than other forms.	Formal application and filing fee required; also, services of an attorney, since qualification is complicated.
Liability of Owners	Liability limited to amount invested.	Liability limited to amount invested.
Continuity	Continuity provided by stockholder-elected Board of Directors; death or departure of stockholders or Directors does not affect entity.	Continuity provided by stockholder-elected Board of Directors; death or departure of stockholders or Directors does not affect entity.
Transferability of Interests	Extensive flexibility for shareholders to sell or transfer interests; some control by present shareholders over prospective shareholders.	Number of stockholders limited by law; among stockholders, flexibility to sell or transfer interests.
Management	Management in hands of stockholder-elected Board of Directors. Their duties and responsibilities are described in the corporate by-laws. Directors answerable to corporate stockholders; also, must file annual report.	Management in hands of stockholder-elected Board of Directors. Their duties and responsibilities are described in the corporate by-laws. Directors answerable to corporate stockholders; also, must file annual report.
Attractiveness for Raising Capital	Limited liability, degree of control and upside potential (resulting in increased shares and more dividends) make corporations attractive investment opportunities.	Because the "Sub-S" Corporation, designed to help new small businesses, is taxed like a partnership, it offers attractive features to a potential investor:
Taxes	A taxable entity, taxes at a lower rate than personal. However, individuals receiving income are taxed at personal rate.	• Business losses flow through to stockholders increasing their personal tax base for absorbing losses; • Distribution to stockholders taxed as dividends, not ordinary income.

LEGAL ISSUES

BANKRUPTCY LAWS AND PROCEEDINGS

INTRODUCTION: WHY YOU SHOULD KNOW ABOUT BANKRUPTCY

Familiarity with bankruptcy laws will be useful to the entrepreneur in three instances:

1. For the owner of a business who has incurred more debt than he will ever be able to repay.

2. For the owner of a business approaching insolvency (the state when liabilities exceed assets) who desires to continue operation, if possible; and,

3. For the prospective buyer of a venture or its assets which has been adjudicated bankrupt.

Although the greater part of this note is addressed to the potential insolvent, the potential buyer will be able to learn what constitutes a bankrupt company, and one section includes a number of questions he should ask before contemplating a purchase.

HISTORY

The Constitution of the United States vests specifically in Congress the power to "establish uniform laws on the subject of bankruptcy throughout the United States," since the founding fathers believed that national standards would offer the fairest treatment to debtor and creditor alike. However, not until 1898 during a national economic crisis was the Federal Bankruptcy Act adopted by Congress; until then, bankruptcy proceedings had been handled in different ways by different states.

The 1898 law provided a lasting foundation for Federal bankruptcy law, though it was amended many times. It was designed to serve two purposes: to give honest debtors an opportunity to start anew to build a firm financial future; and, to give creditors an opportunity to claim certain of the debtor's assets and share in them equally.

Under Federal Bankruptcy Law, Chapters 1—7 established the framework for "straight" bankruptcy proceedings, which provide for a liquidation of the debtor's assets and his subsequent discharge as debt-free. These chapters included the following important guidelines:

—Establishing federal district courts as the bodies responsible
for administering the laws,

—Defining the rights of both debtors and creditors,

—Creating the offices of "referee" - a federally-appointed official
acting as both judge and administrator of the bankrupt, and of
"trustee," a custodian or manager of the debtor's assets, either elected
by the creditors or appointed by the judge, if such a position should be filled,

—Describing in detail the priorities for distributing the bankrupt's
liquidated estate,

—Giving the referee the power to discharge the bankrupt and close
the case.

In 1938, the Bankruptcy Laws were augmented by the inclusion of the Chandler Act, seven chapters of debtor-relief provisions allowing for the "rehabilitation" of the debtor as an alternative to liquidation. These chapters provided for court-supervised "arrangements" for certain classes of debtors to satisfy the claims of their creditors. The chapters most germane to the entrepreneur/businessman were:

Chapter X:	Corporate reorganization
Chapter XI:	Unsecured debt in business cases
Chapter XII:	Noncorporate debt secured by liens on real property (rarely used)
Chapter XIII:	Arrangements for the Wage Earner*

THE NEW LAW

In 1978, President Carter signed into law a new Bankruptcy Code, some provisions of which have already taken effect, and the entirety of which should be in operation by 1984. Though the form of the laws has been revised somewhat (see Table I), the basic philosophy of American bankruptcy law has remained on the whole unchanged. However, there are several interesting revisions.

—The scope of Chapter XIII, relief for the personal wage earner, has been extended in the new Chapter 13 to include any debtor with a regular income, whether he is a wage earner or self-employed. Seemingly, this will allow a self-employed entrepreneur earning a sizable income to avoid liquidation and set his own repayment plan under this revised provision.

———————

*The other chapters included: interstate railroad corporations, VIII; certain public authorities, IX; maritime liens, XIV.

Table I

The United States Bankruptcy Code (Revised 1979): a summary

TITLE I

1. General provisions
3. Case administration
5. Creditors, debtors and the estate
7. Liquidation
9. Adjustment of the debts of a municipality
11. Reorganization
13. Adjustment of debts of individuals with regular income
15. New U.S. trustee concept

TITLE II

Amendments to the U.S. Code on the Judiciary

TITLE III

Necessary changes in legislation

TITLE IV

Interim provisions between 1979-84, when the full new court structure will be in operation

Source: Daniel Cowans, *Bankruptcy Law and Practice,* West Publishing Co., 1980 and 1979.

—The rehabilitation procedure for the business debtor under Chapters X, XI and XII have been combined into a new Chapter 11, which most closely resembles the old X. The business debtor has less leverage; bankruptcy proceedings are no longer exclusively voluntary (as under old XI); and the debtor may be forced to accept an involuntary payback "arrangement" drawn by the court and the creditors.

Also, a number of procedural matters have been revised, the court has been excluded from participating in creditors' meetings, and the word "bankrupt" has been in every instance replaced by the word "debtor."

Table II, comparing the old and new laws, may be useful at this point, for the discussion that will follow.

Table II

Application of U.S. Federal Bankruptcy Laws
before and after the new 1979 Code

Chapter	Parties Covered			Type of Proceedings	
	Personal	Business		Voluntary	Involuntary
		Uninc.	Corp.		
Chapters I-VII (before 1979) Chapter 7 (new U.S. Code)	X X	X X	X X	X X	X X
Before 1979					
Chapter X — Corporate Reorganization			X		X (usually)
Chapter XI — Arrangements for business debtors and non-wage earners		X	X	X	
Chapter XII — Arrangements for non-corporate debtors with liens secured on real property		X		X (usually)	
Chapter XIII — Arrangements for wage-earners	X			X	
New U.S. Code					
Chapter 11 — Business Reorganizations		X	X	X	X
Chapter 13 — Adjustments and debts of individuals with regular income	X			X	

X = Scope of chapter covers this situation.

SOME FIGURES ABOUT FAILURE

What are the odds that a new venture will fail?

A number of discouraging rumors abound. One popular belief is that 90% of all businesses fail in the first year. The "educated guess" most often cited is that 65% of new companies fail in the first five years, and most of the 65% in the first three. No wonder prospective entrepreneurs become disheartened!

However, one respected authority in the field checked some figures himself and reached some more optimistic conclusions.[1]

—Dun & Bradstreet, the statisticians of business, regularly count the number of failures among the approximately three million companies they track. The highest number of failures in the past decade was 43,514--or 53 per 10,000. That's about a half of one percent. In 1979, the rate was 28 per 10,000.

—The Internal Revenue Service, according to the 1980 "Statistical Abstract of the United States," listed approximately 14.7 million businesses which file tax returns, up from 13,979,000 in 1975. Statistics are not kept on the failure rate of this larger population, but startup rates are. If the failure rate approached the 60% rumor rate, let alone the 90% one, the number of startups to explain the growth in new businesses would be astronomical. They are not.

—The "bankruptcy rate" in 1979, reported by the U.S. district courts, was--226,000 filed, 258,000 pending. Of those filed (proceedings had begun) less than 29,000 of the petitions were brought by merchants, manufacturers, or those in business. The vast number were personal bankruptcies filed by employees. 29,000 business bankruptcies is a statistical drop in the bucket.

In addition to the gross figures, a number of small sample studies of business bankruptcies, beginning at startup, have been taken.[2] Based on limited sampling, entrepreneurs do not as a group seem overwhelmingly destined to fail. For example, of 100 Michigan manufacturing firms started in 1960 about a third had failed by 1964 and another quarter were marginally successful. The remainder were doing fine.

All these statistics suggest that notions about business failure need to be reexamined. First, consider the ventures that "go out of business." To be sure, some vanish in the night leaving unhappy creditors in their wake. However, others sell their assets to pay their debts and close their doors on a set of balanced books. And some "go out of business" with a pocketful of cash: long-time proprietors wishing to retire, entrepreneurs who have lost the itch. Going out of business is not synonymous with failure.

---

[1] Albert Shapero, "Numbers That Lie," *Inc.,* May, 1981, p. 16.

[2] Russell Knight, "Bankruptcies by Type of Entrepreneur in Canada," paper in *Frontiers of Entrepreneurship Research,* Babson College, 1981, p. 138.

Next, there are the "bankruptcies," those businesses which formally declare a state of temporary involvency. But, as we will see, a declaration of bankruptcy can indicate that a business wishes to continue to do business, and has declared bankruptcy in order to structure an arrangement by which it can continue to survive.

And finally, there is the issue of failure itself. As more research is done on entrepreneurs, "failure" is being redefined. Not only is it not "bad"--but it may be a necessary preliminary to future "success"!

Recent in-depth studies on successful entrepreneurs reveal that the majority of them failed at least once, and often twice, before learning how to make their ventures go. In interviews, they invariably point to previous failure as the best "learning experience" in their careers, and champion the "right to fail" as an essential ingredient in an entrepreneurial society.

However, entrepreneurs who have failed—and especially those who have been through the public humiliation of bankruptcy proceedings--are the first to declare that failure takes a tremendous psychic toll. Self-esteem can be shattered, marriages can fall apart, friends can disappear, accompanied by physical symptoms of exhaustion and illness. In short, failure is not a pleasurable way to learn.

But it is effective. Those who have failed in the past agree that it takes about three years to recover fully from the experience--to let the dust settle, the wounds heal, the lessons be absorbed, and the entrepreneurial spirit rekindled. In many cases, it is a time to go to work for someone else. Before long the dedicated entrepreneur will be able to count his "failure" as a plus, and a new venture will be born.

ABOUT BANKRUPTCY LAWYERS

This note *presupposes that you intend to hire a lawyer specializing in bankruptcy* should you need to enter bankruptcy proceedings. As one recognized commentator on bankruptcy law admonishes, "Bankruptcy (law) is a highly specialized field, and the best thing a general practitioner can do for his client is to send him to a specialist."[3] The experienced bankruptcy lawyer will guide the bankrupt through a dangerous minefield: under which chapter to file; how to value assets and liabilities; how to negotiate with creditors; if necessary, what kind of liquidation sale to arrange; or, if warranted, how to continue operations during a court-certified credit crunch. An experienced creditor's lawyer will help him to recover a bigger share of his losses. And a bankruptcy lawyer representing buyers of companies in receivership can assess more accurately the true value of the company and the lowest possible price at which it can be purchased.

Bankruptcy lawyers are well paid for their efforts; they are assured of receiving their fees off the top, since the law requires that "Administrative" expenses be met as soon as secured creditors have been reimbursed. At times the bankruptcy lawyer will request a

---

[3]Sidney Rutberg, *Ten Cents on the Dollar,* Simon and Schuster, New York, 1973, p. 87.

percentage of the settlement; on other occasions he will ask for a flat fee. (Disgruntled bankrupts have been heard to remark that paying the lawyer turned out to be more expensive than paying the creditors.) A reputable corporation lawyer or general practitioner can probably recommend a firm they use exclusively for bankruptcy cases. So, if you find yourself in one of the three situations described at the outset, be prepared to pay. Usually, you will get your money's worth.

DEFINITION OF TERMS

To clarify the meaning of some terms used frequently in this note, here are some definitions:

> **PERSONAL BANKRUPTCY**: applies to an individual who files for bankruptcy, though his debt may have arisen because of unprofitable business transactions. Unless otherwise protected, his assets can include those of the business and of his spouse.

> **BUSINESS BANKRUPTCY**: applies to either an unincorporated business or a corporation which files for bankruptcy. In "rehabilitative" proceedings, business and personal bankruptcies fall under different chapters. In all instances, different forms are filed.

> **VOLUNTARY BANKRUPTCY**: The debtor initiates the process.

> **INVOLUNTARY BANKRUPTCY**: The creditors or stockholders initiate the process.

> **"STRAIGHT" BANKRUPTCY**: The debtor's assets (if any) are distributed to creditors with proven claims, and the debtor may be discharged.

> **"CHAPTER" BANKRUPTCY**: The debtor chooses one of several forms of "rehabilitation," in an attempt to repay his unsecured debts over a period of time without being judged "bankrupt."

> **SECURED DEBT**: Debt for which the creditor holds collateral rights: the debtor's house, car, appliances.

> **UNSECURED DEBT**: Practically defined, any debt not secured by collateral: accounts payable, insurance premiums, unsecured loans. Unsecured debt is the only type of debt from which the debtor can seek relief.

COMPOSITIONS: Common law agreements under which creditors can agree to accept partial payment to satisfy their claims.

EXTENSIONS: Common law agreements under which creditors can agree to longer times for repayment.

ARRANGEMENTS: One form of statutory provision under rehabilitative CHAPTER LAW which include both compositions and extensions.

REORGANIZATIONS: Court-imposed arrangements involving both debt and equity interests, large and complex in scope. (Formerly describing corporations filing under Chapter X.)

LIQUIDATION: (in bankruptcy) The settling of financial affairs of a business or individual usually by turning into cash all assets for distribution to creditors. (Distinguished from dissolution, the end of the legal existence of a corporation.)

BANKRUPTCY REMEDIES UNDER COMMON LAW: SOME ALTERNATIVES TO FEDERAL BANKRUPTCY PROCEEDINGS

For both the individual and the businessman, procedures exist under certain state laws to help the debtor repay his debt without declaring bankruptcy. If these work, fine; if not, the debtor cannot be released from his debt and must turn to the federal laws.

Personal Relief

—Debt pooling. Debt pooling means that a debtor turns over a portion of his income to an agent, for a fee, and the agent assumes responsibility for paying back the creditors over time. In certain circumstances, such as a well-run company credit union, this type of organized approach to repayment is sufficient. However, too often, debt-pooling agents are not closely examined by state officials, and may be charging the debtor exorbitant fees without satisfying the creditor's claims.

—Wage Earner Trusteeships. A few states, notably Ohio, have adopted this remedy at a state level; it is essentially the same as Chapter 13 proceedings, with the state court appointing the trustee. If well-administered, proceeding at a local level can be more efficient.

—Compositions and Extensions. As explained earlier, a composition is an agreement between debtor and creditors to repay in part the creditors' claims; an extension is an agreement to pay back over time. At a state level, this type of out-of-court settlement, negotiated by a lawyer, is very effective if the debtor has every expectation of being able to repay the debt.

Business Relief

—Compositions and Extensions. As in personal relief, the out-of-court settlement is also useful for potentially solvent businesses, though the stakes are invariably higher and the creditors more persistent.

—Assignment for the benefit of creditors. In this instance, a debtor may assign to a third party all his exempt assets, which the agent then liquidates for the benefit of the creditors and for himself. Again, this can be a timesaving shortcut to the federal proceedings--but only if the assets satisfy the creditors' claims.

—State court receivership. This remedy is available to corporations on a state level, and the receiver may either liquidate the corporation or attempt to negotiate an arrangement with the creditors.

Since state law varies widely, and certain proceedings are more efficiently administered in some states than in others, it is imperative that your lawyer be entirely familiar with the most effective remedies in your geographical area, so that he can advise you wisely on whether or not to proceed under state law.

BANKRUPTCY PROCEEDINGS UNDER FEDERAL LAW

Personal Bankruptcy

"Straight" Bankruptcy Proceedings, Chapter 7

Before 1979, a debtor who filed a petition under Chapters I - VII, requesting relief from his debts by liquidation of his assets and formal discharge from meeting debts still outstanding, was said to be filing for "straight" bankruptcy. The new law refers to this procedure as Chapter 7 proceedings, but to avoid an excess of already confusing numbers we will continue to refer to the liquidation option as "straight" bankruptcy.

1.*Formal proceedings begin when the debtor files a petition for bankruptcy. The filing of this petition automatically declares him bankrupt, and provides immunity from his creditors. Usually, the debtor files voluntarily, but in a few instances his creditors may force him to. This petition asks the debtor to describe all his assets, all his liabilities, and the exemptions which he legally can retain. The liabilities must be itemized in Schedule A, and include debts secured by law (taxes, employee wages, landlords), by securities, unsecured debts (outstanding bills, personal loans), and liabilities on notes and bills (mortgages). Assets are itemized in Schedule B, and include real estate, personal

---

*The description of "straight" proceedings, both personal and business are based on a report from the Brookings Institute published in 1971, following the procedure under the Bankruptcy Act at that time. As the authors explained, the scheme is greatly simplified and generalized. Since the former procedure will not in great measure be changed, the description, written in 1981, will still serve as a guideline.

property, "Choses in action"(prepaid security deposits), property in expectation or trust, and property which by law is exempt. A summary of these two schedules is then prepared, and the debtor signs the document under oath.

2. The case is then assigned to a referee, who notifies the creditors listed in the petition of the First Meeting. Under the new law, the court may not be present at this, or any other, creditor meeting. At this time, the creditors have a chance to examine the debtor and, if they wish, to ask that a trustee be appointed to take charge of the assets. Frequently, the amounts involved are not worth the creditors' time, and the referee himself examines the debtor, accompanies by his lawyer.

3. Next, the referee decides which of the debtor's exemptions to allow. This depends somewhat on the judgement of the referee and the law of the state. Usually, the debtor is allowed to retain a portion of his salary (if any), the tools of his trade, his car (if it is necessary to his work), his house, and--in some states personal property of his choice up to a given value. Under the new Code, the debtor may choose between a list of existing state and federal exemptions and a list of new exemptions provided in the Code.

4. At this point, the referee initiates the heart of the proceeding: the collection and liquidation of the debtor's estate. He does this either by a sale, or by collecting nonexempt monies such as wages and income tax refunds. (In reality, there is often little to collect, and what can be salvaged goes to pay administrative expenses.)

5. Then, a distribution is made. Assets are distributed in this order:

  -Secured claims

  -Administrative expenses

  -Taxes

  -Priority creditors, falling into categories specified by the Bankruptcy Act

  -Unsecured creditors (In practice, the last two categories
    are treated much the same in small suits.)

6. Finally, the referee certifies the records and sends them to the clerk of the court, discharges the trustee (if any), discharges the debtor and closes the case. The now debtless individual can begin anew; however, he cannot file for bankruptcy again for *six* years.

Rehabilitative Proceedings: "old" Chapter XIII and "new" Chapter 13

Chapter XIII, which covers the personal wage-earner, was included in recognition that close to 50% of personal bankrupts are wage-earners, and that they should be given an opportunity to make an "arrangement" to repay their debts out of income, as an alternative to having their assets liquidated. Again, the process begins with a petition filed by the debtor and the referee calls a first meeting of creditors to negotiate the "arrangement" that the debtor has proposed.

The success of a Chapter XIII proceeding often hinged on the claims of the secured creditors; if they were large and the creditors insisted on repayment in full, it was often beyond the capability of the debtor to repay them in a reasonable period of time, and the unsecured creditors would object, throwing the petition into "straight" proceedings. The advantage to the debtor under Chapter XIII, if he could meet his "arrangement," was a temporary stay against all creditors petitioning for payment after the original filing date. The disadvantage was that the referee would often find a renegotiated arrangement "feasible" if it satisfied the creditors, though the burden on the debtor would be nearly intolerable.

However, the new Chapter 13 appears to make this form of relief much more attractive, both to the debtor who temporarily needs "a port in a storm" and to the creditor who stands to recover more by payback than by liquidation. Chapter 13 is exclusively voluntary and available to all individuals with a regular source of income. One provision limits the liability of co-signer of the debtor's obligations. Another allows a husband and wife to file jointly. A third eases the discharge stipulations. A fourth limits the time of "feasibility" to three years.

For these reasons, the advice of your lawyer as to whether to file "straight" or 13 is crucial.

Business Bankruptcy

"Straight" Bankruptcy Proceedings, "new" Chapter 7.

"Straight" business bankruptcies are very similar to "straight" personal bankruptcies, but because the stakes are usually higher the process is more time-consuming, the creditors more belligerent, and the costs to the debtor substantial. Also, the 'discharge' from debt so desirable to the individual is not desirable or a business which wishes to continue operations, for it trades freedom from debt for liquidation.

However, one study concludes that "straight bankruptcy is attractive to the unincorporated businessman because it is the only federal procedure that discharges him from personal liability for the obligations of the business."[4]

Now, let's see how it works.

1. The debtor business files a petition of bankruptcy, listing all assets and liabilities of the business. If unincorporated, the petition is effectively a discharge from debt.

2. The referee may choose to take steps for early protection of the estate, especially if it is sizable. He may appoint a receiver, either custodial or operating. He may also issue a restraining order, preventing creditors from collecting anything until the process is concluded, which could take several years.

---

[4]Stanley and Girth, *Bankruptcy: Problem, Process, Reform*, The Brookings Institute, 1971, p. 108.

3. At the First Meeting between the creditors and the debtor (the court may not attend, under the new law) the creditors can form committees (which the court is authorized to appoint) according to class and establish priorities among themselves.

4. The collection and liquidation of the estate now proceeds in the manner prescribed by the referee. Since more is at stake, there is considerably more interest in the liquidation--both by creditors and by prospective buyers--than in a personal bankruptcy sale. Under the new law, claims by secured creditors are given much more weight than formerly. Liquidation is through sale and/or collection.

Sales. The referee may recommend a public auction, usually conducted by a private auctioner, or a private sale, conducted through negotiations or sealed bids. In either altenative, let the innocent beware! Auctioners are a group of closely-knit professionals; buyers frequently have inside information about what other buyers plan to bid for and avoid bidding wars. Goods at auction are sold "as is," and the auctioner can tip off a prospective bidder (not you) in advance about the good deals. There is no such thing as a warranty at a bankruptcy sale. Bidding action is fast. If you are bidding on the assets of a company at auction, your lawyer should "know the other players;" he may want to do a bit of pre-bid negotiation. There can be many winners at auction: the auctioner, the trustee, the lawyers, and bidders, and--when it is all over--the creditors. In practice, the greatest beneficiaries of the system are not the creditors, but the people who administer it.

Collections and recoveries. This is the other method of gathering the debtor's assets which the referee will pursue. He will attempt to recover: accounts receivable, money in bank accounts, tax refunds, and utilities deposits. If the amounts, as stated on the petition are small, they may not be worth the time and expense of collecting them--but if not, they are fair game.

6. Repayment then follows: to the secured creditors, the administrators, the government, the employees owed wages, and the unsecured creditors. Administrators never seem to go hungry. Then, once the liquidation and distribution are complete, the referee declares the case closed and the businessman, debt-free, can go out and try again.

Rehabilitative Proceedings

Under the new Code, the business rehabilitation procedures included in Chapters X, XI, and XII have been blended into Chapter 11. This has the advantage of eliminating the debtor's choice of relief and the loss of time in changing from one to the other if circumstances so dictated. However, the thrust of the new chapter will not be welcomed by some parties--especially by the debtor in a smaller business and by the debtor who valued the relief because it was exclusively voluntary. To illustrate the situation, we will look at both the old chapters and the new.

"Old" Chapter XI

Chapter XI was designed for the businessman or corporation who voluntarily wished to arrange with his creditors for a mutually satisfactory pay-back arrangement, while allowing him to continue to run his business and generate income to discharge the debts.

The key provisions of Chapter XI proceedings were: *voluntary* - only the debtor can initiate the proceedings, *business* - a sole proprietor, partnership or corporation, and *unsecured debts* - outstanding bills and the like, and not the interests of secured creditors and stockholders.

This procedure was straightforward. The debtor filed a petition stating his assets and liabilities, along with a plan for repaying them. If the creditors agreed to the plan, and if the referee found it "for the best interest of the creditors" and "feasible," he confirmed the plan. The debtor proceeded with repayment, according to the plan, and the case was closed when the debt was discharged.

Chapter XI proceedings differed from "straight" bankruptcy in several important respects. First, the debtor had to produce a cash deposit after his plan was confirmed, both for administrative expenses and to make the first cash repayment on the schedule. To raise the money, the debtor sold assets not germane to the business or used operating funds, or attempted to borrow it. Second, the creditors had to prove to the referee that their claims were valid, or the referee would disallow them, since the valid claims constituted the framework of the "arrangement." And third, "feasibility" was at the discretion of the referee, and what may have been in the best interest of the creditors was often burdensome to the debtor.

Nonetheless, certain types of businesses found Chapter XI a convenient way of handling a temporary credit crunch when the business was basically healthy. Retail stores with a surplus of inventory, restaurants whose suppliers could be paid only if customers ate there, manufacturing concerns with an unexpectedly wide gap between purchasing raw materials and selling finished goods--all these business concerns benefited greatly from a court-approved, mutually satisfactory payback "arrangement" proposed by the debtor and agreed to by his creditors, because staying in business was the only way they could discharge their debts.

"Old" Chapter XII

"Old" Chapter XII offered debt relief to "non-corporate debtors with secured liens on real property." It was included primarily for the real estate industry, but also for debtors whose assets were primarily in real property, as an alternative to liquidation. The proceedings were initiated voluntarily, and in form resembled those of Chapter XI. However, since two thirds of the creditors had to agree to the debtor's payback "arrangement," Chapter XII proceedings proved to have a low likelihood of acceptance and, as a result, were seldom used.

"Old" Chapter X

Chapter X pertained to only one situation, corporate reorganization. It was designed to protect equity, as well as debt, interests, and proceedings could be initiated by stockholders, or creditors, or the corporation itself.

Chapter X has been described as "major surgery" and differed from other debtor-relief chapters in several ways.

—Both the initiation of the proceedings and the imposition of an arrangement "feasible" for the debtor in that it it provided him a "reasonable prospect for survival" could be involuntary.

—The case was heard by a federal district judge, not a referee, who was joined by a representative of the Securities and Exchange Commission if the debt exceeded $3 million, and frequently if it was less.

—Because both equity holders and creditors were a party to the suit, many interests and their lawyers were party to the procedures, and Chapter X was long and very costly to the corporation. In reality, less than one in four corporations survived Chapter X proceedings in 1964-69.[5]

Even for the surviving corporations, the situation had been changed dramatically. Usually, top management had been fired, the financial structure had been built anew and new stock issued, and operating budgets had been slashed. Inevitably, too, the image of the corporation had been tarnished. Nonetheless, Chapter X provisions were designed for the best interests of the stockholders and the creditors, especially secured creditors, and the drafters of the chapter believed that, in the case of a publicly-held corporation, the interests of creditors and investors were too important to be left to voluntary corporate decisions and corporation-proposed arrangements.

"New" Chapter 11

In general, the debtor relief provisions in the new law appear to favor large businesses with assets untouched by debt at the expense of smaller single-source businesses. This is because new Chapter 13 incorporates many of the lengthy procedural requirements of old X, and time is money--and also because there nowhere remains a business "arrangement" alternative which is exclusively voluntary. A brief listing of some of the new provisions will help to illustrate this thrust.

1. Eligibility includes all the businesses described in "straight" bankruptcy, and still excludes farmers and certain non-profit organizations, but now includes also stockbrokers, commodities brokers, and railroads.

2. Petitions will be heard by a federal district judge, though he may appoint a referee as "master." The court can appoint committees both for creditors and for equity interests, though it may not sit in on their negotiations. Effectively, these provisions make the proceedings more judicial and less administrative.

3. The appointment of a trustee for the debtor no longer depends on the amount of the assets, but rather on the discretion of the court.

4. A debtor may operate his business unless the court rules otherwise; no longer must he ask permission.

---

[5]Stanley and Girth, *Bankruptcy: Problem, Process, Reform,* The Brookings Institute, 1971, p. 145.

5. New rules governing the confirmation of the debtor's "arrangements" strike two ways: no longer can the plan be strictly voluntary (though the debtor is given 120 days to submit his own plan); but, the criteria for feasible arrangements are easier to meet.

6. The Securities and Exchange Commission can no longer be an active party in the proceedings or file an appeal, though it may attend the hearings and raise issues.

It remains to be seen whether the smaller business debtor can effectively use Chapter 11 relief while continuing to operate his business profitably.

BUYING A BANKRUPT BUSINESS — SOME QUESTIONS

For the prospective buyer of a bankrupt business, the information he can learn from the preceding discussion is largely a warning:

--Don't move without a lawyer - a bankruptcy lawyer.

--Don't buy a pig in a poke.

By now, you have a clearer idea of the apparent reasons a debtor will declare bankruptcy, the types of creditors and the nature of their claims, and the disposition of the debtor's assets. Doubtless, you have also gathered that the reasons a company goes bankrupt lie much deeper than the lists of names and amounts of money appearing on the petition.

If you are negotiating with the owner of a company in bankruptcy, what should you be wary of?

—Study the petition with your lawyer to assess the claimed scope of the debt.

—How much debt will be paid back by the purchase price? How many unhappy or reluctant creditors will you inherit?

—Why did the company really go bankrupt? Mismanagement, pure and simple? Loss of an existing market? Shortage of skilled labor? Environmental regulations? You won't find the answers on a petition, and yet you must find them.

—Do you have the capability to reverse or erase the causes of the business failure? If not, no deal is the best deal.

—If you're buying part of the assets of a company which has declared bankruptcy, does a secured creditor already have prior claims on them?

—If you are buying goods and/or equipment at auction, are you willing to take them "as is," without a warrent? Do you have an experienced agent to bid for you?

—Given an alternative, would you prefer to negotiate for a failing business in an out-of-court settlement, or under the scrutiny of a referee in bankruptcy?

A number of other considerations enter into the decision as to whether or not to buy a bankrupt company. A few have been suggested here.[6] Others are treated elsewhere. See the technical note on Acquisitions and Leveraged Buyouts. Also, accounting procedures used to evaluate a bankrupt company and to set a liquidation value for a company are covered in a number of accounting books. For these reasons, they are not covered here.

CONCLUSION

Any entrepreneur whose venture appears to be a candidate for bankruptcy proceedings should consult a bankruptcy lawyer at once. However, the lawyer must understand even more than the laws we have discussed--he must understand you and the potential of your venture. Perhaps your situation is hopeless in the long run, and you should liquidate with dispatch. Perhaps you are psychologically unable to undergo the procedural examinations and disclosures for several months. Or perhaps, all you need for success is temporary relief--spelled Chapter 11 or 13.

In some instances, a conscientious lawyer may suggest that bankruptcy is inappropriate, and will suggest consulting a "turn-around specialist," a consultant with experience in helping small companies to tighten up, redirect, or discontinue parts of their operation which are unprofitable, and to arrange informal payback schedules with their creditors.[7]

Any entrepreneur who is considering the purchase of a bankrupt business is directed to proceed with caution, as well as a lawyer. Bankruptcy laws deal with results, not causes; and the would-be buyer may find that the latter is of more importance in his decision than the former.

Again, this note is intended only as an introduction to bankruptcy laws and not as a how-to manual. The importance of consulting a bankruptcy lawyer cannot be overstated.

---

[6]Rees Morrison, "Shopping for Bankruptcy Bargains," *Inc.,* March 1982.

[7]Herbert Kierulff, "Turnabouts of Entrepreneurial Firms," paper in *Frontiers of Entrepreneurship Research,* Babson College, 1981.

BUSINESS PLANS:
THEIR DEVELOPMENT AND USES

WHAT IS A BUSINESS PLAN?

A business plan is a report written by you about your venture at a particular point in time. Your business plan should describe your venture, WHAT it is, WHO will be active in it, WHY you believe it will be successful, and HOW you intend to implement your plans. It should be a concise, readable, well-written document. It should anticipate setbacks as well as successes. It should be evaluative, not promotional, in substance and tone. And it should be dated, because you will want to revise or rewrite it at different times during the evolution of your venture.

WHY DO I NEED ONE?

You need a business plan for two purposes -- for *internal* evaluation of a venture, both as a checklist and as a timetable for accomplishing stated objectives; and for *external* use, to attract resources -- both financial resources and human ones -- e.g., attracting partners or other entrepreneurial team members if the venture requires them. Let us briefly consider how a business plan can provide valuable assistance in each of these areas.

Internal Planning

Initially, in the pre-start-up phase, writing a business plan is another method of evaluating your venture--a chance to explain, justify, and project your assumptions. During this exercise, you may uncover oversights which are potentially fatal flaws in the original venture concept. You can also work through more than one scenario -- a worst-case projection as well as a best-case one, cost-volume trade-offs, and break-even points under a variety of conditions. A few examples might be:

. My team -- who is going to do what? If we can't cover all the bases, do we need to hire part-time help, such as an accountant or a delivery person?

. My competitive edge -- who is the competition and why do I think I can move in on them? Are they thriving, or is the market generally level? What do they charge? How do I want to position my pricing in that context?

. My physical facilities -- are they in good shape? Big enough to anticipate expansion? Would it be more advantageous to lease or buy?

. My cash flow -- where can I anticipate a cash crunch? If I have a surplus, even briefly, how can I make that money work for me?

Asking these kinds of questions forces us to deal with potentially bad news. For example, there's the entrepreneur who discovered during his business plan rewrite that the warehouse space he had leased for his toy store wasn't big enough to accomodate his pre-Christmas inventory. In another case, an entrepreneur found that he would not be able to remain solvent during year two if his rent were raised, or if fuel bills increased even a moderate amount. The good news is that in both instances the problems were discovered before they happened -- on paper -- and the entrepreneurs involved could take steps to minimize or avoid them.

As your venture gets underway, you will find that portions of your business plan will have to be revised. For example, one team member may have too much to do. Or a shipping delay in raw materials will necessitate a delay in production schedules, which in turn makes your cash flow statement useless. As these changes occur, you should rework your plan. Such revisions can be jotted down on note paper or dictated but should be filed along with the original in a safe place so the revisions can be included when you need to prepare a formal new plan.

When you write your first business plan, you should gather information from everyone involved with your venture. These include both your team (partners, employees, part-time advisors such as a lawyer and an accountant) and those with whom you will be doing business (suppliers, distributors, customers), even though you will share it only with your team. If prepared properly, everyone will know his area of responsibility, agree on goals and objectives, and provide information for establishing production, sales, and financial schedules. The more procedure that you can spell out, the less opportunity for misunderstanding will exist as your venture begins operations.

External Funding

At various points in your venture you will need to attract outside sources of financing. The sources,* and the timing, will change depending on the needs and maturity of the venture, but your business plan will be an important instrument in every instance in which you need to raise money.

Potential investors generally have at least one overriding concern: the bottom line. How much money are you looking for? How long will you need it? What will be the rate of the return to the investor? What are the risks?

Your business plan should give them the answers to these questions. Your bottom line will be evident in the mandatory series of financial projections which are essential to a business plan (income statements, balance sheets, cash flows), but, equally important, you must explain why you believe you will be able to achieve them. This explanation must include a clear description and evaluation of:

1. the concept of your venture;
2. the entrepreneurial team;
3. the market and the competition;
4. why your product/service is distinctive; and
5. what you intend to do with the money you hope to raise.

A recent study of 20 business plans for high-tech ventures, which had been submitted to venture capitalists were rated according to the five criteria above without knowing which plans had been accepted or rejected by the venture capitalists. Of those with minor flaws in any of the five areas, four of five were accepted; among those with severe deficiencies in any area, only two of eight were accepted.[1] But whether dealing with venture capitalists, bankers, or informal investors, a well-drawn business plan can be the single best way to get your venture off the ground.

---

*See note on *Sources of Capital.*

[1]Edward Roberts, "Businesss Planning in the Start-Up High-Technology Enterprise," speech to the MIT Enterprise Forum, April, 1983.

Here are a few issues which potential investors will want to know about:

• *New Products.* Virtually no invention will sell itself. Figures show that less than half of one percent of the inventions listed in the U.S. Patent Gazette between 1975 and 1980 returned a cent of profit to the investor;[2] and it is safe to assume that the lucky .005 who did, owe their success to an adequately financed marketing strategy and an organization which could produce the invention as well as find willing buyers. A business plan which shows how an idea can be turned into a profit is the entrepreneur's blueprint for success. The blueprints on the inventor's desk are not sufficient. When new products are involved, the business plan must explain in simple words why the product is unique, and present a strategy for protecting its uniqueness.

• *New Markets.* A prospective investor is not looking for a "snow job" about millions of potential new customers. He is looking for an active investment opportunity. He's looking for facts, well ordered ones, about who will buy, when and how often. Remember, he is looking for a return on investment, not a charitable deduction. He will have little interest in a business plan that is "too good to be true," or one that fails to anticipate problems about a new market segment.

In the study of business plans mentioned earlier, the chief weakness in all the plans was the failure to understand the potential customer -- who he was, where he was, how to reach him. This omission was often accompanied by a failure to analyze the competition, both present and future, together with strategies for gaining market share from them.

• *Experienced team members.* Lately, much emphasis has been put on the entrepreneurial team -- for good reason. A mixture of skills is needed to successfully launch a venture:

• marketing: how, where, to whom to sell it
• sales: selling and delivering it
• controls: having enough product, people, cash where you need it, when you need it

---

[2]Jeffry A. Timmons, "A Business Plan is More Than a Financing Device," *Harvard Business Review,* March/April 1980.

- financial planning/raising money
- operations/production
- day-to-day administration

An investor will want to know which team member has experience in which areas. In the high-tech ventures mentioned earlier a team of four or more members correlated positively with success. A lead entrepreneur with a Ph.D. did not correlate with success; the lead entrepreneur who understood marketing stood a better chance of success.[3]

Seldom can a new venture include experienced personnel in all these areas, but the business plan must show a concern about these issues and, when possible, the name of a specific person or persons who will join the venture later should be included.

FORMAL VERSUS INFORMAL PLANS

A recent survey shows that most venture capital investors require a "formal" business plan while others are willing to help the entrepreneur develop one. But even if your venture won't require heavy infusions of venture capital, the fact remains that nearly all entrepreneurs need "something on paper" early on: for themselves, for steering their venture, and for prospective investors other than venture capitalists.[4]

Exhibit 1 may be a useful way to visualize when you will need a formal business plan versus an informal one, based on the type of venture and the time during its life cycle. The distinction between an informal plan and a formal plan is one of degree. The informal plan, usually limited to internal use, can be thought of as a checklist or a timetable. A formal plan, on the other hand, is almost exclusively for external use, and is directed specifically to individuals or groups from which you hope to raise money. It should be a written document supported by quantitative data, titled, signed, and numbered, covering in some detail the key aspects of your venture -- past, present and future.

------

[3]See Roberts, op. cit. p. 3. Also his article, "Entrepreneurship and Technology," *Research Management,* July, 1968, pp. 249-266; and Roberts, E.B. and Wainer, H., "Some Characteristics of Technical Entrepreneurs," *IEEE Transactions on Engineering Management,* August, 1971, pp. 100-109.

[4]Jeffry A. Timmons, "Survey of the Most Active Venture Capital Firms," *Frontiers of Entrepreneurship Research* (FOER), Babson College, Wellesley, MA 1981.

Exhibit I

Need for a Business Plan: Which Type and When

	Pre Start-Up		Start-Up		Operating		End (buy-out)	
	Internal	External	Internal	External	Internal	External	Internal	External
Life-style Ventures	I		I		I	F	I	F
Smaller Profit-Oriented Ventures	I		I		F	F	I	F
High Growth Ventures	F	F	I	F	F	F	I	F

F= Formal   I= Informal

THE BUSINESS PLAN: CONTENTS AND ORGANIZATION

There are several sources that discuss the preparation of business plans. One especially useful one, in workbook format, provides a number of "do's" and "don'ts" that reflect "our own experience and reactions to a great many business plans, as well as some of what has been published, on the foibles, pet hates, and preferences of venture capitalists."[5]

> 1. Do keep the business plan as short as you can without compromising the description of your venture and its potential. Cover the key issues that will interest an investor and leave the details of secondary importance for a meeting with the investor. Remember venture capital investors are not patient readers.
>
> 2. Don't overdiversify your venture. Focus your attention on one or two product lines and markets. A new or young business does not have the management depth to pursue a number of opportunities.

---

[5]Timmons, Jeffry, Leonard E. Smollen and Alexander Dingee, *New Venture Creation: A Guide to Small Business Development,* Homewood, Illinois: Richard D. Irwin, Inc., 1977. See Chapter 14, Developing a Business Plan, pp. 417-455.

3. Don't have unnamed, mysterious people on your management team -- that is, the Mr. G., who is currently a financial vice president, who will join you later. The investor will want to know early on who Mr. G. is and what his commitment is to your venture.

4. Don't describe technical products or manufacturing processes in a way and with a jargon that only an expert can understand. A venture capitalist does not like to invest in what he doesn't understand or thinks you don't understand because you can't explain it to a smart fellow like himself.

5. Don't estimate your sales on the basis of what you can or would like to produce. Do estimate carefully your potential sales and from these determine the production facility you need.

6. Don't make ambiguous, vague, or unsubstantiated statements. They make you look like a shallow and fuzzy thinker. For example, don't merely say that your markets are growing rapidly. Determine and delineate past, present, and projected future growth rates and market size.

7. Do disclose and discuss any current or potential problems in your venture. If you fail to do this and the venture capitalist discovers them, your credibility will be badly damaged.

8. Do involve all of your management team in the preparation of the business plan as well as any special legal, accounting, or financial help that you may need.

Other guidelines are directed at specific types of ventures, e.g., the Small Business Administration provides brochures on business plan development for the small manufacturing company, the small construction company, the small service firm.[6] For an overall guideline as to format and length, another expert suggests a maximum length of fifty pages, neatly typed, and a two-page introductory summary (written after you have completed the plan), containing a few brief statements to highlight:

1. your company's origins, activities, management and
   performance,

---

[6]*Business Plan for Small Service Firms* (No. 153), *Business Plan for Small Manufacturers* (No. 218) and *Business Plan for Small Construction Firms* (No. 221) are available free of charge from field offices and Washington headquarters of the Small Business Administration or by writing SBA, P.O. Box 15434, Fort Worth, Texas 76119.

2. any distinguishing features of your product or service,

3. the attractiveness of your market,

4. a summary of your financial projections,

5. the amount of money you now seek, in what form (equity, debt or both), and for what purpose.[7]

Another source, directed primarily to the entrepreneur with a high-tech, fast-growth venture, suggests formatting the business plan so it answers at least ten key questions that sophisticated investors generally ask:

1. *Is the company in an area of emerging technology?* Does the technology have a solid base for growth as measured by the research and development efforts put into the technology, both by this and other companies? If the company thinks its technology is way ahead, is it too far ahead? Where is everyone else? Why? Do I understand the technology and its potential growth? Can it be explained to the customer, the directors and other investors?

2. *Is there a market for the technology or product?* Basically, is there a need demonstrated already? Or will it create a new market? New-market speculation entails the highest risks but the greatest rewards. Does management understand the market and how to exploit it? What's the competition?

3. *Why didn't an established company decide to exploit and market the product?* The entrepreneur may tell me his old company didn't understand him, stifling his inventiveness. This can often be true. It may also be true that the parent company made a market evaluation and determined that the product was not worth exploiting further. On the other hand, maybe the parent company thought it was a good idea but just couldn't invest resources in it.

4. *Is there a natural product line or follow-on technology?* In other words, has the new concept or product or technology a long-range career and reproductive aspects? Is the management flexible and adaptable to change?

———

[7]Brian Haslett and Leonard Smollen, "How to Prepare a Business Plan," p. 55, in *A Guide to Venture Capital Sources,* 7th Ed. Wellesley, MA: Capital Publishing Company, 1983.

5. *Does management have corporate experience?* The key people, particularly the decision-makers, should have experience either as officers or as directors of a profit-making corporation in a technology area. There is always the exception to the rule, but the chief officials should have been around the corporate track so they know what to expect and how to plan.

6. *What are management's goals?* Only to make money? This type of leadership will go over the side quickly -- its goals may be in conflict with corporate and stockholder goals. The entrepreneurs are people who like to run things, organize them and grow them -- as well as have financial incentives.

7. *Does management have a ten-year objective and a five-year operating plan?* These may change with time, but they should always be clearly stated at the outset.

8. *Does management understand and have capabilities for all phases of its operations, from research through production and marketing, as well as support functions -- comptroller, accounting, legal, and so forth?* The missing manager, whom the company is going to hire tomorrow, can always be the weak link in the chain. The full span of experience and authority should be visible at the outset.

9. *Does management understand the nature and use of money?* This is extremely important regardless of how good the ideas or the management are. Money is the fuel that stokes the fire.

10. *Does management have a competent, recognized leader and decision-maker?* Group decision-making may be fine in the textbooks, but it doesn't work very well in a small emerging organization that has to make decisions fast if it is to survive. Above all, the decision-maker should be a good manager.[8]

---

[8]Albert Kelley, Frank Campanella, and John McKiernan, *Venture Capital: A Guidebook for New Enterprises,* Chestnut Hill, MA: The Management Institution, School of Management, Boston College, 1973, pp. 5-6.

Exhibit 2 summarizes many of these questions in checklist form, while noting those topic areas which should be addressed in your plan.

Exhibit 2

Sample Outline for a Business Plan

1. **Introductory page**

   • Name of the business (Is it descriptive? Distinctive? A potential trademark?)

   • Form of business (Partnership? Corporation? Other?)

   • Address and telephone number (Your own home? Office space? Factory?)

   • Summary of purpose of business (the product/service, the market you are aiming for, your goal and what you must do to achieve it. Can you focus your venture this succinctly?)

   • Summary of Capital Needs (present and projected)

2. **The Industry: The Context for Your Venture**

   • The Industry (national, regional, history, projected growth)

   • Your venture (how it fits into the industry context)

   • Key factors for success (both for the industry as a whole and for your venture)

3. **The Management Team**

   • Key management personnel, qualification to participate in your venture based on their past experience

   • Organization chart (Who does what? Who is responsible to whom?)

   • Compensation plan

   • Board of Directors (Are they informal advisors or active participants? What are their qualifications?)

   • Supporting consultants (Lawyer? Accountant? Other?)

4. **Product/Service: What and How**

   • If product: how made? with what? patented? (a production timetable, inventory control procedures, quality control guidelines should all be defined)

   • If service: how performed? with what? plans for attracting the customer? getting him to try? getting his repeat business?

   • Location of venture, and why

   • Rent or purchase — why

5. **Marketing Plan**

   - Size and trends of market, in general
   - Your target segment, and methodology of selection
   - What percent of the market is this? (In absolute size, and in dollar amount?)
   - Competition: list of names and market percentage
   - Your strategy, against the preceding background of facts and projections
   - Pricing
   - Distribution, packaging
   - Promotion
   - Customer Service Plan: product warranties, deliveries, repairs, installations

6. **Financial Plan**

   - Pro forma income statements (monthly for first year, quarterly for years 2 and 3)
   - Pro forma balance sheets (semi-annually first year; annually years 2 and 3)
   - Cash flow analyses (monthly first year, quarterly years 2 and 3)
   - Break-even analysis, under several sets of assumptions
   - Schedule of anticipated capital needs
   - Proposed offering — how much? how used?
   - Desired type(s) of financing

7. **Potential risks**

   - Identify potential weaknesses in topics 2-6
   - Project different outcomes using different assumptions (use electronic spread sheets)
   - Explain what you plan to do if they happen

8. **Supporting documents**

   - Partnership agreements, articles of incorporation
   - Patents, copyrights
   - Rental agreements, buy/sell contracts
   - Agreements with vendors
   - Insurance policies
   - Promotional material, photographs of principals, products, buildings, etc.

The next important step is to *translate your plan into dollars*. Your financial plan should indicate the venture's potential and the timetable for financial viability.[9] Your financial plan must include at least three basic exhibits:

- Profit and Loss Forecasts
- Pro Forma Balance Sheets
- Cash Flow Projections,
  and a break-even analysis
  based on the above.

Details on how to prepare these are provided in *New Venture Creation: A Guide to Small Business Development,* cited previously, and additional information is provided in Chapter 4 of this book. Quantitative Assessment: Numbers for Entrepreneurs. Our purpose here is to describe why these exhibits are important, and to reiterate that translating venture ideas into dollars is the true test of the viability of a venture. If your venture doesn't "add up" in terms of dollars and cents, it isn't going to fly very far.

Profit and Loss Forecast. This is the planning-for-profit part of financial management. Crucial to the projection is the sales forecast, and it may be useful to use a microcomputer and an electronic spread sheet and any one of several programs to prepare several P&Ls under various estimates of sales. Next, sales projections must be weighed against cost of goods sold, and these must be separated into fixed and variable costs. Finally, both pre-tax and after-tax results must be calculated. In order to be useful, the assumptions underlying all the figures must be explained in detail.

Pro-forma balance sheets. The balance sheets are used to detail the assets required to support the projected level of operations and, through liabilities, show how these assets are to be financed. Investors and bankers look to the projected balance sheets to determine if debt-to-equity ratios, working capital, current ratios, inventory turnover, etc. are within the acceptable limits required to justify future financings that are projected for the venture.

Pro forma cash flow analysis. Understanding cash flow, as we point out in Chapter 4, is a core concept for entrepreneurs. You must begin at the beginning: with startup expenses. These can include: fixtures and equipment, starting inventory, leaseholder improvements, utility deposits, legal and professional fees, licenses, advertising, and cash on hand. From the beginning, you must plan to have sufficient cash on hand to cover these expenses as they become due. A cash flow forecast will highlight any significant deficiencies between cash inflows and outflows and give you time to find ways to take appropriate action.

We should remind you again that the advent of the electronic spreadsheet makes it possible for today's entrepreneurs to project all three types of financial statements under

---

[9]This section is based on "The Financial Plan," from *New Venture Creation: A Guide to Small Business Development,* op. cit., pp. 437-41.

a variety of assumptions. This is useful both to the entrepreneur as a manager and to potential outside investors.

Finally, how long does it take to prepare a business plan? We have heard stories of "overnight wonders," but do not recommend this time table. Our best estimate, including time to gather adequate information, both quantitative and qualitative, to prepare analyses under varying sets of assumptions, and to organize the facts and figures into a tightly-structured, well-rounded, readable introduction to your venture is 150 to 300 hours depending on the complexity of the business.

REVIEWING AND PRESENTING YOUR BUSINESS PLAN

Because the development of a formal plan takes so much time, entrepreneurs may be tempted to utilize private consultants for this purpose. This practice can be dangerous if the entrepreneur does not work closely with the consultant to develop the business plan. Remember, it is your business plan and investors will want to know how familar you are with its contents. After all, they are not investing in a consultant but in you and your entrepreneurial team. No doubt their desire to invest will evaporate rapidly if you reveal less than intimate and thorough understanding of your business plan.

How should the presentation be made? First, no formal presentation should be made until you have had your business plan reviewed by impartial individuals. Other members of your entrepreneurial team do *not* qualify in this regard. You might start with your attorney or accountant if they are not full time members of your entrepreneurial team. Members of SCORE, an SBA sponsored counseling services composed of retired executives can also act as a sounding board for embryonic business planners. Depending on where you live, you may have access to one or more public forums, such as the Enterprise Forum sponsored by MIT, which brings entrepreneurs and their business plans into contact with business advisors and even potential investors.

Second, you need to assess if the organization of your business plan is also an appropriate way to organize your presention. This decision will turn on several factors, including the length and complexity of the business plan, the amount of time you have to make a presentation, and whether or not your audience has studied the business plan beforehand. In nearly all instances, you will need to allocate some time exclusively for the preparation of your presentation.

Third, you need to evaluate your presentation skills. If they are weak, you may be able to rely on other members of your team for some support. However, it is very important not to confuse presentation capabilities with other capabilities and responsibilities. For example, your brilliant engineer may be the last one you want to talk about technical matters, particularly if the investors are not strongly versed in your particular technology. Sometimes it pays to have team members from other functional areas explain what might be particularly difficult or complex portions of the presentation--on the rationale that if they can understand and articulate the principal issues, then your audience will also be able to understand them.

SOURCES OF CAPITAL: AN OVERVIEW

AND

INFORMATION ON DEBT FINANCING

INTRODUCTION: INTERNAL FINANCING, DEBT FINANCING AND EQUITY FINANCING

The entire life cycle of a venture is punctuated by a recurring theme--the need to obtain capital at a reasonable price. There are many sources of capital, tailored to meet many different types of capital needs. Knowing where to look is one of the most difficult tasks for the entrepreneur.

He can look within the venture itself for sources of internal financing. Or he can look to the outside for sources of external financing, in order to match his capital needs with a lending source whose business it is to deal with those particular needs. If he needs seed or startup money, he must find lenders who find his concept attractive; if he needs money for growth, he must show that his venture will generate substantial returns for investors over and above the needs of the venture itself; if he needs to borrow cash, he must show convincing evidence that he can repay the loan.

This brief note begins with several general distinctions between different types of funding. Section II provides a specific list of capital sources with brief descriptions of each. Section III provides detailed information on perhaps the most utilized source of capital: debt financing from banks and finance companies.

SOME BASIC DISTINCTIONS

Internal financing is a time-honored method of letting the business itself provide as much as it possibly can. Some of these cash generating strategies include: accelerating accounts receivable collections, optimizing trade credit arrangements, improving inventory turnover, and turning fixed assets into cash. [1] Of course, internal financing assumes you have an ongoing business.

---

[1] "See Internal Financing," *Venture,* June 1983, p. 68, for a further discussion.

External financing does not make this ongoing business assumption. It falls into one of two categories, depending on the way it is lent: *debt financing* and *equity financing*. In essence, debt financing may be defined as an interest-bearing loan, the cost of which has no direct relationship to the venture's sales, profits, or future growth. Equity financing, on the other hand, offers investors an ownership postion in a venture's future and the right to share on some *pro rata* basis in the profits and/or the final disposition of the net assets.

The costs and benefits of each type of financing must be weighed at the time the decision is being made since both are subject to constant fluctuations. A key variable in debt financing is the interest rate, and in 1982 the National Foundation of Independent Business (NFIB) found high interest rates to be the single most important problem in the poor performance of small business.[2] (However, as interest rates fell, poor sales became the major problem.) A key variable in equity financing is the amount of ownership, or shares of stock, that the potential investors demand. The consequences of either choice will make a difference both in the balance sheet and in the amount of control retained by the entrepreneur.

Debt financing and equity financing are not mutually exclusive, and often a combination of the two is a satisfactory solution to an entrepreneur's financing needs.

Another distinction can be drawn according to the degree of participation investors can exercise--*active investors* vs. *passive investors*. Active investors may desire at least an advisory role in your venture and almost certainly a share of the profits. Passive investors generally desire only the repayment of their money plus the agreed-upon rate of return. The following list of sources is divided according to these two categories with the realization that specific circumstances can cause shifts from "active" to "passive" status and vice versa, e.g., "Aunt Minnie" may become very "active" if she thinks the venture is "going under."

SOURCES OF CAPITAL - A LISTING

Active Investors

- You
- Partner(s)
* - Informal Investors
- Family Venture Capital Funds
* - Private Placements
* - Private Venture Capital Firms   *
- Corporate Venture Capital Divisions
- SBIC's and MESBIC's
- State and Local Development Corporations
- Corporate and University R&D Funds

Passive Investors

- Aunt Minnie
- Banks
- Commercial Finance Companies
- Insurance Companies
- Pension Funds
- Purchaser of publicly traded stock

*These particular investors are discussed further in separate notes.

[2]NFIB "The Small Business Economy - 1982," San Mateo, California: National Federation of Independent Business, 1983, p. 2.

A brief characterization of each source will suggest the broad distinctions between them and the types of ventures which might be of interest to each one.

ACTIVE INVESTORS

- You and your venture: Internal financing

How can you maximize the amount of capital your venture is capable of producing? Four sources of internally generated capital should be mentioned here. First, accounts receivable. The failure to receive payments on time can mean that the company does not have the use of those funds and often has to borrow the money instead. However, if your receivables policies are too strict, you may drive clients and suppliers into the arms of your competitors. One strategy, to be used with caution, is offering cash discounts for customers who pay on schedule. However, this option must be costed out and compared to your existing A/R situation before you attempt to implement it.

Second, optimizing trade credit arrangements. This is the opposite side of the coin, where the entrepreneur seeks out vendors who will give him the most flexible payment schedules. If your venture looks promising, a vendor may grant you extended credit in hopes of becoming a prime supplier as your venture grows. In fact, the key to successful credit management is the balancing act between the ability to collect on the earliest date without antagonizing customers with the ability to pay on the latest possible date without damaging the relationship with your creditors.

Third, improving inventory turnover. Inventory that sits in a warehouse is not earning anything; inventory which turns over rapidly is the mark of a company which uses its resources efficiently. A careful review of the ordering and stocking process may turn up savings which can be used for other purposes.

Fourth, turning fixed assets into cash. The lease, rather than buy, option or the subcontracting option may offer your venture a source of cash.

- You--as a source of external financing. How much of your own money are you able, or willing, to invest in your venture? Almost invariably, the initial investment(s) in a venture are made by the entrepreneur himself. You do so because it may be the quickest, easiest, or only way to get started, even if the start is only a systematic exploration of your venture concept. Future investors will look to your investment as an important indicator of how much personal risk you are willing to bear, and of how much faith you demonstrate in your own venture idea.

- A partner, or partners, is the next level of active investors to which you can look. If carefully chosen, partners can help to share the risks and multiply the opportunities for gain--especially if their background and skills are complementary to yours. A prospective partner need not be someone you know already; your informal advisors and business contacts often can suggest potential co-workers and co-investors.

• Informal investors have recently been the subject of intensive research, and a profile of the New England informal risk capital investor has emerged. [3] The "informal investor" is interested in investments between $10 and $25 thousand, usually with other sophisticated investors; he strongly prefers manufacturing ventures, high technology in particular; and he prefers start-ups or first-round financing. He also likes an active role in the venture as a means of overseeing his investment and identifying with the entrepreneur.

• Family partnerships often are attracted to early-stage investments in companies that could affect their lives economically and socially. Some research has shown that certain family investors, as well as some informal investors, are altruistically motivated. If they believe your venture will be of a benefit to society, they will support you even if the growth potential in dollars is not great.

• Private placements describe a larger category of investment opportunities of which venture capital is one example. A qualified private placement is exempted from the Securities and Exchange Commission's requirements on registration, prospectus contents and disclosure documents. However, the legal definition of a "qualified" private placement is not clear-cut. In general, the investor must be "sophisticated" and able to afford a high degree of risk. The entrepreneur must make available all the information the potential investor needs to make an informed judgment about the opportunity. For a fuller discussion of private placement, see the note on the subject.

• Private venture capital firms invest in the range of $250,000 to over $1 million in a venture over a period of 10 years, in return for an equity interest and an expectation of increasing their original investment 5 to 10 times. However, the types of ventures they favor and the amounts they are willing to invest are highly individualized. For example, though high tech is popular, almost 40% of the venture capitalist responding to a recent survey expressed "no preference" for type. [4] You can find venture capital companies listed in a venture capital directory, where their preferences are frequently listed by: type of industry, geographical location, average investment and range, and degree of control desired. [5] Because of the growth of interest in venture capital, the topic will be discussed later in a separate note.

• Corporate venture capital divisions often make their investment in the form of mergers and acquisitions to strengthen or enhance their parent company.

---

[3]William E. Wetzel, Jr., "Informal Risk Capital in New England," *Frontiers of Entrepreneurship Research* (FOER), 1981.

[4]Jeffry A. Timmons, "Survey of the Most Active Venture Capital Firms," *Frontiers of Entrepreneurship Research* (FOER), Babson College, Wellesley, MA, 1981.

[5]Stanley E. Pratt, ed., *Guide to Venture Capital Sources,* 7th edition, Capital Publishing Co., Wellesley, MA, 1981. See: Directories and Indexes for listing of Venture Capital Companies and Underwriters.

• SBIC's (Small Business Investment Companies), are investment partnerships between the U.S. Government and individuals or corporations or municipal or state agencies. They are authorized by the Small Business Investment Act of 1958, later amended, to "motivate and supplement the flow of *private* equity capital and long-term loan funds which small business concerns need for the sound financing of their business operations..." Depending on the interests of the private investors, SBIC's are receptive to a variety of proposals. They are also listed by size and interest in various directories.

• MESBIC's (Minority Enterprises Small Business Investment Companies) provide the same sort of aid exclusively to minority businesses.

• State and local development corporations are often more interested in providing jobs than in the nature of the venture itself, looking for steady growth rather than high-growth ventures.

• Some universities and major corporations make "seed grants" to new ventures involving new technologies or new products of interest to them. They are a valuable resource for the invention/venture.

PASSIVE INVESTORS

• Aunt Minnie, or another close family member, may only want to get her money back when you feel you can repay her--and, for many start-ups, the Aunt Minnies make it possible for a venture to get on its feet and establish a "track record" before approaching another source of funds for second-round financing.

• Life insurance companies are a leading institutional source of long-term debt financing, and invest heavily in corporate bonds and business mortgages. However, these investments are usually limited to large corporate investors with high credit ratings. Their small-business investments are usually done through long-term real estate mortgages; they rarely invest in bonds of small corporations.

Of course, insurance companies may be willing to lend to individuals who hold life insurance policies or residential property mortgages with them, since this offers them a secured lending basis.

• Pension funds have emerged as a very attractive sources of funding in the 1980's for certain sorts of ventures, usually ones whose principals have established a good track record in a growing market. Though managers of pension funds have traditionally been unwilling to put more than a small percent of their capital into venture--in part because they cannot by law make high-risk investments--the regulatory climate is changing, and the vast resources of pension funds may soon be more accessible for venture investments.

• Going public requires detailed compliance with the regulations of the Securities and Exchange Commission, and requires the services of a lawyer experienced in taking companies public.

• Commercial banks and finance companies are treated in more depth in the following section.

COMMERCIAL BANKS AND FINANCE COMPANIES

The commercial bank is the businessman's most frequently used source of temporary funds; the commercial financial company (sometimes referred to as an asset-based or secured lender) is often a source of assistance when the commercial bank is reluctant to extend credit. However, their financing roles are not neatly divided; with the concept of "full-service banking," these--and other lending--institutions are competing for business, and, in fact, may collaborate on joint financing arrangements.

Banks and other lending institutions are required by law to use prudently the funds provided by their depositors and other investors. To protect themselves against possible loss, they usually require from the entrepreneur tangible guarantees, or collateral, in the form of personal property, real estate or equipment owned by the venture, or a co-signer on the note who can guarantee repayment in the event of the entrepreneur's default.

THE COMMERCIAL BANK[6]

TYPES OF BANK LOANS

The concept of the full-service bank--one ready to perform a wide range of banking and lending services--has greatly expanded the types of loans that are available. These include factoring, accounts receivable and inventory financing (discussed under "Commercial Finance Companies"), and equipment loans (discussed under "Equipment Financing"). The more conventional types of commercial bank loans are described briefly in the following paragraphs.

Lines of Credit. When a bank extends a line of credit, it states that it is prepared to lend up to a certain amount of money as long as certain terms and conditions are met. The bank may cancel the line of credit at any time, but banks rarely cancel a line of credit without cause. The borrower may draw funds as he needs them; as a result, interest is generally charged only on the funds actually owed to the bank--although occasionally the borrower is required to pay a commitment fee on the entire line of credit to ensure that the bank will make the loan when requested.

Straight Commercial Loans. Straight commercial loans are short-term loans made for a period of from thirty to ninety days. They are self-liquidating loans used for seasonal financing and buildup on inventories.

Installment Loans. Installment loans may be made for any productive business purpose. Payments are usually made monthly, and, as the obligation is reduced, it is possible to obtain refinancing at more advantageous rates. These loans may be tailored to a business's seasonal financing requirements.

---

[6]The material in this section was excerpted from an AICPA continuing professional education course, "Financial Small Business Clients," and modified for inclusion in this practice aid. It is reprinted here with permission from the authors— the American Institute of Certified Public Accountants. The publication is *Assisting Small Business Clients in Obtaining Funds,* 1982, pp. 27-34.

Character Loans. Character loans are short-term, unsecured loans made to individuals or companies of high credit standing who need the funds for general purposes.

Collateral Loans. Collateral loans are made to individuals or companies who give security in the form of chattel mortgages, stocks and bonds, real estate mortgages, or life insurance.

Bank Credit Cards. Although not thought of as such, the bank credit card is a form of credit. The bank assumes the financing of the retailer's accounts receivable. For the retailer, a major advantage of the card is the ease with which purchases (and hence sales) can be made. A second important advantage is the elimination of concern about enforcing credit policies for such purchases and the consequent reduction in the dollar investment in accounts receivable. Of course, these benefits must be weighed against the costs involved (the discount charged the retailer).

Term Loans. A term loan is a business loan with a maturity of not less than one year and, usually, no more than ten years. Term loans are used in situations in which short-term loans and financing do not adequately meet the borrower's needs. Term loans may be used to purchase new equipment, to purchase an existing business, to establish a new business, to provide additional working capital, to retire a bond issue or outstanding preferred stock, or for other reasons.

BANK LENDING POLICIES

Bank loan officers study the borrower and his financial statements before granting loans. Bankers often require audited or reviewed statements from their borrowers as assurance of the reasonableness of the information contained in the statements. In studying the financial statements, bankers look at the key profitability and credit ratios, inventory turnover, and receivable liquidity. In addition, they are concerned with owner's capital committed to the business and the rate of withdrawal of capital in the form of dividends and salary.

The banker also studies the "C"s of credit--character, capital, capacity, collateral, circumstances, and coverage. In terms of character, he wants to be certain that the borrower will do everything in his power to conserve business assets and provide assurance that his indebtedness will be repaid. The borrower must also have a sufficient amount of his own capital invested in the business and should not expect others to carry his financial burden for an extended period of time. In terms of capacity, the borrower should have some managerial skill so that he will use the funds wisely and profitably. In addition, the borrower should have either such a high credit standing that he can borrow on an unsecured basis or tangible assets that he can pledge to reinforce a weaker credit position. The banker looks for such circumstances as seasonal character of the business, long-run business changes, level of community business activity, the competitive position of the firm, and the nature of the product. Finally, the small business should be covered against losses from such causes as the death of an owner, partner, or principal stockholder, stoppage of operations due to fire, flood, or explosion, theft and embezzlement, and liability suits.

The banker looks for trouble signs in studying the borrower and his financial statements. Here are a number of warning signs that might indicate problems:

- There are heavy inventories relative to sales.
- High dividends are paid, or there are excessive salary withdrawals.
- There are substantial loans to officers.
- A high percentage of receivables is past due.
- Debt is high relative to capital plus retained earnings.
- Investments in property, plant, and equipment are too high.
- The company has an overextended credit position.
- The company's structure is unstable.

BANK LENDING CONDITIONS

Banks usually want the principals of the private or small company to endorse the note personally, and the borrower may be required to maintain a compensating balance with the bank. If the company's position is so weak that it cannot provide assurance that the loan will be repaid, the bank may require the company to ask someone to guarantee the loan.

The rate of interest may vary with the size and term of the loan and the risk involved.

Since term loans are of longer duration, bank lending policies with respect to them are more formal. Generally, a loan agreement is negotiated between lender and borrower, stipulating the terms under which the loan is made. Along with the usual requirements of a loan agreement, it may impose specific limitations on the borrower. It may require that the borrower do one or more of the following:

- Maintain working capital at a specified minimum amount.
- Furnish audited (or reviewed) financial statements at periodic intervals.
- Provide assurance that there is no default of loan provisions.
- During the term of the loan, refrain from certain acts, such as--
  Paying dividends or redeeming capital stock.
  Entering into a merger or consolidation or selling substantially all of the firm's assets.
  Creating or assuming any obligation for money borrowed by the firm, except as provided by agreement.
  Guaranteeing, endorsing, or becoming surety for or on the obligation of others.
  Making capital expenditures in excess of a specified amount.
  Selling receivables with or without recourse.
  Making loans or advances to others in excess of a specified amount at any one time.
  Purchasing securities other than those of the U.S. government.

Term-money lenders usually ask borrowers to pledge collateral security, such as equipment or other property, in order to back up the loan. However, it is the ability of the borrower to repay the loan that is of prime importance. The lender looks at some key ratios, such as the current ratio and the net-worth-to-debt ratio, and is keenly interested in cash forecasts to measure the ability of the company to free cash.

The term-loan agreement is based on the ability of the borrower to repay the loan out of earnings, generally in installments, by maturity of the loan. As long as the borrower complies with the terms of the loan, he has assurance that no payments other than regular installments will be required before the due date of the loan. The borrower has no registration expense--just the costs of securing the loan.

A loan agreement can be revised or modified more readily than a bond indenture or a preferred stock arrangement.

In a term loan, the lender and borrower have a relationship over a relatively long period of time, and the lender can advise the small firm on financial matters.

LIMITATIONS ON COMMERCIAL BANK FINANCING

With the rapid expansion of commercial banks into fields other than short-term, unsecured loans, one might wonder why the bank should not be the source of all required funds. While banks are expanding into many fields, funds loaned out by banks are provided by depositors and, consequently, are subject to very careful management and regulation. Therefore, a bank reviewing a loan application must consider the degree of risk involved and the ability of the borrower to repay. These considerations generally exclude loans to newly started businesses, high risk or venture businesses, and poorly managed businesses (as evidenced by their performance records).

INTEREST RATES

The prime interest rate, which is the rate charged by large banks to their most credit-worthy corporate borrowers, is the base from which interest rates vary. A small business will pay more--perhaps one to two points more. Rates, of course, fluctuate, depending on many circumstances (the supply of money, the state of the economy, government policy, and so on); as these rates vary, the interest rates paid by the borrower also fluctuate.

THE COMMERCIAL FINANCE COMPANY

Commercial finance companies (sometimes referred to as asset-based or secured lenders) usually are asked to provide financial assistance when commercial banks are reluctant to extend credit.

ACCOUNTS RECEIVABLE FINANCING

Accounts receivable financing is an important service offered by commercial finance companies. Under this method of financing, the borrower assigns its accounts receivable to the lender, and they serve as the security for the cash advances made to the borrower. When the borrower collects the accounts receivable, the proceeds are given to the lender, who reduces the borrower's indebtedness; any excess is returned to the borrower.

The borrower is responsible for the collection of its accounts receivable. The accounts may be financed either on a notification basis or on a non-notification basis. When the notification basis is used, the customer is informed of the assignment and is asked to remit directly to the finance company. Under the non-notification method payment is made directly to the borrower by the customer. The non-notification method is more prevalent because it minimizes the possibility that the relationship between the borrower and its customer will be disturbed.

A businessman may enter into an agreement with a commercial finance company or other financial institution in order to accomplish a number of desired objectives. The owner of a business will be able to borrow needed working capital without diluting ownership or control of his business. The businessman may borrow without the necessity of entering into a long-term financing arrangement, which may be unnecessary. The borrower is immediately able to obtain working capital by releasing funds partially frozen in accounts receivable, and working capital turnover is accelerated by the immediate conversion of accounts receivable to cash. The borrower is able to secure a continuous source of operating cash on a flexible basis because advances are made only when cash is needed. Because it can pay its bills more quickly, the borrower may improve its credit standing, effect cash savings by being able to take advantage of cash discounts, or take advantage of profitable opportunities that present themselves.

Before an agreement is negotiated, the lender will make a thorough investigation of the borrower to determine whether to assume the risk of financing the accounts receivable. The accounts receivable themselves are also examined to see if they are acceptable for financing.

A contract is then drawn up between the borrower and the lender, since the two parties anticipate a continuing relationship rather than a single borrowing. The terms of the contract detail certain rules and procedures. The lender is to advance a certain percentage of the accounts that are assigned; the most common amount advanced is 80 percent of the assigned accounts that are not past due, as defined in the agreement. The borrower is to prepare a schedule of all assigned accounts.

If the customers are not notified of the assignment, the borrower collects payment and generally turns the remittance over to the lender intact. If the notification method is used, remittances are sent directly to the lender. When forwarding remittances to the lender, the borrower will usually prepare an accompanying remittance list.

Any accounts overpaid to the lender will be (a) applied on acount and adjusted in the next advance, (b) transmitted immediately to the borrower by check, (c) accumulated and sent to the borrower periodically, or (d) applied to reduce the account.

Interest may be charged until the average clearance date of the remittances that are turned over to the lender--for example, a four-day clearance period may be established.

Rates charged by commercial finance companies on assigned accounts receivable vary widely (as do rates charged by those commercial banks that engage in accounts receivable financing). The finance company's charge is generally computed as a specific rate per day on the amount of funds advanced, plus in some cases a service fee to compensate for the cost of maintaining the account. Graduated rates may be applied as the account grows larger.

FACTORING

In a factoring arrangement, the client actually sells his accounts receivable to the factor. If any of the receivables are uncollectible, the factor is stuck with the loss and has no recourse to the client. Since this is an outright sale of receivables, the client does not incur any debt. This differs markedly from accounts receivable financing, in which the client merely assigns his receivables to a commercial finance company as collateral for a loan; the client remains responsible for any uncollectible accounts, so that the assignment is termed "with full recourse."

Since the account debtor pays the factor directly, most factors require that the invoice bear a notification legend, such as "This account has been assigned to and is payable only to the ABC Factors."

Non-notification factoring, however, is available to businessmen who sell directly to customers in the retail trade. In this type of factoring, the factor purchases the receivables outright without recourse but does not assume the collection function without specific request. The businessman makes collections himself, and the customer is not notified of the factoring arrangements. The fee for non-notification factoring may be less than that charged for notification factoring.

Factoring costs consist of two elements: (1) an interest charge based on funds advanced prior to the maturity date of the invoices and (2) a commission designed to cover the credit and collection services and protection against credit losses.

INVENTORY LOANS

When a business has exhausted its ability to borrow on receivables, commercial finance companies may advance funds on inventory under appropriate conditions at a lesser percentage of value than on receivables. Three methods exist for financing inventory.

The first method, the floating lien, was made possible under the Uniform Commercial Code (UCC); it helped solve the problem of creating a security interest for the lender on a shifting stock of inventory in a debtor's possession. In addition, the UCC made possible the creation of a security interest on property that is not even in existence at the time but that may come into existence or be acquired subsequently by the person creating the lien. Under this method, an inventory security agreement is negotiated by the commercial finance company (or commercial bank) and the borrower, spelling out in detail the obligation of both parties.

Warehouse receipts are commonly used to finance inventory. The borrower delivers goods to a warehouse, which in turn issues a warehouse receipt to the lender. The goods may be placed in either a public warehouse or a field warehouse. A public warehouse is in the business of storing goods for the general public; a field warehouse is one set up at the borrower's place of business. A field warehouse is leased and maintained by a public warehouse, and no one has access to the property placed in it except the authorized employees of the public warehouse.

Finally, trust receipts are evidence that certain goods or property to which the lender has acquired title have been released to the borrower in the trust. Title is retained by the lender until sold and accounted for by the borrower. Trust receipts are used in floor planning, which is a form of financing employed frequently by automobile and appliance dealers. The lender advances a percentage of the invoice price of the shipment. As the goods are sold, the borrower must immediately reduce the portion of the loan applicable to the goods sold.

SUMMARY

At one time accounts recievable financing, factoring of receivables, and inventory financing had a stigma attached to them; it was felt that the business resorting to financing of this kind was in trouble and perhaps on the verge of bankruptcy. While some businesses may feel a perfectly legitimate reluctance to engage in receivables financing or factoring, this type of financing is ideal for many concerns. So important is the potential for growth in this industry that larger commercial banks, in certain parts of the country, are rapidly moving into it, through the acquisition or creation of commercial finance divisions.

EQUIPMENT FINANCING

Equipment financing can be accomplished through sources other than commercial finance companies and can take several forms. It can involve (1) financing of equipment presently owned by the company, (2) financing of the purchase of new equipment, (3) sale-leaseback financing, or (4) lease financing. Each form of equipment financing may be appropriate at different times and under different conditions.

FINANCING OF PRESENTLY OWNED EQUIPMENT

If a company has equipment that is fully paid for and in good condition, it can often obtain funds by pledging the equipment as collateral for a loan. This is usually accomplished under Article 9 of the UCC through the use of a written security agreement on the equipment.

FINANCING OF THE PURCHASE OF NEW EQUIPMENT

Manufacturers of new equipment recognize that it is frequently necessary to provide financing arrangements as part of a sales package. Some manufacturers discount the purchasers' notes at their banks. Other manufacturers act as agents for lending institutions offering installment plans as part of the terms of sale. Under installment financing, title is usually retained by the manufacturer until all payments are made. If the purchaser arranges direct installment financing with a financing institution, a lien on equipment is normally taken by the institution.

SALE-LEASEBACK

The sale-leaseback method of financing has become increasingly popular. A company concurrently sells its property to an insurance company or other investor and leases it back to be assured of continued use or occupancy. The lessee obtains needed working capital, and the lessor obtains a lease commitment that assures him of recovering his purchase price plus interest for use of his money over the life of the lease.

LEASE FINANCING

The leasing of equipment has become an increasingly important method of financing. Without making a substantial cash payment or incurring a large obligation, a company can acquire the use of equipment by merely committing itself to make a specified number of payments. As a result, the number of leasing companies has grown rapidly in recent years, and banks and insurance companies have entered this field.

Any type of equipment can be leased. The lease is usually written on the total customer selling price (including transportation charges and taxes) and is drawn for a period of time. The total amount to be paid is computed by adding finance charges to the total customer selling price.

ON ACQUISITIONS AND LEVERAGED BUYOUTS
SOME CONSIDERATIONS FOR ENTREPRENEURS

A leveraged buyout is a type of acquisition currently in vogue. It is "in vogue" mainly because many of today's corporations carry assets purchased at pre-inflation prices, which have been substantially reduced through depreciation. Their book value is carried at far below replacement cost. Also, the high interest rates of the early 1980's have kept the market value of corporate securities depressed and, as a result, corporate securities often are priced below their deflated book values. These conditions work in favor of the high leveraged buyout by providing ample collateral for an asset-based loan. Also, since inflation tends to increase the backing for the loan, a buyer may reap the benefits of an increased dollar value of the purchased properties vis-a-vis the original loans.

ACQUISITIONS: A CAREER PERSPECTIVE

For several different reasons, entrepreneurs may find that acquisitions, and leveraged buyouts in particular, are advantageous ways to pursue their entrepreneurial careers.

1. *At Career Startup.* Buying a company, whether or not using a leveraged buyout, can provide a number of benefits compared to starting a venture from scratch--it may mean less risk, since the operation has already been started and proven, and/or provides more credibility to customers, suppliers and creditors. Risk can be minimized even further if the prospective entrepreneur(s) are currently members of the company's management team. Leveraging the buyout or acquisition simply means that the entrepreneur can obtain these advantages with minimal capital investment.

2. *As an Effective Way to Continue Your Career.* At some point, one or more of your ventures may need a new direction or new resource. These may include new markets, new management, new technology, new financial resources or new product lines to supplement or complement existing venture activities. Yet, an entrepreneur may be unable to pay for, or borrow, the price of these necessities for *internal* expansion. An acquisition may be the most economical way to generate the needed expansion or diversification, given time constraints.

The "leveraged" notion regarding an acquisition means that entrepreneurs can invest little or none of their own money and a lot of someone else's in order to acquire the assets and/or stock of a company. Simply stated, it works this way: one or more entrepreneurs use the assets of the company they wish to buy as collateral for loans to cover the down payment and for whatever capital they may need for initial operations.

3. *Ending a Venture and/or a Career.* An entrepreneur who wishes to sell one or more ventures, but for tax and other reasons does not wish to realize a lump capital gain--or who wishes to remain with the venture in some capacity--can use a leveraged buyout as a negotiating point to obtain other concessions from a buyer who might not otherwise be able to acquire the company.

LEVERAGED BUYOUTS

Like any acquisition, a successful leveraged buyout is one in which everyone--buyer and seller--should come away winners. However, each situation is unique and each deal must be tailor-made and skillfully negotiated. For this reason, no single recipe for strategic and tactical success exists for all situations. However, entrepreneurs should be aware of certain considerations regarding acquisitions in general and leveraged buyouts in particular.

A veteran in the field of raising and lending outside equity provides some observations on successful leveraged buyouts in which he has participated. They are particularly useful guidelines for entrepreneurs because they go beyond the necessary and important quantitative and qualitative analysis of the company and deal, from his experience, with how to make the crucial "gut decision" to lend funds for an acquisition.

> We have found that the safest leveraged buyout is one that contemplates no management changes whatsoever. A good example of this is a corporate divestiture to the management group that has (and has had for some time) the operating responsibility for the business being divested. Not only is there a zero learning curve, but also the management will have full knowledge of potential problems that are not readily apparent to outsiders seeking to purchase the business.
>
> If an attractive opportunity presents itself and it does not include existing management, the risk is enhanced...The new management must take control and overcome a learning process...We feel more comfortable if the new management has a successful track record in precisely the same business.
>
> When an outside equity investor ventures beyond these parameters, the risk factor will increase dramatically...We do much soul searching.[1]

---

[1]Gregory P. Barber, "The Key to Successful Leveraged Buyouts," in *Guide to Venture Capital Sources,* ed. Stanley Pratt, 1981, p. 90.

EXAMPLES OF DIFFERENT TYPES OF LEVERAGED BUYOUTS

1. At Startup: Manager Turns Entrepreneur

The manager of a customer-print division in an aerospace corporation was told by his CEO that his operation no longer "fit" the corporate strategy, though it was contributing substantially to the bottom line. In the next breath, the CEO suggested that the manager buy the division himself. Each man, with the help of a lawyer, came to terms quickly:

> • The "hard" assets were to be purchased at book value.

> • The parent firm would loan the manager-now-entrepreneur the money secured by the assets and repayable over five years.

> • The new owner would purchase the existing inventory for cash, payable within 90 days.

> • The parent company would supply headquarters service (accounting, purchasing, personnel records) for 90 days, at cost, to ease the transition.[2]

2. Entrepreneur Needs Cash Now

The star of this story is a vice president for mergers and acquisitions in a large accounting firm, who directed his entrepreneurial urge toward providing himself with an outside source of income which would not take too much time away from his job. He heard that a local heat-treating company was for sale, a highly technical process. Though the fellow knew nothing of the technology, he saw no obstacle there, commenting that "my job was to get someone in there who did." Using sound management techniques, he found that he was able to increase the company's earnings by 30% within the first year, and spend a maximum of 3 hours a day to run the company. Most interesting is the way he structured the deal, requiring the minimum investment on his part.

> "In the first acquisition, the heat-treating company, I formed a new corporation, which then bought the stock of the heat-treating company from the owner. I then argued that if the owner claimed his company was worth $475,000, which was the purchase price, and I was going to give him $60,000 down, then the amount he would want security on would be $415,000. To provide that security I offered to pledge the stock of the company he said was worth $475,000,

---

[2]Daryl Mitton, "The Anatomy of a High Leverage Buyout: Roadmap for Transition from Manager to Entrepreneur," *Frontiers of Entrepreneurship Research,* Babson College, 1982.

plus the stock of the new corporation that bought the new stock, plus my personal guarantee on the note, which had significance to him because he had some faith in my personal integrity even though my personal assets to back up the guarantee were small. This left the assets of the company I was buying--the plant, land, equipment, inventory, and receivables--free of encumbrance, except for about $10,000 of accounts payable, so I could borrow against them at the bank. It turned out that these were worth about $800,000. There was cash of about $30,000. I persuaded the old owner to accept half the down payment at closing and the other half a couple months later in the next fiscal year to spread out his taxes. Then I went to the bank and told them I wanted to borrow $30,000, which I would pay back the next day. I gave the $30,000 to the old owner and closed the deal. The next day I filled out the signature cards for the company account to pay off the loan. Then to get working capital as needed and later to meet the other half of the down payment, I simply borrowed against the assets of the company." This process began in June 1974. The deal closed with the first down payment five months later, in October, and the second half of the down payment was made in January 1975.[3]

3. During Operations: An Entrepreneur Needs Special Capabilities

In growth situations, entrepreneurs may not have the time to build in-house capabilities. For this reason, they choose to search for appropriate acquisitions.

Acquisition of a selected number of high-tech companies in California's Silicon Valley was the subject of a recent study. The study surveyed over 250 such firms, all started in the 1960s and found that over 32 percent of them had been merged or acquired by 1980, a higher percentage than those which had survived independently.[4] When analyzed by type of product, the highest percentage of merged/acquired companies looked like this:

Semiconductor Components and Materials	50%
Semiconductor Devices	55%
Computers, Computer Peripherals, Software, Services	57%

————

[3]Karl H. Vesper, *New Venture Strategies,* Prentice Hall, 1980, Chapters 9 and 10: "Acquisition Finding;" and "Acquisition Dealing."

[4]Albert Bruno and Arnold Cooper, "Patterns of Acquisition in Silicon Valley," *Frontiers of Entrepreneurship Research,* Babson College, 1981.

For the entrepreneur, what was the conclusion? The authors believe that "Even relatively unsuccessful firms are attractive acquisition candidates because their expertise is applicable in relatively growing markets." Thus, if you are operating a venture in need of an infusion of special skills, an acquisition may be the solution. Furthermore, if you are short of cash, a leveraged buyout may still provide you with a way to acquire the needed assets.

The authors of the study also noted that the peak acquisition period for the acquired firms was 4 to 7 years after founding--the period during which the often brilliant technical founder found he was a mediocre general manager. If the acquiring entrepreneur is long on managerial expertise and short on technical skills, the potential synergy is strong, and will provide both parties with considerable leverage to attract outside sources of funding—banks, venture capitalists, even pension funds and endowments.

4. At Ending: Entrepreneurs Who Wish to Harvest Their Ventures

The founding family of House of Ronnie, a publicly-held New York-based manufacturer of women's and children's clothing, decided that they desired liquidity over ownership. Carl Marks and Company, a New York securities firm, engineered and financed a buyout in the following way as explained by vice president John Jordan:

> House of Ronnie...had 1980 sales of $62.6 million and profits of $4 million...The $35 million management buyout occurred for two reasons...Apparel stocks traditionally sell at very low multiples, so being a public company just wasn't worth it for them. Also the founding family wanted to cash out. Marks is the sole investor in addition to the management of the House of Ronnie, which sold at 8 times earnings. Five managers put in an undisclosed amount of cash to receive 20% of the company, a percentage that will rise based on their performance.[5]

Though overall management strategy will change very little, Jordan believes that management's new equity will soon result in larger profits. In the meantime, the former owners are busy with new investments.

SPECIAL SOURCES OF FUNDING

As in any situation which requires the entrepreneur to raise capital for expansion or diversification, the entrepreneur must explore a variety of financial sources. In the case of a leveraged buyout, the list is much the same: wealthy backers, banks, investment management companies, venture capitalists, pension funds, and endowments. However, two other sources must be added to the list--the company's employees and the company's former owners.

---

[5]Kevin Farrell, "Yesterday's Managers, Today's Entrepreneurs," in *Venture*. March 1982, p. 50, ff.

A key issue is whether these or other funding sources will desire an equity position-- e.g., as venture capitalists and certain investment banking firms. For instance, Citicorp Venture Capital, Ltd., was started explicitly to lend buyout money in return for equity. Other sources, primarily banks and some privately-held lending operations, refuse to take an equity position. Allen Kerr, EVP of Walter Heller & Company, recently commented, "We feel people in the company (Heller) might be over-willing to lend money to a business in which we have equity."[6] Entrepreneurs must weigh both equity and non-equity financing options on a case-by-case basis.

ACQUISITIONS: STRUCTURING THE DEAL

The act of buying or selling a business entails much more than two parties agreeing on a mutually acceptable price. For instance, how to structure the transaction is often crucial to the final arrangement. The unsuspecting buyer or seller can easily be taken advantage of by a shrewd dealmaker who knows how to structure the final transaction to his or her advantage. In short, the structure of a deal itself has a positive or negative effect on that real price paid for the business.

A multitude of techniques exist for acquiring or selling small or privately held concerns. Various structuring techniques are available, each possessing distinct advantages to the buyer and seller under varying conditions. What structure is ultimately selected will determine often who will benefit the most in these smaller acquisitions. By "structure," we mean the particular configuration of *who* buys *what* and *how* and *when* the purchase is made. "Who" may mean a single individual, a partnership, a corporation or a Sub S corporation on either the buying and selling sides. "What" can mean selected assets, all assets, selected assets and liabilities, or the stock of the legal entity known as XYZ company. "How" can mean purchase using all cash, some combination of cash and notes, all notes, and/or the use of other items of value (property exchanges, employment contracts, etc.). "When" can mean payment of some or all of the funds up front -- before the buyer takes control of the acquired property; or payment may be delayed so it occurs within the year of takeover or is spread over many years (an installment purchase). Obviously the number of possible ways to structure a deal is quite large. Equally large is the number of tangible and intangible factors that influence the final structure of a deal.

---

[6]Dave Lindorff, "Buying a Piece of the Action," in *Venture*, April 1981, p. 34, ff.

VENTURE CAPITAL AND THE ENTREPRENEUR

INTRODUCTION TO THE VENTURE CAPITAL INDUSTRY

Venture capitalists can be defined as "participating investors seeking to add value through ongoing longer-term involvement with continuing business development." This definition highlights three important characteristics of venture capitalists:

- *participating investors.* Venture capitalists require equity participation in the company, and generally expect to take an active advisory role in its day-to-day affairs.

- *ongoing longer-term involvement.* Venture capitalists are not interested in short-term gains but rather in long-term growth, usually in a time frame of 5-10 years.

- *seeking to add value.* Venture capitalists are interested almost exclusively in those ventures where high growth possibilities exist. Since the money at stake is "risk" capital, investors are looking for commensurately high returns. They expect their investments to increase 5 to 10 times over 5 to 10 years. Such returns can be realized only if there is considerable growth potential in the products/services which the venture intends to commercialize.

The venture capital industry is the dynamic driving force in the capital market today because of its focus on promoting new business development. This support may start with the emergence of a new business concept, but it encompasses expansion financing and management/leveraged buyouts as well; in short, it covers the life of the venture from start-up to cash-out: i.e., when the venture is ready to go public or to sell out to other private investors.

The venture capital industry is composed of small groups of individuals with a great deal of prior experience in the investment business. They leave R&D financing to others, and concentrate on identifying opportunities for business growth. They use "other people's money" drawn from investors who usually put their funds into 10-year pools managed by venture capitalists. The venture capitalists then explore a great number of opportunities and settle on a handful of the most promising ones each year, usually never more than they can comfortably monitor and advise. When the pool is cashed out, the venture capitalists typically receive 20% while the original investors receive 80% of the capital gains.

The profits may seem high, but so are the risks. The typical venture capital portfolio consists of "a third, a third, and a third,..." one-third of the investments fail to pay off, one-third break even, and one-third pay off sufficiently to cover the others and still return a handsome profit to the investors. Since the risks are high and the wait is long, experienced fund managers claim that the two essential ingredients for success are bravery and patience.

Most experts believe that there is no shortage of capital formation in this country, but rather a shortage of capital distribution. As catalysts, venture capitalists are attempting both to tap sources of capital, such as pension funds, and to use these funds to back promising entrepreneurial teams working in expanding market niches. In return for their active participation in a venture, they require an equity position, which is why many entrepreneurs refer to them as "vulture capitalists." On the other hand, if the venture is given the time and the financial resources to grow, venture capitalists know there will be more than enough to go around.

HISTORY OF VENTURE CAPITAL

A brief history of venture capital may help to put this unique source of funding into perspective. A widely recognized authority on the topic offers the following chronology:[1]

- Before 1945: *Strictly "informal"*--wealthy individuals and family foundations.

---

[1]Stanley E. Pratt, "The United States Venture Capital Investment Marketplace," a speech delivered at the Symposium on Financing More Innovation at Less Risk, Luxembourg, December 1981. Pratt is editor of *Venture Capital Journal,* the industry's monthly trade publication. This note relies heavily on his collected information.

- 1946-58: *The Pioneering Era,* American Research & Development. General Georges Doriot attracts a small amount of individual and institutional capital to ARD, a professionally managed vehicle for making active investments in selected emerging businesses. The most outstanding choice was Digital Equipment Corporation.

- 1958-68: *Small Business Investment Corporations (SBIC's).* Congress authorizes this new investment vehicle to marry private capital with government funds, to be invested by private managers in growing businesses needing capital infusion. The SBIC Act was the beginning of the "industry." However, professional managers of SBIC's were more interested in short-term performance and frequently lacked the expertise to help a business to grow beyond the first several years. Consequently, the failure rate somewhat discredited SBIC's as responsible investment vehicles for passive institutional investment.

- 1968: *Emergence of small private firms and venture divisions of larger companies.* Boom-boom-economics see undisciplined investment in high-flying companies, frequently offering investors excellent returns but rarely helping businesses to grow in a controlled manner.

- 1974-75: The venture capital market dries up during the depression: bad investments are flushed away, good ones were allowed to develop quietly.

- 1978-?: *The Modern Era.* This period is characterized by careful investment and disciplined growth plus an influx of new funds spurred by the capital gains tax reduction and the redefinition of "prudent investment" with reference to ERISA monies (pension funds) by the Department of Labor. In 1983, at this writing, new money is flooding into venture capital pools because of these factors.

STATISTICS ON THE VENTURE CAPITAL INDUSTRY

- Size by number and type of firm

The following table, current in 1980 and updated to 1983 (see asterisk and footnote), breaks down this information in several useful ways.

Overview of Venture Capital Sources[2]

	Private Venture Capital Firms	Small Business Investment Companies (SBIC s)	Corporate/Industrial Venture Capitalists
Estimated Number — 1980*	100-250	305+	Perhaps 60 in business; 20-30 active (Exxon, G.E., Monsanto, 3M, Inco, etc.)
Principal objectives and motives	Capital gains 25%-40% compounded after tax per year; 5-10 times original investment in 5-10 years	Capital gains same range as private	Windows on technology; tap new talent; acquire new markets; spawn new suppliers; diversification; public relations; use of surplus cash; philanthropy; capital gains
Typical size	$300,000 to $4 million Survey average: $813,000		$10-$15 million not unusual
Stage of ventures sought	All stages 25-35% start-ups more common		Later stages; rarely start-ups; seeking $100-$200+ million
Outside approval	Unusual, perhaps 10-12% of firms		Very common, 75% of decisions; review boards and directors

------

[2]This table is from an article by Jeffry A. Timmons, "Venture Capital Investors in the United States," *Frontiers of Entrepreneurship Research*, Babson College, 1981, p. 201. It also appears in:

David E. Gumpert and Jeffry A. Timmons, *Insider's Guide to Small Business Resources*, Chapter 6, Doubleday: New York, 1982.

*According to Stanley Pratt, (*Guide to Venture Capital Sources*, 1983, pp 19-20) 1983 estimates are:

Private venture capital firms: approximately 150, 60 of which were formed in the last five years.

SBIC's: approximately 356 licensed by the federal government, 200 oriented primarily toward venture capital investments. The remainder function primarily as lending institutions.

Corporate/industrial: This group has grown greatly since 1977, with more than a 75% increase in total dollars committed.

• Dollars in, dollars out

In early 1983, the industry counted some $7.5 billion in total capital committed to various venture funds by investors, over three times the resource committed five years earlier. This infusion is attributable mainly to the reduction in tax rates for capital gains. The following graph shows the increase in *new* private capital being committed *annually* to the total investment pool.[3]

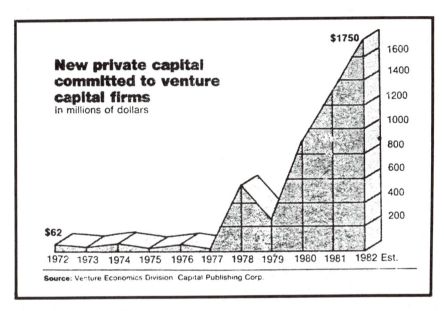

New private capital committed to venture capital firms
in millions of dollars

$1750

1600
1400
1200
1000
800
600
400
200

$62

1972 1973 1974 1975 1976 1977 1978 1979 1980 1981 1982 Est.

Source: Venture Economics Division Capital Publishing Corp.

In 1980, venture capitalists disbursed approximately $1 billion; in 1981, this figure rose to $1.4 billion. Disbursements in 1982 are projected at the 1981 level.[4]

• Geographical distribution

There is a difference between the location of venture capital firms and the locations to which they disburse capital. Venture capital firms are concentrated in New York City, the San Francisco area, Boston, and Chicago, in that order. Yet California attracted 36% of venture disbursements in 1981, while Massachusetts attracted only 15% and New York a modest 6%. The following tables, arranged by both state and region, illustrate these trends.

---

[3]Source: Venture Capital Journal. Reported in *Guide to Venture Capital,* 7th ed., Capital Publishing Co., 1983, p. 19. Graph appeared in the *Boston Globe,* Tuesday, May 3, 1983, p. 39.

[4]*Guide to Venture Capital Sources,* 7th ed., *op. cit.,* p. 9.

The Distribution of Venture Capital Resources
(by Location of Venture Capital firm) as of June 30, 1982

Capital Resources by Leading States[5]
Capital ($ millions)

	1982	% of Total
New York	$1,835	27%
California	1,509	22
Massachusetts	892	13
Illinois	808	12
Connecticut	276	4
Texas	259	4
Ohio	166	2
Minnesota	120	2

Capital Resources by Regions
Capital ($ millions)

	1982	% of Total
Northeast:		
CT, MA, ME, NJ, PA, RI, VT, NY	$3,324	50%
Southeast:		
AL, DC, FL, GA, KY, MD, MS, NC, SC, VA	237	4
Midwest:		
IL, IN, IA, MI, MN, MO, OH, WI	1,179	17
Southwest:		
AZ, CO, LA, NM, NV, OK, TX	397	6
West Coast:		
CA, OR, WA	1,574	23
Total	$6,711	100%

---

[5]*Guide to Venture Capital Sources*, op. cit., p. 21.

The Disbursement Activity of Venture Firms by Total
Number of Financings (where the money went)[6]

	Percent of Total Financings	
	1981	**1970-1979**
California	36%	27%
Massachusetts	15	14
New York	6	8
Texas	5	8
Total	62%	57%
Northeast:		
MA, NH, RI, CT, NY, NJ, PA	31%	33%
Southeast:		
MD, DC, VA, NC, GA, TN, AL, FL	6	10
Midwest:		
MN, WI, MI, OH, IL, IN, MO	10	12
Southwest:		
OK, TX, LA, UT, CO, AZ, NM	12	12
West Coast: WA, OR, CA	39	30
Total	98%	97%

- Identifying the "hot" industries[7]

Five industry sectors have attracted the bulk of venture capital funds because of their exciting growth potential. These are:

- Data communications
- Computer software and peripherals
- Health care delivery and products including medical instrumentation
- The office of the future
- Robotics, and the factory of the future

---

[6]Ibid., p. 22.

[7]"Industries Attractive to Venture Capitalists," E. Roe Stamps IV, in *Guide to Venture Capital Sources, op. cit.*, pp. 65-6.

The following chart from *Venture Capital Journal* shows what specific industries venture capitalists invested in in 1981.

1981 Disbursements by Industry

	Percent of Total Number of Investment	
	1981	**1980**
Communications	11.4%	11.5%
Computer Related	30.0	27.4
Other Electronics Related	14.5	9.6
Genetic Engineering	6.2	4.2
Medical/Health Related	7.0	10.5
Energy	4.9	8.3
Consumer Related	4.9	7.5
Industrial Automation	6.2	4.5
Industrial Products	4.4	3.6
Other	10.5	12.9
Total	100.0%	100.0%

	Percent of Dollar Amount	
	1981	**1980**
Communications	11.2%	10.9%
Computer Related	34.3	25.7
Other Electronics Related	13.1	9.6
Genetic Engineering	11.2	7.6
Medical/Health Related	5.8	9.3
Energy	5.8	19.9
Consumer Related	1.9	3.7
Industrial Automation	5.3	2.7
Industrial Products	3.4	2.0
Other	8.0	8.6
Total	100.0%	100.0%

As the tables show, the concentration of capital in the top four industries increased between 1980 and 1981, the last year on which complete statistics are available. In addition, venture capitalists are backing "niche" business in changing industries, such as FM radio and cable TV. Finally, there is great interest in non-technological but "technology-related" companies, those which offer a product or service which will increase the productivity or marketability of a new technological product.

Another kind of a deal which is increasingly favored by venture capitalists is the management leveraged buyout (see note on leveraged buyouts.). Leveraged buyouts are advantageous to the entrepreneur without much capital of his own, as well as to the venture capitalist--who can purchase equity in a tangible and potentially profitable ongoing enterprise.

- Industry status in 1983

"1983 is going to be the year of the lemons," commented Stan Pratt, publisher of *Venture Capital Journal,* in a recent article.[8] Veteran venture capitalists know from experience that during the 5-10 year growth cycle of their portfolio companies, lemons ripen first--and there are several reasons why 1983 appears to be a difficult year.

> - The venture capital industry has grown dramatically since 1980, bringing to it a number of inexperienced venture capitalists whose choice of ventures and ability to sustain them is of questionable value.
>
> - The percentage of early-stage deals being funded increased tenfold between 1975 and 1981; Pratt estimated 300-400 in 1981 alone. Early-stage deals are traditionally risky.
>
> - The increased competition for deals pushed the price of investment unreasonably high, in some instances.
>
> - A number of start-ups funded in 1980-2 required technological breakthroughs which failed to materialize.
>
> - The slump in the economy added to the difficulty of bringing new ventures onstream profitably and with relative speed.

But, the veterans are not alarmed. Their portfolios always contain approximately 30% non-profitable ventures, and they are prepared to cut their losses where necessary and devote more money and time to the potentially profitable ones. However, some marginal venture capital firms and their marginal ventures may not survive the shakeout.

"After a four-year spending spree, caution is clearly setting in again," remarked one observer. "The number of flops is beginning to show--at least, in proportion to the increased activity--although the appetite for quality start-ups will continue."[9] In fact, the demand for quality investments is so high that fortunate entrepreneurs find they are able to strike harder bargains and retain more equity than in the past. The only danger to the industry, as another observer sees it, is that venture capitalists will treat the high level of turkeys as abnormal--and try to hide it, or that they will throw good money after bad.

---

[8]"The Rising Tide of Venture Capital Failures," Jon Levine, *Venture,* April 1983, pp. 58-64.

[9]*Ibid.,* Jon Levine.

HOW TO APPROACH VENTURE CAPITALISTS

Advice on how to get your foot in the door comes from two excellent sources: from venture capitalists themselves, and from a survey of venture capital firms completed in 1980.

From the Venture Capitalists. First, some don'ts, which most appear to believe:

- Don't bring the wrong proposal to the wrong firm. Venture capitalists tend to be specialists, and if your plan falls outside of their stated area of expertise or their average amount of investment, they may turn you down regardless of the merits of your plan.

- Don't shop around too much. If you have shown your plan to a number of potential investors and it has been rejected, everyone probably knows it; the lending community is small and secrets are few. If asked, don't brush the question aside; explain why you believe your plan was rejected and by whom--your explanation may convince these investors that they can provide the "fit" that the prior investor couldn't. However, judicious shopping is often advisable--not for the purposes of finding the best price, but rather to locate the best quality of support for your venture.

- Don't be inflexible about the amount of control and profit you are willing to share. If a potential investor believes you are too stubborn to form a working partnership he may not bother to continue negotiations.

- Don't bring outside "experts." Bring yourself and the key members of your team; they are as important to the investors as your plan.

Now some do's--not guaranteed to succeed, they warn, but worth consideration. If:

- your management team has a good track record,

- you have been introduced to the firm by a person whose judgement the partners respect, a lawyer or banker, for instance,

- your team has put up much of its own money as part of the financing and is not drawing unreasonably large salaries,

- your chemistry clicks with theirs, and their gut says yes,

then, you are on the way to finding a financial partner.

Further, if:

- you can reasonably predict a growth rate of 30-50% per year,

- the size of the market for the product/service you will be offering is potentially $100 million or more in annual sales in 3 to 5 years,

- your product/service will occupy a defensible market niche,

then, your prospects for finding venture capital are good.[10]

A final comment on the industry: venture capitalists are trying to structure profitable deals and, right or wrong, they generally believe that profitable deals are much more likely to be made with "A" men with "B" ideas than vice versa. If a venture firm sees you and your team as "A" material, they may approach you with a venture opportunity or ask you to identify one and present it to them. Experienced venture capitalists have a nose for entrepreneurial talent, and skillful entrepreneurs should not be surprised if they find they have sold themselves but not their venture to their potential investors.

From a Survey. "Venture Capital Investors in the U.S.: A Survey of the Most Active Investors," 1980,[11] was "an exploratory search...aimed at mapping the activities and practices of the most active firms" in very specific areas. Two of the areas may be of special interest to first-round entrepreneurs.

One set of responses tabulates the ways in which venture capitalists were approached by entrepreneurs on proposals they ultimately accepted:

Best Method to Approach Investor	Number	Percentage
• Letter, mail-in business	12	24%
• Phone-in person	10	20%
• Referral	9	17%
• Doesn't matter	20	39%
	51	100%

---

[10]Stamps, F. Roe IV, "Industries Attractive to Venture Capitalists," in *Guide to Venture Capital Sources,* 7th edition, Capital Publishing Corporation 1983, p. 67.

[11]Jeffry A. Timmons, "Survey of the Most Active Venture Capital Firms," *Frontiers of Entrepreneurship Research* (FOER), Babson College, Wellesley, Ma 1981.

Another set of responses maps answers to the question: "What are the odds of obtaining U.S. Venture Capital?" The answers from 48 respondents follow:

What are the Odds of Obtaining U.S. Venture Capital?"[12]

	High	Middle	Low	Avg.
Number of proposals received per month	50+	26-50	1-25	43
Percent of respondents	19%	40%	42%	

Percentage of business plans funded:	Venture Capital Companies	
	Number	Percentage
less than 1%	16	33%
1% to 5%	29	61%
6% to 10%	2	4%
more than 10%	1	2%
	48	100%

From the entrepreneur's perspective the odds of raising venture capital are still slim. Investors in the survey reported receiving an average of 43 proposals a month, and many receive 50 or more. One-third said they fund 1% or less of these proposals, and 94% said they fund 5% or less of the proposals they review.

WHAT VENTURE CAPITALISTS EXPECT

Venture capitalists are not a homogeneous group -- different firms choose different ventures and for different reasons -- but all of them are looking for two things:

- the Management you have chosen, and

- the Marketplace you have identified.

A number of investors mention a third factor:

- the reputation of your lawyer and your accountant.

They will also want to know the current growth level of your venture. The four categories commonly used are:

0: No ongoing business
1: Seed money, a venture with a prototype or a pilot program, no track record yet.

---

[12]Jeffry A. Timmons, "Survey of the Most Active Venture Capital Firms," *Frontiers of Entrepreneurship Research* (FOER), Babson College, Wellesley, Ma 1981.

2: Growth money, a venture that has started and is looking
   for first round capital infusion.

3: Maturity money, a venture with greater capital needs to
   get it over the hump on the way to its "cash out" point
   where it can go public.

If you have attracted the interest of a venture capital firm, you and your key team members will be invited to a first meeting. To give you an idea of the intensive screening which takes place initially, a set of internal guidelines used by one venture capital firm is provided in Appendix I. This is their "short form."

This form of interrogation should be taken for what it is--an objective framework for analyzing a potential investment. It does not purport to objectify the "feel" of the investors about the entrepreneurs, and this intangible "feel" accounts for a good deal of what happens at the first, and subsequent meetings. If exploration proceeds, there will be meetings at the place of business, so the investors can watch the venture in operation, or, if it is a start-up, so the investors can observe the interaction between the team members and the sense of leadership provided by the entrepreneur.

The foregoing is an example of "major league" venture capitalism. There are other leagues and other types of players. The importance of this type of information to the entrepreneur is to make him aware of the range of possibilities and what to expect, to help him identify the most appropriate source of funds for his particular venture at a particular time.

WHAT IF A VENTURE CAPITALIST TURNS YOU DOWN?

A recent study[13] attempted to track ventures rejected by venture capitalists in order to find if they had been successful in raising capital from other sources after being denied venture capital money, and to obtain more information on whether denial or postponement of venture capital money constituted a serious hindrance to the innovation process. Their data base, of 95 ventures mostly high-tech, provided information which should give heart to a "denied entrepreneur." Here are a few of the findings:

- Of the sample denied funding on one try (as reported by the denying venture capitalist) beginning in 1979, almost 70% were still in business in 1983.

---

[13]"The One That Got Away: A Study of Ventures Rejected by Venture Capitalists," Albert V. Bruno and Tyzoon T. Tyebjee, *Frontiers of Entrepreneurship Research,* Babson College, 1983.

• Subsequent to a denial, a number of firms were able to raise outside capital from venture capitalists and other sources. The mean age of the sample of firms were 4.0 years; on the average the firms made 2.6 attempts to raise capital and were successful 1.5 times on average.

• However, the initial setback did result in delaying venture development in proportion to the amount of money sought, and often ventures had to settle for less money than hoped.

• Nonetheless, the down-scaling of expectations of denied entrepreneurs was not seen as a serious threat to the innovative process.

Although some denied entrepreneurs have harsh words for "vulture capitalists," it is our experience that an initial denial may help to tighten up plans for a promising venture--and, by the same token, may help to abort an unpromising one before it is too late.

APPENDIX I

ANALYTICAL FRAMEWORK[14]

The following outline is an analytical framework that we try to work through in performing due diligence on a potential investment. The overall objective of the *industry analysis* and, subsequently, the *strategic analysis* of a particular firm with that industry, is to gain a more thorough understanding of the certainty of future cash flows deriving from that firm's business activities.

From the analysis, we can place ourselves in a position to judge whether a particular firm's strategic objectives make sense. We can then negotiate the terms of our investment and project a rate of return on our investment according to the certainty we attach to the future cash flows of the company.

A. Industry Analysis

1. **Competitive posture**

   a) Number of firms, size and concentration
   b) Characteristics
      i) Degree of integration; balance; diversification; captive; geographic location; etc.
   c) Market share distribution; changes occurring in
   d) Market growth rate
   e) Methods of competition
      i) Pricing; delivery; quality; flexibility; service; etc.

2. **Cost structure** (typical firm)

   a) Investment requirement — size, frequency, and type
   b) Fixed cost component
   c) Operating cost as % of total cost
      i) Material; labor; overhead; depreciation; margin

3. **Financial Structure** (typical firm)

   a) Size of sales and assets
   b) Margin analysis ⎫
   c) Asset turnover ⎬ ROE components
   d) Leverage ⎭

4. **Supplier/Customer Relationships**

   a) Number and size
   b) Terms of trade
   c) Changes in concentration
   d) Certainty of stability in both

---

[14]Private Source

5. **External constraints**

   a) Political
   b) Legal
   c) Economic cycles
   d) Environmental
   e) Technological

6. **Internal constraints**

   a) Sufficient returns to attract short or long term capital
   b) Availability of skilled labor
   c) Adequate supplies of raw materials

7. **Key success factors**

   a) Cost control
   b) Product design
   c) Technological advances
   d) Quality assurance
   e) Flexibility/Adaptability
   f) Service

8. **Major industry trends and risks**

B. **Strategic Analysis of a Particular Firm**

   1. **Competitive position within industry**

      a) Ranking in size of sales and assets
      b) Market share; recent changes
      c) Key factors in acquiring/maintaining market share
      d) Product characteristics
      e) Adaptability to external and internal constraints

   2. **Market strategy**

      a) Demand analysis
         i) Primary or derived
         ii) Degree of cyclicality
         iii) Price sensitivity
         iv) Customer preferences/requirements
      b) Product policy
         i) Kind of product being sold
         ii) Summary of benefits to customer
      c) Pricing policy
         i) Freedom in setting margins
         ii) Acquiring or maintaining market share
         iii) Different prices for different market segments
      d) Channels of distribution
      e) Method of selling
         i) Personal
         ii) Advertising mix

3. **Manufacturing strategy**

   a) Mechanical process
      i) Degree of automation
      ii) Level of technology
      iii) Organization of process flow
   b) Economics
      i) Cost structure
      ii) Scale economies
   c) Skill requirements
      i) Degree of precision
      ii) Nature of labor force
      iii) R & D levels

4. **Financial strategy**

   a) Capital structure
      i) Appropriateness for margins produced
      ii) Ownership distribution
   b) Access to capital markets
      i) Short and long term; nature of relationships
   c) Nature of supplier credit; customer terms of trade
   d) Historical and pro forma financial analysis

5. **Management structure**

   a) Organization
   b) Resumes
   c) References
   d) Strengths and Weaknesses

6. **Summary of corporate strategy**

   a) How has the strategy been implemented historically and what have been the key changes in that strategy
   b) Is present strategy:
      i) Appropriate to compete in its industry on an ongoing basis
      ii) Consistent with our analysis of industry trends
   c) Is management team suitable for carrying out their corporate strategy

6. **Major risks of the firm**

   a) Business risks
      i) Competitive trends
      ii) Life cycle of products
      iii) Changing needs in the market place
   b) Financial risks
      i) Adequacy of capital structure
      ii) Sufficient availability of credit to suppliers/customers
   c) Suitability of management to accommodate these risks

PRIVATE PLACEMENTS

INTRODUCTION

Financing a new or growing venture is a topic of considerable importance to all entrepreneurs. However, access to funds is limited mainly to private (as opposed to public) sources for the vast majority of entrepreneurs. One source of "private" funds is called Private Placements and one purpose of this note is to provide a better understanding of the role of private placements as a source of equity funds. However, the reader should realize that the term "private placements" is applied across a vast spectrum of long term equity investments often involving large institutional investors and vast amounts of money. Consequently, a general discussion of this concept might *not* be of particular interest to an entrepreneur. Therefore, we have chosen to emphasize those types of private placements which the entrepreneur will find most useful, specifically when:

> • the amount of money to be raised is relatively small, as little as $25,000, and does not exceed $1.5 million;

> • the potential investors are "informal investors," defined as "sources of risk capital other than professionally managed venture capital funds, equity-oriented Small Business Companies (SBIC's), other institutional investors and the public equity markets."[1]

---

[1] Wetzel, William, "Informal Risk Capital in New England," *Frontiers of Entrepreneurship Research,* Babson College, 1981, p. 218.

SECTION 1 - RULES AND REGULATIONS

DEFINITION

A review of the law tells us that a *private* offering of securities is possible under the section 4 (2) exemption clause of the Securities Act of 1933 which exempts the issuer from a public registration under SEC regulations. A private placement as defined in the Act is a "transaction by an issuer not involving any public offering." However, the simplicity of this legal definition has created some ambiguity and confusion surrounding the availability of a private placement exemption.

The ambiguity stems from the fact that the section 4(2) exemption of the Act covers a wide variety of circumstances ranging from the equity financing of small privately held firms (entrepreneurial ventures) among employees, relatives, and/or friends, to the multi-million dollar institutional private placement utilizing high grade debt securities. Difficulty arises when one tries to list and apply the precise requirements of the federal exemption as they relate to the variety of individual transactions. The issue is further complicated by the existence of additional regulations defined in state security laws and "Blue Sky Laws."*

BACKGROUND INFORMATION

Utilization of private placement financing is due partly to certain advantages to the issuer and investor not available in a public offering of securities. While the pros and cons are delineated later, the advantages include the tailoring of terms to meet the special needs of the participants, avoidance of underwriting expenses, and other costs and delays involved in a public disclosure of information which the Securities Act requires of a public offering.

Today, the majority of private placements consist of the sale of long term debt securities by large corporations to institutional investors, i.e., life insurance companies, banks, and pension funds, with the largest life insurance companies purchasing 90% of all privately placed securities.

In spite of the predominance of the large issuer and institutional investor in the private placement market, this method of financing is also popular with smaller issuers and individual investors. The majority of these private placements were in the form of equity issues and were typically made to corporate promoters, officers and individual investors as a means of raising venture capital.

Information about the activities of "informal investors" however, is almost nonexistent. Regarding this source - friends, relatives, customers, suppliers, individual investors - a long-time observer of the risk-capital scene commented:

---

*Blue Sky Laws are state laws intended to stop the sale of fraudulent or visionary stock to the public — "speculative offerings which have no more basis than so many feet of blue sky."

General estimates indicate that most capital for new and emerging business is raised from these informal sources. However, there is virtually no way to identify quantities, much less specific investors that might be interested in such projects.[2]

The gravest concern facing the independent businessman seeking to raise capital through private placement is the uncertainty involved. The availability of an exemption from the Securities Act's registration requirement is often unclear because the statute itself fails to delineate the types of private sales which my proceed without registration.

Since the term private placement is not defined specifically in the Act, the SEC and the courts have been left to determine when a particular sale of securities qualifies for an exemption. To facilitate decisions, the SEC, in 1935, set forth a list of factors to be considered when determining the applicability of section 4(2).[3] At that time, the principal factors to be considered were:

1. The number of offerees and their relationship to each other and to the issuer;

2. The number of units offered;

3. The size of the offering; and

4. The manner of the offering.

On the basis of factual evidence presented regarding these four points, the courts decided whether a transaction constituted a public offering requiring registration.

In 1953, the Supreme Court attempted to define the scope of the private placement exemption in its decision regarding the SEC v. Ralston Purina Co. Here the Supreme Court held that:

"the applicability of Section 4(2) should turn on whether the particular class of persons affected needs the protection of the Act. An offering to those who are shown to be able to fend for themselves is a transaction not involving any public offering."[4]

---

[2]Rubel, Stanley, "Equity Capital," in *Source Guide for Borrowing Capital,* Capital Publishing Co., 1977.

[3]"Reforming the Initial Sale Requirements of the Private Placement Exemption," *Harvard Law Review*, Vol. 86: 403 1972, p. 405.

[4]346 U.S., 119, 125 (1953); SEC v. Ralston Purina Company.

The Court also ruled that the issuer must prove that all offerees had "access to the kind of information which registration would disclose."[5] Finally, the Court rejected the notion that a public offering is tied to the number of offerees. In other words, there was no inherent limit on the number of private placement offerees.

Unfortunately, the Ralston Purina case failed to provide much guidance to issuers and investors. The "able to fend for themselves," and "access to information" factors were too vague to delineate with certainty what distinguishes a public offering from a transaction eligible for the Section 4(2) exemption.

The failure of the SEC and the courts to clarify the relevant factors in applying section 4(2) placed entrepreneurs wishing to utilize a private placement in a potentially precarious legal position. They first had to assess whether a particular sale met the requirements and then they inherited the burden of proving that the sale was proper if it were chllenged by the SEC or a purchaser.

CONDITIONS REQUIRED FOR THE SECURITIES ACT EXEMPTION

In an attempt to clarify and standardize the exemption requirments, the SEC issued the Securities Act Rule 146 in November, 1972. The object of the Rule was to define a set of objective criteria for the private placement exemption so that:

> "any transaction by an issuer which meets all of the conditions...shall be deemed not to be a transaction involving any public offering within the meaning of Section 4.(2)"[6]

The revised conditions imposed by the Rule for a section 4(2) exemption are designed to insure compliance with "the access to information" and "able to fend for themselves" standards of the Ralston Purina decision. In doing so, the Rule defines five relevant factors that will determine a proper private placement. They are:

- offeree qualifications;
- availability of information;
- the manner of the offering;
- the absence of redistribution;
- the number of offerees; number of purchasers.[7]

---

[5]SEC Rule 146, 17 C.F.R. s 230. 146 (1975).

[6]Section 4(2) and Statutory Law; "A Position Paper of the Federal Regulations of Securities Committee," Section of Corporation, Banking, and Business Law of the American Bar Association. *The Business Lawyer,* Vol. 31, November 1975, p. 489. This is the source for much of the information in this section.

[7]SEC Rule 146(d), 37 Fed. Reg. 26137, 26140 (1972)

Any entrepreneur evaluating the feasibility of raising capital through a private placement will simplify the task if he acquires a working knowledge of these interrelated attributes. It is essential that the entrepreneur realize that these factors are not to be regarded as fixed parameters that assure the availability of the exemption but rather practical guidelines for what may constitute a private placement exemption.

In April 1982 a further attempt was made to allow small enterprises to enter the equity market without the red tape of SEC registration--know as *Regulation D*. In essence, Regulation D allows companies to sell stock through a brokerage firm to an unlimited number of investors without having to register the offering. It divides potential equity seekers into two classes: up to $500,000 and $500,000 to $5 million. Although this broker-based opportunity may not have much impact on the smaller venture, for reasons which follow, it defines for the first time in clear terms what constitutes a "sophisticated investor." Here is a paraphrase of an accountant's summary:[8]

ISSUES UP TO $500,000: REGULATION D, RULE 504

- Private offerings in the less-than-$500,000 category - equity and debt issues, limited partnerships in oil and gas ventures, and any type of security - may be sold without registration to an unlimited number of purchasers. (The number of investors was previously limited to 100.) This is because SEC commissioners think that some deals are simply too small to warrant Uncle Sam's involvement.

- Brokerage firms, which previously had no incentive to take part in such deals, are now allowed to charge as high a commission as the market will bear. (Observers expect these fees to be 15-20% of the offering.) This is because the SEC believes that broker-dealer involvement provides safeguards for investors, and wishes to provide them with incentives for using their expertise to aid small businesspeople. However, brokerage firms are not hurrying to take advantage of this opportunity; they cite the economics of handling an issue as small as $500,000 as the primary deterrent.

- Securities sold under the Regulation D exemption are "restricted;" they are marked "unregistered" and may not be resold for two years. For many potential investors, this illiquidity is not appealing.

- Regulation D or not, any sale of stock must also meet the provisions of the securities laws of the states where potential

---

[8]"Reforming the Initial Sale Requirements of the Private Placement Exemption," p. 410.

investors live -- the "blue sky" laws. As these vary greatly from state to state, a broker's attorneys would have to analyze the offering very thoroughly before offering it interstate.

ISSUES OF $500,000 TO $5 MILLION: REGULATION D, RULE 505.

- All companies, closely held or public, may sell unregistered securities up to $5 million under certain conditions:

- The number of investors is limited to 35, only if some of them can not pass a test as "accredited investors."

- The SEC has defined these "accredited (or sophisticated) investors" as those who can fend for themselves without the protection provided by registration as follows:

    Banks; insurance companies; investment companies; pensions plans and tax-exempt organizations such as college endowment funds with more than $5 million in assets; directors and officers of the company raising the equity capital; and individuals with net worth of more than $1 million, or annual income of at least $200,000 for the last two years and an expectation of at least the same amount in the third.

Because accredited investors are expected to get investment information from their own research, there are no requirements for prospectuses, financial statements or annual reports, provided the offering is sold to those who are accredited.

- A company can place unregistered securities with an unlimited number of investors, and, as long as the total offering doesn't exceed $5 million during a 12-month period, with 35 nonaccredited investors as well. However, if known unaccredited investors are among the offerees, the issuing company must provide appropriate documentation.

- If unaccredited investors are inadvertently included and the issue sells out, nobody can be held liable for not providing disclosure documents if the issuing company and its underwriters "reasonably believed" that all investors met the requirement.

OFFEREE QUALIFICATIONS

Except for the specific definition pertaining to a Regulation D offeree, developing a precise test that assures the identification of qualified offerees is very difficult. Generally, however, the offeree may be judged qualified on the basis of sophistication, wealth, and personal relationship to the issuer.

- *Sophistication*

Sophistication refers to the offeree's ability to understand risk. In the words of the regulation, the issuer must have reasonable grounds to believe that "either the offeree or his investment representative has such knowledge and experience in financial and business matters that he is capable of utilizing the information to evaluate the risk of the prospective investment."[9]

Inherent in the above quote is the assumption that a sophisticated offeree is one who does not need the protection of a "public disclosure" of information regarding the placement. However, the entrepreneur must keep in mind that the detail of the information disclosed and the manner in which it is presented will have a direct effect on the offeree's ability to understand risk. Because there are degrees of sophistication among the offerees of a single transaction, the entrepreneur must detail financial disclosures in relation to the offeree's familiarity with the business and industry. In general, the relevant factor is whether the investor can evaluate risk based on the information supplied to him.

- *Wealth*

Wealth refers to one's ability to bear the economic risk of an investment being held for an indefinite period of time. The SEC states that the relevant consideration must be the total amount of money invested and the probability that all or part of it will be lost. The issuer must be aware that the same investor may qualify on a private placement when the chance of substantial loss is minimal, but not on a speculative high risk offer where the chance of total loss is significant. The entrepreneur must keep in mind that risk-bearing ability may require his judgment regarding the general level of inherent risk and not only the total amount invested.

- *Personal Relationship*

The offeree's personal relationship with the issuer includes, but is not limited to: family ties, friendship, an employment relationship, or a pre-existing business relationship. When the offerees have such close relationships with the issuer, the public benefits which would result from the registration of the issue are remote. As a result, these relationships qualify a transaction for a section 4(2) exemption. In addition, the SEC and courts have held that when close personal relationships exist, a decision to make an investment may be motivated by factors unrelated to risk and return. In these circumstances, the offerees do not need the protection of a public registration.

---

[9]"Reforming the Initial Sale Requirements of the Private Placement Exemption," p. 495.

A final consideration concerning offeree qualifications is whether the exemption is available only if every offeree, even those who do not become purchasers, meet the qualification criteria. The legal literature indicates that the court would rule on such a matter based on factors such as the status of the offeree in question, whether the issuer acted reasonably in making the offer to those who were not qualified, and the remedial action, if any, taken by the issuer upon learning of the non-qualified offeree.[10] Under *Rule 146*, the exemption remains even if a sale was made to a non-qualified person as long as the issuer had reasonable grounds to believe, after making reasonable inquiry, that each was a qualified offeree.

In summary then, an offeree is judged qualified on the basis of sophistication, wealth, and relationship. Although it is not specifically required under Rule 146 that the issuer document each offeree's qualifications, such a practice may prove beneficial when any doubt exists given the fact that the burden of proof is on the issuer should the private placement be challenged.

ACCESS TO INFORMATION

The second major condition refers to the scope of and access to information. The issuer may meet this requirement by insuring that each offeree or his representative has equal access to the

> "same kind of information that the Act would make available in the form of a registration statement."[11]

Offerees must also have access to additional information necessary to verify the accuracy of the information they have received. Institutional investors are presumed to have equal access to any information they request because of their "strong economic bargaining power."[12] However, satisfying the information requirement in the case of the small individual investor is more difficult. For example, the use of a broker or dealer as offering intermediaries may be deemed to indicate a "public offering" if it is assumed that unequal information was supplied to the different investors.[13]

For the small business issuer, it is usually adequate to supply information regarding the issuee's financial conditions, the results of operations, and business and management information. In fact, many private placements by small closely-held companies are completed with a minimum of formally documented disclosures. In some instances,

---

[10]"Reforming the Initial Sale Requirements of the Private Placement Exemption," p. 495.

[11]Cox, J., *On Corporations: The Sum and Substance of Law*, Second Edition, 1975.

[12]*Ibid.*

[13]*Q & A, Small Business and the SEC:* Office of Small Business Division of Corporate Finance, Securities and Exchange Commission: March 1980, p. 9.

private placements have been held proper in the absence of reliable financial statements under the conditions that such statements were unavailable and the buyer was still willing to sign a waiver and assume the risk.

To fulfill the requirement, disclosures should whenever possible be made in writing using a structured memorandum, business plan, or by alternative means such as: oral presentation, a tour of the physical plant, inspection of the products, process, and facilities, and finally communications with suppliers, customers, and banks.

Entrepreneurs issuing a private placement may be assuming an unnecessary risk of invalidating the exemption by relying on anything less than well-documented disclosure information particualrly because they are typically dealing with investors of varying degrees of sophistication and wealth. Given this diversity, the issuer of the placement may seek to secure written acknowledgement that the purchaser is aware of the business, industry, and inherent risk factors.

MANNER OF THE OFFERING

Rule 146 addresses a third attribute, i.e., the manner in which the issuer's securities may be privately placed. The securities may be offered and sold only in a "negotiated transaction" that requires that the terms and arrangements relating to the sale "are arrived at through direct communications between the issuer and the purchaser." Naturally, the transaction can take place through the participants' consultants. In addition, the issuer is prohibited from using "any form of general advertising" including but not limited to newspaper or magazine articles, radio or television broadcasting, seminars, or promotional meetings, or letters, circulars, or other written communication. However, the key word in this regulation is *general*. The offer may be communicated through a letter, circular, or memorandum provided that they are directed to "specifically targeted sophisticated investors."[14]

This attribute of Rule 146 is perhaps the least ambiguous of all the regulations that determine the availability of the section 4(2) exemption. Nonetheless, the issuer should be just as cautious in fulfilling this requirement as with the regulations mentioned above.

ABSENCE OF REDISTRIBUTION (RESALE)

Because a private offering is meant to be a long-term investment (the present guideline being at least 2 years), the fourth relevant condition is the prohibition of immediate redistribution by the initial purchasers. Such a resale would constitute a "public offering."

At issue in the resale regulation is the determination of investment intent which refers to absence of the intention to resell the security. Under the conditions of Rule 146, the issuer must secure some documented restriction prohibiting resale. Such documentation

---

[14]*Q & A, Small Business and the SEC:* Office of Small Business Division of Corporate Finance, Securities and Exchange Commission: March 1980, p. 9.

includes, but is not limited to, the endorsement of legends on the stock certificate, (referred to as letter stock or restricted stock) investment non-distribution letters, and/ or stop transfer instructions to transfer agents.

Whatever device is used, it is the issuer's responsibility to secure, before purchase, a signed document of intent from the investor stating that there is no reason in the foreseeable future as to why the security would be sold. Great care must be taken in securing these documents as the presence or absence of them may be the determining factor in the legality of the private placement transaction.

It would be unrealistic to assume that a venture capitalist or any individual participating in a private offering would not at some point in time liquidate the securities. In fact, a large resale market for privately placed securities does exist under regulated conditions. Under the controlled methods of redistribution, there are three different ways the security may be resold:

    i. If the security is later registered.
    ii. If an unforeseeable "change of circumstance" takes
        place after a significant length of time.
    iii. If all of the requirements of SEC Rule 146 are met which are:

        (a) There is an adequate amount of current public information concerning the issuer.

        (b) The issue has been held for at least two years.

        (c) The investor sells no more than 1% of the total issue outstanding during any given six-month period.

        (d) A signed notice of intent to sell the securities is filed with the SEC if more than 500 shares are sold or the total sale exceeds $10,000 in value.

NUMBER OF PURCHASERS, NUMBER OF OFFEREES

Rule 146 provides that issuers may sell securities without registration to not more than 35 persons in any consecutive twelve-month period. But in determining the number of purchases, the issuer may exclude

    "any person who purchases securities from the issuer for cash in an amount not less than $150,000."[15]

---

[15]Liles, Patrick R. *New Business Ventures and the Entrepreneur,* Richard D. Irwin, Inc., 1974, pp. 504-509.

The number of offerees is a much-discussed subject regarding private placements because the Rule's language is not as specific concerning offerees as it is with purchasers. The regulation states that an "unlimited number of persons may be approached about buying the securities, provided they meet the sophistication and wealth requirements and other defined standards."[16]

Legal literature indicates that in the future there will be less concern regarding the number of offerees (provided that this number is not excessive) and the focus of attention will shift to the manner of the offering. For practical purposes, the total number of offerees may be considered relevant primarily as evidence of the manner in which the offering is made.

SUMMARY — RULES AND REGULATIONS

Obviously, none of the foregoing factors-qualifications of the offeree, availability of information, the manner of the offering, the absences of redistribution and the number of offerees/purchasers - standing alone would assure the availability of the section 4(2) exemption. However, compliance with all the factors under Rule 146 will almost assuredly qualify a transaction for the exemption from public registration.

These attributes should never be considered as unrelated or totally self-contained criteria. The issuer must take care to correlate the scope and detail of disclosure information, the manner of the offering, and the qualifications of the offeree in terms of his/her ability to understand and asssume risk. A practical rule should be that all transactions should be planned under the guidance of an experienced attorney and no transaction should be planned to meet just the minimum standards required for the registration exemption.

---

[16]Rubel, Stanley. "Equity Capital," in *Source Guide for Borrowing Capital,* Capital Publishing Co., 1977.

SECTION II

PROS AND CONS OF PRIVATE PLACEMENTS VS. PUBLIC OFFERINGS

Pros:

- No SEC registration or prospectus filing requirment.

- No 20-day waiting period between registration and sale.

- Greater flexibility in tailoring the terms and provisions of the
    the issue to individual investor requirements.

- Significantly lower distribution and reporting costs and fees.

- No public financial disclosure requirements.

Cons:

- The issue has much less marketability.

- A higher return on equity is generally demanded by investors due to
    the lesser marketability.

- Resale cannot generally take place for at least two years
    from the purchase.

- Additional legal liability may exist if an unsophisticated
    person invests.

SECTION III

PRACTICAL INFORMATION

A. *Private Placement Memorandum*

Once an entrepreneur has decided to finance his capital needs through a private placement, the next step is to prepare a private placement memorandum or business plan. This memorandum should be designed to provide extensive analysis and information to the potential investor. While the entrepreneur should strive to interest and sell the potential investor through this memorandum, he must also be aware that it represents a legal document that is the primary source on which investors will base their decisions. Legal proceedings could arise from any falsification, misrepresentation, or omissions in this memorandum. The best way to obtain the confidence and trust necessary for a working relationship with the investor is to identify and highlight problem areas rather than to attempt to hide them. The private placement memorandum can assume a variety of forms, as each entrepreneur tailors the document to fit his particular needs and to intensify the investor's interest.

Due to the restrictions on the number of purchasers in a private placement, it is important that each memorandum be pre-numbered and contain a legend which states that under no circumstances can the document be reproduced or disclosed to outsiders. A log of all memorandum numbers should be maintained by the entrepreneur. This log should account for those documents submitted to investors as well as those unissued. In addition, it should include the offeree's name, the date it was submitted, and other appropriate dates. Once all offers have been extended, a file memo should be placed in the log stating that no offers or contacts were made other than those indicated. Any unissued memorandums should be voided.[17]

B. *Locating Potential Investors*

Once the entrepreneur has identified his investment needs and prepared the private placement memorandum, he is confronted with the task of locating potential investors. This may be the hardest task of all.

Until recently, there have been three recognized sources of information available to entrepreneurs on how to locate investors:

- Financial middleman

- Brokerage houses and investment bankers

- Venture capital firms

Financial middlemen, also referred to as agents, brokers, and finders, can be very helpful in locating prospective investors. They normally have an extensive pool of contacts armed with backgrounds in law, accounting, or consulting. They can be particularly helpful to the entrepreneur who is inexperienced with private placements. Also, they generally are experienced in analyzing business plans and making presentations to investors.[18] Typically, financial middlemen charge a 5% commission on the amount of capital raised and a 2% equity participation. However, brokers frequently take part of their commission in equity, which allows the entrepreneur to obtain more of the valuable cash proceeds while enhancing the broker's upside potential.[19]

Brokerage houses and investment bankers have recently entered the more risky private placement business. Notable investment bankers which have been participating in private placements are Allen & Co. of New York, Hambrecht & Quist of San Francisco, Smith Barney Harris Upham & Co. of New York, Donaldson, Lufkin & Jenrette of New York, and Bateman Eichler Hill Richards of Los Angeles. Several of these firms also have

---

[17]Bill Sloan, "How Middlemen Help Raise Money," *Venture,* February 1981, pp. 50-51.

[18]Dave Lindorff, "Investment Bankers Take the Venture Plunge," *Venture,* January 1981, p. 8.

[19]*Ibid.,* quoting John Knorp, financial advisor for Good Earth Restaurants.

established venture capital investment arms. These investment bankers cite their contacts and visibility in the financial world as their major advantage over competitors. Smith Barney, for example, has 100 sales offices and nearly 1,500 sales representatives around the country.

Investment bankers are often ideal for private placement and venture capital funding because they can not only provide first round placements but also second and third round financing and underwriting of an eventual public offering. Similar to the middlemen, investment bankers normally take part of their compensation in equity. In addition, they normally participate in the venture's management by sitting on the board of directors. This relatively inexpensive consulting service can be of tremendous benefit to the entrepreneur. As one entrepreneur explained, "For us, an investment bank is sort of like a supermarket of the investment business. They can finance us when we start out, help us with interim financing, provide us with talented people for our board of directors, underwrite us when we want to go public, and sell us if we want to be acquired."[20]

The third resource for potential investors are *venture capital firms*. While the investors in these closed-end funds normally participate through the firm itself, some are willing to deal directly with the entrepreneur, and a venture capital firm may be willing to arrange a contact. Thus, consequently, it may be worthwhile for the entrepreneur to approach them. Also, many corporations have venture capital arms which invest in related but non-competing fields. Their motivations may include cultivating a potential merger, supplier or customer. Similarly, the entrepreneur may approach certain wealthy individuals who qualify as "sophisticated." Such individuals are generally more willing to accept risk than the institutional venture capital investors.

As can be seen from the above suggestions on how to locate potential investors, the process is haphazard and chancy. In recognition of this fact, and working with the hypothesis that informal investors represent an important source of risk capital, a study was undertaken in 1980 by Professor William Wetzel and others under the sponsorship of the Office of Advocacy, U.S. Small Business Administration. The results of this report[21] and of a subsequent pilot project to create a regional referral service, Project I-C-E,[22] should be of great interest to entrepreneurs. Some of the findings of the first report, "Informal Risk Capital in New England," are reproduced below:

> The results of this research confirm and document generally
> held impressions that informal investors are a significant
> and appropriate source of risk-capital for technology-based
> investors, and for both emerging and established firms

---

[20]Wetzel, William, "Informal Risk Capital in New England," *Frontiers of Entrepreneurship (FOER)* 1981, p. 218.

[21]Wetzel, William, "Project I-C-E; an Experiment in Capital Formation," *FOER* 1982.

[22]Wetzel, William, "Informal Risk Capital in New England," *FOER*, 1981, p. 219.

without access to traditional venture capital sources or the public equity markets. Informal investors are difficult to reach -- geographically dispersed and tough to identify. Nine months and the assistance of several professional organizations were required to find and collect data from 133 informal investors in New England.

Respondents reported risk capital investments totalling over $16 million in 320 ventures during the five years from 1976 through 1980, an average investment rate of about $3 million per year in 64 ventures per year. The average size of past investments was in the neighborhood of $50,000, while the median investment was about $20,000. Investment goals of respondents over the next two years reflect an expected investment rate of about $5 million in over 100 ventures per year. If the research sample represents one informal investor in five or ten, total informal risk capital financing in New England is in the neighborhood of $15-$30 million per year for 300-500 ventures.[23]

The report concludes:

Informal investors generally learn of investment opportunities through friends and business associates. During the course of this research it was not uncommon to discover that finding one informal investor led to contacts with several others. A network of friends and associates appears to link these individuals. However, the majority of respondents was less than satisfied with the effectivenss of existing channels of communication between bonafide entrepreneurs seeking risk capital and investors like themselves. Over eighty percent expressed an interest in a regional referral service that would permit them to examine a broader range of investment opportunities. These widely held opinions suggest that an appropriately designed regional network linking investors with opportunities could materially improve the efficiency of the informal risk capital market. Confidentiality and timeliness appear to be two essential characteristics of such a network.

Generalizations about a group as diverse as the informal investor population are hazardous. Nevertheless, the data reveal a number of interesting characteristics of informal

---

[23]Wetzel, William, "Informal Risk Capital in New England," *FOER,* pp. 244-5.

investors. Despite the pitfalls, and as a starting point for discussion and further research, the following profile of the mythical, "typical" informal investor is offered:

INFORMAL INVESTOR PROFILE

1. Age 47.

2. Education: Post graduate degree, often technical.

3. Previous management experience with start-up ventures.

4. Typically invests between $10,000 and $25,000 in any one venture.

5. Invests at a rate of approximately once a year.

6. Typically participates with other financially sophisticated individuals.

7. Prefers to invest in start-up and early stage situations.

8. Willing to finance technology-based inventors when technology and markets are familiar.

9. Limited interest in financing established, moderate growth, small firms.

10. Strong preference for manufacturing ventures, high-technology in particular.

11. Invests close to home--within 300 miles and usually within 50 miles.

12. Maintains an active professional relationship with portfolio ventures, typically a consulting role or service on a board of directors.

13. Diversification and tax sheltered income are not important objectives.

14. Expects to liquidate investment in 5-7 years.

15. Looks for rates of return on individual investments ranging from 50 plus percent from inventors to 20%-25% from established firms.

16. Looks for minimum portfolio returns of about 20%.

17. Often will accept limitations on financial return in exchange for non-financial rewards.

18. Learns of investment opportunities primarily from friends and business associates.

19. Would like to look at more investment opportunities than present informal system permits.

Having enumerated the above characteristics, it must be said that exceptions abound. Informal investors are a very diverse group and there are few bonafide opportunities for which an appropriate informal investor cannot be found.

SECTION IV

OUTLOOK FOR PRIVATE PLACEMENTS IN THE 80's

The opportunities and outlook for private placements in the future is closely tied to the venture capital industry in general. In this regard, the September 1980 issue of the *Venture Capital Journal* states that based on the "resurrection in 1978, dramatic growth in 1979, and explosive expansion in 1980, the venture capital industry's current status certainly offers remarkable opportunity."[24] This article also points out that the tremendous growth which has occurred in this area in recent years has done so during a period of national economic down-turn, and projects that "the future for business development may be brighter than at any time in the (venture capital) industry's past." The optimism surrounding this outlook for venture capital and accordingly private placements can be traced to several factors. The venture capital industry is basically one of capital gains. As a result of the government's recognition of the need to stimulate more productive investment in the economy, the capital gains tax rate was reduced in 1978. Perhaps this reduction more than anything has accounted for the recent resurgence in the industry. Summarizing the effect of the 1978 capital-gains tax law, *U.S. News and World Report* cites that six of every ten dollars worth of long term capital gains are currently tax free as compared to the previous ratio of five to ten. More specifically, the maximum tax on long term capital gains is currently 28 percent as compared to 49 percent previously.[25]

Another important factor related to the optimism surrounding the future for private placements and general venture capital opportunities is what *Business Week* labels as "perhaps the most significant policy shift (in Washington) since the creation of the Small Business Administration in 1953."[26] More than 80 new bills were passed by Congress in October 1980 including the regulatory Flexibility Act and the Small Business Investment Incentive Act. These bills were designed to:

1. ease the regulations on small business.

---

[24]"Special report - Business Development Financing 1980 - Opportunities and Concerns," *op. cit.*

[25]"Wallets Open up for Risky Ventures," *U.S. News and World Report*: December 24, 1979, pp. 75-76.

[26]"Bonuses for Small Business," *Business Week,* November 3, 1980, p. 100.

2. ease the regulations on venture-capital firms to make it easier for small businesses to raise capital.

3. spur industrial innovation.[27]

In addition to these, the Reagan Administration has recently proposed additional corporate tax cuts. To the extent that the capital gains tax and federal regulations are eased in the future, the opportunities for private placements should continue to grow.

Finally, regional networks which bring together entrepreneurs and investors, such as Project I-C-E, promise to fill an important gap in equity funds flow -- and to expedite the entrepreneur's role as a technological innovator and/or creator of jobs.

---

[27]"How Washington Spurs High-Tech Companies," *Business Week*, November 10, 1980, p. 98.

PUBLIC OFFERINGS AND THE ENTREPRENEUR

"Going public" is a means of raising capital which the entrepreneur may wish to consider at any stage of his venture: start-up, operating, or ending.* The major determinant in the decision is timing: what is the state of the equity market? and, how "sexy" is my venture vis-a-vis the public market? When the public is in a buying mood, and when interest rates are so high that debt financing becomes almost prohibitive, going public may be the most satisfactory solution to the entrepreneur's capital needs.

This note will discuss first the pros and cons of making a public offering and next the process of doing so.

SHOULD I EVEN CONSIDER GOING PUBLIC?

Some general comments about the prime determinants--the market, your venture and your underwriter--may be helpful in answering this question.

The new issues market, to experienced observers, resembles a roller coaster. One expert remarked:

> The hot new issues markets usually seem to accelerate in the latter phases of a sustained bull market. One was running in late 1961; it collapsed, along with everything else, in May 1962. Another was roaring in 1968-69. What happened to it in May, 1970, is also history. As of mid-1980, a modest new issue market has begun to show some evidence of vigor.[1]

---

*However, there are restrictions on stock transactions involving principal shareholders in new issues...and a lawyer can explain which ones are pertinent to your offering.

[1]Gordon Baty, *Entrepreneurship for the Eighties,* Prentice-Hall, 1981. Chapter 10: Public or Private: What's the Difference?

In April 1983 another observer proclaimed, "The window's open again. Underwriters, flooded by three times as many requests from entrepreneurs seeking to go public today as in 1981, conservatively estimate that 400 companies will go public this year, almost double the 222 that went public in 1982, and not far from the 448 initial public offerings in 1981."[2]

The success of many new issues is highly trendy. Oil and gas and alternate energy companies were hot tickets in 1980-1 and cold turkeys in 1981-2. In 1982 analysts were looking to the following industries for strong growth: telecommunications; medical services and products; consumer services; cable TV and related services; motion picture production; and computer software.[3]

If your venture is hot and the market is good, underwriters will probably beat a path to your door. If this is true, you must select one with care, because the choice of a principal underwriter will influence greatly the acceptance of your issue and the strength of its aftermarket. Look especially at:

• Their track record. Have they underwritten companies like yours before? How many hits and how many misses? Of the hits, how is their continuing market performance?

• Their proposal. Is the underwriter offering "best effort"—to sell as much as they can (and pay themselves first), leaving the rest of the stock without a buyer? All-or-nothing—if X percent of the stock does not sell by a predetemined date the issue will be withdrawn? Or a guaranteed underwiting—a firm commitment to sell the whole offering at a pre-determined price? During hot markets, underwriters blossom; in hard times, all but the best vanish. The entrepreneur needs excellent legal and financial advice before making a final choice.

A logical answer to the initial question is: unless both the market and the industry trends are working in your favor, along with your underwriter, you probably shouldn't worry about going public--for now.

---

[2]"The Window's Open Again," Lori Inannou, *Venture,* April 1983, pp. 36-41.

[3]*Venture Magazine,* "Going Public 1982," and "New Issues Winners and Losers, 1977-81," April 1982, pp. 30.

GOING PUBLIC--PROS AND CONS

Knee-jerk Cassandras counsel against new and growing companies going public for several reasons.

1. It costs too much.

2. It takes too much time away from running the company.

3. It robs the entrepreneur of privacy.

4. It forces the entrepreneur to give up control.

All of these are true--up to a point. If the entrepreneur asks, "As compared to what?", as we are about to do, he will be able to make a more informed decision.

1. *Costs* - The costs of an initial underwriting are estimated at a fourth to a fifth of what you plan to raise. The underwriter's fee is typically 10% of the issue, in addition to 5% or more in other expenses. To these costs should be added: lawyers' fees; accountants' fees; filing fees; printing expenses; and your own time, traveling, and trouble.

Alternatively, however, any method of raising capital costs something--you have to give in order to get. How much would the interest on a bank loan cost, assuming you could get one for the amount you need to raise? What is the cost of a private placement? 15% is a standard fee. What are the costs, hidden and otherwise, of going to a venture capitalist?

And, assuming the public offering is successful, think what you stand to gain--in addition to the capital:

• Liquidity. Your interests can be traded on an open market. In addition, you can use stock, rather than cash, to buy future acquisitions.

• Credibility. A publicly-owned, publicly-accountable company inspires more trust in customers, vendors, and prospective investors.

2. *Time* - Unquestionably, going public takes time. War stories from now-public entrepreneurs abound. Days, nights and weekends are consumed. The elapsed time from the decision to go public to the final approval of the offering can stretch close to a year. "I would never want to live through it again," is a common refrain.

Especially for the brand-new or barely-born venture, the entrepreneur's time is a key consideration. He or she needs time to devote to the business, or they may have nothing to go public with. However, raising capital from other sources takes time as well. Sources must be located and screened. Business plans must be prepared. Presentations must be made. The question to answer is, "How much time can I afford to spend raising money?"

3. *Privacy* - Going public involves a full and intimate disclosure of you and your

company. The initial prospectus must contain everything of concern to a potential non-sophisticated investor: who is going to get paid how much, who the major shareholders are, the track record of principal management--and opinions about the viability of the venture from a lawyer, an accountant, and you. "Due diligence" in presenting issues of fact and of opinion must be taken initially; failure to do so may result in a negligence suit.

In addition to the disclosure, statements must be filed annually (or more often) with the IRS, and an annual report must be sent to each stockholder. The publicly-held entrepreneur has nowhere to hide.

But, where can you hide when dealing with a banker? Or a venture capitalist? These fellows want to be kept closely informed, too. In addition, your lawyer and your accountant need to know the state of your affairs, if you are running a business with sound groundings. Here, the question might be, "How much privacy do I need?"

4. *Control* - Giving up equity seems to be the fear of every entrepreneur, and yet it is part of the capital-raising process. You must be prepared to give up equity to raise money in a public offering, or in a venture capital partnership, or in a private placement. Giving up equity, some would argue, is not the issue; rather, it is the ability to make decisions quickly in what you perceive as the company's best interest, that you may give up, to some extent, by going public.

In the publicly-held company, every stockholder is an owner, and decisions must be made in *their* best interest. Should profits be distributed in the form of dividends or plowed back into the company? Should a key manager be fired because his operation is temporarily floundering? Should you test an unproven but potentially attractive new market? Should you spend money for R&D now...instead of for marketing? In a privately-held company, you would have more freedom to decide these questions. As the CEO of a publicly-held company you are responsible first to your board of directors and next to your equity holders. You may find that consensus is as important as intuition.

Ask yourself, "How important is it to my venture that I be able to call all the shots exactly as I see them, and do what I want to do when I want to do it?"

FILING TO GO PUBLIC

There are four basic ways to take a company public which we will discuss here:

- the standard and time-consuming S-1 offering,

- a relatively new and simpler S-18 offering for companies wishing to raise up to $5 million,

- a Regulation A offering for companies wishing to raise up to $1.5 million, and

- an Intrastate offering for local businesses seeking local financing.

A fifth procedure, the Private Placement, is discussed in a separate note.

The Securities Act of 1933 requires that all public offerings be registered with the Securities and Exchange Commission (SEC)* unless specifically exempted. Exemptions include "Regulation A" offerings, intrastate offerings and private placements.

In addition, public offerings are regulated at the state level by the state's own "Blue Sky Laws" which differ from state to state. A public offering must satisfy both sets of regulations.

SEC-registered S-1 Offerings - Here is a thumbnail description of the standard S-1 registration procedure described by the partner of a respected investment banking firm.

> (After a number of prospective underwriters have made presentations to the board) a selection is made by the board and management and the formal process commences.
>
> When the preparation of the underwriting is to begin, an "all hands" meeting is held involving the company management, the managing underwriter, company counsel, underwriter's counsel, and auditors. At this time, a time schedule is laid out for the demanding task of preparing the registration statement to be filed with the SEC as well as the subsequent events that will involve the marketing of the proposed issue. A part of the registration statement is the prospectus, ("red herring") which will be distributed publicly, and which describes the company's history and operations in some detail. The preparation of the registration materials will typically take 30 to 60 days, a time period that may be extended if necessary, to accommodate the completion of an audit. (Recognizing that some companies wishing to go public are still in the R&D stage, the SEC has issued a special set of guide lines for "Companies in the Development Stage." Because of lack of a track record, each and every financial transaction must be described in detail, as most agreements among principal shareholders. The purpose, as in most SEC regulations, is to protect the investing public against misrepresentation and fraud.)
>
> Once the registration statement is filed with the SEC, the preliminary prospectus is printed and the marketing process commences. At this time, the underwriter will invite other investment banking firms into the underwriting syndicate,

---

*List of terms and definitions common in the securities industry is included in the Glossary of this note.

and the final syndicate may be composed of 50 to 70 firms. As these firms accept positions in the syndicate their salesmen begin to talk with clients and furnish them with a prospectus. Meanwhile, the managing underwriter will typically organize a series of presentations by company management in various key cities where significant institutional or individual investor interest can be found. Perhaps a half dozen to a dozen cities will be visited over a period of one to two weeks.

At the same time the SEC processes the registration and ultimately responds (usually within three to four weeks) with a series of comments, questions, or requests for additional information. The prospectus is then modified as needed to conform with the SEC request, and when the SEC is satisfied with the content, it will permit the issue to become effective.

Immediately prior to the offering becoming effective, the underwriter and the company have the last of a series of price discussions and set the price of the offering, which will then be incorporated into an amended prospectus. The revised prospectus with the price amendment then becomes a final prospectus that is printed and distributed after the offering has become effective. As soon as the offering is effective, sales can be confirmed by the members of the syndicate to their clients. Prior to effectiveness, they can do nothing more than take indications of interest.

The final step will be the closing, generally five business days after the offering becomes effective. At this time, the money changes hands and the offering is completed.[4]

Exhibit 1 provides a sample timetable for this process which covers approximaterly 90 days. This amount of time can be lengthened easily by any number of factors and/or delays associated with your particular situation.

Finally, the S-1 offering must also be in compliance with the Blue Sky Laws of the state in which it is registered. Usually, the procedure can be simplified by filing a "coordinated" registration with the state authorities; however, some states have more stringent regulations than does the SEC, and it is the responsibility of the underwriter to be sure the issue is in compliance with state rules.

––––––––––

[4]Peter Wallace, "Public Financing for Smaller Companies," article in *Guide to Venture Capital Sources,* 5th ed., ed. Stanley Pratt, Capital Publishing, 1981.

S-18 Offerings - The S-18 offering procedure is relatively new, and permits the offering to be filed at the regional SEC headquarters, rather than in Washington. It is intended to simplify the procedure of going public for companies wishing to raise up to $5 million. However, a number of conditions must be met, including: securities must be sold for cash; the company must be incorporated, and do business principally, in the U.S. or Canada; the company may not be an investment company or a limited partnership.[5]

Regulation A Offerings - "Reg A's" are a simplified version of S-1's, designed for the smaller company wishing to make a smaller offering. The prospectus is reviewed at the regional SEC office, and may not be distributed to the public until SEC comments have been received and answered; in other words, this "red herring" has been screened.

Regulation A offerings are available to companies wishing to raise up to $1.5 million (recently raised from a ceiling of $500,000).[6] If the company has less than 500 shareholders and fewer than $1 million in assets, it is not required to file certain quarterly and annual reports with the SEC regional office. The trend in recent SEC policy has been to extend this "mini-registration," making the procedure easier for the company wishing to go public and less time-consuming for the SEC at both the national and regional offices.

As in a standard offering, Regulation A offerings must also comply with "Blue Sky Laws" of the state in which the offering is made.

Intrastate Offerings - Intrastate offerings were designed for local businesses seeking local financing. An intrastate offering was intended to simplify the process of going public by removing the SEC from jurisdiction and handling registration at the state level. The rule, as amended, covers companies in which 80% of its gross revenues are derived from, 80% of its assets are located in, and 80% of the offering is used within one state. (Rule 147)

However, the intrastate offering has been abused, and consequently the SEC has attempted to restrict its use as much as possible. For this reason, the advice of a lawyer is critical if this well-intended "short-cut" is chosen.

WHAT HAPPENS *AFTER* I GO PUBLIC? ANATOMY OF THE SECURITIES MARKETS

- Primary Markets vs. Secondary Markets

The economic functions of securities markets are twofold, and it is important for the entrepreneur to understand the distinction.[7]

---

[5] *Venture Magazine,* "The New Issues Boom," Dave Lindorff, December 1980.

[6] *Venture Magazine,* December 1980, *op. cit.*

[7] Stanley S. C. Huang, *Investment Analysis and Management,* Winthrop Publishers Inc., Cambridge, Massachusetts, 1981. Chapter 3.

Primary markets deal with newly issued securities. They involve the entrepreneur, the managing underwriter, and a syndicate of other investment bankers whom he has put together. The managing underwriter generally guarantees the sale of a new issue at an agreed-upon price, and agrees to deliver the total proceeds (less commission) to the entrepreneur by a specific date. In some instances, the underwriter may insist upon a "best effort" deal, where he sells only what he can and returns the unsold stock to the entrepreneur. In either instance, the entrepreneur takes whatever financial proceeds he receives from the public offering and gets on with building his venture.

Secondary markets deal in existing securities, providing marketability and liquidity for stockholders. In secondary markets, direct financial benefits accrue only to the holders of the stocks and the dealers and brokers who take commissions on the sale; none of these monies go to the entrepreneur.

The performance of a stock in the secondary markets is affected by two factors: the reputation of the managing underwriter plus the quality of the initial market he is able to attract; and the financial performance of the venture itself.

Although entrepreneurs are often concerned mainly about the sale of the initial public offering they should also be concerned with the "after-market" for their stock. Initially the managing underwriter plays an important role here. With your stock, which he now owns, the underwriter "makes the market" with other of his associates, attempting to provide sufficient depth on both the buy and sell sides to insure liquidity for even large stockholders, usually taking a 10% commission on each sale. He keeps the potential buyers and sellers informed with up-to-date information about your venture and its industry.

- Secondary Markets: Over-the-counter (OTC) and Organized Exchanges

Existing securities (securities bought previously by investors from the issuing corporation) can be resold in the secondary markets. There are two types.

The *OTC market* is the broadest of all markets for securities. It is not centrally located, but rather composed of a network of dealers linked by teletype and telephone. It is a negotiated market, as distinguished from the exchanges which are auction markets. Many OTC stocks, with their bid and asked prices, are listed daily in newspapers and other financial publications.

The vast majority of initial public offerings (IPOs) are traded over-the-counter for at least an initial "seasoning" period. When the ventures reach a certain size and meet other qualifications they can, if they choose, apply to an organized exchange, either regional or national.

The "penny stock market" is not an "official" entity, and is mentioned here to clarify its status. "Penny stocks" are any stocks which sell for less than a dollar, and there is a

[8]Stanley S.C. Huang, *Investment Analysis and Management,* Winthrop Publishers Inc., Cambridge, Massachusetts, 1981. Chapter 3.

publication listing activity in penny stocks. A number of these, primarily speculative oil and gas issues, are traded actively in Denver--and Denver has the reputation of being a "penny stock exchange," though in fact Denver does not have a regional exchange organized for the exclusive purpose of selling penny stocks.

The *organized exchanges* are of two types: regional and national. In terms of relative importance, the New York Stock Exchange (NYSE), a national exchange, is clearly the most important, representing (in 1975) 80% of total share volume. The American Stock Exchange (AMEX), the other national exchange, accounts for about 10% of the activity, and all other activity (including regional exchanges) make up the remaining 10%.[8] However, depending on the circumstances, regional exchanges can be important for an entrepreneur seeking a broader base of exposure.

Regional exchanges - Regional exchanges provide a regulated market for OTC stocks; each exchange has its own criteria for membership and charges a listing fee. The principal regional exchanges are: Boston, Midwest (Chicago), Pacific, Philadelphia/Baltimore/Washington, and Cincinnati.

Regional exchanges employ specialists who maintain a fair, orderly and competitive market and steady a stock's performance. As a result, the spread between the bid and asked price is usually closer than in the OTC market.[9] In addition, most regional markets list some of their stocks nationally.

To give some idea of the range in membership qualifications from region to region--

> Boston has a listing fee of $3500 and an annual membership cost of $500.

> Philadelphia has a listing fee of $5000 and an annual membership cost of $1000.

> Pacific Exchange has a listing fee of $5000 and an annual membership cost of $750.

Regional stock exchange do not deal exclusively in regional stocks. Some West Coast companies who desire a marketplace in the East and are not prepared to join a New York exchange choose an exchange in the East or the Midwest and vice versa. In addition, some of the regional exchange members also belong to the NYSE or AMEX. Finally, a regional listing does not prevent a stock from being traded between brokers off the exchange.

National Exchanges - There are two: The New York Stock Exchange (NYSE) and the American Stock Exchange (AMEX). To be eligible for trading at these levels, a company must show a minimum of $400,000 in pre-tax earnings for AMEX and a minimum of $2.5 million for the NYSE.

---

[9]*Venture Magazine,* "Is a Self-Underwriting Worth It?", July 1981, p. 12.

Exhibit 1

SAMPLE TIMETABLE

The following is a sample timetable to be used as a guide in a public stock offering:

	Tentative Agenda and Time Schedule
July 18	Meeting of Board of Directors to receive and act upon proposals for stock offering.
July 29	Prepare Registration Statement and other corporate documents hereinafter referred to.
August 10	Financial Statements made available by accountants. Send Registration Statement to printer.
August 14	Execute Registration Statement and mail to SEC.
August 17	Registration Statement filed with SEC.
August 17-21	Meeting of Board of Directors of (the "Company") at which following action is taken: (a) Adopt Amendment to Articles reclassifying stock; (b) Authorized execution of Agreement and Plan of Reorganization between the Company and its stockholders; (c) Adopt Amended By-laws. Increase number of directors; (d) Ratify preparation and filing of Blue Sky applications; (e) Elect additional officers. Prepare and file Blue Sky applications.
August 24-28	Tax ruling received.
August 27	Special meeting of stockholders of Company is to be held approving the matters previously adopted or approved by the Board of Directors, and electing new directors. File certificate of amendment to articles of incorporation.
September 4-8	Deficiency memorandum received from SEC.
September 4-10	Note: This is predicated upon receiving the deficiency memorandum at the end of 20 days. This date varies depending upon the time schedule of the SEC at the time of filing. Prepare and file Amendment No. 1 with the SEC.
September 8	Due diligence meeting of underwriters.
September 14	Issue new temporary stock certificates evidencing the stock recapitalization. Procure, affix and cancel Federal documentary issuance and transfer tax stamps. File report of issuance of shares. Execute agreement among stockholders.

Special meeting of Board of Directors of Company authorizing execution of Underwriting Agreement, fixing price and authorizing appointment of transfer agent and registrar.

Execute Underwriting Agreement.

Prepare and send price amendment to SEC.

Complete Blue Sky qualification.

September 15   Price amendment is filed and Registration Statement becomes effective.

September 16   Public offering of stock by Underwriters.

Release press release on notice of receipt of order of Commission. Underwriters' counsel mails 25 copies of Prospectus to SEC (Rule 424(c)).

Managing Underwriter informs Sellers as to names, denominations in which shares are to be issued, with copy to transfer agent.

September 23   Closing date.

Source: Winter, Elmer L. *A Complete Guide to Making A Public Stock Offering*. New Jersey: Prentice Hall Inc., 1970.

A SHORT GLOSSARY OF
SECURITIES TERMINOLOGY

Annual Report: A company's statement of financial and other activities which, by law, must be sent to its shareholders once a year.

Blue Sky Laws: A popular name for state statutes providing for the regulation and supervision of securities offerings and sales, for the protection of citizen-investors from investing in fraudulent companies.

Cold comfort letter: A letter from an accountant to management, stating his opinion of the financial statements included in the prospectus.

Convertible debentures:: Bonds or debentures issued with the privilege of converting them into common stocks at a later date; an investment alternative attractive to investors particularly in start-up companies.

Due diligence: The legal standard defining the responsibility both of management and the underwriter to include all relevant material in the disclosure document.

Insiders: Management and 10% equity security holders. Insiders must report their transactions in the company's equity securities to the SEC annually, or, in some cases, quarterly.

IPO: Initial Public Offering.

NASD: National Association of Securities Dealers, Inc., a self-regulatory body which enforces its own regulations upon its members (in addition to SEC and state regulators).

Opinion letter: A letter from a lawyer to management, stating his opinion of the legal issues raised in the disclosure document.

OTC: Over-the-counter — a decentralized system for trading shares of publicly-held stock, where trades are reported between individual brokers.

Prospectus: A disclosure document prepared by a company intending to raise equity capital; submitted to prospective investors, and to the SEC (if the company intends to make a public offering) as part of the registration statement.

Red herring: An advance copy of the prospectus to be filed with the SEC preceding an issue of securities. The copy is marked in red ink, "not a solicitation, for information only."

Rule 144: For private placements, Rule 144 states that securities cannot be sold unless a public market already exists, and the securities must be fully paid for and held for two years. Form 144 must be filed with the SEC before any transaction can be made.

Rule 147: In intrastate offerings, Rule 147 defines the circumstances under which a company may qualify for this alternative.

SEC: The Securities and Exchange Commission, the federal body with which all public offerings must be "registered" unless an exemption is available. Established by the Securities Act of 1933.

SEC-Exemptions: Regulation A Offerings, Intrastate Offerings, Private Placements.

Sophisticated investors: For private placements, the definition of those eligible to invest. Sophisticated investors are distinguished from the general public, on the assumption that their greater understanding of securities transactions enables them to understand more fully the degree of risk they assume when making the investment.

Stock options: The guarantee that a prospective investor can purchase a particular number of shares for an agreed-upon price on or before a particular time; usually used as an incentive for management.

Tombstone ad: A notice, circular or advertisement of a stock offering containing language to the effect that the announcement is neither an offer to sell nor a solicitation of an offer to buy any of the securities listed. The actual offer is made only by the prospectus.

Warrant: An order or draft payable on presentation when funds are available, or at a fixed date with interest if so ordered; underwriters often demand warrants from client companies as part of their compensation.

10 K: Annual disclosure form
10 Q: Quarterly disclosure form
 8 K: Current report

By law, these forms must be filed with the SEC by publicly held companies.

DIRECT MARKETING TECHNIQUES
INFORMATION AND CONCEPTS FOR ENTREPRENEURS

"Trial offer - absolutely free. Satisfaction guaranteed or your money back."

If you cannot resist reading offerings of this sort when they appear in your mailbox, you know how effective the sales strategy of direct marketing can be. As an entrepreneur, you should know about direct marketing because it is possible that the concept may play some part in your overall marketing strategy, or in that of your competitors. This note will introduce you to the concept and the key elements of the strategy.

SOME BASIC DEFINITIONS

What is Direct Marketing? The Direct Mail/Marketing Association (DMMA), after struggling to describe the term as comprehensively as possible, proposed the following definition:

> Direct Marketing is the total of activities by which products and services are offered to market segments in one or more media for informational purposes or to solicit a direct response from a present or potential contributor or customer by mail, telephone or other sources.[1]

Another expert in the field puts it more bluntly:

> (A) recent development in the (mail-order) business is the use of the fancy new name "direct marketing." One of the advantages of the term is that it doesn't exclude telephone selling, as does the name "mail-order business." But the main purpose of the new name is to impress potential investors with a new, exciting image of the business. Since most people don't know the name "direct marketing," we'll stick to "mail-order business."[2]

---

[1]Richard Hodgson, *Direct Mail and Mail Order Handbook,* Dartnell Publishing Company, 1977.

[2]Julian Simon, *How to Start and Operate a Mail Order Business,* McGraw-Hill, 1981, p. XIV.

In this note we'll use the term "direct marketing," by which we mean a sales technique used by all businesses which deal with customers at a distance, without face-to-face selling.

At this point, a few more definitions may be useful.

Direct Mail is a special type of direct marketing, in which a mailing piece is sent directly to a targeted group of customers to generate orders. (Direct mail includes catalogues, flyers, and letters.)

Mail order describes the way the customers order the merchandise (though, as was pointed out earlier, the telephone is included as well). The product solicitation may be in the form of an advertisement in a publication, an ad on the radio or TV, designed to attract customers whose names are not yet known to the merchant offering the goods--or it may be a direct mail solicitation, as described above.

In this note we'll concentrate on the basics of direct mail marketing--direct marketing efforts which focus on direct mailing as the primary method of generating sales.

BACKGROUND: THE DIRECT MARKETING EXPLOSION

Mail-order has been an effective method of selling for many years. Catalogues and flyers sent to prospective customers have generated sales of every sort. Customers liked the convenience, the uniqueness of the product, the price--and the anticipation of waiting for the merchandise to arrive.

In the 1960s, however, mail/phone order sales expanded rapidly. Solicitations, and orders, soared. The reasons usually given for the boom are these:

> The computer and its ability to print lists on labels and write "personalized" letters;

> The modernization of the U.S. Postal Service and the introduction of zip codes;

> The popularity of credit cards;

> The increase in working women, with less time to shop and more money to spend;

> The increase in gasoline prices and the inconvenience of parking near stores in many downtown areas.

Direct mail found its way into a number of businesses where it had not been before. Retail outlets mailed catalogues and flyers to their customers as a way of expanding store sales and profits. Industrial companies used direct mail to restructure their sales forces, in some instances reducing the size of an inefficient organization while increasing sales.

Service industries, especially insurance and real estate, used direct mailings to expand their lists of potential customers, and to cut down on unprofitable "cold calls." Billions of mailing pieces filled an increasing number of mailboxes every year.

The 1970s witnessed some refinements in the use of direct marketing techniques. One was the emergence of a more specialized approach to targeting potential recipients of direct marketing efforts. This refinement was represented by the "specialty catalogue" companies, presenting a small collection of merchandise chosen to appeal to certain targeted groups--for example, "upscale" urban professionals, gourmet cooks, fly fishermen. The impetus was provided by Roger Horchow, a successful buyer for Neiman-Marcus, whose "Collection" of tasteful merchandise was made available exclusively by mail to a group of proven shop-by-mail buyers, beginning with a nucleus of credit-card holders and charge-account customers of luxury stores. Based on the success of the Horchow Collection, many retail stores introduced their own mail-order collections, often operated separately. A few other exclusively mail-order operations attempted to emulate Horchow, though this proved a risky proposition--"a ticket to going bust," as one authority termed it--and more than one entrepreneur went bankrupt in the attempt to start up and operate a full-scale mail-order business.

Statistically, how big is the mail-order boom? Since mail-order is a method of marketing and not necessarily a business in itself, broadly-based statistics about its effectiveness are difficult to compile. However, reports from a number of different sources confirm that the boom is booming, and is responsible for an increasing number of sales each year. Here are a few examples:

> In 1978, total sales for gifts and home furnishings through direct marketing grossed over $2 billion.
>
> Mail-order sales, as a whole, are growing at an annual rate of 8 to 12 percent, and show no sign of declining.[3]
>
> A recent A.C. Nielsen poll shows that 66% of the respondents buy from mail-order catalogues at least once.
>
> L.L. Bean, a sporting goods store in Maine which depends heavily on catalogue sales, grossed $9.9 million in 1970 and $115 million in 1980.
>
> J.C. Penney, which started a catalogue business from scratch to augment its retail sales, showed in the first half of 1979 a 4% increase in store sales and a 26% increase in catalogue orders.

---

[3]Maxwell Sroge, "Establishing a Mail Order Business," articles collected by *Encyclopedia Britannica, Inc.,* Library Research Service, Chicago, IL 60611.

You know something big is happening when the Federal Trade Commission gets interested. They did in 1975, and passed a series of regulatory measures designed to protect the consumer against dilatory mail-order operators. The FTC stipulated that:

> Merchandise must be received within 30 days, unless otherwise specified. If not, prompt refund must be made upon request. After 60 days, a full refund must be made automatically.

In addition, an increasing number of suits have been brought against fraudulent or misleading mail-order solicitations by two government watchdog agencies--the U.S. Postal Service and the Food and Drug Administration.

No matter where you look, the evidence of a boom in direct mailing is unmistakable.

ADVANTAGES OF DIRECT MAIL MARKETING

The explosion in direct mail marketing is based not only on changes in consumer lifestyles and shopping habits but also on some fundamental advantages unique to the technique itself. The DMMA has identified a number of these, the most important of which are listed here:

1. Direct mail marketing can be targeted at specific individuals or organizations identified as prime prospects, and the solicitation can be made personal to the point of being absolutely confidential.

2. The solicitation is a single advertiser's individual message and is not in competition with other advertising and/or editorial material.

3. It can be controlled for specific jobs of research, reaching small groups, testing ides, appeals, reactions.

4. It can be produced according to the needs of the advertiser's own immediate schedule and can be timed to coincide with supplementary promotional efforts.

5. It provides an effective means for the reader to act or buy through response devices difficult to employ when using other media such as space ads or radio and TV spots.

KEY FACTORS IN A DIRECT MAIL MARKETING CAMPAIGN

1. Identifying the Customer

The entrepreneur who has developed a product he desires to sell by direct mail solicitation must somehow *identify his potential customers by name.* He cannot rely upon an anonymous customer who just happened to be walking by a display of his merchandise, such as in a retail store. Nor can he rely upon the personal contact which a face-to-face salesman can use to turn an anonymous face into an interested buyer. For the mail-order entrepreneur, a general profile of his hoped-for market is not enough; he must know their names and where they live.

Here is one example of a successful initial effort:

"Annie Hurlbut is an anthropologist who, when she was at Yale, spent her sophomore summer working at an archeological dig in Peru. There, she encountered the alpaca, a cameloid animal related to the vicuna and the llama...The alpaca is raised mainly for its extraordinary wool, which is lightweight, warm, and grows naturally in a variety of colors, from white to beige, brown and gray.

"Ms. Hurlbut returned to Peru again as a graduate student in anthropology, but this time for her thesis research on women who sell in primitive markets. Among their wares were handloomed alpaca garments, which were warm and practical but not exactly stylish.

"So, Annie Hurlbut turned designer. She worked with Peruvians to design sweaters with more flair so they would be more acceptable to North American women. With her first stock, she returned to the Hurlbut farm in Tonganoxie, Kansas, and started a mail-order catalog business called, "The Peruvian Connection," with her mother as a partner. They produced a catalog and some ads and with this Annie Hurlbut was in the mail-order business.

"Some of Annie's early ads were as primitive as the natives. And the first 'catalog' was really no more than an amateurish flyer. But the first ads and catalogs sold enough merchandise to pay the bills with some left over to reinvest. Clearly, alpaca styled by Annie and woven by Peruvians overcame any lack of sophistication in mail-order techniques. Annie Hurlbut's sense of style, plus alpaca's uniqueness worked. Annie learned quickly that the secret to building a mail-order business was in developing a customers file as quickly as possible, and then to offer those customers other items."*

Though one would like to know more about how Annie compiled her first mailing list, it is reasonable to assume that she relied upon friends, professional colleagues, and friends of friends--and advertisements. One can also surmise that her list produced a high yield of responses, though it may have been small in numbers, because of the personal way she had chosen her potential customers. Regardless of the details, however, Annie successfully compiled a nucleus of NAMES which she converted into buyers of Peruvian alpaca.

2. Developing the List: Two Ways

For many entrepreneurs, Annie's methods of identifying customers would be too slow. Assuming they have compiled a profile of their would-be buyer, they should explore two proven strategies for reaching their market:

- Renting or buying lists
- Advertising in selected media, especially publications.

---

*Bob Stone, *Advertising Age*, January 5, 1981.

List Rental. The traffic in lists is a lucrative byproduct of the mail-order boom. Entrepreneurs calling themselves "list brokers," are so numerous that they are classified separately in the Yellow Pages. Some of the lists identify specific groups of people: charge account customers of retail stores, credit card holders, subscribers to certain publications, professional associations, and alumni groups. Some are based on voting lists and zip code numbers. Others are composite lists, tested and refined, and classified by average order size. Specific lists are usually rented for a flat fee; composite lists are priced according to their yield. (For example, a list with $15 average order size can be rented for about $30 per thousand names, with a standard minimum of 5000 names; a list averaging $60 an order may rent for $80 per thousand names.) The entrepreneur will soon find that the art of renting and swapping lists is highly developed, and that nurturing and maintaining a good list is an important element of success.

Here are several illuminating incidents.

One publisher who has long been considered a direct marketing sage, Ralph Ginsburg, former publisher of "Eros," is so enamored of list rental income that he relies on it as the sole profit-producer for his publications. Upon the introduction of a new magazine, "American Business," at $1 a year, Ginsburg informed an interviewer that each of his customers would receive 110 mailing pieces from other companies renting his list that year! "We're essentially in the list business," he says. "It's the list business that bails out the whole company."[4]

And:

The list is one of the most, if not the most, important ingredient for success in direct marketing. Some marketers insist that the right list will sell anything. To illustrate, a Boston-based company preparing to release its first catalogue rented 12 of the most proven, most expensive lists. They arrived, ready for mailing, on self-adhesive stickers, and as the marketing manager looked them over, he discovered that one man's name was on every single list. He learned two things in a hurry. First, the immense value of a list made up of names like that of the duplicated man. Second, the cost savings to the company of computerized duplication elimination, which would soon pay for itself in subsequent mailings. By the way, that man did buy from that catalogue and continued to buy thousands of dollars of merchandise for the next several years.[5]

Advertising. The second way to add names of potential customers to your list is by advertising--in national or regional magazines and in newspapers. The trick is to find the right publications for your products, the ones your potential customers read.

Advertising serves two purposes: to generate sales, and to attract inquiries; and some experts would argue that the promotional purpose is the most important one. Top mail

---

[4]Michael Stedman, "Direct Marketing" (unpublished).

[5]*Ibid.*

order operators say they don't expect to make a profit on the sale that pulls in the customer's initial order. All they hope to achieve with those sales is to cover the costs of the advertising and build their mailing list.[6] A typical advertisement would feature one product, a bit of lively description, and a line saying, "For more information, write to..." If successful, new names should start arriving in your mailbox soon after the ad appears.

Responses to ads are also tools for your market research. Which publications produced the greatest response? Which sold the most merchandise? Which products (if you are advertising more than one) were the most popular? To capture this information, you should key each response with a code identifying where it came from.

Your choice of publications requires a feel for who your customers are and some knowledge of the publishing world. *ABC, the Audit Bureau of Circulation,* collects and certifies circulation figures on a wide variety of publications. However, quality will pay off before quantity in most instances. The more specialized the publication, the greater concentration of potential customers will see the ad. Since advertising rates vary greatly, initial efforts must often be a trade-off between optimum placement and the pocketbook. You need to experiment to see what works the best.

A final word on good lists. They must be constantly augmented and refined in order to remain productive (a 25% annual turnover is standard in the industry). It is essential to develop an efficient system for keeping lists current--and for adding information about the source of the customer and the number of purchases he makes. If affordable, a computer is a great boon. In any event, list-keeping is so crucial to mail order that Roger Horchow prescribes that a minium of 10% of the overall budget be allocated to that activity.

The Telephone. The telephone is an increasingly important method of communication between mail-order firm and customer--in both directions.

First, the customer can call in orders. Telephone consultants believe that the 24-hour-a-day option provided by telephone ordering is one of the most powerful advantages of direct marketing. The "800" number plus the credit card make it easy for the customer to place an impulse order, and once a customer has tried ordering by phone he is much more likely to form the habit. Surveys show that the use of an "800" number will increase sales 25% to 30%, thus paying for itself in a short period of time. Your telephone number should be prominently featured in both your catalogue and your advertising.

Second, the entrepreneur can call out. A well-designed telephone marketing campaign can sell certain products, especially magazine subscriptions, very effectively. A telephone survey can also be useful before launching a new product. Telephone follow-ups on orders produce needed information quickly. However, a word of caution from a veteran mail-order entrepreneur:

> While it might be more prudent for a small, cash-tight
> business to develop its own initial direct mail campaigns,

---

[6]"Making Good in Your Own Mail-Order Business," *Changing Times,* October 1980.

most experts agree that telephone marketing is best left to the pros.

3. Preparing the Mailing Piece[7]

The overall appearance of your mailing piece is a primary determinant of success in the mail-order field. Particularly because of the increasing competition in the marketplace, the first impression created in the prospective buyer's mind is crucial. This section, and the next, will discuss how to prepare and evaluate your catalogue.

The total visual presentation begins with the cover. A generally accepted rule of thumb is that no selling is done on the front cover, but the back cover is space well used for displaying items. Other "hot spots" include the inside front and back covers, the center spread, the page facing the order form, and pages 3, 4, and 5. The following chart shows how page placement of an item can affect sales. (See Table 1)

Table I
Catalog Layout

Catalog Page Numbers	Percent Above Average Sales
1- 9	58%
10-19	60%
20-29	55%
30-39	47.5%
40-49	37.5%
50-59	35%

Source: Bursk, Edward C. and Stephen A. Greyser, *Advanced Cases in Marketing Management*, Prentice-Hall, Englewood Cliffs, NJ, 1966, p. 95.

Whether to group merchandise by particular categories is another controversy in the catalog field. Some operators arrange their books this way and others advise against it lest a catagory turn off a reader and prevent him/her from reading the rest of the catalog. Most, however, advocate use of a particular theme. Examples are a special sale catalog, an all luxury item catalog, a catalog of gifts for men, etc.

Color is a major cost item and should be given careful thought. Most, but not all, items sell better when pictured in color. However, both the cost of color separations and of high-quality coated paper required for color printing are of such magnitude that they need to be weighed carefully against such factors as expected sales volume per run, number of catalogs printed per run, and number of runs scheduled per year.

---

[7]Collins, Dun and Mateau, "Marketing Through Mail Order Catalogs," Portions of Sections 3 and 4 are used with permission of a student paper, done at Babson College, Fall 1980.

Most statisticians can prove that a relationship exists between thickness of the catalog and sales. In general, the thicker the book the better. Better to reduce the overall size of the catalog than to reduce the number of pages to where the book resembles a flyer more than a catalog. Some catalog houses use different sizes at different times of the year.

Precise descriptions are essential to compiling a mail order catalog. The copy should include sizes, materials, color selections, etc., along with some selling copy. The catalog should also include a clear and simple statement of your guarantee.

Various sales stimulators can be employed to increase the success and profitability of a catalog operation. Among these are:

- Overwraps - (paper sleeves which fit over the catalog, announcing a special bonus)
- Telephone orders
- Incentives for early orders
- Bank cards
- Free trial periods
- Free gifts or discounts tied to size of order

A critical element of successful catalog layout is the order form. It should have sufficient space for number and description of the item, size, color, dollar amount, and imprinting where appropriate. Nothing should be left to chance.

Finally, a word must be said about catalog costs in general. Costs fall into three categories: set-up, printing and mailing. Set-up includes writing and typesetting copy, photographing merchandise, having line drawings made, and doing layout -- the work of a graphic artist. Printing costs include many variables: overall catalog dimensions, number of pages, type, weight and finish of paper, color separations (if used), type of ink (regular or metallic), type of binding, type of cover, to mention only the most obvious. Mailing costs continue to rise, and the weight of the catalog is a factor here. In addition, the price of printing and affixing address labels must be included. A "good" catalog is vital to certain direct mail operations, but it does not come cheap.

4. Tracking Profits

Key decisions must be made about the catalog which will affect its future, such as which merchandise to display and how many pages the catalog will be. Once the items have been chosen, tracking the catalog's success becomes of greatest importance.

Space is extremely valuable and more space should be allocated for the more profitable items. Two measures of profitability are used:

GIPM — Gross Item Profitability Measure

NIPM — Net Item Profitability Measure

Let us look at an example to see how this works:

Picture requires	3 square inches
Copy requires	2 square inches
Cost/catalog square inch	$2.20
Therefore, space costs =	$11.00
Selling Price	$5.20
Cost	$2.40

If we sell 1,354, our sales are	$ 7,041
Cost of goods sold =	3,249
Advertising cost	1,100
Gross	$ 2,692

Our gross item profitability measure is 38% of sales and this should be calculated and tracked for every item in the catalog to see if it is more or less profitable than other items. The net measure would be figured by assigning a portion of the operating costs (making adjustments for different shipping costs and storage costs). Both measures should be used to track the attractiveness of an item and they should be used for planning the next catalog edition.

Another item which should be carefully calculated is the average sales return per catalog. This will help determine the worth of particular lists and make projections about the long term viability of the operation. Assume planning and projections result in an estimated response rate of 1.5% for all catalogs sent, and an average order size of $42. The resulting response factor is 63¢ (.015 x $42). However, if the response rate were in fact only 1.2% and the average order size $66, the response factor would be 79.2¢ per catalog. On the other hand, with a 1.2% response rate and an average order size of only $48, the response factor is only 57.6¢ (See Table II for the required equations.)

Table II

Required Order Size

$$S = \frac{A + (G+C) R}{R} \quad 1.00 - P$$

S = average order size required
A = advertising cost per thousand
G = current average COGS per order
C = average cost of fulfillment and all other applicable cost minus advertising and COGS
R = expected responses per thousand
P = profit required

Markup on Costs

$$M = S \times P$$

M = markup
S = average order size required
P = cost of goods sold

5. Calculating the Dollar Value of a Customer

Another important profit measurement is the Dollar Value of a Customer. This figure indicates the total profit (not volume, but profit) that a customer will bring you over time. It is important as a standard against which to evaluate the promotional costs associated with attracting customers -- advertising and others. Without knowing the dollar value of a customer, you cannot know if the dollars spent in promotion are contributing to profit.

The dollar value of a customer, exclusive of promotion, may be calculated as follows:

- The dollars of revenue you expect to get from the customer in each year.
- The cost to you of filling each of his orders.
- Your "cost of capital," that is, the worth to you today of a dollar in net revenues a year or two hence.

The simplest example would be a one-shot purchase:

> ...say a camera sold by Bell & Howell from a Diners Club list mailing...The revenue from the first sale is all that Bell and Howell will get from the customer. And the costs of the camera are relatively easy to figure because they all will be incurred immediately. And you do not need to know the "cost of capital" because all the revenues and costs will occur within a short time...So the value of a customer to Bell & Howell is simply the sales price minus the cost of goods sold and the cost of servicing the order. (Notice that the cost of the advertisement that solicits the customer is NOT included in this calculation of the value of a customer.[8]

Based on the above, Bell & Howell could compare the cost of preparing and running the advertisement, divided by the number of orders, to the profit per camera sold. If the expense did not cover the profit, the promotion resulted in a net loss, regardless of the number of cameras sold.

However, life is seldom so simple. Repeat customers are the backbone of successful mail-order solicitation, and their value extends over time. Therefore, dollar value per customer must be based on the amount of merchandise the customer is expected to buy over time. It is easy to see that a proven customer who will provide a steady source of income is worth spending more for initially--and that to calculate dollar value on an initial purchase alone is to risk scrapping promotional activities that may pay off handsomely over time.

---

[8]Julian Simon, *How to Start and Operate a Mail Order Business,* McGraw-Hill, 1981, p. 106.

6. Overall Profitability: Goals and Projections

Profitability in the mail-order business is a function of accurate planning and forecasting. Goals should be set, and step-by-step implementation should be worked out prior to set-up. Some specific examples will help to illustrate.

Roger Horchow suggests that a profitable income statement should look like this:

Sales	100%
Operating Costs	10%
Merchandise	50%
Catalogue	24%
Fixed Overhead	6%
Profit before Taxes	10%
Taxes	5%
Profit after Taxes	5%

Let us assume that your annual budget breaks down approximately this way. That is still no guarantee of profitability, as Horchow is quick to add, even if your sales projection is accurate. Day-to-day success depends on two important projections: costs, and cash flow.

Costs. A general list of costs associated with each item on the balance sheet would include the following:

Catalog: printing and paper, photography, typography, envelopes or wraps, order blanks, labels, postage, list rental, labor.

Merchandise*: cost, warehousing, shipping, insurance

Operating costs: order processing and fulfillment, carrying costs of inventory, list maintenance, packing and shipping, advertising

General fixed overhead: rent and lights, telephone, salaries, office supplies, dues and subscriptions, interest, taxes.

But what about:

- returned merchandise (e.g., 20% for ready-to-wear items)
- merchandise that must be replaced because it arrived at the customer's address damaged

_____

*Some mail-order concerns "drop-ship" merchandise, which means that the supplier actually stocks and ships your product.

- bad debts
- lost shipments
- bank charges
- management costs--a buyer-consultant, advertising designer, accountant
- indirect labor (truck drivers, supervisors, etc.)

Failure to anticipate every conceivable cost, including those caused by Murphy's law, can bring down the business. One useful technique for avoiding disaster is to run numbers under three different sets of assumptions--best case, worst case, and something in the middle--to help you identify the circumstances under which failure is inevitable.

Cash flow. Failure to provide adequate cash flow is the entrepreneur's nemesis. One sadder but wiser mail-order entrepreneur comments:

> The easiest thing in the world is to boost sales dramatically with a direct marketing program that generates losses faster than cash. Virtually no direct marketing business in retail can start out profitably. The trick is to roll over the new customers fast enough for a reorder so that the negative cash flow doesn't force the business into bankruptcy before it starts turning a profit--and that typically takes two to three years.[9]

A drop-shipper allows you to draw on his inventory and ships individual mail orders to your customers. You do the advertising, receive the orders, and send them to the supplier along with the proper remittance (you keep the difference between the advertised price and the wholesale price charged by the drop-shipper). The advantages: you don't have to invest in inventory and you don't have to pay packing and shipping costs. The disadvantages: you earn less money per sale; in effect, you're sharing the profits with the drop-shipper.[10] To bridge the gap between expenses and receipts, especially in the beginning before receipts start to flow steadily, a cushion of capital is usually necessary. How large the cushion should be is difficult to say; it depends on the operation. An entrepreneur selling one item by direct marketing as a sideline to a business he has already established may need just enough to cover the cost of the mailing--he is the "How I Started a Business with $500..." person you read about in ads for how-to books. On the other hand, an entrepreneur starting up a large-scale mail-order operation will need considerably more, upwards of $100,000.

---

[9]Michael Stedman, "Direct Marketing," (Unpublished).

[10]See "Basics for Money Makers: Mail Order," *Income Opportunities,* December-January 1981.

The aim of the cash flow chart, and the capital cushion, should be to minimize the cash crunch described above: where today's receipts are needed to pay for merchandise shipped several months ago, and the money required to pay for the goods you are shipping today lies in a dim and uncertain future. This situation is a treadmill to oblivion.

Again, it will be helpful to prepare cash flows under varying assumptions--to identify potential cash crunches before they happen, and to plan ahead to offset them.

FRANCHISING

INFORMATION AND CONCEPTS FOR ENTREPRENEURS

> The Franchise offered an opportunity to own, and yet not to own, a risk and yet to be cautious. It democratized business enterprise by offering a man with small capital and no experience access to the benefits of large capital, large-scale experiment, national advertising, and established reputations. It also democratized and leveled consumption by offering the same foods and drinks and services in all sorts of neighborhoods, across the country. It created new forms of independence. It lessened the differences between times and places, between ways of selling and buying anything and anything else. It added new ambiguities to the relations among buyer and seller and maker. It altered the experience of things, and created another frontier of vagueness.
>
> Daniel Boorstein
> *The Democratic Experience*

INTRODUCTION: SCOPE OF NOTE

This note presents an overview of franchising for the entrepreneur whose venture may cast him into either of two roles: the franchisor (one seeking to multiply his concept), or the franchisee (one buying the right to operate the venture from the owner of the idea). The note recognizes that the perspective of the franchisor is greatly different from that of the franchisee, and examines the key considerations in franchising from both points of view.

Franchising, here, is treated as a start-up alternative to an independent venture, though the entrepreneur should be aware that franchising may arise as an issue at a later time in the lifestyle of a venture. As a start-up alternative it is evaluated in terms of different venture objectives.

DEFINITION

A franchise can be defined as a contract to distribute and sell goods and services within a specified area. The word *franchise* evolved from the old French word for "free", implying a special privilege. It was extended to mean the right to vote, and, further, to the right of an inventor to allow others to use his invention. The term gained recognition in this country with the advent of the mass-marketed automobile and the decision of the manufacturing companies to distribute their products to the public through certain independent businessmen on whom had been conferred the "special privilege" of selling their cars. A contract stating the rights and obligations of both parties became necessary in order for the manufacturers to assure that profits were returned to them regularly in return for providing cars to dealers. This contract, defining the terms of the franchise, is still at the heart of the franchise method of doing business.

RECENT BACKGROUND: FEDERAL TRADE COMMISSION LEGISLATURE

In the past generation, franchising expanded far beyond a form of business used exclusively by automobile manufacturers and a few others. By 1980, franchising accounted for almost a third of *all* retail sales. According to U.S. Department of Commerce statistics of that year, over 500,000 establishments were "franchises" with combined sales exceeding $300 billion -- a sales increase of 18% since 1978, and of hundreds-fold since the first auto dealers became semi-dependent entrepreneurs.

Franchising also became recognized by the American Bar Association as a distinct area of anti-trust law. The explosive growth of franchising began in the fast food industry, and rapidly spread to everything from real estate to eyeglasses. The boom was so sudden that a uniform body of regulations could not keep up with the action. The legal status of franchising under the federal anti-trust laws had not been adequately defined, and state legislation and court decisions varied widely. Almost without exception, the franchisee who believed he had been treated unjustly was the loser in subsequent adjudication; the franchisor had ultimate control of the inventory utilized by the franchisee, as well as the power to operate a two-tier distribution system, whereby a company store could provide direct competition for a franchisee. In addition, if the franchisee failed, the franchisor could maintain the option to reacquire or resell the operation. If the franchisee broke any part of the original contract in an effort to better his own situation, he was found to have violated his contractual obligation to the franchisor, and thus had no recourse to bring legal action against him.

In 1971, California rewrote its state anti-trust rules to give franchisees access to meaningful means of relief from unfair franchisor restrictions, and by 1978 many other states had followed suit. Recognizing, at last, that franchising had assumed national proportions, the Federal Trade Commission drafted a new set of rules governing the establishment of franchises in 1978, and it became law in 1979.

The rules are designed to protect both parties involved, especially the franchisee, from entering an agreement under false or misleading pretenses. Basic disclosure documents, covering 20 categories of information, must be presented and discussed at the first meeting between the two parties where the possible purchase/sale of the franchise is discussed. However, the rule does not regulate the substantive terms of the franchisor/franchisee contract, nor does it require registration or approval from the FTC.

The disclosure rules apply only to two types of franchises, defined in the rule and summarized below:

> 1. Package and Product Franchises. The three elements common to these types of franchises are: distribution of goods or services associated with the franchisor's trademark; significant control of, or significant assistance to the franchisee's method of operation; and required payments by the franchisee to the franchisor. Examples of package franchises are fast food chains, car washes, tax preparing services. Product franchises usually involve distribution rights for the franchisor's product -- door-to-door cosmetics, brushes, certain tablewares, the Encyclopedia Britannica.
>
> 2. Business Opportunity Ventures. This category is covered by the rule if each of the following three elements is present:
>
> (a) The franchisee sells goods or services supplied by the franchisor or its affiliate, or by suppliers with which it is required by the franchisor to do business.
>
> (b) The franchisor secures retail outlets or accounts for the goods or services, or secures locations for vending devices or racks, or provides the services of a person to do either.
>
> (c) The franchisee is required to pay the franchisor or an affiliated person in order to obtain or commence the franchised business.

The most common examples of business opportunity franchising are distributorships, rack jobbing and vending machine routes. In these ventures, the franchisor contracts with the franchisee to be a distributor for goods or services usually provided for a third party; the franchisee pays a fee in return for the franchisor's guarantee of pre-selected locations or routes, the product/service to be distributed, and the necessary expertise so to do.

The disclosure rules do *NOT* apply to a number of other types of franchises, including:

• Fractional franchises, when an established distributor adds a franchised product line to its existing repertoire;

• Leased departments, when independent retailers rent space in a larger retail establishment to sell their own product exclusively;

• Oral agreements, when there is no written evidence of financial or other guarantees on the part of either party.

The new rules are an important step in regulating the franchising industry, but many experts argue that they do not go far enough -- the exclusions are too broad, and the FTC has no power to prohibit unfair practices written into the disclosed documents. Nonetheless, every franchisee should be aware of his right to see a disclosure document, and every franchisor must prepare one with the most current information available. It should go without saying that any prospective franchisee or franchisor should consult legal counsel knowledgeable in franchise law before seriously considering a venture of this nature.

To underscore the entrepreneur's need for legal advice, there are technicalities caused by the new rule which go beyond it. The federal rule remains silent on certain points covered by pre-existing state laws, and some state laws go beyond the federal mandates. The following table *(Exhibit I)* gives some idea of the overlapping inherent in the present circumstances, and the necessity for finding a lawyer familiar with all relevant bodies of law - federal, state, and local.

Exhibit I

State Requirement	FTC Requirement	Franchisor must comply with
Disclosure of item X	(silent as to item X)	State Disclosure
Disclosure of item X	Disclosure of item X	FTC Disclosure Requirement
Disclosure of item X	Disclosure of items X, Y, Z	Both
Prohibits disclosure	Disclosure of item X	FTC Requirement
Registration; escrow	(silent as to items)	State Requirements
Disclosure by Franchisor X	(silent as to Franchisor X)	State Requirement
(silent as to Franchisor X)	Disclosure by Franchisor X	FTC Requirement
Disclosure by Franchisor X	Disclosure by Franchisor X & Y	State and FTC Requirement

THE TWO-WAY STREET

In a successful franchise the most important ingredient in the success has proved to be symbiosis -- that state of ongoing interdependence between franchisor and franchisee where each provides certain essential ingredients for the other. This symbiosis, or mutualism as it is often called in the extensive literature on the subject, will be a recurring theme in this note. Here, we will look briefly at the specific needs of each party, to see where the symbiosis lies.

The Franchisor. For the entrepreneur who has come up with a profitable way to sell or distribute goods or services, franchising offers a way to finance growth and generate revenue. The revenue comes from the fees paid by the franchisee; the growth comes from attracting an increasing number of franchisees to open new outlets.

However, unlike the administrator of a single operating entity the franchisor must monitor every single unit in his chain, since the franchise is no stronger than its weakest link. This requires controls at many levels. But if the control is not balanced by incentive and support for the franchisee, the unit will not produce as expected. The balance is delicate.

Characteristics of a successful franchisor usually include: a high degree of managerial ability; extensive knowledge of the marketplace; extreme sensitivity to cost and quality control; the ability to motivate people -- in short, a benevolent dictator.

The Franchisee. In contrast, the franchisee is usually looking for a risk-protected entrepreneurial opportunity, in which he can manage a business with an accepted name and image, receive training and other assistance, and put up a limited amount of capital as an entry fee. A recent survey in which franchisors were asked to describe the ideal franchisee suggests that financial soundness, with savings beyond the franchise fee, some college education, and previous experience operating any kind of business is desirable. Personality requirements include cheerfulness and cooperation; thinking ability, communicative skills and prior knowledge of product or equipment are not vitally important. If an entrepreneur fits this "good soldier" profile he may find that franchising is the most advantageous way to begin his career -- it is less risky than starting from scratch and less expensive than buying out a going concern.

However, a would-be franchisee should also consider the potential disadvantages: the enforced conformity to pre-set standards, the profit-sharing requirement; the vulnerability of the franchise as a whole if one unit performs poorly. The good franchisee is one who understands and accepts these conditions.

THE FRANCHISED START-UP: PROS AND CONS

What are the advantages and disadvantages -- for both franchisor and franchisee -- in a franchised start-up? The following list provides a number of considerations, and will serve as a framework for the subsequent discussion of The Franchise Checklist.

The Franchisor Start-Up (contrasted to the independent start-up)

Advantages

- Built-in sources of capital through franchise fees
- Self-financed incremental growth
- Cost savings through quantity purchasing
- Less risk when experimenting with new operating methods (using a single outlet as a test case)
- Less need for a large corporate administrative staff
- Additional sources of capital through franchisee lease-back: real estate, equipment

Disadvantages

- Vulnerability at the weakest link in the franchise chain
- Difficulty of raising outside capital until concept is proven
- Profits shared with franchisee and generally less than company owned units
- Control of operation reduced, and much more costly, as operation grows
- Conflicts between franchisor and franchisee more frequent than between corporate headquarters and company-owned outlets

The Franchisee Start-Up (contrasted to the independent start-up)

Advantages

- Less experience needed
- Less capital
- Established name and consumer image
- Operations training
- Locational analysis
- Ongoing assistance in management, R&D, personnel supervision, marketing
- Cooperative advertising
- Lower apparent failure rate

Disadvantages

- Dependence on franchisor
- Lack of control over franchisor's policies
- Limited exit flexibility
- Vulnerability to weakest link
- Profit and incentive conflicts with franchisor

THE FRANCHISE CHECKLIST

The following list of topics is discussed from two points of view -- the franchisor and the franchisee.

PRICING/FINANCING

As a franchisor, the price you set for each franchise must be related to its value. The value offered is in the form of market size and saturation, expected growth, and cost of services provided to the franchisee.

A franchisor may decide to have a several-tiered pricing strategy, depending on market size and services provided, in order to attract a variety of franchisees with varied expectations. A low initial fee usually implies that the franchisor desires quick expansion through easy entry. This strategy could be used in the early years of a franchise when the franchisor wishes to attract a substantial market share. It could also be used if the franchisor were aiming at the "mom and pop" franchisees with an expectation of slow but steady growth. In contrast, if the franchisor wishes to attract only franchisees with a strong capital position, he will set the initial fee high in an attempt to discourage investors with inadequate resources. This strategy may include a slow start-up period, requiring extra capital for the franchisor at the outset.

In addition to determining the initial price, the franchisor must make a series of other pricing decisions, including the amount and type of annual franchisee fees and the charge for the centralized goods and services he plans to provide. His strategy will be determined to a great extent by his priorities among three objectives: generating capital, maintaining control, and minimizing franchisor-franchisee conflict. Here are some of his alternatives, and the implications:

- Charging franchisees a flat fee. This provides the franchisor a known amount of dollars per franchise. Its effects on the franchisee are twofold: if he fails to meet the payment he may lose the franchise, but all earnings above the payment are entirely profit to him -- a powerful incentive.

- Charging franchisees a fixed percentage of sales. This provides the franchisor with a less predictable income. It also may produce franchisor-franchisee conflict. It would be in the franchisor's interest to have the franchisee maximize sales; the franchisee wishing to maximize his profit may prefer a sliding scale of percent of sales owed the franchisor.

- Charging the franchisee other annual assessments, including territorial rights. Unless these are clearly stated at the outset, and reasonable in amount, they may oppress the franchisee.

- Renting real estate and equipment to the franchisee. For the franchisor, this is frequently a necessity because of the high cost of land and certain expensive pieces of equipment (photography development, dry cleaning, for example). The franchisee may be grateful for this leaseback arrangement; however, he may resent it if he feels he is being overcharged.

• Selling equipment, raw materials and promotional aids to the franchisee. For the franchisor, selling directly to the franchisee has several advantages: a dependable source of revenue, and a dependable means of quality control. However, this is the area in which the independent-minded franchisee may be the most unhappy, especially if he believes he can buy the same quality of goods cheaper on his own. The franchisor must weigh carefully the benefits to him against the risk of antagonizing franchisees and stifling their motivation to increase both sales and profits.

From the franchisee's point of view, the price of the franchise and the ongoing fee structure must be evaluated against the earning potential and the risk. He must determine the extent to which the following considerations are met:

• Has the concept been tested thoroughly and adjusted? Is the concept now a proven and viable operation, allowing people with little or no experience in a given area to learn about that business rapidly and to own and operate that business?

• Is the failure rate among the system's franchises low and explainable?

• Are key services provided by the franchisor -- not only initially but on an ongoing basis: management training, accounting, personnel management, marketing research? What ongoing value does the franchisor provide that is unique or unusual?

• What economies are provided by the franchisor's central purchasing and manufacturing capabilities that offer significant cost savings?

• Does the system provide a recognized product/service to a known market? How does the system cultivate customer goodwill?

• Is the location of the franchise desirable?

The franchisee's assessment of the franchise in all of these areas will help him to determine whether the asking price and other fees are "fair." It should be repeated that the most successful franchisees are those who do not have to overextend themselves financially at the outset; if the fee is steep for your checkbook, perhaps you are looking at the wrong franchise.

SELECTION: THE FRANCHISOR-FRANCHISEE PARTNERSHIP

The issue of selection is crucial for both the franchisor and the franchisee. The franchisor must solicit, select and recruit the best franchisees possible for his venture. The franchisee must find the proper franchise partner for himself, under terms with which he is comfortable.

Some franchisors have found that the proper selection of a franchisee can be expensive but it is one of the key to building a strong system. The selection process has been called by some experts "the single most pervading operating problem in franchising."

Experience has shown that the franchisor should draw a profile of a successful franchisee. The skills essential to success should be established. The skills and aptitudes required to run a franchise which offers tax consulting services are different from those required to run a fast-food service.

A simple and practical technique has been to begin with a list of the activities the franchisee must do. The list then becomes the basis for understanding the skills and personality types that will maximize your chances for success; once you know who you're looking for they will be easier to find. Advertising in newspapers and trade publications are common ways to attract franchisees.

From the franchisor's point of view, as we have seen, the most attractive franchisees are those with substantial credit, some prior business experience, and a high desire to cooperate. But what about your needs as a franchisee? You should make a list, too. Include such items as desired income, financial security, location of job and desirable working hours, desired degree of autonomy, amount of assistance needed. In a sense, you are paying someone to be your boss -- and you should be satisfied about your end of the deal.

THE FRANCHISE CONTRACT

Since the passage of the FTC Disclosure Act franchisors are on notice that they must come to the bargaining table with all cards face up, and franchisees must be sure to ask a number of important questions. During this process, a lawyer is of utmost importance -- at least one for each party.

The following list of questions has been compiled by a group of franchisees; they believe that failure of a prospective franchisee to ask these questions invariably leads to a less than satisfactory situation after the contract is signed.

- The three most important considerations in buying a franchise are "location, location and location"...how do you select these?

- What is the preliminary fee for the territory and what is its basis - population, potential, etc.? Is it exorbitant given ROI analysis available?

- Is there a "hidden" cost called a site survey fee to determine the optimal site in a territory?

- What inventory and/or products provided by the franchisor does the contract commit the franchisee to - how much is necessary for start-up and what are the terms? What inventory levels are required?

- What advertising and promotion is required by both parties in the contract and what is only "verbally agreed to?"

- What freedom does the franchisee have with slow turnover items, or low profit margin items in the inventory, stock, or product line?

- What insurance and maintenance charges can be expected? Who is liable in the case of a suit?

- Are the training and technical aid programs adequate?

- How quickly can repairs and supplies be delivered when needed?

- Is there any system, formal or informal, for preferential treatment or prices for franchisees?

- Has the franchisor over-estimated or exaggerated the profit and earnings picture for the first critical months?

- Is the franchisee likely to find himself bound to rigid contract terms while the franchisor's commitments are vague?

- Is there any guarantee of price stability for supplies or does the contract include some phrase to the effect that "prices are subject to change without notice"?

- Are territorial rights closely defined or are there "house accounts" that cut seriously into the market?

- Is the renewal clause and length of time of contract clearly defined?

- Is there any imposition of sales quotas which give the franchisor the right to cancel if quotas are not met? If there are quotas, are they reasonable?

- Are the accounting and control systems too cumbersome and designed primarily to keep the franchisor informed?

• Is the franchise a negotiable asset?

• Is there any fine print allowing the franchisor to control title for any essential equipment?

• What does the back door look like - is there a sell-back provision in case of failure?

The contract, the hub of the franchise agreement, should address each of these points, and both parties, with the help of their lawyers, should be in agreement upon each of them.

CONTROL AND STANDARDIZATION

The franchisor will attempt to control each franchise to the extent that consistency throughout the system is necessary to promote the goodwill of end users. As Harold Wattel explained in a 1968 issue of the *Journal of Retailing*, "The glue that holds any franchise system together is standardization." Most franchisors want to control franchisees in the area of physical appearance, quality of product or service, inventory prices, and product line. The purpose is to create a consistent image in the consumer's mind which in turn, by design, creates goodwill and return business.

Quality control is a critically important factor in the managing of a franchise system. A franchisor does not want a product that varies depending upon which franchise a customer chooses to frequent. A bad experience at one franchise outlet will taint the consumer's perception of the quality of product or service across the entire franchise system. Franchisors, therefore, frequently adopt specific requirements stated in a company manual itemizing operational steps in running the franchise. The franchisee is usually required, by contract, to abide by these stipulations and procedures. The franchisor may choose to use inspectors to monitor a franchisee's compliance.

For the franchisee, the rigors of quality control can be valuable -- but they can also become stifling if not properly understood. First, although a franchisor may wish to maintain a uniform pricing policy, the franchisee must have the flexibility to adapt to special circumstances in his territory. Special conditions can include the amount of competition, the local tax structure, and local vendor fluctutions if the franchisee is not entirely supplied from a central warehouse. Most franchisors understand this, and include a suggested retail price to which franchisees must adhere "as closely as possible."

Second, if a franchisee comes up with what he perceives as a better way to do something, the terms of this contract should reward him for sharing this information with the franchisor, on the "all ships rise with the tide" theory. Quality control should never stifle initiative and worthwhile innovation.

TRAINING

The training program offered by the franchisor should have two goals -- it should help the franchisee gain understanding and confidence in running his new business, and it should enable the franchisor to inculcate the necessary standardization criteria into the new franchisees while taking the measure of their individual strengths and weaknesses for future reference.

There are many excellent "up front" training programs, and because these programs are an important part of the sales pitch, few franchisors neglect this part of the training process. The programs vary from home-study courses, to on-the-job training under the supervision of an existing franchisee, to a formal curriculum of courses -- and most of them combine formal knowledge with on-the-job experience before the franchisee is allowed to start operating.

However, an equally important aspect of franchisee training is too often neglected -- the follow-up programs, providing additional opportunities to learn about various aspects of the business as the franchisee grows into it. With rare exception, ongoing training programs are the hallmarks of successful franchises.

ONGOING SERVICES PROVIDED

Training is but one feature of the ongoing services provided by successful franchisors, for they have found that continuing service is critical in building and maintaining strong franchisees. These services include centralized advertising, employee incentive programs, special promotions, and research and development assistance. Here are a few services a franchisee might expect:

> Advertising assistance is explicitly provided for in many franchise contracts, but terms vary widely. Often, the franchisor will advertise nationally and the franchisee will advertise locally on a cooperative basis; the agreed-upon fee for this option should be specified in the contract. Also, the franchisor may supply the franchisee with customer giveaways and other inducements.

> Motivational bonuses are offered by many franchisors. These might take the form of a free trip for a franchisee who exceeds his quota, or a bonus check for the franchisee to award to his most industrious employee.

> Management services are often provided by regular visits from the franchisor's representatives, who use the visits both to assist the franchisee and to report on his activities.

Most franchisors assist franchisees in complying exactly with uniform accounting practices, enabling them easily to compare franchise performance. Some franchisors employ consultants and development specialists, enabling the franchisee to adapt to market conditions as soon as trends are spotted in ways he never could have foreseen on his own.

An annual convention of franchisees is a valuable way to assure good ongoing relationships between franchisor and franchisee, and serves also to let franchisees compare notes. These meetings, sponsored by the franchisor, should enable the franchisee to:

- have achievement recognized and rewarded;
- be updated on the status of the system;
- elect new members to an association executive committee;
- establish committees as needed;
- have new programs explained;
- have their enthusiasm renewed; and,
- air any discontent.

SITE LOCATION

The franchisee's selection of a site location is critical -- site alone can make the difference between average and superior performance, and occasionally between success and failure. The selection begins with a particular city or town, then a neighborhood within the city or town, and finally the actual site.

Recognizing the importance of site selection, many franchisors have made location analysis a sophisticated science, and are eager to help the franchisee with the choice. At least, the franchisor will suggest criteria for site locations, and require the franchisee to obtain an independent feasibility study to determine the suitability of the site for the proposed venture.

Many types of information are used in site selection. Here is a partial list:

- Standard Market Statistical Area data, demographic statistics about the area compiled by the Census Bureau

- Local Chambers of Commerce, Industry Associations, planning commissions, community opinion leaders -- people who are involved in the future of the community

- Traffic counts

- Adjacent sources of customers, such as office buildings, schools, residential developments

- Where the competition is located

- Access and visibility from the street

- Zoning restrictions -- setbacks, signage, licenses to do certain sorts of business (liquor, especially)

- Aerial photographs and road maps

STRATEGIES

The entrepreneur who chooses franchising as his venture strategy *must* be sure that the options it offers coincide with the objectives he has set for his venture. The chart below categorizes strategies for both franchisor and franchisee in terms of venture objectives, and serves as the framework for the remarks which follow.

	Life Style Venture	Smaller Profitable Venture	High Growth Venture
Franchisor	Usually Not Applicable	Regional distribution	National distribution
Franchisee	"Smaller" franchise • Lower initial price • Predictable earnings	"Larger" franchise or several "smaller" franchises • Higher initial price • Possibility of higher earnings	Usually not applicable

The Franchisor. An entrepreneur desiring a life-style venture will probably not choose to be a franchisor. The inherent growth potential of franchising, coupled with the administrative burden of monitoring a group of franchisees, make this alternative overly ambitious. However, these same qualities will make franchising appealing for a smaller high profit venture or a larger high growth operation. The decision between regional and national distribution is one of degree. A regional chain offers an easier venture to monitor, one less vulnerable to differences in economic trends and buying patterns across the country. A national start-up is, in essence, no different from an independent high-growth start-up, with the same sorts of capital needs, profit potentials and risks, and national marketing strategies.

Though the entrepreneur with regional ambitions will be satisfied with his regional niche, the entrepreneur with national aspirations may choose to start regionally. This will give him an opportunity to refine his concept, develop the capability to attract and train competent franchisees, and gain favorable recognition locally -- providing a fine track record for obtaining further capitalization.

The Franchisee. An entrepreneur seeking a lifestyle venture with a minimum of capital risk is an ideal franchisee. He can shop around for a franchise tailored to his desired lifestyle and his pocketbook. He can receive help both at the start-up and during operation. And, regardless of the growth of the chain as a whole, the franchisee need not build his own volume of sales (and consequent growth-pains problems) beyond the quota imposed by the franchisor.

The entrepreneur with greater financial ambitions may also choose to be a franchisee, but he should adopt a different strategy. He must be prepared to risk more up-front capital, with the intent of doing one of the following:

- Buying a single, expensive franchise with a high projected volume of sales

- Buying two or more franchises with moderate projected sales and profit margins -- i.e., building a small chain of franchises within the system and operating it.

- Buying and improving individual franchise units and selling them at a profit.

The entrepreneur seeking a high growth venture would be an unhappy franchisee. A franchisee must accept limits on his autonomy and a ceiling on his earnings opportunity as the trade-off for a less risky and more structured venture -- and these sacrifices are unlikely to appeal to the entrepreneur seeking a high growth venture.

PLANNING FOR SUCCESSION

Transferring leadership from one person to another is both a problem and an opportunity for entrepreneurial ventures that have become established entities. Recent statistics shed light on the magnitude of the potential problem: the average life of all companies, counting only those which have survived at least ten years, is 24 years.[1] This average age suggests that a great many ventures do not make the transition beyond the era of the founder. After the early crisis of venture startup, the first succession often becomes the next most critical moment that threatens the continuity of a venture.

For the founder who wishes to ensure venture continuity the task of finding and grooming the right successor is not an easy one. But despite the odds, the first succession can be navigated successfully. Moreover, an effective transfer of leadership will not only ensure continued venture existence, but it can extend and improve the quality of leadership as well. How to plan and implement a successful succession is our subject in the following pages. Here we argue that a successful succession depends on correctly understanding at least three factors: 1) the type of succession desired; 2) the context of the succession; and 3) the alternative strategies for succession and how to implement them.

ENTREPRENEURIAL VERSUS MANAGERIAL SUCCESSION

The most important decision a founder must confront when thinking about the transference of leadership, in our view, is the choice between an entrepreneurial successor versus a managerial successor. The distinction between the two types of successors is actually quite straightforward:

- Entepreneurial succession occurs when a new leader is given effective majority control of a venture and is a chief executive officer as well;

- A managerial successor, by contrast, does not own or receive a controlling interest in the venture and in effect works for others who have control of the company.

---

[1] Leon Danco, "The Unwritten Laws of Family Business Continuity," University Service Institute, 1978.

This distinction does *not* concern styles of management. In fact, a managerial successor may have an entrepreneurial flair and ultimately take a company in new directions. Yet, by definition, entrepreneurial activity pursued by a managerial successor must first be sanctioned by those with effective ownership control -- e.g., the founder who remains chairman of the board, or other owners who hold a majority equity interest. In our view, ownership is the crucial distinction in determining the hierarchy of power within most ventures, and defines the successor's latitude for action and flexibility of decision-making. Ownership implies ultimate control and/or sanction of *strategic* decisons made by a managerial succccessor, if the latter is even allowed to make such decisions.

The distinction between strategic decisions and operating decisions is a tricky one, for no clear-cut dividing line exists. What is a strategic decision under one set of circumstances can be an operating one under another set of circumstances. Generally speaking, however, a strategic decision sets a future direction for the venture, and thereby defines what the company's business is. Operating decisions often translate strategic decisions into action. Yet how strategic decisions are realized may be so critical to the survival or success of the enterprise that these implementing actions may also be termed "strategic." Hence we often hear executives speak of a "strategic policy" or a "strategic plan" which is needed to achieve a strategic goal or objective.

A further confusion often develops around the notion of importance, e.g., all *important* decisions must be strategic ones. In fact, some operating decisions may be quite important without affecting the direction or nature of the venture's business. For instance, the construction of a multi-million dollar plant is no doubt an important decision for any venture. But it is not necessarily a strategic decison if, for example, sixteen other plants just like it have already been built in various parts of the United States. On the other hand, the construction of the seventeenth plant may represent a strategic decision if, for example, it is the *first* production facility to be built outside the United States and represents for an enterprise "a new direction" of geographic diversification abroad.

Our purpose here is not to define in detail what constitutes strategic decision-making in every instance. Others have written tomes on the subject and entire courses are devoted to the topic. Our point is simply that even among owners and managers apprised of the concept of strategy, a good potential exists for confusion and ambiguity about what is strategic versus operational. For those (probably the vast majority) who do not have a clear handle on the strategy concept, the potential for confusion is undoubtedly ever higher. What may be seen by a managerial successor as operational may, because of its potential impact, be considered strategic by the venture's owners. This ambiguity can be a source of considerable friction between managerial successors and those who control the venture. An implication is that a managerial successor will rarely be able to make a strategic decision unless the venture's owners agree and give their approval.

However, obtaining such agreement or consensus takes time. The process of reaching an agreement may also require concessions before a consensus is reached. In either instance, the freedom to lead in an entrepreneurial fashion has been lost the moment one *must* explain a decision and obtain even implicit approval to proceed.

The implication of these distinctions is that the venture's founder is making a strategic decision of extreme importance when he determines *the type of successor* who will best carry on the venture. Whether the founder realizes it or not, he or she:

- will seek *de facto* an entrepreneurial successor if the founder is prepared to relinquish both his controlling equity interest and the strategic decision-making power which accompanies it.

- will seek a managerial successor if the founder believes that his continuing presence in a controlling role is essential to the survival of his venture.

An important factor in this decision will be the number, frequency and magnitude of strategic decisions the founder sees the venture requiring in the future. One contention is that a frequent number of strategic decisions favors succession by an entrepreneurial successor. Where few strategic decisions are contemplated, a managerial successor may be more appropriate.

However, a number of other factors bear on the choice of successor, and these will be discussed in the following section -- the context of succession.

THE CONTEXT OF SUCCESSION

Five aspects of the context of succession seem particularly important to us. They include:

A. The *time* available for succession.

B. The entrepreneur's *future aspirations* and likely role vis-a-vis the venture.

C. The *type of venture* involved in terms of sales and profit goals.

D. The number and relationship of other potential entrepreneurs and general managers associated with the venture.

E. The "friendliness" or support of the environment regarding succession.

THE TIME AVAILABLE FOR SUCCESSION

The duration of the "pre-succession period"--the time when an entrepreneur begins to proactively plan for succession to the actual moment of succession or changing of the guard -- can vary considerably from non-existent or almost so to many decades. The actual time available, however, can greatly affect the probabilities of a successful succession.

For example, an unforseen crisis may occur when a founder suddenly becomes incapacitated and someone must be found to take his place. What are the chances of a successful succession under these conditions? Evidence correlating successful leadership transfer with crisis situations is highly unsystematic at this point. Examples can be found of a spouse, other family member, or close friend who have risen to fill the shoes of the incapacitated entrepreneur. A limited study[2] identified one reason why a succession under these circumstances can succeed. The reason is that the venture is large enough and structured enough to support an unexpected change of leader. In other words, the venture already has developed a size and degree of internal momentum which enables it to exist independently of the entrepreneur, at least for some period of time. If the venture is smaller, as most are, the ability to survive an unexpected crisis is quite weak. At best, the successor will maintain operations on the level they were before the founder's departure; however, if no changes are made, the result is usually a gradual decline unless a new leader can be found.

A second type of crisis occurs when an entrepreneur realizes suddenly that retirement is at hand and there's been no prior planning for succession. Because the founder has left himself little time to plan for succession one of two things is likely to happen. The founder may choose the most available person regardless of ability, or reject the idea of succession altogether and opt to dissolve the venture and sell the assets. If our founding entrepreneur takes the former route and chooses a successor based on availability, the chances of having the venture survive into the second generation are abysmal.[3] Unfortunately for many small ventures, the head-in-the-sand approach to succession by the founder appears to be the chief cause of their demise; the business may be healthy but the pool of qualified leaders, for either entrepreneurial or managerial succession, is nil.

A longer pre-succession period implies that the founder has planned both for his own exit and for the implementation of a succession plan. The length of this period varies from venture to venture; too much time can be as bad as too little.

The remainder of this note assumes a non-crisis situation regarding succession - one with sufficient time for the founder to plan the type of succession he or she wants and provide the means to implement it.

PERSONAL GOALS: THE ENTREPRENEUR'S DESIRES AND NEEDS

What are the entrepreneur's own desires and needs for the future? A thorough assessment of one's personal situation is a prerequisite to any decision about succession. An entrepreneur can begin by dividing these needs into three groups and asking the following questions, bearing in mind that he can opt for an entrepreneurial succession, a managerial succession, or the discontinuance of the venture.

---

[2]David Ambrose, doctoral thesis, University of Nebraska, Omaha, 1980.

[3]Leon Danco, *Beyond Survival,* Cleveland, Ohio: The University Press, 5th edition, 1979, pp. 143-69.

1. *The venture as a continuing career.*

Do I want to retire? If so, when? How old am I now and how many more years do I want to run the show? If you, and your venture, are young the succession issue may not yet be germane. If you have a "life-style venture" and intend to die in your boots, you may decide to let the venture die with you. However, if you want to establish a family-owned company to provide careers for your children and grandchildren, your interest in planning succession will become more immediate — choosing and grooming an heir-apparent, and/or making provisions for a successor until the new generation is ready to assume control.

2. *The venture as a source of income*

What are my financial needs? If you are young, with a wife and small children, you may depend entirely on the growth and health of your venture for income -- and seek an entrepreneurial "partner" who could continue it if you were suddenly unable to do so. If you are older, and planning to retire, you will have to assess your venture's capability to support both you and a successor. If other family members are dependent on your venture for income, a third set of provisions for continuity will have to be defined. In short, your need for income will affect directly your approach to succession.

3. *The venture as contributor to your community*

How does my venture affect my community, and vice versa? Am I providing a heritage of jobs and services which, as a responsible citizen, I feel obliged to perpetuate after my time?[4] If your venture has become an integral part of the community fabric, you will have to choose the type of successor best equipped to carry on this function.

A personal assessment of this type should help the founder to place his own needs within the context of his particular venture in terms of the degree of leadership and control he wishes to maintain, and the length of time he wishes to maintain it. If he comes to believe that, at some future time, his needs and the perpetuation of the venture can best be served by stepping aside, he may choose to do so in one of three ways:

1. Retirement: complete separation from the venture

2. Exit to begin another venture: complete separation from original venture

3. Resigning from day-to-day operations

   - Assuming a strategic planning role as chief executive officer and retaining control;

---

[4]Stanley Davis, "Entrepreneurial Succession," *Administration Science Quarterly,* December, 1967.

- Conducting an independent R&D operation, or undertaking a consulting assignment, but relinquishing top management control to the new leader;

- Operating a new acquisition or diversification, over which he maintains control beneath the "total venture" umbrella.

An entrepreneurial succession, is recommended when the founder must pursue alternatives 1 and 2, though this choice does not guarantee a successful continuation of the venture. Nonetheless, the founder leaves all control in the hands of his successor.

The possibilities for entrepreneurial succession in the case of alternative 3, however, are apt to be less successful because of the ambiguous tie which remains between the founder and his venture, for he often finds that he cannot confine himself to his new role. Let us examine the difficulties of each one.

The founder who retains strategic control, typical of a managerial succession, is likely to interpret his "strategic" powers more broadly than the new president would like, and the successor feels impotent to carry out his duties in the founder's shadow. The situation may be ameliorated by an active Board and a managerial successor who has earned the respect of the venture's employees, a strategy which will be discussed later.

The founder who becomes a researcher or consultant to his/her former venture also appears to be a less than successful strategy. One business adviser estimates that, although the founder's formal contract is typically drawn for a five-year period, the relationship lasts on average only a year and a half. The primary cause of the breakdown appears to be that the former owner cannot remain at a distance from the operation of the venture, despite the most explicit wording of the "consulting" contract.

The founder who is given control of a subsidiary operation seems to prosper in direct proportion to his distance from the main operation. The less reliant he is on capital or on direction from the original venture, the better his chances for success in the new environment, as well as the chances for success of his successor to the parent venture.

VENTURE GOALS

The context of succession also seems to be influenced considerably by existing and future goals for the venture in question. Prior research has shown that most ventures can be classified by their founders as either "lifestyle ventures" with lower sales and profit aspirations or "smaller profitable ventures" with lower sales but high profit goals. Very few ventures fall into the "high growth venture" category with both high sales and ultimately high profit aspirations.[5]

----

[5]Robert Ronstadt, *The Entrepreneurial Career Pathways of Babson Entrepreneurs,* Unpublished Manuscript, Board of Research, Babson College, Wellesley, MA, 1982; also by same author, "Initial Venture Goals, Age, and the Decision to Start an Entrepreneurial Career," *Proceedings of Academy of Management,* 1983.

The implications for each of these three venture types regarding succession are summarized in the following chart, which shows the likelihood of success associated with the choice of one or the other type of successor. (See Table 1) For example, the founder of a life-style venture will have the most difficulty in finding a qualified successor of either sort because the venture itself offers the least potential for both growth and profit. Because the venture is a reflection of the founder's interests and expertise, it is often unlikely that a candidate will be found to manage its future. The only possible candidate will be a person who mirrors the founder's own skills and goals, who is probably also looking for a chance to be his own boss now, not five or ten years down the road. Even if a candidate is identified, lifestyle ventures seldom have the financial resources to sustain a successor for very long. In the case of a smaller profitable venture, the founder seeking an entrepreneurial successor must contemplate future growth or diversification in order to provide the strategic opportunities and challenge a potential candidate will require; if his venture does not hold this potential, his choice will be limited to a competent manager capable of perpetuating the mission of the venture as the founder conceived it. Clearly, the high-growth venture -- with greater opportunities for growth and profit -- is the most likely environment to breed a successful successor of either sort; the choice depends on the founder's own future aspirations. Unfortunately, as stated earlier, this type of venture is the scarcest.

Table 1

	LSV	**SPV**	**HGV**
Entrepreneurial Succession	**Unlikely:** Need to find someone with same "lifestyle" orientation.	**Possible:** If new diversification foreseen or major expansion of existing business.	**Possible:** But difficult given usual diffusion of equity and power associated with growth.
Managerial Succession	**Unlikely:** Business cannot support non-equity based salary.	**Possible:** Maintenance of existing business.	**Usually Very Possible:** Given size of internal organization and/or ability to attract a professional outsider.

LSV = Life Style Venture
SPV = Smaller Profitable Venture
HGV = High Growth Venture

HUMAN RESOURCES: OTHERS ASSOCIATED WITH THE ENTREPRENEUR AND THEIR GOALS

At some point, the founder must change his focus from the general to the specific -- from "What type of successor" to specifically "Who will be my successor?" This question can be painfully revealing.

As the founder looks around for a potential candidate, he hopes to find: a person with the *capability* to be an entrepreneur or manager; and a person who has, or who can receive, the necessary *experience* to succeed in the new leadership role as entrepreneurial or managerial successor.

Let us look at some typical situations:

- In the case of "one-man" operations, there is normally no one readily available.

- In the case of most lifestyle ventures and/or smaller profitable ventures, a group of functional managers may exist. But they are usually the same age as the founder and have reported to him throughout their careers. Often they have had no experience in general management.

- In some instances, family members are present in the company but they are either too old or too young ... or not interested in a leadership role.

- Some ventures may be dynamic enough to attract potential successors, but they have never been given the chance to learn how to lead; the founder has guarded his strategic decision-making privilege as closely as his majority ownership.

The founder, after looking inside his own venture to see who might be a potential successor, must then ask a key question: Does anyone here really want to be an entrepreneurial successor, and all it implies? Or are the most likely candidates more inclined by orientation and experience to be managers (albeit with a healthy bonus or even some equity participation)? Depending on his findings, and on his desires for a successor, he may decide to look outside for future leadership.

ENVIRONMENTAL FACTORS

Environmental factors also play an important role in defining succession. Here we can distinguish between three types of factors:

1. The general economic environment

2. A specific industry environment

3. The local geographic environment (the town or city where the venture is located).

Research has shown[6] that growth (or the potential to grow) in the venture itself enhances the posibility of a successful succession -- expanding activities create new jobs, and bring in new blood; responsibilities must be delegated and an organization must be built to sustain the growth of the venture. In this context, two key questions that relate to succession must be asked:

● How rapidly is change occurring in any or all of these three environments? Rapid change often implies a need for strategic decision-making and an entrepreneurial successor.

● How important is the venture in terms of its impact on any of these three environments? If it is very important to any of them, you may receive support for your efforts to find a successor, whether he or she be an entrepreneurial or managerial successor.

STRATEGIES FOR SUCCESSION

Choosing a Scenario

There are four basic types of successions. We have already defined the first two to some extent. They are:

1. Entrepreneurial Succession: where the long-term needs of the venture indicate a corresponding need for an entrepreneurial successor, or at least as far as the founder can foresee.

2. Managerial Succession: where the long-term needs of the venture suggest a managerial successor, or at least as far as the founder can foresee.

3. Entrepreneurial Succession followed by Managerial Succession: a short period of initial growth is foreseen, followed by an era of stability and gradual evolution. Here the founder may need to enlist the agreement of the entrepreneurial successor to give up the reins at a later but clearly foreseeable date.

4. Managerial Succession followed by Entrepreneurial Succession: either

> ● a short period of stability and strengthening is required before entrepreneurial growth and/or diversification can proceed, or,

> ● the founder decides to test and develop an outsider or "unknown quantity" before turning over the entrepreneurial reins.

---

[6]C. Roland Christensen, *Management Succession in Small and Growing Enterprises,* Harvard University, 1953; and Stanley Davis, *op. cit.*

Choosing a Person

As a guide in selecting a successor, a venture's founder can think in terms of three criteria:

- Entrepreneurial successor/Managerial successor

- Inside the firm/Outside the firm

- Family/Non-family

Graphically, the range of possibilities is shown below. (Table 2) As a conceptual framework, these possibilities should help the founder structure and clarify his thoughts on an ideal successor. Practically, however, his choice is limited by the available pool of candidates.

Table 2

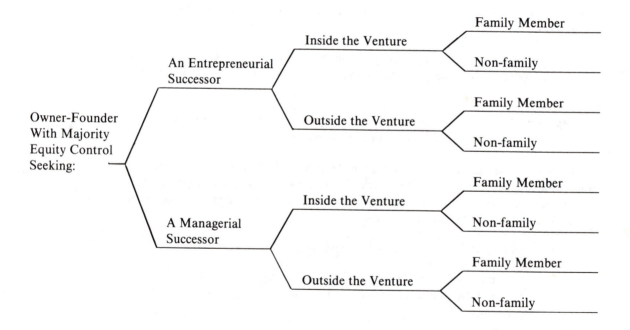

Experienced observers have studied the pros and cons of many of these alternatives. Here are some of their findings:

Insider/Family

This is the "Crown Prince" strategy. At some point the founder decides to select a family member, most often a son or nephew, to succeed him with the intent of delegating to him first gradually the operational responsibilities and eventually strategic powers and ownership. A key to success is the chemistry between founder and heir apparent. The founder must also be able to turn from a leader to a coach, from a doer to an advisor. The "prince" must respect the founder's creation and be sensitive to his possessive feelings, but he must also be able to exercise his entrepreneurial flair to initiate change. One aid for training an heir is a carefully planned "training program" which will expose the successor to every aspect of the venture over a period of time. In some instances, seminars and workshops designed for the young heirs of business owners may provide him with additional perspective.[7]

The potential pitfall is timing; the founder often prolongs the "training period" unnecessarily and holds fast to the reins of authority. There are many examples of heirs apparent growing well into middle age while waiting for the "old man" to step aside.

It is understandably difficult for the creator of a venture to relinquish control--even though he knows his successor needs the latitude to make and implement his own decisions, even if they are not always good ones. The founder/owner is often emotionally involved with his venture to a degree which makes "rational" training for a successor difficult. The venture is an extension of himself -- his baby as well as his mistress -- and he often has a deep-seated desire to hang on to it. In addition, psychologists have documented the inherent subconscious resistance and mistrust in a father-son business relationship.[8]

Nonetheless, in a small venture especially, this option may be the most satisfactory, or even the only solution.[9]

The "Crown Prince or Princess" is intended to be an entrepreneurial successor since he or she expects to receive majority ownership at some point.

Insider/Family or Non-Family

This choice is based on meritocracy. It begins early in the life of the venture with the founder's decision to recruit and train a small group of executive managers, family members and/or others, to fill positions at every level in the organization. This strategy assumes a rate of growth which can support new managerial talent. It avoids the pitfall of getting stuck with a nucleus of "old boys" resistant to change; it encourages an ongoing infusion of new blood; it distributes responsibility over a wider base; and it enables the founder to build an experienced management team capable of producing a successor. The founder assumes that, in time, a natural leader will emerge. Once identified, the founder will delegate to a potential successor an increasing amount of operational responsiblity as soon as he can handle it, while stepping back to concentrate on strategic planning. In time, he will relinquish that responsibility as well.

---

[7]Leon Danco, *Beyond Survival, op. cit.* p. 79.

[8]Harry Levinson, "Conflicts that Plague Family Businesses," *Harvard Business Review,* Mar/Apr 1971.

[9]Leon Danco, *Beyond Survival, op. cit.*

Outsider/Family

A number of founders choose to groom their heirs apparent by having them work for someone else first,[10] letting them make their initial mistakes out of daddy's sight. Some experts on family succession believe that this approach is an optimal solution: it avoids father-son friction during the learning process, and it broadens the son's range of experience. This option assumes a venture large enough to allow the son to work elsewhere first, and a cadre of management who can tolerate the idea that they will never be president.

Outsider/Non-Family

If the founder has no one in his venture who is ripe to succeed him, he often looks outside for a professional manager -- with the help of his lawyer, his banker, and his Board of Directors. Much has been written about professional managers[11] and, contrary to some opinions, an MBA from a prestigious business school is no sure ticket to success — rather, familiarity with the type of business, with the business itself, and a knowledge of the specific role of a successor appear to be more pertinent criteria for success. Professional managers often are hired on an interim basis (which can be as long as 10 to 15 years) until an heir apparent has matured. In these instances, the professional manager may be offered a small minority equity position with the understanding that their function is mainly operational; major policy decisons are usually made by the Board, which may include the entrepreneur/founder.

Outsider/Non-Family

Another type of outsider is the turn-around specialist who is experienced in rescuing ventures from impending financial difficulty. Customarily, this person demands more control in the form of equity in order to do what he believes necessary, and the entrepreneur choosing this type of successor must keep a low profile, or resign altogether. This successor usually plans to hand the rejuvenated venture to another leader, either managerial (if he wishes to retain ownership) or entrepreneurial (if he wishes to move on to another venture).

Outsider/Non-Family

This approach is the "adopted son" strategy. In the absence of a legitimate heir, a founder will occasionally find a younger person with the right talents and bring him into the venture as his assistant, on the understanding that the "adoptee" will grow into both the presidency and the ownership of the venture. In a small venture, or one with a handful of older executives, an entrepreneur anxious to perpetuate his enterprise may find this solution successful.

---

[10]Leon Danco, *Inside the Family Business,* Cleveland: University Press, 1980, pp. 455-67.

[11]Duncan and Flamholtz, "Transition from Entrepreneurship to a Profesionally Managed Firm," *AMACOM,* 1982;
Robert Donnelley, "The Family Business," *Harvard Business Review,* July/Aug 1964.

Insider/Non-Family

This is the "caretaker" strategy. If the founder finds the gap between his planned retirement and his heir's coming of age too wide, he may appoint his second-in-command to keep the business going, with the understanding that the course not be altered and the captaincy be of limited duration. If effected in an atmosphere of understanding, a capable "caretaker" can be the key to the venture's survival into the second generation.

IMPLEMENTING THE CHOSEN STRATEGY: INGREDIENTS OF SUCCESS

Observers of the succession process have noted certain ingredients which contribute to smooth transitions. Heading the list, as we have noted, are two:

> •. The founder himself -- his willingness to accept the issue as an integral part of his strategic planning and his ability to move from leader to coach to retiree.**

> • The type of venture and the environment -- specifically a growing enterprise in a growing market, attractive to new management and active community support

Yet, several other factors are present in most successful successions and we shall look at these now.

**One school of thought popular in the 1960's maintained that the owner/founder of a venture was temperamentally unable to make the transition from leader to manager/coach/advisor, that there was no such thing as a "back-seat entrepreneur."

This theory was based on studies of leaders and managers,[13] and concluded that certain qualities present in entrepreneurs (antisocial, mercurial, willful) were antithetical to those needed by a successful manager. Others building on this base, questioned that a founder/entrepreneur was even capable of selecting and training a successor.[14] However, recent studies[15] suggest that an owner/founder who can operate a venture long enough to create something worth preserving also has the ability to adapt his skills to the changing needs of the venture, and is entirely capable of planning for a future that does not include him.

Nonetheless, all research indicates that it is difficult for the creator of a venture to relinquish control -- the disagreement is over the degree of difficulty.

[13]Abraham Zaleznik, "Leaders and Managers," *Harvard Business Review,* May/June, 1977.

[14]Christensen, *op. cit.*

[15]Ronstadt, *op. cit.*

The Board of Directors

A working Board of Directors can be a venture's most valuable asset in times of stress -- such as succession. A conscientious board can take upon itself the responsibility of "providing for the profitable continuity of the firm."[12] Specifically the Board can broach the subject to a reluctant founder; help him define his objectives in light of the continued profitability of the venture; help in the search for a successor; mediate between founder and successor; and even help the founder ease into retirement.

A working board is not to be confused with the token board -- Aunt Minnie, the founder's golf partner, and the family dentist, who are as a rule uncritical yes-men. A working board is a group of peers -- other risk-taking business-people, non-competitive outsiders, people of integrity and experience in various aspects of management. A working board meets regularly and generally is salaried It reviews the policies and operations of the venture regularly, including the performance of the founder. It listens closely to the founder and others, but its primary responsibility is to the venture as a whole.

It is the founder's responsibility to create an active board, and the task is not easy. Much has been written about creating a board -- composition, size, length of term -- and about the differences between an effective board and a token one. Most experts agree that a formally organized board is appropriate for ventures:

- with sales approaching $1 million, or

- when multiple levels of management become necessary and the review process cannot be carried out by one person alone, or

- when continuity of the venture becomes an issue.

Good outside directors are hard to find, and it takes courage for a founder to enlist the support of those who may disagree with him on strategic issues, but a founder's best chance of ensuring continuity may be a board if the venture is large and dynamic enough to support a higher level of expertise.

Taking Care of the Family

A founder may have financial responsibilities to family members which can be met only through the profitability of the venture, and yet believe (often rightfully so) that his dependents should have no say in how the venture is run. Or, a founder may wish to maintain control of the stock, yet be unable to do so without placing unbearable burdens on his estate. How can he eat his cake and have it too?

---

[12]Danco, *Beyond Survival*, p. 137.

A solution may be estate planning, with the consultation of a lawyer and an accountant specializing in this field. Much has been written about estate planning for the entrepreneur,[16] and a few ideas are listed below, to suggest the range of possibilities:

• In the case of management succession, when you wish to maintain a controlling interest. You can give your stock, over time, in equal (minority) blocks to your heirs, to lessen the burden on your estate and to preclude a controlling majority stockholder in the near future.

• In the case of entrepreneurial succession, you can provide for family members by establishing a category of non-voting stock which will give them potential income but no control.

Professional estate planners, with full knowledge of your particular situation and needs, can tailor a plan appropriate for your ongoing financial responsibilities to family members.

"Cleaning House"

In some ways, preparing your venture for a successor is like selling a house -- you want to be sure that everything is in working order and that the instructions on how to make things work are clear. You may know that the best way to get the furnace started is to kick it, but your successor will be cold on more than one morning if you don't explain the system to him carefully.

Regarding your venture, a good place to start is with the accounting system. Is your procedure clear? Are the books up to date? If you do not have a reliable outside accountant, should you get one? Another area to check is purchasing and inventory control. Is the system comprehensible to an outsider? Would it collapse if the production manager weren't there to look in the right shoebox?

This is not the time to initiate new systems -- leave that to the successor -- but it is the time to be sure what you have can be understood by someone else.

Timing

The duration of the pre-succession period and the timing of the succession itself depends to a great degree on the choice of successor. Based on the discussion above, different options require different time frames.

---

[16]Philip Dawson, "Succession Planning," newsletter, Center for Family Business, JA 1982.

• Grooming a successor from the next generation -- a crown prince, a son working elsewhere, an "adopted son" -- can only begin when the person is old enough - late teens or 20's, making the founder middle-aged. Ideally, the duration of the training period should be long enough for the successor to learn the ropes but no longer; at that point, he should start assuming responsibilities. Ideally again, the heir should be fully in charge of operations at the time the transition is made. Unfortunately, we do not live in an ideal world.

• The meritocratic successor requires much less lead time, if the entrepreneur builds his team along with his venture. In fact, if he plans to exit the venture and begin another, his successor could be developed within several years.

• The "Outsider"—professional manager or turn-around specialist—may require even less time to find, provided that the founder has an active search committee (the board and other professional advisors) to help him. This strategy is frequently chosen because it is expedient, and the founder does not have the luxury of taking time to develop a successor.

• The inside "Caretaker" is quickest of all, though the founder is apt to lose in dynamism what he gains in speed.

When should the founder step down? Every venture is different; every founder is different. If the founder is able to put the future of his venture in front of his self-interest, he may be able to make a better determination. With the advice of an outside board, he will gain still a better perspective.

CONCLUSION

The issue of succession plays an important part in the long term future of an established venture. Entrepreneurs must confront the interrelated questions of stock/strategic control and management responsibility if they wish their ventures to continue and prosper after they have ceased to be active. Because succession implies the transfer of control, it is a highly emotional decision for an entrepreneur to make. Given the emotionally charged nature of the issue, considerable care must be taken to analyze carefully the type of successor desired, possible ways to implement the choice, and the probability of achieving a smooth transition.

Index of Names

Index of Subjects

Index of Cases and Authors

Index of Technical Notes